SINATRA

SINATRA

RICHARD HAVERS

DK

LONDON, NEW YORK, MUNICH, MELBOURNE, DELHI

For Ron Accosta, 'The Hollywood Bible', who never ever gave me too much information.

Produced for Dorling Kindersley by
The Bridgewater Book Company Limited,
The Old Candlemakers, West Street, Lewes,
East Sussex BN7 2NZ

Creative Director Terry Jeavons
Senior Art Editor Michael Whitehead
Editors Susie Behar, Sara Harper, Alison Bolus
Designers Anna Hunter-Downing,
Kevin Knight, Barbara Zuniga
Editorial Director Robert Yarham
Project Manager Stephanie Horner
DTP Ginny Zeal, Christine Engert
Proofreaders Philippa Smith and Kathy Speer
Indexer Ursula Caffrey

At Dorling Kindersley
Senior Designer Mabel Chan
Designer Jerry Udall
Senior Editor Victoria Heyworth-Dunne
DTP John Goldsmid
Picture Researcher Maria Gibbs
Production Joanna Bull

Editorial Direction Andrew Heritage
Managing Editor Debra Wolter
Managing Art Editor Louise Dick
US Editor Vicki Arkoff

First published in Great Britain in 2004
by Dorling Kindersley Limited
80 Strand, London WC2R 0RL
This edition published in 2007
A Penguin Company
2 4 6 8 10 9 7 5 3
Text Copyright © Richard Havers, 2004
Compilation Copyright © Dorling Kindersley Limited, 2004

A CIP catalogue record for this book is available
from the British Library

Colour reproduction by GRB, Italy
Printed and bound by L. Rex Printing Company, China

ISBN 13: 978-1-40531-461-9
ISBN 10: 1-40531-461-3

For our complete catalogue visit

www.dk.com

CONTENTS

OREWORD

AS WORLD WAR II IN EUROPE WAS ENDING Frank Sinatra recorded 'The House I Live In' – the song was for his film about racial tolerance; in it he asks, "What is America to me?" Then, and as it has been ever since, the question is, "What was Frank Sinatra to America?" It's particularly so because for the next 50 years he lived the American dream. Frank has been described as imperious, gregarious, a lonely man, a family man, profound, loyal, ruthless if crossed, effervescent, obsessive, a mobster, a communist, a conservative, prejudiced, fighter for the downtrodden, intransigent, quick-tempered, brilliant… he was all of these things, and he was so much more. It's as an entertainer who shaped a career as a singer that lasted longer than he, or anyone else, thought it was possible for a singer's career to last that makes Sinatra so fascinating. At the same time he was no great actor, and yet he made some great movies and won an Academy Award. Frank was an icon to those in search of the dream.

For many years, and it still happens today, singers have been hailed as the next Frank Sinatra. While it's easy to understand why it's done, it's futile… there will never be another. When I interviewed Bill Miller, Frank's pianist for five decades, he said, "He just wanted to be Frank Sinatra, and he became Frank Sinatra." To me this is the very essence of the man. Frank fashioned his own persona, created his own world, which is what made him unique. Too many biographies of Frank ignore his contemporaries, those who breathed the same air (even if it wasn't so rarefied). In so doing they downplay his achievements.

Most of us could not have been a part of Frank's ring-a-ding world; we had to content ourselves with being his subjects. But from wherever we looked, it seemed like a gasser. This book explores the world he created and the landscape in which he lived. It's about people, both the ordinary and the extraordinary, the peripheral and the essential, his influences and those he inspired. It's about Frank and life in Sinatraland.

"He was more than just a singer, he was a cultural expression of a whole nation's sense of style. He was our notion of class and elegance."

JIMMY WEBB

RICHARD HAVERS
May 2004

INTRODUCTION

FRANK SINATRA WAS (UNNEGOTIABLY, AS I SEE IT) the greatest interpretive musician of the 20th century. By interpretive I mean that he took what others had written or composed, and swept across the country, allowing his vivid personality, his musical genius, his untrained actorial impulse, to spread universal emotions into the longing souls of millions of people, many of whom spoke no English but were able to receive and understand what Sinatra was expressing, and to eventually regard him iconically. Mostly, he chose songs of a high order, crafted by men and women with the schooling, wit, and discipline to create songs of integrity and beauty. These songs became Sinatra's currency. They were his tickets to command performances, stadium sellouts, nightclub near-riots as the people pushed forward trying to get in, to place themselves as close to the music as they could.

Sinatra's warm decency is there on the records, his very humanness is alive, sparkling with candor. His syncopation, his technical cool under the pressure of novelistic punctuation—he is the only singer I've ever heard who could sing a semi-colon—and his energy, so essential for those long lines delivered in one unheard intake of oxygen-lines that lead to the next part of the story, as if in prose—all these amazing graces collaborated on well over a thousand recordings, leaving a vital American presence on the waters, the cities, the ashes of mankind. If you read me as hyperbolic, so be it. There are few who warrant such an outpouring. Sinatra is two of them.

JONATHAN SCHWARTZ

Jonathan Schwartz's recent memoir, All in Good Time, was published by Random House in March 2004. Jonathan can be heard in New York on NPR's WNYC-FM and nationally on XM Satellite Radio.

1861-1939

An American
Dream

Frank Sinatra, the only son of first-generation Italian immigrants, had a family background like hundreds of thousands of others. He was born in Hoboken, New Jersey, in the second decade of the 20th century and spent his formative years across the Hudson River from New York City. Being Italian was central to Frank's life and the very essence of his personality. His family and upbringing gave him his drive and commitment to his career. It affected well-documented aspects of his personal life, and ultimately led to his realization of the American Dream — a dream shared by millions like him.

WHAT A VIEW
An immigrant family standing on Ellis Island, having just passed the immigration examination, stare over at the New York skyline in the early part of the 20th century.

LEAVING HOME FOR THE NEW WORLD, SICILY, c.1900

"When land appeared on the sixteenth day after leaving the port of Naples, it was so fascinating to me that I wanted to shout for joy because now I was coming to the beautiful America. After a couple of hours we began to see the outline of the American shore and buildings. The Statue of Liberty... was inviting us to come over."

MARIA DEVENEZIA, *A GRAIN OF SAND*

$\mathcal{F}$ROM THE OLD
TO THE NEW

Emigration from Italy to the United States did not happen as a result of one single event. It began as a slow burn and peaked in the ten years either side of 1900, during which time nearly four million people took the decision to leave their homeland and travel thousands of miles across the Atlantic to America. Whatever their situation, it cannot have been an easy choice for anyone.

It was the nature of Italy during the 19th century, with its poverty, political instability, and poor infrastructure, that forced people to make the difficult choice to emigrate. Before 1861, Italy was not a nation but a loose assemblage of states which, from as early as 1500, had been subject to foreign rule.

In 1796, Napoleon invaded the Italian peninsula, but his regime fell in 1815, leaving "Italy" as a loose assemblage of independent states. The Hapsburgs ruled the Kingdom of Piedmont, which consisted of most of Savoy, Sardinia, and Piedmont, and the Duchies of Tuscany, Parma, and Modena. The Pope reigned over

THE OLD WORLD
Palermo Harbour in 1864, from where Frank's father's family probably began their journey to America.

the Papal States of Bologna, Ancona, and Rimini, and, from Naples, the Bourbons ruled the Kingdom of the Two Sicilies.

During his brief reign, Napoleon was responsible for introducing ideas of national unity, and revolutionary groups like the Carbonari and Young Italy (republican groups seeking unification) started to form. There followed a period of political upheaval and revolution that finally led to unification in 1861. With the support of revolutionaries such as Garibaldi, Victor Emmanuel II was eventually crowned King of Italy.

Although now one country, Italy was still divided into distinct regions and peoples. Italy also suffered from debt, poverty, limited natural resources, a largely agricultural economy, and little or no transport infrastructure.

The gulf between the developed, urban north and the rural south hampered attempts to move forward. By the 1880s, a more pronounced socialist ideology was evident among the workers in the cities, though this outlook had not spread to the more feudal south. Successive coalitions tried to govern, but from the late 1800s right up until the start of World War I, Italy was a nation in crisis, making it a country that many people were only too happy to leave.

LAND OF OPPORTUNITY

Emigration to America began as a trickle in the late 1840s, and by 1870 around 20,000 people had left Italy bound for America. However, over the following 20 years an estimated 355,000 Italians went to the United States. Initially it was mostly northern Italians who made the journey. Faced with increasing economic problems at home, the number of émigrés increased. Between 1890 and 1914, nearly four million Italians went to *l'America*. Overpopulation, high taxation, food shortages, unemployment, and a desire to own property were all factors in driving migration to "the land of the free". The growing popularity of the steamship also played a part, as did the "agents" who got their cut of the 20 lire per head it cost to make the trip.

ITALY DIVIDED
A 19th-century map shows Italy as a collection of independent city-states, dukedoms, and monarchies before it became a unified state in 1861.

1861–1939

PASSAGE TO AMERICA
American entry visas were issued on immigrants' passports only after a rigorous inspection at entry ports such as Ellis Island.

As emigration from southern Italy grew, people tended to head for the big cities, such as New York or Chicago, or for destinations on the East Coast. Previously many northern Italians had settled in mining towns across the United States.

It was not just to the United States that Italians emigrated, however. Many went to Argentina, Uruguay, Brazil, Australia, and Canada. Families bearing the name Sinatra are known to have emigrated from Sicily to Australia and Argentina.

Even after 1916, Italians continued to move to America in significant numbers: more than one million people left Italy during the quarter of a century before America's entry into World War II.

THE GREAT DIVIDE

Frank Sinatra's maternal grandparents lived in Genoa during the latter part of the 19th century. By the mid-1890s, Genoa was the recipient of an economic upsurge that affected what was known as the industrial triangle of the north which had at its points Milan, Turin, and Genoa. Traditional crafts were changing and giving way to new forms of industry.

For Frank's maternal grandfather, Signor Garavente, a lithographer, this shift persuaded him, and many others, to leave for a new life in America.

While Genoa was at the heart of the Italian industrial revolution, Frank's paternal grandparents' home of Sicily – the largest island in the Mediterranean – seemed to have been forgotten by the central government.

Throughout the 19th century, Sicily was in open revolt against just about any form of government. There was hostility between the rich landowners and tenants on the one hand, and the rest of the population on the other. In many municipalities (*communes*), the local mayor was often also the largest local landowner. He had a virtual monopoly, along with his friends, in controlling the job market and the wages and conditions in which people were expected to live.

This situation led to the rise of the Sicilian Fasci (translated literally *fasci* means bundles). These self-help, mutual-aid groups offered resistance against the oppression by the rich. In 1893 they quickly spread throughout Sicily, and before long strikes, violence, and arson were increasingly commonplace throughout the island. The Fasci were soon

THE START OF A NEW LIFE
Immigrants, having passed through the immigration procedures, await the ferry to carry them over the harbour to New York City around 1900.

joined by radical intellectuals, a situation that began to worry the local landowners and the Italian government. Against a background of promised reform, the Fasci were dissolved in 1894, and up to 1,000 people were deported. However, the series of promised reforms simply consolidated the landowners' control of their own land as well as any uncultivated parcels of land. The peasants were deprived of voting rights through the electoral roll revisions. In the new climate of power, the poor had little option but to knuckle down or depart. Many chose the latter, and emigration from Sicily rapidly escalated.

A TRAVELLER'S TALE

MARIA SAPORITO DEVENEZIA, BORN IN AVELLINO NEAR NAPLES, SOUTHERN ITALY, IN 1896, EMIGRATED TO THE UNITED STATES AGED 14. SHE RECALLS THE LONG VOYAGE.

"The ship was not allowed to enter port (Naples) as a precautionary measure against contamination by cholera. The ship anchored three miles away from the city and I went on a rowboat and had to ascend the ship by means of a ladder.

Once on board, supper was our first meal. I was glad to approach the window dispensing the food. The food was placed in the container furnished us when we came aboard. The container and utensils had to serve us for the whole voyage and we had to wash and care for them.

… During the night the girl sleeping on the berth next to mine woke up. She said, 'Maria, please come to the women's room. I feel sick.' The lady on the lower berth was vomiting. After seeing so many people sick, I felt sick too…

Next morning the most magnificent panorama spread before our eyes. The city of Palermo, capital of Sicily, lay in the full splendour of the sun bathed

in the blue water of the Mediterranean Sea. The reason we had come here was to pick up some cargo and more passengers. The new passengers stared at our group….They were strangers to us and we were strangers to them. Their dialect was different from ours. We who embarked in Naples never mixed with the passengers from Sicily. …We came from Naples and were Neapolitan and they came from Sicily. They were Sicilians. The feeling aboard was that we were two people instead of one.

When land appeared on the sixteenth day after leaving the port of Naples, it was so fascinating to me that I wanted to shout for joy because now I was coming to the beautiful America. After a couple of hours we began to see the outline of the American shore and buildings. The Statue of Liberty with the light high in her hand was inviting us to come over."

FROM *A GRAIN OF SAND* BY MARIA DEVENEZIA

SHIP OF HOPE
Princess Irene, typical of the ships used to bring immigrants to the US, lies at anchor off Ellis Island in the late 19th century.

1861–1939

LOST IN TRANSLATION

What's in a name? Many immigrants arriving in the United States found that their names were unusual, difficult to pronounce, even a hindrance. Whether you were Russian, Hungarian, Dutch, Swedish, German, Italian, or from wherever, the new world often meant a new name. In addition, entries on the Ellis Island forms were sometimes misspelled or the surname of a stepfather was employed instead of the natural father; the putative father's name may have been used for an illegitimate child; or a maiden name instead of a married name.

Sometimes just a nickname would suffice. One Ellis Island immigrant who failed to understand the questions, but just kept grinning, found his surname was put down as "Smiley". It was not only surnames that got lost during this process – Christian names were also changed.

According to Frank Sinatra's "Certificate and record of birth" of 17 December, 1915, his father was Anthony Sinestro (born in the US), and his mother Dolly Garaventi. Anthony's occupation was listed as "chauffeur" (age 22); Dolly's as "housewife" (age 20). It seems most likely that the clerk executing the birth certificate was as careless as the immigration authorities in recording family names. Research reveals that no one called Sinestro landed at Ellis Island prior to 1915, but that 206 men, women, and children named Sinatra arrived there between 1892 and 1910. In *Frank Sinatra – an American Legend*, Nancy Sinatra says that her great grandparents, John and Rosa Sinatra, were born in Agrigento in Sicily and took their son, Anthony Martin Sinatra, to America soon after his birth (this would have been in the mid-1890s). As grape growers in rural Catania, she says, their prospects were not good and they decided to leave. ("Grape growers" should not be deemed to imply ownership of vines – it is more likely they tended the vines of an oppressive Sicilian landlord.)

The only record of an Antonio Sinatra of about the right age arriving at Ellis Island is on 21 December, 1903, when a 9-year-old boy arrived on board the *Città di Milano* from Naples. His place of residence was given as Perlanno, a likely misspelling of Palenno in Sicily. He arrived with two sisters, Angela aged 7 and Dorotra aged 4 years and 11 months. (Many years later Frank referred to his father's sister, Dora; could this have been Dorotora?)

THE REGISTRY ROOM
For many immigrants to Ellis Island this was their first taste of America prior to going through the immigration procedures.

There is no mention of a mother or father travelling on the same boat, although a 46-year-old married woman, Pierta Saghabeni, is next to them on the passenger manifest and came from the same town. Further research of the Ellis Island immigration records and the ship's manifests reveals a Giovanni Sinatra arriving in America on 27 March, 1902. This 26-year-old married man travelled on the *Calabria* from Naples and came from Termini, in Sicily. He travelled with a Michelle Sansone, a married woman, aged 23, who also came from Termini. Could they possibly have been married and travelled nine months ahead of their children to get settled? Neither of these names appears to relate to John and Rosa Sinatra who Nancy says are Frank's grandparents. To add to the mystery, every other source names Frank Sinatra's maternal grandparents as John and Rosa. Some claim that John was an Americanization of Giovanni. According to Nancy Sinatra, Frank's mother's family name is Garavente. Nancy says the misspelling (Garavanti) on the birth certificate

arose because of a non-Italian clerk mistaking the pronunciation. Natalie Catherine Garavente was born around 1895 and travelled to America with her parents when she was just two months old. Other sources report that her middle name was Della, hence the derivation "Dolly". Nancy Sinatra does not definitively say when the family arrived. She contents herself with the fact that Natalie was the daughter of a well-educated lithographer from Genoa.

The records from Ellis Island reveal no Garavente family or similar arriving from Genoa around the mid- to late 1890s. A number of men and women named Garaventa travelled from Genoa during the 1890s, but none appears to have travelled with children and there are few couples among the passenger lists.

To add a twist to the tale, in 1941 Frank filled out a form for the police when at MGM Studios in which he stated that his mother was born in Hoboken (rather than arriving in the United States as a young child). Frank also stated that he was born in 1917, even though his birth certificate indicates 1915.

The young first-generation Italian-Americans, Anthony (known as Marty) Sinatra and Natalie (known as Dolly) Garavente were Frank's parents. Exactly when both families arrived in America at the turn of the century is unknown. What is known, however, is that both families settled in Hoboken, New Jersey, and there Frank's parents met and fell in love.

> 66 We know from experience that records of entry of many aliens into the United States contain assumed or incorrect names and other errors. 99

CLEAN BILL OF HEALTH
Immigrants who arrived as steerage or third-class passengers had to undergo a health inspection before an entry visa would be granted.

HOBOKEN AND LITTLE ITALY

Like so many places in the United States, and particularly on the Eastern Seaboard, Hoboken is a city whose name appears to have originated from Europe. The European Hoboken was an industrial city on the Scheldt River in northern Belgium, which became part of Antwerp in 1983. It is possible that the Flemish people who emigrated to the United States had an influence in the naming of the city.

When Henry Hudson sailed up the river that bears his name in 1609, a crew member made a note in the ship's log of a high rock. Later, Dutch settlers called the rock "Hoebuck", meaning high bluff. To Native American Indians the area was "Hopoghan Hackingh", or "Land of the Tobacco Pipe", as they carved pipes from the local rock. Then in 1658 the Dutch Governor of Manhattan, Peter Stuyvesant, bought the land between the Hackensack and Hudson rivers. In 1784, Colonel John Stevens, Colonial Treasurer of New Jersey, bought the land at a public auction, and it was Stevens who decided to call the area Hoboken.

The town quickly became a resort for well-heeled New Yorkers, and by 1820 the waterfront area was transformed into a recreation area. As many as 20,000 New Yorkers would sometimes make the trip for Sunday picnics.

HOBOKEN BROWNSTONES IN THE 1920S

"*I came to America because I heard the streets were paved with gold. When I got there I found three things. First, the streets weren't paved with gold. Second, they weren't paved at all, and third, I was expected to pave them.*"

ANONYMOUS ITALIAN IMMIGRANT

ON THE WATERFRONT
Hoboken's dockyards, facing the West Side piers of Manhattan; this was later the setting for the film On The Waterfront *(1954) which reflected the corrupt influence of the Mob and the unions who controlled the dockyards.*

Twenty-five years later, the first organized baseball game took place in Hoboken. The wealthy Astor family built a summerhouse on Washington and Second Street, making Hoboken fashionable long before it was functional. Charles Dickens wrote about his visit to Hoboken in 1842: "Then there lay stretched out before us, to the right, confused heaps of buildings, with here and there a spire or steeple, looking down upon the herd below; and here and there, again, a cloud of lazy smoke; and in the foreground a forest of ships' masts, cheery with flapping sails and waving flags. Crossing from among them to the opposite shore, were steam ferry-boats laden with people, coaches, horses, wagons, baskets, boxes: crossed and recrossed by other ferry-boats: all travelling to and fro: and never idle." (*American Notes*)

John Stevens, the city's "founder", was an amazing man whose interests ranged from engineering to town planning. He obtained one of America's first patents for a steam engine, and in 1804 his ship, the *Little Juliana*, steamed across the Hudson between New York City and Hoboken. Four years on, his steam-powered *Phoenix*, an ocean-going vessel, was launched. Soon his attention switched to trains, and in 1825 he designed the first steam locomotive in the US, which operated on a circular track in the city. By the time he died in 1838, Hoboken was establishing itself as a transport centre. Development was rapid in the mid-18th century, and under Stevens's Hoboken Land & Improvement Company the grid street plan formed. On 28 March, 1855, Hoboken became a city in its own right.

The city expanded rapidly between 1860 and 1910, and its proximity to Ellis Island made it a convenient place for many immigrants to make their home. The first

major ethnic group to decide to settle in Hoboken were the Germans, and their mother tongue soon became the dominant language in the city. Next came the Irish, and then the Italians – including the Garavente and Sinatra families. Other nationalities that settled in Hoboken included Yugoslavs, Greeks, Belgians, Dutch, Syrians, Spanish, and Turks.

The proximity of Hoboken to New York, just a short boat ride across the Hudson, was perfect, and before long the waterfront became a major transatlantic port for shipping lines, including North German Lloyd and Holland America. Two years after Frank Sinatra was born, the city became the embarkation point for the American Expeditionary Forces heading to Europe in World War I.

NEW YORK, NEW YORK
A turn of the century panoramic view of Manhattan and Brooklyn as seen from New Jersey. Hoboken and Jersey City are in the foreground; the newly-constructed Brooklyn Bridge in the distance.

Over three million soldiers left America for Europe from the port, giving rise to the slogan: "Heaven, Hell or Hoboken… by Christmas."

THE ITALIAN COMMUNITY

Any immigrant arriving in the United States faced a huge challenge. The changes and adjustments that had to be made in order to settle in the new country were enormous, and for the Italians it was no different from anyone else.

At the peak of immigration at the beginning of the 20th century, ethnic quarters formed in nearly every town where there was a sizeable number of arrivals. Dozens of cities had their "Little Italy", home to Italian immigrants. Hoboken was no different.

The Italian communities were largely self-contained and inward-looking, and a reliance on their own culture became something of a safety net; they were mistrustful of new ways. They relied on their methods of doing things, in particular how they found work. The *padrone* system, in which the boss found employment for the workers, transferred from Italy to America with ease. It was of course a racket. Three principle

THE BUSTLE OF LITTLE ITALY
Mulberry Street, in New York City, around 1900. This was typical of many close-knit Italian communities in cities throughout the eastern part of the United States.

factions exerted influence over the local population: leaders of local commerce, the Catholic Church, and the *padrones* — of which the last two, as everyone knew, held the real power.

The Italian communities gained strength throughout America with their direct and obvious links to the Catholic Church in Rome. It was not only the Italian immigrants, of course: Poles, Slovaks, and Hungarians also joined the American Catholic Church in great numbers. The strength of the Irish Catholic lobby was also significant. However, the language issue meant that Italians frequently decided to build and congregate in their own churches, rather than worship at the English-language Irish churches.

The *padrone* system was an integral part of the culture of the extended family that Italians brought with them to the New World. Normally, it was a relatively harmless form of nepotistic self-help. However, for some, and at its most extreme, it transformed itself into the Mafia.

The organization has roots that go back much further than the period at the end of the 19th century that witnessed the real thrust in migration from southern Italy to America. *Mafia* is a Sicilian word for bragging and specifically a hostility towards the law. For two thousand years, Sicily had been an occupied country. Over the years, the feudal nature of the island led to the formation of "secret societies" that ran virtually every aspect of life. The Mafia exerted its influence, whether it was on a grand political scale or against individuals.

In the 1920s, the Italian dictator Mussolini subdued the Sicilian Mafia in order to consolidate his own powerbase on the island. The only escape route really was a boat trip to the United States – and so business meetings were now held in the close-knit ethnic areas of New York, Chicago, Philadelphia, and further afield.

One immediate problem faced by the early Italian gangs was the fact that the Irish criminal fraternity had their own protection in place, as most police in New York and the surrounding area were Irish.

The American Mafia – the Mob – as we know it today did not really become a reality until the end of Prohibition in 1933. Up until then it had been localized within districts and communities. Local organizations dealt with local situations, which might sometimes have strayed over into neighbouring territories. Turf wars and gangland killings in cities throughout America became common as the gangs fought for supremacy.

During the Prohibition, a period of criminal consolidation, when gangsters such as Al Capone ruled the streets, operating techniques were fine-tuned, and tensions and rivalries grew, giving rise to gang warfare. Inevitably bars, whether they were run by Irish, Jews, or Italians, became the focal point for much of the crime. But whatever the strength of other ethnic criminal elements, it was Italians, and among them Sicilians in particular, who came to dominate the underworld.

In spite of its criminal nature, the Mafia was often respected by the public as much as it was feared. That respect is one of the main reasons for the longevity of organized crime in America. By paying off police, judges, and politicians, the Mafia maintained the balance of power. In its perverse way, it kept the peace, curried favour, solved local disputes, and effected the age-old *padrone* system.

MARTY, THE PRIZEFIGHTER

Hoboken in the early years of the 20th century must have been quite a place. Old photographs show a city with its fair share of smart and affluent buildings, with the bustling and dirty waterfront forming its eastern boundary. The docks and port facilities provided much of Hoboken's economic wealth, as well as directly or indirectly employing many of the 70,000 people who were living there by 1910.

Nancy Sinatra says that Marty's father, Giovanni (John) Sinatra, like many immigrants at that time, never did learn to speak English. His first job was as a boilermaker, and later he worked in the American Pencil Company. The German immigrant community dominated the city in which the Garavente and Sinatra families made their home. Hoboken had its own German newspaper, there were *biergartens* (Jerome Kern's 1929 musical, *Sweet Adeline*, was set in one of the city's beer gardens), and the Germans were definitely at the top of the social heap in the first decade of the 20th century. This state of affairs came to an end with World War I, when natural suspicions removed the German community from the top spot, making the Irish the new power in Hoboken.

Marty Sinatra's first job appears to have been at a cobbler's. He took up prizefighting around the same time, and apparently Dolly Garavente even sneaked out of her house disguised as a man to watch him, since in those days women were banned from such events. Marty fought Dolly's brother Dominic (known as "Champ") although no one is quite sure who won, because both men claimed victory until they died. Nancy describes her grandfather as "quiet and gentle" – not ideal attributes for a prizefighter. There are conflicting stories as to exactly how long Marty continued to fight, but all the time he did he fought under the pseudonym of Marty O'Brien (the name of his manager). The reason for this was simple: back then in Hoboken you were better off being Irish than Italian. Marty, like his son in later years, hated to be called "a WOP", a term derived from the immigration process when the letters WOP on a ship's manifest meant "without papers". It was also derived from the southern Italian dialect word *guappo*, meaning a braggart.

HOBOKEN POPULATION

When Frank Sinatra was born in Hoboken, the city's population was at its highest. As it declined, so its affluence grew.

1855	7,000
1865	15,000
1900	59,000 (20% Germans)
1910	70,324
1920	68,166
1930	59,261
1940	50,115
2000	38,577 (due to redefinition of city limits)

RAGPICKERS' ROW
The tenement conditions, in which many immigrants lived on Manhattan, were cramped and deprived. Hoboken, on the Jersey shore, was slightly more salubrious.

1861 - 1939

PENCIL FACTORY
Franks's father Marty earned $11 a week in the American Pencil Company factory.

MARTY AND DOLLY SINATRA
Against her parent's wishes Dolly married Marty Sinatra on 14 February, 1913 in the City Hall, Jersey City. This photograph was taken at the second ceremony, attended by both families.

Precisely when Dolly and Marty first met is not known, but what is abundantly clear is that Dolly's parents were against their relationship from the outset. Calling himself Marty O'Brien did not fool Mr and Mrs Garavente. Genoese did not marry Sicilians; and they thought the Sinatras were as far below them in the Italian pecking order as it was possible to be.

Despite her parents' opposition, the romance blossomed and Dolly and Marty were soon talking of marriage, an early indication of Dolly's single-mindedness. The Garaventes were so set against the idea they refused to host the wedding – a very strong stance, considering the family values of Italian culture. The couple's solution was simply to marry anyway, and they chose Valentine's Day 1913 for their civil ceremony at the City Hall in Jersey City. Marty declared himself to be an "athlete" on his marriage certificate. Dolly's family bowed to the inevitable (another indication of her forceful personality?) and a second ceremony took place. The couple began their married life as one of eight families in a four-storey tenement at 415 Monroe Street in central Hoboken.

HOME SWEET HOME

When Frank first found fame in the 1940s, many stories were circulated about where he was born and brought up, and they all had a tendency to paint a rather dour picture of his home. While Hoboken was far from paradise, it was certainly not a bad place in which to live. For many of the immigrants, including the Sinatras, it was better than life in the old country. While Hoboken's Little Italy was not as good looking, or as affluent, as the districts where the Germans and the Irish lived, it was home; and perhaps more importantly, it was a community.

The tenement in which Marty and Dolly lived was torn down years ago, as were many similar buildings in Hoboken's Little Italy. The Sinatras shared a bathroom in the hallway and had cold running water, but they also had the comparative luxury of several rooms. Many families had to live, sleep, and eat in just one room.

In addition to being tiny (she weighed just 90 lb and stood less than 5 ft tall), Dolly Sinatra had two other physical qualities that set her apart from most other residents of Little Italy: she had blonde hair and blue eyes. This allowed her to pass herself off as Irish, as "Mrs O'Brien", when she wanted to, which had definite social advantages. She also benefited from the fact that she spoke all the Italian dialects, another distinct advantage in the class-ridden Italian community.

Reports vary as to just how long Marty carried on fighting, and how significant any prize money was to the family income. At least one source said he fought up until 1926, when a broken wrist forced his retirement. Given the fact that Marty was asthmatic, it may well be questionable that he would still be fighting in his mid-30s.

Whether he was working as a boilermaker, chauffeur (as it says on Frank's birth certificate), or at some other odd jobs, it appears that the family never went hungry, as Marty's mother ran a small grocery store and kept the family supplied with a few extras.

A STAR IS BORN

Dolly fell pregnant and Frank was born on 12 December, 1915 at the Monroe Street apartment. Given Dolly's small frame, it was amazing that her baby weighed in at a massive 13 lb 7 oz! The birth was difficult not just because of baby Sinatra's size but also because he was in the breech position. The doctor used forceps and damaged the baby's neck, cheek, and ear, as well as puncturing his eardrum. A further complication was that the baby wasn't breathing. Nancy says that his grandmother, an experienced midwife, held him under the cold running water until he breathed his first breath. Interestingly, she says that her grandmother Rose did this, and elsewhere she refers to Marty's mother as Rosa. From this we can probably assume that Rose was Mrs Garavente. Such were Dolly's problems with her son's birth that she was never able to have any more children.

On 2 April, 1916, four months after Frank's birth, Marty was at St Francis Holy Roman Catholic Church for the christening. Dolly was not well enough to attend. The godparents were to be Frank Garrick and Anna Gatto. Frank worked for the *Jersey Observer* and his uncle Thomas was a Hoboken police captain; good connections in a city where connections mattered.

A story that has circulated for years claims that there was some confusion at the christening, and that the priest, instead of naming the baby by his parents' chosen name of Martin, called him Frank after his godfather. Some have speculated that it was a sign of Marty's weakness that he couldn't speak up when the priest got his own son's name wrong, yet nothing could be further from the truth.

Checking the "Certificate and record of birth", it states "Francis Sinestro", although some people believe it says "Frank" not "Francis". While the clerk may have recorded the surname as "Sinestro" instead of "Sinatra", he

THE FIRST
Frank with grandma Rose shortly after he was born. It is the first picture of the man who was one of the 20th century's most photographed people.

certainly didn't confuse "Francis" and "Martin". This certificate was issued five days after Frank was born, and four months before the christening. At the end of World War II, Dolly and Frank, in an effort to clear up the confusion over the birth certificate, had a new set of papers drawn up. On this form, "Frank Sinestro" has become "Francis A. Sinatra", "Dollie" Garavanti becomes "Natalie", and Anthony gets his middle "M" for Marty. Interestingly, Nancy Sinatra says that this is the last time that anyone will "fail to recognize the name of Francis Albert Sinatra", yet there is no mention of "Albert", just that rather

BABY FRANK
The photograph is taken from the side where the scars made by the doctor's forceps are not visible.

> 66Heaven, hell or Hoboken… by Christmas99
>
> WORLD WAR I SLOGAN

non-committal initial A. For a man who lived so openly and so long in the glare of the publicity spotlight, there is still some mystery to Frank's early life.

HOBOKEN GOES TO WAR

One year after Frank's christening, the United States officially entered World War I, and Hoboken, more than almost any other American city, was affected by what became known as "the war to end all wars". President Woodrow Wilson signed the declaration of war at the White House on the afternoon of 6 April, 1917. From the start of the conflict in Europe three years earlier, Wilson had struggled to maintain the United States' military neutrality. Involvement became inevitable, however, when Germany announced that it would attack, without warning, all ships, whether enemy or neutral, found near British waters. America was further threatened when a telegram was intercepted between the German

Foreign Minister and the Mexican Foreign Office, in which a military alliance was proposed. The German ambassador to Washington left America with his staff on 14 February, 1917; they sailed from Hoboken aboard the SS *Frederik VIII*.

Between 1914 and 1917, 17 German ships were immobilized at Hoboken piers under harbour neutrality acts. One of these, the symbolically named *Amerika*, was seized and turned over to the Navy for conversion to a troop transport ship. Originally completed in October 1905, the ship spent the first nine years of her life on the Hamburg–America Line service between Germany and the United States, mostly sailing to Hoboken. Then, in late October 1917, she was renamed USS *America* and began active war work, carrying troops across the Atlantic to France. On 15 October, 1918, just before departing for another trip, the transport ship sank alongside her pier in Hoboken. The 1st Infantry Division is the oldest

LIBERTY BONDS
The United States Government needed to raise money to help the war effort, and did so under the banner of "Help Win the War." During World War I, Boy Scouts sold 2,350,977 Liberty Loan bonds, totalling $147.8 million.

continuously serving division in the United States Army. It was enacted into the US Army as Headquarters, First Expeditionary Division, on 24 May, 1917. Three weeks later, the first units sailed from Hoboken to France.

By mid-1917, the government had seized Hoboken's piers for military use. While this was clearly necessary, it had the effect of cutting the city's tax revenues by hundreds of thousands of dollars almost overnight, though the city did finally receive some recompense decades later. The citizens of Hoboken were also dealt a more personal blow: all bars within half a mile of the port were closed, so that, in effect, Prohibition came early to Hoboken. Further, the German parts of the city were placed under martial law, and many Germans were sent to Ellis Island, where they were interned for the duration of the war; Germans left Hoboken in their thousands.

ANXIOUS INVESTORS, NEW YORK, 1931

A LIFE LESS ORDINARY

Frank's childhood in Hoboken has been the subject of much conjecture, and reliable sources are difficult to come by, with recollections clouded by the years that have passed since. Although relatively unscathed by the Depression, the Sinatras were directly and indirectly affected by the Volstead Act of 1919, which outlawed the sale of alcohol across much of the United States.

Mobsters, bootleggers, gamblers, Tommy guns, sharp suits, and speakeasies are just some of the things that come to mind when we think of America during the Prohibition era of the 1920s and early 1930s. In fact, Prohibition was a long-gestating notion advocated first by the US Temperance Movement, and taken up in 1869 by the Prohibition Party.

ALCOHOL OUTLAWED

The 18th Amendment to the US Constitution was eventually proposed in 1917 and became law in 1919. Adopted by every state except for Connecticut and

> 66 Alcohol may be man's worst enemy, but the bible says love your enemy. 99
>
> FRANK, MANY YEARS LATER

"This great Nation will endure as it has endured, will revive and will prosper. So first of all, let me assert my firm belief that the only thing that we have to fear is fear itself — nameless, unreasoning, unjustified terror, which paralyses needed efforts to convert retreat into advance."

PRESIDENT ROOSEVELT'S INAUGURAL ADDRESS, WASHINGTON D.C., SUNDAY 4 MARCH, 1933

Rhode Island, the amendment limited the production of alcohol, and the Volstead Act was brought in to enforce compliance. On 29 January, 1920, Prohibition became law. Illegal trafficking in and production of alcohol (bootlegging) became a huge underground industry over the following decade, one that was controlled in the cities by organized criminal gangs and in rural areas by small-time crooks, who ran their own illicit stills.

By 1926, the illegal alcohol trade was estimated to be worth $3.6 billion. Bootlegging was at the heart of the criminal underworld, and was used as a means to branch out into other lucrative criminal, and non-criminal, activities. By October 1928, the Mayor of New York was becoming increasingly concerned at the lawlessness and gangsterism that Prohibition generated. Organized

DOWN THE DRAIN
Law enforcement officers destroyed shipments of illicit alcohol.

gang leaders across the United States, particularly Al Capone in Chicago, were becoming increasingly powerful and rich as a result of their activities. (Capone is reported to have made $60 million in one year from alcohol sales alone.)

Eventually, a presidential committee concluded that although alcohol consumption had originally been reduced, levels had risen again, and crime was rife: Prohibition was clearly not working. On 5 December, 1933, it was repealed by the 21st Amendment to the US Constitution.

AN ITALIAN ANOMALY

Much that has been written about Frank's childhood is in fact a case of history being rewritten as Frank first became a star, and then a legend. Frank himself helped to refashion elements of his own story. When this is weighed alongside the recollections of "close personal friends", often dispensed many years later, it is clear to see that there is a great deal of scope for confusion regarding what Frank's early years in the 1920s were really like. One thing is obvious, however: Frank was very different from most other children in his neighbourhood, because he was an Italian rarity – an only child. Many years later, he told his daughter Nancy after she had her first child, "I hope you'll consider having another baby. It was very lonely for me. Very lonely."

By 1920, Italians outnumbered Germans in Hoboken and the infant Frank grew up in a household that was in many ways like that of any other Italian family. His

THE KING
Frank, aged 9, shown here with his unidentified Queen, was crowned the May King of Hoboken.

GOING DRY
During Prohibition, many restaurants and clubs ran illegal backroom drinking parlours.

1861 1939

NICE SLACKS
Frank and his mother, Dolly, on holiday possibly in the Catskill Mountains sometime around 1928.

66 They didn't have much time for Frankie. I think he was always underfoot. 99

ONE OF FRANK'S COUSINS, REFERRING TO HIS PARENTS

father was scratching a living prizefighting and working in the docks. With the onset of Prohibition, Marty also did jobs for the bootleggers.

Dolly worked in a sweet factory, dipping chocolates and marking them as to their flavour, but she had also begun to take an interest in politics. Whether it was a heartfelt interest or one that was born out of the sense of opportunity that being well connected offered is unclear. She became the organizer for the Democratic Party in the ward where the Sinatras lived. The Mayor of Hoboken was Patrick Griffin, who would later be replaced by Gustav Back and then, in 1930, by Bernard McFeely. Both Griffin and McFeely were Irish, and Dolly was particularly close to McFeely, whose power base was extended through his family. His brother was the Superintendent of Schools, while another brother was Chief of Police – useful allies in a small, politically motivated city. There has been talk of Dolly wanting to run for mayor and of Marty telling young Frank he had to do something "to stop his mother". This seems a wildly exaggerated story; being connected was one thing, power was something else.

Dolly was also a midwife and an abortionist. As Frank found fame, there have been things written that feign shock at this illegal activity, but it was probably a lot more common than we now like to think. Before the 1960s and the introduction of the contraceptive pill, a practical approach took precedence over pregnancies. Many people have said that Dolly was a decent woman who did more good than harm, but in politically-charged Hoboken, with its ethnic rivalries, it was unthinkable that anyone would have universal appeal, least of all strong-willed Dolly.

One aspect of Dolly that everyone agrees upon is her use of bad language – she was someone who seemed capable of introducing a swearword into practically any sentence she uttered. Hoboken was no upscale place, and so for people to comment on Dolly's language must have meant that it was particularly colourful. It would be yet another influence on Frank himself. She was a character, a dominant character, and one who clearly liked to be seen as important. Her influence on Frank has been hotly debated; but since he was an only child, and a son at that, it is hardly surprising.

HOLIDAY TIME
Frank sitting in front of his guitar-playing mother on vacation in the Catskill Mountains in 1925 with family and friends. It was the traditional way, and a traditional place, to get away.

As Dolly Sinatra's influence in the neighbourhood began to grow, so did the family's standing. Details are vague, but at some point during the 1920s Marty opened a pub, which he named "Marty O'Brien's" after his boxing pseudonym. It may have stemmed from Marty's earlier involvement with bootleggers. "He was one of the tough guys," said Frank in 1986. "His job was to follow trucks with booze so they weren't highjacked." Frank says that he was three or four when his father did this. This seems unlikely, since Prohibition didn't start until he was four so perhaps it was some time in the early days of Prohibition when the Sinatras opened their bar on the corner of Fourth Street and Jefferson. Dolly's connections were obviously good enough to put her and Marty in this position, although it is not clear whether the bar was theirs or if they simply managed or fronted it for someone else. These were unusual times and the whole spectre of organized crime was at the forefront of the illegal booze business. Dolly used the bar as an "office" for her various activities, and the bar obviously improved the couple's position within the Italian-American community of Hoboken.

In the summer of 1927, Marty began working at the Hoboken Fire Department. Dolly's connections probably helped to get him the job and then almost certainly secured his promotion to captain – a most unusual thing for an Italian in what was an Irish-dominated sector. Around this time, the Sinatras moved to a three-bedroom apartment in Park Avenue. This was only about ten blocks from Monroe Street, but it was a lifetime away from the hustle and bustle of the tenement lifestyle that young Frank had grown used to.

FRANKIE GROWS UP IN HOBOKEN

Frank's childhood is a mess of contradictions. There are as many different views as to how tough it was, how bad Frank was, how good he was, how neglected, or how much he was doted upon, as there are books on Frank Sinatra. One thing that practically everyone agrees on, however, is the fact that little Frank spent less time with his parents than he did with his grandmother and aunts. "They didn't have much time for Frankie, I think he was always underfoot", said one of Frank's cousins. But he thought Frank "was warm, he wanted friendship. Frankie was really a soft, kind boy." Another childhood friend with years of hindsight said, "What's with this 'poor little Frankie' crap? He was tough as nails." So what is the truth? Frank was no different from any other child growing up then. He was good, bad, weak, and strong; he had fun, he cried. It was an exceptional childhood in only one way, his lack of

THE TALKIES

THE JAZZ SINGER WAS NOT THE FIRST SOUND FILM BUT IT WAS THE ONE THAT STARTED IT ALL; TO PARAPHRASE AL JOLSEN, "YOU AIN'T HEARD NOTHIN' YET".

WARNER BROTHERS' "supreme triumph", as the film was called, opened in the US on 6 October, 1927 and starred Al Jolsen as a black-faced minstrel. It became the first "talkie" to be shown in Britain, opening at the Piccadilly Theatre in London's West End on 27 September, 1928.

Not everyone thought talkies had a future. Charlie Chaplin gave them three years, saying they were a passing novelty. "Who the hell wants to hear actors talk?" was an even more scathing put-down by H M Warner of Warner Brothers Pictures. The *Film Spectator* took a more pragmatic view, "If I was an actor with a squeaky voice I would worry."

PARTIAL TALKIE
Largely silent, the film included a few talking sequences but, significantly, featured musical numbers.

siblings. Frank was undoubtedly taunted by other children because he had no brothers to stand by him when times got rough. Although there are stories of him fighting back when he was called a wop or some other ethnic slur, he was probably not that tough a child. But it was in these formative years that much of his character was created, notably his determination, and his self-sufficiency – first and foremost Frank was a loner.

There are tales of Frank indulging in petty thieving from "Five and Dime" stores. Others say he had nothing to do with it. Frank himself, many years later, said, "We started hooking candy from the corner store. Then little things from the Five and Dime, then change from cash registers, and finally we were stealing bicycles." True or false? If he did, he probably never got caught.

DRESSED FOR SUCCESS

The move to Park Avenue pushed the Sinatras up the social scale and young Frankie out of his own "neighbourhood". The taunts got worse as he got older, too. Apparently, Dolly had dressed Frank in "Little Lord Fauntleroy" suits from a very young age and the trend to spend money on Frank's clothes continued unabated. It is said that he even had his own charge account at a local menswear shop. This apparently gave rise to the nickname "Slacksey O'Brien" in recognition of his prodigious collection of trousers. Yet when people said that Frank was better dressed than other kids in his neighbourhood, it all came down to the only-child syndrome. What Italian family with an average of five children (sometimes ten or more) had the kind of spare money to clothe their children in such an extravagant way?

In the US, the cradle of baseball, it is said that Dolly founded a baseball team for Frank to play in, calling it "The Turks Palace". There is a picture of Frank wearing his baseball shirt, with "Turks" on the front. According to some people, this was his street gang's name, though this could be another story embellished with hindsight.

In every book written about Frank there is little said about his schooling, for one simple reason: Frank and school did not get on particularly well. In fact, it seems that he skipped a lot of school, which was not an unusual thing to do at the time. (In the New York area, Italian children were the most likely to play truant of any ethnic grouping.) After elementary school, Frank attended David E Rue Junior High School in 1928. Nevertheless, his diploma, issued on 28 January, 1931, shows that 'Francis Albert Sinatra' completed his course.

HIGH HOPES
1927/8 Frank aged about 12 in his baseball gear, naturally enough, acting out his mother's aspirations for Frank's success in the national game.

THE DEPRESSION

"PRICES OF STOCKS CRASH IN HEAVY LIQUIDATION, TOTAL DROP OF BILLIONS", "PAPER LOSS $4,000,000,000", "2,600,000 SHARES SOLD IN THE FINAL HOUR, RECORD DECLINE"… THE HEADLINES COULD NOT ANTICIPATE THE IMPACT OF THE WALL STREET CRASH.

To HAVE LIVED THROUGH the Depression in America must have been a life-changing experience that would affect aspects of one's thinking forever. The Depression touched, and in some cases devastated, every stratum of society, but as always it was the poor at the bottom of the heap who had nowhere to go, neither up nor further down. The very words "Wall Street Crash" still create a feeling of unease and impending doom. These fears can be traced to the period that followed the first crash on 24 October, 1929. What was undeniable is the fact that the Sinatras felt the effects of the Depression far less than many, although they like everyone bore witness to the fact that it impacted on every aspect of life – from business to entertainment. The poet W H Auden described the 1930s as "A low dishonest decade." The US economy had gone into recession some six months before the October crash, yet no one forecast its severity or even dared to imagine the consequences. In fact the Depression lasted for much of the 1930s, becoming the longest and most severe ever experienced by the Western world.

The fall in the value of American stocks and shares was catastrophic; by 1932 they were worth 20 percent of their 1929 value. While individuals suffered most, banks and other financial institutions were for a long while in free fall. By 1933 nearly half of America's 25,000 banks had collapsed, at the same time almost 30 percent of the working population were jobless. Collapse on this scale produced a nationwide loss of confidence, and led to drastically reduced spending. It was more a case of "panic not-buying" with spending on non-essentials cut to a minimum, with even essentials becoming luxuries. As a consequence, production fell too; by 1932 output had fallen by 54 percent. The result was a level of industrial, commercial, and personal misery that has never been repeated in the developed world.

The US President, Herbert Hoover, publicly underestimated the impact of the Depression. In 1930 he told Americans to remain confident, "The fundamental business of this country, that is, production and distribution, is on a sound and prosperous basis". Hoover's opponent in the 1932 Presidential election was Franklin D Roosevelt. What FDR offered the electorate was short on specifics; although he had one key advantage… he was not Herbert Hoover. Roosevelt's big idea was the 'New Deal', a series of social and economic reforms and job-creation schemes. While Roosevelt may not have ended the Depression he was credited by many with saving their job, their home, even their lives. No American President since has so dominated the US political landscape: Roosevelt, re-elected three times, died in office in April 1945 aged 63.

The impact of Roosevelt's social and economic reforms during the 1930s came to an end after the United States entered World War II in December 1941. However, the war economy of the next few years set the US on a course of rapid growth which led to the "boom years" of the late 1940s and 1950s which transformed the US into the largest and the most powerful economy in the world.

ON THE BREADLINE
A queue of unemployed men and women receiving soup and slices of bread in an outdoor breadline during the Great Depression in Los Angeles, California.

ONE CAREFUL OWNER
Walter Thorton offers his flashy roadster for $100 after he lost everything in the Stock Market Crash of 1929. The glamour of the 1920s rapidly turned into the desperation of the 1930s.

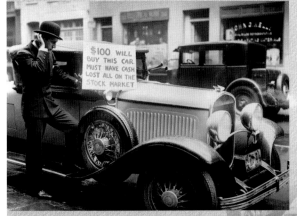

NO PARTICULAR PLACE TO GO
An evicted couple sits on the kerb surrounded by their furniture and belongings during the Great Depression, Los Angeles, California, 1937. The New Deal did not solve everyone's problems.

PLAYING HOOKY, HOBOKEN SHIPYARDS, 1920S

"What are the band conductors seeking? I think they want, and will eventually get, a straight singer who will be able to moderate his voice down to crooning and strike something between the present 'whisper' and a more mezzo-forte tone ... I consider Crosby the best link in the 'chain of crooners'."

KENNETH WYNNE, *MELODY MAKER*, APRIL 1934

SCHOOLING OR SINGING

During 1931, Frank went to A J Demarest High School, where he and schoolwork continued their nodding acquaintance. He spent much of his time impersonating singers he heard on the radio and talked of wanting to be one himself. In the light of events, it is impossible to be certain if this was just a typical childhood dream or a burning ambition.

Singing, whether in class or to impress his friends, played an increasing role in Frank's life. He had been in the choir of St Francis Church since the age of 11; how devoted a chorister he was has never been ascertained.

It appears that Frank was at High School for just 47 days, making it probable that he was expelled. It was possible that his parents didn't even know of his expulsion. According to his cousin, "He played hooky for a whole year before Aunt Dolly ever knew he was out of school." After his early exit from Demarest, Frank enrolled at Drake

SEAT OF LEARNING
A J Demarest High School was not a place with which Frank became that well acquainted.

FERRY ACROSS THE HUDSON
The Hoboken ferry terminal was for every New Jersey resident, the adolescent Frank among them, a gateway to the glamour of Manhattan.

Business School in Hoboken, but this lasted just a term and soon he was out looking for a job. In later years, it has been said that Marty told Frank "You have to get a real job – no music business." This again may be a subtle rewrite of what actually happened.

Listening to the crooners on the radio inspired Frank. At first it was Rudy Vallee and Russ Columbo, even before Bing Crosby, who fired Frank's dreams, but a career as a singer was nothing more than a fantasy at this time. Shortly after Frank's schooling came to an end, the family were on the move again, clearly bucking the trend during the Depression years. They went to 841 Garden Street, a three-storey, four-bedroom home – with a real dining room! While the Sinatras may have struggled with the payments, it was a demonstration to the world that they were doggedly moving on up; Garden Street was in the Irish part of town.

KEEPING THE DAY JOB

It seems that one of Dolly's brothers got Frank a job in Teijent and Lang's shipyard. According to Frank, it was hell: his job was to catch white-hot rivets while hanging over a four-storey shaft. On the third day, he got really scared. "I was hanging onto that rope and that burning rivet went by me like a bullet, singeing my shoulder." That was enough, Frank quit and began making the trip over to New York each day to unload boxes for the book publisher Lyons and Carnahan on 16th Street. But soon it was back to the docks, this time to work for United Fruit Lines.

Frank's lack of steady employment exasperated Marty, and he threw 16-year-old Frankie out of the house to fend for himself. Despite Marty's own lack of formal schooling, he was desperate for his son to do the right thing and get an education. "My old man thought that anyone who wanted to go into the music business must be a bum," Frank told writer Robin Douglas-Home in 1962. Frank's lack of ability or interest in a proper career, as well as his ambitions in other directions, were all behind his failure to hold down a steady job. For a while he lived in New York City to avoid any further problems at home.

By late 1932, Frank was back home in Hoboken, and although a steady job still eluded him, he had began to sing on some nights with little groups of musicians in various Hoboken bars and clubs. He was on his way, probably unsure which way, but for Frank anywhere was better than where he was.

According to Frank, he was working with little combination bands by late 1932 and into 1933. "I was making nothing, but it was great experience. I was using a megaphone like Rudy Vallee, and guys would throw pennies and try and get them in my mouth." While this was valuable experience, it was not moving Frank along as quickly as he wanted. He borrowed $65 from his parents (some say his mother paid for it out of her part-time abortion business) and bought a small portable PA system. He also invested in sheet music of popular songs. Having his own sheet music

> **"**You have to get a real job – no music business.**"**
>
> MARTY SINATRA,
> AFTER FRANK QUIT BUSINESS SCHOOL

RUDY VALLEE

"Heigh-Ho everybody, it's Rudy Vallee …"

RUDY VALLEE, 1901–1986

RUDY VALLEE, BORN HERBERT PRIOR VALLEE IN 1901 IN VERMONT, WAS ONE OF THE FIRST CROONERS. HE BEGAN EVERY PERFORMANCE WITH THE IMMORTAL WORDS "HEIGH-HO EVERYBODY".

He learned to play the alto saxophone and clarinet before joining the navy. Later, after going to University (Yale), he went to England and played in the Savoy Havana Band at the Savoy Hotel on London's Strand. His first record came out in early 1921 but he came to prominence on returning to America. He was famous for singing through a megaphone and adopted his famous "Heigh-Ho everybody" introduction from playing at New York's Heigh-Ho Club. With the help of the radio, the *Rudy Vallee Hour* attracted well over 100 million listeners at its peak and, after his appearance in the film *The Vagabond Lover*, Rudy became a sensation.

Rudy continued to appear in films during the 1930s (he made 33 in all), including *Gold Diggers in Paris*. He continued with films in the 1940s although his role shifted from the romantic lead to a more of a character actor. During World War II he led a Coast Guard orchestra and had a No 1 hit in 1943 with 'As Time Goes By', a song he had first recorded in 1931. After the war, Hollywood, radio, and TV had the benefits of his talent. In 1961 Rudy stared in the smash Broadway hit, *How To Succeed In Business Without Even Trying*; the show ran for four years. He continued to appear in films until the mid-1970s, and performed almost up to his death in 1986.

A saxophone that belonged to Rudy Vallee was sold to a Little Rock attorney as a gift for the then Governor of Arkansas, Bill Clinton.

BEST-KNOWN RECORDINGS
'Honey' 1929
'Stein Sing
(University of Maine)' 1930
'Brother Can You Spare
A Dime' 1932
'Vieni, Vieni' 1937

1861 1939

NEW SKYLINE
In late 1930 the view
of New York City from
Hoboken changed when
the Empire State
Building was built.
The 1,245 ft tall,
102-floor skyscraper
was opened on 1
May, 1931 by
President Hoover.

NEW SKYLINE
In late 1930 the view of New York City from Hoboken changed when the Empire State Building was built. The 1,245 ft tall, 102-floor skyscraper was opened on 1 May, 1931 by President Hoover.

gave him an advantage over other singers: "If a local orchestra wanted to use my arrangements, they had to take singer Sinatra too. Nobody was cheated. While I wasn't the best singer in the world, they weren't the best bands either." Songs like Bing Crosby's 'Just One More Chance' and 'I Found a Million-Dollar Baby (in a Five-and-ten Cent Store)' were among those that Frank performed. Having his own sheet music also demonstrated, even that far back, how Frank thought about what he did, and approached his career with a degree of professionalism that few others adopted.

Getting bookings cannot have been easy to begin with, and Dolly's political connections may have come in useful once again. Frank secured some bookings at Democratic meetings and social events, as well as at gatherings of the Hoboken Sicilian Cultural League — an interesting sobriquet?

For a day job, Frank got work through his godfather, Frank Garrick, in the dispatch department of the *New Jersey Observer*. It wasn't long before a job came up in the sports department. Popular myth has Frank working as a reporter. Given his scholastic achievements, it stretches credulity somewhat. It is more likely that he worked as a copy boy, running errands, filling inkpots, and doing what boys rather than men do. With his ambitions elsewhere, it seems that the inevitable happened and Frank lost his job. The story goes that no one among the Sinatras ever spoke to Frank Garrick again.

Quite what Frank was doing for money, apart from singing, during the latter part of 1933 and 1934 is unclear. Maybe his home

situation and the money from his evening singing gigs was enough. One thing is for sure: Frank would have continued to keep abreast of the top songs of the period, and Bing Crosby's especially. Bing's 'June in January', 'Love in Bloom', and 'Little Dutch Mill' were all very big hits in 1934.

Kenneth Wynne noted the Crosby phenomenon in an April 1934 piece in *Melody Maker*, headed 'Mike Singing of the Future': "What are the band conductors seeking? I think they want, and will eventually get a straight singer who will be able to moderate his voice down to crooning and strike something between the present 'whisper' and a more mezzo-forte tone... I consider Crosby the best link in the 'chain of crooners'."

LOVE IN LONG BRANCH

Frank is said to have spent the summer of 1934 at the house of his mother's sister, Josephine Monaco, but if he was working, how could he have spent the whole summer there? In any event, a pretty, dark-haired girl of 17, Nancy Rose Barbato, from Jersey City, was also staying in Long Branch on the Jersey shore. She was on holiday with her father Mike, his brother Ralph, and sister Kate and their families. The story goes that while Nancy was sitting on the front porch giving herself a manicure, the 18-year-old Frank came along and began to sing to her, accompanying himself on his ukulele. According to daughter Nancy, "One thing led to another and they started going out together."

Stepping out with Nancy meant that Frank was under pressure to find a job from both his own father and Nancy's. Frank began working for Mike Barbato, a plastering contractor. Not surprisingly, his heart was not in it, and this lack of enthusiasm combined with his late nights from his part-time singing gigs meant that he was forever falling asleep at work and generally doing a poor job. The problem was, according to Nancy's father, no job meant no Nancy. Stories abound of Frank dating other girls at the time, so perhaps he was uncertain that he could stick at plastering.

A REGULAR GIG

Singing at social clubs like the Cat's Meow and the Continental Bar on Hoboken's First and Hudson Street and the Oval Bar on First and Washington Street kept Frank busy, and it began to get him recognition, which was as important to young Frank as anything.

By 1935, Frank was singing songs like 'Blue Moon', sung first by Kenny Sargent with Glen Gray & the Casa Loma Orchestra and then by Helen Ward with Benny Goodman's Orchestra, and 'Sweet and Lovely', which Russ Columbo and Bing Crosby had helped to make popular. He had also got a more regular gig, at the Union Club at 600 Hudson Street. Once again, Dolly had exerted her "patronage" on another Italian to do her family a favour. According to the Union Club's owner, Joseph Samperi, times were tight: "We could afford to pay him $40 for five nights a week, but we couldn't wire the place for sound." This means that there was no possibility of radio stations doing remote recordings from the club. With hindsight, the $40 pay sounds a little exaggerated for the time.

THE UNION CLUB
In 1935 this was one of Frank's first regular gigs, hardly the acme of glamour but a solid experience.

RUSS COLUMBO

"The Romeo of Radio" RUSS COLUMBO, 1908–1934

RUGGIERO EUGENIO DI RUDOLPHO COLUMBO WAS BORN ON 14 JANUARY, 1908 IN CAMDEN, NEW JERSEY. HE WAS, LIKE FRANK SINATRA, THE SON OF ITALIAN IMMIGRANTS, POSSIBLY FROM NAPLES. HIS IS A STORY OF WHAT MIGHT HAVE BEEN.

At 6 ft tall and with deep brown eyes, black hair and weighing 170 lb, Russ Columbo was the epitome of the tall, dark, handsome Italian man. Reported to have had some surgery on his chin and nose to improve his chances at movie stardom, it is also probable that he wore a hairpiece to disguise his receding hairline.

His family moved to Los Angeles in 1924. Russ learned to play the violin and performed with several bands, including Professor Moore's Orchestra at the Hollywood Roosevelt Hotel and Slim Martin's Orchestra at the Pantages Theatre in Hollywood. He joined Gus Arnheim's band as a violinist in 1927. Later, Bing Crosby became the band's singer, and he encouraged Russ to sing. When Bing left the band, Russ took over his singing spot.

Russ went to New York in 1931 with his own band and landed a recording contract with RCA and spots on the radio with NBC. From there it was a short step to stardom. He became known as "The Romeo of Song", "The Singing Valentino", and "Radio's Revelation", and from 1931 until 1934 he rivalled Bing Crosby and Rudy Vallee as the most popular crooner, reputedly earning $500,000 per year. He recorded as a violinist and a vocalist and was branching out successfully into films at the time of his death on 2 September, 1934.

Russ's death has been the subject of much speculation. Was it suicide, murder, or just a tragic accident? The official verdict was a tragic accident. Russ's friend Lansing Brown, a leading Hollywood photographer, was striking a match on an antique pistol that he believed to be unloaded. The gun went off and a bullet ricocheted off a desk and struck Columbo in the head.

Rumours within Hollywood, however, declared that Russ and Lansing were lovers, and that Russ may have caused an irreparable breach when he announced that he and Carole Lombard, with whom he had been romantically linked, were to marry. (Just two days before his death, he had been to the premiere of his first starring film, *Wake Up and Dream*, with Carole, which could have been the final straw for Lansing.) The truth will never be known since all three took their story to their grave. What is known, however, is that thousands attended the church for the 26 year old's funeral, and Bing Crosby was one of the pallbearers.

BEST-KNOWN RECORDINGS
'You Call It Madness, But I Call It Love' (Columbo's theme song) 1931
'Goodnight Sweetheart' 1931
'As You Desire' 1932

BIGGEST FILMS
Broadway Through a Keyhole 1933
Moulin Rouge 1934
Wake Up and Dream 1934

SWINGING WITH THE BIG BANDS

The evolving sound of the Big Bands as they entered the 1930s was heaven to the teenaged Frank's ears. Their music heard on the radio helped to lift a weary public's spirits in the face of the Depression. Frank was taking his first tentative steps in the world of singing and was hugely influenced by the sounds of the bandleaders and, of course, Bing Crosby.

It was an era when swing was *the* thing. The Dorseys, Count Basie, Benny Goodman, Les Brown, Duke Ellington, Woody Herman, Glenn Miller, Artie Shaw, Paul Whiteman, and Harry James are all names that epitomize the big band era. With more than a hint of nostalgia, we think of it as an age that had everything. There was glamour, excitement, style in abundance, and more than a hint of romance.

The big bands were, first and foremost, dance bands. They first found success in the 1920s, blossomed in the 1930s, and reached their peak in the 1940s before declining throughout the 1950s. The zenith of the big

DANCING TO THE PAUL WHITEMAN ORCHESTRA,
HOTEL BILTMORE, NEW YORK, 1934

TOMMY DORSEY
Between 1938 and 1943 Tommy's band got the runner's up spot four times on the Billboard College Survey of America's favourite big bands.

"If I wrote history and could pocket a moment for me, It would be singin' with the big bands."

BARRY MANILOW, FROM 'SINGING WITH THE BIG BANDS'

bands era ran from about 1935 to the early 1950s. Changing tastes, the birth of rock 'n' roll, and the advent of television all played a part in their waning popularity. While many bandleaders became household names, their singers often became even more famous. Hundreds of singers started out that way. Some, such as Frank, went on to bigger things; others simply sank without trace.

The importance of the big bands lay not just in their role of "introducing" a number of important singers but in the fact that they bridged the gap between "hot jazz", as popularized by men like Louis Armstrong and Jelly Roll Morton in the 1920s, and a more "acceptable" style of playing. For white Middle America, the big bands were a window on black rhythms, a chance to listen to a jazzier style of playing without crossing the line. The big bands lifted jazz from the roughest dance halls and brothels to the supper clubs, nightclubs, and even the concert halls frequented by a more affluent audience.

THE NEXT BIG SWING

Bands like Louis Armstrong's in the 1920s would have typically been five or seven strong, which is why the bands that began to find prominence in the 1930s were called big bands. Generally they were about 15 strong, but could be as large as 25 and as small as ten. By mid-decade they

SHEET MUSIC
In the heyday of the big bands, sheet music still sold in big numbers; gramophones were still a luxury.

generally comprised three trumpets, three trombones, four saxophones, and four-piece rhythm section (drums, double bass, guitar, piano). To this a couple of clarinets were sometimes added. A decade on, a typical band had grown to four trombones, four trumpets, five saxes, and a four-piece rhythm section. Some bandleaders experimented with French horns, flutes — even violins.

Not every band from the 1920s was small. Paul Whiteman led an impressive and large band throughout the decade, more of a show band than a dance band. By the late 1920s his band included the Dorsey brothers, the brilliant guitarist Eddie Lang, and cornetist Bix Beiderbecke. He also employed excellent arrangers including Ferde Grofé (who wrote the 'Grand Canyon Suite') and Bill Challis. Bing Crosby and the Rhythm Boys got their break with Whiteman. While his band began to sound somewhat anachronistic by the 1930s, his importance as both a training ground and an inspiration should not be underestimated.

Today, we are so used to groups of musicians using amplification to beef up their sound that many people have never ever seen or heard a big band in all its live glory. In the ballrooms, clubs, hotels, and theatres of the late 1930s it must have been a revelation for their audiences. Not least because the reproduction quality of radios and gramophones in the 1930s failed miserably to do justice to the excitement and power of a live band in full cry. For the singers it must have been a wonderful feeling to be "out front" as the big band laid down its musical accompaniment.

A LOCAL HERO

Jersey City's Loew's Theatre, "the most lavish temple of entertainment in New Jersey", had cost $2 million to build and had opened in

SINGERS WITH THE BIG BANDS

Many singers in the 1930s and 1940s started out like Frank, in a big band.

ARTIST	BAND
Fred Astaire	Leo Reisman
Harry Babbitt	Kay Kyser
Mildred Bailey	Paul Whiteman Benny Goodman
Rosemary Clooney	Tony Pastor
Perry Como	Ted Weems
Vic Damone	Dean Hudson
Doris Day	Bob Crosby, Les Brown
Ray Eberle	Glenn Miller
Bob Eberly	Jimmy Dorsey
Ella Fitzgerald	Chick Webb
Helen Forrest	Artie Shaw Harry James
Rita Hayworth	Xavier Cugat
Billie Holiday	Count Basie
Lena Horne	Charlie Barnet
Peggy Lee	Benny Goodman
Jack Leonard	Tommy Dorsey
Ella Mae Morse	Freddy Slack Jimmy Dorsey
Helen O'Connell	Jimmy Dorsey
Anita O'Day	Gene Krupa Stan Kenton Woody Herman
Dinah Shore	Leo Reisman Xavier Cugat
Ginny Simms	Kay Kyser
Mel Torme	Artie Shaw
Sarah Vaughan	Earl Hines, Billy Eckstine
Dinah Washington	Lionel Hampton

THE BIG BANDS' BIGGEST HITS

BAND	HIT
Artie Shaw	Begin the Beguine
Benny Goodman	Sing, Sing, Sing (With the Swing)
Glenn Miller	In the Mood
Tommy Dorsey	I'll Never Smile Again
Duke Ellington	Take the A Train
Jimmy Dorsey	Besame Mucho
Les Brown	Sentimental Journey

1861–1939

1929. All 3,100 seats in its spectacular interior were undoubtedly full on the night that Frank saw his hero, Bing Crosby, starring in a show there. "I thought… he looked so easy… in those days he had such an easy style. I thought if he can do it as easy as that, then, I'm going to take a whack at this myself," said Frank in 1958, recalling the moment. One thing that Frank recognized immediately, however, was that he had to be different. He couldn't just be "another Crosby", he had to find something that set him apart, made people take notice of his talent and recognize that he also had something special to offer his audiences.

Throughout 1935 Frank worked harder than ever at finding and perfecting his "style". He continued to play small places around Hoboken and New Jersey, but he was a long way from receiving any serious recognition. He was little more than a very local hero. Frank knew a vocal group in Hoboken called the Three Flashes, who were getting along a little better than him. They were working with Harold Arden's Orchestra at the Rustic Cabin in nearby Englewood Cliffs. According to member Frank Tamburro, "Frank hung around us like we were gods or something." Frank was useful to the band too, as he had the use of a car and could drive them to the Cabin.

Some time in the summer of 1935, a man came to the Rustic Cabin who was working for Major Bowes, the host of a New York-based talent show that was broadcast on the radio. *The Original Amateur Hour* offered performers a shot at the big time, and literally thousands of hopefuls (30,000 in 1934, the first year) tried out for the show. Bowes' man wanted the Three Flashes to appear in a couple of movie shorts that the Major was making. Frank, of course, saw an opportunity, but was unable to persuade the three others to let him in on their act. He turned to Dolly, who performed her usual magic and persuaded the others that Frankie would be a useful addition to their group.

The two black-and-white movie shorts took the best part of a week to film at Biograph's studio in New York's Bronx. Released as *Major Bowes' Theater of the Air*, the two scenes that featured Frank were called 'The Night Club' and 'The Minstrel'. The Three Flashes did the singing and Frank acted as a waiter in one, and in the other, in black-face make-up, he was part of a chorus of singers, making no significant vocal contribution.

THE HOBOKEN FOUR

The introduction to Major Bowes encouraged the Three Flashes to try out for the *Amateur Hour* in their own right. Naturally, Frank wanted to be a part of that too. It could be that both Frank and the Three Flashes applied separately to appear on the show but somehow or other they got together and rather than calling themselves the Four Flashes they settled on the Hoboken Four. It is even likely that the Major decided on their name. Before appearing on the radio competition proper they still had to audition and so, on 31 August, 1935, they sang 'The Curse of An Aching Heart'. A strange choice of song, given that it had been a hit for Will Oakland, an exceptionally high countertenor, in 1913. The audition was successful and they decided for the actual contest to interpret 'Shine', a more appropriate hit song from 1932, by Bing Crosby and the Mills Brothers. Broadcast from the stage of New York's Capitol Theatre, the Hoboken Four were introduced by Bowes as "singing and dancing fools"; the audience loved them. In the theatre, a giant audiometer was used to measure the applause (very scientific!).

> "Some day that's gonna be me up there."
>
> FRANK, SEEING BING CROSBY AT LOEW'S THEATRE

COURTING COUPLE
Frank and Nancy snapped during their courtship. He already displays a relaxed pose in front of the camera.

BING CROSBY

"The song that Crosby sings, these foolish things remind me of you."

FRANK SINATRA FROM THE 1945 RECORDING 'THESE FOOLISH THINGS'

FRANK'S LITTLE NOD TO BING CROSBY, THAT HE ADDED TO HIS 1945 RECORDING OF 'THESE FOOLISH THINGS', WAS A NICE TOUCH. WHILE BING WAS HIS RIVAL, IT WAS ALSO BING WHO, ABOVE ALL OTHERS, HAD INSPIRED "THE KID FROM HOBOKEN". PEOPLE TALKED OF THE "BATTLE OF THE BARITONES" BETWEEN BING AND RUSS COLUMBO, BUT EVEN ALLOWING FOR COLUMBO'S UNTIMELY DEATH, THERE WAS ONLY ONE WINNER.

Born Harry Lillis Crosby, the fourth of seven children, in Tacoma, Washington, on 2 May, 1903 (throughout his life, Bing claimed 2 May, 1904, as his birth date), he was nicknamed Bing after a comic strip character in the *The Bingville Bugle*.

Bing's family moved to Spokane and by 1920 he went to College to study law and joined a local group called The Musicaladers to play drums. In 1925, Bing and Al Rinker (The Musicaladers' manager) headed for Los Angeles to play vaudeville. In 1926, orchestra leader Paul Whiteman offered them a job, along with Harry Barris, and they became known as Paul Whiteman's Rhythm Boys. In 1930 they appeared with Whiteman in *The King of Jazz*, but during the filming Bing was arrested for drunk driving and soon after Whiteman let the trio go. They got a job with Gus Arnheim's band at the Cocoanut Grove in Los Angeles. In November, 1930, Bing and The Rhythm Boys recorded 'Them There Eyes' but it was in February, 1931 that 'I Surrender Dear', a song written by Harry Barris and performed solo by 27-year-old Bing, won him national recognition. Spotted at the Grove by film producer Mack Sennett, Bing was hired to star in six comedy shorts and then Columbia Broadcasting System began giving him regular radio airtime. This, combined with a record run of performances at the Paramount Theatre in New York City in 1932, made Bing a star.

RECORD SELLER

Crosby's relaxed, effortless style was the perfect antidote to the Depression. He employed his humour to good effect on radio and in films, making him hugely popular with the public. His records sold in large numbers, which did a great deal to help the beleaguered recording industry. Crosby took full advantage of electronic amplification allowing him to develop an intimate style of singing, rather than having to belt out a song to be heard. The way he 'sold' a song made him unique; Frank Sinatra developed it into an art form.

Bing recorded over 1,600 songs and sold 500 million records, the majority for Decca between 1934 and 1955. Ill health was a problem during the latter years of the 1960s but after he had a cancerous lump removed from his lung in 1973 he gained a new lease of life; he recorded extensively and played concerts that lasted over two hours. His last concert, at London's Palladium, was four days before he died on 14 October, 1977, on a golf course in Spain.

Bing, unlike many of his peers, was an astute businessman. His investments included real estate, mines, oil wells, cattle, music publishing, television, and motion picture production companies. When he died he was worth in excess of $150 million. His disciplined approach to business was mirrored in the way he led his private life, one that was very much at odds with his relaxed and informal approach on screen and in song.

CROSBY AT THE MOVIES

Bing made *The Big Broadcast* in 1932 and appeared in over 100 movies in all. By the mid 1940s he was the number one American box office attraction, winning an Oscar in 1944 for *Going My Way*. His most popular films, apart from the musical *White Christmas* (1954), were those when he played straight guy to Bob Hope and Dorothy Lamour, the 'Road' movies, starting with *The Road to Singapore* in 1939 and ending with *The Road to Hong Kong* in 1962. One of his best performances was in 1954 as an alcoholic husband opposite Grace Kelly in *The Country Girl*.

BIGGEST HITS... BESIDES 'WHITE CHRISTMAS'

'June in January' 1934
'Pennies from Heaven' 1936
'Sweet Leilani' 1937
'Only Forever' 1940
'Swinging on a Star' 1944

SINGING BY EAR
Despite his mastery of the popular music idiom (song), Bing Crosby never learned to read music.

THE HOBOKEN FOUR
*Fred Tamburro and Pat Principe are
on Major Bowes' right, James
Petrozelli and Frank on his left.*

Listeners to the radio were asked to call the station and register their votes. Legend has it that the quartet from Hoboken won with the largest ever number of votes in the history of the contest. Major Bowes offered them a contract with one of his touring units. These groups of performers appeared in vaudeville theatres all over the United States, and the foursome travelled as part of touring unit number five for the next few months. Earning $50 a week each plus their keep must have been pretty good for the young hopefuls.

They started out in Des Moines, Iowa, on 15 September, 1935. Two days later they were in Wichita, Kansas, before criss-crossing the country, reaching Vancouver, Canada, in early November. Pictures that Frank sent home to Dolly show he was taking his quest for stardom seriously: he was wearing a trilby hat and smoking a pipe, looking very like Bing!

Ironically, after playing Bing's home town of Spokane, things reached crisis point for the four boys from Hoboken. According to Morton Gould, the deputy Musical Director on the tour, Frank and the other three argued frequently. In Spokane, Frank was on the receiving end of a beating from Tamburro. That was enough for Frank, being ragged was one thing, beaten up another, he headed home to Hoboken; stardom would have to be put on hold.

FRANK GOES SOLO

Stardom for Frank meant his own personal stardom, and that was probably at the root cause of the dissent with the other members of the Hoboken Four. Frank unquestionably was the bigger talent, and knew it. In later years, Frank talked of being homesick, of missing his girl and family. Truth is, if it had been going better for him on the road – better that is in the sense that he was achieving what he wanted – he would have stuck at it. But clearly he was just one of the four, even though he had gradually become the front one. Any hint of failure by Frank as a result of leaving Major Bowes' tour was talked down. It was more of a case of them being unable to keep up with him.

Back in Hoboken, Frank, his portable PA system, and his drive for success were once again to the fore. He sang at Italian weddings, clubs, and bars in Hoboken, and even got into black-face make-up again to appear as part of a minstrel show at a New Jersey fire station. All in all, 1936 must have been a frustrating time for Frank. Having put his toe in the waters of success, he must have felt he had taken a step backwards. There is talk of him performing on local

radio stations during the year. It may also have been in the summer of 1936 (though others say it was not until 1938) that Frank first visited a New York vocal coach to help sort out some of his diction problems. John Quinlan, an Australian (Frank says he was Irish!) ex-opera singer, saw the potential in Frank, and his work with him had superb effects on improving his diction and enunciation. He gave Frank one piece of advice that he certainly grew to appreciate, even if it took a little while for its full effect to blossom: "You can't sing what you don't understand."

In early 1937, Frank had a piece of luck when his cousin Ray Sinatra, who played in the house band for NBC radio, got Frank an audition. Frank got the job and began to appear on a daily 15-minute spot, for which he was paid just 70 cents a week. It can only have been the exposure that made it worth it. Also appearing on the show was another young hopeful by the name of Dinah Shore.

On 12 May, Frank appeared on another amateur show, *Town Hall Tonight*, hosted by comedian Fred Allen. Frank, backed by a Dixieland band, The Four Sharps, performed 'Exactly Like You' on the ukulele. The song had recently been a hit for Benny Goodman's trio featuring Lionel Hampton on vocal. Eight years later, Frank reprised his performance, this time singing with the Nat King Cole Trio. It was an early example of a recurring theme throughout Frank's long career. He would often revisit songs, on record and through radio and television performances, giving the listener the chance to see how he could take the familiar and imbue it with something fresh and new.

It may have been as early as August 1937, but could have been in 1938, that Frank heard of an opportunity. The Rustic Cabin needed a singing waiter, and who better than Frank? He got the job and, as he recalled many years later, it was great experience. "The piano player and I performed from table to table between sets. I would push his little piano around, he'd play and I'd sing. I never stopped, I showed people to tables, I sang with the band, I sang in between sets. But I didn't mind. Because I was learning." There was another advantage, too. A new resident band was Bill Henri and his Headliners, and they performed on radio WNEW's *Dance Parade*, which was broadcast from the Cabin. Frank, dressed to match the band in a white jacket and little bow tie, was out front. Frank was back on the radio. As Jimmy Rich, Station Director of WNEW, recalled: "Whenever we had an open spot we put him in. Hell – he was offering to sing for free."

COURT AND SPARK

It was while working at the Rustic Cabin that Frank had his first brush with law and order. Despite "going steady" with

Nancy, Frank seems to have been playing around a bit. On 26 November, 1938, two police officers from nearby Hackensack, New Jersey, arrested Frank after he had finished his closing set with Bill Henri. They took him to the police station and charged him with "a breach of promise". Apparently, 23-year-old Frankie had been seeing a girl called Antoinette Della Pente and had promised to marry her. There was one slight complication, however: Antoinette was already married. Undeterred, she then had Frankie charged with "committing adultery", and he was again arrested at the Rustic Cabin, three days before Christmas 1938. The following day, the *Hudson Dispatch* ran the headline 'Songbird Held on Morals Charge'. The case came to court on 4 January, 1939, and Frank was remanded to appear before a grand jury 20 days later, when the case was dismissed.

It cannot have been an easy time for Frank or Nancy, especially since they were to be married on 4 February. Nancy asked Frank if this girl was the first, to which Frank replied "No, but she's the last." Harry Schumann, one of Bill Henri's Headliners, recalled Frank at the Rustic Cabin: "He had more broads around than you ever saw. I'd think to myself what do they see in him. …But when he opened his mouth you knew. He had that charisma that went right out to every gal in the room."

Frank and Nancy's wedding at Our Lady of Sorrows Church in Jersey City was a swish affair. Frank was in full morning dress, looking every inch the happy bridegroom. After the wedding, they moved into a rented three-room apartment at 487 Garfield Avenue that cost $42 a month. One of the people that Frank

WHERE IT ALL BEGAN
The Rustic Cabin, Englewood Cliffs, where Frank got his first really big break. The Cabin is long gone and a petrol station now stands on the spot.

hung around with at the time was a saxophonist by the name of Frank Mane. The two of them would spend time at Bayonne's Sicilian Club, a haunt for local musicians. Mane told Frank that he was forming a ten-piece band in order to make some recordings, and Frank asked to go along to the session. On 18 March, 1939, they went to Harry Smith's Recording Studio in Manhattan. Sinatra's best man at his wedding, Don Rigney, was the drummer, and it was Mane's intention to record just instrumentals. After cutting several, including 'Flight of the Bumblebee', there was still studio time remaining. Frank asked his friend if he could cut a song. They decided to do 'Our Love', based on the melody for Tchaikovsky's *Romeo and Juliet*, for which Mane must have had the sheet music.

There was never any intention by Mane, or Sinatra, to do anything with these recordings. Mane just wanted to hear what his band sounded like. He kept the master recordings and did absolutely nothing with them, even after Frank became famous. In fact, the recording itself become something of a legend and added yet more disinformation to the story of Frank's early life. Countless books, including daughter Nancy's own, talk of Frank recording 'Our Love' the day before Nancy Barbato and he got married and young Frank giving it to her as a troth of his love. Legend is often so much better than reality.

❝Songbird Held on Morals Charge❞

HEADLINE IN THE *HUDSON DISPATCH*, CHRISTMAS 1938

ON THE RECORD
The Bergen County Sheriff's office mugshot taken on 27 November, 1938, after Frankie was arrested at the Rustic Cabin.

THE BIG BANDS

THE BIG BANDS' GOLDEN YEARS BEGAN IN THE LATE 1930S, JUST AS FRANK CAME ALONG. BIG BANDS WERE RARELY OFF THE CHARTS AND THEY GENERATED TREMENDOUS EXCITEMENT WHEREVER THEY PLAYED. FOR A WHILE THEY *WERE* POP MUSIC. THE BAND LEADERS AND THEIR SINGERS WERE THE EPITOME OF CHIC IN AN AGE OF COOL AND SOPHISTICATION FOLLOWING THE AUSTERITY OF THE DEPRESSION. AS FRANK SAID MANY YEARS LATER, "IN THOSE DAYS, WORKING WITH A BIG BAND WAS AT THE END OF THE RAINBOW FOR ANY SINGER THAT WANTED TO MAKE IT." FRANK WAS LUCKY TO WORK WITH TWO OF THE BEST... AND THEY WERE FORTUNATE TO WORK WITH FRANKIE.

THE HOLLYWOOD PALLADIUM
The Tommy Dorsey band with vocalist Frank Sinatra performing at the Hollywood Palladium's opening night on 31 October, 1940.

THE PARAMOUNT THEATRE, NEW YORK, TIMES SQUARE, NEW YORK

"I was listening to the car radio, and my date says, 'Oh, listen to that. It's Dick Haymes.' And I said, 'No, Dick Haymes doesn't sound that good.' Then they announced it was Frank, singing 'All or Nothing at All'. I said, 'Told you.' And that was my first introduction to Frank."

BILL MILLER, FRANK'S PIANIST FROM 1951

WHEN HARRY MET FRANKIE

"We don't have a singer," said the manager at the Rustic Cabin, one day in late May or early June 1939. "We have an MC that sings a little bit." This is how 24-year-old Frank Sinatra very nearly missed out on becoming the boy singer with the Harry James Band.

Harry James's first wife, singer Louise Tobin, who was packing to leave town to play some dates with her boss, Benny Goodman and his band, was listening to the radio when she heard Frank on the WNEW *Dance Parade* from the Rustic Cabin. She and Harry were both staying in a New York hotel, since he had a booking at the city's Paramount Theatre, the 5000-capacity "bastion of elegance on tawdry Times Square", as one New York paper described the place. The next night, Harry drove over the George

GOLDEN TRUMPET MAN
"He made it all possible," said Frank when bandleader Harry James died in 1983.

Washington Bridge and headed for the Rustic Cabin. "I asked the manager where I could find the singer", Harry later said. Interestingly, it may have worked out very differently as Frank recalled many years later he had asked Glenn Miller for a job shortly before Harry James heard him. Miller hired Bob Eberle and so he gave Frank a polite rebuttal along the lines of "Don't call me, I'll call you." Many years later, Frank recalled his days on WNEW to Leonard Feather of *Metronome* magazine: "Boy, was that a routine, it sustained everybody but me. I was on four local stations and sometimes had it planned so I'd be on the air somewhere or other every three hours all through the day. But the only money I got out of the whole thing was 70 cents carfare from Jersey to the Mutual studios. On top of the 18 sustainers a week."

After his wedding to Nancy, Frank resumed his role as waiter, albeit a singing one, at the Englewood roadhouse on Route 9W in New Jersey. He and Nancy were living on $50 a week in their Garfield Avenue apartment. This was not that much of a struggle, since the average family income at the time was closer to half that. Nancy was bringing home the same as Frank from her secretarial job at American Type Founders, and while most of her money went on household bills, Frank's wages supported his "fetish", as some have described it. With his mother's spoiling of young Frankie and his grandmother's taste for Little Lord Fauntleroy suits, they had inadvertently created a clothes-horse. His excesses even drove him to bounce a cheque on a neighbour who owned a clothing store. The way Frank saw it was that he needed the clothes – his image was important if he was to succeed.

HARRY'S NEW BOY SINGER

Frank went over to New York City and rehearsed with Bob Chester's band at Steinway Hall. On his nights off from the Rustic Cabin, he would work on his vocal technique by visiting New York's nightclubs, such as the Uptown House, where he saw Billie Holiday and Mabel Mercer. He was particularly enamoured with the latter's enunciation and strove to emulate her clever interpolation of song lyrics. Twenty years later, Frank told the *Melody Maker* that he "…first heard her [Billie] standing under a spotlight in a 52nd Street jazz spot. I was dazzled by her soft, breathtaking beauty." He also talked of Ethel Waters, "whose feeling for the blues and great warmth touched me deep down; I shall never forget her."

Frank could not believe that Harry James had come out to the Rustic Cabin. It was a Monday night and normally Frank would have been off. But the band's girl singer "asked me to change nights – she had a date," recalled Frank in 1945. He chose to sing 'Begin the Beguine' that night; it had topped the charts for Artie Shaw at the end of 1938. According to Harry, "I felt the hairs on the back of my neck rising. I knew he was destined to be a great singer."

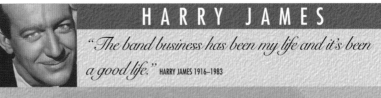

HARRY JAMES

"The band business has been my life and it's been a good life." HARRY JAMES 1916–1983

TRUMPETER AND BANDLEADER HARRY JAMES WAS THREE MONTHS YOUNGER THAN FRANK SINATRA BUT, BY THE TIME FRANK JOINED HIS BAND, HIS REPUTATION AS ONE OF THE GREAT TRUMPET PLAYERS WAS WELL ESTABLISHED.

Born in Albany, Georgia, on 15 March, 1916, where his parents were working with The Mighty Haag Circus, Harry's middle name was Haag. He began playing professionally with his father's circus band (his mother was a trapeze artiste) when he was very young. He worked in a rival circus band in his teens, before the family settled in Beaumont, Texas, where he attended school.

RISE

At 15, Harry joined Joe Gale's orchestra and in 1935, Ben Pollack, for whom he composed 'Peckin', which spawned a dance craze, hired him. He got his big break in late 1936, when he joined Benny Goodman's band. He backed Ella Fitzgerald on Goodman's January 1937 No 1 'Goodnight, My Love'. Harry had his first hit in February 1937 with 'One O'Clock Jump', which had been composed and originally recorded by Count Basie. It was this success that convinced Harry James to go out on his own. Having continued with Benny Goodman for the rest of the year, Harry formed his own band in 1939, on $4,500 borrowed from his former boss.

Frank Sinatra joined Harry James in June 1939; their most famous recording was 'All or

MR AND MRS JAMES
Harry James and actress Betty Grable, the GIs' favourite pin-up girl, stayed together for over 20 years before their marriage ended in 1965.

Nothing at All', which they cut on 31 August, 1939, (it went to No 1 in 1943 having been re-released by Columbia). After Sinatra's departure for the Tommy Dorsey band at the beginning of 1940, Harry James really hit his stride. His first hit of 1940 was 'Ciribiribin' (They're So In Love), which became his theme tune. For the next seven years, James was rarely off the charts, with hits that included 'Skylark', 'I'll Get By', 'I'm Beginning to See the Light' and 'It's Been a Long, Long Time'. Harry met the film star Betty Grable at Chicago's College Inn shortly after Frank had left his band and they married in 1943.

REVIVAL

While most Big Bands went into decline in the 1950s, Harry kept his band at the very top. He played coast-to-coast tours, as well as the casinos in Las Vegas, Reno, and Lake Tahoe well into the 1960s. With a Big Band revival in the 1970s, James toured Europe, and also played one-nighters, Disneyland, and cruise ships. Right up until just before his death from cancer, the Harry James band was a sell-out attraction. He died in Las Vegas on 5 July, 1983, 40 years to the day that he married Betty Grable in the same city.

Harry was the slightly younger of the two men, but he impressed Frank, not only because he offered him a year's contract at $75 a week – three times Frank's earnings at the roadhouse – to come and sing with his band, but also because Harry was a "name" and he was already gaining a good reputation with his new band. Harry's band had played their first gig at the Benjamin Franklin Hotel in Philadelphia four months previously. Harry had also been around, having played with Benny Goodman's band and also recorded under his own name in 1937 with members of the Count Basie and Duke

IN THE STUDIO WITH HARRY JAMES

HARRY JAMES AND HIS ORCHESTRA, WITH FRANK ON VOCALS, RECORDED JUST TEN SONGS. THE FIRST TWO WERE CUT ON THE AFTERNOON OF 13 JULY IN NEW YORK CITY, PRIOR TO AN EVENING SHOW AT THE ROSELAND BALLROOM.

ANDY GIBSON ARRANGED 'From the Bottom of My Heart' and 'Melancholy Mood' and both were issued on the Brunswick label a month before it was absorbed into the parent company, Columbia. The songs were probably cut at 550 Fifth Avenue, but no one can precisely recall which New York studio was used. Just 5,000 copies were pressed.

COLUMBIA RECORDING CORPORATION

William Paley founded the Columbia Broadcasting System in 1928. Among the investors was the Columbia Phonograph System, who made record players. By 1938, CBS were branching out from radio through their acquisition of the American Recording Corporation, who were known as ARC. By this time, ARC also owned the Columbia Phonograph System as well as a clutch of record labels that included OKeh, Vocalion, and Brunswick. The new corporation was renamed The Columbia Recording Corporation. The eight recordings by Harry James and Frank Sinatra that came out after that initial Brunswick release all appeared on the Columbia label.

SINATRA SESSIONS

On 17 August, Frank cut 'My Buddy' and 'It's Funny to Everyone But Me'. Two weeks later, on 31 August, 'Here Comes the Night' and 'All or Nothing at All' were put down. Six weeks later, on 13 October, 'On a Little Street in Singapore' and 'Who Told You I Cared?' were recorded. The final two sides were recorded in Los Angeles on 8 November: 'Every Day of My Love' and a vocal version of 'Ciribiribin (They're So in Love)'. 'Ciribiribin' was written in 1898 and had originally been adapted by Harry James as his theme song. 'On a Little Street in Singapore' became a hit for Jimmy Dorsey in January 1940. Ozzie Nelson and his Orchestra also recorded 'Who Told You I Cared?' with a vocal by Harriet Hilliard. They had a minor hit with the song in December 1939. In 1952, Ozzie and Harriet, who were married, began a long-running television show; their son, Rick Nelson, became a star in the 1950s and 1960s. Harriet was already pregnant with Rick when 'Who Told You I Cared?' entered the

charts. Artie Shaw's version of 'Melancholy Mood' reached No 8 in October 1939.

It was common practice in the 1930s and 1940s for many different bands and singers to record versions of the same song. Publishers and their pluggers hedged their bets in getting different vocalists and bands to be recorded.

ALL OR NOTHING AT ALL

None of the five records featuring Frank was a hit when they were first released in 1939 and 1940. The most popular at the time was 'All or Nothing at All'. Written by Arthur Altman and Jack Lawrence, it sold around 8,000 copies (at the time, 15,000 would have been considered a minor hit). Unusually for a Big Band record with a vocal, Frank sang almost the whole way through the song – singers were often limited to a couple of choruses.

The song was given to Harry James by Lou Levy, the head of Leeds Publishing. Lou also gave it to two other bandleaders, Jimmy Dorsey and Freddy Martin. Jack Lawrence, the song's lyricist, recalled Frank's original version, "...the way he attacked that song, and what he did with the breath control and the wonderful phrasing that he used even in those early days." He refers to the original version, because Frank actually recorded the song on three more occasions (1945, 1961, and 1966). There was a fifth recorded one, a disco version that Frank cut with Joe Beck in February 1977, but, apart from being included on a complete set of Frank's Reprise recordings, it has never officially been released... thankfully. The 1945 version was recorded for the film *A Thousand and One Nights*.

'All or Nothing at All' became Frank's second big hit when it got to No 2 on the *Billboard* chart in September 1943. It had been re-released to cover a shortage in recorded material during the Musicians' Union strike.

Although it was not recorded until the end of August, Frank had been honing the song on live shows since early July, almost as soon as he began singing with Harry. It became a staple of Frank's 1940s' radio shows and then a popular live number throughout the

1960s and on to the 1990s. It became one of Frank's seminal songs. It is very likely that Frank performed 'All or Nothing at All' during Harry James's stint in Atlantic City in 1939, and he certainly sang this classic song at one of his very last concerts, 55 years later, at the Sands in Atlantic City in November 1994.

Besides releasing 'All or Nothing at All' in 1943, Columbia capitalized on Frank's success by releasing 'On a Little Street in Singapore', 'Every Day of My Life', and 'It's Funny to Everyone But Me' in 1944; all three songs were minor hits.

HARRY JAMES AND HIS ORCHESTRA WITH VOCAL CHORUS BY FRANK SINATRA

'From the Bottom of My Heart' (B Hays/ A Gibson/M Beck/H James)
'Melancholy Mood' (V Knight/W Schumann)
'My Buddy' (G Kahn/W Donaldson)
'It's Funny to Everyone But Me' (J Lawrence)
'All or Nothing at All' (J Lawrence/A Altman)
'Here Comes the Night' (F Loesser/H Edelstein/ C Hohengarten)
'On a Little Street in Singapore' (P DeRose/WJ Hill)
'Who Told You I Cared?' (G Whiting/B Reisfield)
'Ciribiribin (They're So in Love)' (A Pestalozza/ R Thaler)
'Every Day of My Life' (H James/M Beck/B Hays)

All songs arranged by Andy Gibson.

> 66 He was anxious... on the playbacks Frank would sit there saying 'Oh I missed that,' or 'I should have done this or that'. 99
>
> MICKEY SCRIMA – DRUMMER WITH HARRY JAMES

Ellington bands. Harry had experience, and it showed. It has been said that Frank went to the Paramount Theatre the night after Harry signed him and that they performed together. He was certainly at the Paramount to see Harry James and his Melody Makers, but probably didn't perform. It is much more likely that there was a week of rehearsals to work up the numbers Frank was to sing and to acquaint him with Harry's style, which was very different from what he was used to at the Rustic Cabin. There may have been a club date at the Waldorf-Astoria, but the most frequently quoted debut for Frank with Harry James is 30 June, 1939, at the Hippodrome Theatre in Baltimore, Maryland. Two of the songs that Frank sang that night were 'Wishing', a current hit from the film Love Affair, and 'My Love for You'.

FRANKIE SATIN?

Almost as soon as they met, Frank and Harry had a disagreement. Harry felt that the name Sinatra was not ideal for his new singer – it was too Italian – and suggested changing it to Frankie Satin. "Change it? You kiddin'?" is how Frank's reply has been reported, or perhaps paraphrased. Many years later, Frank said "If I'd done that, I'd be working cruise ships today." Harry's other singer had already changed her name from Marie Antoinette Yvonne Jamais to Connie Haines, which in her case was sensible move. The 18-year-old Connie had joined Harry a matter of days before Frank joined the band, having replaced Bernice Byers. Frank was an immediate hit with the girls; Connie Haines later recalled, "After the first show the screaming started in the theatre and those girls came backstage."

From Baltimore, the band went back to New York's Roseland Ballroom for much of July and August. Around the end of July and the beginning of August, there was a stint at the Marine Ballroom on Atlantic City's Steel Pier. Harry James and the band would open up with his theme song 'Ciribiribin' and then Connie and Frank would perform between band numbers such as 'Shorty George', 'Indiana', 'Two O'Clock Jump,' and 'I Found a New Baby' (Harry's first but minor hit record). Connie and Frank would perform Connie's main featured song 'White Sails (Will Find a Blue Lagoon)', Frank did 'Melancholy Mood', 'My Love for You', and 'From the Bottom of My Heart,' which he had recorded with Harry James at their first session together two weeks earlier in New York.

Frank was happy because the band was often featured on the radio broadcast from the Steel Pier and the Roseland.

MABEL MERCER
Born in England in 1900 and brought up in North Wales, Mabel Mercer was one of Frank's earliest inspirations. She died in 1984.

For two weeks from 19 August Frank and Harry's orchestra played every afternoon at the New York World's Fair in Queens. On most nights it was back to the Roseland. It was during this spell that Frank got his first serious mention in the press. George T Simon, the editor of *Metronome* magazine, had gone to the Roseland to see Harry James. As Simon was leaving, Harry's manager, Jerry Barrett, went running after him and asked "How do you like the new singer? The boy wants a good write-up more than anybody I've ever seen, so give him a good write-up will you because we want to keep him happy with the band and that's the only thing that will make him happy." Fortunately for everyone, Simon found it easy to say something good. In the September *Metronome* he wrote, "Featured throughout are the very pleasing vocals of Frank Sinatra, whose easy phrasing is especially commendable." While Frank was making progress with his vocals, it is fair to say on those first recordings he sounds somewhat tentative. Harry told him, "Keep the bottom filled up". He also told him he should exercise and that skipping would help his breathing technique.

> 66 With a few exceptions, every major pop singer in the US during her generation has been touched in some way by her genius. 99
>
> **FRANK SINATRA ON BILLIE HOLIDAY**

> 66 Bending those notes, that's all I helped Frankie with. 99
>
> **BILLIE HOLIDAY**

FRANKIE ON THE BBC

In July 1939, tensions in Britain were rising with the threat of war with Germany. On 19 July, 1939, Harry James's band broadcast on BBC radio. Reporter Mike Butcher tuned in, not expecting much because he was unimpressed with Harry's records featuring Bernice Byers. "You'll understand how pleasantly surprised I was when between a real killer-diller workout on 'Beer Barrel Polka' and some similarly depressing manifestations of the Swing era's worst aspects a male singer announced as Frank Sinatra came on with the sentimentally affecting 'From the Bottom of My Heart ' and 'To You'." This was the first time Frank was heard in Britain.

LADY DAY
Her singing inspired countless singers over the years, but Billie Holiday's life was a tragedy.

1939–1942

military service, and that included both Frank and Harry.

Connie Haines had left Harry James's band after the Atlantic City gig in early August at a time when their finances were at a precarious level, despite the constant working. Frank was also anxious about his progress towards stardom, especially the speed of it. His friend Hank Sanicola, a song plugger, was encouraging him to stay with Harry's band, and in the short term Frank agreed. At the time, Harry James told *Downbeat* magazine, "He considers himself the greatest vocalist in the business. Get that! No one ever heard of him. He's never had a hit record. He looks like a wet rag, but he says he is the greatest."

HARRY JAMES'S BAND
"A band that kicks as few have ever kicked before." George T Simon, Editor, Metronome *magazine September 1939. Frank is seated next to the guitarist.*

As the band was coming to the end of its run at the World's Fair, the crisis in Europe erupted as Germany invaded Poland. Many Americans were worried about how the war would affect them, including many of the boys in James's band. If the US was to get involved in the war, which was very possible, they would be eligible for

BOOGIE YOUR WOOGIE

A week after Germany's blitzkrieg on Poland, Harry James and the band began a four-week booking at the Sherman Hotel in Chicago, in the Panther Room (later renamed the College Inn). Besides James and Frank, there was equal billing for the trumpet-playing singer in the band, Jack

Palmer. Also on the bill, which ran from 10:00–3:00 am, were the Boogie Woogies – the brilliant black pianists Meade Lux Lewis, Albert Ammons, and Pete Johnson. The three pianists had starred in the 'From Spirituals to Swing' concerts that John Hammond (who later discovered Bob Dylan) staged at New York's Carnegie Hall at Christmas 1938. Lewis, Ammons, and Johnson had become overnight stars with white people, whereas before they had been playing almost exclusively to black-only audiences.

The craze for boogie woogie was quickly picked up by the Big Bands. One of the first big hits of the Big Band era, and a four million-seller, was 'Boogie Woogie' by Tommy Dorsey and his Orchestra. This was actually 'Pinetop's Boogie Woogie', first recorded in 1928 by Clarence 'Pinetop' Smith. Tommy Dorsey had been quick off the mark to capitalize on the craze for boogie woogie that was sweeping the nation in the wake of the 'From Spirituals to Swing' concerts. Dorsey's recording had staying power: in 1943, 1944, and 1945 it was reissued and sold well each time. Boogie woogie was not confined to Big Bands either: in 1941, one of the best-selling records of the year was the Andrews Sisters with 'Boogie Woogie Bugle Boy'.

When it was time for Frank to sing, Jim Bacon, a Chicago reporter who had accompanied the actress Betty Grable to the Panther Room, said, "Every girl left her partner on the dance floor and crowded round the microphone on the bandstand. He was so skinny the microphone almost obscured him." It was during Harry's band's run at the Sherman that the name Frank Sinatra first appeared in *Billboard*. The write-up said, "Harry James and his Orchestra numbers 17

people using instrumentation of seven brass, four sax and four rhythm. Featured vocalists are Marie Carroll (Connie Haines's replacement), Frank Sinatra, and Jack Palmer."

After Chicago, the band were due to head west to the Palomar Ballroom in Los Angeles. Unfortunately, it burned down one night while the Charlie Barnet band were playing; they were lucky to get out with most of their instruments intact. A hasty booking was arranged for Harry's band at Victor Hugo's, a restaurant on Sunset Boulevard. Nancy joined Frank for the trip to Los Angeles, and the two of them shared a two-bedroom apartment with drummer Mickey Scrima. "We never had an argument, we just enjoyed each other's company. It was tough then because no one had any money," Scrima later recalled. "Nancy would cook for us… beans and wieners." There was another complication: Nancy was pregnant. It was a hand-to-mouth existence and the thought of another mouth to feed obviously concentrated Frank's mind – especially as the booking at Victor Hugo's turned into a fiasco. The restaurant

ROSELAND BALLROOM
The home of the "Dime-a-Dance" nights in New York City, on Broadway between 51st and 52nd Street.

BOOGIE WOOGIE BOYS
Albert Ammons (left) and Pete Johnson were two of the greatest exponents of boogie piano. Albert's signature number was 'Boogie Woogie Stomp'; Pete's was 'Roll 'Em, Pete'.

usually booked "sweet" bands, such as Guy Lombardo, and Harry's hot style of playing, even with the addition of Frank's ballads, was not what the diners there were used to. As for the management, a half-empty restaurant was not what they were used to. According to Harry, "They didn't like us and refused to pay us." Ironically, the owner of the restaurant fired them while Frank was singing 'All or Nothing at All'. He started yelling, "Stop! No more! Enough!" A booking at the Paramount Theatre in LA was hastily

arranged, followed by a week in San Francisco before the band headed for Chicago, playing one-nighters as they went cross-country. At the Chicago Theatre they were booked with the Andrews Sisters. Here again, Frank Sinatra did not impress the manager, though it wasn't his singing that was a problem: it was Frank in his ill-fitting band uniform that did it. "Take that little scarecrow out of the show," he insisted. Harry was equally insistent, "He's my singer, he stays in." Unfortunately, for Harry, Frank had other plans.

DICK HAYMES

"... I became a superstar when I was too young to handle it." DICK HAYMES IN 1976

ASK ANYONE TODAY WHO DICK HAYMES WAS AND THEY WILL EITHER LOOK BLANK, OR SHRUG, AND PERHAPS SAY HE WAS VERY NEARLY ONE OF THE GREATEST SINGERS OF THE 20TH CENTURY.

Dick was born in Buenos Aires, Argentina, on 13 September, 1916, to a father of Scottish/Irish descent and an Irish mother (a former musical comedy star) who had been raised in the US. Shortly after Dick's birth, the family moved to the US. When Dick was two, his parents separated, and his mother took him and his brother to live in Paris, where she opened a dress shop and they attended school. The Depression forced the family to move back to New York in 1930, and Dick's mother took up singing and acted as a vocal coach while Dick went to Military Academy. When he left school in 1933, Dick headed for Hollywood, where he formed his own group and worked on an LA radio station and as an extra and stunt man for MGM. He dived from a mast in the 1935 version of *Mutiny on the Bounty*.

In 1939, anxious to try to get a career going as a songwriter, he went to Harry James with some songs, which was good timing because Frank had just quit to join Tommy Dorsey. Harry auditioned him as a singer, was impressed with his baritone voice, and offered him the job. With a little handover period with Frank, he quickly settled into Frank's old job and became a firm favourite with Harry's fans.

One problem for Dick was women. By the time he left Harry James to start his own band in early 1942, he had already been married twice and he was just 26. His first wife, a singer called Edythe Harper, was never

mentioned to his five other wives. His own band floundered as its members were drafted into the Forces. Just before the Musicians' Strike, he had three hits with Benny Goodman that certainly gave him a timely career boost, and a chance to follow Frank a second time when he joined Tommy Dorsey's band in late 1942.

His first major hit was in July 1943 when he made No 1 with 'You'll Never Know' – an a cappella version with the Song Spinners. After a year-and-a-half with Tommy, he quit, this time to go solo with Decca Records and to host his own radio show. He also got a contract with 20th Century Fox to make movies, including *Four Jills and a Jeep*, *Billy Rose's Diamond Horseshoe* and *State Fair*. In 1947, Dick left Fox and joined Universal for two films, including *One Touch of Venus* (1948) with Robert Walker and Ava Gardner.

DOWNHILL SLIDE

Other problems were surfacing in his life. He was drinking heavily, and his inability to handle money was proving to be a threat to his marriage. Despite everything, his recording career was in good shape, and he had a string of Top 10 hits, some with Helen Forrest, Harry James's old singer. Up until 1949, he was rarely off the charts. He married again in 1949, to Nora Eddington, Errol Flynn's ex-wife. In every other respect it was downhill by this time – a lack of decent movie

roles, a radio show that lasted a season, and then the end of his recording contract with Decca in 1952. By this time, his run of big hits was well over.

Then, in 1953, his third marriage ended, amid very bad drink problems, and he fell in love with Rita Hayworth, one of the movies' legendary beauties. They got married, and when Rita went to Hawaii to film, Dick went too. The only problem was that he was stopped from re-entering the US because he had registered as a resident alien during the war (partly to avoid being called up). The immigration people wanted to deport him to Argentina. His marriage to Rita lasted just two years; both took to drinking, and the environment of huge back tax problems, alimony payments to two ex-wives, and a career going nowhere were hardly conducive to a happy marriage. He married again in 1956, to Fran Jeffries, his singing partner on the nightclub circuit, and this lasted six years, by which time he had moved to Ireland to "sort his life out". He married for the sixth and

HARRY'S VOCALISTS
Both Helen Forrest and Dick Haymes sang with the James band after Frank left to join Tommy Dorsey. Helen had two No 1s with Harry in 1942: 'I Don't Want To Walk Without You' and 'Sleepy Lagoon'.

final time in Ireland, and when he went back to the US in the 1970s to launch a comeback it was not to be. Then tragedy struck, and Dick was diagnosed with cancer. He died on 29 March, 1980, in Los Angeles.

BIGGEST HITS
'Idaho' with Benny Goodman Orchestra (No 4, 1942)
'You'll Never Know' (No 1, 1943)
'I'll Get By' with Harry James's band (No 1, 1944)
'Long Ago (and Far Away)' with Helen Forrest (No 2, 1944)
'I'll Buy That Dream' with Helen Forrest (No 2, 1944)
'Little White Lies' (No 2, 1948)

Like Frank, Dick had his biggest hit after he left Harry James, when 'I'll Get By' was released during the Musicians' Strike in 1944.

FRANKIE AND HARRY
Frank held Harry in great esteem
and they remained friends for the
next forty years.

THE GENTLEMAN OF SWING

Tommy Dorsey's singer Jack Leonard decided to leave his boss in late November 1939, despite (or perhaps because of) having been voted the number one male band vocalist in the *Billboard* poll of 1939. Some time during 1937, Frank had taken Nancy to see Tommy Dorsey's band, with Jack Leonard crooning. While they were dancing, Frank said to Nancy. "See that singer guy? One day I'll be sitting where he's sitting."

Some have speculated that in fact Tommy Dorsey took the initiative and asked Frank to join him, replacing Jack. However, this seems highly unlikely because Frank was still learning his craft. It sounds more like history rewritten with the benefit of knowing how successful Frank became. Jimmy Hilliard, who worked for CBS in Chicago, had previously told Tommy that he should check Frank out. Fortunately, both Tommy's band and Harry's were in Chicago at Christmas to play at a benefit for Ed Kelly, the mayor of the city. Tommy's manager slipped a note to Frank, asking if he would meet Tommy in his suite the following afternoon.

> **66** Even without lyrics, Tommy made it sound so musical that you never lost the thread of the message. **99**
>
> FRANK ON TOMMY

TOMMY DORSEY
Dubbed "the sentimental gentleman of swing", Tommy Dorsey was the first band leader to successfully combine "sweet and swing".

DORSEY FAN FEVER, C.1940

"I first met Sinatra around 1939. I was playing trumpet with Charlie Barnett's band and we met up with Harry James's band. Frank was just another guy then… not outstanding at all."

BILLY MAY , BANDLEADER AND FRANK'S FUTURE ARRANGER

When they met at the hotel, Tommy offered Frank $125 a week – an offer that Frank did not hesitate to accept. With Nancy pregnant and work with Harry's band still uncertain, it was an easy decision for the ambitious singer. Tommy's band was number two in the land, after Benny Goodman's, and there was no shortage of ballrooms and hotels wanting to book them. Frank went straight to the Chicago Theatre where Harry was getting ready for the night's show. Frank paced around Harry's dressing room while Harry sat reading a magazine. Eventually, Harry asked him what was up. Frank liked Harry, and if the offer had come from any other band, he would probably have stayed put. When Frank told Harry of the offer and that he wanted to accept, Harry agreed on the spot and they ended their business relationship on a handshake; Harry effectively tore up his contract. Many years later, Harry recalled the incident, "Well, if we don't do any better in the next few months or so, try to get me one too."

THE ROAD GOES EVER ON

Before Frank left, the band had an engagement to fulfil in Buffalo, New York, at Shea's Theatre. Also on the bill were the comedian Red Skelton and a trampoline act featuring Burt Lancaster (before he made it big in Hollywood). After the last show, the band bus departed for Hartford, Connecticut. Frank was left standing there, about to embark on a new career with new people, but with fond memories of his time with Harry. "I stood alone with my suitcase in the snow and watched the taillights of the bus disappear. Then the tears started, and I tried to run after the bus." According to Mickey Scrima, "As far as the band was concerned, the only guy who thought this guy (Frank) had a real future was Harry James." Frank must have felt nervous. He would be expected to perform at a whole new level with the Tommy Dorsey organization.

Frank had to get himself to New York City and to Grand Central Station to take the train to Chicago and then another to Rockford, Illinois, to join up with the Dorsey band. Frank's first gig with Tommy was in Rockford on 26 January 1940. He sang 'My Prayer', a big hit for Glenn Miller, and then 'Marie', a big hit for

---

TOMMY DORSEY

"Tommy was great at showcasing soloists and singers. Tommy's presentation was superb." FRANK

TOMMY DORSEY GOT HIS BIG BREAK PLAYING WITH THE PAUL WHITEMAN ORCHESTRA BEFORE FORMING HIS OWN BAND WITH HIS BROTHER JIMMY. BETWEEN 1938 AND 1943, TOMMY'S ORCHESTRA WAS ONE OF THE TOP THREE MOST POPULAR IN THE US.

Born Thomas Francis Dorsey Jr on 19 November, 1905, in Shenandoah, Pennsylvania, his father, a part-time musician and miner, first taught Tommy the trumpet, before he switched to the trombone. His brother Jimmy (born 29 February, 1904) was also taught the trumpet, and he later switched to the clarinet and saxophone.

The two brothers led their own bands – Dorsey's Novelty Six and Dorsey's Wild Canaries – before playing with the Scanton Sirens in the early 1920s. In 1928, Tommy and Jimmy founded the Dorsey Brothers Orchestra. Their first minor hit was 'Coquette' in June 1928, and for the next six years they had a few sporadic and minor hit records. In late 1934, they signed to Decca and found real success. In 1935, the band released numerous records and had two No 1 records, 'Lullaby of Broadway' and 'Chasing Shadows'. The Dorseys' innovative sound was an inspiration to many and the way they combined a big sound with a real dance band rhythm made them very popular.

Tommy, who had a quick temper, argued with Jimmy one night while on stage and stormed off, leaving the orchestra to Jimmy. Tommy took over the Joe Haymes Orchestra and the brothers vied to be the best, a contest Tommy won, but not by a lot. Tommy worked with brilliant and respected arrangers including Sy

Oliver, Carmen Mastren, Paul Weston, and Axel Stordahl; good singers were also eager to sing with the band that was the perfect vocal platform. Jack Leonard, Jo Stafford, Edythe Wright, Connie Haines, Dick Haymes, and Frank all handled vocals for Tommy's band.

In 1942, Dorsey hired Artie Shaw's string section to give his sound something of a revamp but in truth, the decline in the Big Band sound, albeit a slow one, had begun.

BIGGEST HITS

'Alone' 1936
'Once in a While' 1937
'All the Things You Are' 1939
'I'll Never Smile Again' 1940 (with Frank Sinatra and the Pied Pipers)
'There Are Such Things' 1942 (with Frank Sinatra and the Pied Pipers)

THE TOMMY DORSEY ORCHESTRA
Frank is third right, top row (between the two female vocalists), in this promotional handout for the band. No doubting who's boss.

In the 1950s things looked up for a while – the Dorsey band even had its own television show, where Elvis Presley made his TV debut on 28 January, 1956, singing 'Blue Suede Shoes' and 'Heartbreak Hotel' with them. Ironically, it was rock 'n' roll that really finished off the Big Bands. But before Tommy could witness this shift in popular taste, he died on 26 November, 1956. Jimmy only lived until 12 June, 1957. Their legacy of recordings is among the greatest of the Big Band era.

Dorsey introduced him. And he came on and sang 'Stardust' and it was quite an experience. You knew after eight bars that you were hearing something just absolutely new and unique. Up until then, the great sound you were looking for was always the Crosby sound." Although this was obviously said with hindsight, Frank confirmed what Jo was saying; "I was cold-shouldered by that whole band, apart from Jo Stafford."

After the relaxed, easygoing, and friendly feel of Harry's band, Tommy's was a very different situation. Dorsey was tough, volatile, and a strict disciplinarian – nothing was left to luck in his quest for big band supremacy.

ROMANTIC VIRTUOSO

The day after Frank's first recording with Tommy, the band began a week-long engagement at the Lyric Theatre in Indianapolis, Illinois, where Frank was billed as a "Romantic Virtuoso". After a three-week booking at Frank Dailey's Meadowbrook Club on Pompton Turnpike in Cedar Grove, New Jersey, and more recording sessions in New York, the band played three weeks at the Paramount Theatre in New York. For Frank it must have been justification for his decision to go with Tommy. The Paramount was considered the best big band venue in America, and, what's more, Frank was singing to the biggest crowds in his career to date.

The Paramount Theatre at Times Square on Broadway and 43rd Street was billed as the "Home of New York's Greatest 2 for 1 Show". For the price of admission, the audience got to see a movie (when Frank appeared that first time it was *The Road to Singapore*), and a whole host of live entertainment. Tommy Dorsey, his Trombone and his Orchestra featured in order of billing, Bunny Berigan "World's Hottest Trumpet" (Harry James may well have disputed that); Buddy Rich, at the drums; Frank Sinatra, Baritone, and Pied Piper Quartette. Also on the bill were Winfield and Ford, Stepping Stars of Harlem, and Red Skelton, the comedian.

As the band's run at the Paramount was ending, the war in Europe was gathering pace. On the last day of their engagement, 9 April, Germany invaded Denmark and Norway; a month later, Holland and Belgium succumbed to the German blitzkrieg. For Frank and the Dorsey band,

MOVIE MOMENT
Frank, Jo Stafford, and the Pied Pipers, with Joe Bushkin at the piano, on the set of Ship Ahoy.

BUNNY BERIGAN
Bunny was a great trumpet player who started his own band in 1937, but his lack of business acumen and his choice of material soon forced him to disband it. Described as a man with "no enemy but himself", he was an alcoholic. He ended up playing with Tommy Dorsey and was with him when Frank joined. He died on 2 June, 1942.

Tommy in 1938. Others have said that Frank's first show was at the Palmer House in Chicago, while Jo Stafford thinks that the first song he sang was 'Stardust'. According to one member of Tommy's band, "The guy actually looked into a mirror and pinched himself." Even Frank may well have found the whole thing difficult to believe. Almost immediately, Frank was in the studio with Tommy to cut their first sides together on 1 February. Dorsey and his 15-piece band backed Frank singing 'The Sky Fell Down' and 'Too Romantic'. The latter song was from the Bing Crosby and Bob Hope film *The Road to Singapore*. 'The Sky Fell Down' was arranged by Axel Stordahl, who was one of Tommy's regular arrangers. It was the first time that Frank and Axel worked together, the start of one of the most fruitful relationships of Frank's career.

Frank had to be on his mettle because the boys in the band were in need of some impressing. "They loved Jack Leonard, and I think they were saying 'Well let's see what he can do'", Frank later recalled. Tommy's other vocalists were three guys and a girl, known as the Pied Pipers. They had started out as an octet in 1938 but by the time Frank joined they had reduced to the quartet of Chuck Lowry, Billy Wilson (Clark Yocum replaced Billy in April 1940), John Huddleston, and Jo Stafford (John and Jo were married). To begin with, only Jo Stafford seemed to appreciate Frank's singing: "I was almost entirely unfamiliar with him. In fact I never laid eyes on him until he actually walked on stage for the first time. We were sitting on the stage when however, it was very much business as normal. They were in and out of the studio in New York cutting songs such as 'Fools Rush In (Where Angels Fear to Tread)', 'East of the Sun (and West of the Moon)', and 'Imagination'.

A little under three weeks after the band finished their run at the Paramount, Frank had his first hit record with the Tommy Dorsey Orchestra. Recorded on 4 March, it was a song written by Johnny Burke and Jimmy Van Heusen and arranged by Axel Stordahl. 'Polka Dots and Moonbeams' was the second song written by Van Heusen that Frank cut (the first being 'Shake Down the Stars', recorded a week earlier). It would be the first of many hit recordings of Jimmy's songs by Frank. Others included 'Nancy (with the Laughing Face)', 'I Thought About You', and 'Come Fly With Me'. 'Polka Dots' made No 18 in the *Billboard* chart for just one week on 27 April, 1940. In 1961, Frank made a tribute album to his old boss, entitled *I Remember Tommy,* and did a new version of the song arranged by Sy Oliver, one of Tommy's old arrangers.

SHOWMANSHIP

Although things were going well for Frank, it was not all good news. *Billboard* magazine reported: "He's a good ballad singer, but nil on showmanship." At the same time, their College Survey showed that Frank was at No 22 on the list, while Tommy Dorsey's former singer, Jack Leonard, was at No 2; Ray Eberle, Glenn Miller's vocalist, was at No 1 (none too surprising, given the supremacy of the Miller band).

Personally for Frank things were very much on the up when Nancy gave birth to their daughter Nancy at the Margaret Hague Maternity Hospital in Jersey City on 8 June, 1940. According to daughter Nancy's reminiscences many years later, Frank missed the birth because he was

CONNIE HAINES

"Call her a trouper, for that's one of the outstanding qualities." CRITIC ROBERT W DANA

CONNIE WAS JUST 18 WHEN HARRY JAMES HEARD HER REHEARSING IN A MUSIC PUBLISHER'S OFFICE; HE IMMEDIATELY OFFERED HER A JOB. SHE WAS CALLING HERSELF YVONNE JASME AND IT WAS HARRY JAMES WHO CHANGED HER NAME.

Born Marie Antoinette Yvonne Jamais in Savannah, Georgia, on 20 January, 1922, Connie had been "discovered" on Fred Allen's

radio talent show, which broadcast from New York's Roxy Theatre (the same one that young Frank had tried out on).

After leaving Harry James, Connie joined Tommy Dorsey, and then quit to sing on Abbott and Costello's radio programme. She went on to have a few minor solo hits, away from the Big Bands, in the late 1940s. During her career she has made more than 200 recordings for Decca, Capitol, Mercury, and Columbia. She even recorded for Motown Records on an album of songs written by Smokey Robinson.

Over the course of her career, Connie Haines played Broadway, Las Vegas, and Disneyland, made movies, appeared on television and radio, and was still performing in the 21st century – not bad for a "cornball" from Savannah.

away working in Los Angeles. Frank himself claims he was at the Hotel Astor, "I hated missing that. It was just a taste of things to come, man. When I think of all the family affairs and events I would miss over the years because I was on the road." In tribute to his boss, Frank and Nancy asked Tommy Dorsey to be godfather to their baby. Frank's relationship with the rest of the Dorsey

THE DORSEY ORGANIZATION
"When I was a kid and Sinatra was singing with Tommy Dorsey I loved him then."

RAY CHARLES

FRANK, BUDDY AND TOMMY DORSEY
Frank, Buddy Rich, and Tommy Dorsey appeared to be getting along just fine when this picture was taken.

band settled down. According to Frank, "For maybe the first five months I missed the James band. So I kept to myself, but then I've always been a loner – all my life. Eventually I shared a room with another loner, Buddy Rich." Buddy was the third big ego in the band, and as Frank's reputation, and billing, grew larger, Buddy became less and less enamoured with their singer. Things got off to a bad start when Dorsey introduced his new singer to his drummer: "I want you to meet another pain in the ass," he reportedly said. One night in June, back stage at the Hotel Astor in New York, things came to a head. Jo Stafford recalls: "Buddy called Frank a name and Frank grabbed a heavy pitcher filled with water and ice and threw it at Buddy's head. Buddy ducked. If he hadn't, he probably would have been killed or seriously hurt. The pitcher hit the wall so hard that pieces of glass were embedded in the plaster." On other occasions their simmering bad feeling boiled over and they actually took to swinging punches.

Buddy was not Frank's only *bête noire*. In April 1940, Tommy offered Connie Haines a job with his band, which, given the strengths of the vocal department, must have made it a little crowded at times. Connie picked Tommy over Glenn Miller, who had offered her $200 a week; she, like Frank, felt that Tommy was the man to be with: "He was a starmaker."

Connie, just 4 ft 11 in tall, later recalled that Frank would not let her share the same microphone so she, in retaliation, would pick a guy in uniform in the audience and sing just to him. This had the dual effect of getting the audience going and annoying Frank. Connie would also dance the lindy or boogie when she was not singing, which also proved popular with the boys in the crowd, Frank's usual retort was, "Do your thing, cornball."

TECHNIQUE AND TANTRUMS

Whatever difficulties and frustrations Frank felt were far outweighed by what he identified as the advantages of singing with Tommy Dorsey. The most important thing for Frank was what he was learning from his boss. People have said that Frank copied Tommy's style of dressing, his manner of speaking, even his temper tantrums – all of which may have been true. But what was far more important was what Frank learned about vocal technique from Tommy's

trombone playing. "The thing that influenced me most was the way Tommy played his trombone. He would play it all the way through, seemingly without breathing, for eight, ten, maybe sixteen bars. I used to sit behind him on the bandstand and watch, trying to see him sneak a breath. But I never saw the bellows move in his back. His jacket didn't even move. Finally I discovered that he had a 'sneak' pinhole in the corner of his mouth – not an actual pinhole, but a tiny place where he was breathing. He'd take a quick breath and play another four bars with that breath. Why couldn't a singer do that too?" Well Frank did, and "The Voice" was born. This technique of taking a breath in the middle of a note without "breaking" the note was also a trick of American Indian singers.

It was not just by watching that Frank learned breathing control. He started to go running on the track at the Stevens Institute in Hoboken. He would run for a lap and then trot for a lap, all the while building his stamina. He even sang while he ran to control his breathing better.

> **66** Frank was the chairman of the board even back then – he had the healthiest ego! **99**
>
> CONNIE HAINES

FRANK IN 1941
"Singing with the Big Bands is like lifting weights – you're conditioning yourself."

He also went swimming and did lengths underwater, "thinking song lyrics to myself as I swam, holding my breath." Tommy also offered Frank some advice: he told him to listen to Bing Crosby. "All that matters to him is the words," said Tommy, "and that's the only thing that ought to matter to you." This was solid advice to which Frank paid attention for the rest of his career.

THE LONG AND WINDING ROAD

A month or so after the contretemps with Buddy Rich at the Hotel Astor and the birth of Nancy, Frank recorded 'I Could Make You Care' from a movie called *Ladies Must Live*. It was written by Sammy Cahn, a man who, like Jimmy Van Heusen with whom he later collaborated, was to figure large and long in Frank's career. According to Sammy, Frank's marriage was already showing signs of wear and tear, as the initial euphoria of Nancy's birth began to fade. "He told me how unhappy he was being a married man. I gave him the George Raft Syndrome. 'George Raft has been married all his life, put it this way — you're on the road all the time, you at least can go home to clean sheets.' He kind of understood that."

One thing that everyone found difficult was the sheer slog of life on the road, particularly when they were doing one-night stands. One night they might be at the Raymore Ballroom in Boston and the next it was at the Van Cleve Hotel in Dayton, Ohio. As Connie Haines recalled, "We would all travel on one bus — a broken down old Greyhound bus — and there would be just four females — Jo Stafford, Tommy's secretary, me, and my Mum. Later, Mum had to give guardian status to Tommy Dorsey as I was still underage! The band were all real gentlemen. Tommy would always sit me upfront, right behind the driver. Most of the time on the bus, we would all sleep. Once I smelt smoke, and I yelled out 'Fire!', and Tommy came to me and said 'Don't worry! It's just the Blue Room Boys!' Joey Bushkin was known a bit for that sort of thing, but really there was never much." According to Jo Stafford, it was hell. "Most of the time you never even saw a bed. Maybe once every couple of weeks. The rest of the time, you slept and dressed on the band bus. A different city every night. Sometimes really long hops. Once, after an unusually long trip the bus rolled into town real early one morning and there were all these college students waiting to greet us. And I had my hair up in curlers, all rumpled, and I overheard one kid say, with terror and pity in his voice, 'My Gawd! I think that's Jo Stafford!'"

One aspect of all this that must have tested Frank was the cleanliness, or lack of it, when travelling on the bus. According to his band mates he was "sensationally fastidious". "He used to change his shirt every day. Sometimes he took two or three baths a day. Also damned if he'd eat from a dirty plate." This sounds almost quaint 60 years on, but life was very different then. The strain on any singer's vocal chords must have been intense,

I'LL NEVER SMILE AGAIN

FRANK'S FIRST NO I WAS not strictly speaking a solo hit, and that's not just because Tommy Dorsey's name appeared on the label in the largest type. Tommy Dorsey and the Pied Pipers, along with Frank, using an arrangement by Fred Stulce, Tommy's alto sax player, recorded 'I'll Never Smile Again' on 23 May, 1940.

Ruth Lowe, the piano player with Ina Ray Hutton's all-girl band, wrote the song following the death of her husband Harold Cohen in 1939, a few weeks after they wed. At least, that's the PR story. Ruth's song won a song-writing contest in her native Canada and had been played by Percy Faith on Canadian radio; a demo was made shortly afterwards. When offered the song by a publisher, Tommy initially passed on it, and Glenn Miller recorded it and released it in April 1940, when it failed to make an impression.

Tommy decided to cut the song, and because there was a celesta (a small keyboard instrument in which hammers strike steel plates to produce an ethereal, bell-like sound) in the studio, someone suggested that Joe Bushkin, the band's new pianist, should use it. The effect, when coupled with the sweetest of vocals from Frank and the Pied Pipers, with Jo Stafford to the fore, proved irresistible; it was the first recording made by Frank together with the Pied Pipers. It made the charts at the end of June 1940 and climbed to the top a month later, staying there for 12 weeks. Only Glenn Miller's 'In the Mood' had stayed at No I for as long in the previous decade.

Typically, for Frank, it was a song that was to keep turning up throughout his career. Soon after the initial hit, it was rerecorded for the film *Las Vegas Nights*, in which the Tommy Dorsey band appeared. Frank did it again for his radio show in 1945, on which Tommy Dorsey and the Pied Pipers were guests. In 1959, Frank cut a slower, moodier, middle-aged version of the song with Gordon Jenkins

for his album *No One Cares*. It sounded just as good, maybe even better. In 1965, he cut another version for his album *A Man and His Music*, which was a fairly faithful reproduction of the original hit version. In 1982, 'I'll Never Smile Again' was inducted into the Grammy Hall of Fame.

THE BILLBOARD CHARTS

While we have referred to "hit records" and "chart positions", the pop chart was, up until July 1940, far from an exact science, and even after that it can only be said to have got better.

The first pop chart was a list of the top vaudeville songs, published in 1913 by the magazine *Billboard*. The radio show *Your Lucky Strike Hit Parade* began in 1935 and ran until 1959, featuring the top fifteen songs of the week. In 1935, *Billboard* began running a chart called Your Hit Parade. Before this, charts made up of record company sales and sheet music sales had been carried. Your Hit Parade was far from definitive, but it did include radio airplay information. In late 1938, *Billboard* began a new chart, a survey of the most popular records on US jukeboxes.

On 20 July, 1940, *Billboard* magazine ran its first bestselling records chart, which was a far more accurate indication of the taste of the nation. Even then, *Billboard* ran separate bestseller and jukebox favourites on a regional basis, which showed that it was very often a different taste, depending on where you lived. Somewhat appropriately, the first No I on the new *Billboard* best sellers list was 'I'll Never Smile Again'.

Given the rivalry between Tommy and his brother Jimmy, it was ironic that at No 2 on the bestsellers' list was the Jimmy Dorsey Band with their version of 'The Breeze and I'.

JO STAFFORD

"The unfound star." FRANK SINATRA, MAY 1943

SHE HAS BEEN CALLED ONE OF THE MOST IMPORTANT FEMALE VOCALISTS OF ALL TIME, YET TODAY NEITHER HER NAME NOR REPUTATION WOULD REGISTER WITH MANY UNDER THE AGE OF 65. SHE WAS THE NO 1 RANKED SINGER OF THE PRE-ROCK ERA.

Jo Stafford had more than 70 *Billboard* Top 30 hits as a solo artist as well as a number as a member of the Pied Pipers. During her solo career, she topped the charts on five occasions between 1945 and 1954.

Born in California on 12 November, 1920, Jo studied classical music, intent on becoming an opera singer. The Depression put paid to that plan, so she and her sisters began singing on a Los Angeles radio station as the Stafford Sisters, as well as singing in a 1937 Fred Astaire movie. When they broke up, Jo found work with the stylish harmony group the Pied Pipers. In 1938, the eight-piece group began working with Tommy Dorsey on radio but were fired by the show's sponsor, who did not like them. In 1939, by which time they were a four-piece, Dorsey offered them a job, and success was just around the corner. The Pied Pipers stayed with Dorsey until Thanksgiving Day 1942, when, in one of his frequent rages, he fired them. In early 1943, Jo went solo with Capitol Records and had her first hit in January 1944.

At Capitol Jo worked with Paul Weston, the label's A&R director, and the two ended up marrying in 1952. Her World War II recordings were very popular with servicemen,

which won her the nickname "GI Jo". During the 1950s, Jo had her own television series, as well as recording several albums with her husband as Jonathan and Darlene Edwards. They parodied a very bad lounge act and won a Grammy for their efforts.

Jo semi-retired from showbusiness in 1966 and stopped working completely in the late 1970s, making only one more public appearance: in December 1990, she appeared with the Hi-Lo's at the Society Of Singers' Salute To Frank Sinatra along with Tony Bennett, Peggy Lee, Ella Fitzgerald, Connie Haines, and many others.

BIGGEST HITS
'Candy' No 1 1945
'Temptation' No 1 1947
'My Darling, My Darling' No 1, 1948 (with Gordon MacRae)

ALWAYS BUY CHESTERFIELD
RIGHT COMBINATION WORLD'S BEST TOBACCOS PROPERLY AGED

> 66 Take the jackets off, we got another programme to play. 99
>
> **TOMMY DORSEY**

but, on the other hand, if you could last the course you came out stronger. Luckily Frank was blessed with good equipment. "I had real strong pipes in those days," he would say years later. Frank's training regimen coupled with life on the road just made him get better and better. What was amazing was that he appeared to do it all so effortlessly. Joe Bushkin, who had recently joined the band, had the job of rehearsing Frank on any new material (Frank could not read music). It created a bond between them and they remained good friends.

The bond was perhaps strengthened because at the time Bushkin was another who had regular run-ins with Buddy Rich. One night Bushkin was late for a show, so late that they had already started, and when he arrived, Tommy stopped the band and said, "You used to play with us." Joe was also in the wrong uniform – it was a Tuesday, the day they changed into the light suits. Joe was fined the regular fine of having to buy the whole band a drink. As the

waiter approached with wine for everybody Joe told him to "cancel the wine". He said he was not paying because every night that Tommy was away Buddy Rich had been late and he, Joe, was not paying until Buddy paid first. "Afterwards Buddy and I went out in the park and beat the shit out of each other. Well, it was a fighting band", said Bushkin, later. Tommy came running out and tried to stop the fight, not because he was worried about two of his star turns, but because he was concerned about their clothes: "Take the jackets off, we got another programme to play."

Between July and September 1940, the Tommy Dorsey band deputized for Bob Hope on an NBC radio show. At the same time, Frank and the band were in and out of the New York studio cutting more sides. The exposure on the radio certainly helped with record sales. 'Imagination', 'Fools Rush In (Where Angels Fear to Tread')', 'All This and Heaven Too', 'The One I Love (Belongs to Somebody Else')', 'Love Lies', and 'The Call of the Canyon' all made the *Billboard* bestseller's list over the summer and all featured Frank, as well as the Pied Pipers on the first four songs. 'I'll Never Smile Again' reached No 1 three weeks after they began their run.

FORTUNE AND FAME

In October, Tommy Dorsey's band headed west to California, and Hollywood in particular. They were there to film a sequence for a Paramount comedy, *Las Vegas Nights*, for which Frank was paid the standard extra's rate of $15 a day. At the same time the band, along with Frank, Connie Haines, and the Pied Pipers, were appearing on a new weekly radio show for NBC called *Fame and Fortune*. Frank's numbers included 'Marie' (Jack Leonard's big hit with Tommy Dorsey), 'I've Got a Restless Spell', 'Our Love Affair', and 'Shadows in the Sand'. The gimmick behind *Fame and Fortune* was a competition for aspiring songwriters to send in their efforts for Frank to sing on air; the winner getting $100 for the song. The first show was broadcast on 17 October at 8:30 pm. The show's announcer introduced the winners with words to inspire others: "The second spot in our *Fame and Fortune Show* is always saved for the romantic Frank Sinatra. Take Frank's voice and a swell ballad like this one, and you have the perfect twosome." Tommy Dorsey, along with Frank, recorded two of the winners, 'Oh Look At Me Now' and 'You Might Have Belonged to Another' in January 1941. According to *Variety*, "fortunately for the listeners the program includes only one sample of this solicited stuff." The report went on to comment on the craftsman-like job done by Tommy on the first week's winning entry, 'I've Got a Restless Spell'.

While Dorsey and the band were in Hollywood they took the time to record. Among the sides that Frank cut was 'Stardust', along with the Pied Pipers, which made No 7 in January 1941. Frank's recording added to the tally that makes this one of the most recorded songs of all time. He also indulged in some extra-curricular activities while he was in LA. No doubt appearing in his first proper movie, albeit as an unbilled artiste, had a positive effect on his libido. Staying at the Plaza Hotel on Vine Street was a far cry from Hoboken and the band bus. Frank met, and began to spend time with, a pretty blonde actress called Alora Gooding, and before the week was out she had moved into Frank's room at the hotel. By any number of accounts Frank's head had been turned by the glamour of it all, and he had convinced himself that he'd fallen in love. Nancy apparently found out about this affair in a good deal more detail than she had about the other times that Frank had played away. Apparently her reaction was a mixture of hurt and pragmatism. She was at home, which was a good home, her husband earned well, and what happened when he was away did not come home with him. In truth, it was another step along the street of dreams that would end in divorce, but for now it was just a long and winding road.

THE TEMPLE OF TERPSICHORE

It was not only filming and a radio show that had brought Tommy Dorsey out to the West Coast. He was also there for the opening of a prestigious new venue in Los Angeles, the million-dollar coral and chrome Palladium Ballroom. Prior to the Palladium opening, the Dorsey band played the Paramount along with the Dorothy Lamour film *Moon Over Burma*. According to the *LA Times*, "The Jitterbug's delight, Tommy Dorsey and his musical gang opened at the Paramount yesterday (18 October), easing in with the alluring 'Song of the Nile' which gave no hint of the racket to come. There are only a few 'merciful passages in all that pitiless storm of sound', to quote Mark Twain. Making special hits were trumpeter Ziggy Elman and drummer Buddy Rich. Warbling nicely were the Pied Pipers and Frank Sinatra, while Connie Haines turned out to be one of those throat-splitting blues singers."

The Palladium's opening night was two weeks later on Thursday 31 October, Hallowe'en. Fifty searchlights combed the skies and limos dropped off a parade of stars to be at the opening. But it was not just stars who attended: the place was filled to capacity. Over 8,000 people (all paying $1) were somehow jammed in, and it was Tommy Dorsey's trombone that heralded the opening at 8:30 pm. An hour or so later, the lovely Dorothy Lamour helped Tommy cut the ribbon that encircled the band platform. Many people who could not get in watched outside as Mary Astor, Claude Rains, Alice Faye, Ida Lupino, and Gracie Allen and George Burns arrived. Two days or so after the opening, during a speech in

1940 ON THE JUKEBOX

FRANK'S CHART HITS WITH TOMMY DORSEY

'POLKA DOTS AND MOONBEAMS'
Johnny Burke & Jimmy Van Heusen
27 April, No 18, 1 week

'SAY IT'
Frank Loesser & Jimmy McHugh
25 May, No 12, 3 weeks

'IMAGINATION'
Jimmy Van Heusen & Johnny Burke
22 June, No 8, 6 weeks

'I'LL NEVER SMILE AGAIN'
Ruth Lowe
29 June, No 1, 18 weeks

'FOOLS RUSH IN (WHERE ANGELS FEAR TO TREAD)'
Johnny Mercer & Rube Bloom
10 August, No 17, 2 weeks

'ALL THIS AND HEAVEN TOO'
Eddie DeLange & Jimmy Van Heusen
10 August, No 15, 2 weeks

'THE ONE I LOVE (BELONGS TO SOMEBODY ELSE)'
Gus Kahn & Isham Jones
31 August, No 15, 4 weeks

'LOVE LIES'
Joseph Meyer, Carl Sigman & Ralph Freed
31 August, No 17, 1 week

'THE CALL OF THE CANYON'
Billy Hill (from the film Rhythm on the Range)
21 September, No 18, 3 weeks

'TRADEWINDS'
Cliff Friend & Charles Tobias
21 September, No 10, 4 weeks

'I COULD MAKE YOU CARE'
Sammy Cahn & Saul Chaplin (from the film Ladies Must Live)
12 October, No 18, 1 week

'OUR LOVE AFFAIR'
Arthur Freed & Roger Edens (from the Busby Berkeley film Strike Up the Band)
9 November, No 5, 3 weeks

'WE THREE (MY ECHO, MY SHADOW, AND ME)'
Dick Robertson, Nelson Cogane & Sammy Mysels
30 November, No 3, 5 weeks

Artie Shaw
VICTOR'S FAMOUS CLARINETIST-MAESTRO

The inaugural *Billboard* bestsellers' chart at the end of July 1941 really marks the dawn of the modern pop era, with the added relevancy of Frank Sinatra singing on his first No 1 record. The sales of records up to this point had been fewer than many have since speculated. The sales of sheet music were a significant part of the whole music industry, and for a long time records supplied to jukeboxes were a significant part of the money earned by record labels. Joining the Dorsey band when he did was a case of perfect timing.

Quite apart from his No 1 and his first chart entry with 'Polka Dots and Moonbeams', it was a good year all around for Frank Sinatra. Thirteen hits and a total of 53 weeks on the *Billboard* bestseller's chart was no mean achievement. Clearly the selling power of Tommy Dorsey's band should not be underestimated, nor the added appeal of the Pied Pipers. During the year, Frank Sinatra featured on 34 sides released with the Tommy Dorsey band.

The information to compile this and future explanations of the success of Frank Sinatra's recordings is taken from Joel Whitburn's *Pop Hits 1940–1954* (and subsequent volumes). Joel's invaluable work in compiling the data into a series of books has been done through analysis of the three *Billboard* pop singles charts that were in operation at this time: the bestseller's, the jukebox and the disc jockey charts. This is why information may differ between the peak positions of certain records as reported on *Billboard*'s three pop singles charts versus other contemporary magazines. These charts are a more accurate reflection of the overall taste of the nation because they take into account airplay and jukebox popularity, which, back in the days when many could not afford phonographs, was a more accurate barometer.

TOP OF THE POPS

The most successful artist in the US during the year was Glenn Miller and his Orchestra, who topped the charts on eight separate occasions, for a total of 24 weeks. Of his hits, 'In the Mood', which stayed at No 1 for 12 weeks, and 'Tuxedo Junction', which managed 9 weeks, were the most successful. Other big sellers were Bing Crosby's 'Only Forever', which stayed at No 1 from October until December, when it was replaced by 'Frenesi' from Artie Shaw and His Orchestra which topped the charts for 13 weeks.

Tommy Dorsey
VICTOR'S INCOMPARABLE SENTIMENTAL GENTLEMAN

THE PALLADIUM

LOCATED ON SUNSET BOULEVARD, THE NEW BALLROOM IN 1940S LOS ANGELES WAS THE PALLADIUM. DESCRIBED BY THE PRESS AS THE "TEMPLE OF TERPSICHORE" AND "EVERYBODY'S NIGHT CLUB", THE PALLADIUM WAS SOPHISTICATION ITSELF.

IT WAS THE VISION of film producer Maurice "Maury" Cohen, who wanted to create the world's largest dining and dancing palace. The silver and pearl-grey interior with coral accents was designed by Frank Don Riha, who also created a coordinated light show in harmony with the music. According to Connie Haines, "Of all the places we played, I think I liked the Hollywood Palladium best. It was a huge place with everything just right." The Palladium had a 12,000 sq ft oval-shaped dance floor, with a balcony that ran the length of each side of the dancing area. It could accommodate 6,000 dancers, doing the Lindy Hop or the Suzie Q, while another 1,000 could dine in comfort. Its main bar and circular cocktail lounge had a 50-ft diameter redwood dome. For the underage dancers, there was a 200 ft milk bar.

"I never ate there; it was too expensive for me. I was in the service and used to go there with a navy blue kerchief covering part of my USNR T-shirt and my black GI shoes, self-shined... civilian guys usually wore a necktie

EVERYBODY'S NIGHT CLUB
The Palladium is still operating today and has become an important location for movies. Among those shot there have been *The Bodyguard*, *1941*, and *The Blues Brothers*.

with either a suit or sport coat and slacks. Girls usually wore what I'd call cocktail dresses. It cost 50 cents to get in and drinks were 40 cents, but I bought never more than one because I had virtually no money!" said Bert Moore, who was a Palladium regular while serving in the US Navy.

Marion Wallien also remembered the Palladium. "My date and I drove there in his father's car, a yellow and black, two-tone Studebaker with four doors. The only one of its kind in Glendale, it stuck out like a sore thumb. It was one of the great thrills of my life, even though I didn't dance much. At the start of each set there would be couples 'just standing' at the bandstand. By set's end no one would be dancing, everyone would be either holding hands swaying with the music, that's if you were just on a date, but if you had 'it going on' the boy would be standing in back of his girl holding her around the waist listening to Frankie, the Pied Pipers, and Tommy Dorsey's band. The bar was roped off, even now when I see a velvet rope I think of the Palladium. I used to have just one coke in a glass, with ice, that had a small little umbrella in it. The crowd was mostly young people 20 or under. I always stayed till the very end, 'till the last dog was hung."

Philadelphia, President Roosevelt denied that the US was to go to war. Just under two weeks later, he was re-elected as president in an unprecedented third term in office. Frank was still in Los Angeles during the elections, staying there until at least 28 November.

WAR AND WORK

Frank was back home in Hoboken by mid-December. He had an important task to carry out on 17 December – the completion of his Draft Board form regarding his suitability for military service. Along with hundreds of thousands of young American men, Frank filled out the form – known officially as the Selective Service Questionnaire – and when it came to the bit about his physical condition, he wrote "To the best of my knowledge, I have no physical or mental defects or diseases." No doubt his running at the Stevens Institute and his swimming made him feel, despite his thin frame, that he was in pretty good shape. Despite the progress of the war in Europe and President Roosevelt's speech about not involving the US in the conflict, Frank and many others probably hoped that they would not be called upon to fight. Two weeks after Frank filled out the questionnaire, Roosevelt told Americans in a radio broadcast that the US was "the arsenal of democracy".

The events that would unfold in the coming year would, of course, bring the US into the conflict with Germany, as well as with Japan. Frank's answers to the Selective Service Questionnaire would later become the subject of an FBI investigation and his conduct a matter of scrutiny by both the press and the public in a potentially highly damaging time in his career. The day after Frank filled in the questionnaire, he was on stage with the Tommy Dorsey band, the Pied Pipers, and Connie Haines at New York's Paramount Theatre for an engagement that ran for almost a month. One afternoon, during their run at the prestigious venue, the band were in the studio working on a couple of numbers – Joe Bushkin and John DeVries's 'Oh Look at Me Now' and 'You Might Have Belonged to Another' by Pat West and Lucille Harmon; both had been winners on *Fame and Fortune*. It was the first time that Frank and Connie featured on a recording as a duet. In the event, 'Oh Look at Me Now' reached No 2 in March 1941, where it spent six weeks. For most of that time it was kept from the top spot by 'Amapola (Pretty Little Poppy)', recorded by Tommy's brother Jimmy. It must have rankled.

With *Fame and Fortune* coming to an end on 10 April, it was one-night stands throughout the East Coast and the Midwest that took up most of the spring and summer of 1941. Among the many one-night stands was one at the Benjamin Franklin Hotel in Philadelphia on 16 May. It was the Ivy Ball for Penn State University, and the Dorsey Band shared the bill with Woody Herman's Band. On 27 June, Frank and Tommy Dorsey were in the studio in New

York cutting four sides. Three days later, Germany broke its pact with Russia and invaded the country—an invasion that would end in humiliation for Hitler's forces at Stalingrad. A war that would involve the US was seeming ever more likely.

Back on the home front, demand for Tommy Dorsey recordings featuring Frank was on the increase. While the Dorsey band did not have a chart topper during 1941, the records generally reached higher positions than those during the previous year. This had a positive effect on Frankie's earnings, and Tommy was by this time paying his singer $400 a week. But things were coming to a head for American involvement in the war in Europe when, in July, President Roosevelt informed Congress that US troops had landed in Iceland to prevent the country from falling into German hands. (Iceland was vital to the seaborne trade between Britain and the US, and the deployment of US Marines helped to free up British troops that had hitherto formed the country's garrison.) The Dorsey band on its tour of the Midwest must have been worried about the effects, both professionally and personally, of war with Germany. By the end of July, there was a looming threat in the West as Japanese troops invaded French Indochina, and threatened Thailand and Cambodia. Both Britain and the US denounced Japan as an aggressor.

On 27 August, the Dorsey band began another engagement at the Paramount in New York City. This three-week run was for Frank proof of his burgeoning stardom, as girls mobbed him and his vocal spots became the high points of the band's show. It was probably on this engagement at the Paramount that Connie Haines saved Frank's life. "The stage would come up from the pit… up really high, and after it would go down again. One time, after we had closed with 'I'll Never Smile Again', we were going down and three girls grabbed Frank's tie and wouldn't let go. He was hanging there. I ran over and screamed and hit out at their hands. Tommy ran over too and joined in too, and we got him away!"

NEW HORIZONS

It was around this time that Frank started to consider a career away from Tommy Dorsey. To this point it was the Big Bands and their leaders that were the stars. Frank sensed that there was an opportunity to strike out and become his own man. George "Bullets" Durgom, Tommy's road manager, had been hearing that radio stations were reluctant to play Tommy's recordings that did not feature Frank. Of the 15 Tommy Dorsey records that made the charts in 1941, only three did not have Frank singing on them. A number of other releases by the band failed to chart at all.

A month after the run at the Paramount, the band travelled cross-country doing one-nighters and went back for a spell at the Palladium in Los Angeles. Despite the fact that Tommy felt they were not paying him enough, it was still a lot more than he could get for most venues. There was also another movie featuring the band to be made called *Ship Ahoy*. While they were in California, the Japanese attacked Pearl Harbor and Germany declared war on the US.

LAS VEGAS NIGHTS

Released in the US on 24 March, 1941, this 90-minute long black-and-white Paramount movie was directed by a Hollywood veteran of the silent screen, 46-year-old Ralph Murphy. Starring Phil Regan, Bert Wheeler, and Constance Moore, it featured the Tommy Dorsey Band playing themselves. When Frank sings 'I'll Never Smile Again', his vocals are largely obscured by dialogue. Not quite a case of blink and you'll miss him, but pretty close. The movie also featured 'Dolores', which made it to No 7 at the end of April when it was released on record.

He sings prettily in an unphotogenic manner.

GEORGE T SIMON, *METRONOME* MAGAZINE

OPENING NIGHT
The Hollywood Palladium's opening night. According to band leader Les Brown, "It was the hottest place around."

BLUEBIRD BEAT

The talk around every American table at Christmas 1941 was about the war and how it would affect individuals and families alike. Casualties in World War I had been on the low side for the US when compared with the European countries. However, the shock of the attack on Pearl Harbor and of a war on two fronts struck deep into the psyche of Americans.

With Christmas over, it was back to work for Frank, and business as normal with two recording sessions sandwiched before and after Christmas 1941, one on 22 December and the other on 29 December. On the later session, Frank and the Pied Pipers recorded 'Moonlight Bay' for *Ship Ahoy*, although when the movie came out it is Connie Haines who can be seen in the place of the Pied Pipers' Jo Stafford.

Early in January 1942, Frank made his first step towards freedom from Tommy Dorsey, although it was more artistic than contractual. At RCA's Hollywood studio, between 2:00 and 5:15 pm, Frank recorded four

FRANK AT BLUEBIRD
Frank recorded four songs for the Bluebird label on 19 January, 1942, at RCA's Hollywood Studio.

AMERICA DECLARES WAR, 8 DECEMBER 1941

"You can quote Sinatra as saying that he believes it is wrong for anybody to own a piece of him and collect on it when that owner is doing nothing for Sinatra."

FRANK TO REPORTERS

songs with an orchestra conducted by Axel Stordahl. Some of the players were drawn from Tommy's band, including Fred Stulce, Pied Piper Clark Yocum playing guitar, and, for the first time, there were strings on a Frank Sinatra record. The four songs were 'The Night We Called It a Day', 'The Lamplighters Serenade', 'The Song Is You', and 'Night and Day'. Henry Myerson, the Victor A&R man who supervised Frank's first solo session, commented, "Frank was not like a band vocalist at all. He came in self-assured, slugging on that first date, he stood his ground and displayed no humility, phoney or real." There may well have been an element of bravado in Frank's stance, because in reality his vocals are less self-assured than those he made soon after – or just before for that matter.

THE BUDGET BLUEBIRD

These records were to be released on Victor's "budget" label, Bluebird. It has been suggested that in some way Frank did this behind Tommy's back. This is totally false, since on the Union contract for the session it says at the bottom, "Property of Tommy Dorsey". It has also been mooted that Tommy "tricked" Frank into having these records released on Bluebird so that Frank got less money. Given the nature of Frank's contract with Tommy, it would also have meant that Tommy got less money too. It may have been Machiavellian chicanery by Tommy in order somehow to exert control over his protégé; it may also have been Victor thinking they were more likely to sell more records at a lower price (Bluebird records were 35 cents, Victor's 75 cents). Whatever the reason, it had the effect of giving Frank's career a further boost, despite some poor initial reviews of the recordings.

Frank was obviously excited by his new records. Axel Stordahl related: "I'll never forget when we got the advance dubs on the first two sides. Frank had a room in the Hollywood Plaza on Vine St opposite the Brown Derby. We sat in it all afternoon of a sunny day, playing the two sides over and over on a portable machine. Frank just couldn't believe his ears. He was so excited, you almost believed he'd never recorded before."

Even before any of the Bluebird recordings were released Frank had the idea of sending them to Manie Sacks, the head of A&R at Columbia Records. Manie was sufficiently impressed to agree to sign Frank once he was free of his contract with Tommy Dorsey. Frank was likely to have been quite confident of achieving his aim and was probably unaware of the contractual difficulties he would face with the savvy Tommy Dorsey.

In March 1942, 'Night and Day' was released. This Cole Porter song from the 1931 Broadway musical *The Gay Divorcee* had been a No 1 for

1941 ON THE JUKEBOX

FRANK'S US CHART HITS WITH TOMMY DORSEY

'STARDUST'
Hoagy Carmichael & Mitchell Parrish
4 January, No 7, 1 week

'OH LOOK AT ME NOW'
Joe Bushkin & John De Vries
1 March, No 2, 12 weeks

'YOU MIGHT HAVE BELONGED TO ANOTHER'
Lucille Harmon & Pat West
22 March, No 16, 1 week

'DO I WORRY?'
Stanley Cowan & Bobby Worth
12 April, No 4, 3 weeks

'DOLORES'
Louis Alter & Frank Loesser
26 April, No 7, 2 weeks

'EVERYTHING HAPPENS TO ME'
Matt Dennis & Tom Adair
3 May, No 9, 1 week

'LET'S GET AWAY FROM IT ALL PARTS 1 & 2'
Matt Dennis & Tom Adair
10 May, No 7, 2 weeks

'YOU AND I'
Meredith Wilson
30 August, No 16, 3 weeks

'I GUESS I'LL HAVE TO DREAM THE REST'
Harold Green, Martin Block & Mickey Stoner
4 October, No 15, 3 weeks

'THIS LOVE OF MINE'
Sol Parker, Hank Sanicola & Frank Sinatra
25 October, No 3, 16 weeks

'TWO IN LOVE'
Meredith Wilson
20 December, No 9, 1 week

'A SINNER KISSED AN ANGEL'
Ray Joseph & Mack David
20 December, No 20, 1 week

Frank's recordings with Tommy in 1941 were, on the face of it, less successful than in 1940. However, he did score with eight Top 10 records and of those two, 'Oh Look At Me Now' (a winner on *Fame and Fortune*) and 'This Love of Mine' were significant hits. 1941 was a year in which the Big Bands still dominated. Frank had not yet broken through as his own man, he was still Tommy Dorsey's boy singer.

'This Love of Mine' is one of the very few songs that Frank had a hand in writing. Sol Parker was 21 in 1941 when he took a song he had written to a friend of his who then took it to Frank and Hank Sanicola. "My friend played it on the piano and I sang it," Parker recalled. "And there was a skinny little Italian kid, stroking his chin and listening. When we were done, he said, 'Let's make it more commercial.'" After a little tinkering, it became 'This Love of Mine' and earned Parker, from his third share of the royalties, around $300,000 over the years.

Other big hits in 1941 were Artie Shaw's 'Frenesi', Jimmy Dorsey's 'Amapola (Pretty Little Poppy)' and 'Green Eyes', 'Daddy' by Sammy Kaye, and 'Piano Concerto in B Flat' by Freddy Martin (an arrangement of Tchaikovsky's piano concerto). Every song that made No 1 on the bestsellers' list was from a Big Band, as was just about every record that made the Top 10.

THE FIRST GOLD DISC

On 10 February, 1942, on a Chesterfield (cigarettes) radio show, Glenn Miller was awarded the first 'Gold Disc' for sales of over one million of a recording. 'Chattanooga Choo Choo' had made No 1 for 9 weeks at the end of 1941 and beginning of 1942. The record had sold 1.2 million on the Bluebird label, the same label that Frank would record his first truly solo records with.

METRONOME POLL

Frank was voted No 1 male vocalist in the music magazine *Metronome* poll. Helen Forrest was voted the top female band singer.

"One of the charms about Frank was that he wasn't like a boy singer in the band. This guy was more like a saxophone soloist, or an instrumentalist. That was the feeling we got with Frank, and we loved playing with him."

JOE BUSHKIN

GLENN MILLER
Regardless of where Tommy Dorsey saw himself in the pantheon of bandleaders. Miller is now the name that people most widely recognize.

THE RIVALS

SHORTLY AFTER 'NIGHT AND DAY' CAME OUT FRANK ACHIEVED SOMETHING HE PROBABLY DREAMED OF WHEN HE FIRST JOINED TOMMY DORSEY, BUT COULD NEVER REALLY HAVE IMAGINED HAPPENING.

IN THE 1941 *BILLBOARD* survey of the most popular male band vocalists, Frank went from No 22 to No 1, knocking Ray Eberle from the top spot. Interestingly, Frank headed a list of singers who would scarcely raise an eyebrow of acknowledgement today:

Ray Eberle

1 Frank Sinatra (Tommy Dorsey)
2 Ray Eberle (Glenn Miller)
3 Bob Eberly (Jimmy Dorsey)
4 Harry Babbitt (Kay Kyser)
5 Kenny Sargent (Glen Gray and the Casa Loma Orchestra)
6 Bon Bon (Jan Savitt)
7 Tommy Ryan (Sammy Kaye)
8 Bob Allen (Hal Kemp)
9 Larry Cotton (Horace Heidt)
10 Sully Mason (Kay Kyser)

Ray Eberle and Bob Eberly were the Eberle brothers. Bob got a job with Jimmy Dorsey and changed his name because radio announcers could not pronounce it. Glenn Miller asked Bob if he had any brothers, which is how Ray got a job with the Miller band. Ray's career was hurt by the war, where he served in the Army. He never regained his popularity after 1945. Glenn Miller fired Ray in late 1942, apparently for turning up late for rehearsal. Ray always insisted he quit, mainly over money, because the band were getting more than him. He later sang with Gene Krupa's band, and with Tex Beneke's Glenn Miller Orchestra in the 1970s.

Harry Babbitt's popularity can be attributed to the popularity of Kay Kyser's band, which he joined in 1937. He joined the Navy in 1944 and, like Eberly, never got back on track.

The Casa Loma Orchestra was one of the first "Swing" bands. It was led by saxophonist Glen Gray and Kenny Sargent, a sax player who branched out into vocals when the band signed to OKeh records. In 1939, Sargent had been runner-up to Tommy Dorsey's vocalist, Jack Leonard.

The unusually named Bon Bon sang with Russian émigré Jan Savitt's band and both appeared in a number of movies. Savitt died in 1948 and Bon Bon was never heard of again. Tommy Ryan, Bob Allen, Larry Cotton, and Sully Mason owe their positions as much to the popularity of their bandleader bosses as their own fan base or talent. Tommy Ryan had made No 1 in January 1940 with 'Dream Valley', but he was just one of the vocalists with 'Swing and Sway with Sammy Kaye'. By this time, Hal Kemp's band were very much on the wane, and Bob Allen with them. Hal, along with Bob, had a number of big hits in 1937–8, but not another after May 1941. Larry Cotton was a very minor player, as was Hal Heidt's band.

EBERLY BROTHER
Big Band vocalists Bob Eberly and Helen O'Connell pictured with Jimmy Dorsey's Orchestra in 1939.

Leo Reisman's Orchestra with Fred Astaire in early 1933. Fred Astaire reprised his role in *The Gay Divorcee* for the 1934 movie, which also starred Ginger Rogers.

The song proved to be a perfect vehicle for Frank, although it only reached No 17 on the *Billboard* chart at the end of March, spending just three weeks on the bestseller's list. Tommy and Victor's hunch was probably right in releasing it, coupled with 'The Night We Called It a Day', on Bluebird. It may not have charted at all if it was not for its lower price than regular Victor (and Tommy Dorsey and Frank Sinatra) records.

'Night and Day' has become synonymous with Sinatra; some have even called it "an obsession". Frank probably sang it more than any other song during his career. He recorded it again less than eight months later for the film *Reveille with Beverly*. It is fascinating to listen to both versions to hear how Frank had improved. He sounds altogether more confident on the soundtrack version, closer to "The Voice", and a little further from Frankie.

JIVEY JUVIE LAND

A month after recording his first solo sides, Frank was back in the studio in Hollywood with Tommy Dorsey, Connie Haines, and the Pied Pipers cutting three songs from the movie *Ship Ahoy*. Soon after this session Frank told Tommy it was his intention to leave, but he was in no hurry and intended to stick around through the end of the year. Tommy's reaction has not been recorded, but it is probable that he thought Frank might change his mind, or that things might change Frank's mind. For one thing, it was not singers who were the stars, it was the bands, or at least that was the way that Tommy Dorsey saw it. He also had another card up his sleeve that might have made him pretty relaxed about the whole idea, but for now he was keeping that one to himself.

Just before Tommy Dorsey and the band returned to New York from the West Coast, they played their first date in San Francisco at the Golden Gate Theatre. It was a week-long run and, typically for many of their dates, it included a movie as well. This was the RKO picture *A Date With The Falcon*, starring George Sanders and Wendy Barrie.

"With jivey juvies hanging from chandeliers, mere mention of Dorsey's name in a screen trailer started a demonstration at the opener. As curtains parted with the leader tromboning the theme, hepsters split the joint wide open. Dorsey took it with quiet dignity… Pied Pipers resume with 'Embraceable You', after which Elman takes over on 'When Angels Sing'. Lad figuratively blows his brains out. Elman and drummer Buddy Rich then monopolize 'Hawaiian War Chant' with their duet interlude. For no particular reason Elman then takes the sticks while Rich does a tap routine which gets by only because he can do no wrong. Frank Sinatra then baritones 'Without A Song' for

SHIP AHOY
Short on plot and long on song and dance (and legs!) best describes this movie, which was released in May 1942. Frank was there purely as a member of the Tommy Dorsey Band.

smash returns. During his second, 'This Love of Mine', the Dorsey trombone quartet moves in for some nice stuff. Following 'Beguine', Dorsey's trombone works again in 'Never Smile Again' together with Sinatra and the Pipers. Sinatra finishes his stint with a deadpan version of 'South of the Border' which pleased the mob although corny… Biz excellent!" (*Variety*, 4 March, 1942)

At the end of March, 'Night and Day' made the charts and the band began yet another month-long engagement at the Paramount Theatre in New York City. According to Tommy's arranger Sy Oliver, Frank had learned well from the boss, and not just about breath control. "Even then Frank had that spark, that great belief in himself, and you knew he was going to be big. When he walked out on that stage, you knew he was in charge. Tommy was like that." This must have been a double-edged sword for Tommy. On the one hand, a

---

ON DISC

There are seven officially recorded versions by Frank of 'Night and Day'.

Studio versions
- 19 January, 1942, with Axel Stordahl, 78 rpm release
- 18 September, 1942, with Morris Stoloff, soundtrack of *Reveille for Beverly*
- 23 October, 1947, with Axel Stordahl, unreleased at the time
- 26 November, 1956, with Nelson Riddle, 45 rpm release and on the album *A Swingin' Affair*
- 22 November, 1961, with Don Costa, Reprise album *Sinatra and Strings*
- 15 February, 1977, with Bill Miller, arranged by Joe Beck, 45 rpm release

Live version
- 5 June, 1962, with Bill Miller leading a sextet, Reprise album

success such as Frank's was good for business, Tommy's business, and he increased his collateral with theatres and ballrooms across the country. But on the other hand, there was the little question of ego. Tommy is reported to have said "Let him go? Might be the best thing for me. Anyway I could get another crooner... Dick Haymes." During the 1940s, many musicians felt that Dick Haymes was Frank's equal when it came to vocal ability, although most thought Frank could interpret and phrase a lyric better.

A few days after *Ship Ahoy* was released on 15 May, 1942, Frank was in the studio with Tommy recording more material, and there was an added impetus to this session. Over the course of the next six weeks they cut ten sides. It was the last time Tommy Dorsey would be in a recording studio in 1942, and the last time Frank would record with the band. The American Federation of Musicians was expected to strike, and all the major labels and bands were stock-piling recordings to tide them over what was anticipated to be a long strike, although they would have made more if they had known just how long it would last. On these recordings, Dorsey added a string section, a move made popular by the likes of Artie Shaw and Harry James. They are not the best recordings by Frank and Tommy Dorsey, and it is almost as though they are trying to work out a way of working with strings. 'Be Careful, It's My Heart' is the best of these sides, while 'In the Blue of the Evening' is something of a confused and muddy mess. Dorsey later admitted that using strings was a tax write-off, not a serious shift in where he was taking his sound.

In protest at the number of jukeboxes there were in the US (225,000 in 1939), James Caesar Petrillo, President of the American Federation of Musicians, declared that records were "the number one scab". He and his members felt that records and record companies were taking work away from musicians. The AFM strike in 1942 included instrumental soloists and studio players for all the major labels. Their motive was to persuade record companies to create a trust fund to compensate musicians who might lose live work as a result of records played on jukeboxes and the radio. The strike would not end until 1944. During this period, AFM members supposedly recorded no music, though there were some clandestine sessions designed to bolster the output of some of the bigger selling stars.

As a result of the strike, union musicians were paid royalties on record sales as standard practice; prior to this point it had been a privilege for a fortunate few. Session musicians had been paid a flat fee for a session. Because of the war, there was a shortage of shellac and some of the metals used in record making. These shortages meant that the record companies were in no great hurry to settle. In fact, they concentrated their efforts on fewer releases and increased their profits.

THE SUMMER OF '42

Tommy Dorsey and the band had been kept busy touring in the spring of 1942, and, along with their recording schedule, which anticipated the strike, there was the need to consider what they would do to supplement their income from recording. At that time, the musicians themselves would be less affected by a reduction in recording, as they did not get royalties. There was the loss of session fees to be considered, but these would have been only a small, though welcome, part of their income.

After playing at the Forum in Quebec and a spell at the Hotel Astor in New York City, Tommy and the band had the chance to replace Red Skelton while he had a summer break from his radio series, beginning 8 June. There were also dates in Detroit, Baltimore, Washington, Philadelphia, Akron, and Chicago. *Billboard* reviewed their appearance at the Chicago Theatre on the afternoon of 17 July. As well as the Tommy Dorsey Band the theatre was showing a movie, *The Great Man's Lady*, and featuring an acrobatic duo, Lane and Ward, along with an impersonator, Paul Regan: "Tommy Dorsey is here on his annual visit, this time exhibiting a ten-piece string section (including a girl harpist) in addition to his regular money-making group, featuring Frank Sinatra and his ballads, Ziggy Elman and his trumpet, Buddy Rich and his drums, the Pied Pipers (three men and sexy Jo Stafford) and their vocal harmony, plus the maestro's famous sweet slide horn.

"The boys dish out oldies, new hits as well as Dorsey trademarks ('Song of India', 'I'll Never Smile Again'), all placed in the proper spots and delivered in the usual Dorsey standard. A definite highlight, and doubling in the role of sub leader, is Ziggy Elman, the boy with the hot trumpet who is a familiar name to the jitterbugs judging by the applause greeting him. He takes a featured part in several numbers, delighting his followers. Frank Sinatra is another band natural, possessing a strong tenor voice that treats ballads with more than normal polish. From the standpoint of appearance, however, he could use a few extra pounds (and the blue spot doesn't flatter him either) stays on for several numbers and stays on for the closing tune, 'Tallulah'. Most of his numbers are embellished with rhythmical support from the Pied Pipers, who work in fine harmony. On their own, earlier in the bill, they score with 'Embraceable You' and a military melody. The string section gets its inning in the melodic arrangement of 'Sleepy Lagoon'. Otherwise, it plays a minor second to the brass and reeds." (*Billboard*, 25 July, 1942)

66As a teenager, I would go to see the Tommy Dorsey Band. It was sheer joy! The band was spectacular – the best white band until Woody Herman's. The singers would be at the back, and they'd wave around and look lively. The whole thing was very theatrical and was a musical thrill!99

JOHNNY MANDEL – ARRANGER WHO WORKED WITH SINATRA IN THE 1960S

MANIE SACKS
Frank's mentor, Sacks worked at Columbia Records and was instrumental in signing him to the label when he left Dorsey.

AXEL STORDAHL

"He is one of the single most beautiful men I ever met…" SAMMY CAHN

BORN IN STATEN ISLAND, NEW YORK, JUST TWO YEARS BEFORE FRANK, AXEL WAS OF NORWEGIAN ORIGIN AND HIS REAL NAME WAS ODD STORDAHL…SO IT'S EASY TO SEE WHY HE CHANGED IT.

"In every conceivable way, Stordahl was more than Sinatra's first conductor and musical director but the man who helped popular music's greatest vocalist lay the foundation for his entire career." So said author Will Friedwald on the notes of the Columbia legacy recordings of Frank Sinatra. That's how important Axel Stordahl was to the singer.

"Sinatra might have to do some worrying if he hadn't Axel Stordahl to make certain every song he sings is made for the voice." Billboard Year Book 1944

Axel started out playing trumpet with the Bert Block band, and then joined Tommy Dorsey in 1936. Tommy allowed him to develop his arranging skills and Axel soon became a dab hand at arranging ballads, which is not to say he couldn't swing when he needed to. Although he worked a great deal with Frank over the next decade he also worked with Bing Crosby, Doris Day, Dean Martin, Eddie Fisher, and Dinah Shore. He married the singer June

Hutton (Ina Ray Hutton's young sister). June had replaced Jo Stafford in the Pied Pipers. Axel arranged twice as many songs for Frank as any other arranger, although those that appeared on record number around 300, the same as Nelson Riddle.

Axel worked with Frank in 1961, having spent most of the 1950s working separately. He died on 30 August, 1963, in Encino, California.

AXEL AND FRANK
It is difficult to believe that the prematurely bald Axel Stordahl was just two years older than Frank. Here they are pictured going over a lyric together.

STRIKE VOTE
James Caesar Petrillo, the President of the American Federation of Musicians, addressing his members during the AFM strike in 1942.

After using strings on the pre-strike recordings, Tommy decided to take them on the road to augment the sound. This took the band to 25 players, plus the four Pied Pipers, Connie Haines, Frank, and Tommy. The costs of keeping such a large band on the road must have been huge. Tommy had a fuller list of bookings than many other bands, but it still must have focused his mind on the possible downsides of losing Frank; although Tommy undoubtedly thought of himself as the bigger star, the bigger draw – and maybe he was justified in thinking that way.

Relations between Tommy and Frank had obviously changed after Frank had informed him of his intention to leave. Having got Manie Sacks' agreement to a Columbia contract, there was the small matter of extricating himself from his Tommy Dorsey contract, which Tommy had shaped in his own favour and to which Frank, desperate to get ahead in the big time, had probably not paid enough attention at the time of signing.

Frank referred to his contract with Dorsey as "a ratty piece of paper", with good cause. It called for Frank to pay Tommy 33 per cent of whatever he would earn after he left Tommy's employ, not just for a year or two but for the rest of his career (though few expected to have singing careers that lasted for decades). There was another twist: Tommy expected Frank to pay another 10 per cent to his agent.

AN AXEL TO GRIND

The affair was not completely one-sided, however. Frank had offered Axel Stordahl a job as his "arranger" and effectively his musical director, long before there were such people. It's unclear just how much Axel was earning with Tommy but reports have suggested it was more than Frank which shows how much he was valued. Frank, though, was shrewd and offered Axel $600 a week. The value of a man such as Axel Stordahl was his ability to take a song and turn it into a hit. In an era when song pluggers and publishers often got a number of different artists to record their songs, it was the arrangers who often made them hits, made them different. Frank was astute in taking Axel with him, and whatever he paid him to begin with was repaid many times over in helping make Frank's renditions of songs, which in the hands of others were

> 66 'Sinatra'd' was the past tense of a verb meaning 'to cut up into several financial pieces'. 99
>
> **WALTER WINCHELL, COLUMNIST**

1939-1942

TIPS ON POPULAR SINGING

"NEVER BE CARELESS WHEN LEARNING NEW SONGS. IF A CERTAIN PHRASE DOESN'T SOUND AS IT SHOULD TO YOU, GO OVER IT AGAIN AND AGAIN UNTIL YOU ARE PERFECTLY SATISFIED." FROM *TIPS ON POPULAR SINGING*

SOMETIME IN 1941 Frank and his vocal coach, John Quinlan, found the time to write a 32-page book, *Tips on Popular Singing*. As it says above, it was clear that Frank followed his own advice. In many respects the book offers an insight into Frank's personal mantra when it comes to his singing and his career.

The book was published at the end of 1941 and offered for sale at 75 cents (between $8 and $10 today). Popular Westerns and paperback novels were selling at between 15 and 25 cents. The book was actually one of a series published by Tommy Dorsey's company. One of the other titles was *The Modern Trombonist – A Complete Method for the Trombone* by Tommy James. In Britain Frank's book was on sale for 2 shillings and 6 pence, Tommy's for 12 shillings and 6 pence!

There is an introduction in the book, a word of commendation, by Tommy Dorsey: "From the standpoint of convention, it would seem rather bizarre for me to step out of my role as an orchestra leader and master of ceremonies in the field of entertainment and enter the realm of belle-jetties, even in a minor capacity. But the subject matter of *Tips on Popular Singing* appealed to me so forcibly that, when I was requested to write an opinion on it I immediately

followed up on the idea." He went on, "Frank Sinatra, who is a member of my organization, is an unusually talented, conscientious artist. Through his interpretive qualities, he has not only brought success to himself, but he has made many hits for the various music publishers and, of course, has brought pleasure to thousands of listeners. *Tips on Popular Singing* features mouth positioning diagrams for vowel enunciation and 16 vocal exercises, along with other more general advice from Frank and his vocal coach."

The book's preface says "Mr Sinatra's marvelous success is due, to a great extent, to the careful and systematic approach given him by Mr Quinlan, one of America's leading voice teachers." The likelihood is that Frank continued to take lessons well after the initial coaching he received in the late 1930s. The introduction encourages people wishing to take up singing to listen to the Vallees, the Columbos, the Crosbys, as well as the Eberlys and the Leonards – a nice nod to his mentors and rivals. Interestingly, while Frank never really lost his New Jersey accent when speaking, Quinlan got him to enunciate clearly when he sang.

could make it big without his help. Such was the level of rancour between the two strong-willed men that ever since there has been gossip that it was pressure from Frank's "gangster" friends that got him out of the punitive deal. Initially, Frank was paying off his "debt" to Dorsey, but after six months he decided enough was enough. Frank found a good entertainment lawyer in Henry Jaffe, a friend of Manie Sacks, and some serious wrangling commenced on both sides. As Frank said to reporters at the time, "You can quote Sinatra as saying that he believes it is wrong for anybody to own a piece of him and collect on it when that owner is doing nothing for Sinatra."

ONE CAREFUL OWNER

Tommy sued Frank, and in return Jaffe threatened to have some of Tommy's broadcasts stopped through pressure from the American Federation of Recording Artists, helped by the fact that Jaffe was also their lawyer. Some militant Sinatra fans even started picketing theatres where Dorsey was appearing. In the end, the dispute was settled in August 1943, when Frank agreed to pay Tommy $60,000. Frank did not actually have that kind of money. He relied on an advance ($35,000) from Sonny Werblin and Norman Weiss at MCA (Frank's new agent), and Columbia Records ($25,000), against his future earnings. Frank was confident, and MCA and Columbia felt it locked him into them. Everyone had confidence in Frankie's potential. Even after the deal was finalized, GAC continued to get 10 per cent of Frank's earnings for the balance of his GAC contract period; probably it was MCA that lost out for this period. As Frank succinctly put it, "I now own myself."

Many years later, in Mario Puzo's 1969 novel *The Godfather*, there is a story that has similarities to the Frank and Tommy saga. Mario claims that he heard the stories and used them as the basis for constructing his story. The whole business of Frank and his "friends" putting the squeeze on Tommy was not helped by Tommy himself, who claimed, a decade later, that there was pressure from people to resolve the situation. The legitimate story of Jaffe and MCA working out the whole thing sounds much more credible. If any of Frank's so-called heavy friends had been involved, then why did Frank end up paying Tommy anything at all?

During his time with Tommy Dorsey – a little over two years – Frank recorded over 90 songs. It was an incredibly important time for Frank, which he would later acknowledge. No doubt both men felt a good deal of resentment in the immediate aftermath of the singer's departure, although in truth Tommy probably felt he could get along just fine without the Hoboken upstart, however good he thought he was. But, and it was a very big but, this was a turning point in the history of popular music, just like when the rock and rollers came along in the 1950s or the beat groups in the

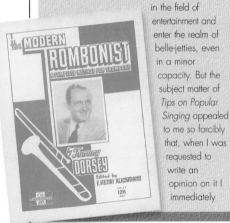

"Keep the feet dry and avoid sitting in a draft."

FROM *TIPS ON POPULAR SINGING*

merely mediocre, hit records. Along with everything else, there was ego involved here too. Frank wanted his name in the largest type on those 78 rpm pieces of heavy shellac. If it was his talent and popularity that sold them, then why shouldn't he?

The problem with the contract hinged around the fact that when Frank signed in 1940, his deal was with General Amusement Company, and his deal with Tommy included an advance in excess of $15,000, which is one reason why Tommy had the "lean" on future earnings. Dorsey, while he was sure that he would have no trouble replacing Frank, was in no small measure miffed that Frank thought he

1960s. The singer was about to become king (or queen) and the bandleader relegated to supporting player. Obviously the talent and popularity of Frank Sinatra were vital to this process. When any phenomenon comes along, every other record company tries to find its own act to rival the success of the supposed top dog. For a long while it would be Frank Sinatra, and the next "Frank Sinatra". There was also the issue of the Musicians' Union strike, which was another nail in the coffin of the Big Bands. Frank could make records without backing musicians, Big Bands couldn't.

Frank officially announced his departure from Tommy Dorsey on 28 August, 1942 at the Circle Theatre in Indianapolis. On 3 September, he bade farewell to the band on air on his last broadcast with Tommy Dorsey. He handed over to Dick Haymes. It was pure synchronicity, having done the same thing when he left Harry James's band. A week or so later, Frank was gone, and things would never be quite the same again in the Dorsey band. Ironically, four months later, in the second week of January 1943, Frank was again at No 1 with Tommy Dorsey and the Pied Pipers. 'There Are Such Things' was one of the sides recorded before the Musicians' Union strike, with a string section. It is far from a classic and today it is difficult to see why it was so big. Perhaps Frankie really was that popular, but then again it might have been Tommy… after all, it was his name that was writ large on the Victor recording.

> 66 Remember, he was no matinée idol. He was a skinny kid with big ears. 99
>
> **TOMMY DORSEY**

1942 ON THE JUKEBOX

Tommy Dorsey's ability to pick a song was another great musical lesson that Frank learned from his boss. During his career, Tommy had well over 200 hit recordings, something you cannot do without good ears. In 1942, Tommy, like everyone else, was hampered by the Musicians' Union strike. Despite that, Tommy, with Frank, still had nine *Billboard* hits, and another No 1.

During the year, Frank Sinatra featured on 21 sides released with the Tommy Dorsey Band. 'How About You' came from the Busby Berkeley musical *Babes on Broadway*. This hit version was arranged

WOODY HERMAN
Woody took over the leadership of the Isham Jones Band in 1936 and went on to have over 50 hits.

by Paul Weston, Jo Stafford's future husband. Fifteen years later, Frank remade it for his classic album, *Songs for Swingin' Lovers*. 'Just as Though You Were Here' is one of those Sinatra songs that probably deserves a better place in his canon. The Axel Stordahl arrangement brings out the best in the song. 'I'll Take Tallulah' is far from a classic and is interesting because Tommy Dorsey can be heard on vocals. Ferde Grofé had been an arranger with Paul Whiteman's Orchestra in the 1920s and composed the music for 'Daybreak' in 1926 as part of his 'Mississippi Suite'. Harold Adamson added the lyrics. Not everyone was totally convinced by Frank. *Metronome* magazine was less than enthusiastic about Frank's singing on 'The Song is You': "He is not an impressive singer when he lets out — that's a cinch."

> 66 Sinatra hits the bull's eye squarely with his relaxed, effortless ways and smart phrasing. Bluebird has a terrific bet here… and a potential juke winner. 99
>
> *DOWNBEAT* REVIEWING 'NIGHT AND DAY'

MUSICAL ICON
The jukebox was pivotal in the careers of so many performers from the 1940s and later.

FRANK ON THE US CHARTS

'HOW ABOUT YOU'
Burton Lane & Ralph Freed
28 February, No 16, 3 weeks

'NIGHT AND DAY'
Cole Porter
28 March, No 17, 3 weeks

'THE LAST CALL FOR LOVE'
Burton Lane, Yip Harburg & Margery Cummings (from Ship Ahoy)
20 June, No 20, 1 week

'JUST AS THOUGH YOU WERE HERE'
John Benson Brooks & Eddie DeLange
25 July, No 3, 9 weeks

'I'LL TAKE TALLULAH'
Burton Lane & Yip Harburg (from Ship Ahoy)
8 August, No 18, 1 week

'BE CAREFUL, IT'S MY HEART'
Irving Berlin
29 August, No 15, 3 weeks

'TAKE ME'
Rube Bloom & Mack David
26 September, No 5, 3 weeks

'THERE ARE SUCH THINGS'
George Meyer, Stanley Adams & Abel Baer
14 November, No 1, 24 weeks

'DAYBREAK'
Ferde Grofé & Harold Adamson
7 November, No 10, 2 weeks

BILLBOARD'S BESTSELLERS CHART
Glenn Miller's gold-winning disc, 'Chattanooga Choo Choo', was No 1 at the start of 1942 and it stayed there for another five weeks. Glenn would reign at the top of the charts for the next three months, first with 'String of Pearls' and then 'Moonlight Cocktail', apart from one week when Woody Herman's rendition of 'Blues in the Night' briefly toppled him. For the rest of the year it was first Jimmy Dorsey's 'Tangerine', then Harry James and 'Sleepy Lagoon', followed by Kay Kyser's 'Jingle Jangle Jingle', before Miller once again made it to the top with '(I've Got a Gal in) Kalamazoo'. Then, in the week of 31 October, Bing Crosby's 'White Christmas' climbed to the top to stay there for the rest of the year. It was as if Bing, 'The Old Groaner', was somehow signalling the end of the Big Bands' domination of the chart. Never again would they get back in such control. The singers were about to take over.

1942–1946

THE SULTAN OF SWOON

MANY OF FRANK'S RADIO SHOWS OPENED WITH COLE PORTER'S 'NIGHT AND DAY'; ITS LOVELY LYRICS SET THE TONE FOR HIS APPEARANCES AS WELL AS HIS APPEAL TO HIS FANS IN EVERY STATE IN AMERICA. IT ALSO APTLY DESCRIBES FRANK'S CAREER WHICH, ONCE HE TURNED SOLO, WOULD EVENTUALLY BECOME LIKE NIGHT AND DAY. FROM THE HIGHS OF TOPPING THE CHARTS, THE ADULATION OF THE BOBBY-SOXERS, HIS TRIUMPHS ON THE POLLS, AND HIS AWARDS IN THE MIDDLE YEARS OF THE 1940s, TO HIS SLOW SLIDE AS THE DECADE DREW TO A CLOSE. IT IS A FASCINATING STORY OF A POP IDOL, THE FIRST REAL POP IDOL. FRANK WAS MODELLED IN THE STYLE TO WHICH WE HAVE GROWN ACCUSTOMED, BUT BACK IN WARTIME AMERICA IT WAS ALL VERY DIFFERENT.

THE FAITHFUL
The girls who went to see Frank were true fans, queuing for hours on end. Song Hits magazine offered anti-swoon mints to the queue, but the fans came to do Frankie justice with the full quota of swoons, so they refused.

POP'S BIG BANG

BOBBY-SOXERS AWAITING THEIR IDOL, MARCH 1946

Frank's last show with Tommy Dorsey was at the Circle Theatre in Indianapolis on 10 September, 1942. To mark the occasion, Tommy's recording of Irving Berlin's 'Be Careful It's My Heart', from Bing Crosby's film *Holiday Inn*, with Frank on vocals, entered the *Billboard* charts.

While Frank's departure from Harry James had been tinged with sadness and fond memories, leaving Tommy was an altogether different affair. Quite apart from the wrangling over his contract, he was less a part of "the band" – with Tommy Dorsey he was part of an "organization". It has even been reported that Tommy told Frank, "I hope you fall on your ass", which is an indication of the level of bad feeling felt by both sides. But, as Frank commented on many occasions throughout the remainder of his career, he had much to thank Tommy for – not just for giving him the opportunity to get ahead but also for what he learned from the tough bandleader, both professionally and personally.

CRUISING COUPLE
Things were looking up for Frank and Nancy. With fame came money and with money came its trappings.

> "Frank Sinatra was the 20th century. He was modern; he was complex; he had swing and attitude. He was the big bang of pop."
>
> BONO, LEAD SINGER OF U2

As the old adage goes, timing is everything, and Frank felt he had done his stretch with Tommy. It was finished business; his period with Dorsey had reached its natural conclusion. Frank Sinatra was ready to conquer the world, to become a big star; he was going to be nobody's boy singer. In an interview ten years later for *Metronome,* Frank made a startling revelation: "I don't think I ever told anybody this before, but the reason I started out on my own when I did was because I wanted to make sure I got there as a single before Bob Eberly did. I knew that if that guy ever did it first, I'd never be able to make it the way I did. That Eberly, he sang so rich and so pure, it used to frighten me. I knew he'd be too much for me if he ever got started on his own before I did."

GOING TRULY SOLO

A few days after leaving Tommy Dorsey, Frank went to Los Angeles. He was there on 17 and 18 September with Axel Stordahl to record 'Night and Day' for the Columbia Pictures film *Reveille with Beverly.* Despite the strike, there was no ban on musicians working on film soundtracks, so Frank was back in the studio for the first time in two months with an orchestra.

He got $1,000 to film a sequence that featured six women pianists. While he was in LA, he went to NBC Radio looking for a job. He wanted to be a "staff singer" for the network, but they

turned him down, deciding to stick with their resident vocalist, Johnny Johnstone.

Back in New York, Frank's priority was to get his "act" together. Working with Dorsey meant that, for the most part, he had had his songs chosen for him. Song pluggers and their publishers would have been very keen on having the nation's number two orchestra leader play and record their songs. Frank on his own, however, was a slightly different proposition. Having Axel Stordahl and a contract with Columbia were a major asset, but the Musicians' Union strike meant that there was something of a hiatus for everyone. Frank, like every singer and bandleader, would need radio, in addition to any live shows, more than ever before to sustain popularity. For the rest of September and October, he worked on a twice-weekly show, *Reflections* for CBS, which was broadcast from New York on Tuesdays and Thursdays. Manie Sacks, having signed Frank to Columbia, called William Paley, head of the Columbia Broadcasting System, and told him that Frank was going to be "the hottest thing that ever hit". It was just the right kind of exposure for Frank.

Frank was a guest on a number of other radio shows prior to Christmas 1942. While he continued to perform songs that he had

RADIO CITY
The NBC studios Radio City, on Sunset and Vine, Los Angeles, during the 1940s.

❝He weighed 120 pounds soaking wet – 20 of which was hair.❞
BENNY GOODMAN ON FRANK

1942–1946

THE KING OF SWING
Benny Goodman in 1938 with Tommy James on trumpet (third from left).

66They call me an overnight success. Don't make me laugh.99

FRANK SINATRA, 1944

recorded with Dorsey, he did others that were new to him, including 'A Touch of Texas', 'Please Think of Me', 'Velvet Moon', 'Everything I Have Is Yours', and 'Rose Ann of Charing Cross'. The last was written by the delightfully named Kermitt Goell, who wrote many songs with very little success, and Mabel Wayne. Mabel co-wrote 'It Happened in Monterey', which Frank recorded over a decade later with Nelson Riddle. Several of these songs and many others that Frank sang on the radio were already hits, or popular by other artistes: 'A Touch of Texas' with Freddy Martin, Shep Fields' rendition of 'Please Think of Me', and 'Velvet Moon' by Frank's old boss, Harry James. Frank also did some of his old Dorsey hits, including 'Just as Though You Were Here' and he never missed a chance to sing 'This Love of Mine', his composition with Hank Sanicola and Sol Parker.

Given his many radio appearances and the success of his recordings with Tommy Dorsey, Frank was rarely off the airwaves during the last quarter of 1943. In addition to the radio shows, Frank returned to working live. One of his earliest solo bookings was a few miles to the west of Hoboken, at the Mosque Theatre on Broad Street in Newark, New Jersey. Opened in 1925, the Mosque accommodated 2,880 people and was the biggest venue in the city. In this impressive building, built by the Ancient Order of Nobles of the Mystic Shrine, Frank performed on the 70-foot wide stage. There are no reports of how

many people turned up at Frank's show, but there is ample evidence that those who did greeted Frank enthusiastically and made him feel right at home.

Frank's agent, who had secured the booking quickly, went to work on Robert A Weitman, the manager of the Paramount Theatre in New York, and therefore one of the most influential entertainment men in the city. Somehow Hank Sanicola and Harry Romm, a booker at the agent General Amusement Company, persuaded Weitman to drive out to Newark to see Frank's show. It was reported later that not since Rudy Vallee had Weitman seen a singer who induced so much squealing from the young girls in the audience. Now that Frank was free of Dorsey's shackles, he could explore his own act, developing every little gesture and nuance for maximum impact. The Dorsey shows were carefully planned and choreographed; nothing was supposed to upstage Tommy. While it had been acceptable for Frank and Connie Haines to vie for attention against each other, Tommy was boss. Frank's ability to work an audience had been evident while he was with Tommy, but from here on in it was this remarkable gift that helped him to establish his reputation – a talent that never deserted him when faced with an audience.

Weitman was impressed enough to offer Frank a booking at the Paramount for the end of December, which Benny Goodman was to headline. It has been said that

Benny Goodman exclaimed, "Who the hell is Frank Sinatra?" when asked by Weitman if he would mind the young singer being added to the bill. Given Frank's performance on the *Billboard* band vocalist poll and his hit records with Dorsey, his comment either beggars belief or shows a wry sense of humour. Benny was said to have lived very much in a world of his own; maybe he did, but that is taking it too far. Benny Goodman also recorded for Columbia, Frank's new label, and it is likely that they influenced Weitman to book Frankie.

OVERNIGHT SENSATION?

Benny Goodman's booking at the Paramount was to run for four weeks from 30 December. It was the tried-and-tested formula of a two-for-one show; the featured movie was *Star Spangled Rhythm* starring Victor Moore and Betty Hutton. The appeal of the film was increased by the addition of Bob Hope, Bing Crosby, Veronica Lake, and Rochester, along with a whole host of other Paramount Pictures stars. The live entertainment featured "the King of Swing", Benny Goodman and his famous orchestra. There was also his young vocalist, Peggy Lee, while the Radio Rogues along with Moke and Poke provided the laughs. Frank was billed as an extra-added attraction, with the slogan "The Voice That Has Thrilled Millions". After Benny had worked his way through numbers like 'Taking a Chance on Love' and his theme song, the wonderful 'Let's Dance', and Peggy had performed 'Why Don't You Do Right?', it was time for Benny Goodman's introduction, which was somewhat low key: "and now, Frank Sinatra".

It has been reported that at that first performance the place was full with 5,000 chanting, screaming fans. Various eyewitnesses said the crowd was going mad, chanting "F.R.A.N.K.I.E.". It has also been said that Nancy Sinatra was in the audience, and she must have found it all quite amazing, and also a little disconcerting, to have so many young girls chanting her husband's name. While there is no doubting Frank's success at the Paramount, it would seem more likely that the hysteria as it is now reported was not at this level from day one. It seems inconceivable that it could happen virtually overnight. What would be more believable is the fact that George B Evans, the man whom Frank hired as his press agent, worked a little magic.

George B Evans was 40, an experienced PR man with an office at 1775 Broadway in New York, whose clients included Duke Ellington, Jane Froman, and Glenn Miller. When the run at the Paramount began, another man was handling Frank's PR, who seems not to have taken Frank as seriously or treated him as well as he would have liked. In any event, George went to the Paramount early in the run, saw the initial signs of Sinatramania and was, like many of the young girls, impressed by what he saw. People have since said that Evans was the biggest thing ever to have happened to Frank, a notion that is hard to refute.

George's plan was simple. He hired some girls and coached them in the antics that were to become famous as "the Sinatra swoon". At the same time, he showed Frank how to use the microphone, as both something to help him stay standing and as something to caress and to touch. While sex had been a part of Frank's stagecraft for some time, it increasingly took centre stage in the coming years. It was all carefully choreographed, even down to the moments that the girls should scream out. At certain points in certain songs a girl would yell out suggestive answers to the lyrics that Frank was singing. Before long, the sheer infectiousness of the girls was influencing larger and larger numbers in the crowd – hysteria was just another scream away. Evans also

> 66 Frank sang four songs, all in the bedroom style he favoured at the time. Songs like 'These Are Such Things' and 'She's Funny That Way'. Of course there was an encore. 99
>
> **NEIL MCCAFFREY,** *THE NATIONAL REVIEW,* LOOKING BACK IN 1975

BOBBY-SOX BABIES
"Plain lonely girls from lower-middle-class homes" is how E J Khan Jr, of The New Yorker described the bobby-soxers.

FRANKLY SPEAKING
George Evans' original press release about Frank read: "Likes the colors blue and brown, hates evening clothes, prefers sports clothes. Is sentimental especially about Nancy and Little Sandra, music, and his parents."

gave away free tickets to some girls who were still on Christmas vacation from school. All in all, he did what every great PR person does: he created the story; and before long the newspapers were doing the job for him. "Five Thousand Girls Fight To Get A View Of Frankie" was one headline.

SWING SHIFT

The run at the Paramount was gruelling. There were six or seven shows a day and 11 on Saturdays. Shows started in the morning, some even before 9:00 am. The early shows came about as a result of the shifts worked during the war. The need for increased production meant that many production lines were working around the clock, and many more people, often women (given the need for men to fight), worked shifts. These were not regular shifts, but something known as swing shifts. They worked a week or a month on early shift, then the same on the late shift, and finished the swing through the shifts with a night shift. The day shift was 7:00 am to 4:00 pm, second shift was 4:00 pm until 1:00 am, with the graveyard or third shift from 1:00 am until 7:00 am, though times could vary by an hour or so from factory to factory. In addition, people had more money to spend, with less and less to spend it on. Entertainment was a prime candidate for their disposable dollars.

Frank wore big floppy bow ties that Nancy made for him, and before long she had to work overtime to replace the ones that eager fans had ripped from around his neck. His suits took a beating too. He lost jacket after jacket as fans just grabbed and pulled at whatever they could. The fact that there were so many shows a day meant the theatre's management was faced with the task of clearing the place after each performance. This became a battle of wills and a test of stamina, because girls simply stayed in their seats for performance after performance, oblivious to the fact that there were others outside trying to get in (and costing the Paramount money because they could not resell the seats). Some even took food in to last them the day. The younger, more vociferous, teenage girls were known as "bobby-soxers" as they wore ankle-length white socks, known as bobby sox, and often saddle shoes. As Hilda Kubernik recalled 50 years on: "I lived in Chicago and was a big fan of Frank. I had seen him at WMAQ in Chicago when he did a radio show with Tommy Dorsey and so I was determined to go to New York to see him at the Paramount. I caught the train from Chicago at 4:30 in the afternoon, which arrived in New York the next morning around nine. My cousin, who lived in Brooklyn, met me at the train station and we went straight to the Paramount. We stood in line around the block and eventually got in. Frank was amazing; I was not a screamer I just sat there paralyzed. We stayed and watched every performance until they threw us out at around 10:30 or 11. Then my cousin and I caught the subway back to her house where I stayed. I left Sunday and was back home in Chicago Monday morning. Looking back I think what was important was that he was there when we needed somebody."

There may be grounds for questioning the full extent of the initial reaction to Frank's shows, but none for arguing with the fact that his popularity grew quickly and it was genuine. According to Peggy Lee, she and Frank would lean out of the dressing room window to see the crowds of swooners, "like swarms of bees down there in the street, just waiting for a sight of Frankie". Peggy got 'flu during her run at the Paramount and Frank showed her great kindness. "I'll especially never forget what he did for me in the middle of his greatest triumph… he could have been too busy but he wasn't", is how Peggy wrote of Frank in her autobiography. Within a couple of weeks, Frank's four-week run had been extended to eight. Benny Goodman had another booking and so Johnny Long and his Orchestra, who were doing well in the charts with '(As Long as You're Not in Love with Anyone Else) Why Don't You Fall in Love with Me?', were drafted in to back Frank.

EVANS' SINATRATICS

Elements of the press were naturally sceptical about Frank's effect on the predominantly teenage female fans. George Tucker of Associated Press wrote somewhat cynically asking if someone was paying for these girls to demonstrate. This got George Evans into a flurry of self-righteous indignation; he even offered to give $1,000 to charity if anyone could prove that he paid the girls. He did, however, admit he took some of the Sinatratics (as he christened them) to the basement of the Paramount to coach them to know exactly when to scream. According to *Time* magazine, "Not since the days of Rudolph Valentino has American womanhood made such unabashed public love to an entertainer."

While George's efforts were the impetus for what happened, the speed with which Frank became so popular was a revelation to everybody, even to Frank, who had a full

*Yours
Frank Sinatra*

YOUR HIT PARADE

WITH THE POWER OF TELEVISION AND THE INTERNET TODAY, IT MAKES IT DIFFICULT TO IMAGINE HOW IMPORTANT THE RADIO WAS TO PEOPLE DURING THE 1930S AND 1940S. FOR MANY PEOPLE, ESPECIALLY THOSE WHO LIVED IN RURAL AMERICA, IT WAS THEIR WINDOW TO A WORLD OF NEWS AND ENTERTAINMENT.

FRANK HAD FIRST WORKED on the radio when he was at the Rustic Cabin, but it was a very hit-and-miss business and his appearances were unable to generate the level of exposure to turn young Frankie into a star. As soon as he joined Harry James and then Tommy Dorsey, the radio became important to Frank in exposing him to millions of listeners across America.

LUCKY BREAK

Almost as soon as Frank left Tommy, he began appearing on various American Forces Radio programmes, but it was the day before Valentine's in 1943 that Frank first appeared on the radio show that would help catapult him to superstardom. *Your Hit Parade* was a simple concept that featured the biggest songs of the moment performed by the studio band and a male and female singer. Mark Warnow conducted the band to begin with and Frank's female partner was Joan Edwards. The downside for Frank with these shows was that it restricted him to the hit songs of the week, regardless of their quality or suitability to his vocal talents. As Leonard G Feather wrote in *Metronome* in May 1943, "Right now he's pretty happy about the whole thing. The 'Hit Parade' gives him national publicity, even if it doesn't give him a real personal build-up."

THE VOICE OF AMERICA

Listening to the show became a weekly ritual for many teenagers like Bill Konrad, who lived just across the border from Detroit in Windsor, Canada. "On Saturday nights, a group of about ten of us would gather at the home of three sisters, crowd around the radio and listen to *Your Hit Parade* before bouncing off to the dance at the Masonic hall. A half hour of the popular hits of the week, with Frank singing three or four songs, including what they called 'A Lucky Strike extra', it was sponsored by a cigarette company, Lucky Strike. They were innocent days. Some of the songs I remember were 'Accentuate the Positive', 'Coming in on a Wing and a Prayer', and 'Pistol Packin' Mamma'."

Another teenager, Ginny Gates, living in New York City, had a very different memory of the show. "They announced that Frank Sinatra would talk on the telephone to anyone who bought a war bond. We called in, my sister and I, and left our number. At one o'clock in the morning, the telephone rang. HIMSELF calling back. We were scared to death, and excited and fell all over ourselves. I was just 9 years old; she was 12. It was just a few words of thanks but it was the most thrilling memory I have of my childhood."

According to Billboard, *Your Hit Parade* holds its audience minimum age to 18 years to try and reduce the interruptions and

Lucky Strike
PRESENTS
"YOUR HIT PARADE"
Starring— *Frank Sinatra*
America's Singing Sensation
LUCKY STRIKE MEANS FINE TOBACCO
So round, so firm, so fully packed...
so free and easy on the draw

A FAN
Lucky Strike gave away this tobacco leaf-shaped "fan for my fans" to the audience at Frank's shows, no doubt to alleviate the effects of a swoon.

SOUNDSTAGE
This picture of Frank and the orchestra and singers from *Your Hit Parade* was probably staged for promotional purposes. The real thing got increasingly rowdy as the Sinatratics screamed and shouted through some broadcasts.

chaos generated by Sinatra's younger fans. The news is, of course, not well received by the teenagers affected."

Frank stayed on the show until December 1944, when he left. Even before moving on he did other radio shows, including a weekly *Songs By Sinatra* which first aired in October 1943. In August 1944, there was the weekly Vimms Vitamins-sponsored *Frank Sinatra in Person*. Frank went back to *Your Hit Parade* in September 1947, finally leaving in May 1949. It's no exaggeration to say that without Frank's radio appearances, he would not have become the star that he did.

> ❝When I was growing up in the 1940s you could turn a radio on and they would play you a Country and Western, a Muddy Waters, a Mahalia Jackson, Johnny Otis, a Count Basie, Frank Sinatra. I mean they played all kinds of music, not like it is today. You turn on the radio, you hear the same tune.❞
>
> BUDDY GUY, 2000

tank of self belief. Many have hypothesized as to why it happened. Psychiatrists have studied the phenomenon, other performers tried to mirror what he did, and a multiplicity of managers encouraged their rising stars to try to emulate "The Voice". The truth is that Frank had learned well from his time with Harry James and Tommy Dorsey. He had been developing his stagecraft, working on his little mannerisms and making everything he did on stage count. People have talked about the way Frank seemed to sing just to them, holding them with his blue eyes. There is no question that some of it was gift, but an awful lot more of it was sheer hard work and determination.

THE VOICE

While George Evans is generally credited with naming Frank "The Voice", others have said that it was Harry Kilby, Frank's agent. It was certainly Harry who had added the strapline "The Voice That Has Thrilled Millions" to the Paramount billing.

In fact there's an element of truth on both sides. Kilby's slightly overblown statement definitely came first but it was probably Evans who had the savvy to shorten it to "The Voice". Whoever it was, it certainly stuck. Critics were soon likening his voice to "worn velveteen", or, as one said, "it was like being stroked by a hand covered in cold cream". Fans wondered whether he tucked his voice under his armpit between numbers; another said he had musk glands where his tonsils ought to be.

THE SINATRA EFFECT

George Evans defied the first rule of PR – there is no such thing as bad publicity as long as they spell your name right. He crafted a whole new section of the dictionary to describe the Sinatra effect. Besides dubbing him "The Voice", and calling the girls "Sinatratics", he called Frank "Swoonatra". In what was an unsubtle linking of the effect that Frank had on some of the girls, he called it "Sinatraism"… and undoubtedly many had these "isms". It's just a pity he never wrote a book on image-making; it would have become a bestseller. Much of what he did were old tricks of the trade: inventing stories about Frank's growing up, taking a few years off his age, running competitions with radio stations under the guise of Frank Sinatra Day, adding noughts to what Frankie was earning and being paid, playing up the happy family angle, and never missing an opportunity to get his boy's name in the papers. Evidence of Frank's popularity was everywhere, especially in the number of local fan clubs that were formed. They grasped every titbit that George Evans fed them, and, of course, they also bought Frank's records – not that there were any new solo ones available.

With the passing of 60 years, it is sometimes difficult to unravel fact from fiction. Was there really a Frank

THE HOLLYWOOD BOWL

THE HOLLYWOOD BOWL

"Sinatra… is the new idol — the man who, in a few months, has stepped from the role of band singer into a solo spot on a major network show, top billing in one of New York's fashionable night clubs, and a publicity build-up which now has him out on a limb as the biggest thing since Crosby."

LEONARD G FEATHER, *METRONOME*, MAY 1943

THE SUIT
Frank in his dressing room at the Paramount. "His weight sometimes dropped to 128 [lb], which made him only a shade fatter than a microphone."
Earl Wilson, 1940s journalist.

Sinatra Fan and Mahjong Club – a club at which a group of middle-aged Jewish women got together to play mahjong and listen to Frank's records? Over the course of the next few years, everyone wanted to say that they had been at that first Paramount show, or at least there during the first week. Over the decades, memories fade and a little embellishment goes an awfully long way. Given the fact that Frank played the Paramount a number of times in 1943 and 1944, it is probable that people adjusted their truth. But one thing always holds true: when someone as big as Frank Sinatra comes along, everyone is either a fan or they loathe him.

During his run at the Paramount, Frank was voted No 1 male vocalist in the *Downbeat* poll, a position Bing Crosby had held for the previous six years. When the run came to an end on 20 February, Frank was a genuine star, maybe not as big a star as George Evans would have people believe, but he was very big. Maybe it was not pop's big bang, but the sound of Frank would be heard all over the US. Frank was about to create radio waves, and along with a little help, as well as some hindrance, from the big screen and the newspapers, the opening chapters of his legend were about to be written.

MOVE ON UP

Frank and Nancy had moved once before, from their two-bedroom apartment on Garfield Avenue to a bigger one on Bergen Street in Hasbrouck Heights, a few miles northwest of Hoboken but it was still nowhere for a star to be living! Frank's earnings had shot up, giving the couple a far greater choice of where to live. However, Frank's earnings had not risen from the $750 or so a week he was getting at the start of the Paramount run to the $25,000 a week by the end of the eight weeks,

◀◀ REVEILLE WITH BEVERLY

WHILE FRANK WAS at the Paramount Theatre, this black-and-white Columbia movie had its release on 4 February, 1941. Frank appeared singing 'Night and Day', in a scene that has been described as "cut-price Busby Berkeley". The picture was a budget production ($350,000), running for just 78 minutes with a slight plot that featured various artistes introduced by Ann Miller as an Armed Forces DJ. Others to appear in this Charles Barton-directed film included Count Basie, Duke Ellington, Bob Crosby, Freddie Slack, and Ella Mae Morse. After Frank's success, it got a re-release and grossed around $3 million.

❝His voice is pleasant... a kind of moaning baritone with a few trick inflections. ❞

JOHN T MCMANUS REVIEWING *REVEILLE WITH BEVERLY*

as some have suggested. It would be a while before Frank was really earning over $1 million a year. Apart from anything else, he was still paying Mr Dorsey and his agent a good slug of his earnings.

Frank and Nancy's new home was a $25,000 two-storey, seven-room house at 220 Lawrence Avenue in Hasbrouck Heights. They had moved to the small town some time in 1941, and, as its name suggests, it was a step up from Hoboken. Their next-door neighbours were Dr Joseph Latona and his wife Nancy (Latona was the Sinatra family doctor). According to Nancy Latona, their arrival made life a little difficult. Fans were always around the house. "They wrote love letters to him with lipstick on his garage door, they all wanted to catch a glimpse of him. The whole intersection was constantly blocked with traffic."

A month after he began appearing on *Your Hit Parade*, and three weeks after the Paramount run finished, Frank was booked to appear in a nightclub. Manhattan's Riobamba Club was on East 57th Street and it too turned out to be another sell-out engagement. It was a very different audience from the "bobby-soxers" at the Paramount: more sophisticated and less liable to scream. For his appearance at the fashionable Riobamba he was paid $750 a week, which certainly supported the argument for the lie regarding his Paramount wages reaching $25,000. The club was in some financial trouble, possibly because its owner, Louis Lepke, a hit man for the Mob, was in prison awaiting execution. In Louis' absence, his wife was running the club. A few months after Frank appeared there she gave another young singer a break. He was named Dean Martin. Topping the bill at the club was Sheila Barrett, a singer and comedienne, along with Walter O'Keefe, a veteran monologist and comedian. Frank was again billed as a

PHENOMENAL FRANKIE
E J Kahn's book about Frank was the first biography of the singer and identified, presciently, his enormous impact.

"specially added" attraction, much, apparently, to his annoyance. There was also a group of chorus girls known as Russell Patterson's Magazine Cover Girls.

OPENING AT THE RIOBAMBA

Frank was by all accounts nervous in this new environment; it had been a while since he had sung in a club. "I had to open the show walking round the tables and singing. There was no stage or anything and the dance floor was only as big as a postage stamp." He was backed by a band led by pianist Nat Brandwynne and began his set with 'Night and Day'. He went on to sing 'Embraceable You', 'You'd Be so Nice to Come Home to', 'Where or When', and 'As Time Goes By' to the highly appreciative audience, but with none of the reaction he had had at the Paramount. A regular black bow tie to go along with Frank's dinner jacket replaced Nancy's colourful homemade floppy ones. It was a smart move by Frank's agent to book him somewhere that could only diversify his appeal. Leonard G Feather recorded the reaction at the Riobamba in *Metronome* in May 1943: "'Shut up, will you? Sinatra's singing!' The beautiful and bejewelled young lady turned away from her escort, nose in air, as a respectful hush

settled over the Riobamba. A smart, over-sophisticated nightclub crowd fixed its attention on the thin young man with the progressive ears, who had just stepped to the microphone. You can hardly be surprised at the young lady's reluctance to let her escort talk while Sinatra was working. For Sinatra, my children, is the new idol – the man who, in a few months, has stepped from the role of band singer into a solo spot on a major network show, top billing in one of New York's fashionable night clubs, and a publicity build-up which now has him out on a limb as the biggest thing since Crosby."

Robert Dana, writing in *Dining and Dancing*, was less impressed. "Frank Sinatra is a living advertisement for an arranger's skill. He has a good, but not a very good, voice. The trick of his success is in timing the phrasing of the lyrics to give the music additional feeling and meaning. Sometimes it amounts only to a *tour de force*, but an effective one."

Frank's success at the Riobamba proved he had a greater all-around pulling power than just with the bobby-soxers. His profile was building. George Evans and Columbia Records must have been very pleased. He was getting coverage in not just the New York press but also *Life* magazine and the *Saturday Evening Post*. A cover feature on *Billboard* on 27 March was a coup for George Evans: "The best way to describe Frank Sinatra and record his amazing

FRANK'S FIRST STADIUM
Frank rehearsing at New York's Lewisohn Stadium with Max Steiner, the conductor, on Frank's right. George Evans looks on.

1943 ON THE JUKEBOX

In 1943, Frank spent 84 weeks on the *Billboard* charts, but only 29 of those weeks were truly as a solo artist; the remaining time was spent on recordings by either Harry James or Tommy Dorsey. This must have irked both Frank and Columbia, his new label. There was naturally a delay for Columbia in getting new recordings made because of the musicians' strike. When they found a way, by recording Frank a cappella with the Bobby Tucker Singers, they were on a tough mission to try to compete with recordings that the public were more used to hearing, even given Frank's soaring popularity. One reason for the success of Frank's records with James and Dorsey was the success of the bands themselves. Taking nothing away from Frank, it gave the records greater selling power with the increased fan base; Big Bands were still very popular.

BIG TIME FRANKIE

Frank took over the No 1 spot from Bing Crosby's 'White Christmas' on *Billboard*'s 26 January bestseller's list with 'There Are Such Things'. The Tommy Dorsey recording had been released in November 1942 and worked its way up the chart to No 2 by the first week of 1943.

Frank had his second No 1 on the bestseller's list for 1943 with 'In the Blue of the Evening' on 21 August, again with Tommy Dorsey. This song originally came out in September 1942, having been recorded at a session on 17 June, 1942. Backed by 'A Boy in Khaki: a Girl in Lace', with a vocal by Jo Stafford, it failed to make any impression on the chart. With the shortage of material created by the musicians' strike and Frank's new-found popularity, it was hastily re-pressed with 'It's Always You' on the b-side and rush-released at the end of June, 1942. 'All or Nothing at All' with Harry James made No 2, with 'In the Blue of the Evening' at No 1.

'You'll Never Know' came from the film *Hello, Frisco, Hello*, starring Alice Faye. Frank's version of the Oscar-winning song, backed by the Bobby Tucker Singers, was his first release on Columbia. It was also, one suspects, something of a disappointment to him, despite making No 2 on the *Billboard* bestseller's chart. Not only was it kept from the top spot by 'In the Blue of the Evening', it was also outsold by Dick Haymes's version of the song on Decca.

THE MILLS BROTHERS
This family group from Piqua, Ohio, had five No 1 singles in all, including 'Tiger Rag' and 'Dinah' in the 1930s.

Haymes's version stayed at No 1 for four weeks and occupied the No 2 spot for an additional two weeks. Dick's version was ranked the 5th most popular song of the year (Frank's version was ranked 15th); 'In the Blue of the Evening' was ranked 6th.

Given that 'Sunday, Monday, or Always' came from the film *Dixie*, starring Bing Crosby, then it is perhaps not too surprising that Bing's version outsold Frank's a cappella rendition. Bing's version stayed at No 1 on the bestseller's list for seven weeks, making it the third most popular recording of the year.

Frank's last two hits of 1943 were both sides of a record featuring songs from Rodgers and Hammerstein's landmark musical *Oklahoma*. The musical was first staged on Broadway on 31 March, 1943, at the St James Theatre with Alfred Drake, Joan Roberts, and Celeste Holm (who would later appear with Frank in the film *High Society*). *Oklahoma* ran for 2,212 performances on Broadway, breaking all records; it opened in London in 1947 (where it ran for 1,500 nights).

BOBBY TUCKER SINGERS
Bobby Tucker was a pianist who assembled "his singers" to accompany Frank a cappella on his first Columbia recordings. There were between 12 and 17 Bobby Tucker Singers, and together with Frank they cut 12 sides for Columbia during the strike. The arranger on these sessions was Alec Wilder — "The Professor", as Frank called him. Frank would work with Wilder at various times in the future. While the records Frank made a cappella are good, they are not a patch on his recordings made with an orchestra. A good example of the difference is on 'Close to You' recorded in June with the Bobby Tucker Singers, and again in December with Axel Stordahl and the Bobby Tucker Singers on a V-Disc taken from a rehearsal for a CBS radio show. Frank sounds more relaxed and gives an altogether more convincing performance with the orchestra behind him. Not that the a cappella recordings are bad; in fact the version of 'People Will Say We're in Love' gives Frank's voice a great deal of room to breathe. The warmth of Frank's voice is wonderful.

BILLBOARD'S BESTSELLER'S CHART
The year belonged to Harry James. His recording of 'I've Heard That Song Before' featuring Helen Forrest become the number one song of 1943. It topped the bestseller's list for 13 weeks. Harry and Helen also held the top spot with 'I Had the Craziest Dream' for two weeks. Add to this his performance with Frank of 'All or Nothing at All', and a

number of other hit records pushed Harry to the top of the big band rankings.

After a couple of quieter years on the bestseller's list, Bing Crosby bounced back in 1943 as the best performing artist of all. 'Sunday, Monday or Always' was his biggest hit, but 'Pistol Packin' Mama' with the Andrews Sisters and 'People Will Say We're in Love' with Trudy Erwin both did very well. The big surprise of the year was the re-emergence of the Mills Brothers, whose recording of 'Paper Doll' went to No 1 for 12 weeks (four of them in 1944). The Mills Brothers had been very popular in the early 1930s, having had No 1 recordings with 'Tiger Rag' (1931) and 'Dinah' (1932), as well as a string of other big sellers. On virtually all their records up until 1950 they had no instrumental accompaniment other than a guitar.

IN GOOD COMPANY
The *Billboard* Chart for 16 October, 1943.

FRANK ON THE US CHARTS

'IT STARTED ALL OVER AGAIN'
Carl Fischer & Bill Carey
13 February, No 4, 13 weeks

'ALL OR NOTHING AT ALL'
Arthur Altman & Jack Lawrence
19 June, No 2, 18 weeks

'IN THE BLUE OF THE EVENING'
Alfred D'Artega & Tom Adair
10 July, No 1, 17 weeks

'IT'S ALWAYS YOU'
Jimmy Van Heusen & Johnny Burke (from The Road to Zanzibar)
17 July, No 6, 7 weeks

'YOU'LL NEVER KNOW'
Harry Warren & Mack Gordon (from Hello, Frisco, Hello)
31 July, No 2, 13 weeks

'CLOSE TO YOU'
Al Hoffman, Jerry Livingston & Carl Lampl
2 October, No 10, 1 week

'SUNDAY, MONDAY OR ALWAYS'
Jimmy Van Heusen & Johnny Burke (from Dixie)
18 September, No 9, 4 weeks

'PEOPLE WILL SAY WE'RE IN LOVE'
Richard Rodgers & Oscar Hammerstein II from Oklahoma
9 October, No 6, 9 weeks

'OH WHAT A BEAUTIFUL MORNING'
Richard Rodgers & Oscar Hammerstein II from Oklahoma
27 November, No 15, 2 weeks

NATIONAL

POSITION Last Wk.	This Wk.		
1	1.	SUNDAY, MONDAY OR ALWAYS —BING CROSBY Decca 18561	
2	2.	PAPER DOLL —MILLS BROTHERS Decca 18318	
3	3.	PISTOL PACKIN' MAMA —AL DEXTER Okeh 6708	
4	4.	I HEARD YOU CRIED LAST NIGHT —HARRY JAMES Columbia 36677	
8	5.	YOU'LL NEVER KNOW —HAYMES-SONG SPINNERS Decca 18556	
5	6.	YOU'LL NEVER KNOW —FRANK SINATRA Columbia 36678	
9	7.	PEOPLE WILL SAY WE'RE IN LOVE —FRANK SINATRA Columbia 36682	
7	8.	ALL OR NOTHING AT ALL —JAMES-SINATRA Columbia 35587	
6	9.	IN THE BLUE OF THE EVENING —TOMMY DORSEY Victor 20-1530	
—	10.	PEOPLE WILL SAY WE'RE IN LOVE —BING CROSBY Decca 18564	

1942 – 1946

career is to say that he is the biggest threat in years to Bing Crosby's reign as King of the Vocalists." It went on to discuss Frank's appearances on *Your Hit Parade* and his career with Dorsey before finishing up: "He has the headwaiter goofy trying to keep the crowds in check at the Riobamba Club. The music industry has nominated Sinatra as its No 1 topic of conversation. Young, good looking, and heavily romantic on the vocal side, Frank Sinatra has given his wife and child a bale of reasons to go in for hero-worship."

A booking at the Meadowbrook in Cedar Grove in April continued to build on his success in Manhattan. Frank also helped out his old friend Harry James, who was playing the Paramount. Harry was so exhausted from his hectic schedule as well as running the band that he was taken ill during his band's month-long booking. Frank sang with the band while Harry rested; you doubt he would have done the same for Dorsey!

FLAG WAVING

On 16 May, Frank was at the 'I'm an American Day' in New York's Central Park, singing 'God Bless America' along with other stars. It was a war bond rally, a popular fund-raising effort during World War II that was often fronted by singers and film stars. The war bonds attempted to pull on the heartstrings of patriotic citizens to lend their money, particularly because these bonds offered a lower rate of return than market rates. For entertainers left at home by the war it was their chance to "do their bit".

Two days later, Frank was at Madison Square Garden in New York to perform at a rally in aid of Greek war relief, and then it was back to the Paramount on 26 May for another month of sell-out performances. This time they were paying him $2,500 a week (although it went up to $3,100 by the end of the four weeks). Frank had told Leonard Feather of *Metronome* about the booking, "Gene Krupa's band will be there, so I'm adding five strings of my own. I'm crazy about strings for a vocal background. Tell you the truth, if James had had strings at the time I was with the band, maybe I'd never have left."

FRANKLY SURPRISING
Frankie goes to Pasadena. Fortunately, RKO took their prop department steps to the station just in case the fans found out about Frank's arrival.

Unfortunately for Frank, and Gene, the drummer bandleader was arrested in San Francisco for possession of marijuana and he got 80 days in jail for his trouble. Robert Dana again criticized Frank Sinatra's performance, this time in a review in the *New York World Telegram and Sun*. He even made the mistake, as far as Frank's fans were concerned, of comparing him, somewhat unfavourably, with Dick Haymes. Mr Dana was subjected to some pretty strong fan mail: "You had the audacity to say that this jerk could compare with our Frankie… Do you know he sings 'Black Magic' to us? We spent five days in the first row of the Paramount through all shows until after midnight. We have all his records and we never miss his radio shows. We love him more than our own fathers and brothers. Dick Haymes stinks on ice. We will go to see him only if fortified with rotten tomatoes. We saw Dick Hamyes (sic), and not one woman swooned. Not one man looked mad. You have every right to say Dick Haymes is the best singer you ever heard, but you cannot say Frank is artificial."

Just after Frank opened his third solo run at the Paramount, he appeared on the radio show *Broadway Bandbox*, backed by the Bobby Tucker Singers. Just over a week later he was in the studio at Columbia's Liederkrantz Hall in New York City, again with the Bobby Tucker Singers. They were there to record Frank's first solo sides for his new label. The only thing missing was an orchestra. Columbia had decided to record Frank a cappella because of the continuing strike. They needed to get their protégé's records into the stores and on to the jukeboxes. While the radio was important – it made the sponsors money and earned the artistes a little – it did nothing for the record company coffers. The strike had gone on longer than anyone expected and every label was running out of stockpiled records to release.

FRANKIE GOES TO HOLLYWOOD

Having completed his month at the Paramount, Frank spent the next six weeks working mostly on radio shows, including *The Stage Door Canteen*, *Broadway Bandbox*, and continuing, of course, to appear each week on *Your Hit Parade*. He appeared on stage again with Benny Goodman. This time it was a Saturday afternoon gig at the Mall in New York's Central Park. It was an event sponsored by The American Legion to which people took their old records, which were then sold for scrap.

On 3 August, Frank appeared at New York's Lewisohn Stadium with the Philharmonic Symphony Orchestra conducted by Max Steiner in front of 7,500 fans: "no sell out", as *Life* magazine reported. They also said that Frank "got under the skin of the orchestra at rehearsals". The *New York Sun* noted the voice was "rather nondescript"; the *Herald Tribune* was a little less harsh: "pleasant voice, satisfactory projection, excellent diction". But Frank's mind was on other things. He was off to

Hollywood for a shot at a real career in the movies, rather than the cameo roles he had so far experienced.

The story goes that Frank left New York's Grand Central Station on the *20th Century Limited* bound for Chicago, where he had to change both train and station to catch the *Santa Fe Chief* to Union Station in Los Angeles. With him were George Evans, Hank Sanicola, and Axel Stordahl as well as some other unnamed people (it was the early days of the Sinatra entourage). Somewhere along the route, it was decided they should disembark at Pasadena, 9 miles east of Los Angeles, to avoid the anticipated throng of fans that would be there to meet him. Word somehow got out that Frank was going to leave the train in Pasadena, however, and according to Frank, the crowd at the station that was there to meet him on 11 August was enormous: "There must have been 5,000 kids mashed against the car. It was exciting, but it scares the wits out of you, too."

Nice story, but while it is partially true in the detail, it is far from true in the overall effect of Frank's arrival in Hollywood. Frank did indeed arrive in Pasadena with his entourage, but the arrival had been planned by RKO to exploit the photo opportunity; the studio even "whispered" the news over the radio. Frank was never to have arrived at Union Station. RKO had a group of their own "comely starlets" at Pasadena's station to meet Frank. The crowd, far from numbering 5,000, more likely amounted to no more than a few hundred. Press reports talked about there being "twenty of Pasadena's finest trying to keep the horde of ecstatic swooners from stampeding". "One starlet, Patti Brill, is crying. 'Oh she got squashed in the rush,' somebody explained. Sinatra interrupts the interview to determine that Patti ain't lost an arm or leg," is how another reported the scene. RKO had even taken along a stepladder for Frank to stand on so that everyone could get a better look at their new star. Who can blame them? They needed to capitalize on their investment, and so careful "media management" was the order of the day. In fact, it was lucky that the RKO people were there at the right time and day, since, according to their own press release, Frankie was travelling on the *20th Century Limited*.

The day after Frank arrived in California there was an amazing coincidence. A letter was received by the FBI from a resident of San José, California, that compared the frenzy being created by Sinatra with the actions of Hitler! "Last night I heard *Lucky Strike* produce more of this hysteria. I thought how easy it would be for certain minded manufacturers to create another Hitler here in America through the same influence of mass hysteria!" The remainder of the letter smacks of someone who

WAR BOND
War bonds were issued by the US government during World War II to raise money for the war effort.

66Mr Sinatra's baritone had little real volume and little carrying power beyond what the amplifier gave it, and it was utterly inadequate in 'Ol Man River', but the singing was definitely unique in the matter of style, and the singer's pleasant and friendly and somewhat dreamy personality matched it.**99**

NEW YORK TIMES
WEDNESDAY, 4 AUGUST, 1943

1942-1946

has a somewhat tenuous grasp on reality. This is the earliest document that exists on the FBI files about Frank Sinatra – but it was the beginning of what was to be an awful lot of filing for someone at their headquarters in Washington. The FBI, like many in the US, were about to take more than a passing interest in Frank remaining at home rather than doing military service. Many people, more often than not men, and service personnel at that, began to make disparaging remarks about the man whom they saw as not altogether doing his patriotic bit. For George Evans it would become a long-running battle that would exercise his damage-limitation skills to the hilt.

BOWLED OVER

Frank, of course, was completely unaware of the letter from "Disgruntled of San José". His first engagement on his trip out west was at the Hollywood Bowl on Saturday 14 August with the Los Angeles Philharmonic Orchestra. The Bowl was having a financial crisis, and someone had the bright idea of staging this concert to get the venue out of the red. The first part of the evening, which began at 9:00 pm, was given over to "light classics", including Rimsky-Korsakov's 'Dance of the Comedians' from the *Snow Maiden* and 'A Night on a Bare Mountain' by Mussorgsky. Nancy Sinatra must have been thinking of Axel Stordahl, because she refers to it as "Night on a Bald Mountain". For the classical portion of the evening, Vladimir Bakaleinikoff conducted the orchestra, while Morris Stoloff had the baton for Frank's songs.

At the Bowl, Frank, billed as a baritone soloist, dressed in a white dinner jacket and began his half of the evening's entertainment with 'Dancing in the Dark', and included among his programme 'It's Always You', 'Night and Day', and his current hit song 'All or Nothing at All'. He finished the evening with two songs not scheduled in the printed programme: 'The Song Is You' and 'She's Funny That Way'. It was a triumph for all concerned. With an audience of 10,000 (some have said 18,000, which was the Bowl's original capacity, but the wartime seating was restricted to 10,000) paying between 75 cents and $2.20, the Bowl's financial worries were eased (the show grossed $12,500) and Frank had presented himself to another stratum of the musical community, although it is doubtful whether many of the audience were there for Mussorgsky or Rimsky-Korsakov. According to *Variety*, most were "adolescent Sinatrics ready to shriek, squeal, gurgle or giggle on the slightest provocation". They went on to say: "As he was whisked away by a flock of traffic cops, there was a final chorus of gurgles, mingled with masculine sounds redolent of night-blooming raspberry."

"Mr Swoon Bowl debut Super, what kids want. "

VARIETY, 16 AUGUST, 1943

Two days after the Hollywood Bowl show, Frank and Harry James were reunited, for one night only. They played *The Hollywood Canteen* radio show in front of an audience of mostly servicemen. Naturally they performed their big hit. By this time, Harry's band was more of an orchestra with the addition of a string section. Any antipathy that the GIs may have felt seemed to ebb away as Frank said by way of introduction, "Well, at least nobody in this crowd is going to faint."

Almost immediately it was time for Frank to get to work on his first starring movie role in *Higher and Higher*. While it was a step up from the cameo roles, it has to be said that RKO, whose picture it was, were the least financially sound of the major Hollywood studios, as well as the smallest. Harry Kilby at GAC had negotiated the deal for Frank, and it gives a measure of Frank's standing in early to mid-1943. He was to be paid $25,000 for his first picture; from then there would be a doubling of his fee for each subsequent film. He was contracted to make seven in all, which meant he would be earning $1.6 million for his seventh film – either RKO were very confident of his success or doubtful of their long-term future.

Filming *Higher and Higher* took place at RKO's studio on the corner of Melrose Avenue and Gower Street and was scheduled to last eight weeks. Frank was to play himself in the film and was to appear alongside Michèle Morgan and Jack Haley; all in all it was not the most exciting career move. In September, while Frank was filming, he met his hero, Bing Crosby. Filming for Frank finished earlier than anticipated, and RKO told him he would be needed back in Hollywood in December to work on his next picture. Louella Parsons, a William Randolph Hearst nationally syndicated columnist, who always claimed "a story wasn't a story unless I got it first", reported that Frank told her at Ronald Reagan and Jane Wyman's party that his next RKO picture would be *Mr Cinderella*. Returning home to Hasbrouck Heights at the end of September, it was not long before Frank was back at his day job. On 1 October he was in New York City, to appear in the Wedgwood Room of the Waldorf-Astoria Hotel for what was another carefully thought-out career move.

SINGING FOR HIS SUPPER

As Frank began his two-month run at the world-famous hotel, the 46-year career of the legendary *maître d'hôtel*, Oscar Michel Tschirsky, was coming to an end; he was the man who invented the Waldorf salad and Thousand Island dressing. For over a century the Waldorf-Astoria Hotel in New York has been a symbol of the American dream. Frank's run at the hotel coincided with the 50th anniversary of the second Waldorf-Astoria, one of the city's best Art Deco buildings. When it was opened it was the largest hotel in the world. Frank's booking was the

BOWLED OVER
"I want to thank you from the bottom of my heart... I don't see why there shouldn't be a mixture of all kinds of music at any bowl or auditorium. Music is Universal."
Frank in his closing speech.

1942–1946

MONDAY AT THE CANTEEN
Frank with Harry James at the Hollywood Canteen, 16 August, 1943.

fulfilment of the first stage of his campaign to conquer the US. As venues come, they did not get any more prestigious in the 1940s. The Wedgwood Room, with its blue-and-white décor, was elegance personified – far more upmarket than the Riobamba. But, as Frank later quipped on radio, the Waldorf-Astoria room was so named because "If they could wedge another person in, they would." But even with them wedged in, it still only accommodated fewer than 300 people, so the numbers that got to see Frank were limited.

CAFÉ CRÊME

The cream of New York's society frequented the Waldorf and not everyone among the New York press corps thought that Frank, accompanied by Nat Brandwynne's Orchestra, could carry it off. The critic Earl Wilson was one of them. However, he had to admit that Frank had done it. The day after Frank opened at the Wedgwood on I October, Wilson's column ran under the headline "Sinatra wins the sceptics in opening at the Waldorf". Amongst the crowd on that opening night was Cole Porter, and he heard Frank sing 'Night and Day'. Sammy Cahn had also written a parody of 'Don't Blame Me'

aimed at the bobby-soxers. "I don't blame the guy who threw an egg at me, if my gal swooned, I'd do the same as he. It's tough to sing. I wish they'd do the same to Bing."

Later Frank told Earl Wilson how nervous he was. "If I hadn't been, I'd be a self-satisfied guy, and that would stink." Later others followed Wilson's lead in praising Frank's performances. Elsa Maxwell, the queen of New York society columnists, who had previously referred to some of Frank's fans as "emotionally unstable females" did an about turn: "He has found a setting to show off the sweetness of his voice." While the Wedgwood Room was more used to hosting a ritzy clientele, there were some diehards who went to see Frank, despite the $2 cover charge. To accommodate them, the Waldorf printed extra menus for Frank to sign and give away. After he had finished at 2:00 am one night, which was the usual time, a 17-year-old girl, Marion DePlasco from the Bronx, showed off her extra prize. It was Frank's handkerchief, which she had taken from his pocket. "I asked him if I could, and he didn't say no," she said. She announced that it had some cologne on it. "Aw, I wants to smell it," cried some of her friends. "Let me smell it, too," said others. "I'm going to frame it and I'm going to keep it close to me all the time," declared Marion.

V-DISCS

ON 17 OCTOBER, 1943, FRANK, AXEL STORDAHL, AND THE BOBBY TUCKER SINGERS WERE IN CBS'S NEW YORK CITY PLAYHOUSE NO 3 REHEARSING FOR THEIR LAST *BROADWAY BANDBOX* APPEARANCE. THEY WERE ALSO WORKING FOR THE ARMY.

THIS WAS TO BE FRANK'S first V-Disc release, a recording specially made for distribution to active service personnel. Between October 1943 and November 1947 Frank recorded 55 songs for V-Discs, of which all but six were released at the time.

'V' FOR VICTORY

V-Discs came about because the musician's strike drastically reduced the supply of new recordings to the forces. Army sound engineer Lieutenant George Robert Vincent approached the War Department with the idea of making records especially for the troops. In July 1943, he joined the music section of Army Special Services to develop the Victory or V-Disc (a name apparently coined by Vincent's secretary). Vincent's first task was to secure a waiver on royalties and fees from both the record companies and the unions. From his office on East 42nd Street in New York City, Vincent quickly won the support of the recording industry. RCA Victor pressed the first V-Discs in New Jersey and the initial shipment of 53,400 discs, in boxes of 25 records, took place on 1 October, 1943. V-Discs were different from normal 78-rpm commercial records. They were 12 inches in diameter, whereas commercial records were 10 inches. They usually had more grooves per side, which meant up to six minutes of music could be put on one side.

VIRTUALLY INDESTRUCTIBLE

On Frank's first V-Disc (V-Disc 72A/B) there was 'I Only Have Eyes For You' on side A and 'Kiss Me Again' and 'Hot Time in Old Berlin' on the other. V-Discs were manufactured on virtually unbreakable vinyl for good reason. Apart from the distances they had to be shipped, they had to withstand being played on phonographs in barracks, mess halls, and infirmaries from the English home counties to the North African desert and to a Pacific atoll. Many V-Discs were similar to Frank's rehearsals for a radio show – recordings where there was no audience. Sometimes they were commercial recordings, or un-issued takes and film soundtracks. Some recording sessions used unusual combinations of musicians. Sgt Tony Janak, a former recording engineer for Columbia Records, undertook recording sessions in concert halls, in jazz clubs, in apartments. "In the beginning we chose material from broadcasts and the files of the record companies that were contracting on the project. Then we got into doing live sessions of our own: [we] were always dreaming up new recording dates. We recorded at Columbia Records, RCA Victor, NBC, World, and Carnegie Hall with Louis Armstrong, Tommy Dorsey, and Duke Ellington; jazz at the Metropolitan Opera House and Stuyvesant Casino; at West Point with the Military Academy Band."

SCRAP MAN
Frank in New York's Central Park receiving old records to be sold for scrap to raise money for the war effort.

At the end of the war, Vincent left the army, but V-Discs continued, at a reduced rate, until May 1949. In six years there were 8 million V-Discs shipped to the forces on over 900 different titles containing over 3,000 recordings. Most V-Discs and their masters were destroyed as promised. Some did find their way back to the US and other places, helped by their robust manufacture: the Library of Congress in Washington, DC, has almost a complete set.

> 66 Hi ya men! This is Frank Sinatra. I hope you like these tunes that I've chosen to do for you on these very wonderful V-Discs. I hope you get as much a kick out of hearing them as I get from doin' 'em. 99
>
> **FRANK INTRODUCING 'I ONLY HAVE EYES FOR YOU'**

After 22 days of his 60-day run at the Waldorf, and having had a thorough investigation by the press as to the depths of his talents, the likelihood of his professional longevity, and the intensity of his fans' love and affection, Frank faced another examination of a totally different kind. On Friday, 22 October, 1943, he went to Jersey City to see Dr Povalski, a Local Board Examining Physician for the US Army. Frank was there to ascertain his suitability for military service. It was not just a physical examination and induction – there was also a questionnaire to be answered, similar to the one Frank had already filled out in 1940. One question asked, "What physical or mental defects or diseases have you had in the past, if any?" Frank's one-word reply was "No". Frank was passed fit for call-up by the Army. In normal circumstances, it would be expected that this would follow shortly thereafter, given the crucial stage in the war effort against both Germany and Japan.

The threat of call up must have played on Frank's mind, but it may well have been kept at the back of it by sheer hard work. Not only was he appearing nightly at the Waldorf but he was also keeping up a steady stream of radio shows. In addition to American Forces Radio Shows, guest appearances on other shows, and *Your Hit Parade*, he was also doing *Broadway Bandbox*. When the latter show went off the air, an even better showcase for Frank's talent, *Songs by Sinatra*, replaced it almost immediately. This 15-minute programme aired on Sunday nights and was first broadcast on 24 October, 1943. It featured the Bobby Tucker Singers, with Axel Stordahl conducting the orchestra (radio shows, like live performances, were not being affected by the musicians' strike). It went on air at 7:15 pm and used as its theme Frank's co-composition 'This Love of Mine'. Each week three or four other songs were showcased. On that first show, Frank did 'Paper Doll', the current big hit by the Mills Brothers.

THE WEDGWOOD ROOM AT THE WALDORF-ASTORIA, NEW YORK, 1946

*F*RANKIE FEELS THE DRAFT

Frank's success at the Wedgwood Room brought greater attention to his every move. It was no longer just bobby-soxers who couldn't get enough of Frank and what he was up to. His profile in New York was sky-high and his radio work gave him a good deal of awareness across the US. But he was not alone in this.

Dick Haymes had out-gunned Frank on the charts with 'You'll Never Know', and by the time Frank's run at the Waldorf-Astoria came to an end, Bing Crosby had four records in the *Billboard* bestseller's Top 10, while Frank had just one. There was also talk of another young Italian who was showing promise – the former barbershop owner, Perry Como. It is important to put Frank's success into context. Some who have written and spoken of Frank in the subsequent 60 years would have you believe it was a one-horse race. There was Frankie and a very long way back was the rest of the field. Some of this is a result of

DRAFT REGISTRATION
Men line up at their voting station in St. Paul, Minnesota, to register for the draft under the Selective Service Act.

"*Frank Albert Sinatra is physically and/or mentally disqualified for military service by reason of: 1. chronic perforation (left) tympanum; 2. chronic mastoiditis.*"

CAPTAIN J WEINTROB, MD, ASSISTANT CHIEF MEDICAL OFFICER

where Frank ended up in the pantheon of performers, some is from blinkered adulation for the man, and some just set out to distort the truth. In reality, when people fail to acknowledge the talent and variety of the competition, it diminishes Frank's achievement. While his success was real and being dubbed "The Voice" was one thing, being *the* voice was something else. There was also the little matter of Frank's military service.

UNFIT FOR DUTY

In the event, there was to be no call-up. Somehow, between 22 October, when Frank was examined in Jersey City, and 9 December he went from being fit to unfit, suitable to unsuitable for military service. The *New York Times* had carried a piece on 6 November, saying he had been passed as I-A, and talked of him being called up in January. Ira Caldwell, chairman of the Selective Service Board, said he had been assured by the singer's manager that Frank would not appeal. Yet on his Physical Examination and Induction form, stamped by Captain J Weintrob, MD, Assistant Chief Medical Officer, it stated that Frank was classified as 4-F (unacceptable for service for medical reasons). "Frank Albert Sinatra is physically and/or mentally disqualified for military service by reason of: 1. chronic perforation (left) tympanum; 2. chronic mastoiditis." In the physical examination results, it added that the 5ft 7½ in, 119 lb singer was listed with emotional instability under a heading of "Mental".

The press were keenly interested in Frank's call-up status and it had been reported in some newspapers that he had a pre-induction physical two weeks prior to his examination proper and therefore Frank knew he was going to be classed as 4-F. The chief clerk of the Hudson County Draft Board, Mrs Mae Jones, was questioned about this and she denied that anyone ever had a pre-induction examination. She felt that because Sinatra continued to make plans for his new radio series that people felt he somehow knew the outcome of the examination. She suggested it was because he had been examined by his own doctor prior to the military physician. However, it does seem amazing that Frank could have gone from being an eligible candidate for military service to such an ineligible one.

The FBI thought so, too. The decision on whether Frank was to be called up drew a good deal of ongoing media attention of the "will he, won't he" variety, especially when Frank was asked to appear at the New Jersey Draft Board once again on 8 February. The next day, Frank was insisting "I think I'm in." Three days later, he left for Hollywood after being told of his 4-F status, telling waiting newsmen "I'm dying."

At the end of December 1943, a letter arrived at the *New York Mirror* addressed to Walter Winchell, the paper's columnist and one of the most influential newspapermen of his day. He also happened to be a good friend of the fine, upstanding head of the FBI, J Edgar Hoover. Winchell lost no time in sending the letter on to Hoover. Winchell's informant suggested that the FBI was investigating a report that Frank Sinatra had paid $40,000 to the Newark doctors who examined him. The money was supposed to have been paid by Frank's business manager. It also went on to say that a former school friend of Frank's said he had "no more eardrum trouble than General MacArthur".

The irony of the whole situation was that the FBI was not actually investigating Frank, but it soon would be. J Edgar got Assistant Director Mickey Ladd, the head of the FBI's Domestic Intelligence division, on the case within the month. February became a pretty busy time around the FBI office in Newark, New Jersey. Captain Weintrob, who had stamped Frank's 4-F, was questioned by the FBI on 23 February. The captain stated that he had examined Frank's ears and found the perforation and the mastoiditis and had rejected him personally. He went on to say that this was very much against the wishes of Sinatra himself. Weintrob's letter to his commanding officer included details of Frank ear problems and it also went into other matters.

"During the psychiatric interview the patient stated that he was 'neurotic', afraid to be in crowds, afraid to go in an elevator, makes him feel that he would want to run when surrounded by people. He had somatic ideas and headaches and has been very nervous for four or five years. Wakens

HERE?
"Frank Sinatra, painter of tone poems, signs paper before leaving his draft board in Newark, New Jersey. Speaking of his rejection, the singer said: 'I am very unhappy about it. If I had been accepted, I would have preferred the Army or Marines.'" Quoted from the original press release distributed with the photograph.

❝Army Swoons – Sinatra is 4-F❞

THE *NEW YORK POST*

1942-1946

HIGHER AND HIGHER

"GOOD MORNING, my name's Frank Sinatra". Cue the swooning...

When *Higher and Higher* opened at cinemas across the US in early January 1944, audiences had to wait 25 minutes from the opening credits for Frank's first on-screen words. This RKO movie had "B" written all over it, from the sets to the actors; even the songs were not that inspiring.

Some of the movie's failure can be blamed on Tim Whelan's wooden and unimaginative direction, but the hard-up RKO Studio ought to shoulder their share, too. The French actress Michèle Morgan and Jack Haley (the Tin Man in Judy Garland's *Wizard of Oz*) were modest actors, which helped Frank to stand out. Originally written by Rodgers and Hart as a Broadway show starring Haley, it ran for only 108 performances in New York.

The plot concerns scullery maid Michèle Morgan's unrequited love for valet Jack Haley. Frank plays himself to sing some songs at a Butler's Ball. Frank's only reason to be in the film, apart from the money-spinning opportunity it created,

was to act as a friend to Marcy McGuire's character, who has a "thing" for Mel Tormé... the plot is as thin as that!

Of the songs written by Jimmy McHugh and Harold Adamson, two stand out above the rest: 'A Lovely Way to Spend an Evening' and 'I Couldn't Sleep a Wink Last Night', but this was small compensation.

The studio hyped it well. "The voice that's THRILLING THE WORLD teamed with a half dozen popular top-flight comedians in a glittering, glorious musical show..."

The critical view seems to have been split across east–west lines. Frankie's hometown media were less enthusiastic than Tinseltown. The *LA Times* said "He plays himself and appears more at ease than we expected", but *The New York Herald* was less applauding: "His ugly, bony face photographs well; his voice registers agreeably enough and he handles himself easily". The *New York Times* stated that "Frankie is no Gable or Barrymore". Frankie had deserted them for the glitter of Hollywood and he was out of favour.

SONGS

'A Lovely Way to Spend an Evening'
'I Couldn't Sleep a Wink Last Night'
'I Saw You First' (duet with Marcy McGuire)
'The Music Stopped'
'You Belong in a Love Song'
'You're on Your Own' (with cast)
All songs written by Jimmy McHugh and Harold Adamson

"The cinema captures an innate shyness in the singer who has uniquely become an idol of the airlanes and the bobby sox trade."
THE HOLLYWOOD REPORTER

tired in the a.m., is run down and undernourished." This is how Weintrob described Frank's condition. He concluded that Frank suffered from "psychoneurosis" but decided to soften the blow of psychoneurosis by substituting the words "emotional instability" instead. Special Agent in Charge Sam McKee relayed this information to FBI headquarters from the Newark office. Despite what appeared to be some misgivings by the FBI about how Frank had changed his story, they closed the case.

"BUGLE-DEAF FRANKIE BOY"

The same could not be said of the press. They began acting like a dog with a new bone in early 1944. Unsurprisingly perhaps, the Army's own newspaper, the *Stars and Stripes*, derided Frank as a "coward". Another paper, slightly more humorously but no less pointedly, called him "Bugle-deaf Frankie Boy Sinatra".

Given his career, and everything else we now know of Frank Sinatra, it does defy credulity to accept that he was ever emotionally unstable in the way described in the captain's letter. As for the mild mental illness ascribed to the "repression of unconscious conflict or fantasy rather than present sexual frustration", which is how psychoneurosis is described in the dictionary, you can make up your own mind.

There was one other side effect of all this investigation. The FBI learnt of Frankie's bad boy past – his arrest for "seduction" back in 1938 and being charged with adultery. Under J Edgar Hoover, the FBI had a penchant for investigating celebrities, which in some way explains how the memos and letters about Frank's military status and earlier misdemeanours became the first pieces of paper in FBI files on Frank. These papers would eventually number many, many thousands. Its appetite for investigating Frank Albert Sinatra remained voracious for many years. The FBI had an ally in all those members of the press who saw it as their patriotic duty to work with J Edgar Hoover's men. The favour was often returned by the FBI.

Of course, all this was going on behind the scenes. It was almost undoubtedly quite unknown to Frank. He was busy getting on with his own life, working on the radio, performing on stage in some week-long bookings in Pittsburgh and Philadelphia, and enjoying the fact that his new film, *Higher and Higher,* was released in major US cities exactly a week after his 4-F classification. Frank himself was reported to have "looked disappointed" when he could not join up. He was even quoted as saying "I was planning to ask for the Marines if they'd have me."

At the beginning of 1944, Frank was not the most popular singer on the stage, or actor on the lot, or voice on the radio, with the majority of the press. Frank was trying hard to take Bing Crosby's advice and just ignore what the press said. George Evans received an award from *Billboard* magazine for the "Most Effective Promotion of a

Single Personality"; no one could argue with that. He had crafted Frank's image and a new year meant new things, new places, and new challenges.

THE EGO HAS LANDED

Despite the hullabaloo about Frank's military service, or lack of it, January 1944 was a case of business as normal. A new radio series, *The Frank Sinatra Show*, presented by Vimms Vitamins, premiered on 5 January, which was broadcast every Wednesday night. Axel Stordahl conducted the orchestra, and the Bobby Tucker Singers, who for this show became known as the Vimms Vocalists, were featured on the show. Frank had to go to LA to work on his new RKO film, *Step Lively*, and so it was broadcast from Hollywood, which is how he came to miss the birth of his second child.

Franklin Wayne Emmanuel Sinatra was born on 10 January at the Margaret Hague Maternity Hospital in Jersey City. With Frank several thousand miles away, it was left to George Evans to use the moment to best effect. The day after the birth, an immaculately made-up Nancy was surrounded by photographers while she lay in bed holding their baby son and a large photo of Frank, so that the press could make the most of this photo opportunity. He was named Franklin after President Roosevelt and Emmanuel after Frank's friend at Columbia Records, Manie Sacks; the name Wayne remains a mystery.

Two days later, according to *Radio Life*, the second *Frank Sinatra Show* in the series was the scene of some West Coast

"COLUMBIA SQUARE" C.B.S. STUDIOS HOLLYWOOD, CAL. 59

"Sinatrantics". The show was broadcast from the CBS Radio Playhouse at 1615 North Vine in Hollywood. Apparently, fans were gathering outside the theatre from as early as 6:45 am. The show went out at 6:00 pm for half an hour, so they had a long wait. "I'd like to sing one of my favourite songs to my little son in New Jersey. So pull up a chair, Nancy, and bring the baby with you. I want him really to hear this," said Frank on air just after Frank Jnr was born. It would be over two months before he went back east to see the family.

FRANK & GINGER
A newspaper advert for Frank's first Vimms-sponsored show, at CBS's Radio Playhouse in Los Angeles.

FRANKLIN MEETS FRANCIS
George Evans engineered a great photo op with Nancy and Frank Jr.

FRANK SINATRA
FOR THE FIRST TIME TONIGHT
IN HIS OWN HALF-HOUR
Presented by VIMMS
THE VOICE all America loves
Frank's guest tonight:
GINGER ROGERS
with BERT WHEELER and the
VIMMS VOCALISTS and ORCHESTRA
SINATRA singing
the songs you like best
WCAU-9:00 P.M.

NAT KING COLE

"Ultimately only Nat King Cole rose to challenge him." DEREK JEWELL FROM *THE POPULAR VOICE* COMPARING COLE TO SINATRA

WHILE FRANK SINATRA WAS WOOING NEW YORK, ANOTHER CROONER WAS CREATING QUITE A BUZZ OF HIS OWN. A NUMBER OF SINGERS HAVE BEEN CALLED THE SEPIA SINATRA; NO ONE DESERVED TO BE MORE THAN NAT COLE.

Nat Cole's family moved from Montgomery, Alabama, where he was born in 1917, to Chicago around 1919. After singing in church – his father was a preacher – he made his recording debut in 1936 with his brother Eddie's band, The Solid Swingers. At 19, he left Chicago and moved to Los Angeles, the beginning and the end of 'Route 66', one of Cole's biggest hits from 1946. He played piano in a revival of Eubie Blake's revue, *Shuffle Along*, and after the show folded Nat formed his own trio with bassist Wesley Prince and guitarist Oscar Moore. As the King Cole Trio they got a residency at the Swanee Inn on North La Brea Avenue, just south of Hollywood.

He recorded as King Cole's Swingsters in 1939 and then in July, 1942, with saxophonist Lester Young and bass player Red Callender. Among these sublime sides were 'I Can't Get Started', 'Tea For Two', and 'Body and Soul'. The impeccable performances and especially Cole's piano playing show his jazz credentials.

In November 1942, the King Cole Trio recorded 'That Ain't Right' went to No1 on the R&B charts. The following year, 'All For You' repeated the success and also crossed over to the *Billboard* chart. National recognition came in early 1944 with 'Straighten Up and Fly Right', and from then on Cole was rarely off the *Billboard* bestseller's list. Cole had arrived, and via a very different route from Frank Sinatra.

Cole's enunciation was just as clear as Frank's, but his playing as part of a trio was very different from the big band that was Frank's comfort zone. While Cole worked with big studio orchestras from around 1946, his earlier work owed more to juke joints than ballrooms and concert halls.

Cole's jazz leanings, blues undertones, and silken voice appealed to everyone. His influence spread to piano players like Errol Garner, Bill Evans, Charles Brown, and Ray Charles. He had signed for Capitol Records in 1943 and for the next two decades Cole was one of the biggest things on the R&B charts, and no slouch on the mainstream *Billboard* charts, as his records increasingly crossed over to the white audience. Interestingly, one of his best-known songs, 'Unforgettable' (recorded in 1951), was not one of his biggest single releases. He was one of the first black performers to get his own radio series (1948). In the 1950s and 1960s Cole, like Frank, recorded with both Nelson Riddle's and Gordon Jenkins's orchestras.

Cole, a heavy smoker, developed lung cancer, which cut short his career in 1964. He died the next year, aged 47. In March 2000, with Ray Charles as his presenter, Nat King Cole was inducted into the Rock and Roll Hall of Fame.

BIGGEST HITS
'(I Love You) For Sentimental Reasons' (No 1, 1946)
'Nature Boy' (No 1, 1948)
'Mona Lisa' (No 1, 1950)
'Too Young' (No 1, 1951)
'A Blossom Fell' (No 2, 1955)
'Ramblin' Rose' (No 2, 1962)

The Frank Sinatra Show was a typical 1940s radio variety programme. It featured compère Jerry Lester, some comedy, and of course Frank singing, and not just his hits but also other big songs of the moment. A measure of Frank's increasing stature were the guests that the show attracted. In the five months (until the regular summer break) in which it was on the air, WC Fields, Ida Lupino, Alan Ladd, Judy Garland, Lana Turner, and Gene Kelly were among the stars who "dropped by".

Shortly after Frank Jr's birth, Frank sang at a benefit for the Jewish Home for the Aged at a hotel in Los Angeles. It was a typical showbiz affair supported by the great and the good of the movie and entertainment industry, many of whom were hoping for continued success to avoid ending up there themselves.

One of the greats who bought a ticket was movie mogul Louis B Mayer, the last "M" in MGM. The story goes that Frank sang 'Ol' Man River', and reduced Louis to tears. The song came from the 1927 musical *Showboat*, and was written by Oscar Hammerstein II and Jerome Kern for Paul Robeson to sing in the original Broadway production. Back then no one, not even Hammerstein (who was mighty liberal for the time), saw anything wrong with having the son of a former slave sing the words, "darkies all work on the Mississippi." Frank had introduced the song into his repertoire in 1943 and he sang it at the Hollywood Bowl five months before his performance in front of Mayer. According to daughter Nancy, Frank refused to sing "darkies", substituting "Here we" instead, which was one reason why Louis was so moved. There is no question that Frank did take out the offending word when he came to record it, although he had sung "darkies" at the Hollywood Bowl. Whatever the truth about Mayer's reaction to Frank's performance of the song, he was reported to have lent over to an aide and said "I want that boy." And in Hollywood, what Louis wanted, Louis got.

CLUBBING

Having "gone Hollywood", Frank found it suited him. He could do just about what he pleased without interference from his family. While he had dined out regularly in New York at the Stork Club and spent nights well into the wee small hours at the Copacabana Club, he was still a married man. Although Frank probably got away with more than most married men, he still had a wife and children at home. George Evans was often tested to the limit in keeping Frank's "family man" image untarnished by the press. Even though Nancy may have continued to adopt the reverse of the George Raft principle, it would not have looked good if Frank had been caught out on the town with some girl on his arm in New York soon after his son's birth. Los Angeles allowed him far greater scope. Dining out, often as part of a large group, allowed Frank to have fun and maintain a veneer of respectability. After all, he had to be seen around town – it was all part of the image.

Filming *Step Lively* began at the end of January, and soon after Frank signed a five-year contract with MGM, negotiated by MCA, and worth $1.5 million. The power-broking business was working to Frank's advantage. The contract gave George Evans the opportunity for some fun with the media. He announced that Frank was now the highest-paid entertainer in the world! Given the fact that the contract was over five years and the salaries that the top stars earned in Hollywood, it was just the kind of thing that Evans relished. Twenty years later, Frank told writer Robin Douglas-Home that his earnings were not quite as spectacular as Evans and others had made out. "The first year on my own I made $650,000, the second $840,000, the third $1,400,000." That first year was 1943.

MEDIA WEB

In the middle of all this activity, the media were as usual weaving their web. With the war effort increasing and many more soldiers, sailors, and airmen being sent to the front line, it was inevitable that Frank's classification of 4-F rankled with the ordinary servicemen, some of whom were probably being, albeit inadvertently, fed stories by their loved ones at home. They were also reading about the type of life Frank led, a life that was as far away from their own as was possible. It led to newspaper stories with headlines such as "Sinatra I-A with US girls, rated 4-F by Army Doctors." As the writer William Manchester later noted, "I think Frank Sinatra was the most hated man of World War II." I think to be fair he should have added "– by men".

In fact, the problem of Frank's lack of military service just got steadily worse. The *Stars and Stripes* continued to talk of cowardice on Frank's part, a masthead to which other newspapers were more than happy to nail their colours. It must have made Frank angry in the extreme. No doubt he and George Evans debated what was best for Frank's image. Should he go overseas to entertain the troops or stay at home and do his bit through war bond rallies? It was decided that Frank was better off at home, given the likelihood of hostilities breaking out between the troops and Frank. When certain sections of the media started to suggest that Frank was actually a "commie", it all began to get even more ridiculous. But it was a taunt that tainted Frank for many years.

At the same time as all this was going on, Frank made his first appearance on *Command Performance*. The show was produced by the War Department for transmission by shortwave to the troops overseas; "each and every week until it's over, over there". Frank,

like everyone else, did the show for free. "A mighty fine new customer of ours, a swell guy," is how Dinah Shore introduced Frank on his debut on *Command Performance*'s second-anniversary broadcast. Frank sang 'Speak Low' and duetted with Bing in a good-hearted comedy routine, "This is the guy I dreamed about, this is the guy the gals used to rave about," sang Frank. They finished up with 'People Will Say We're in Love'.

In early March, people in Britain were beginning to take a little more notice of Frank. In the *Melody Maker* under a headline "Analysing the *Downbeat* Poll", there was some incredulity at Frank's achievements. "That readers of the erudite *Downbeat* should have chosen Frank Sinatra as their favourite male vocalist may possibly surprise British readers, and that they should have chosen him by 4,099 votes to Bing Crosby's 3,942 may surprise them still more. Anyway, there it is…"

Back in Hollywood, Frank was probably totally oblivious to the coverage he was getting in Britain;

MAYER FROM MINSK
Louis B Mayer, born in Minsk in Belarus, epitomized the American Dream. Originally a scrap merchant, he became a cinema manager, then went into film distribution. He formed a production company, Metro-Goldwyn-Mayer, with Sam Goldwyn in 1924 and became one of Hollywood's most influential movie moguls. By 1944, when he signed Sinatra, the MGM studios in Culver City, LA (bottom), was one of the landmarks of Hollywood, with a restaurant to cater for the stars (below left).

the world was a very much bigger place then. He was also busy working on another movie, albeit little more than a cameo for the Treasury Department. He appeared in *The Road to Victory* singing his old friend Joe Bushkin's 'Hot Time in the Town of Berlin'. Frank eased into the great Stordahl arrangement as the announcer said, "No programme would be complete in 1944 without The Voice… Frank Sinatra." This wonderful period piece romps along in a jaunty celebration of war; lyrics such as "They're goin' to take a hike through Hitler's Reich" make it hard not to laugh.

Two days after filming his appearance, he was back on the radio with Gloria DeHaven, his co-star from *Step Lively*, in the Screen Guild Theatre production of *The Gay Divorcee*. These radio shows were adaptations of movies and during their life span, which lasted from 1939 to 1951, featured just about every star in Hollywood. The shows were charity affairs with the actors working for nothing, donating what would have been their fees, paid by the shows' sponsor (Lady Esther cosmetics), to the Motion Picture Relief Fund. Frank performed his hit

song 'Night and Day', along with 'I'll Follow My Secret Heart', and 'The Continental'. Frank made two more appearances on the show during the 1940s.

With the continuing success of Frank's radio appearances and filming going well, life, even with the antagonism of the press, was pretty good. Hollywood was one long round of parties and nights out with beautiful people. At one party he met Peter Lawford, another actor contracted to MGM, but that was just about the only way in which the two men were similar; that and the fact that they were the two youngest people at the party. According to Peter, "He was a tough little Italian son of a bitch and for some reason that persona appealed to me. We made a strange combination, with me being the ever so ever so son of a British knight of the realm and him with his brash, cocky, and often arrogant attitude and friends in the Mafia. But we hit it off." Given that this was said many years later, the idea of Frank having Mafia contacts at that point might be taken with a pinch of salt. No doubt Frank's attitude may have hinted at "friends in low places", but it was probably hindsight that made Lawford talk that way.

FROM EAST TO WEST

George Evans was increasingly aware that Frank's lifestyle in Hollywood could, and probably would, land him in deep, as well as hot, water. Living in the ego capital of the world is never easy, especially when you have an inflated self-image. Frank was a prime candidate for problems. Evans knew he had to get some stability back into Frank's life, and the only way to do this was to try to ground his wayward client. He started working on Frank, telling him that he needed his family to be in California. George Evans also had Nancy giving him grief back in New York. Frank working on *Step Lively* and broadcasting from the West Coast meant that she did not see him for months on end, so that now she did not even have the benefit of an errant husband who came home at least sometimes.

When Frank did go back for his son's christening, things finally came to a head. It wasn't that Nancy was bursting with enthusiasm for a move to California (she at least had a support network around her in New Jersey), but she was a pragmatist and she agreed to the move, so it was left to Frank to find them a home. Frank wanted to

SAMMY CAHN & JULE STYNE

"Sammy's words fit my mouth better than anybody else." FRANK

ANY PERFORMER WHO DOES NOT WRITE HIS OR HER OWN MATERIAL HAS TO RELY ON OTHERS. APART FROM A HANDFUL OF SONGS HE CO-WROTE, FRANK HAD TO DO JUST THAT THROUGHOUT HIS CAREER. WHEN HE WAS A MEMBER OF THE DORSEY BAND, IT WAS HIS BOSS WHO CHOSE MOST OF THE MATERIAL. WHEN HE WENT SOLO, SAMMY AND JULE SOON BECOME TWO OF FRANK'S MOST FAVOURED WRITERS.

Once Frank went solo and started to "make it", publishers were eager to get their material performed, recorded, and released by "The Voice". Frank's relationship with Hank Sanicola, who was a song plugger, must have helped. He had access to material and presumably a good pair of ears, too.

Frank first met Sammy Cahn when he was working with Tommy Dorsey. It was through Sammy that Frank met Jule Styne and before long they became a very effective partnership. The first song of Sammy's that Frank performed was one he wrote with his writing partner at the time, Saul Chaplin, called 'I Could Make You Care', and he cut it with Tommy Dorsey in 1940. Frank would go on to record over 120 of Sammy's songs.

EARLY DAYS
Sammy Cahn was just a couple of years older than Frank and had been born in New York. His was the classic rags-to-riches story of a poor Jewish boy brought up in a tenement on New York's East Side. The family were immigrants from Galicia in northern Spain. After school, Sammy worked as a meat packer and a cinema usher and he began writing songs when he was about 16. Sammy had learned to play the violin as a child, but soon he met pianist Saul Chaplin and Sammy's skills as a lyricist came to the fore.

Their first major success was a song commissioned by the Jimmie Lunceford Band. Called 'Rhythm is Our Business', it became a big hit and Cahn and Chaplin were on their way, soon writing for Ella Fitzgerald and Andy Kirk and His Clouds of Joy, a band that featured the brilliant Mary Lou Williams on piano. The pair moved to Hollywood, and, in the early 1940s, Sammy began writing with Jule Styne. It wasn't long before they were being described as "Frank Sinatra's personal songwriters". "One of the brightest and most melodic of the new song-writing teams is Sammy Cahn and Jule Styne," said Frank on his radio show. As Tita Cahn, Sammy's widow once said, "Sammy saw himself as Frank, without the voice, without the looks."

Jule Styne was ten years older than Frank and was born in London. His family emigrated to the US in 1913, and by the age of nine Jule, a child prodigy, was playing piano with the Chicago Symphony Orchestra. By his late teens he had switched his allegiance and was leading his own dance band. Moving first to New York and then

to Hollywood, he got by as a vocal coach as well as doing some arranging. Daryl Zanuck at 20th Century Fox advised him to take up songwriting and Jule got a job with Republic Pictures in 1940 and almost immediately began working with Frank Loesser. Two hits soon followed: 'Since You' and 'I Don't Want to Walk Without You Baby'. Jule began working with Sammy after Loesser joined the Army.

GREAT DAYS
Sammy and Jule's first compositions especially for Frank were for his movie *Step Lively*, and the first song of theirs he recorded was 'As Long as There's Magic' on 31 January, 1944. It was the first of more than 30 songs by the partnership that Frank recorded over the next four decades. The majority of the songs were cut during the 1940s and, given Frank's work in the movies, it is none too surprising that they were often featured in films.

In the summer of 1946, Frank cut three classic Styne and Cahn compositions. Unusually, 'The Things We Did Last Summer' was not from a movie and Frank took it into the *Billboard* Top 10 later that year. Six days later, he recorded 'Guess I'll Hang My Tears Out to Dry', which Sammy and Jule had written for the 1944 stage show *Glad To See You*. Frank's recording was released in 1949 but it failed to chart. It achieved its true status when Frank recorded it again in 1958 with a new arrangement by Nelson Riddle. The third of these songs was 'Time After Time'

from Frank's movie *It Happened in Brooklyn*. It was a sensitive reading of a song that also got the Riddle treatment in 1957. Both are excellent, but the later recording just shades it. One lovely song that many have overlooked is 'You're My Girl', which Frank cut in 1947. It was written for the Broadway show *High Button Shoes*.

Recognition for Sammy and Jule's writing came when they won an Oscar for 'Three Coins in the Fountain', which Frank cut in 1954. Frank also recorded two Christmas songs that have over the years become definitive of the genre: 'Let It Snow, Let It Snow, Let It Snow' (1950), although he had sung it on the radio as early as 1945, and 'Christmas Waltz' (1954).

A big hit for Harry James in 1942, 'I've Heard That Song Before' was recorded by Frank in 1961 and sums up the essence of Sammy Cahn and Jule Styne's songwriting: strong yet easy melodies topped off with crafted lyrics:

"It seems to me I've heard that song before
It's from an old familiar score
I know it well that melody."

THE END
Sammy and Jule's partnership came to an end in the early 1950s, not for any reason other than that Jule wanted to concentrate his efforts in the theatre and so stayed in New York. Not that it stopped them writing together for a while, but the geographical distance between them slowed their collaborative efforts. Sammy was more at home in Hollywood so he stayed on the West Coast. Jule's success in the theatre included writing the musical *Funny Girl*, which launched Barbra Streisand's career in the early 1960s. Sammy began working with Jimmy Van Heusen and together they wrote a prodigious number of songs for Frank Sinatra. "I stayed in Hollywood. Frank put me and Jimmy together. Why, I don't know. Maybe he thought I'd be good for Jimmy's lacy melodies. A couple of days later, the phone rang. 'Sam, Frank.' 'Frank, Sam.' 'I want you to write a song with Van Heusen called 'The Tender Trap'.' Then Van Heusen called, and we started to write."

PRACTICE TIME
Frank, Richard Whorf (director), Jule Styne (playing piano), and Sammy Cahn rehearse songs for 'It Happened in Brooklyn'.

1942–1946

THE HOUSE IN TOLUCA LAKE

"Once John the courteous colored butler has let me in you find yourself standing in a sun soaked flagged patio with a fountain in the middle of it." Eleanor Harris, contemporary journalist, on visiting the Sinatra residence.

be near the studios. He also wanted privacy, so he settled on a home in the San Fernando Valley. 10051 Walley Spring Lane, a pink stucco house in Toluca Lake, was not far from where both Bing Crosby and Bob Hope had homes. The Mediterranean-style house had once been home to the silent-screen actress Mary Astor.

A few days before the Allies liberated Rome, the Sinatras moved out to California, staying first at Castle Argyle in Hollywood while their new home was made ready. It was to be the beginning of a whole new era for the family. Whereas the house in Hasbrouck Heights had been accessible to just about every bobby-soxer who had a mind to drop by and scrawl something on the garage, or even, as did happen once, break in and steal some fan mail and other family items, the new home was secure. It was one that befitted a star of Sinatra's stature and it had the benefit of a wall all around it to keep out the unwanted.

Almost as soon as the family arrived in Los Angeles, Frank started work on his first MGM movie, *Anchors Aweigh*. Frank was permitted to work at MGM's Culver City studio because of the clause in his RKO contract that allowed him to be "loaned out" to other studios. (RKO borrowed some MGM contract players in return.) The film was a musical comedy co-starring Gene Kelly. With George Evans based in New York, it meant that he was not always around to take care of things. The solution was to hire a guy named Jack Keller to look after Frank out on the West Coast. Jack was quickly put to work when Frank got upset with some aspects of filming and told a reporter "Most pictures stink, and the people in them too." This was hardly guaranteed to ingratiate Frank with Louis B, MGM, Gene Kelly, or Kathryn Grayson and the others working on *Anchors Aweigh*. Jack wrote a suitably apologetic letter, which he got Frank to sign, and then set about getting it published to avoid any backlash.

The atmosphere during shooting was not helped by Frank's insistence that Sammy Cahn work with Jule Styne on the music for the film. Unfortunately, Joe Pasternak, who was producing this first outing for Frank and MGM, objected to Sammy, and threatened to halt filming. "They even came to me to persuade him (Frank) not to use me. I agreed. I said I'm sure we can work together some other time, let's give it a miss", said Sammy. "Be there Monday", was Frank's categoric reply.

Sammy was, and the movie got made. Frank got his way in an early example of his ego and his will combining to get what he wanted.

One person with whom Frank got along really well was Gene Kelly. Later Frank would tell people that Gene "was one of the reasons I became a star". Gene coached Frank on the dance routines, which were incredibly tiring. He worked on Frank, making each routine succeed by allowing for Frank's limited abilities. Frank lost a lot of weight off a frame that was already sparsely covered. Gene joked that Frank "set dancing back twenty years".

Because of his filming schedule, Frank had to cancel a booking at the Riobamba in July, but his radio work continued unabated. Just over a week after filming on *Anchors Aweigh* commenced, Frank appeared again at the Hollywood Bowl. It was the Academy Night, and he performed 'And Then You Kissed Me', a Cahn and Styne song from *Step Lively*, which premiered three days later.

FRANK ON THE AIRLANES

With *Anchors Aweigh* in the can, Frank's main activity continued to be his own radio shows, as well as guest appearances on other programmes. Among the latter was *Mail Call*, a programme for US servicemen, which was recorded live and shipped overseas. On one show, Frank appeared with one of his early heroes, Rudy Vallee. Frank and Gloria DeHaven sang 'Come out, Come out, Wherever You Are' from *Step Lively*, and Frank alone did 'Begin the Beguine'. On 16 August, a new series that went under the name *Frank Sinatra in Person* began its run. Vimms Vitamins must have been pleased with their previous deal, as they were again the sponsor. On that first show, Frank's last number, before the show's closing theme ('Put Your Dreams Away (For Another Day)'), was written by Cole Porter for the 1936 film *Born to Dance*. It was 'I've Got You Under My Skin', considered by most to be Frank at his up-tempo best when he finally recorded it with Nelson Riddle almost 12 years later.

A month after the first airing of *Frank Sinatra in Person*, Frank was starring in *Your Hit Parade* where the studio orchestra included a young trombone player called Nelson Riddle. It was the first time they worked together, and while Frank was probably oblivious to Nelson's presence, he was certainly unaware of how inexorably entwined their careers would become.

Frank finished completely with *Anchors Aweigh* on Tuesday 5 September when he recorded 'I Fall in Love Too Easily' for the film's soundtrack. A few weeks later, he went to New York, and while he was there he did some of his radio shows from CBS in New York. He also went to Toots Shor's restaurant, across from Madison Square Garden. Toots and Frank had been friends for a while, and Frank, when he was in the city, was often to be found at the place, which was more like a saloon than a restaurant. People would stop there on their way out to eat somewhere else – it was that kind of place. Although women were allowed in, they were not encouraged; it was very much men only. In fact, if anyone turned up with their wife or girlfriend once too often, they were generally put on the "not wanted" list.

TEA WITH TOOTS AND THE PREZ

Shor told Frank that he had been invited for tea at the White House. Frank was a big admirer of President Roosevelt, despite the Democrats' seeming antipathy towards the Italian-American community. President Roosevelt had earlier asked FBI Director J Edgar Hoover to compile a list of anyone who was a threat to national security. By June, 1942, 1,521 Italian aliens had been arrested by the FBI. Frank's mother Dolly saw this as a slight and had berated Frank when he came out in support of Roosevelt in 1941.

The Democratic National Committee Chairman, Robert E Hannegan, was in Toots Shor's bar when he suggested that they went to Washington to meet the President. The next day, 28 September, 1944, Toots, Frank, and comedian Rags Ragland flew from La Guardia airport to Washington DC. On meeting Frank, the President is said to have looked him over and turned to his secretary, Marvin McIntyre, and said, "Imagine this guy making them swoon. He would never have made them swoon in our day, right?" If nothing else, it proves that times never change. Every older generation reacts negatively towards the singing and acting heroes of a younger generation. It's one of life's rules.

After tea with the President, Frank and his friends had their picture taken leaving the White House. The whole thing was reported very positively from Frank's standpoint, and it probably did no harm to the President's position, although inevitably some newspapers took the opposite view. The *Baltimore Sun* called it "a cheap little publicity stunt". Frank contributed $7,500 to Democratic Party funds, which may have been the first such contribution he had ever made, and certainly the first of any substance. It was his first real brush with serious power, and it proved to be a seductive process. Just as Dolly had done in the 1920s when she was a local organizer for the Democratic Party, Frank found he rather liked it, so much so that the rest of his life would be peppered with such incidents, many on a far grander scale. But who's to say who was the seduced and who was the seducer on some of those later incidents?

Just over a month later, Roosevelt and his running mate Harry S Truman won the election by a landslide. Opponent Thomas Dewey could not even hold his home state of New York. As Frank was leaving the White House he had been asked if he wanted President Roosevelt to win the upcoming election, "You might say I'm in favour of it", he replied. With Roosevelt's victory, he proudly wore a big badge saying "I told you so".

STEP LIVELY

THIS MOVIE'S MAIN MOMENT of notoriety is Frank's first on-screen kiss. Gloria DeHaven is on the receiving end of the lips. RKO had confused Frank with Shirley Temple, resolutely decreeing that he was not to undertake such a lewd act in his first film. Maybe they had been clever because *Look*, the family magazine, devoted a whole four pages to the subject of "the kiss".

The black-and-white movie, directed by Tim Whelan, is a remake of an earlier RKO production called *Room Service*, starring the Marx brothers. The original, released in 1938, did badly, losing RKO over $300,000 (a small fortune at the time). RKO were obviously seeking to recoup some of their losses, which were compounded by the fact that they had paid $255,000 for the film rights in the first place.

Step Lively was originally to be called *Manhattan Serenade* (a much better title for both a movie and a song). A good cast that included George Murphy, Gloria DeHaven, Adolphe Menjou, and Eugene Pallette surrounded Frank.

After the less than inspiring music for *Higher and Higher*, Frank made sure things were better on this movie by using Sammy Cahn and Jule Styne. Their numbers, while not blockbuster material, were certainly a vast improvement. The songs include 'As Long as There's Music', 'Come out, Come out, Wherever You Are', 'Some Other Time' with Gloria DeHaven, and 'Where Does Love Begin?'. All four songs were recorded with the RKO Orchestra, which was conducted by Constantin Bakaleinikoff, whose brother had the baton at the Hollywood Bowl.

The plot is somewhat dire, even by the standards of wartime Hollywood. Sinatra is cast as Glen, a country bumpkin who wants to become a playwright. He ends up in New York, and the main focus of the story revolves around a dud cheque and Sinatra's attempt, along with a cast of actors, to put on a play. The fact that bumpkin Glen has, after all, got a wonderful singing voice that saves the show is the pay off, plus the fact that he falls in love with Christine (Miss DeHaven).

> **❝**Sinatra's name on the marquee is sufficient to guarantee lipsticky posters on the outside, moaning galleryites within.**❞**
>
> *TIME* MAGAZINE

THE COMB
Gloria DeHaven is on Frank's left. He nicknamed her "The Comb" because she never stopped attending to her hair.

When Frank got back to New York from Washington, he stayed around for the next two weeks because he was due to open at the Paramount on 12 October for another extended run. The theatre even billed him as the 'Theatre's Greatest Discovery'. While Frank's appearances at the Paramount had always been enthusiastically received since going solo, the October 1944 engagement was the big one. It was his first appearance in over a year at the venue favoured by the bobby-soxers. Some must have thought that Frank had deserted them in favour of the upscale nightclub crowd, and, more to the point, they knew that he had left them to live in Los Angeles.

HEADLINING AT THE PARAMOUNT

On 11 October, Times Square was a seething mass of people, all anxious to get into the Paramount to see the first show of the morning. It was estimated that 10,000 were there (some said 25,000, others 30,000, but both sound like an exaggeration). The first 3,600 to get in clearly had an advantage, because until they left no one else was going to get in. As it happened, most chose to stay put. According to the *New Republic* on 6 November, 1944, "only 250 came out when the second show started". To control the mob outside the theatre there was a large number of police (estimates in this case varied from 150 to 700), including reservists, detectives, traffic cops, and a dozen mounted men. The *New York Times* printed a letter from Anne Helen Van Messel on 16 October, 1944, saying, "Is there no way to make those kids come to their senses? The time they are waiting outside the Paramount Theatre could be used for other purposes for instance, to help us win this war."

It was the standard 2-for-1 show, featuring the movie *Our Hearts Were Young and Gay*; Eileen Barton, the regular singer on *Your Hit Parade*; Pops and Louie, two dancers; impressionist Ollie O'Toole; Raymond Paige and his Orchestra; and Frank. Inside the Paramount, the mostly female audience had come prepared for a day out. Many had sandwiches and fruit to eat and most were pent up from not seeing Frankie for so long. You could feel their passion for the return of their conquering hero. One parent even tried to buy a place in line for their daughter while other girls used subterfuge to get closer to the front of the line. A mother standing near the front of the line

with her daughter said she had to be there as the teenager had threatened to kill herself if she was kept at home. Although over 80 per cent of the audience were female and around three-quarters of them were aged 12 to 16 there were guys there to see Frankie, too.

One young man took apparent umbrage at Frank and threw several raw eggs during his closing number, 'I Don't Know Why I Love You Like I Do'. The stocky, blue-suited Alexander J Dorogokuputz was lucky to escape relatively unscathed when he was set upon by screaming and scratching "Sinatranshis". A dozen uniformed officers saved him and, after Frank declined to press charges, they escorted the young man to the safety of the subway and a short trip back to his home in the Bronx. He subsequently admitted that he had been paid $10 by a reporter to throw the eggs. The following day, encouraged by these egg-throwing antics, a group of sailors threw tomatoes at the huge billboard that was atop the Paramount's entrance. The portrait of Frank got covered in red blotches, making it look as though he had a dose of some communicable disease.

These scenes in the autumn of 1944 were the zenith of Sinatramania; they would never be repeated. Of course, this is not to say that Frank's popularity did not increase, but it subtly shifted away from the teenagers to a wider audience. Frank himself summed it all up in a way that suggests he understood as well as anyone his own dynamic: "There was great loneliness. I was the boy in every corner drugstore, the boy who'd gone off, drafted to the war." This pivotal moment in Frank's career would account for his enduring legend to many women (and not a few men). They saw Frank as the embodiment of their youthful conflicts, and not just the tensions on the world stage. It was the first skirmish between the "pop generation" and the more staid among the population who had been brought up in the first half of the 20th century. It was no wonder that so many people found it shocking: nothing quite like it had ever happened on such a scale before. While men such as Valentino, in particular, and Bing aroused a certain level of youthful ardour, it was all somehow a little more reserved than the madness of Sinatramania. "Just what does Frank Sinatra have that causes such demonstrations? The answer is that the cause lies not in what Frankie has, but in what his admirers have, which is a mild case of mass hysteria," was how Robert Sullivan put it, writing in the *New York Sunday News* on 5 November, 1944.

FRANKIE GOES INTO BUSINESS

While Frank was at the Paramount, he spent some time establishing a new business venture with Hank Sanicola and Ben Barton. They had formed the Barton Music Corporation after Ben Barton had got to know Frank when he brought him 'Close To You' back in early 1943.

Hank was quoted as saying "Frank has long been desirous of becoming a business executive." Ben Barton was the father of the singer Eileen Barton.

Almost as soon as the run at the Paramount ended, Frank was in the recording studio. The musicians' strike ended on 11 November and, three days later, Axel Stordahl, along with the full CBS studio orchestra and the Bobby Tucker Singers, was at the Leiderkrantz Hall. With an eye to the holiday season, they cut 'White Christmas', along with three other songs, which would all be released over the next eight months.

One of the songs was Sammy Cahn and Jule Styne's 'Saturday Night (Is the Loneliest Night of the Week)'. Six days earlier, Frank had made a visit home to LA to record the song with Harry James and his Orchestra for the soundtrack of a short film, *All Star Bond Rally*, a US Treasury film to promote the sale of war bonds and also starred Bing Crosby, Harpo Marx, and Betty Grable; Harry and Betty were married by this time. In the movie, Harry uses the same arrangement that Axel put together for Frank's CBS session. Frank is introduced in the movie as "Mr Swoon himself, the ol' collapso singer himself..."

After two more sessions at CBS's New York City studio, Frank returned home to California for Christmas. Besides more radio, there was one pre-Christmas recording session in Hollywood. After the enforced veto from working with a studio orchestra, Frank, like every other singer, was making up for lost time. He had cut 17 tracks in just over a month.

1942–1946

LOUIS JORDAN

"A great musician, and way ahead of his time"

BB KING, 1999

IN 1944 THERE WAS A NEWCOMER TO THE WHITE-DOMINATED *BILLBOARD* CHARTS – A MAN WHO HAD WORKED WITH ELLA FITZGERALD IN THE 1930S, WHO WOULD BECOME KNOWN AS THE KING OF THE JUKEBOXES. HIS NAME WAS LOUIS JORDAN.

JORDAN WAS BORN in 1908 and followed his father into the famed Rabbit Foot Minstrels, playing saxophone. He formed his Tympany Five (although there were usually eight or nine members in the band) in 1939. Jordan's music was christened "Jump Blues" – a fusion of both jazz and blues. Louis scored his first R&B hit in October 1942 on the Harlem Hit Parade. His big break came in the late summer of 1944 with 'GI Jive'. His popularity meant that his bookings increased. *Downbeat* magazine reported in August 1944, "Due to the band's popularity with both white and colored audiences, promoters in larger cities are booking the Jordan quintet for two evenings: one to play a white date and the other a colored dance."

For the rest of the decade, he was huge on the R&B charts and had a strong showing on the *Billboard* chart. Jordan took on board the sounds of the big bands and boogie woogie, as well as Louis Armstrong's Hot Fives and Hot Sevens. Songs such as 'Caledonia', 'Choo Choo Ch'Boogie', 'Ain't Nobody Here but Us Chickens', and 'Stone Cold Dead in the Market Place' (with Ella Fitzgerald) were big hits with both black and white audiences.

Louis Jordan could justifiably be said to have been at the birth of rock 'n' roll; later, Chuck Berry would "borrow" licks and lyrics from Louis' work. His career tailed off during the 1950s, and although he continued to perform right up until the 1970s, it was a time when people were not so interested in their musical roots. He died of a heart attack in 1975 and was inducted into the Rock & Roll Hall of Fame in 1987, a fitting, if belated, tribute to one of the greats of both black and white music.

BEST-KNOWN RECORDINGS
'GI Jive' (No 1, 1944)
'Choo Choo Ch'Boogie' (No 1, 1946)
'Ain't Nobody Here But Us Chickens' (No 1, 1946)
'Saturday Night Fish Fry' (No 1, 1949)

At the session in Hollywood on 19 December, a trumpet player named Billy May was in the orchestra; it was the first time he had worked with Frank. A few days later, Frank sang 'Don't Fence Me In' on *Your Hit Parade*. "Axel asked me to help out on some of the arranging – pressure of work, I guess – Cole Porter's 'Don't Fence Me In' was the first one I worked on," said Billy May. It would be over a decade before Frank and Billy would create one of the seminal relationships of Frank's career.

The recordings at CBS studios marked a subtle shift in Frank's recorded output. Now that he was no longer a regular member of a touring big band, the orchestras were made up of some of the best players around, but it was a shifting group of players, especially because recording switched between the East Coast and the West. For this session Axel Stordahl had assembled a 35-piece orchestra. There were 3 trumpets, 3 trombones, a French horn, 5 sax and woodwind players, 12 violins, 3 violas, 3 violincellos, 1 harpist, a pianist, guitarist, bass player, and drummer… bigger even than a big band. At the

FULL ORCHESTRA SESSION
Frank at Columbia's Liederkrantz Hall Studio in New York City, a former German Beer Hall. It was a great facility measuring 100 ft long, 60 ft wide and 30 ft high. This shot was taken on 14 November 1944 when Frank cut four songs – including 'White Christmas'.

time, Frank was playing live shows with smaller backing bands, a fact that was hardly noticed by his fans. However, there was no question that almost imperceptibly, albeit inevitably, the importance of recordings was taking over from live performances. The spread of the jukebox and the availability of an increasing number of phonographs was what the Musicians' Strike had hoped to address. In reality, however, the strike, along with the war, had helped to bring about the demise of the big band. The singer was becoming the star; the bandleader would never again be pre-eminent.

In the *Billboard* Top 10 artists back in 1941, every place was taken up by a bandleader. By the following year it had dropped to eight; by 1943, just five were bandleaders and, now, in 1944, it was just three. While they would recover slightly in 1945, when a post-strike flurry of big band recording brought renewed sales, they still managed to fill only five of the top places. And from then on it just got worse. Frank, Dick, Perry, Dinah, Ella, and Bing were all at the big band wake.

1944 ON THE JUKEBOX

FRANK ON THE US CHARTS

'I COULDN'T SLEEP A WINK LAST NIGHT'
Jimmy McHugh & Harold Adamson
12 February, No 4, 14 weeks

'A LOVELY WAY TO SPEND AN EVENING'
Jimmy McHugh & Harold Adamson
18 March, No 15, 3 weeks

'ON A LITTLE STREET IN SINGAPORE'
Peter DeRose & Billy Hill
13 May, No 20, 1 week

'EVERY DAY OF MY LIFE'
Harry James, Morty Beck & Billy Hays
27 May, No 17, 2 weeks

'I'LL BE SEEING YOU'
Sammy Fain & Irving Kahal
27 May, No 4, 17 weeks

'NIGHT AND DAY'
Cole Porter
2 September, No 15, 3 weeks

'IT'S FUNNY TO EVERYONE BUT ME'
Jack Lawrence
28 October, No 21, 1 week

'WHITE CHRISTMAS'
Irving Berlin
30 December, No 7, 2 weeks

This was not such a good year on the *Billboard* charts for Frank. His eight hit records spent just 42 weeks on the chart, precisely half the number achieved in 1943. Of these, three were recordings with Harry James from 1939, one with Tommy Dorsey, and another was a re-release of his first solo hit, 'Night and Day'. Given the prolonged musicians' strike, it is easy to explain his lack of hits. Most of Frank's recording activity during the year was for films or V-Discs. Twenty-two sessions took place during the year and the ones done after November at the end of the musicians' strike yielded some very impressive releases in early 1945.

Frank's lack of releases and related lack of chart success was not shared by other performers... someone has to have the hits! It was another outstanding year for Bing Crosby, who dominated the charts as no one had done since Glenn Miller in 1940. Bing Crosby's stellar year was a result of the phenomenal success of a Jimmy Van Heusen and Johnny Burke song, 'Swinging on a Star', which held the top spot for nine weeks. Add to this two No 1 records with the Andrews Sisters, 'Don't Fence Me In' and 'Hot Time in the Town of Berlin', along with three more solo Bing Crosby No 1 records, and it is easy to see why he reigned supreme in 1944 when it came to record sales.

While the release of the Harry James sides, recorded four years earlier, and the old Tommy Dorsey recording must have frustrated Frank, at least this time around his name was on the label as the star. Not that Frank was eclipsing his old boss in 1944. Harry was No 4 on the year's best performers' table. His version of 'I'll Get By (As Long as I Have You)' with Dick Haymes on vocals had spent six weeks at the top of the bestseller's list. It had also helped Dick to make No 6 on the same table, three places above Frank. Six

other recordings had charted for the Harry James Orchestra. Columbia had been shrewd in releasing the Frank and Harry James's sides as it benefited both performers. It meant that Harry James had only just failed to be the most successful bandleader on the *Billboard* charts — an honour that belonged to Jimmy Dorsey.

There was also a relatively new name on the *Billboard* charts, that of Ella Fitzgerald. While Miss Fitzgerald was no newcomer herself to recording (she had scored in 1941 with 'Five O'clock Whistle'), this was her first sustained run on the bestseller lists. Her two No 1 recordings, 'Into Each Life Some Rain Must Fall' and 'I'm Making Believe', with the Ink Spots, had helped both of them become hugely popular in 1944. 'Into Each Life...' was No 1 on the jukebox chart; 'I'm Making Believe' was No 1 on the bestseller list, as well as topping the Harlem Hit Parade. The latter song came from the movie *Sweet and Lowdown*, starring Benny Goodman.

THE R&B CHART

From October 1942 until February 1945, the US Black Music chart was called the Harlem Hit Parade. From 1945 until June 1949, there was a chart known as the Juke Box Race Records, and from May 1948 there was a concurrent chart known as the Best Sellers Race Records Chart. From June 1949 these two charts continued to run in tandem, but instead of being called race records they were known as rhythm 'n' blues records... and the R&B chart was born.

THE ANDREWS SISTERS
The trio became known as "America's Wartime Sweethearts".

VICTORY CELEBRATION, TIMES SQUARE, NEW YORK, AUGUST 1945

"You need only to talk to Frank Sinatra for five minutes to realize how very sincere he is in his fight to help children."

LOUELLA PARSONS, *LA EXAMINER*, 30 SEPTEMBER, 1945, WRITING ABOUT *THE HOUSE I LIVE IN*

TEACH YOUR CHILDREN WELL

Frank's contract with CBS for *Your Hit Parade* ended as 1944 came to a close; he had featured on the show since February 1943. Many people had begun to feel that the programme had done all it could do for him, but there is no question that it had been a great opportunity for Frank to build his profile as a solo performer.

It had, however, probably been doing more for the songs themselves than for Frank's own career. After all, he was more often than not performing songs that were hits for others and therefore, apart from his fee for doing the show, there was little direct benefit. There were other practical issues too. With Frank resident in Los Angeles, and spending an increasing amount of time on his film work, he wanted to switch the show from New York. This was unacceptable to CBS. Frank was earning $2,800 a week for the show but it was costing him $4,800 a week to broadcast from LA. Frank was due to start receiving $4,000 per week on 20 January, but CBS refused to pay this and the connection charges from LA, so a mutual termination was the only outcome. This probably suited everyone. CBS hired an opera singer, Lawrence Tibett, and the fact that his name has now virtually been forgotten in part justifies the argument that the show did more to promote the songs, and the sponsor, than ever it did to

EXIST FRANKIE
Leaving the CBS Radio Theatre studios in New York was not easy. With only one exit it was not difficult for fans to know where to wait.

further the career of its star. Frank's last show was on 30 December, 1944, and within a few days he was back on the air when his own *Frank Sinatra Show*, sponsored by Max Factor, began broadcasting on 3 January, 1945; Rudy Vallee was his special guest. This was just a new sponsorship deal and a small title change from his old *Frank Sinatra in Person* show sponsored by Vimms Vitamins.

PATRIOT GAMES

By the end of January, 29-year-old Frank (although George Evans had two years knocked off his age at this point) had two records on the charts: 'If You Are but a Dream' and 'I Dream of You (More Than You Dream of Me)'. He was also back in the studio for the first of 12 recording sessions during 1945. In early February, he left by train and headed east for an appointment with the draft board in New Jersey. As the *Washington Times-Herald* reported, "Frank Sinatra, crooning idol of the bobby-sox set, is to appear before his draft board for possible reclassification." A few days later, the *New York Daily News* announced in a headline, "Whee-ee! Swoon! Frankie's now in 2-A." The Army had decided that he was in a job "necessary to the national health, safety, and interest", as well as being physically unfit to serve.

It is difficult to see why the draft board did this. If anything, it fuelled elements of the media in what seemed like a vendetta against Frank for failing to serve his country properly. Headlines such as "Is Crooning Essential?" left no doubt as to how they felt. Somewhat more bizarrely, on 5 March the New Jersey Draft Board announced that there had been a mix-up and Frank was, after all, classified as 4-F. "First in the hearts of his countrywomen but just 4-F to his New Jersey draft board" said the *LA Herald Express*. People from across the US wrote letters, journalists fumed, and even GIs serving overseas complained. As he was now confirmed as 4-F, he could be drafted into essential war work... Frank in a factory could have been interesting.

It was another episode in the saga that would continue for several years, Frank's lack of a sense of duty, as some saw it, was a potentially crippling blow to his popularity. Before long, this media interest in Frank's patriotism would rear its ugly head under the guise of "Is Frank a commie?" As the old saying goes, this one would run and run.

Radio continued to be Frank's main focus of activity. Besides his own show, he appeared on *GI Journal*, *Command Performance*, and on one aimed at teenagers starring Louise Erickson called *A Date with Judy*. His appearance on *Command Performance* on 15 February was a comedy special, 'Dick Tracy

LA MARTINIGUE
Frank on a night out with friends at La Martinigue nightclub in New York City, following his physical examination by selective service on 10 February, 1945.

in B Flat', also starring Bing Crosby, Bob Hope, Dinah Shore, Jimmy Durante, Judy Garland, and the Andrews Sisters. Frank shared a comedy song with Bing and Bob.

It was not long before Frank was back in New York for another recording session and a personal appearance of a very different kind. The *Daily Worker* of 17 March announced that Frank had been invited to speak at the World Youth Rally at Carnegie Hall on 21 March, which was staged under the auspices of "American Youth for a Free World". What is strange about this affair is that the FBI's special agent who covered the meeting makes no reference to Frank being present. However, in May 1945, the International Workers Order would distribute a pamphlet entitled 'Thoughts of an American', which supposedly had excerpts from the speech that Frank made. While Frank may or may not have been there, his involvement in politics was getting to be an issue, and one that was to increasingly tax George Evans. It was one thing to get involved with the president's re-election, and to give a donation to his campaign (although at the time it was less usual than now for entertainers to do such a thing), but it was quite another to be involved in "fringe" political activities. While it cannot be said that Frank Sinatra was close to President Roosevelt, such a large donation would have ingratiated him with the Democratic Party machine. However, all this would have counted for less when, three weeks after the World Youth Rally, President Roosevelt died.

MAKING FRIENDS ON SUNSET

Following this spell in New York, it was back home to Los Angeles – not that Frank appears to have spent as much time "at home" as one would expect. He was becoming even more of a socializer, meeting up

> **"** Here's your host for tonight, the Voice himself, in the flesh; what there is of it. Frank Sinatra. **"**
>
> ANNOUNCER ON *COMMAND PERFORMANCE*, 8 MARCH, 1945

HOLLYWOOD NIGHTS

Frank was regularly out on the town when home in LA. Here he is with a young Peter Lawford at the Players Club.

with the likes of comedians Phil Silvers and Jack Benny, and eating out at his favourite restaurants: Chasens, Romanoffs, and the Players Club on Sunset Strip, run by the film director Preston Sturgess. To the west of Hollywood lay a strip of land through which ran Sunset Boulevard, and this was known as "Sunset Strip". For a while, this was an area that lay "unincorporated" and came under the jurisdiction of the County of Los Angeles Sheriff's Department. During Prohibition, the City of Los Angeles had had somewhat stricter licensing laws than those that applied in the Strip, making this the ideal place to build a club.

Frank would often bump into some of the biggest names in movies at the Players, which is where he met Humphrey Bogart and his wife, Lauren Bacall. On their first encounter she said to Frank, "They tell me you have a voice that makes girls faint. Make me faint." Frank told her that he was taking the week off. It was the beginning of a firm friendship between the beautiful actress, the Hollywood hard man, and Swoonatra.

SUNSET BOULEVARD

NBC's Radio City is on the far right of this shot taken in 1945.

Other firm friendships were the kind that gave George Evans and Jack Keller sleepless nights. Frank had got to know many of the young, unattached Hollywood beauties. Lana Turner and Marilyn Maxwell had both spent more time than a single gal ought to spend with a married man – a fact that the newspapers had become aware of, and some of Hollywood's most vicious columnists would exploit to their advantage. One wrote, "What blazing new swoon crooner has been seen night clubbing with a different starlet every night?" Yet another was even more pointed, "I wonder if the wonder boy of hit records tells his wife where he goes after dark." On one of Frank's nights on the town in April 1945, he met a woman who was to be both his muse and very nearly his ruin: the gorgeous and sexy 22-year-old Ava Gardner.

This was not the first time they had met. According to Ava, in her biography, she had met Frank several years earlier when she was 19 and still married to Mickey Rooney. In early 1945, Ava had been seeing Howard Hughes, owner of RKO Pictures. Howard's oppressive nature was not in tune with young Ava's idea of a fun relationship, and the whole thing had cooled by the beginning of spring. Ava was one of those women with such self-confidence that she would turn up at the Mocombo without an escort, although sometimes she and Lana Turner went out on the town together (an awesome concept). While Frank may have been attracted by the vivacious Ava, nothing happened between them. It could have been that Frank was more attracted at that time to Lana Turner, known affectionately as "the sweater girl". In any event, within a couple of months Ava had met the bandleader Artie Shaw, recently returned from wartime service, and by October 1945 they were married. Nancy kept up appearances telling Louella Parsons, "I couldn't believe it, only millionaires made millions. All I could think of was the time six years before when we had spaghetti without meat sauce because meat sauce was more expensive."

HOLLYWOOD WENT TO WAR

WHILE MANY ACTORS, SINGERS, AND MUSICIANS JOINED THE US ARMED FORCES, OTHERS WERE, FOR WHATEVER REASONS, INELIGIBLE FOR COMBAT. MANY WHO COULD NOT SERVE IN UNIFORM DID SO THROUGH THE AUSPICES OF THE UNITED SERVICES ORGANIZATION.

IT WAS THROUGH THE USO that many of the biggest stars in the world of entertainment sang, joked, and danced their way through battle fronts around the world. The USO was formed in 1941 following a request from President Roosevelt for an organization to coordinate civilian war efforts for the benefit of the troops. The six civilian agencies were the Salvation Army, Young Men's Christian Association (YMCA), Young Women's Christian Association (YWCA), National Catholic Community Services, National Travelers Aid Association, and the National Jewish Welfare Board.

Throughout the war the USO dealt with the needs of the forces in myriad ways. These included service personnel clubs, among them The Hollywood Canteen, which was the inspiration behind the film of the same name. It is when it came to entertaining the troops that the USO is best known. From 1941 to 1947, USO Camp Shows gave 428,521 performances. By 1945 there were over 700 shows a day to audiences (which could number in excess of 15,000 and as few as 25), all around the world. Over 7,000 entertainers gave their services. Some were world famous stars; others almost completely unknown. Among the best known of the USO entertainers was Bob Hope. Others included Bing Crosby, German expatriate Marlene Dietrich (whose 'Lili Marlene' was a hit both sides of the front line), The Andrews Sisters, Andre Kostelanetz, and, of course, Glenn Miller and his Army Air Force Orchestra.

In 1947 the USO had all but disbanded, but with the coming of the Korean War in 1950 it was revitalized, and is still very active today in every corner of the globe where American forces can be found.

BOB HOPE

The king of the USO shows is doing what he likes best, entertaining the troops on the island of New Georgia in the Solomon Islands on New Year's Day, 1944.

NONCHALANT FRANKIE

Frank with Phil Silvers (centre) and pianist Saul Chaplin in their USO uniforms have difficulty leaving a New York restaurant just prior to embarking on their trip to Europe to entertain the troops.

HOLLYWOOD IN UNIFORM

Of the Hollywood stars who "joined up" it seemed that the Air Force was the most popular service. Clark Gable became a major and flew B.17 Flying Fortress missions across Europe. James Stewart flew both B-17 and B-24 bombers and was awarded the Distinguished Flying Cross. Charles Bronson was a tail-gunner. Actors Tyrone Power, Lee Marvin, and Glenn Ford served in the Marines, while Jackie Coogan flew gliders for the Army Air Corps; Douglas Fairbanks Jr and Eddie Albert served in the Navy, and Gene Autry was a Flight Officer in Air Transport Command. 1950s Western star Andie Murphy was America's most decorated soldier in World War II; he killed 240 Germans and won the Congressional Medal of Honour.

On 30 April, with Russian troops closing in on his Berlin bunker, Adolf Hitler killed himself. The end of the war in Europe swiftly followed. President Truman and the American military machine were left to focus on the final defeat of the Imperial Japanese forces.

OPPORTUNITY KNOCKS

The end of the war in Europe did not mean an immediate return of US forces, however. The logistics of moving so many people would take weeks of preparation and months to complete. But it did mean that there were an awful lot of troops with more time on their hands, and the need to entertain them became of prime importance. This gave George Evans the opportunity to relieve some of the tension surrounding Frank's own military situation. Evans talked to Phil Silvers about the idea of doing an overseas tour to entertain the troops. It would also have the added benefit of getting Frank out of Hollywood for a while, allowing the engine of gossip time to cool.

Before the tour, there was some filming to be done that was quite different from any Frank had undertaken before and that was close to his heart, as he had demonstrated

through his political activities. On 10 May Frank appeared as a guest on Dinah Shore's *Birds-Eye Open House* show and sang 'You'll Never Walk Alone', which he had recorded ten days earlier with Axel. Two days before Dinah's radio show Frank recorded two songs for a new film project entitled *The House I Live In*. He spent two days filming this ten-minute short in the middle of the month. Its message of racial equality and anti-semitism was absolutely up to the minute, given what the Allied troops had discovered in the German concentration camps. Frank helped devise the idea with producer–director Mervyn LeRoy, although according to Jack Keller it was not Frank's original idea. "George Evans and I encouraged this newly developed social conscious. We convinced him to make a film entitled *The House I Live In*, which caused a lot of people to sit up and take notice." It would prove to be something of a bittersweet pill for Frank. It would win a special Oscar, but at the same time it fuelled the whole "Frank's a red menace" brigade among the media. One of the major ironies in all this red scare nonsense was the fact that Howard Hughes, who was obsessive in his hatred of "reds", bought RKO in 1948 and Frank continued working for them.

> " The man solely responsible for the sale of 18 million bottles of smelling salts in the United States. "
>
> DINAH SHORE INTRODUCING FRANK ON HER *BIRD'S EYE OPEN HOUSE* RADIO SHOW

1942-1946

ANCHORS AWEIGH

Lucky singstress Kathryn Grayson — with two such guys as Sinatra and Kelly after her heart!

66 On Waves of Song, Laughter, and Romance. 99

MGM PROMOTION FOR THE FILM

THE PREMISE FOR THE storyline of the film is a thinly veiled piece of wartime patriotism. Frank and Gene play a couple of sailors on leave in Hollywood. Against the realities of the war, this is pure Hollywood whimsy, a world where song and dance reign supreme. Frank plays Clarence Doolittle, a former assistant choirmaster, and Gene Kelly is Joseph Brady. Frank is shy and retiring while Gene is the outgoing one. The plot concerns Gene's efforts to get Kathryn Grayson to fall in love with Frank. The "twist" comes when Gene and Kathryn's characters realize they are falling in love. Meanwhile, Clarence falls for a girl from Brooklyn, played by Pamela Britton.

Gene Kelly's dancing is superb, and he helps Frank "get by", often making the routines simpler to accommodate Frank's abilities, or lack of them. As Frank graciously admitted, "I was born with a couple of left feet, and it was Gene and only Gene who got me to dance." In one scene, where Frank and Gene leap from bed to bed, it took 72 takes, admittedly done over a couple of weeks. You have to feel for Frank, being asked to dance with a genius, a similar feeling to you being asked to sing a duet with Frank.

Frank's numbers in the film, mostly composed by Sammy Cahn and Jule Styne, are 'What Makes a Sunset', 'The Charm of You', 'I Fall in Love Too Easily', 'We Hate to Leave', 'If You Knew Suzie', and 'I Begged Her', the last three with Gene Kelly. Frank also performs Brahms' 'Lullaby', often called 'The Cradle Song'. All the songs were recorded in Hollywood between June and September 1944 with the orchestra conducted by George Stoll.

Anchors Aweigh was the film that did most to launch Frank's career in the UK – that and his appearances on the BBC *Command Performance* radio shows.

The controversy that surrounded Frank for some of his negative remarks about Hollywood, MGM, and some of his co-stars took some careful handling by Jack Keller. Some have argued that this was the start of Frank's downward drift, and in particular his deteriorating relationship with the press. As always, it is far more complex that that, but it was one of those unfortunate little incidents that would stick around. Not that it affected the way the film was received by the critics, helped probably by the distance between Frank's remarks and the film's release. The film got an Oscar nomination for Best Picture (difficult to see why) and Gene Kelly was nominated for Best Actor.

STILL LIFE
Gene Kelly and José Iturbi look on as Frank clinches the deal with Pamela Britton.

While Frank was filming, broadcasting, and recording, Phil Silvers was preparing the tour to Italy and North Africa. He had already been overseas with the USO and knew the ropes. Later he recalled that the whole thing was a case of bad timing. He had just married the 21-year-old former Miss America, Jo-Carroll Dennison "I was still on my honeymoon with Jo-Carroll. Yet Frank was a pal. If he needed me, I had to help." Luckily, Jo-Carroll understood: "He [Frank] knew that he finally had to go, but he was scared. He had heard rumours that the guys were really going to let him have it. There were reports that they were going to throw eggs at him and make fun of him for not being in the service."

The touring party put together by Phil included Fay MacKenzie, an actress and singer, and Betty Yeaton, a dancer. Saul Chaplin was drafted in to accompany Frank on the piano; as Sammy Cahn's old writing partner, he and Frank knew each other from the Dorsey days.

Even by agreeing to go on the tour, Frank gave the press the opportunity to attack him, saying he was only going because the war was over. It was a no-win situation. Over the years, people peddling the story that the FBI had prevented him from going overseas because of his communist activities have not helped Frank's case. Nothing in the FBI files that have been released (and far worse has been released) indicates that during the war years the Bureau gave Frank's politics a thought. It is true that before the decade was out they would become an issue. Back in 1945, it would appear that the criticisms of Frank had some justification.

FRANK CROSSES THE WATER

The German surrender had taken place on 7 May, so when the party arrived in Rome by air from Casablanca the war had barely been over for a month. Phil Silvers was amazed when Frank told him he wanted an audience with the Pope. He was even more amazed when he told Phil that he intended to tell him some home truths about some of the Church's activities in the US, although there is no real evidence to suggest that Dolly had told Frank to tell the Pope to legalize abortion, as some people have suggested. The audience was arranged through the American Envoy to the Vatican. The Pope seemed to be unaware of Frank's singing talents (he thought Frank sang opera) though he had heard of Bing Crosby. The Pontiff imparted a benediction for Nancy and the children.

Phil 'Glad to See You' Silvers and Frank had worked out a skilful way of hopefully avoiding any antipathy or hostility towards Frank from the Forces audience. Phil presented Frank as the butt of his jokes. He ribbed him about his weight, his ears, even the fact that he could not sing. "I know the food here is lousy," cracked Phil as Frank walked onstage, "but this is ridiculous." It worked really well; reverse psychology put Frank at an advantage. He sang 'Nancy (with the Laughing Face)', the song written by Phil Silvers and Jimmy Van Heusen for little Nancy's fourth birthday. Frank had recorded it a year earlier as a V-Disc, and it had become a firm favourite with the troops. Frank played the show for laughs, even allowing Betty Yeaton to carry him off stage. Stanley Phippard, a serviceman who watched the show, commented: "I took my men to a USO show at an outdoor amphitheater 'somewhere in Italy.' It was needed and deserved relaxation. The great (and sadly forgotten) comic Phil Silvers was warming up the crowd when he called out for that 'skinny little Italian kid' to come down to the stage and 'sing a few songs.' And that kid was sitting right next to me the whole time. Sinatra gets up, walks to the stage and sang for an hour. That was the best performance I have ever seen. He barely cast a shadow, he was so skinny, but boy could he sing."

Even the newspapers had to agree that Frank had turned the thing around. According to the *New York Times,* "His box score? No swoons, two screams, seventeen request numbers. The singer kidded himself throughout the program and had the audience on his side all the way." *Yank, The Army Weekly* (Mediterranean Edition), on 6 July, had a slightly more "on the spot" feel to it: "The Sinatra show opened its two-weeks Italian tour in Rome on June 21. It was a good show by USO standards and the GIs liked it. Fay McKenzie sang a few songs, Betty Yeaton danced, and Phil Silvers pulled a succession of gags, most of them funny. Nobody swooned

when "The Voice" opened up, but nobody threw any tomatoes either." During his USO tour, Frank played 17 shows in front of 97,000 service personnel in ten days.

True to Frank's reputation as something of a Jekyll and Hyde, when it came to dealings with the press, he undid most of the good he had done by going overseas on his return home. On arrival in New York on 6 July, he criticized the organization of the trip. The *Stars and Stripes* naturally took umbrage, declaring that Frank was "hardly an authority on either the military or the workaday show business". Frank's defence was that the troops had asked him to "beef about the shows they'd been getting". There is no question that Frank was somewhat too strident in his criticism, especially given his track record on the draft and

THE ARMY SPEAKS
"To the Italian girlfriends of the GIs, Sinatra proved to be just another tenor, while the WACs [Women's Army Corps] in the audience were less enthusiastic. 'We're not babies,' said one WAC. 'Took him a long time getting here,' said another."
Yank, The Army Weekly, *6 July, 1945.*

1942 1946

FRANK AND JUDY

Frank appeared on Judy Garland's radio show, A Date with Judy, in February 1945.

the lack of support from the press over his military service and for what they saw as "his patriotic duty". But there is another aspect on a more human level. This was Frank's first trip overseas, and not just any trip, but one to countries ravaged by war and lacking the sophistication of life at home. Marlene Dietrich, a veteran of several long and gruelling USO tours probably summed it best of all: "You could hardly expect the European Theater [of war] to be like the Paramount." While Frank was definitely a little naïve, and there was clearly a case for "The Voice" needing to be a little more prudent, no one could deny his sincerity and his generous nature. He had collected several hundred messages and telephone numbers from soldiers while he was away. He took three days to phone every one of them through to their families from his Waldorf-Astoria suite. It would probably only have taken two days if most people had believed it really was Frankie on the phone. As it was, he had to spend a long time convincing them.

NANCY (WITH THE LAUGHING FACE)

IT MAY NOT BE one of his greatest or his most loved songs, or even one of his biggest hits, but it is one of those songs that people most associate with Frank Sinatra, particularly those who got to know him through listening to the radio in the 1940s. Frank continued to sing the song in concert right up until the 1980s; at President Ronald Reagan's Inaugural Gala in January 1981 he sang it to Nancy Reagan with adapted words.

Written by Jimmy Van Heusen and Phil Silvers, it had begun life as something of a joke. Phil was at a party at Johnny Burke's house, one of Van Heusen's regular lyricists, when he had said that Johnny's wife was "Bessie with the laughing face". Phil quickly worked up the lyrics and he and Van Heusen took them to Frank with the idea of giving it to him as a present for little Nancy's birthday.

Frank loved the idea, and the song, and he used it on his radio programmes in 1944, including his last *Frank Sinatra Show* on 14 June before the traditional summer break, when Lana Turner was his guest. On Saturday 8 July, he cut it with Axel Stordahl conducting the orchestra at

KFWB studio theater on Melrose in Hollywood, along with six other songs for release as V-Discs. It was this recording that became so popular with the troops on active service overseas. After the success of the song with the troops during Frank and Phil's USO tour, Frank went back into the studio in August 1945 and recorded two takes of the song, both of which were subsequently released on different formats.

In the middle of some of these negative comments and press speculation, Frank had a success. Amid the euphoria at the war's end – the second atomic bomb had been dropped on Nagasaki on 9 August – *Anchors Aweigh* came out and was very well received. It became one of the top films of the year and fully justified Louis B Mayer's commitment to Frank. Of course the film was also a triumph for Gene Kelly. His involvement was as much a reason for its box office success and a far greater reason for its artistic achievement. Frank took a lot of ribbing about his role in *Anchors Aweigh*, but he took it all in good heart with remarks such as, "Besides, I made a perfect sailor. Who else could get out of those jeans without unlacing them?"

RADIO, RADIO

On 15 August, Frank was a guest on a one-hour Victory Celebration special of *Command Performance*. Bing Crosby and Frank shared a comedy spot and a duet on 'You are My Sunshine', before Frank appropriately sang 'The House I Live In'; his performance received an amazing ovation. Before Frank sang he was asked by Crosby, "Are you in good voice?" He certainly was; it is a great performance in which Frank draws on some hidden emotional depths to bring out the best in the song.

A week later Frank was in the studio cutting it for his Columbia release. On the same day, he also recorded 'Nancy (with the Laughing Face)'. Frank's radio work over the summer was limited to appearances as a guest on radio, which included both Bob Hope and Danny Kaye's show. Frank also appeared on a AFRS *Command Performance* along with Victor Borge on 30 August. He was back a week later, this time with Bing Crosby, Bob Hope, and Judy Garland. Listening to these old radio shows, it is amazing how much ribbing Frank took about his weight. Even Judy and Bob Hope were in for a dig. "The choice for my next lead has narrowed down to two men, Bing Crosby and Frank Sinatra," said Judy. "Well so far you've got a man and a half. Which shall it be, flesh or fantasy?" was how Hope saw it.

Frank's last Max Factor-sponsored programme had been in May and his new show aired on 12 September. Called *Songs by Sinatra* and sponsored by Old Gold Cigarettes, it was broadcast every Wednesday. Besides Axel Stordahl as his music director, Frank was reunited with the Pied Pipers, who by this time had split from Tommy Dorsey. The first song that Frank sang was 'Night and Day', which remained as his theme until the series ended in June 1946. Each week there was a guest; Peggy Lee, Dinah Shore, Gene Kelly, the Andrews Sisters, Louis Prima, Marilyn Maxwell, Nat King Cole, and Tommy Dorsey all appeared before 1945 was over.

During this time, Frank was sometimes being too forthright in his comments, and his politics were beginning to get a little tricky. George Evans must have worried about what Frank was going to say and do next, but it was in fact partly down to Evans that Frank had become more outspoken in his views. George wanted Frank to be seen as more than just a singer. As early as November 1944, Robert Sullivan of the *New York Sunday News* interviewed Frank who was plainspoken in his comments about race and religion. He showed Sullivan his medallion with St Christopher on one side and the Star of David on the other. "I'm not the kind of guy who does a lot of brain work about why and how I happen to get into something. I get an idea – maybe I get sore about something, and when I get sore enough I do something about it," Frank told Sullivan. The film roles were a vital part of the plan, but so was his involvement with some left-of-centre organizations, and while George may have felt professionally challenged in having to deal with this, he was personally shoulder-to-shoulder with Frank. Of course, this was manna from heaven for the Republican press, especially the Hearst organization. Their newspapers were home to some of the more vitriolic columnists, among them men such as Westbrook Pegler (who sounds more like a Dickensian villain than a 1940s newspaperman).

When *The House I Live In* was released in September 1945 it was, on the whole, well received, for who could not support its message? The majority of the press made positive comments and many members of the public who saw it were also right behind Frank and his message of tolerance. The worst that some could find to say was that he had smoked a cigarette during the film – a sure-fire stimulus to youth crime. However, it was what it encouraged certain groups to do that got Frank into trouble with the dreaded Pegler and others of his ilk. It was the attention of the press that brought Frank back into the sights of the FBI, for J Edgar Hoover hated communists almost as much as he publicly hated homosexuals. It was all going to get very interesting, since it was this environment that probably drew Frank into closer contacts with the Mafia – an organization that did not exist, according to Hoover, but one that knew of Hoover's own homosexuality.

FRANK THE SUBVERSIVE

Two weeks after *The House I Live In* came out, Frank appeared again at the Hollywood Bowl. On 22 September, there was a "For the Wounded" concert. Mervyn LeRoy was involved in the organization of this charity event, and Frank appeared along with Dinah Shore, Bing Crosby, Jack Benny, Bob Hope, and Jack Haley. For the finale, Frank, Bing, and Dinah Shore sang excerpts from Gershwin's *Porgy and Bess*. What is surprising is that there is no mention in the FBI files of this open act of subversion. A few days earlier, the *Daily Worker* had announced that Frank was to be the sponsor of the World Youth

THE HOUSE I LIVE IN

❝Last night I caught you in a movie short, I'm proud of you Frank, 'cos that short will make a big contribution to the cause of tolerance.❞

GENE KELLY, 28 NOVEMBER, ON *SONGS BY SINATRA*

WITH A SCREENPLAY by Albert Maltz, a card-carrying member of the Communist Party and soon to become one of the renowned "Hollywood Ten" of the McCarthy era, and a title song by Lewis Allen and Earl Robinson, the film came out on 11 September, 1945. Everyone involved donated their time, and the money that the film generated was given to various charities. As *Variety* said at the time "A short subject to make everyone concerned feel proud."

The story is a simple one. Frank interrupts his rehearsals for a radio show to talk to a group of kids about the dangers of prejudice and anti-Semitism. While the film looks somewhat old-fashioned today, there is no arguing with the sentiment. Frank's message holds good. "Look, Fellas, religion makes no difference except maybe to a Nazi or somebody equally as stupid. Why, people all over the world worship God in many different ways. God created everybody. He didn't create one people better than another."

The song that Frank sings, 'The House I Live In (That's America To Me)' was arranged by Axel Stordahl and recorded for the movie on 8 May, 1945, VE Day in Europe. Frank's was not the original version of the song; the black gospel group The Golden Gate Quartet were featured singing the song in the movie *Follow The Boys* in 1944.

In early 1939, Billie Holiday opened at Café Society in New York City, her first real taste of stardom. During her residency she recorded Lewis Allen's anti-lynching protest poem set to music. Her own label refused to release 'Strange Fruit', and when it came out opinion was sharply divided on the song, but there is no doubting its impact.

While Lewis Allen's words for 'The House I Live In' may have lacked some of the impact of his earlier work, in its own way it was both important and relevant. It was important for Frank to be making this stand, and it was no publicity stunt. Frank showed integrity, a trait that would remain throughout his career, and his life. Frank also sings 'If You Are But a Dream' in the movie. In 1998 'The House I Live In' was inducted into the Grammy Hall of Fame.

A RAY OF LIGHT
"Its value lies in just one element; the unquestionable sincerity of this chap Sinatra, a sincerity that shines through his performance like a clear ray of light."
Downbeat,
1 November, 1945

Conference scheduled to be held in London from 31 October to 9 November, 1945. Later reports in FBI files suggest that Frank helped to raise funds to send a number of the US delegates to the event, which the FBI regarded as an "international communist-dominated youth organization". They are not specific as to how he did this. These reports appeared several years after the event, and it must be remembered that they were compiled during the dawning of the Cold War, when the whole spectre of McCarthyism was rearing its ugly head. This was the beginning of a period of intense debate throughout the US, Frank's involvement was real, and while the use of his name may not always have been with his agreement, his politics were to provide the backdrop to his career over the next few years. This milieu may well have had a bearing on his popularity as well as the work that he was offered.

BACK TO SCHOOL

Spurred on by George Evans's liberal tendencies, it was decided that Frank should capitalize on the positive press generated by *The House I Live In*. Given the negative feelings about Frank's lack of military service, this was the perfect antidote. It should also be said that Frank clearly identified with the message of racial tolerance himself: he was in no way going along with it for purely altruistic reasons. But, as is nearly always the case, mixing entertainers and politics is a high-risk strategy. Not only did Frank lack any political organization behind him, but the press had already set up their entrenched battle lines. Frank spoke about tolerance to an integrated class at a school in Harlem, New York City, in late October, but it was a trip to Gary, Indiana on 1 November that raised the stakes.

A strike at Froebel High School in the city had begun on 18 October, brought on by a group of "anti-negro" students objecting to having to share their classrooms with black students. The principal of the school was seen as "pro-negro", and the whole situation had boiled over into a strike by the students. Various local business people and others who were attempting to start an all-white parent-teacher association fuelled the situation. According to the FBI, the sitting PTA was made up of

MORAL MESSAGE
Frank talking to high school students in their auditorium on the wrongs of racial intolerance.

whites and blacks, and was chaired by the wife of the local Communist Party organizer – a perfect recipe for the commie-bashing crew. When Frank arrived at the Memorial Auditorium with Jack Keller and George Evans, the tension was palpable. The mayor was there as well as churchmen, business leaders, and other local worthies. Some of the business people in the town were seen as being behind the whole affair, encouraging the white students in their action.

Frank walked on stage and just stood there, staring at the audience, most of whom were yelling and shouting. Frank stood with his arms folded for several minutes until he got complete silence – sometimes showbiz and politics do mix. "I can lick any son of a bitch in this joint," were Frank's opening words. From then on he had them on his side. He proceeded to lambast them for their lack of tolerance. He also specifically attacked Joseph Lach, an undertaker whom he claimed was a prime mover in the strike, along with a man named Julius Danch, who was also City Hall custodian. Such was the embarrassment of the people on the stage that Father Grothaus, the pastor of a local church and Director of the Catholic Youth Organization, walked off; and while the mayor remained, he looked highly uncomfortable throughout. The upshot of this was that the strike continued. The following day, Frank was in Philadelphia talking to a group of people on the importance of tolerance. This time his audience, at a hotel, was more friendly, allowing Frank to talk without interruption. The end result of all this was that Frank increased his standing with liberal organizations but the downside was that the FBI really began to take an interest in him.

A week after the Gary High School debacle, Frank was back in New York, doing what he did best: singing. He began a six-week engagement at the Wedgwood Rooms, at the Waldorf-Astoria. Each night, backed by Dick Stable's 22-piece band, he would finish with his show-stopping rendition of 'Ol Man River'. Among his other numbers were 'Paper Moon', 'It Might as Well Be Spring', 'Laura', 'It's Been a Long, Long Time', and 'How Deep is the Ocean?'; several of which he had never recorded. One night Cole Porter was there to catch Frank sing 'Night and Day'; the Waldorf was that kind of place. Celebrities, the well heeled, and the cream of New York Society all caught Frank's performance. In between there were some more recording sessions, and on 8 December 'Nancy (with the Laughing Face)' entered the chart for a two-week run. One week later, 'White Christmas' was given another release. This time, it climbed higher than the previous year and reached No 5 on the chart. The year ended with *Modern Screen* naming Frank the most popular screen star of 1945, which in some ways compensated for the somewhat lacklustre performance of his recordings on the charts.

1945 ON THE JUKEBOX

FRANK ON THE US CHARTS

'IF YOU ARE BUT A DREAM'
Nat Bonx, Moe Jaffe & Jack Fulton
27 January, No 19, 1 week

'SATURDAY NIGHT (IS THE LONELIEST NIGHT OF THE WEEK)'
Jule Styne & Sammy Cahn
3 February, No 2, 12 weeks

'I DREAM OF YOU (MORE THAN YOU DREAM I DO)'
Jule Styne & Sammy Cahn
27 January, No 7, 5 weeks

'WHAT MAKES THE SUNSET'
Jule Styne & Sammy Cahn (from Anchors Aweigh)
5 May, No 14, 1 week

'DREAM'
Johnny Mercer
2 June, No 5, 7 weeks

'I SHOULD CARE'
Axel Stordahl, Paul Weston & Sammy Cahn (from Thrill of Romance)
23 June, No 8, 2 weeks

'IF I LOVED YOU'
Richard Rodgers & Oscar Hammerstein II (from Carousel)
8 September, No 7, 2 weeks

'YOU'LL NEVER WALK ALONE'
Richard Rodgers & Oscar Hammerstein II (from Carousel)
15 September, No 9, 1 week

'DON'T FORGET TONIGHT TOMORROW'
Jay Milton & Ukie Sherin
10 November, No 9, 4 weeks

'NANCY (WITH THE LAUGHING FACE)'
Jimmy Van Heusen & Phil Silvers
8 December, No 10, 2 weeks

'WHITE CHRISTMAS'
Irving Berlin
15 December, No 5, 4 weeks

In terms of weeks spent on the chart Frank was slightly less successful than in 1944, but with 11 hits that was an improvement. In all he spent 41 weeks on the *Billboard* charts with 'Saturday Night (is the Loneliest Night of the Week)' by far his best selling song. Frank first performed it with Harry James and His Orchestra on the *All-Star Bond Rally* film, and cut his hit version a week later with Axel, following the end of the Musicians' Strike.

The Johnny Mercer song, 'Dream' was Frank's other big hit of 1945. It is a lovely song that perfectly suited Axel Stordahl's arranging skills. 'If You are But a Dream' was originally recorded for a V-Disc and was Frank's first recording after the Musicians' Strike. It was adapted from the melody of Anton Rubinstein's 'Romance', and was featured in *The House I live In*. The two songs from Rodgers and Hammerstein's musical *Carousel* appeared on the same record that came out in August. The musical was a huge success on Broadway starring John Raitt, the father of blues singer Bonnie Raitt. A new departure for Frank was his recording, 'Don't Forget Tonight, Tomorrow' with the Charioteers. This four-man black group had first recorded ten years earlier and was very popular from appearing on Bing Crosby's *Kraft Music Hall* radio show.

THE COLLEGE SURVEY

On the *Billboard* College survey Frank came No 2 to Bing Crosby, and Dick Haymes was third. On the charts in 1945 Frank did manage to climb up to No 5 for overall annual performance. He was beaten by Bing, bandleaders Sammy Kaye and Harry James, and just pipped for fourth place by Perry Como, whose recording of 'Till The End of Time' stayed at No 1 for ten weeks. Como's recording of 'If I Loved You' had also out-performed Frank's. Frank was voted *Metronome's* "Act of the Year": "Ever since *Metronome* has known him, and especially during 1945, we have been impressed with the way he believes in himself, with his courage, with his direct approach to his fellow men..."

The Andrews Sisters had the top song of the year with 'Rum and Coca Cola', which like Perry Como's hit also stayed at number one for ten weeks. Doris Day had her first hit records in 1945 with bandleader Les Brown. 'Sentimental Journey', one of the best known songs from the big band era, held the top spot for nine weeks, and this was followed by 'My Dreams are Getting Better All the Time', which was No 1 for seven weeks. 'Do Do', as she was nicknamed, stayed with Les Brown's Orchestra until 1948 when she went solo. Other newcomers to the chart included 31-year-old Billy Eckstine from Pittsburgh. His first solo hit, 'A Cottage For Sale', made No 8 in the autumn of the year.

SONGWRITERS

Sammy Cahn was the most successful songwriter of the year with 23 hits; four were by Frank. He had 19 in partnership with Jule Styne. Almost as successful was Johnny Mercer, whose 21 hits included 'On The Atchison, Topeka and Santa Fe', 'Dream' (a bigger hit for the Pied Pipers than for Frank), and 'Laura' by Woody Herman and several other performers.

BILLY ECKSTINE
He had been singing for four years with Earl Hines and his Orchestra before breaking through in 1945.

THE IMPORTANCE OF BEING EARNEST

The following year, 1946, was a year of professional triumphs and personal difficulties. Frank's relationship with organizations that some considered subversive was attracting more and more attention. His marriage to Nancy was showing increasing signs of strain, and people were openly talking about Frank's philandering. On top of everything, sections of the press took every opportunity to attack him. Despite it all, Frank released some of his most successful records of the 1940s and he won an Oscar.

OSCAR NIGHT, MARCH 1946

"I cannot bear to let anything lick me. If it's hard — if I dread it — I can't rest until I've made myself go through with it."

FRANK, OCTOBER 1945

OSCAR NIGHT
Frank and Nancy at Ciro's on 11 March, 1946. Frank steals a glance at his Oscar.

Early in the year, an increasing number of reports began appearing in newspapers about Frank receiving awards from various organizations. In December 1945, he had received a citation from the National Conference of Christians and Jews for his "contribution to the cause of religious tolerance and unity among Americans". At the luncheon in New York where he received the award, David O Selznick, the Hollywood producer, had spoken about "demagogues, rabble-rousers and hate-mongers seeking to exploit post-war dislocations and nerves".

Frank's stance was clearly one that was shared by others in Hollywood. Now in January, at the "New Masses" dinner, Frank won another award, this time "for his courageous fight on behalf of all minorities". A month later, Frank was elected Vice Chairman of the Board of Directors of the Independent Citizens Committee of Arts, Sciences, and Professions (ICCASP), a pro-communist group, according to the FBI. On 11 February, after a nationwide poll, Frank was among a group of six white and 12 black people to be honoured in "Negro History Week" for their contribution to national unity. In some cases, including the "New Masses" award, Frank was not even there to receive his citation, nor was he necessarily asked if he wanted it. Organizations liked to "attach" themselves to the famous and the influential in order to further their own ideals. In the case of the ICCASP, Frank's involvement was real, and it was because friends were involved and he agreed with their philosophies.

PARANOIA

The problem for Frank, and others like him, was the post-war paranoia with communism, or anything that vaguely resembled it. The FBI and some newspaperman worked hand in hand to link many of the pro-Jewish organizations with communism, a strange scenario given the Nazis' exploits. Frank even went to the annual ball of the Free Italy Society in the Kastritta Hall on North Broadway, New York. Hadn't there just been a war against fascism? This group was supposedly anti-fascist, which, in the minds of many, made them de facto communists. Ironically, Frank's recording of the theme to *The House I Live In* entered the charts in mid-January, so there were undoubtedly some people who listened to its message and were influenced by it.

It was not just the US press that was anti-Frank, however. On 19 February, it was announced by concert impresario Harold Fielding that he had abandoned plans to have Frank visit London for some concerts. There had been adverse press in the UK against spending dollars on US entertainers while the post-war "dollar shortage" prevented the importation of food such as dried eggs.

March was a busy month for Frank, very much back to business. On 6 March, the *Los Angeles Times* columnist Edwin Schallert announced that Frank was to play the lead in a new Arthur Freed romantic comedy for MGM called *Jumbo*

(which never happened). The following day, Frank, along with Frank Ross, the producer, and Mervyn LeRoy, the co-producer and director of *The House I Live In*, collected their Special Academy Award at the Oscar ceremony. Frank must have felt at least partially vindicated in his stance against prejudice, although the FBI and some sections of the press were still not convinced. Throughout the remainder of 1946 there was a gathering momentum in their investigation and interest, all of which would have a significant impact on Frank's career, and life, for the next five years.

ON THE ROAD AGAIN

A week after winning his Oscar, Frank began work on a new movie, *It Happened in Brooklyn*. This was his second film for MGM and the first under his new five-year contract arrangement with the studio. Frank was to be paid $260,000 per year, and he won several unusual clauses in the contract, including a relaxation of the studio's rigorous morals clause. As well as starting work on his own movie, Frank was given a cameo part in another MGM film, *Till the Clouds Roll By*. In this film about the life of composer Jerome Kern, who had died the previous year, he sang 'Ol' Man River', and got some hostile press for his trouble. It may well have been Louis B Mayer's doing that he performed the song, having heard Frank sing it two years previously at the benefit for the Jewish Home for the Aged. For his performance in the film, which starred Robert Walker as Kern, Frank was dressed in a white suit, surrounded by an all-white orchestra. When the movie was released in December 1946, *Life* magazine called Frank's performance "a high point in bad taste."

In the week in which Frank's first album, *The Voice of Frank Sinatra*, entered the charts, he played the Golden Gate Theatre in San Francisco on a "2-for-1" show. Sharing the bill was the film *Riverboat Rhythm*, starring Leon Errol as a riverboat captain and orchestra leader Frankie Carle playing himself. The Pied Pipers, who were having a run of their own hit recordings, and Axel Stordahl and the Radio Orchestra completed the bill. This was the first live show for Frank in quite a while, and it began a series of dates in different cities, including Philadelphia (opening with 'The Girl That I Marry', which he'd just recorded, for 10,000 fans at the Convention Hall), New York, Detroit, and Chicago. Frank was paid $41,000, a record for an entertainer appearing in the windy city. (His basic fee was $25,000, plus 50 per cent of whatever the house grossed over $60,000.)

This was not a specially arranged tour to promote the album. Back then, the concept of touring and selling records off the back of live shows had not really been worked out. In Philadelphia, after his opening number, Frank continued with 'September Song' (not recorded until July 1946), 'I'm Sorry I Made You Cry' (recorded October 1946), 'Soliloquy' (recorded 3 April) and then about a dozen other songs. The radio continued to be the medium for exposing artistes, and

66 I haven't always believed in Frank, but I have always believed in his sincerity. 99

LOUELLA PARSONS

1942-1946

ALL WHITE
Frank, surrounded by a full orchestra all dressed in white, on the set of director Richard Whorf's film Till the Clouds Roll By.

Frank's weekly *Songs by Sinatra* continued to be his showcase to the nation as a whole. At this time, Frank had never played shows outside the main West Coast and East Coast cities and key northern centres such as Chicago.

DOWN TOWN

When Frank arrived at the airport in Detroit around midnight on 8 May, there was a large group of fans waiting for him, which he somehow managed to elude. Around 2:00 am, a crowd started gathering at Detroit's Down Town Theatre, where he was due to perform his first set around 10:00 am. Since it was a schoolday, the police quickly got involved, checking the ages of girls, especially those who looked under 16, of which there appeared to be a large number. Truant officers later arrived to carry on the checks, much to the girls' disgust, and they soon started berating the officers. In the FBI files, it stated that parents and others were appalled by what had gone on, and one had gone so far as to suggest that "Sinatra should be lynched" – the person had obviously not seen *The House I Live In*. The memo in the files had a hand-written notation by Hoover: "Sinatra is as much to blame as the moronic bobby-soxers."

But it was not just girls who were there, or who found Frank's performance exciting. Bill Konrad, a 17-year-old Canadian living in Windsor, Ontario, had driven across the river that formed the border with America: "Frank had a flair for the dramatic even then. After the movie the theatre went dark and two green florescent drum sticks were all you could see keeping time to 'Night and Day'. Frank sang a few lines, the lights went up and he ran out on the stage to a roaring waiting crowd of teenagers. It was some 60 years ago but I remember the drama of the performance. He sang 'Sunday, Monday or Always' and he apologized for having a raw throat but we didn't care – it was Frank Sinatra. I remember Frank asking the kids to go down the street and see Tex Beneke, who had taken over the Glenn Miller band. In a chorus they said, 'No, we want you, Frankie.'"

A week later, Frank was at Madison Square Garden to speak at a Veterans' American Rally, yet another communist front group according to the FBI. A few days later, the *Daily Worker* had Frank denying he was delivering bobby-soxers into the hands of communism. It was all getting rather ridiculous.

THE VOICE OF FRANK SINATRA

COULD FRANK'S FIRST ALBUM HAVE BEEN CALLED ANYTHING ELSE? IT CAME OUT THREE DAYS BEFORE THE OSCAR CEREMONY AND WENT INTO THE CHARTS TWO WEEKS LATER...

Nowadays, many still refer to CDs as albums, and certainly most called the Long Playing $33^{1}/_{3}$-rpm record an album. The reason is simple. Major artists had sets of 78-rpm recordings that were packaged together in a cardboard casing and sold as an 'album' of their recordings. Frank's was not the first album, but it was the first to be thematically arranged, something of a recurring theme throughout the remainder of his career. The four records had a wonderful cohesion, and as Columbia have reissued a CD of the album you can relive the experience; it certainly stands the test of time.

The Voice of Frank Sinatra was probably conceived by Columbia in isolation from Frank. Whether he and Axel were specifically asked to record the songs included in the album, or whether they were just collected together from the two recording sessions, is not known. If it had been the intention to release the album why did they wait over four months to record the second set? There were five other recording sessions between 30 July and 7 December. The July session took place in Hollywood from 8:00 in the evening until 11:30 (you couldn't record songs like this during the day), and is arguably the single best four-song session of the 1940s (quite why they didn't stick to Hollywood for the second set is difficult to understand). Everything at the first session is perfect. It's as though Frank is living every moment of those songs. You 'feel' the emotion. The 'sound' of the studio adds to the atmosphere, the arrangements (all eight songs were done by Axel Stordahl) and the playing of the studio orchestra is flawless.

Another significant difference between these sessions and regular recording sessions is the size of the accompanying orchestra. It is not even an orchestra but a nine-piece group consisting of flute/oboe, two violins, cello, viola, piano/ celeste, guitar, bass, and drums. It all adds to the intimacy of the album and creates a significant difference to Frank's normal 78-rpm releases. Given the difference in costs of an album versus a normal release it is as though they are aiming at the Waldorf-Astoria crowd rather than the regulars at the Paramount, a conscious effort to move Frank's appeal onwards.

The album was like a trip down memory lane for Frank – the newest song was 'You Go To My Head', from 1938, and the oldest George and Ira Gershwin's 'Someone To Watch Over Me' from 1927. It was also a nod towards Frank's hero Bing Crosby, who was still beating him in the popularity stakes. Bing had recorded 'Try a Little Tenderness', 'Paradise', and '(I Don't Stand) a Ghost of a Chance' in the 1930s, as well as co-writing the latter. Another of Frank's mentors, Billie Holiday, had recorded 'These Foolish Things' in 1936 with jazz pianist Teddy Wilson and His Orchestra.

Among the many myths about Sinatra and his achievements is that this album topped the first ever *Billboard* chart. That honour belongs to Nat King Cole, whose album *King Cole Trio Collection of Favorites* went to No 1 on 24 March, 1945, a full year before Frank's album came out. *The Voice of Frank Sinatra* did stay at the top (the album chart was just a Top 5 until August 1948) for seven weeks in 1946, spending a total of 18 weeks on the charts.

As one fan, Harry Agoratus, put it: "You had to be a teenager when *The Voice of Frank Sinatra* was released on 78s. It was as if a bombshell exploded. We had never heard any singing like this from the other crooners of the day; Bob Eberle, Crosby, Como et al. The idol of the bobby-soxers was a SINGER! We were not sophisticated enough to understand things like phrasing and breath control, we only knew that this was what singing is supposed to be. From our standpoint it was; it made us Sinatra fans."

SONG LINES

Chart US No.1 (7 weeks) 18 weeks on the chart. First charted 23 March, 1946

Although this album came out originally as four 78-rpm discs, it did get a release as a 10-inch LP. This is the running order.

SIDE 1

1. 'YOU GO TO MY HEAD'
(J Fred Coots & Haven Gillespie) 30 July, 1945, Hollywood

2. 'SOMEONE TO WATCH OVER ME'
(George & Ira Gershwin) 30 July, 1945, Hollywood

3. 'THESE FOOLISH THINGS'
(Jack Strachey, Harry Link & Holt Marvell) 30 July, 1945, Hollywood

4. 'WHY SHOULDN'T I'
(Cole Porter) 7 December, 1945, New York City

SIDE 2

1. 'I DON'T KNOW WHY'
(Fred Ahlert & Roy Turk) 30 July, 1945, Hollywood

2. 'TRY A LITTLE TENDERNESS'
(Harry Woods, Jimmy Campbell & Reg Connelly)
7 December, 1945, New York City

3. '(I DON'T STAND) A GHOST OF A CHANCE'
(Victor Young, Ned Washington & Bing Crosby)
7 December, 1945, New York City

4. 'PARADISE'
(Nacio Herb Brown & Gordon Clifford) 7 December, 1945, New York City

MY FIRST ALBUM
Frank shows off his "first album" to a Columbia executive, watched by Manie Sacks.

Back home in Los Angeles, Frank was at the Hollywood Bowl for the second annual Music for the Wounded concert, on 26 August. Sponsored by the Musicians' Association of Los Angeles, it was a prestigious affair. Besides Frank and Axel Stordahl, there was Lena Horne, Marilyn Maxwell, Igor Stravinsky, Leopold Stokowski, and composers David Rose and Sigmund Romberg. Englishman David Rose had already found fame for his composition 'Holiday for Strings', and would later compose that immortal homage to disrobing, 'The Stripper'.

Between regular radio appearances, rallies, and live shows Frank was also busy making *It Happened in Brooklyn*. Filming had shifted to New York in mid-June and continued there for the next month. Frank seems to have been less than disciplined, sometimes not turning up for shooting when he was required. After the Hollywood Bowl concert, there was more filming to be completed in LA, but again Frank absented himself, this time to go to the aid of his friend Phil Silvers. Phil had been booked to appear with Rags Ragland at the Copacabana Club in New York on 9 September. Rags had died quite suddenly two weeks before, and Phil, despite the loss of his friend, had agreed to go ahead. Frank, knowing how hard Phil would find it, went to New York and arrived shortly before the start of the show. The two men continued where they had left off when they entertained the troops with the USO. The hour and 45 minute "routine" earned them an ovation. Phil was eternally grateful, recalling, "gratitude embarrassed Frank. I looked for him to thank him for this expression of love and friendship and he was gone – back to Hollywood, where he had caused a two-day delay because of this gesture."

Back in LA, Frank continued filming, but so did the frustrations. Jimmy Durante, his co-star, was getting tired of the interruptions and so he took to not turning up on some days; then, in retaliation, Frank would not show up. On 1 October, Frank made a trip back to New York to appear in *A Tribute to Al Jolson*, where he sang 'Rock-A-Bye-Your-Baby' à la Jolson.

> **"The Voice is one of the world's most precious uninsured properties."**
> *THE NEW YORKER*, OCTOBER, 1946

LOUELLA PARSONS
She and Hedda Hopper were the queens of Hollywood gossip columnists... cross them at your peril.

An FBI intelligence report dated 13 September reported that Frank was one of the sponsors of the American Crusade to End Lynchings, of which Paul Robeson, the black singer, was the chairman. The organization was planning a "pilgrimage" to Washington DC on 23 September of a parade "led by colored and white veterans." The report went on to say, "This red pageant is another communist-engineered demonstration designed to spread unrest and distrust in the American way of life." Draw your own conclusions but to me it simply says that segregation and the type of conduct that such an ideology encourages causes all kinds of base behaviour, with lynching as its most vile. Frank should have been applauded, not pilloried. These were indeed strange days. America was a very different place in 1946 and would remain so well into the 1960s.

MOONLIGHT SINATRA

One reason for Frank's behaviour was that his personal life was growing increasingly messy. He had started an affair with the actress Marilyn Maxwell early in the summer, and it had reached the point where George Evans was becoming seriously worried about its impact on Frank's career. While he did not have a morals contract in his MGM contract, Marilyn did. Evans put the squeeze on her, threatening to expose the affair and in so doing ruin her career. It did the trick, but it failed to stem all the bad publicity. Rumours of Frank's on-set antics, and his frustrations with the movie's script and his absences, were told to Louella Parsons. She set about Frank in her inimitable style, chastising him and warning him that MGM might dump his contract. Frank, in the style to which he was growing accustomed, sent her a telegram warning her to stop lecturing him. It was no good: Frank did not have enough ink to take on the papers.

With his affair with Marilyn Maxwell over, Frank's thoughts switched to Lana Turner. For while Marilyn was pretty, Lana was gorgeous. She was 26, recently divorced, and the talk of the town. In the age of Hollywood glamour, Lana was among the most glamorous. Frank became smitten, acted like a teenager, and set about wooing her. Frank knew Lana well, but their casual relationship grew into an intense affair towards the end of the filming. The fact that he was married seemed to be of little consequence. He told Nancy that he was leaving their home, and apparently told her why. Far from keeping their affair private, a concept that neither Frank nor Lana grasped too easily, they went out together to places where they would not be missed. Frank was even saying that he was going to marry Lana. George Evans could no longer ignore what was happening, nor deny it. He fielded press questions, all the time insisting, "there's no talk of divorce". Interestingly, in the case of Frank's marital problems, Louella Parsons was actually quite sympathetic to Frank. On 7 October she wrote in the *LA Examiner*, "I think Frank has done his best to be a good family man and still remain the glamorous figure he's been in the public eye."

On 9 October, in the middle of all his troubles, Frank appeared on his own radio show along with Louis B Mayer. Mayer was there to give Frank his award from *Modern Screen* magazine as the most popular star of 1946. Louis started out by saying, "Let me welcome you to the MGM family." "I'm proud to be in that family sir," replied Frank. (One can only imagine what conversations went on backstage between the two men. Mayer would have been furious with Frank for what he was up to.) Mayer presented Frank with a bronze bust sculpted by Jo Davidson.

Lana and Frank went to Palm Springs and stayed at the home that Lana owned in the desert town. The press interest failed to die down. Whether Lana decided that the whole thing had got out of hand, or whether she was worried that it might affect the affair she was also having with married actor Tyrone Power, is unclear, but she began to deflect criticism, saying that she "had never broken up a home." From everything that has been written about Lana Turner, it seems that sex was her thing, and if Frank had confused sex with love that was his problem (he wasn't the first, nor would he be the last). Two weeks later, on 23 October, Frank and Nancy got back together in a very public way. Phil Silvers, who liked them both, arranged for Nancy to be at Slapsie Maxie's on Wilshire Blvd, one of the most famous celebrity watering holes in Los Angeles. Phil was appearing at the nightspot and he got Frank up on stage, totally unaware that Nancy was even there. Phil pointed to where she was sitting, at which point Frank sang 'Going Home'. They spent the evening together before leaving in a cab. Frank was going home. While Frank may have been confused about his feelings for Lana, he was apparently going off

FRANK AND LANA TURNER
At 26, the actress Lana Turner was as stunning a woman as Hollywood could conjure up. The original "Sweater Girl", she remained a Hollywood siren throughout the 1950s.

the idea of a permanent relationship. Lana was devastated that she was the one who had been dumped – that was normally her prerogative. It was her reputation and her image that she was more concerned about. Rather like a spurned teenager, she bombarded Frank with calls, remonstrating with him for what he had done, until apparently he had to have his number changed.

Four days later, Frank was in the studio with Axel cutting three songs, the first of which was Sammy Cahn and Jule Styne's romantic song from *It Happened in Brooklyn*, 'Time After Time', which includes the lyric: "Time after time I tell myself that I'm so lucky to be loving you."

At 30, Frank was no model husband. He had been married for seven years, and it appears that he had a continuous itch. In his world of glamour, bobby-soxer adulation, and friends who told him how great he was,

SLAPSIE MAXIE'S
Max was a former light heavyweight champion of the world and a character actor after he retired from the ring.

1946 ON THE JUKEBOX

FRANK ON THE US CHARTS

'OH WHAT IT SEEMED TO BE'
Bennie Benjamin, George Weiss & Frankie Carle
16 February, No 1, 17 weeks

'DAY BY DAY'
Axel Stordahl, Paul Weston & Sammy Cahn
16 February, No 5, 10 weeks

'FULL MOON AND EMPTY ARMS'
Ted Mossman & Buddy Kaye (melody from Rachmaninoff's Piano Concerto No 2)
13 April, No 17, 2 weeks

'THEY SAY IT'S WONDERFUL'
Irving Berlin (from Annie Get Your Gun)
18 May, No 2, 14 weeks

'THE GIRL THAT I MARRY'
Irving Berlin (from Annie Get Your Gun)
1 June, No 11, 2 weeks

'ALL THROUGH THE DAY'
Jerome Kern & Oscar Hammerstein II (from Centennial Summer)
18 May, No 7, 3 weeks

'FROM THIS DAY FORWARD'
Mort Greene (from This Day Forward)
13 July, No 18, 1 week

'FIVE MINUTES MORE'
Jule Styne & Sammy Cahn (from Sweetheart of Sigma Chi)
3 August, No 1, 22 weeks

'THE COFFEE SONG'
Dick Miles & Bob Hilliard
28 September, No 6, 12 weeks

'THE THINGS WE DID LAST SUMMER'
Jule Styne & Sammy Cahn
26 October, No 9, 6 weeks

'SEPTEMBER SONG'
Kurt Weill & Maxwell Anderson (from Knickerbocker Holiday)
21 December, No 8, 3 weeks

'WHITE CHRISTMAS'
Irving Berlin
28 December, No 6, 3 weeks

This was the year of the crooners on the *Billboard* charts. The big bandleaders were finally beaten, not quite into submission but getting there. Bing, Frank, and Perry Como held the top three places on the annual assessment of performance. There was very little to choose between them with Bing on 995 points, Frank on 947, and Perry amassing 884. Frank went one better than the previous year, charting 12 recordings during the year, and, more significantly, his records spent 95 weeks on the chart, more than the previous two years added together.

Listen to Frank's first No 1, 'Oh What It Seemed To Be', today and it sounds so nostalgic. Even back in 1946 it probably seemed that way. It was written by Bennie Benjamin, George Weiss, and bandleader Frankie Carle, whose own version ran neck and neck with Frank's rendition. At 30 years old Frank was on the cusp of being unable to get away with singing such a pretty, innocent little song. On the other hand, both 'Five Minutes More' and 'The Coffee Song' are comparative rarities from the period — up-tempo rhythmical songs. Frank's other records were fairly predictable fare. The two songs from the hit Broadway musical starring Ethel Merman, *Annie Get Your Gun*, were safe recordings. Given the success that Frank had on the charts it is somewhat surprising that his hit records from 1946 are among the least exciting bunch of recordings from the 1940s. The eight songs that made up his first album, which came out as 'Oh What It Seemed To Be', made the top of the charts, and are paradoxically among his best recordings of the decade.

Two of the hit recordings from the year stand out as being very different from the rest. 'The Things We Did Last Summer' and 'September Song' give the impression of a change within Frank. Both are more mature records than either of his two biggest sellers of the year. 'Summer' has a greater affinity with Frank's regular output from the period, unsurprising given the fact that they were written by his old mates Sammy and Jule, but Frank still sounds like an older, wearier man. 'September Song' is decidedly different; a song of reflection and, if anything, Frank was too young to

do it total justice, but with the lovely Axel Stordahl arrangement he comes very close. Nineteen years later Frank remade it with Gordon Jenkins, and he nails every last emotion of this beautiful song. You know he has lived every moment. Both songs are markers for what will be.

On the *Billboard* College Survey Frank came No 2 to Bing Crosby and Perry Como was third, perfectly replicating their performance on the *Billboard* chart. For Dick Haymes, his challenge effectively dried up in 1946, and while he continued to have hits he would never be in the top flight again. On the *Metronome* poll Frank was No 1. *Melody Maker* commented on the fact in January 1947: "Frank Sinatra holds on to the male throne securely, runners up being Nat King Cole, Billy Eckstine, and Bing Crosby in that order. In view of 'father' Bing's undisputed popularity in America today these results must be seen as an indication of how far he has strayed from the realms of pure dance music."

At 21 Mel Tormé headed the list of artist debuts in 1946 with his version of 'Day by Day'. The top recording of the year was the Ink Spots with 'Gypsy', which occupied the top spot for 13 weeks, making it one of the top ten sellers of the decade. It was originally a big hit in Britain, having been written by Englishman Billy Reid. Of the bandleaders who did well during the year it was mostly the lesser-known names, Sammy Kaye, Les Brown, Guy Lombardo, and Freddy Martin. Following Glenn Miller's death in December 1944, Tex Beneke took over running his old boss's orchestra; they were billed as Tex Beneke with the Glenn Miller Orchestra. Tex Beneke also had a sizeable hit with 'Five Minutes More'.

the reality of life at home was not easy to handle. In the world of showbiz glitz, Frank just couldn't take the commitment and responsibilities of marriage. His self-discipline when it came to his singing and his career is what had got him to the top, and he could resist almost anything except temptation.

MR UNCO-OPERATIVE

There was filming to be completed, and Frank was still being difficult. He left early one day to appear on the Burns and Allen radio show, then went into the studio to cut some more songs. This incident and the others that had gone on throughout the making of the film resulted in an award of a different kind for Frank. The Hollywood Women's Press Club voted him the Least Cooperative Star Award for 1946, a complete turnaround from the previous year, when they had given Frank an award for Outstanding Achievement in Industry Relations Award for his work in juvenile delinquency — what a difference a year can make. It is fair to say that some of what was written about Frank was baseless allegation, often motivated by politics, and written by those with a vested interest. They just wanted to attack Frank for everything he stood for. What is not right, as some have suggested, is that Frank was simply misunderstood and the target for unwarranted attacks that prompted him to defend himself. In early December, Frank even sent a sizzling telegram to the *New York Daily News* drama critic, Erskine Johnson, saying, "Just continue to print lies about me, and my temper — not temperament — will see that you get a belt in your vicious and stupid mouth." Johnson, in his column, offered to fight Frank at Legion Stadium in a benefit affair. At 200 lb, Johnson probably felt pretty confident.

Frank had brought much of his bad press upon himself, particularly over his affair with Lana Turner. In an age when the public was more judgemental about the morals of the rich and famous, Frank had breached a cardinal rule, quite literally. Leaving his wife and children was indefensible to many, particularly to the Catholic community. Going back gave him temporary respite, but it was another factor in the direction that Frank's career would take over the coming years. But whatever the longer-term prospects, his success on the charts in 1946 showed that his star was in no way waning with the majority of the public, especially the younger ones... but they were growing up.

FANS

THE TERM FAN IS SHORT FOR FANATIC, WHICH THE DICTIONARY DESCRIBES AS "A MAD PERSON". SOME WOULD SAY IT APTLY DESCRIBED THE PEOPLE, MOSTLY WOMEN, WHO FOLLOWED FRANKIE IN THE EARLY DAYS.

IN JANUARY 1944, ARTUR RODZINSKI, the conductor of the New York Philharmonic Orchestra, said, "Boogie woogie which appeals to hep cats is the greatest cause of delinquency among American youth today." It's somehow comforting to know that back then things were no different. While this was not specifically aimed at Frank, or his fans, he took the criticism personally and responded in his own inimitable fashion: "Nuts!" said Frank.

Rodzinski had been rounded on by none other than Leopold Stokowski, the eminent conductor, who praised the absorption of boogie woogie, jive, and swing into American art music. He had also singled out Frank for special praise. "Individualistic phrasing of Frank Sinatra's singing is not based on imitation but on initiative." While this may not be completely true, the gist of the maestro's comments held good. As fan "worship" Frank could ask for no higher praise. But more often than not it was Frank's fans who came in for as much scorn as the singer himself; throughout the 1940s they were both Frank's doing and his undoing.

The fact that Frank's fans were made to feel like "they were something" was the key to Frank's success, particularly during the war years, years that seem both far away on the one hand and yet not so far when you listen to Frank sing. Though they were now "in the last century", they might as well have been a thousand years ago when compared to

today … but was it all that different? After Frank's appearance at the Paramount in October 1944, there was a mixed response to the frenzy of the bobby-soxers. The conservative, middle-aged (anyone over 30), and the establishment seemed to view Frank as a menace and, at best, something that would soon go away. Fans naturally closed ranks around their idol and there were even a few clearly thought out views expressed in the newspapers. Frank's gift then, and for most of the remainder of his career, was that he made it all so personal. He made every woman believe he was singing just to her, while every man felt it was him up there singing.

"We must try to understand the American youth. They are accustomed to a youth free of care; however, they accept their duties of manhood and womanhood when adulthood arrives. Therefore let these bobby-soxers snatch a few moments of swooning from Sinatra in this hectic atmosphere of war. Let's have more faith in these youngsters and thank God that they line up for a Sinatra instead of for a Hitler."

> Narciso Puente letter to the *New York Times*, 16 October, 1944

This letter neatly encapsulates Sinatramania, a typical outpouring of affection for a teenage idol. In

ADORATION
At every show that Frankie played in the early days he was given gifts by his adoring Sinatramaniacs – a tradition that would continue throughout his career, only later it became bottles of booze.

the 1940s this was an all-new phenomenon, but one that has been repeated on thousands of occasions since. But these were feelings heated by the cauldron of war in which millions of America's young women saw Frank as the embodiment of the nation's manhood. While it is clear that at 120 lb he was perhaps not everyone's idea of "Mr Perfect", that's not the point. When has being a "star" ever had anything to do with reality? Groomed for stage or screen, what you see is what you get; it has absolutely nothing to do with real life. It's an irresistible cocktail that seduces the emotions. Few have done it better than Frankie.

FAN CLUBS
Frankie had many fan clubs across the USA of which "The Sigh Guy" was just one.

Scooperoo! Inside intimate experiences with swoonsational Frank!

SIGHINGLY

O
U
R
S

...e Visit Toluca ......
...ndid Close-ups.
...ve! We interview Eileen Barton

"The Sigh Guy"

Marie Salamone
Active Member
Feb 1946
Date of Expiration
Pam Walker
President

"The Voice That Thrills Millions"

> 66Mr Sinatra, the self-confessed savior of the country's small fry, seems to be setting a most peculiar example for his hordes of pimply, shrieking slaves.99
>
> ROBERT RUARK

1946-1952

TWILIGHT TIME

IN THE POST-WAR YEARS, FRANK WENT FROM HUGE
STAR TO FADING STAR. HIS FALL FROM GRACE
OCCURRED AS HIS PRIVATE LIFE INCREASINGLY BECAME
PUBLIC PROPERTY, AND MANY AMERICANS WERE NONE
TOO HAPPY WITH WHAT THEY SAW. THE GUERRILLA
TACTICS OF THE PRESS ESCALATED INTO OPEN WARFARE,
BUT IT WAS FAR FROM A ONE-SIDED AFFAIR. FRANK HAD
A BIG HAND IN HIS OWN DOWNFALL MOST PARTICULARLY
WHEN IT CAME TO HIS CHOICE OF FRIENDS, WHICH
WERE SOMETIMES AT DUBIOUS BEST. AT THE START OF
THIS PERIOD, FRANK'S RECORDS WERE STILL SELLING,
HIS FILMS WERE INCREASINGLY IMPORTANT TO HIM,
AND HE WAS ABOUT TO FALL IN LOVE. BUT WITH
HINDSIGHT IT'S EASY TO SEE THAT THIS ADDED UP TO
A NEAR LETHAL CONCOCTION; ONE CONJURED UP
FROM PRIDE, BAD LUCK, BETRAYAL, CHANGING TASTES,
AND A WOMAN SCORNED.

SINATRA IN LONDON
Crowds outside the London Palladium July 1950.

HAVANA MOON, LET ME ALONE

A few days before Christmas 1946, Benjamin "Bugsy" Siegel (with a name like that, of course he had to have Mafia connections) flew to Los Angeles in an attempt to persuade Frank, Jimmy Durante, and Lana Turner, among others, to go to a party in Las Vegas. Siegel, who the FBI described as "a prominent hoodlum operating on the West Coast", was involved with the Flamingo Hotel in Las Vegas, which was due to open on 26 December.

At the party, Frank was not in evidence, although George Raft, Lucille Ball, and a number of other Hollywood stars made the trip. The FBI thought for a while that Frank may have even invested in the hotel, but this proved baseless.

Three days later, Frank and Nancy were having a party of their own at home in Toluca Lake. All was going well until Nancy noticed a diamond bracelet that Marilyn Maxwell was wearing. Nancy had earlier found the bracelet in the glove compartment of their car but had said nothing to Frank, guessing that he was going to give it to her as a New Year's present. The fact that Marilyn had obviously been given the bracelet by Frank, and was now wearing it, enraged her. Nancy confronted Marilyn, who walked out: the festive mood turned ugly. Nancy disappeared into the bedroom,

VIRTUDES STREET, KNOWN AS "SIN STREET", HAVANA 1947

'ROUND MIDNIGHT
Frank, with the Page Cavanaugh Trio, typically recording late at night on 15 December, 1946.

> *"Giggle of the week, funnier than any café comedy are the alibis of Frankie Boy's stooges trying to explain how come the self-appointed shining example to American youth was reported mixed up socially with Lucky Luciano."*
>
> LEE MORTIMER, *NEW YORK DAILY MIRROR*

and it put a damper on the whole evening. It seemed that Frank and Nancy's reconciliation was to be only temporary.

It has been suggested that Frank had originally bought the bracelet for Lana Turner, but after their break-up he had simply given it to Marilyn instead. Whatever the truth of the matter, it does show Frank to have been foolish not just with his emotions but also with his money. It was a sign of Frank's impetuosity – a trait that would play an increasing part in his difficulties over the coming years.

FRANKIE GETS A GUN

January 1947 was the usual round of radio shows and the occasional recording session, but Frank still found time to pen a letter to Henry Wallace, the editor of *New Republic*, to say "Mutual respect, whether it's on the slum level of one little kid for another or at the top of the ladder where it's one government for another, one race for another or one belief for another is nothing but tolerance." Frank was clearly in the mood to continue his fight against racial prejudice. In an unconnected move, he also obtained a permit to carry a gun, or, as the *Los Angeles Times* reported on 21 January, "Frankie packs a rod". Later Frank told columnist Hedda Hopper that he had bought the gun for Nancy as protection when he was away from home.

A week later, *Variety* reported that Frank intended to quit his Old Gold-sponsored radio show, *Songs by Sinatra*, and return to a more lucrative contract on his Lucky Strike show, *Your Hit Parade*, at a reputed $7,500 per week. It seems, however, that Old Gold exercised some muscle to keep Frank to his three-year contract, which still had a year to run. Having decided to stay with Old Gold, Frank took three weeks' sick leave following his 29 January show. *Variety* said that he "may sit it out in Florida", but Frank had more exotic – and dangerous – locations in mind. He had accepted an invitation to stay at a Miami Beach home belonging to the Fischetti family.

The three Fischetti brothers, Rocky, Charlie, and Joe, were reported to be cousins of Al Capone, and Frank had probably got to know them in late 1945 or early 1946. He had certainly visited their mother with brother Charlie in Brooklyn while he was filming *It Happened in Brooklyn* in June 1946. He had even been asked by them to help Joe and Charlie get hotel reservations in New York towards the end of the year. The Fischettis sent him boxes of handmade shirts for his trouble.

How much Frank knew about the Fischettis' activities is conjecture, but it would be difficult to believe that he had no idea of what type of men they were. They may have appeared to him simply as better connected and more "glamorous" versions of the Hoboken hoods he had grown up with. It was also true that men with gangster connections would have owned many of the places that Frank had worked in since the earliest days of his career. That was just the way it was back then.

In mid-January, proof of the appeal of Frank was evidenced by T-Bone Walker, the brilliant black guitarist and singer, who had his first hit record with a song called 'Bobby Sox Blues'. It contains the wonderful lyric: "Ask you for some loving, you say 'what would Frankie say?' Bobby sox baby, I've gotta let you go. Head's full of nothing but stage, screen and radio."

Bobby-soxers were the last thing on Frankie's mind when he flew from LA to New York and from there to Miami on the last day of January. After spending a week or so at the brothers' Florida house, they all flew to Havana to meet Lucky Luciano, head of the Mafia. Luciano had been in exile in Cuba since he had been run out of the US. In these pre-Castro days, Cuba was a haven of gambling, drugs, and just about anything else that was illegal. Luciano had called a meeting there of all the major Mafia players.

IN PRINT
Frank gets finger-printed for his gun licence in January 1947 by Deputy Sheriff Bob Rogers.

> ❝Mutual respect, whether it's on the slum level of one little kid for another or at the top of the ladder where it's one government for another, one race for another or one belief for another, is nothing but tolerance.❞
>
> **FRANK, IN A LETTER TO THE *NEW REPUBLIC***

No one really knows how much Frank knew about the true purpose of this get-together, or whether he simply believed the story that Luciano later told his biographer: "It was to honour an Italian boy from New Jersey named Frank Sinatra." Besides the meetings attended by Mafia men, there were dinners, gambling, a visit to the horse-racing track, and late-night drinking sessions at which Frank was present. While one might consider him to have been naive to go to Havana in the first place, it is clear that he did not exactly rush away either; one could argue that nobody would wish to offend such powerful people by leaving early. Since that time, Mafia members, including Luciano himself, have spoken of their admiration for Frank, their involvement in his early career, and what he did while in Havana, though some of this is clearly fabrication – a case of a quick dip in the pool of reflected glory. After several days, Frank left and flew to Mexico City to join Nancy for a holiday.

> **It was all a coincidence.**
>
> FRANK EXPLAINS THE CUBAN AFFAIR

LUCKY GETS FRANKIE

The fact that we know about this incident at all has a lot to do with luck. Robert Ruark, a reporter with the Scripps-Howard chain, happened to have been in Havana at the same time on a totally unconnected visit. On 20 February in the *Washington News* under his by-line was the headline "Sinatra is playing with the strangest people these days." George Evans, Frank's press agent, probably telephoned Frank in Mexico to break the news. In his article, Ruark tells of Frank being seen "night after night with Luciano at the Grand Casino Nacional". This single story became the root of all the stories about Frank and the Mafia, which continued throughout his career.

Other newspapermen quickly jumped on the bandwagon. Lee Mortimer of the *New York Daily Mirror* even contacted the FBI, privately and quietly, to ask for their help with background information on Frank. In exchange, Mortimer gave the FBI a picture of Frank taken in Cuba; his motive was to secure the FBI's help in identifying the other man in the shot. Mortimer spared no punches: "Giggle of the week, funnier than any café comedy are the alibis of Frankie boy's stooges trying to explain how come the self-appointed shining example to American youth was reported mixed up socially with Lucky Luciano." Just for good measure, Mr Mortimer had been digging around in Frank's past and had found out about the pre-war New Jersey sex case charges, which he didn't hesitate to write about, despite the fact that the charges had been dismissed. It is easy to imagine how angry Frank was at these revelations. Did he for one moment consider himself partly to blame? Robert Ruark was unrelenting: "Mr Sinatra, the self-confessed savior of the country's small fry seems to be setting a most peculiar example for his hordes of pimply, shrieking slaves."

One of the first stories to do the rounds was that Frank took $2 million cash to give to Luciano as a gesture of friendship. This is absurd. For a start, Frank did not have that kind of money. (Much of the talk about his earnings was exaggerated, as is often the case in the entertainment world.) Lee Mortimer, whose boss was newspaper proprietor William Randolph Hearst, with whom Frank had had run-ins in the past, saw it as his "patriotic" duty to attack Frank's politics and, just as important, to expose his lack of "morals". Frank's explanation of the Cuban affair – that "it was all a coincidence" – probably sounded as implausible then as it does today, but Frank went on the defensive, declaring "I was brought up to shake a man's

IT HAPPENED IN BROOKLYN

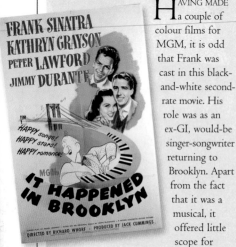

FRANK SINATRA
KATHRYN GRAYSON
PETER LAWFORD
JIMMY DURANTE

HAPPY songs!
HAPPY stars!
HAPPY romance!

MGM's
IT HAPPENED
IN BROOKLYN

DIRECTED BY RICHARD WHORF · PRODUCED BY JACK CUMMINGS

HAVING MADE a couple of colour films for MGM, it is odd that Frank was cast in this black-and-white second-rate movie. His role was as an ex-GI, would-be singer-songwriter returning to Brooklyn. Apart from the fact that it was a musical, it offered little scope for Frank. What MGM were thinking about when they cast Frank as an ex-GI, given all the fuss about his military status, one can only imagine. There was a serious side to the story in that many ex-military personnel were facing a return to civilian life; perhaps it was thought that the film would strike a chord. Maybe they were just testing the true depths of the appeal and talent of their star.

MGM drafted in Richard Whorf as director and Jack Cummings as producer. Neither was top-drawer talent – choosing Cummings may have had something to do with him being Louis B Mayer's nephew.

Despite these unpromising aspects, the film is not all bad. The pairing of Frank with Jimmy Durante (one that would often be repeated on radio) works really well: the chemistry between the two was palpable. Kathryn Grayson is Frank's co-star and their chemistry is non-existent. Grayson's role as an opera singer, which includes some scenes from Delibes' opera *Lakmé*, is flat,

whereas Durante is a huge success, with his humour and character shining from his every scene. English actor Peter Lawford, an MGM contract player who Frank had already befriended, also features but his performance is lacklustre at best and absurd when he sings and dances. The only reason to note his presence is his subsequent involvement in the Sinatra legend.

Filming was affected by Frank's marital troubles and his somewhat less than cooperative nature, but it actually works better than probably anyone had dared hope. Frank should be remembered in this film for giving a solid and sometimes very good performance. Any inadequacies in the film are not Frank's.

When the film premiered in New York on 13 March, 1947, the critics were, on the whole, positive. "Sinatra becomes a smoother performer every time out," said *Newsweek* in what was a fairly representative review. Naturally, Lee Mortimer thought otherwise, "This excellent and well-produced picture bogs down under the miscast Frank (Lucky) Sinatra." Clearly he was at a different movie; but the film still lost over $100,000.

The musical element was helped immensely by the fact that old friends Styne and Cahn were back on the case. The songs included 'Whose Baby Are You?', 'The Brooklyn Bridge', 'I Believe' (with Jimmy Durante and Bobby Long), 'Time After Time', 'The Song's Gotta Come from the Heart' (with Jimmy Durante), 'La ci Darem la Mano' (with Kathryn Grayson), and 'It's the Same Old Dream'.

Frank was required to play the piano in the film, and he appeared to be synching to the playing of 17-year-old André Previn; it was the first time their paths would cross but not the last.

hand when I am introduced to him without investigating his past." Normally a situation like this ends when either the target lies low and allows the spotlight to pass over him or another story comes along that takes the media's fancy. Frank did not lie low, and he was soon to be firmly in the media spotlight again, for all the wrong reasons.

L'AFFAIRE MORTIMER

A month after the "Havana incident", there was some respite from the bad press for Frank when *It Happened in Brooklyn* premiered. Almost without exception the reviews were favourable, although inevitably the one to break ranks was Lee Mortimer's. "Miscast Frank (Lucky) Sinatra, smirking and trying to play the leading man," was how he saw it. Following on from Mortimer's attacks on Frank for his visit to Cuba, this must have been the final straw, and he made it clear to friends that he wanted to "knock Mortimer's brains out".

Three weeks later, on the evening of 8 April, Frank met some friends – Lennie Hayden (MGM Musical Director), Irving "Sarge" Weiss (song publisher), Bill "Doc" Sexton, and singer Luanne Hogan – for dinner at a popular Hollywood nightspot, Ciro's on Sunset Strip. Coincidentally, the 42-year-old Lee Mortimer was also there, although he later claimed he had no idea that Frank was too, until he left. Mortimer was dining with band singer Kay Kino. After Mortimer had finished his meal, he got up and left. As he did so, Frank also got up from his table, along with three of his friends, and followed Mortimer. On the pavement outside Ciro's, Frank hit Mortimer. Definitely not a case of

the shit hitting the fan, but it was about to for Frank.

The *Los Angeles Times* broke the story, saying "Frank Sinatra, bobby-sox idol, was involved in one of those Hollywood fisticuffs last night", while the *Daily News* carried a picture of Mortimer holding his chin and being fingerprinted. A media frenzy ensued, with everyone trying to get to the truth of what really happened. Had Frank got several men to hold Mortimer while he hit him? Had he called him a homosexual? Did Frank have to be hauled off him as he was threatening to kill Mortimer? Had Mortimer said to Kay Kino, "there's that dirty dago"? Was it the result of Mortimer's comments about Frank's relationship with Luciano, or was it because he called Frank's bobby-soxer fans morons? Whatever the precise motive, whatever the real facts of what happened, it landed Frank in court.

The *New York Times*, in a piece datelined Hollywood 9 April, said "Frank Sinatra was arrested in the middle of a tune today and hauled off to court, where he pleaded not guilty to a charge of hitting Lee Mortimer. The singer accused the columnist of insulting him." Frank had, in fact, been in the middle of rehearsing for his *Songs by Sinatra* radio show at CBS Vine Street Playhouse when two detectives arrived with an arrest warrant. Ironically, he was singing 'Oh What a Beautiful Morning'. They took him to Beverly Hills Justice Court, where Judge Bert P Woodward set a jury trial date of 28 May and

"LUCKY" LUCIANO
Born Salvatore Lucania in 1896, he was one of the most powerful Mafia Dons both before and after his exile from the US in 1946.

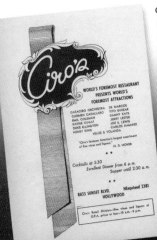

CIRO'S ON SUNSET
One of the places to be seen in the 1940s and early 1950s, Ciro's closed in 1957 and reopened as the Crazy Horse in the 1960s. After several more changes in name it became The Comedy Store in the 1980s.

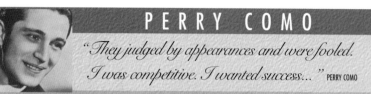

PERRY COMO

"They judged by appearances and were fooled. I was competitive. I wanted success…" PERRY COMO

TELL PEOPLE TODAY WHAT A HUGE STAR PERRY COMO WAS DURING THE 1940S AND EARLY 1950S AND THEY WILL BE AT THE VERY LEAST SURPRISED. ON THE *BILLBOARD* CHARTS, HE WAS WAY AHEAD OF FRANK, PARTICULARLY IN TERMS OF HIS NO 1 HITS.

The former barber's shop owner, born Pierino Como on 18 May, 1912, in Canonsburg, Pennsylvania, had his first professional engagement with Freddy Carlone's band in 1933. By 1936, Perry was the featured vocalist with the Ted Weems Orchestra and his first recording was on 15 May, 1936, when they cut 'You Can't Pull the Wool Over my Eyes' and 'Lazy Weather'. Perry and the band were featured on the popular radio show *Beat the Band*, and continued to record sporadically, without much success, until 1942, when they broke up.

On going solo, Perry, who *Metronome* said "imitated Crosby to the nth degree", signed for RCA Victor, and during 1943–45 he had a number of hits, without any big ones. His big break came in late 1945, when 'Till the End of Time' made No 1 and stayed there for ten weeks. Between the summer of 1945 and 1954, he had 73 *Billboard* chart hits, beating everyone, including Bing, who could muster only 70, and Frank, who had 58. Quite simply, Perry was the biggest recording star of the post-war, pre-rock 'n' roll era.

In the period 1940–54, Perry was the third most successful artist on the *Billboard* chart after Bing and Glenn Miller; Frank was fifth and the Andrews Sisters fourth. Perry had 11 No 1 records, while Frank had three solo No 1s in the same 15-year period. Even post-1954, Perry continued to be very popular, notching up a further 50 chart singles from 1954 to 1974, including three more that topped the chart.

PERRY IN THE MOVIES

Like just about every other singer from the period, Perry tried his hand at the movies, though, as was so often the case, they proved to be lightweights. His first was in 1944, when he appeared in *Something for the Boys*, which starred Phil Silvers, Vivian Blaine, and Carmen Miranda.

Perry's appeal was, as one reviewer so succinctly put it, that "he made vanilla fashionable". His laid-back style was the total antithesis of rock 'n' roll and much of the music on American jukeboxes. With a penchant for recording (although personally disliking) novelty songs, Perry came to define "middle of the road" and the negative connotations that it conjures up. His seemingly endless run of television shows during the 1950s provided Perry with a string of hit singles and albums.

After almost disappearing from view during the 1960s, Perry made something of a comeback in the 1970s with a television series, his first live shows in almost two decades, and a hit record. 'It's Impossible' made No 10 on the *Billboard* chart and No 4 in the UK. While he struggled to follow its success in the US, Perry had two huge UK hits in 1973 with 'And I Love You So' and 'For the Good Times'. Perry died peacefully in his sleep on 12 May, 2001, at home. A year later, he was awarded a lifetime achievement Grammy award.

BIGGEST HITS

'Till the End of Time' (US No 1, 1945)
'If' (US No 1, 1951)
'Don't Let the Stars Get in Your Eyes' (US No 1; UK No 1, 1952)
'Wanted' (US No 1, 1954)
'Catch a Falling Star' (US No 1, 1958)
'Magic Moments' (US No 4; UK No 1, 1958)

Singers of the Year: Jo Stafford and Perry Como

fixed bail of $500. Frank's new gun permit was suspended. Neither Frank nor his attorney could produce the money. "Uh, I'm a little short today," said Frank. Newsmen and others in the public gallery passed the hat and enough was collected for Frank to walk free. Frank told waiting reporters, "He gave me a look, it was one of those contemptuous 'who do you amount to looks'. I followed him outside. I hit him. I'm all mixed up." Any temporary mix up in Frank's mind was quickly clarified when his attorney and George Evans told him he could be facing six months in jail. "Six months – God forbid," said Frank. The might of Hearst's newspapers swung into action to support Mortimer, and soon it was clear that this was a

fight that Frank could only lose. While Frank struck a pose when interviewed – "It was all over in about 15 seconds, I hit him right on the jaw. It's the only place I know to hit a man and knock him down" – there was no way he could win. Amid rumours and accusations of threats against Mortimer, the papers kept up a relentless barrage against Frank. In one article in the Hearst-owned *Los Angeles Examiner*, it accused Frank of attacking ex-GI Mortimer, challenged him about his involvement with Luciano, questioned his stance on racial tolerance, and, for good measure, dared Frank to deny that he "travelled with communists or communist front organizations". About the only thing they failed to challenge him on were his marriage problems of six months earlier, when he had an affair with Marilyn Maxwell.

One thing all the papers agreed on was that the two men were well matched, with Frank weighing in at 130 lb and his opponent at 135 lb, although when Kay Kino and Nat Dillinger, a Hollywood photographer, told the District Attorney that 200-lb Sarge Weiss had held Mortimer, things did not look good for Frank. *Time* magazine struck a more balanced view, saying "Hearst papers gave the story headlines and space almost fit for an attempted political assassination. Mortimer suddenly attained the stature of Dreyfus."

COMMUNISTIC FRANKIE

To add to Frank's problems, MGM boss Louis B Mayer was rattled. He may have been big in Hollywood but he knew that Hearst wielded more power, and he needed Hearst's papers to say good things about his other stars, and his movies. Mayer told Frank and George Evans that there was no choice but to settle with Mortimer. It cost Frank $9,000. Mayer also told Frank that he needed to be a supplicant to the Hearst family newspapers. Frank objected, of course, but without an MGM contract his earnings would have taken a huge tumble. To add insult to injury, Frank was ordered by the court to apologize publicly to Mortimer. Frank acknowledged his "keen regret" for striking him "without provocation", and went on to say that Mortimer had made no remarks about him. It must have been very difficult for Frank to have to say these things, especially given the vicious nature of some of Mortimer's insults.

With the Mortimer incident if not behind him, at least pushed into the shadows by the Hearst papers calling off their dogs, Frank could at last get back to work. Ironically, two days after the fracas, Frank flew to New York to receive the Thomas Jefferson Award for his fight against racial intolerance. Receiving his award at the Waldorf-Astoria, it must have crossed Frank's mind that it was a confusing world. Here he was doing what he thought was right,

HOLDING COURT
Lee Mortimer, not looking too damaged, looks down on a supplicant Frankie at the Beverly Hills Court on 9 April, 1947.

SINATRA ARRESTED, FREED ON BAIL IN FIGHT

A FLOWER FOR FRANKIE
Fans gave Frank a carnation outside the courthouse when he was bailed over his fight with Mortimer.

fighting prejudice, yet many lambasted him for being a "Red" or at least a "fellow traveller", as the FBI euphemistically put it. As Frank had said to the *Daily News* in New York on 15 April, "I'm as communistic as Winston Churchill."

While there was a lull in proceedings between Hearst columnists and Frank, it was very much a public lull. Behind the scenes, Lee Mortimer was actively seeking information from the FBI. On 13 May, Mortimer talked about Frank with Clyde Tolson at the FBI (Tolson was also J Edgar Hoover's lover). In a memo to Hoover, Tolson said, "I told Mr Mortimer that, of course, he realised that we could not give him any official information or be identified in this matter in any manner, which he thoroughly understands." Mortimer gave Tolson a picture of Frank taken in Cuba, talked about Frank's association with Willie (Moore) Moretti, a man well known in New Jersey for his connection to the Mafia, and enquired about Frank's pre-war sex arrest and the fact that an estate car belonging to Frank was in the possession of a man who had been arrested for narcotics smuggling from Mexico. Things were not going to get any better for Frank.

In April, Frank appeared at Carnegie Hall with an orchestra conducted by Skitch Henderson in an afternoon show. A week later, Frank made his first professional solo appearance in Texas. He appeared in Galveston along with Jack Benny, Phil Silvers, Alice Faye, and Gene Autry to benefit victims of a disaster in nearby Texas City. Between 16 and 18 April, a fire and subsequent explosion on a French freighter, *Grandcamp*, which was carrying the explosive ammonium nitrate, destroyed much of the city. At least 516 people were killed and over 3,000 injured. That week, it

> ❝[Frank] isn't a well boy. And I bet that when he's feeling well again, we'll hear no more about his temperament.❞
>
> **LOUELLA PARSONS,** *MODERN SCREEN*

1946–1952

CIRCLE 7-6143 GEORGE B. EVANS PRESS AND PERSONAL REPRESENTATIVE 1775 BROADWAY • NEW YORK CITY

PR

Maybe if George Evans had been based on the West Coast he would have had a greater chance of exacting a steadying influence on Frank.

was announced that Old Gold were dropping Frank from their radio show. Their advertising agency said that there was a decline in ratings and it was a "cold business decision". Ray Vir Den of the Lennon & Mitchell Agency said that Frank's activities outside the entertainment business had not influenced their decision, although he went on to say, "naturally we are not happy about such publicity". They felt that they were paying too much for Frank, given the size of the ratings. Then in May, things seemed to be looking up, since Frank's recording of 'Mam'selle' entered the charts and reached the top, his first for almost a year. Maybe there was truth in the old adage that there is no such thing as bad publicity, just as long as they spell your name right! However, it was to be his last chart-topping single for a very long time.

In the same week as Frank was dumped by Old Gold, it was announced that he had been cast in the role of an idealistic priest for his new RKO picture, *The Miracle of the Bells*. The press found plenty to say about this, chiding Frank for attempting to pass himself off as a better person through an association with a make-believe persona. Hearst columnist Westbrook Pegler was, as usual, happy to pillory Frank: "Sinatra and the movie industry might more honestly dramatize his own life as it is lived and his influence on the cult of the bobby-sox."

UPS AND DOWNS

Frank began filming his new movie in mid-August. In the midst of filming he began a new radio series, or rather returned to an old one: Frank was back on *Your Hit Parade*, sponsored by Lucky Strike. It is a measure of how Frank's fortunes had declined from the heights of 1946 that he was

back on the radio singing other people's songs rather than his own – hardly indicative of a man at the very top of his profession. The first broadcast was on 6 September, and appearing with him were Ken Lane and the Hit Paraders; for 11 weeks Doris Day was the regular female vocalist. *Metronome*, reviewing his return to the show, was about as scathing as one can imagine, considering it had crowned him 'Act of the Year' two years earlier: "The show is alternately dull, pompous and raucous. Frank sings without relaxation and often at tempos that don't suit him or the song. Axel plays murderous, rag-timey junk, that he, with his impeccable taste, must abhor. And poor Doris Day, making her first real start in commercial radio, is saddled with arrangements which sound as if they were written long before anybody ever thought of having a stylist like her on the show… Frank sounds worse on these Saturday nightmares than he ever has since he first became famous…"

Unsurprisingly, it was reported that Frank's yearly earnings were down to less than $1 million. Although this was by no means a catastrophe for Frank, it was certainly not good news for a man with a prodigious spending habit. It was reported that in the previous year he had given away 300 gold cigarette lighters costing $150 each, a cool $45,000 worth, and even if he did get a bulk-purchase discount, that is still a lot of after-tax income. His "Little Lord Fauntleroy" habit had continued from his childhood, and his wealth enabled him to continue supporting it. Reports talk of 50 suits, 25 sports jackets, 100 pairs of trousers, and 60 pairs of shoes.

In part, the reduction in Frank's earnings could be attributed to the cutback in his work during the year, part of which was due to his commitment to political causes. Although George Evans had encouraged Frank with his causes, and may even have suggested that Frank became more overtly political as a "career move", this idea seems, when coupled with some of Frank's other activities, to have had a negative rather than a positive effect. Frank was going to need to draw on his vast reservoir of self-confidence to overcome his predicament. Even his old supporter E J Khan noted in an article in the July 1947 issue of *The Coronet*, "Some people are worried that Sinatra could become a permanent institution, and they may get some comfort from the fact that his income has been declining."

CONSPIRACY THEORY?

Before and during the filming of *The Miracle of The Bells*, there had been a concerted effort by Frank, probably encouraged by George Evans, to rehabilitate himself with sections of the press. Interviews with columnists Hedda Hopper and Louella Parsons attempted to draw a line under the difficulties that Frank had recently been experiencing. Frank was open in talking about what had happened between himself and Nancy; he spoke of "his terrible state of mental confusion". He went on to talk about his trip to

FAMILY MAN

At the Stork Club in New York, Frank, Nancy, and the children portray a united front against the rumours of a rift.

SONGS BY SINATRA VOL. I

IN THE MIDST OF ALL his troubles on a personal level, Columbia issued Frank's second 78-rpm album in April. It again featured eight songs that did not appear as "single" releases. This album was far less successful than Frank's first album, and not just because it was released at a time when his popularity had begun to wane ever so slightly. It's clear from the recording dates that this is not a carefully crafted "concept", more an opportunity to release some tracks that had gone unreleased. There are over two years between the recording of the earliest and the most recent tracks on the album. It was repacked as a 10-inch vinyl album in 1950. While it is something of a ragbag of songs there are some good songs here, particularly the final track, 'I Concentrate on You'.

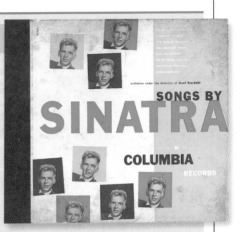

SONGS BY
SINATRA
COLUMBIA
RECORDS

SONG LINES

Recorded: Hollywood. Chart: US No 2, 7 weeks on the chart. First charted 17 May, 1947. The running order is for the LP released January 1950.

SIDE 1

1. 'I'M SORRY I MADE YOU CRY'
(N J Clesi) Recorded 24 October, 1946.

2. 'HOW DEEP IS THE OCEAN'
(Irving Berlin) Recorded 11 March, 1946. This song, along with 'She's Funny That Way' and 'Embraceable You', were

all recorded again in 1960 for Frank's *Nice 'N' Easy* album.

3. 'OVER THE RAINBOW'
(Harold Arlen & Yip Harburg) Recorded 1 May, 1945.

4. 'SHE'S FUNNY THAT WAY'
(Richard Whiting & Neil Moret) Recorded 20 December, 1944.

SIDE 2

1. 'EMBRACEABLE YOU'
(George & Ira Gershwin) Recorded 19 December, 1944. The earliest song on this album, and it suffers by compari-

son with the later tracks. You can hear such a difference in Frank's voice. It is one of those songs that is great to compare to "Capitol Frank". His version recorded with Nelson Riddle in 1960 brings out the lyric in a way that this version does not even get close to doing. Some songs you just have to be a bit older to sing.

2. 'ALL THE THINGS YOU ARE'
(Jerome Kern & Oscar Hammerstein II) Recorded 29 January, 1945.

3. 'THAT OLD BLACK MAGIC'
(Harold Arlen & Johnny Mercer) Recorded 10 March, 1946. Frank's first version of a song he later used in *Meet Danny Wilson*.

4. 'I CONCENTRATE ON YOU'
(Cole Porter) Recorded 10 January, 1947. You can hear the beginnings of Frank's more mature voice on this track.

Havana and how "such innocent acts are so distorted, you can't win, if you break your heart trying". Other articles supported Frank, but some definitely did not. However, his old adversary Westbrook Pegler was not one with whom they attempted any rehabilitation — not that they would have succeeded with the man who took self-righteousness to the level of an art form.

In early September, Pegler wrote a column deriding Frank for his activities under the headline "Silent Sinatra lets publicists repolish him". Apart from the fact that Frank was far from silent, the article said nothing new. Pegler simply re-ran the details of the "Havana affair" and damned Frank for having a gun licence when he "had not carried arms against the Nazis", for failing to visit Europe for the USO when fighting was going on, for consorting with gangsters — even for earning

FRANK SINATRA DAY AT HOBOKEN, 1947
Frank receives the key to Hoboken from the Mayor, Fred De Sapio. A proud Dolly and Marty shared in the rain-sodden celebration of Frank Sinatra Day.

PICTURE NEWS
It's Color and Action 10¢

WIN $1,000 IN CASH PRIZES

BAD NEWS
Lurid stories like this in contemporary comics and popular magazines all added to Frank's problems during this period.

1946–1952

a million dollars, "most of which would be taxed away". As a last resort, he attacked those journalists who wrote in support of Frank as people "who publish prattle". This rant continued in his column over the next three days. He brought up the morals charge (when Frank had been accused of breach of promise and committing adultery back in December 1938) and contested Frank's age (which had, indeed, been reduced by George Evans by two years). Pegler's approach was that lying about one's age made you just the sort of person that would consort with criminals. He even tried to make a case that linked Frank's donation to the Democratic campaign to the change in his draft board status from fit to unfit for military service.

POLITICALLY INCORRECT

Two weeks later, on 26 September, Pegler went for broke: "There's a weird light playing around Sinatra. Hitler affected many Germans much the same way and madness has been rife in the world." It is one thing to have a crank write letters claiming that Frank's radio programmes had a similar effect to Hitler's broadcasts, but for a "respected" columnist in the *Los Angeles Examiner*, and across the US via the Hearst newspaper network, to make such assertions was at best bizarre and at worst conspiratorial. Pegler was very deliberately making a case against a political opponent, mainly through a distortion of the facts and some outright exaggerations. The full text of his columns makes for amazing reading. It is clearly the political angle that motivated this attack, with all the other self-righteous pontificating being little more than a smokescreen behind which he damaged Frank's reputation and image.

While Pegler's writing probably had little effect on Frank's fans, it would have had an effect on others, some of whom might play a part in Frank's career. There is enough circumstantial evidence, especially when the FBI and Lee Mortimer's conversations are taken into account, to make a case for a right-wing conspiracy against Frank. However, from everything that is available from FBI files and such information that is in the public domain, there is no hard evidence of a right-sided plot to discredit or destroy Frank. It would be yet another conspiracy theory to add to many others. While Frank could never be dubbed "the voice of reason", his detractors' voices were a long way from truthful. However, there can be no doubt that all this harmed Frank, and it began to affect him much sooner than he could have anticipated, if he

TOP RATED RADIO SHOWS, SEPTEMBER 1947

In the month that Frank returned to *Your Hit Parade* he at least boosted the show's ratings: the previous month it had ranked 15th most popular radio programme.

(1) Walter Winchell
(2) Mr District Attorney
(3) Lux Radio Theatre
(4) Edgar Bergen & Charlie McCarthy
(5) Your Hit Parade
(6) Break The Bank
(7) Judy Canova
(8) Take It Or Leave It
(9) Suspense
(10) Blondie

MOVIE SINGER
The fact that Frank was billed as "MGM's singing star" indicates the increasing importance of the films he was appearing in.

anticipated it at all. It seems, though, that Frank was not completely preoccupied with such thoughts. One night he was at a club, Paul's Marquis, where he told the owner that he had invented a picture frame with a level bubble to ensure that the picture was always hanging straight!

A DATE WITH SAMMY

In many books and articles it has been widely reported that Frank played New York's Capitol Theatre in May 1947. In fact, Xavier Cugat and Guy Lombardo were the consecutive headliners at the theatre at which Frank had appeared 12 years before, on Major Bowes' *Amateur Hour* as one of the Hoboken Four. Nancy Sinatra says of this supposed May appearance: "Dad said he'd rather book an up and coming trio he'd heard about. The kid in it works with his Dad and his Uncle. I don't know his name." Nancy was not wrong, just six months too early. The opening act for Frank's run, which began on 13 November, was the Will Mastin Trio, a black comedy, song, and dance act that included the 22-year-old Sammy Davis Jr. Frank had first met them when he was singing with Tommy Dorsey some time in 1941, and the then 16-year-old Sammy had never forgotten that Frank had come over especially to shake his hand. In late September 1945, Frank and Sammy met again, only by this time Sammy had just been discharged from the Army. He went to the CBS playhouse in his dress uniform, so he could stand in the servicemen's line, to see Frank perform in his radio show *Songs by Sinatra*. Afterwards, Sammy managed to get to talk to Frank, as he recalled in his autobiography: "God, he looked like a star. he wasn't much older than a lot of us, but he was so calm, like we were silly kids and he was a man, sure of himself, completely in control." Frank remembered Sammy and offered him a ticket for the next week's show. After it, Sammy went backstage and chatted some more. Frank decided that he wanted Sammy, his dad, and Will Mastin to open for him in New York for $1,000 a week, which for the trio was a great deal of money. According to Sammy, "We were a $300 a week act then". Sid Piermont, the head of Loew's booking agency, told Frank they could save on the budget, "we can get the Nicholas Brothers for $1,000." All this in part explains why Sammy had such a special thing for Frank: he came through when Sammy and his family needed help. In Sammy's mind he owed Frank his career.

SAMMY DAVIS JR

"Sammy Davis will be remembered as one of the greatest entertainers America's ever seen." QUINCY JONES

BORN ON 8 DECEMBER, 1925, IN HARLEM, NEW YORK CITY, SAMMY DAVIS JR HAD MORE TALENT THAN IT SEEMS POSSIBLE FOR ONE MAN TO POSSESS. HE COULD SING, DANCE, AND ACT, HE WAS A GREAT MIMIC, AND HE WAS FUNNY.

An all-round entertainer in the vaudevillian tradition, Sammy Davis began performing as part of the Will Mastin Vaudeville Troupe before his fifth birthday. They later renamed themselves Will Mastin's Gang Featuring Little Sammy, in recognition of junior's pulling power. Sammy had some coaching from the legendary Bill "Bojangles" Robinson, and on one occasion the Gang opened for Tommy Dorsey, which is where Sammy first met Frankie. After the war, Sammy, his father, and his adopted uncle performed as the Will Mastin Trio. At a time when they most needed it, they began to get better work – and one man who helped them was Frank Sinatra.

SAMMY GOES SOLO

In 1954, Sammy got his break as a solo artist, signing for Decca Records. His first chart hit came when 'Hey There' from *The Pajama Game* reached No 18 in early autumn of that year. With 'Hey There' still on the charts, Sammy had a car accident on his way back to Los Angeles from Las Vegas, where the trio had been performing. He lost an eye and very nearly the will to perform. Frank Sinatra helped Sammy on the road to recovery, and in June 1955 his solo album, *Starring Sammy Davis Jr,* got to the top of the *Billboard* album charts and stayed there for six weeks. Sammy had arrived, in his own right. Three Top 20 US singles in 1955 confirmed his status, and Sammy went on to make his Broadway debut in the musical *Mr Wonderful* the following year. In the late 1950s, Sammy confounded many, especially some of the black community, when he converted to Judaism. "I don't know what the conversion did for Sammy, but it sure confused my Mother," said comedian Buddy Hackett, at the time.

SAMMY IN FILMS

In 1958, Sammy resumed his film career, appearing in *Porgy and Bess* as the character Sportin' Life. Membership of the Rat Pack confirmed Sammy's status as America's favourite black all-round entertainer, although his marriage in 1960 to the blonde Swedish actress Mai Britt caused controversy in parts of the United States, where racial segregation was still seen as the one true way. In the 1960s, as well as appearing with Frank in *Ocean's Eleven, Sergeants Three,* and *Robin and the Seven Hoods,* he starred in Bob Fosse's 1969 musical *Sweet Charity.* In 1972, Sammy had his biggest hit with 'The Candy Man' song, from the film *Willy Wonka and the Chocolate Factory,* which topped the charts.

Even though he had his own television series in the 1970s, his career was on the wane, and by the 1980s his only real earning potential was in cabaret and the casinos. Towards the end of the decade, in 1988, Sammy toured with Frank and Dean Martin in what was billed 'The Ultimate Event'; when Dean Martin pulled out, Liza Minnelli took his place. Sammy's last screen performance came in 1989 in *Tap,* for which he was much acclaimed.

SPORTIN' LIFE

Sammy in the role from Gershwin's *Porgy and Bess* that helped to further his career.

MR ENTERTAINMENT

Sammy Davis Jr pictured on stage in 1960 at a benefit concert demonstrating that it is possible to sing, dance, and drink all at the same time.

Sammy, a lifelong smoker, died of cancer on 16 May, 1990, aged only 64. He has been called driven and yet was mild-mannered. He was also viewed as a man "standing on the edge". His love for Frank Sinatra went very deep, and some have even referred to this as submissiveness. Whatever the truth of their relationship, Sammy certainly did have a lot to thank Frank for.

BIGGEST HITS

'Something's Gotta Give' (US No 1,1955)
'What Kind of Fool am I' (US No 17, 1962)
'The Shelter of Your Arms' (US No 17, 1963)
'The Candy Man' (US No 1, 1972)

66 He was a complex, touchingly lonely man, driven by strange demons and difficult passions, often disappointed. But he was a phenomenon for all that – and he was never idle. 99

THE HOLLYWOOD REPORTER

1946–1952

VIC DAMONE

"The singer with the best vocal equipment in the business." FRANK SINATRA

FRANK'S VERSION OF 'I HAVE BUT ONE HEART' TRAILED ANOTHER ON THE CHARTS BY A SINGER WHO ALSO HAD ITALIAN ANCESTRY: VITO FARINOLA, WHO WAS BORN IN BROOKLYN ON 12 JUNE, 1928.

Inspired to sing by his mother, a piano teacher, Vito dreamed of a career in music. He worked as an usher at New York's Paramount Theatre, where he was encouraged by Perry Como. As Vic Damone, he won the Arthur Godfrey Talent Scouts show on CBS radio, and after a booking at La Martinique he actually ended up on stage at the Paramount backed by Stan Kenton's Orchestra. Signed to Mercury Records, his first recording was 'I Have But One Heart', and it climbed to No 7 on the *Billboard* chart in the summer of 1947.

While Vic, by his own admission, was inspired by Frank Sinatra, he had a voice that was very special and he also had the looks to go with it. He topped the charts in 1949 with 'You're Breaking My Heart' and had a string of hits over the following few years. MGM signed him to a movie contract in 1951; his first appearance was in the musical *Rich, Young, and Pretty* (as André Milan). He was called up for military service soon afterwards.

On leaving the army, Vic appeared in cabaret, accompanied by a young pianist whom he met while doing military service. The pianist's name was Burt

Bacharach. In 1955, Vic appeared in the MGM musical *Kismet* with Howard Keel and Ann Blyth. In 1956, he had his biggest hit for several years when 'On the Street Where You Live' made No 4 on the *Billboard* charts, where it stayed for 25 weeks. He topped the UK bestseller's list with the same song two years later, helping to establish him as a firm favourite with British audiences.

Vic Damone headed down the Las Vegas route in the late 1960s, having also had a very successful career on his own television variety shows.

On the personal front, he married the actress Pier Angeli (who had been James Dean's girlfriend) in 1954, but they divorced in 1958. He married again in the early 1960s, this time to Judy Rawlins, who died in 1973. His third wife was Diahann Carroll, who he married in 1987.

After suffering a stroke in 2000, Vic Damone gave his last concert performance in February 2001 in West Palm Beach, Florida. Fittingly, his last song at the concert was Harry Warren's 'An Affair to Remember', which was a hit for him in 1957. His performance of this classic has never been bettered.

FIRST MOVIE
Vic (right) appeared with Jane Powell and Fernando Lamas in the 1951 MGM musical *Rich, Young, and Pretty*, a frivolous romance set in Paris, France.

BIGGEST HITS
'Again' (US No 6, 1949)
'You're Breaking My Heart' (US No 1,1949)
'My Truly, Truly Fair' (US No 4, 1951)
'On the Street Where You Live' (US No 4; UK No 1, 1956)
'An Affair to Remember' (US No 16, 1957)

PEARL BAILEY
The Melody Maker *headline of their review of the recording said: "Frankie and Pearl teamed by a genius". It did nothing on the charts, however.*

Given Frank's personal problems, it was ironic that the featured film during his Capitol Theatre run was *Her Husband's Affairs* starring Lucille Ball. On a professional level, this was far from a triumphant homecoming. The *New York Times* said that with Frank Sinatra on the bill, not much attention would be paid to the film, and that is why such a lightweight affair had been booked; "Frank Sinatra, take it away", is how they previewed his appearance. In fact, he didn't. The crowds were smaller than expected and reviews not so enthusiastic, even ignoring the bad ones perpetuated by Mortimer and his sympathizers. By the end of the second week, Mortimer reported, "The crooner, expected to pile up new highs, almost hits a new low. His second week (in which he missed no performances) was a sickly $71,000, half of the advance estimate." The comment is probably factually correct, Frank was on the wane. As one writer put it, "Frank was not *the* Voice, just a voice." Given all that had happened in the recent months, perhaps it was not altogether surprising.

There were other factors too. It is easy to forget now that, back in 1947, Frank was not a legend, not the Chairman of the Board, the leader of the Rat Pack, or any other of the many epithets that have been bestowed upon him. He may have been "the Voice", but he was essentially a pop singer, and, like every other pop singer since, he was subject to the changes in taste of an unusually fickle audience. Some people grow older with their idols, while many move on, dropping their adolescent heroes as they mature. The main wave of hysteria that surrounded Frank had been from the bobby-soxers, but they had now matured. There was an inevitability in Frank's changing audience that no amount of good or bad publicity could alter. He was, like many who have competed in the same field, at the point where he had somehow to change.

There were two options. Frank had to develop an appeal outside of music – and the movies were the obvious arena, although so far the material had been less than impressive – or find a way of changing his style to build a new audience. Sixty years ago people did not envisage a career in pop music; it was just something you did for a while before moving on to live the rest of your life. Whether Frank had a real sense of what the rest of his life might be like is impossible to know. He may have seen himself as principally a movie star, or perhaps he saw himself becoming a businessman (he talked of and had already made some investments). Frank's disappointing showing in New York by no means signalled the end of a career. In the same way that he was no overnight success, neither would he disappear overnight.

Frank's desire to become a businessman got him involved as co-promoter of a heavyweight boxing bout between Jersey Joe Walcott and Joey Maxim on 23 June, 1947, in Los Angeles' Gilmore Stadium. When Walcott won, it earned him a fight against Joe Louis, the Brown Bomber, on 5 December, 1947, in Madison Square Garden. Coming two days after the end of the Paramount run, it was a welcome diversion for Frank. The Brown Bomber won on points, although many thought Walcott should have won. It is said that Joe Louis apologized to Jersey Joe as he left the ring.

During Frank's run at the Capitol Theatre he did several recording sessions, including an unusual one on 8 December. He and the jazz singer Pearl Bailey, backed by a septet conducted by Axel, recorded 'A Little Learnin' is a Dang'rous Thing', which subsequently spread over two sides of a Columbia 78. It was one of Frank's earliest duets after he went solo, and in style and feel it was a long way from his normal output. You can almost imagine that he did it just to irritate the right-wing lobby. When the record was finally released in 1949, the *Melody Maker* said "Somewhere in America there's a lad with an imagination that amounts to genius [for teaming the two singers]". It could definitely be seen as a signpost to the future.

Whatever Frank felt about his apparent lack of success in New York, it did not seem to affect him over much. As Hedda Hopper had written a few months earlier, he'd turned tone deaf to criticism. He was approaching his 32nd birthday, Nancy was pregnant again, and his performance on the charts was far from great.

1947 ON THE JUKEBOX

FRANK ON THE US CHARTS

'THIS IS THE NIGHT'
(Lewis Bellin & Redd Evans)
1 February, No 11, 1 week

'THAT'S HOW MUCH I LOVE YOU'
(Eddy Arnold, J Graydon Hall & Wally Fowler)
8 March, No 10, 5 weeks

'I BELIEVE'
(Jule Styne & Sammy Cahn) from It Happened in Brooklyn
3 May, No 5, 6 weeks

'TIME AFTER TIME'
(Jule Styne & Sammy Cahn) from It Happened in Brooklyn
17 May, No 16, 1 week

'MAM'SELLE'
(Edmund Goulding & Mack Gordon) from The Razor's Edge
10 May, No 1, 10 weeks

**'I HAVE BUT ONE HEART
(O MARENARIELLO)'**
(Johnny Farrow & Marty Symes)
20 September, No 13, 2 weeks

'SO FAR'
(Richard Rodgers & Oscar Hammerstein II) from Allegro
8 November, No 8, 1 week

For the first time in five years, Bing Crosby failed to top the *Billboard* annual performance chart; in fact, he slipped below Frank on the listings. But then again, Frank had also slipped. Perry Como was the most successful of the solo singers, although even he was beaten by two bandleaders: Eddy Howard and Ted Weems, Perry Como's former boss, were No 1 and No 2 respectively.

Frank had signed a new five-year contract with Columbia in July, which at the time of its negotiation must have seemed like a guaranteed success for the company. With Frank's return to *Your Hit Parade* in September, it must have been galling that one of the first songs he had to perform was 'I Wonder Who's Kissing Her Now', a huge hit for Perry Como with Ted Weems and His Orchestra. Frank himself could only just scrape into the chart with the Anglo-Italian song 'I Have But One Heart (O Marenariello)'.

With Frank's records spending just 26 weeks on the chart, it meant that his performance in 1947 was the worst so far of his solo career. Even his solitary No 1 was the least successful of his three solo chart toppers of the 1940s. 'Mam'selle' came from a 1946 film adaptation of Somerset Maugham's *The Razor's Edge*. The film's director, Edward Goulding, also wrote the melody of the song. This lovely song was a huge success during the month of May, with no fewer than five different versions making the charts. Besides Frank's version, there were others by Dick Haymes, Dennis Day, the Pied Pipers, and Art Lund that made the Top 10, with Lund's rendition proving to be the most successful of all. Frank revisited the song in 1960 with Nelson Riddle and improved on the 1947 Axel Stordahl arrangement.

'Time After Time' is another song that Frank recorded again later in his career. It is also one that has continued to be popular with many singers in the years since Frank first recorded it. His 'hit' version was

Wherever you go it's fun to play WURLITZER MUSIC!

America's favorite nickels worth of fun

JUKE JOINT
Jukeboxes had been around since 1900 but by this time they had reached a level of sophistication that made them an indispensable part of any entertainment establishment.

not taken from the movie soundtrack, and is a better recording than the one that was used in the film. It has become a minor "standard", with a vast number of recorded versions by Carly Simon, Ella Fitzgerald, Jack Jones, and Etta James among others. There have even been two more hit versions, one by Frankie Ford in 1960 and another by Chris Montez in 1966.

'That's How Much I Love You' was a fairly radical shift in presentation for Frank. It was recorded with pianist Page Cavanagh's trio, which included Lloyd Pratt on bass and Al Viola on guitar.

UPBEAT
1947 was the last year of the 1940s in which the readers of *Downbeat* voted Frank the "male singer of the year". He had previously won the award in 1941, 1942, 1943, and 1946.

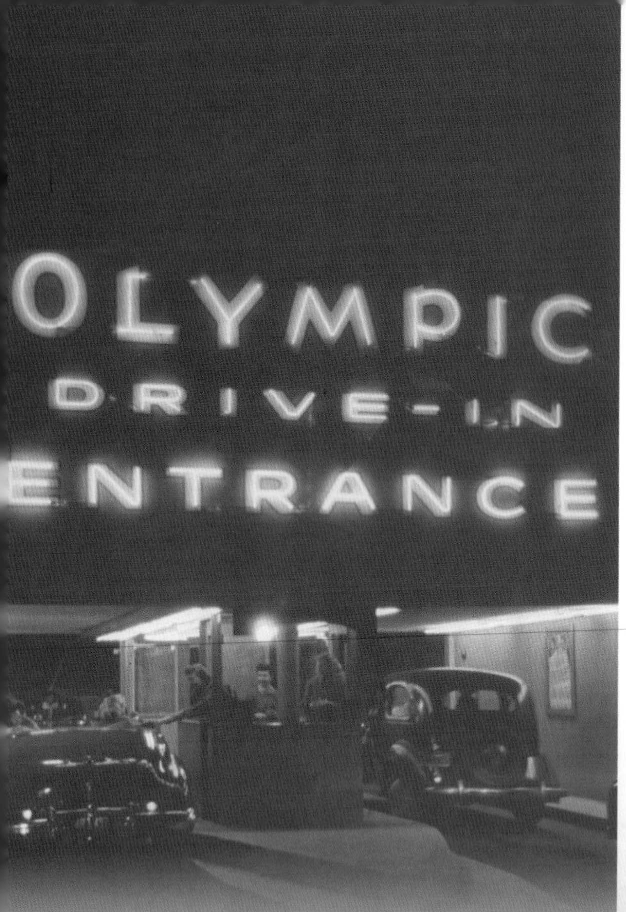

AUTOMOBILE CULTURE, HOLLYWOOD 1951

"He had a thing in his voice I've only heard in two other people – Judy Garland and Maria Callas. A quality that makes me want to cry for happiness."

AVA GARDNER ON FRANK

DOWNHILL FROM HERE

For the first time in four years, a new year began without a Sinatra record on the charts, and the prospects for more hits were hampered by the prospect of yet another musicians' strike. Frank's earnings came from his recordings, along with his film work and his weekly appearances on *Your Hit Parade,* and so this strike would eventually cost him a considerable sum in lost royalties.

Since Frank's return to *Your Hit Parade* in autumn 1947, there had been an initial upturn in listeners, but by early 1948 the figures had dropped again. The show was now sitting at No 18 on the Nielsen ratings for January, and it slipped lower as the year progressed.

One clear illustration of Frank's decline in popularity was the drastic reduction in column inches that the mainstream press now devoted to his activities. In the past, Frank had become accustomed to being front-page news, but now his fans had to search through the papers for the smallest of mentions. A less obvious example, at least to the public, of how bad things were getting was the slowing to a trickle of any mentions in FBI files. Frank's menace, as some had seen it, had passed. To the supporters of the "American way of life", Frank's

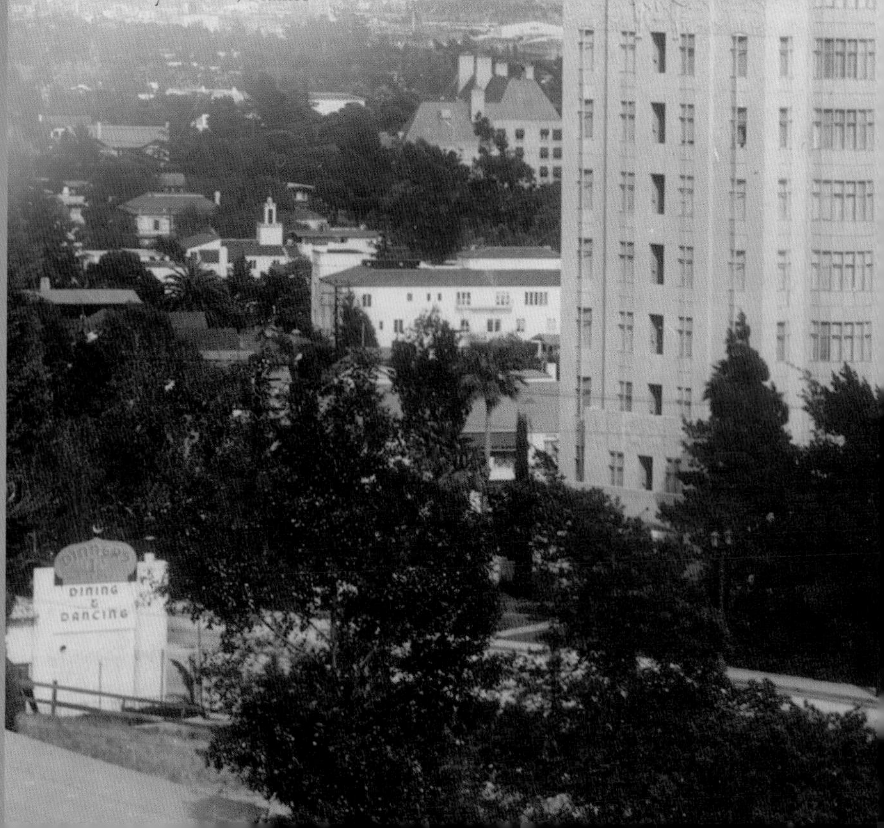

power lay in his ability to reach the young and impressionable bobby-soxers. In actual fact, Frank was showing less of an interest in overt politicizing. He was, however, showing a marked rise in covert activities, and with one woman in particular.

Frank was spending more and more time away from home, not in New York or on tour somewhere but in an apartment he maintained at Sunset Towers in Hollywood, where he was taking a definite interest in one of his near neighbours. "Ava, can you hear me Ava? Ava Gardner we know you're down there. Hello Ava. Hello," is how Frank initially made contact with the beautiful yet wild actress. A few weeks later, his almost teenage-like enthusiasm for her eventually led him to ask her outright for a date.

Ava was living in an apartment that was literally in the shadow of Sunset Towers, with Mearene (Reenie) Jordan, her maid and good friend. According to Ava's autobiography, she already had a thing for Frank – not the man himself, but the voice: "He had a thing in his voice I've only heard in two other people – Judy Garland and Maria Callas. A quality that makes me want to cry for happiness." Despite knowing that he was married, being aware of his reputation, and having an "aversion to married men", Ava agreed to the date. She found his enthusiasm "boyish face, bright blue eyes and his incredible grin" invigorating. This was the start of an affair that would eventually be Frank's downfall, leading to his darkest hour; and yet, paradoxically, this relationship would help him eventually to return to the limelight.

Frank was not finding life easy during this time, and his temperament was showing signs of wear and tear – and no more so than when he went to the premiere of *The Miracle of the Bells* in San Francisco. He went only when reminded of his contractual obligation to do so, and wrought revenge on RKO by running up an enormous hotel bill. Hedda Hopper reported that he ordered 88 Manhattans and left the cocktails untouched on the waiter's trolley when he checked out four days later.

MARRIED BACHELOR

For most of 1948, Frank was living his unusual "married bachelor" lifestyle, with one major interruption. The birth of the Sinatras' third child came in the early hours of the morning on Father's Day, 20 June. Frank and Nancy had been hosting a party at their house the evening before, when Nancy started to have the first signs. Frank drove her to the Cedars of Lebanon Hospital in Hollywood, where Christina was born around 2:00 am. Frank returned to the party, which was still in full swing. Everyone was playing charades and Frank soon joined in. To announce the birth, he acted out an hourglass figure and held up his fingers to indicate the baby's weight. While he was obviously happy with the new addition, it would prove to be a short-term return to happy families.

A month after Tina's birth, Frank was back at work. *Take Me Out to the Ball Game*, his latest MGM movie with Gene Kelly, took up a lot of his time between July and October, and recording sessions were almost non-existent because of the Musicians' Union strike.

A HUNK OF RELIGIOUS BALONEY
This is how columnist Hedda Hopper described the film in which Frank had his first non-singing role, in a movie that was a little too trite to be true. Frank was disappointed with the result and he clearly had higher hopes for his portrayal of the priest, Father Paul. Producer Jesse Lasky contacted the Catholic Church to garner its approval before finally offering Frank a contract. Frank himself, in an unrelated act, donated his $100,000 pay packet to the Church.

SUNSET TOWER
Frank's apartment in this Hollywood landmark must have had a stunning view over downtown LA. It is now the Argyle Hotel.

THE MUSIC BIZ

1948 SAW TWO SIGNIFICANT DEVELOPMENTS THAT WOULD FUNDAMENTALLY CHANGE THE WAY IN WHICH THE RECORD INDUSTRY OPERATED.

THE FIRST TAPE RECORDER

The first invention affected the way in which records were made in the studio, when Ampex, an obscure Californian manufacturer, brought out its first tape recorder. It was based on the Magnetophon, and very soon their 300 and 350 models become the industry standard for recording studios.

THE BIRTH OF THE LP

The second innovation would transform the way in which music was both reproduced and sold. Columbia, Frank's label, gave a press conference at the Waldorf-Astoria on 21 June, 1948, to launch the 33⅓-rpm "Long Playing" record. While there was great secrecy surrounding the launch, Columbia still had over 100 titles ready to release by 1 July. At their Dealer Conference in Atlantic City on 21 June, a company executive gave a speech while an LP of Tchaikovsky's *Nutcracker Suite* was playing, which everyone could see via a large mirror suspended above the turntable. At the end of the 18-minute side (more than four times longer than an existing 78-rpm record), the crowd gave a standing ovation. Within a year, one million American homes would have the equipment to play LPs: the revolutions revolution had begun.

LPs were being sold at $4.95 each, and to encourage sales of the necessary turntables to play them, a Philco player was sold for $29.25 with three free LPs – a neat piece of marketing. Frank benefited from all this in that his LP, *The Voice of Frank Sinatra*, was released as Columbia CL6001. The first classical LP was the Beethoven Violin Concerto with Nathan Milstein, Bruno Walter, and the Philharmonic Symphony of New York.

In October, Columbia simultaneously released a 78- and 33⅓-rpm album entitled *Christmas Songs by Sinatra*. It included his hit rendition of 'White Christmas' along with 'Jingle Bells', 'Silent Night', 'Adeste Fideles', 'O Little Town of Bethlehem', 'It Came Upon a Midnight Clear', 'Have Yourself a Merry Little Christmas', and 'Santa Claus Is Coming to Town'. It managed just a week on the charts, getting to No 7. It was to be Frank's last hit album for five years.

In late autumn, Frank began working on another film, this time for RKO. Filming *Double Dynamite* took up most of November and December, but it was to be another lamentable movie that not even the charms of Frank's co-star, Jane Russell, could save.

Shortly after work began on *Dynamite*, Frank's last RKO "spectacular", *The Kissing Bandit*, had its release on 19 November to terrible reviews. These reviews, coupled with making what he must have realized was a pretty dire film with Jane Russell, mean that this must have been a very depressing time for Frank. Being under contract to the studios meant that he had to make these films, but it is still hard to understand why the material offered to Frank was so bad. Was it that the film companies didn't think it was worth wasting good material on a fading star? Worse still, did they think that he wasn't capable of anything more substantial? In the case of *Double*

DOUBLE DYNAMITE

Jane Russell and Groucho Marx along with Frank give you an indication of how bad this movie was.

COVER GIRL

Patti Page was just 21 when she was featured on the cover of Downbeat. *Six months later, she had her first* Billboard *hit. Patti was born Clara Fowler but took her stage name when she appeared on the Page Milk Company radio show. Her style of singing began to replace Frankie's in the popular music charts.*

DOWN BEAT

December 29, 1948

Duke, Stan, Hamp—Win Place, Show
(See Page 1)

Recording Starts Again
(See Page 1)

BG, Barnet Bands Bop
(See Page 2)

On The Cover
Patti Page

K. L. AND CANADA
25 cents
FOREIGN 36c

Dynamite, judgment and reason probably didn't come into it, as RKO's major shareholder and *de facto* owner, Howard Hughes, of course, was somewhat prejudiced. In the end, it was Hughes who decided to postpone the film's release, whatever its assets, so no one would get to see it until 1951.

WHAT A RELIEF

For Frank, 1949 must have come as something of a relief – things had to look up. On the recording front they did, for he was able to get back into the studio after the musician's strike ended. Frank's performance on the *Billboard* chart was also improving, at least on the surface. After his disastrous movie releases of 1948, there were some positive signs and even a success to trumpet. On the home front, however, things were far from good, because Frank had bumped into Ava Gardner once again.

BAD BANDIT

Just about as bad is it gets is how Frank's 1948 film has been described, and they're right; he hated it too. " He contributes little", said the New York Times.

1948 ON THE JUKEBOX

Frank's poor record sales in 1948 and just six weeks on the *Billboard* charts were in part due to the Musicians' Union strike, which shut down recording for almost the entire year. However, everyone was labouring under the same circumstances and others had a better time on the charts, so it would be wrong to think that Frank was just unlucky in some way. Records like 'All of Me', released in April, simply failed to impress and therefore to chart. Some artists ingeniously had the orchestral track recorded outside the US and then added their vocals in an American studio. But there was no denying that 1948 was a tough year; as *Downbeat* put it, "there was a coast to coast slump for everyone".

Of Frank's three hits, 'Nature Boy' was by far the most successful, but it was still a far cry from what he had come to expect. In fact, the release of 'Nature Boy' seems a curious decision. Frank cut the record a cappella with the 20-strong Jeff Alexander Choir on 10 April, 1948, after they appeared on his Lucky Strike broadcast, *Your Hit Parade*, and copies were delivered to Los Angeles' DJs three days later. A week after Frank recorded his version, Nat King Cole's version entered the *Billboard* chart, for his was the original rendition of 'Nature Boy', cut before the musicians' strike. Capitol had originally released the song as a b-side and it wasn't until WNEW in New York started playing the song on heavy rotation that it was switched to the a-side. Besides Frank's and Nat's versions, two others charted in 1948. Sarah Vaughan's version spent a week on the charts in July, while one by Dick Haymes outdid his old rival by spending

five weeks on the chart, although it only got to No 11. In Britain, Mantovani and His Orchestra, The Joe Loss Orchestra, Jack White and His Orchestra, Turner Layton, and Dick James all released versions of the song. This is a typical tale of a 1940s song, when numerous recordings were cut and it became something of a race to see who would have the "hit version". In the past, it had often been Frank's records that were the winners. In the case of 'Nature Boy', Nat King Cole justifiably won the contest with what was a far superior rendering, and one that captured the public imagination.

THE NATURALIST

The composer of 'Nature Boy', eden ahbez (he liked his name spelled in lower case), has been called a premature hippie. Legend has it that he lived underneath the first "L" of the "Hollywood" sign on Mount Lee in the Hollywood Hills, existing on a diet of nuts and berries. Ahbez was born Alexander Aberle in Brooklyn, New York, in 1908. He had composed his song about a "very strange enchanted boy... who wandered very far, only to learn that "the greatest gift... was just to love and be loved in return." One day he approached Nat King Cole's manager and gave him a manuscript copy of the song. Cole recognized the old Jewish melody of the song ('Schwieg Mein Hertz'), but he liked the words and decided to record it. After it was recorded, the publishers of the original song settled with ahbez for a share of the royalties. Ahbez had already given away shares in the song to Cole's valet, for helping him to gain access to Cole's manager, and a further 12½ per cent share to another man who also helped him, leaving ahbez with 75 per cent. Nat King Cole recorded another of his songs, called 'Land of Love', and in the 1960s ahbez even made a couple of records himself. He died in March 1995 in Los Angeles after being hit by a car.

Male Singer—Not Band	
Billy Eckstine	1,419
Frankie Laine	1,174
Bob Crosby	884
Frank Sinatra	841
Herb Jeffries	577
Bing Crosby	479
Mel Torme	294
Perry Como	264
Dick Haymes	128
Vic Damone	101
Clark Dennis	89
Alan Dale	63
Bill Lawrence	47
Jack Leonard	30
Art Lund	30
Johnny Desmond	28
Gordon MacRae	22
Tony Martin	21
Andy Russell	20
Val Tino	17
Artie Wayne	16
Jack Smith	15
Pat Terry	15
Bobby Breen	13
Johnny Mercer	13
Jerry Sellers	12
Donnie Day	11
Morton Downey	10
(None under ten votes listed.)	

CAPITOL RECORDS

Nat King Cole recorded his version of 'Nature Boy' back in August 1947 for the Capitol label. It went on to sell over two million copies and helped to make 1948 Capitol's year. Their records topped the *Billboard* charts for over half the year, making them by far the most successful label of the year. Besides 'Nature Boy', they had No 1 records with Pee Wee Hunt's version of 'Twelfth Street Rag' (8 weeks), Jo Stafford's 'My Party' (1 week), Margaret Whiting's 'A Tree in the Meadow' (5 weeks), and Peggy Lee's 'Mañana' (9 weeks). Although the label had had eight previous chart-topping records in the 1940s, four of which were by Johnny Mercer, one of the label's co-founders, 1948 was the year that established Capitol as a major label. To round the year off, there was the first showing on the *Billboard* charts of a 31-year-old called Dean Martin. His Capitol recording of 'That Certain Party' with his partner Jerry Lewis crept in at No 22 for just one week in December.

In a *Downbeat* Poll for Best Male Vocalist of 1948, Frank came 4th, after Billy Eckstine, Frankie Laine, and Bob Crosby. Numbers 5–10 were Herb Jeffries, Bing Crosby, Mel Torme, Perry Como, and Dick Haymes. The real stars of 1948 were the Andrews Sisters. They had no huge individual hit records but managed to chart a total of ten in all. Other women also did well, including some relatively new faces. Peggy Lee's 'Mañana' was at No 1 for 9 weeks, a feat equalled by Dinah Shore's 'Buttons and Bows'. Doris Day had four hits, including the chart-topping 'Love Somebody' (a duet with Buddy Clark).

1946–1952

MGM staged a photo shoot to mark the company's 25th anniversary, and both Frank and Ava were invited to appear in the posed picture. "Hurricane Ava" – as some newspapers called her – and Frank chatted, and then a month or so later they met again, this time in Palm Springs. Ava was renting a house in the desert town, and she met Frank at a party. "I suppose we were rushing things a little the last time we met," said Frank. "*You were* rushing things a little", replied Ava. She sounds in control at this point, and it's doubtful whether she ever really lost this emotional upper hand. A few weeks later, they met for dinner in Los Angeles; then they went to Ava's house in Nicholas Canyon and made love. "We became lovers

forever – eternally. Big words I know. But I truly felt that no matter what happened we would always be in love. And God almighty things did happen." This is how Ava described the beginnings of their relationship in her autobiography. Ava was to be the great love of Frank's life, a lost love and one that almost destroyed him.

LOSSES ALL ROUND

There was another loss for Frank around this time, that of the trusting relationship with George Evans. Precisely when their professional relationship ended is unclear, if indeed it ever did. Some say it was as early as autumn 1948, This was the time of an alleged incident when

MGM STUDIO STARS OF 1949

LEFT TO RIGHT: FIRST ROW: Lionel Barrymore, June Allyson, Leon Ames, Fred Astaire, Edward Arnold, Mary Astor, Ethel Barrymore, Spring Byington, James Craig, Arlene Dahl. SECOND ROW: Gloria DeHaven, Tom Drake, Jimmy Durante, Vera-Ellen, Errol Flynn, Clark Gable, Ava Gardner, Judy Garland, Betty Garrett, Edmund Gwenn, Kathryn Grayson, Van Heflin. THIRD ROW: Katharine Hepburn, John Hodiak, Claude Jarman Jr, Van Johnson, Jennifer Jones, Louis Jourdan, Howard Keel, Gene Kelly, Christopher Kent (Alf Kjellin), Angela Lansbury, Mario Lanza, Janet Leigh. FOURTH ROW: Peter Lawford, Jeanette MacDonald, Ann Miller, Ricardo Montalban, Jules Munshin, George Murphy, Reginald Owen, Walter Pidgeon, Jane Powell, Ginger Rogers, Frank Sinatra, Red Skelton. FIFTH ROW: Alexis Smith, Ann Sothern, J Carroll Naish, Dean Stockwell, Lewis Stone, Clinton Sundberg, Robert Taylor, Audrey Trotter, Spencer Tracy, Esther Williams, Keenan Wynn, and, bottom right... Lassie the Dog.

PEGGY LEE

"Miss Peggy Lee knows how to swing."

LOUIS ARMSTRONG

PEGGY LEE HAD BEEN SINGING WITH THE BIG BANDS SINCE 1936 BUT IT WASN'T UNTIL THE MID-1940S THAT SHE BROKE THROUGH IN HER OWN RIGHT TO BECOME ONE OF THE BEST SINGERS OF HER GENERATION.

She was born Norma Jean Egstrom in Jamestown North Dakota on 26 May, 1920 and endured a difficult childhood as her mother beat her. At 16, she was singing with Jack Wardlow's band and joined Benny Goodman's band in 1941. The first hit to feature her sexy vocals came in late 1941 when 'I Got it Bad and That Ain't Good' from the Duke Ellington revue *Jump for Joy* spent a week on the charts. For the next year Peggy's voice was on every jukebox in the country as she sang with Goodman's band. It was in early 1943 that she shared the stage with Benny Goodman at Frank's first Paramount gig, so she was able to view the Frankie phenomenon at close quarters. After marrying composer and guitarist Dave Barbour she left Benny to go solo. Her first solo hit, in late 1945, was 'Waitin' For The Train To Come In' on the Capitol label. More hits followed before 'Golden Earrings' almost topped the chart in November 1947. By the end of 1948 Peggy was second only to the Andrew's Sisters as the most successful chart star.

Peggy displayed a natural talent for acting (she always gave highly interpretive performances in her singing career as well) and in 1950 she starred in *Mr. Music* with Bing Crosby. Her most notable film was *Pete Kelly's Blues* (1955) which won her an Oscar nomination for her portrayal of a woman's breakdown. She appeared in the 1953 remake of the *Jazz Singer* and sings on the soundtrack of Walt Disney's cartoon *Lady and the Tramp*, for which she also composed some of the music.

PEGGY ON SCREEN

In 1957 she made an album with Frank conducting the orchestra. With Nelson Riddle arrangements she does

a beautiful version of Kern and Hammerstein's 'The Folk's That Live On the Hill'. It is as the performer of sultry songs that Peggy Lee will be best remembered, and there is none better than Little Willie John's 'Fever'. Her 1958 rendition is definitive, one of those songs that just hits the right spot.

Peggy's career in the 1960s and beyond was sometimes hampered by ill health and by 1989 she was in a wheelchair, but still actively involved in a court case with the Disney Corporation over royalties for her 6 songs featured in the video of *Lady and the Tramp*. In 1994, she sold out London's Royal Festival Hall with the Brandenburg Symphony Orchestra, performing from her wheelchair. She recorded over 700 songs, made 59 albums and was nominated for 12 Grammy's; she was recognized with a lifetime achievement award in 1995. Peggy Lee died aged 81 at home in Los Angeles on January 22, 2002.

BIGGEST HITS

'Why Don't You Do Right' (US No 4, 1942 (with Benny Goodman)
'Mañana' (US No 1, 1948)
'Lover' (US No 3, 1952) .

❝Her wonderful talent should be studied by all vocalists; her regal presence is pure elegance and charm❞

FRANK SINATRA ON PEGGY LEE, 1994

TAKE ME OUT TO THE BALL GAME

Having been a priest and a bandit in his two previous films, the options left for Frank were becoming decidedly limited. MGM, were less than impressed with Frank's box office earnings, especially as they had paid him over $300,000, decided that another injection of Gene Kelly into Frank's film career was called for. Frank and Gene were cast as baseball players in the first decade of the 20th century (at least there was a tenuous link to Hoboken!) Originally they were to be joined by Judy Garland, but she withdrew from the early stages of filming. The producer, Arthur Freed, who was an associate producer on *The Wizard of Oz*, chose the veteran Busby Berkeley to be the Director. Unfortunately, Berkeley was engaged in a battle with the bottle; in the event it proved to be Berkeley's last director's job. Both Gene Kelly and Stanley Donan ended up doing some of the directorial duties. Busby's influence was certainly in evidence, just watch the swimming pool sequence featuring leading lady, Esther Williams (MGM's "star of the moment"). While she was no singer or actress, Williams was great in the water. Kathryn Grayson was the other female star.

Given some of the problems during the build up, the film actually turned out rather well. It has been described as "modest", but this somehow judges it from the perspective of hindsight. For its time, it was a good movie which met with a positive response from

the public, even if the critics were a little less kind. "It involves Frank Sinatra and Gene Kelly in a whirl of songs and dances that are easy to forget," said *Time* magazine. More importantly, it grossed over $4 million, making MGM a handsome profit, as it cost less than half that to make. The question was, would it be enough to keep MGM interested in renewing Frank's contract once *On the Town* was finished?

Frank had just one solo song in the film, Roger Eden's, Betty Comden's, and Adolph Green's 'The Right Girl For Me'. Other numbers, like 'Yes Indeedy', 'O'Brien to Ryan to Goldberg' and the title song all feature Gene Kelly. To be fair, the film's success lay not in the strength of the musical material, but in the sum of its parts. In Britain, the film was known as *Everybody's Cheering*, so as not to confuse people with baseball.

Frank and Ava drove around Palm Springs firing a .38 revolver from their car, although given every other piece of – albeit flimsy – evidence, it is more likely that it was a year later in 1949. Frank supposedly demanded that Evans fire Jack Keller, his West Coast man, but Evans, a man of principle, refused to do so. It is probable that they continued their relationship through 1949, but it was increasingly strained given everything that was happening between Frank and Ava, coupled with the fact that Nancy was trying to get Evans to "resolve" the situation, which must have placed an intolerable burden on the PR man. It was clearly a no-win situation for the astute publicist who had done so much to guide Frank's career and his chaotic personal life. Whatever the precise details of the situation, Frank must have felt it too. He owed a great deal to Evans, and they had been together for a long time. While his ego was largely intact, it is inconceivable that someone of his undoubted intelligence should not have some form of debate going on in the back of his mind. But Ava and her charms were a powerful draw, and as we all know love does funny things to men.

Frank had begun dance rehearsals for his new movie, again with Gene Kelly, in the third week of February 1949. These rehearsals were much more intense than for *Anchors Aweigh*, and stretched Frank and Jules Munshin, their co-star, to the limit. Shooting for *On the Town* commenced on 28 March, just as *Take Me Out to the Ball Game* was going on general release. The cast and crew shifted to New York on 5 May, although Frank was at least a day late, since he was in the studio on 6 May recording 'Let's Take an Old Fashioned Walk' with Doris

TOBACCO KING
This tatty Billboard *cover seems the perfect way to illustrate the depths to which Frank had sunk.*

Day in Hollywood. A couple of days before filming commenced in New York, Frank, Gene Kelly, Jules Munshin, and the other principals from the film were in the studio recording 'New York, New York', the Leonard Bernstein, Betty Comden, and Adolph Green song.

May also saw Frank's final appearance on *Your Hit Parade*, on the 28th, since he had been dropped by the sponsor, Lucky Strike. There was speculation that Frank had fallen out with the company. As his new album, *Frankly Sentimental*, hit the shops, he was busy recording a

promotional disk to be sent out to NBC radio affiliates for his new Lucky Strike-sponsored radio show, *Lite Up Times*. Frank sang 'Night and Day', 'It All Depends on You', and 'Again' on the disc, which was designed to encourage local radio stations to take the five-nights-a-week 15-minute show. It was to go out on air on 5 September at 7:00 pm, starring Metropolitan opera singer Dorothy Kirsten alongside Frank. It has been said that it is a sign of how far Frank's ratings had slipped that he was prepared to appear five nights a week, although the fact that the show was taped in Hollywood meant that Frank did not actually have to be in the studio every week night. The new show did put to rest the rumour that he had fallen out of favour with Lucky Strike, although it was considered something of a demotion from *Your Hit Parade*.

At first it was reported that Frank was to get just $2,500 a week for his work, and he was cleared to appear on the show only after protracted negotiations between Henry Jaffe, his solicitor, and MGM, who had the right of veto on any of Frank's radio work. Later reports said that his pay was $10,000 a week, which would actually have been a small rise compared to his pay for *Your Hit Parade*, which had required only one appearance a week. Frank's fall from favour was amplified more fully on a trip

to Richmond, Virginia, in early November. *Billboard* reported that Frank was in town for three days and was pictured on the roof of Thalmeimer's department store. During his stay, 6,500 people turned out to see Frank crowned as "The Tobacco Festival King". It was another one of the low points in his 1940s career.

In the same issue, *Billboard* reported that Lucky Strike was considering a television version of *Lite Up Times*, starring Benny Goodman; it was again notable that Frank was not being considered for the job. However, given the fact that there were only two million television sets in America at that time, Frank may not have been unduly upset. Radio still reigned supreme, although not for long.

LOSING TOUCH

In early August, *Variety* reviewed Frank's new release, 'It All Depends On You' backed by 'I Only Have Eyes For You': "Sinatra may not have a revival hit in either of these two standards." Three weeks later, an item in the same paper suggested that Frank had begun rehearsing songs again. It was clear that people recognized that Frank was no longer the force he had once been. Perhaps even Frank himself might have been a little concerned that he was losing his touch.

"THE COVER VOICE"
An article in UK magazine Picturegoer *about Frank discussed how popular he was with British teenagers. A planned concert run at the London Palladium in 1949 had to be cancelled despite the box office having been "bombarded with enquiries".*

FRANKLY SENTIMENTAL

Frank's fourth album came out as a 78-rpm package and a 10-inch vinyl disc in June 1949. It contains one absolute classic performance, in 'Body and Soul', and several more that show Frank at his 1940s best. It is an indication of how far he had slid that it failed to make the charts or excite the critics. In fact *Downbeat* was especially harsh when it reviewed the album in August: "Expertly done but Sinatra could never have become a name on

this… For all his talent, it very seldom comes to life."

The fact that the most recent of the recordings on this album were 20 months old would seem to indicate that Columbia felt that Frank's earlier work was of a higher standard. Like his other albums, it was made up of songs that were not "hits". Unlike his previous album, which was also cobbled together, this one is a wonderfully crafted selection that works as an entity.

COLUMBIA MASTERWORKS RECORDS | LONG PLAYING MICROGROOVE

MANUFACTURED IN CANADA BY SPARTON OF CANADA, LIMITED

FRANKLY SENTIMENTAL
FRANK SINATRA
with quintet accompaniment
and orchestra under the direction of
AXEL STORDAHL

Body and Soul | One For My Baby
Laura | Guess I'll Hang My Tears Out To Dry
Fools Rush In | When You Awake
Spring Is Here | It Never Entered My Mind

CL 6059
Nonbreakable Vinylite

SONG LINES

Recorded New York, except 'One For My Baby' and 'Guess I'll Hang My Tears Out to Dry', which were recorded in Hollywood. Chart: It failed to make the album charts.

SIDE 1

1. 'BODY AND SOUL'
(Johnny Green, Frank Eyton, Edward Heyman & Robert Sour) Recorded 9–10 November, 1947. This features some brilliant trumpet playing by Bobby Hackett. It's an old song from the 1930s play *Three's a Crowd*. It is one of two songs on the album that Frank didn't re-record and release later in his career, 'When You Awake' being the other. He did have a crack at 'Body and Soul' in 1984, when Bob James did the arrangement, with Quincy Jones producing. It certainly came nowhere close to matching the masterful performance that Frank gave nearly 40 years earlier… which is why it wasn't released. It stands as one of the high points in his 1940s canon.

2. 'LAURA'
(David Raksin & Johnny Mercer) Recorded 22–23 October, 1947. This beautiful melody, written by David Raksin (who as an arranger had worked with George Gershwin and Charlie Chaplin), is one that gets in your head and stays there. Frank did this song from the 1944 movie of the same name again in 1957. This version is way better, his younger voice for once more suitable to the feel of the song.

3. 'FOOLS RUSH IN'
(Rube Bloom & Johnny Mercer) Recorded October, 1947.

4. 'SPRING IS HERE'
(Richard Rodgers & Lorenz Hart) Recorded 31 October, 1947.

SIDE 2

1. 'ONE FOR MY BABY (AND ONE MORE FOR THE ROAD)'
(Harold Arlen & Johnny Mercer) Recorded 11 August, 1947. This saloon song, as it would become known, had originally been used in the 1943 film, The Sky's The Limit. This original version lacks the world-weariness that Frank would bring to it on his later recordings.

2. 'GUESS I'LL HANG MY TEARS OUT TO DRY'
(Jule Styne & Sammy Cahn) Recorded 30–31 July, 1946.

3. 'WHEN YOU AWAKE'
(Henry Nemo) Recorded 5–6 November, 1947. This song had been recorded by Frank when he was with Tommy Dorsey. This second reading was one of the few times that Frank went back to something and didn't improve on it. Neither did he do the song again, either at Capitol or Reprise. It is very much a period piece that lyrically and melodically wouldn't travel.

4. 'IT NEVER ENTERED MY MIND'
(Richard Rodgers & Lorenz Hart) Recorded 5–6 November, 1947.

> 66His voice still had the seamless, carefully articulated meaningful quality that could make everyone feel that he was sending a private message to him or her99
>
> **BILL GOTTLIEB, COVERING A 1947 RECORDING SESSION FOR *DOWNBEAT***

HIGH FLYER
If you wanted to know where the original idea for Frank's Come Fly With Me *album cover came from, look no further.*

FRANK IN BRITAIN

FRANK'S BRITISH SHEET MUSIC HITS

1946 (July–Dec)
'HOMESICK THAT'S ALL'
'OH WHAT IT SEEMED TO BE'
'DAY BY DAY'
'FIVE MINUTES MORE'

1947
'THE THINGS WE DID LAST SUMMER'
'TRY A LITTLE TENDERNESS'
'AMONG MY SOUVENIRS'
'TIME AFTER TIME'

'MAM'SELLE'
'THEY SAY IT'S WONDERFUL'
'OH WHAT A BEAUTIFUL MORNING'
'I'LL MAKE UP FOR EVERYTHING'

1948
'THE COFFEE SONG'
'THE GIRL THAT I MARRY'

1949
'WHILE THE ANGELUS WAS RINGING'

Frank's first solo release in Britain was 'A Lovely Way to Spend An Evening', from the film *Higher and Higher*. Released on the Columbia label (DB2141) in May 1944 it was followed 13 months later by Frank's recording with Harry James of 'All or Nothing At All' (Columbia DB 2145). There followed a steady stream of Frank's 78 rpm on the Columbia label.

With the war over and the availability of shellac once more in plentiful supply for the manufacture of records, Frank's release in Britain came thick and fast. After 'All or Nothing at All' came out in June there were another eight releases before the end of the year. In 1946 a total of 10 Frank Sinatra records hit the shops. Given the late entry of Frank into the British record selling business it is none too surprising to find that some of his recordings were "old" US releases. His third British release was 'You'll Never Know' backed by 'Sunday Monday or Always' which came out in June 1945. It had been a hit in America in the summer of 1943. Some British releases had two American 'A-sides' back to back, which of course made them a better buy for the British public and of course increased the sales. In some other cases British releases were records that had failed to make the American charts. 'When Your Lover Has Gone' paired with 'She's Funny That Way' from September 1945 being a good example.

SHEET MUSIC CHART

Britain, unlike the US, did not have record charts in the 40s. There was a sheet music chart of sorts and it is the only published data as to what records were hits. The first sheet music chart was available for the week of July 26, 1946 and even that was simply listed alphabetically. Just like in the US many artists released versions of the same song and Frank was no different. In Britain it was often the case that Frank's "hit" records were different from his stateside hits. Frank's popularity in Britain was as a result of his recordings and his films, there was no Sinatramania promulgated by the bobby-soxers. It is interesting that the drift downwards in popularity in America was mirrored in Britain. Given the fact that the 1946 "chart" only covers half the year, Frank's popularity in his first 'full year' of British releases was probably on a par with 1947. His allure to British audiences was ably aided and abetted by BBC radio. Following the Easter weekend of 1947 *Melody Maker* were even complaining that there should be more British talent played on the radio, saying, "it should have been tagged Easter with Bing, Frank, Inks and Mills." Frank's eventual drift downwards in popularity in the US at the end of the 1940s was mirrored in Britain.

As filming for *On the Town* finished, Frank played three dates at Atlantic City's Steel Pier over the weekend of 24 June supported by the Page Cavanaugh Trio. There followed two weeks of personal appearances in Canada before Frank headed back to the West Coast for a month's holiday. The Sinatras also moved from Toluca Lake to a $250,000 new home at 320 Carolwood Drive in Bel Air, where Walt Disney was a near neighbour.

On 10 and 14 July, Frank was in a New York recording studio cutting six songs that perfectly illustrated his current problems. 'It All Depends On You' and 'Bye Bye Baby' neatly sum up his dilemma over Ava and Nancy. Add to these 'Every Man Should Marry', 'If I Ever Love Again', and 'We're Just a Kiss Apart', and you have the soundtrack to Frank's summer of 1949. These sessions occurred almost exactly a decade after he cut his first record on 13 July, 1939, with the Harry James band, as he started out on his climb to fame and fortune. A lot had certainly happened in those ten years. With the decade coming to a close, Frank's old sparring partner, Lee Mortimer, declared that "The Swoon is real gone… the bobby-soxers had merely grown up and grown out of Sinatra."

1949 ON THE JUKEBOX

Frank's 59 weeks on the charts made 1949 a vast improvement on 1948, and the end of the musicians' strike meant that he could get back in the studio. In actual fact, 1949 was Frank's third best year of the decade in terms of weeks spent on the *Billboard* chart, and the second best of his solo career (in 1943 four of Frank's hits were with Harry James or Tommy Dorsey). But the figures mask the real truth: Frank's popularity was clearly not what it was. With his highest entry reaching only No 6, it meant that it was far from a stellar performance. Frank's rating at the end of year had him at a very unlucky No 13, well behind Perry Como (the year's top performer), Bing Crosby, and Frankie Laine.

Further evidence of Frank's decline in popularity lies in the fact that every song of his that made the charts was well beaten by one or several rival versions. It was almost as though Frank was going through the motions, recording what he was given and showing little originality in the choice of material. *Downbeat* even took Frank to task for some "off-pitch" notes in 'Some Enchanted Evening' and was highly critical of his rendition of 'Bali Ha'i'.

A record release with Frank's name on it was no guarantee of success either. In April, he released 'Night After Night' backed by 'The Right Girl for Me', but neither charted, despite the latter song coming from *Take Me Out to the Ball Game*. As the *Billboard* review said, "Sinatra isn't up to one of his more persuasive efforts here." Sadly, that could be taken to apply to the whole year.

Both the Rodgers and Hammerstein songs came from the hit Broadway show *South Pacific*, which starred Mary Martin and Ezio Pinza. None of Frank's other recordings is from the pens of any of his favoured writers. Of interest is the fact that the melody of 'Sunflower' was later used as the basis of the song 'Hello Dolly'. Frank recorded 'Sunflower' along with a small combo (steel guitar, guitar, bass, and drums), very much in a Country and Western

vein. It was cut on 6 December, 1948, Frank's first session after the Musicians' Union strike ended.

PERRY'S YEAR

With 15 hit records and two chart-toppers, 1949 was very definitely Perry Como's year, though former Dorsey band member and Pied Piper Jo Stafford pushed Perry hard, taking 14 records into the *Billboard* chart. Perry's first No 1 of the year was 'A You're Adorable', which very much summed up the Como vocal approach — he had none of Frank's intensity and was a quintessential light and easy-going singer. Besides Jo Stafford, two other female vocalists had a good year: Margaret Whiting just edged ahead of Evelyn Knight on the end-of-year points list. Evelyn had two No 1 records in the year, 'A Little Bird Told Me', which spent seven weeks at the top, followed by 'Powder Your Face With Sunshine'.

DISC WARS

In response to the challenge of Columbia's 33-rpm LP, RCA decided to take a different approach: they concentrated their research and development efforts on an alternative to the 78-rpm "single". RCA decided on 45 rpm for their singles by taking 78 and subtracting 33. A key player in RCA Victor's launch plan was a Blues singer named Arthur Crudup. The first 45 rpm in Victor's R&B series was 'That's All Right', recorded in September 1946, having already been released on 78 rpm. Some dynamic marketing executive had the idea of colour-coding the RCA releases: 'That's All Right' came out on orange vinyl, popular music on blue, and country records, rather appropriately, on green. While 'That's All Right' did get some airplay on black radio stations, it again failed to chart. But for a certain Mr Elvis Aron Presley, 'That's All Right' would have been no more than a footnote in recording history. Elvis covered the song in 1954 at Sun Studios with Scotty Moore and Bill Black, and while it was nothing more than a local hit, it put Elvis on the map… and gave not a few problems to Frank, Perry, and Co.

THE HITS

'SUNFLOWER'
(Mack David)
19 March, No 14, 5 weeks

'SOME ENCHANTED EVENING'
(Richard Rodgers & Oscar Hammerstein II)
11 June, No 6, 13 weeks

'THE HUCKLE-BUCK'
(Andy Gibson & Roy Alfred)
11 June, No 10, 14 weeks

'BALI HA'I'
(Richard Rodgers & Oscar Hammerstein II)
2 July, No 18, 5 weeks

'LET'S TAKE AN OLD FASHIONED WALK' (WITH DORIS DAY)
(Irving Berlin)
6 August, No 17, 6 weeks

'DON'T CRY JOE (LET HER GO, LET HER GO, LET HER GO)'
(Joe Marsala)
8 October, No 9, 12 weeks

'THAT LUCKY OLD SUN'
(Beasley Smith & Haven Gillespie)
29 October, No 14, 4 weeks

THE BRUNETTE

"Frank is through, in a year from now you won't hear anything about him."

GEORGE EVANS, CONFIDING TO THE
CRITIC EARL WILSON

In September 1949, *Newsweek* ran a piece about Frank's new Lucky Strike radio show. (Significantly, most of the report focused on his co-star, Dorothy Kirsten.) "The sometimes unruly crooner, whose exuberance over rapid fame has left him in staggering financial debt, could look to the show as a good boost back up the money trail." During the autumn, the show was just about Frank's only work, aside from sporadic recording sessions.

Frank was in New York City recording *Lite Up Times.* A few days later, on 8 December, Frank and Ava went to the opening night of the musical *Gentlemen Prefer Blondes,* starring Carol Channing, and from that moment their relationship became all too public. Without question, Frank very definitely preferred brunettes. The following evening, at Radio City Music Hall, Frank attended the premiere of *On the Town.* George Evans wasted no time in telling Frank that he had to keep Ava out of the spotlight if he wanted to have any chance of hanging on to his deal with MGM, a threat that equally applied to Ava's own MGM contract. Within a month, *On the Town* was breaking box-office records at Radio City, but in all honesty its success was largely due to Gene Kelly's performance and not to Frank's. Three days later, on Frank's 34th birthday (although his age was still being publicly quoted as 32), Jack Entratter, the manager of the Copacabana, threw a party. This time Ava stayed on the periphery to avoid any chance of being caught in an compromising photograph. Frank's friends were getting increasingly concerned about his behaviour. Just before Christmas, Frank got a telegram from Mafia man Willie Moretti: "I am very much surprised what I have been reading in the newspapers between you and your darling wife. Remember you have a decent wife and children. You should be very happy. Regards to all." Professionally, the year ended badly too, when Frank fell to No 5 on the *Downbeat* male vocalist poll, beaten by Billy Eckstine, Frankie Laine, Bing Crosby, and Mel Torme. As one critic noted, "The old screamers are now in their sedate twenties. And without hullabaloo, Frank's voice doesn't seem quite so potent."

Twelve days into the new decade, Frank was back on stage, his first concert appearance in two years. Hartford, Connecticut, was the venue. With Frank's record sales lower than ever and his film and radio work tailing off, it is surprising that Frank grossed over $18,000 for his two days at Hartford, or so it is claimed, though recent examination of both *Variety* and the *Hartford Courant* reveal no mention of this gig. At this point in his life, however,

AVA GARDNER
"Face of an angel, body of a goddess".

Frank probably did not care how much he got paid. He was so infatuated with Ava, so in love, so besotted by her, that he was suffering lover's negligence. While their affair was undoubtedly a tempestuous one, their volatile personalities making for a heady cocktail, it was passionate too. As the song says, "the best part of breaking up is when you're making up", and Frank and Ava did a lot of both. Interestingly, it was pure chance that allowed Frank and Ava to be together at the beginning of 1950. She had been due to leave to film in Europe in early January, but James Mason, her next co-star, was delayed making another film and so shooting was postponed. Perhaps if Ava had left in January then their affair might, like Frank's many others, have been just another affair, instead of an all-consuming passion.

THE END OF A PARTNERSHIP

George Evans was becoming increasingly frustrated at his waning influence on Frank, much like a parent feels for an errant son. Despite his best efforts, George could do little to control Frank's image once his affair with Ava had gone beyond the point of no return, and the relationship between the two men deteriorated. Sadly, fate foiled any chance of a reconciliation when George Evans died of a heart attack, aged just 48, at his home on the morning of 26 January. Friends said that the problems with Ava had really affected George, even though he was used to dealing with Frank's women.

Frank and Jimmy Van Heusen were in El Paso, Texas, en route to Houston when they heard of George Evans's death. Frank immediately flew to New York for the funeral on Friday 28 January at Park West Chapel. While Frank's professional relationship with George had effectively already ended, his death must have hit Frank harder than just about anything that had ever happened to him. Evans had, after all, been like a surrogate father, one who gave Frank direction, encouragement, and stability, which were the kind of things that his real father, Marty, couldn't provide. Whatever their arguments, Frank must have realized just what a loss George was going to be, and it was only a matter of days before it became apparent just how big a loss. With the affair with Ava racing along at full speed, a crash was inevitable.

DRAMA AND MELODRAMA

After the funeral, Frank headed back to Texas to fulfil his engagement at the newly opened Shamrock Hilton in Houston. One night, Frank and Ava, along with Jimmy Van Heusen, went to a restaurant. A photographer from the *Houston Post* headed towards their table. Realizing what was about to happen, Frank jumped up and moved to stop

> 66 Evans was credited, although disputed in some quarters, with the exploitation device that sent Frank Sinatra sky-rocketing. 99
>
> GEORGE EVANS' OBITUARY, *VARIETY*, 27 JANUARY, 1950

I MARRIED A COMMUNIST
The Communist witch-hunts of the McCarthy era, and the whole "red menace" threat permeated Hollywood in the early 1950s. There were many victims.

the man, or grab his camera. Ava started screaming, and next morning it was all over the *Houston Post*, and from there it was picked up by newspapers from coast to coast. Any lingering doubts about Frank and Ava that anyone, anywhere in the United States, had had were gone. For Nancy it was the final straw. Her Catholicism had kept her from seeking a divorce, but she immediately started the ball rolling towards a permanent separation. Nancy announced on Valentine's Day 1950 that she and Frank were separating: "married life with Frank has become most unhappy and almost unbearable".

It seemed that things couldn't get much worse but, just like in the movies, they did. Back in Hollywood, Frank cut two songs on 23 February. The first, with Jane Russell and the Modernaires, 'Kisses and Tears', was intended to promote the film *Double Dynamite*, although in the event, the film's release was delayed until December 1951. (With the press railing against Frank and Ava, RKO must have thought that an earlier release would be a waste of time. Frank's portrayal as "heartless" and Ava's as a "home wrecker" did not make for good box office returns.) The other song Frank cut that night was 'When the Sun Goes Down', which includes the lyrics "I'm feeling low, mighty low, I wonder why. I wonder why,

why am I such a lonely guy. A man is such a fool to be alone when the sun goes down." In many respects, this lyric sums Frank up: he needed Ava, and in Frank's mind it was Ava who was going to make everything alright. Throughout his life, the need not to be alone was one of his most defining characteristics.

It wasn't just in America that things were going downhill. In the 11 February edition of the UK's *Melody Maker*, a reporter criticized Frank's song 'It Happens Every Spring', saying "Sinatra makes the worst of it. He intones what surely must be about his most indifferent vocal to date. Frankie frankly sounds as though the whole business was a bore." In the same issue, a reporter bemoaned the death of George Evans, the man "who made Sinatra".

ARTFUL DECODANCE

A week or so later, Frank and Ava were in New York staying at the Hampshire House; it seemed as if they were taunting the press and public with their flagrant behaviour. "Stars staying at same hotel" said one paper – this was, after all, 1950, and morals were publicly, if not privately, very different. Frank and Ava attempted to defend themselves against the attacks by both saying, in their own way, that Frank and Nancy's marriage was over long before Ava came along. It was probably true, but would Frank have left Nancy for anyone other than Ava?

Their tempestuous affair had one of its first peaks, or troughs, at the Hampshire House. The elegant Art Deco building on Central Park South, with its rose-coloured marble floors in the lobby, was the inappropriate setting for one of Frank's more outrageous stunts. Frank and Ava shared a suite, maintaining at least the pretence of separate bedrooms with an adjoining living room. Ava had gone to see her ex-husband, Artie Shaw, and his girlfriend – an act guaranteed to bring on an attack of Italian jealousy. Frank went over to Artie's apartment, and after a minor row Ava headed back to the Hampshire House alone. She went to bed but was woken by the telephone; it was Frank: "'I can't stand it any longer. I'm going to kill myself – now.' Then there was a tremendous bang in my ear, and I knew it was a revolver shot. I threw the phone down and raced across the living room and into Frank's room. I didn't know what I expected to find – a body? And there was a body lying on the bed. Oh God was he dead? I threw myself on it saying 'Frank, Frank.' The face, with a rather pale little smile, turned toward me and the voice said, 'Oh hello'." Frank had fired a single shot into the mattress, trying to muffle it further with a pillow. A stupid, overly dramatic thing to do, and one that nearly got him into more trouble than he bargained for. Others at the Hampshire House had heard the shot and soon there was banging at the door asking if Frank was OK. "Gunshot, what gunshot?" said Frank, who managed to convince the police that nothing had happened. In her autobiography, Ava said that Frank

DEDICATED TO YOU

Frank's fifth Columbia album came out in March 1950, just prior to his run at New York's Copacabana club. It was another with a loose theme, but a less cohesive one than his previous efforts. Columbia delved even further into the vaults for this selection. The oldest recording was five years old and the newest still over three years, and in some cases it shows. Like its predecessor, it failed to trouble the charts and was released as a 78-rpm album set as well as a 10-inch LP. The big album at this time was Doris Day and Harry James's *Young Man With A Horn* from the movie loosely based on the life of trumpeter Bix Beiderbecke.

SONG LINES

Recorded: New York ('The Music Stopped', 'Strange Music', & 'None But The Lonely Heart'), the remainder in Hollywood. Chart: it failed to chart.

SIDE 1
1. 'THE MUSIC STOPPED'
(Jimmy McHugh & Harold Adamson) Recorded 29 October, 1947.

2. 'THE MOON WAS YELLOW'
(Fred Ahlert & Edgar Leslie) Recorded 27 August, 1945.

3. 'I LOVE YOU'
(Edvard Greig, George Forrest & Robert Wright) Recorded 30 July, 1946. This and the album's next song came from the hit Broadway musical *Song of Norway*, about the life of Norwegian composer Edvard Greig.

4. 'STRANGE MUSIC'
(Edvard Greig, Robert Wright & George Forrest) Recorded 22 October, 1947.

SIDE 2
1. 'WHERE OR WHEN'
(Richard Rodgers & Lorenz Hart) Recorded 29 January, 1945. This recording sounds well

out of step with the rest of the album and you marvel at Columbia putting out a five-year-old song.

2. 'NONE BUT THE LONELY HEART'
(Peter Ilyich Tchaikovsky & B Westbrook, Edward Brandt & Gus Kahn) Recorded 26 October, 1947.

3. 'ALWAYS'
(Irving Berlin) Recorded 9 January, 1947.

4. 'WHY WAS I BORN?'
(Jerome Kern & Oscar Hammerstein) Recorded 27 December, 1947.

ON THE TOWN

THE INSPIRATION FOR WHAT has been described as the East Coast version of *Anchors Aweigh* was Leonard Bernstein's ballet *Fancy Free*. MGM had secured the film rights even before the show hit Broadway in December 1944. Apparently, Louis B Mayer was a little hasty in paying the $250,000 for the rights, because when he saw the stage show he described it as "communistic".

It was Gene Kelly's determination to appear in the movie version that got the project rolling; he even persuaded Mayer to allow him to make this his directorial debut. Kelly wanted Frank and Jules Munshin to reprise their success in *Take Me Out to the Ballgame*. Frank was at first a little reluctant, perhaps because he was acutely aware that he was playing second fiddle to Kelly. Despite the fact that Frank was regarded as having second billing, however, advertising at the time showed Frank alongside Kelly.

Unusually, Kelly wanted the whole thing shot on location in New York, making it an even more ambitious project. Arthur Freed, the head of MGM's musical unit, was far from happy with Bernstein's music, and so only four of his pieces were included in the final film, including 'New York, New York'. Additional lyrics and music were commissioned from Roger Edens, Betty Comden, and Adolph Green; Comden and Green also wrote the screenplay.

The challenge of learning what Gene Kelly described as "real dancing", rather than what he had done in *Anchors Aweigh*, was daunting, but Frank accomplished the task, learning his routines quickly. His real headache was down to his appearance: Technicolor film was far less forgiving of the lines on his face and his noticeable lack of hair. A hairpiece was demanded by MGM, and Frank agreed. Frank also had some padding put in his sailor suit to round out his rather non-existent buttocks.

The simple story concerns three sailors – Gabey (Kelly), Chip (Frank), and Ozzie (Munshin) – "on the town" in New York on a 24-hour pass. Gabey falls for a girl he thinks is a top model, when all she does is work at Coney Island. Retiring Chip gets involved with a lady cab driver, while a gorgeous anthropologist views Ozzie as a perfect example of a "prehistoric man". The film is made up of some great music and some wonderful location shots, making it a visually and aurally stimulating film rather than one of real substance. Kelly was rarely less than brilliant when he danced, and while Frank gets no solo songs to sing, the material is strong enough to raise it well above anything else from the period. The reviews were certainly good: "Never before has any motion picture grossed as much in one day in any theatre anywhere," reported the *Motion Picture Daily*.

CAST & CREDITS

Gene Kelly	Gabey
Frank Sinatra	Chip
Betty Garrett	Brunhilde Esterhazy
Ann Miller	Claire Huddesen
Jules Munshin	Ozzie
Vera-Ellen	Ivy Smith, "Miss Turnstiles"

Directors	Stanley Donen, Gene Kelly
Producer	Arthur Freed
Cinematography	Harold Rosson
Original Music	Leonard Bernstein, Roger Edens

ON THE TOWN
Left to right: Vera-Ellen, Gene Kelly, Ann Miller, Jules Munshin, Betty Garrett, and Frank Sinatra

AVA GARDNER

"She can't act, she can't talk, she's sensational."

CONSENSUS OF OPINION ON AVA'S SCREEN TEST

AVA LAVINIA GARDNER WAS A RARITY BECAUSE SHE KEPT HER OWN NAME WHEN SHE BEGAN WORKING IN FILMS. BORN IN GRABTOWN, NORTH CAROLINA, ON 24 DECEMBER, 1922, HER PARENTS BARELY MADE A LIVING FARMING TOBACCO.

By the time she was 17 years old and 5 ft 6 in tall, green-eyed Ava was stunning. Her sister Bappie's husband, Larry Tarr, a photographer, took pictures of Ava when she visited them in New York City. He put one in the window of his studio, which attracted the attention of MGM. She signed to the studio in 1941, for the fee of $50 a week, and remained under contract to them for the next 17 years.

She married Mickey Rooney in 1941, having met him while touring the MGM lot. Sadly, the marriage to one of Hollywood's biggest stars would last just 17 months. Soon after her marriage, Ava appeared in *We Were Dancing*, the first of many small parts during the next three years, often with little more than a line of dialogue. (Initially, her Southern accent was so strong that she needed voice lessons.) Her first solid part came in *Whistle Stop* (1946), with George Raft. In the same year, she was "lent" to Universal Studios to film the successful *The Killers* (for which she earned $350 a week). After her divorce from Rooney, she married bandleader

Artie Shaw in 1945, despite being pursued by film producer Howard Hughes; the marriage lasted little over a year. According to *Time* magazine in September 1951, "She is far from being the most beautiful babe in the Hollywoods. Her figure is not the best (she is a trifle skinny and her legs are only average.)"

Despite – or perhaps because of – notoriety through her short-lived marriages and involvement with Frank Sinatra, it took until 1953, when John Ford cast her in *Mogambo*, for her star to rise high: she was nominated for an Oscar. Indeed it has even been said that MGM simply used her as a means to add gloss to enhance some of their weaker movies. This was something that inevitably affected Ava's confidence in her own abilities.

In 1954, she made *The Barefoot Contessa* and two years later starred in *Bhowani Junction*. Disillusioned with Hollywood, she moved to Spain before settling in London in the late 1960s. Her last major role to receive critical acclaim was in 1964's *Night of the Iguana*.

Although considered by many to have been the most beautiful actress in Hollywood, Ava almost certainly failed to realize her potential; it's as though she almost tried to belie her looks. After moving to London, she worked only occasionally, and then just for the money. She had a stroke in 1989, after which Frank took care of her medical and personal costs. Ava died of pneumonia in London on 25 January, 1990, at the age of 67. She was buried in Smithfield, North Carolina, in the family plot.

INTIMATE DATA ON YOUR FAVORITE STARS, AND OVER 90 EXCITING PICTURES

SCREEN ALBUM 1/-

DELL

Special

SHIRLEY TEMPLE SCRAPBOOK

Ava Gardner

66 If I were a man I wouldn't like me. **99**

AVA GARDNER, IN HER AUTOBIOGRAPHY

SCREEN GODDESS
Ava was what the movie press adored – a beautiful face who loved the camera.

should have won an Oscar for his performance. Fortunately their co-habiting at the same hotel came to an end when Ava left New York for her first trip outside the US: she was finally to begin filming with James Mason on *Pandora and the Flying Dutchman* in England and Spain. Frank stayed behind to open at the Copacabana on 28 March, the start of a busy month. He was recording his nightly *Lite Up Times* radio show, as well as appearing three times a night at the club and on top of that there were some recording sessions at which he cut nine songs, more than he had recorded in the previous five months.

THE VOICE-LESS

For the first time in his career, Frank was having trouble with his voice. One critic noted, "He's letting the orchestra drown out his inability to reach the romantic peaks of his songs." The *Herald Tribune* gave Frank a lacklustre review: "Whether temporary or otherwise, the music that used to hypnotize the bobby-soxers – whatever happened to them anyway, thank goodness? – is gone from the throat. Vocally, there isn't quite the same old black magic there used to be when Mr Sinatra wrenched 'Night and Day' from his sapling frame and thousands swooned… He relies on what vocal tones are operating effectively… He uses carefully made musical arrangements during which the orchestra does the heavy work at crucial points."

Finally, on 26 April, disaster struck: Frank lost his voice. It happened at about 2:00 am during Frank's last show of the night. 'I Have But One Heart', dedicated to Ava, went fine, but then during his second song, 'It All Depends on You', he went for a high note and… zilch, "nothing came out, absolutely nothing. Just dust", is how Frank later recalled the incident. Skitch Henderson, who conducted the band on *Lite Up Times*, was backing Frank and he for one was not surprised, "Frank was burning the candle at both ends." The cigarettes, the whisky, the late nights, the stress of his separation from Nancy, the pressure from the press, and, on top of everything, Ava being away. Frank, who went deathly white, quickly left the stage, where he began coughing up blood, out of sight of the audience. The 70 or so people in the Copacabana must have wondered what was happening. A doctor who came to check Frank told him he had haemorrhaged his vocal chords and would have to remain silent for a week. Tricky for anyone – a mountain for Frank.

As it happened, the bad press for the Copacabana shows was the least of Frank's worries; he was about to be fired by MGM. Frank's behaviour and the old morals clause have often been quoted as the cause, but Frank was no worse than many actors and even a good deal better than some when it came to his off-screen behaviour. The most likely reason is simply that Frank was a fading star. The success of *On the Town* owed little to Frank, according to the critics, and even less in Louis B Mayer's eyes. All in all, Frank's performances for MGM had failed to bring in the money they had been expecting, which gave them reason enough to fire him. There was also the little matter of Frank's big mouth. A few months earlier, Mayer had hurt himself in a riding accident. One day, at lunch in the MGM canteen, Frank made fun of Mayer's accident, saying it was more likely that he'd fallen off Ginny Simms (an actress who was Mayer's mistress). When Mayer heard that Frank had made fun of Ginny, he is said to have been incandescent. Mayer confronted Frank, who was taken aback that he had even heard his comment, saying "I want you to leave here, and I don't ever want you to come back again." When your luck runs out it is easy to think that people and events are conspiring against you, and in Frank's case they may well have been. There was also talk that Frank's agent was unhappy about continuing to represent him. For now, these threats came to nothing, but Hollywood was a small town where behind-the-scenes ripples make for very big waves.

TOTEM OF THE TEARFUL

Frank's response to his vocal problems was to go to Miami for ten days' rest in the sun before heading for Spain to join Ava on location. He had to cancel a booking in Chicago, which strained his relationship with MCA still further, although he went to the trouble of having a statement issued saying he was taking "a voice vacation". Frank was probably drawn to Spain for two reasons – he loved and missed Ava, but he may also have heard that she was having an on-set fling with a Spanish actor, Mario Cabre, who played a bullfighter in the movie. Cabre even wrote a poem about Ava, which would be published in 1951: "In my breast you will still remain/With a throbbing that recalls you/London will see you arriving/With your waist slim like a palm tree."

According to Ava, they only went to bed once, but this news was hardly likely to placate Frank. When he arrived in Tossa de Mar, Cabre was, diplomatically, well out of the way shooting in another area.

After a week in Spain, Frank flew back to California via Paris and New York. Frank was anxious to see if he would be granted a divorce, but there was no softening in Nancy's attitude. So it was back on a plane to New York in time for Frank to make his first television appearance, on Bob Hope's television show, *Star Spangled Review*. Looking tanned and a lot better than on his last public engagement, at the Copacabana, Frank did a great performance of 'Come Rain or Come Shine'. He also did a couple of comedy skits, one in which he played Bing Crosby, along with the show's other guests, Peggy Lee and Beatrice Lillie. At one

RELAXED
After ten days in the Florida sun, Frank, looking tanned and healthy, leaves New York's Idlewild airport for Spain, and Ava.

IT'S A CAMERA
Jimmy Van Heusen showing Ava his camera in Spain, watched by Ava's co-star Sheila Sim and Frank.

1946 1952

THE STRATOCRUISER
Back then air travel really was for the rich and famous, and definitely not for "poor people". On the Stratocruiser the really rich and famous, like Frank and Ava, travelled in first class on the upper deck. They would slip downstairs to the lower deck for a drink at the cocktail bar.

point Frank asks Bob how he looks…"like a breadstick with legs," says Hope. Half a decade later, when Frank was interviewed by Ed Morrow, he thanked Hope for coming to his rescue when his career was in such jeopardy. Coming so soon after the problems at the Copacabana, it is easy to see why he held such views. Or was it all part of some latter-day myth making? Many years later, Frank told interviewer Arlene Francis "I didn't speak for forty days,

MITCH MILLER

"Keep it simple, keep it sexy, keep it sad." MITCH MILLER

BORN ON 4 JULY, 1911, IN ROCHESTER, NEW YORK, MITCHELL MILLER HAD PIANO LESSONS BEFORE SWITCHING TO THE OBOE. AFTER GRADUATING IN MUSIC, HE BEGAN HIS CAREER WORKING FOR THE CBS SYMPHONY ORCHESTRA, LATER TURNING SOLO.

After recording in the first half of the 1940s with Andre Kostelanetz and Percy Faith, Miller joined Mercury Records as Head of A&R, signing Frankie Laine and Patti Page. Goddard Lieberson, the President of Columbia, an old college friend of Miller, enticed him away to run their A&R after Manie Sacks quit. Miller continued the formula he had begun at Mercury and continued to be extraordinarily successful, with everyone, that is, except Frank Sinatra.

Miller worked with Guy Mitchell, Doris Day, Tony Bennett, Jerry Vale, Rosemary Clooney, and Johnny Ray. He also took Frankie Laine to Columbia, where he had over 30 *Billboard* hits. Miller also had a recording career of his own, scoring a No 3 hit with 'Tzena, Tzena, Tzena' in 1950. By the late 1950s, he was recording a series of albums entitled *Sing Along with Mitch*, which later spawned a television series. The "sing along with Mitch" concept was as far away from

rock 'n' roll as you could imagine, and it was this factor that ultimately brought about his downfall at Columbia. There was need for change, and Miller couldn't or wouldn't; he even turned down Buddy Holly for a recording contract.

With Columbia's fortunes in decline, it was a jazz and blues producer named John Hammond who helped with Miller's eventual demise when he signed a young singer named Bob Dylan. Miller left the company and, apart from recording light orchestral works, he virtually disappeared. His legacy is a tarnished one, but he was the man for a while. When Frankie Laine topped the UK charts for 27 weeks in 1953, they were all produced by Mitch Miller, and three other Miller-produced records made the top of the charts in the UK during the same year, giving him an incredible 38 weeks at No 1. This is a record for a producer and one that will probably never be beaten.

for forty days I didn't say a single word." As Frank told *Playboy* in 1963 "When I sing, I believe, I'm honest." Not everyone thought that Frank was right for television: "If TV is his oyster, Sinatra hasn't broken out of his shell", said *Variety* on 5 June. Three weeks later, as President Truman was ordering American troops into Korea, Frank was in the studio cutting Lead Belly's 'Goodnight Irene' and 'Dear Little Boy of Mine' with the Mitch Miller singers… they were ghastly records. Having cancelled his planned shows in Britain in 1949, Frank finally made it to the UK on 30 June, 1950; appropriately he was booked into London's Palladium. There was a certain amount of indecision about the proposed concerts, but no doubt the money was appealing, and by early July the press confirmed that Frank would appear from Monday 10 to Sunday 23 July. A picture on the front of *The Melody Maker* "snapped at rehearsals" shows a smiling Frank looking thinner than ever.

FRANK IS IN THE AIR

According to *Variety* on 5 July, "American Airlines is awaiting reports on the feasibility of installing pianos in its overseas Stratocruisers, following an experimental songfest led by Frank Sinatra last week aboard the London-bound Continental Mercury. Sinatra sang to and with passengers, with Ken Lane, his accompanist, playing piano. Music was piped from the lower to the upper main passenger deck. Songs were also broadcast from the plane to the crew of the US Coast Guard floating weather station Charlie, stationed about 900 miles from Newfoundland. Early reports indicated passengers liked the idea, but no decision on installation of pianos will be made until complete reports are in."

The Melody Maker also made another announcement: "A few hours previously Frank had received confirmation of the US television and radio contract that puts him above even Bing Crosby as the world's highest paid singer – a $1 million contract with the Columbia Broadcasting Company of America." While this statement was essentially true, what it omitted to say was that this was not a $1 million deal as such, but rather a (potential) five-year contract worth $200,000 a year for Frank's television shows. Still, the way the paper put it made Frank sound very successful, which is what media hype and showbiz gloss are all about. When Frank started his

concerts in London, it must have been like turning the clock back, since the British equivalent of the bobby-soxers were out in force for the first night. The press, as usual, was sharply divided as to his appeal. Harold Hobson writing in the *Sunday Times* made some very astute observations: "People who simply put Frank down as 'the Voice' are missing the point. It is not the voice but the smile that does such enormous, such legendary execution … the shy deprecating smile, with a quiver at the corner of the mouth. To a people whose ideal of manhood is husky, full blooded and self reliant he has chosen to suggest that under the crashing self assertion, man is only a child, frightened and whimpering in the dark." While it may be a touch hyperbolic, it did get to the heart of Frank's appeal. A US paper assessed the situation succinctly, saying, "Sinatra big box office in UK". Frank would remain forever "big box office" in Britain. The *New Musical Express* reporter was a little more straightforward: "I watched mass hysteria. Was it wonderful? Decidedly so, for this man Sinatra is a superb performer and a great artist. He had his audience spellbound." The *Daily Express* called him "The Ambassador of Miserabilism," and said, "He is thin-faced, tired looking, carries that world-weary look which comes of being so long a totem of the tearful."

Frank, backed by Woolf Phillips and the Skyrockets Orchestra, was still not in the best of voice, but with Ava in London to wrap up her filming it at least meant that he was feeling less stress in that direction, although on 15 July he had to leave the stage after performing the 'Soliloquy' from *Carousel* "looking tired and grey" said *The Times*. The following night Frank flew to Blackpool to play the Opera House: his fee was $5,000.

Ava's presence in London and the openness of her affair with a married man even aroused the ire of the clergy. One minister used his sermon to address declining moral standards: "painted trollops who worship at the shrine of Saint Ava Gardner" is how he put it. It really was another world back then. Ironically, Mack Miller, Frank's publicist, wrote to American journalist Hedda Hopper on 15 July, eulogizing over Frank's success in Britain in a three-page letter that sounds alternately desperate and fantasizing to show how popular Frank was in Britain.

Frank arrived home as 'Goodnight Irene' was entering the charts. The record made it to No 5. It was another of his records that probably sold more because of the song than for Frank's performance, since it was a cover of the Weavers' (a group led by Pete Seeger) version of a 1930s Lead Belly song. Gordon Jenkins and His Orchestra accompanied the Weavers, and they stayed at No 1 for 13 weeks. In August, Frank was back on stage in Atlantic City and went to a radio station to be interviewed by Ben Heller, who used to play with the Harry James band. Heller played 'Goodnight

TV NATION

IN 1950 THERE WERE 10.5 MILLION SETS IN THE US, BY 1957 THERE WERE MORE THAN 47 MILLION. TELEVISION WAS A CATALYST FOR CHANGE, RADICALLY INFLUENCING HOW PEOPLE BOTH HEARD AND *SAW* MUSIC.

AS THE DECADE WORE ON, Frank's TV appearances represented the music of an older generation Elvis, in the early days, had to be filmed from the waist up to spare the delicate sensibilities of the American public, there was never any hesitation in showing Frank from head to toe. *The Frank Sinatra Show* premiered on the CBS television network on October 7 1950; TV turned out to be the least successful aspect of Frank's career. It was also a case of bad timing given the state of his career and personal life. Columbia may have seen it as some sort of last ditch effort to kick start his career. It aired on Saturday nights from 9:00 until 10:00 pm head to head with NBC's *Your Show of Shows*. Accounts of Frank's on set antics, possibly fuelled by jealousy for what Ava may or may not have been doing, paint a dismal picture. Producer Irving Mansfield claimed, "He hated to rehearse, and refused to discuss the weekly format. Usually he ignored the guest shots entirely." He was often three hours late for rehearsals. As the *New York Times* saw it "Sinatra walked off the TV high dive but unfortunately fell into the shallow end of the pool". While the *Herald Tribune* saw "a surprisingly good actor but a rather bad emcee".

Your Show of Shows first aired in February 1950 and ran until 1954; it starred Carl Reiner, Sid Caesar and Imogene Coca. *TV Guide* named it as one of the greatest shows of all time, influencing television, film, and comedy theatre. The writers who got their start on the show included: Woody Allen, Mel Brooks and Neil Simon.

Axel Stordahl conducted the orchestra and Frank's show regularly featured the former lead singer of the Pied Pipers, June Hutton. On January 27 1951 Frank announced Axel and Jane's engagement on screen. This first series ran until June 9 1951, and the second series began on October 9 1951, it finished on June 11 1952. It would be five years before Frank had another regular series. The best thing about the show was the music. Frank not only used Axel's arrangements, but also George Siravo, who would feature prominently in his early Capitol career.

Guests on the first series of *The Frank Sinatra Show* included Georgia Gibbs, Phil Silvers, Don Ameche, Dick Haymes, Frankie Laine, Dagmar, Lionel Hampton, and Eileen Barton (who had been regular on the radio series *Frank Sinatra in Person*). On the second series Perry Como, Frankie Laine, the Andrews Sisters, Jack Benny, Louis Armstrong, and Tennessee Ernie Ford all appeared.

FRANK'S SHOW
The show was fairly predictable fodder. It featured Frank singing, showing off his comedic skills, as well as guests in what now seem like dated sketches.

HAVE I GOT A SONG FOR YOU

Mitch Miller meeting Frank in New York prior to a fateful recording session.

THE FABULOUS FIFTIES

In 1950 the population of the United States was a little over 150 million people. Post-war unemployment was on the way down and dropped from 5.3 per cent in 1950 to 2.9 per cent in 1952. A wave of optimism swept the nation with the dawning of the new decade.

Radio continued to be a powerful medium, although one that was less and less relevant to Frank. During the decade the number of radio stations grew from under 3,000 to nearly 4,000, offering listeners greater choice. The growth in car ownership meant more people listened to the radio, and it was especially the young who felt the power of radio.

Despite the efforts of Frank, and many others who dedicated their lives to the cause of anti-racial segregation, the early part of the decade was still one of terrible discrimination. In 1952 the University of Tennessee admitted its first black student and the US Supreme Court upheld a decision to ban segregation on trains; a significant move as rail accounted for almost half of US domestic travel. Two years later the Supreme Court unanimously decided that segregation was unconstitutional. It would take one of the greatest leaders of the modern world, Martin Luther King Jr, to facilitate further change.

Irene' and said to Frank, "Hey, that's a nice tune." "You wanna bet…. Naw, it's really cute." "You ought to do a lot of songs like that." "Don't hold your breath," was Frank's emphatic reply. It cannot have pleased Mitch Miller, who had replaced Manie Sacks as Columbia's head of A&R, to hear their star run down his own records. Ironically it became Frank's biggest record of the year.

Frank was now shuttling back and forth between Hollywood and New York. In California, he and Ava rented a beach house to avoid the prying press, where they tried to get their lives together. Break-ups, new relationships, and divorce are all stressful situations even when no third parties are involved. New relationships that come hard on the heels of a marriage, or are the cause of a break-up, often flounder and fail even without the level of external pressure experienced by Frank and Ava. While they were not "easy" people, it is hard not to feel some level of compassion for them. With hindsight, we know that Frank was destined to become an even bigger star than Ava, but it is all too easy to forget that, back then, he had little idea of what was happening or any inkling of what his future would be. He was living his life in a goldfish bowl, surrounded by an inquisitive American media, and to make matters worse, tensions between Frank and Ava sometimes got reported, which probably caused yet more arguments. On one occasion, Ava reportedly said cruelly "He's a has been." At this point he wasn't quite, but he was well on his way.

SEPARATE WAYS

While Frank was in New York, the break-up from Nancy was coming to a legal head back in California. On 28 September, at a court in Santa Monica, Judge Orlando Rhodes granted a sobbing Nancy maintenance on her separation from Frank. She had testified that Frank had humiliated her by going to their Palm Springs home, with its F-shaped swimming pool, for weekends without her. She was granted custody of 10-year-old Nancy Jr, 6-year-old Frank Jr, and 2-year-old Tina, and she got the house in Holmby Hills, its contents, a 1950 Cadillac, furs, jewellery, and a third of Frank's income up to $150,000 per annum. Thereafter she got 10 per cent and was never to receive less than $1,000 per month. Frank got to keep his 1949 Cadillac, a jeep, the $180,000 house in Palm Springs, oil interests in Austin, Texas, and his recording royalties. The latter, of course, were much reduced and were set to get a great deal smaller.

One small piece of detail in the court report speaks volumes about Frank and goes to the heart of his character. There was mention of a $10,000 emerald necklace that Frank bought for Ava when he went to Spain; Spanish Customs even impounded it for a while. When he travelled home via Paris, he bought Nancy a gold charm bracelet. This much cheaper gift may have been prompted by guilt, although they were already separated, but it shows how

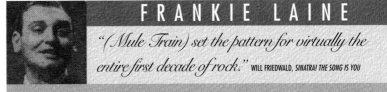

FRANKIE LAINE

"(Mule Train) set the pattern for virtually the entire first decade of rock." WILL FRIEDWALD, SINATRA! THE SONG IS YOU

NO ONE, CERTAINLY NOT FRANK, EQUALLED THE RECORD SET BY THIS MAN WHEN HE TOPPED THE BRITISH SINGLES CHART IN 1953 WITH 'I BELIEVE'. IT'S A RECORD THAT WILL NEVER BE BEATEN.

Born Francis Paul LoVechio on 13 March, 1913, in Chicago's Little Italy, he was the oldest of eight children of Sicilian immigrants. After singing in a choir he won a competition on a radio station, which is when he was persuaded to change his name to Frankie Laine.

At 19, he won a dance marathon in Atlantic City and later took up singing. By 1937, he had joined the Frankie Carlone Band, replacing Perry Como. He moved to Los Angeles, where he worked on a wartime factory line while singing at night. He first recorded for the Exclusive label in 1945, before Mitch Miller signed him to Mercury in 1947. He scored his first hit in March of the same year with 'That's My Desire'. Before the decade was out 'That Lucky Old Sun' and 'Mule Train' both topped the charts.

He had 59 hits on the *Billboard* chart and was also very popular in Britain. Among his many UK hits were four No 1 records. In 1953, he topped the British charts for a record 27 weeks.

In 1959, he sang the theme for the TV series *Rawhide*, starring Clint Eastwood. Fifteen years later, Mel Brooks advertised for a 'Frankie Laine-type' voice to sing the title song for his new movie, *Blazing Saddles*. Frankie Laine applied and got the job! He retired in the mid-1980s.

BIGGEST HITS
'That Lucky Old Sun' (US No 1, 1949)
'Mule Train' (US No 1, 1949)
'The Cry of the Wild Goose' (US No 1, 1950)
'Jezebel' (US No 2, 1951)
'I Believe' (US No 2; UK No 1, 1953)

very complex Frank was – how he still sought Nancy's approval, even while selfishly pursuing what he wanted, which was Ava.

There was no doubt at all that the separation was rough on the children. Daughter Nancy recalled crying herself to sleep, having been told by her mother, "Daddy's just on the road again". Tina, by her own admission, was too young to remember what was really happening, although she later recalled that she had to deal with "this very nice man coming through our lives from time to time". Meanwhile, Frank Jr had no inkling of what he would have to try to live up to.

MITCH AND MITCHELL

Most of the autumn of 1950 was taken up with the television series of *The Frank Sinatra Show*, which was made in New York, along with a few recording sessions. By mid-November, Ava was back in Hollywood to start work on her new movie, *Showboat*. The animosity that existed between Frank and Mitch Miller, the Columbia A&R boss, reached a crescendo around this time.

Miller met Frank, Hank Sanicola, and Ben Barton at the airport early one morning and took them to the studio to cut two songs, 'The Roving Kind' and 'My Heart Cries for You'. The musicians were all booked and everything set up in anticipation of Frank's arrival. After listening to what

SING AND DANCE WITH SINATRA

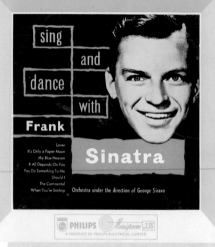

sing and dance with Frank Sinatra

Lover
It's Only a Paper Moon
My Blue Heaven
It All Depends On You
You Do Something To Me
Should I
The Continental
When You're Smiling

Orchestra under the direction of George Siravo

PHILIPS Minigroove 33⅓
A PRODUCT OF PHILIPS ELECTRICAL LIMITED

REFLECTED GLORY
This 10-inch album came out in Britain in October 1954 on the Philips label (they marketed Columbia's material in Britain). It was the first example of a rival label trying to "capitalize" on Frank's new-found success. It was released the month before Frank's second Capitol album.

❝We've got a lot of Jazz things I'd like you to watch for.❞
FRANK TO BEN HELLER ON RADIO IN ATLANTIC CITY, 1950

ALTHOUGH FRANK'S FINAL COLUMBIA ALBUM CAME OUT AS A 78-RPM PACKAGE AND A 10-INCH VINYL DISC, IT WAS THE FIRST CONCEIVED SPECIFICALLY FOR THE NEW LP FORMAT.

APPARENTLY, MOST OF IT was recorded over two days in April 1950 (14th and 24th) with George Siravo conducting the orchestra. Apparently, because there is some doubt that Frank did these sessions on those days. After all, it was just two days after the second session that he suffered his vocal haemorrhage. Listening carefully to the songs it is possible, in a few places, to hear the strain in his voice. According to Charles Granata's excellent book, *Sessions with Sinatra*, Frank overdubbed his vocals later. Mitch Miller was the source of this information and it was done secretly to avoid any problems with the unions.

It was Miller who got Siravo to write the arrangements on this album, which means he was far from all bad! It proved to everyone that Frank could swing, and you wonder whether it was this album that may have been at the back of Alan Livingston's mind when he signed Frank two and a half years later. Seven of the songs on the album appeared on *Sinatra's Swingin' Session* with Nelson Riddle in 1961.

In *Billboard* on 24 December, 1949 there was a fascinating article under the headline "Sinatra's Pioneering Thoughts on LP Pop Tune Production" It talks of Frank being the first noted pop artist to voice his theories on the fact "that LP calls for new orientation and pioneering. (It) calls for an entirely new approach to recording – from the artists' point of view." He said that people were still thinking of LPs as they thought of 78-rpm albums. "Artists and A&R men will have to pioneer in the use of script material in conjunction with music, the representation of musical sketches, commentary, narrative and mood music. Twenty minutes of "time" on each side will call for much more of a production package." It shows how far ahead Frank was in his thinking. It can only have added to his frustration with Mitch Miller and Columbia. It must also have been maddening that at the very moment that the LP was on the up, Frank was on the down. None of Frank's last three Columbia albums hit the charts.

SONG LINES
Recorded: New York. Charts : It failed to chart.

SIDE 1

1. 'LOVER'
(Richard Rodgers & Lorenz Hart) Recorded 14 April, 1950. This track, like many on this wonderfully upbeat album, is something of a homage to Sy Oliver's arrangements when he was working for Jimmy Lunceford.

2. 'IT'S ONLY A PAPER MOON'
(Harold Arlen, Billy Rose & E Y Harburg) Recorded 24 April, 1950. Frank had been doing this song on radio since the mid-40s with an almost identical arrangement. His familiarity with the material helped him deliver a great performance.

3. 'MY BLUE HEAVEN'
(Walter Donaldson & George Whiting) Recorded 24 April, 1950. This track really swings. It is the one where you can hear some fragility in Frank's voice. Apparently Frank so liked the feel on this version that he decided not to go back and try and better his vocal.

4. 'IT ALL DEPENDS ON YOU'
(Ray Henderson, B G DeSylva & Lew Brown) Recorded 10 July, 1949. This track had Hugo Winterhalter conducting the orchestra, although it was still a George Siravo arrangement.

SIDE 2

1. 'YOU DO SOMETHING TO ME'
(Cole Porter) Recorded 14 April, 1950.

2. 'SHOULD I'
(Nacio Herb Brown & Arthur Freed) Recorded 14 April, 1950. If you want evidence of Frank's lack of buyer appeal, then there is no better track than this. Frank swings as hard and as well as he does on any track from the Capitol era. Swinging Frank was just not something that the public wanted.

3. 'THE CONTINENTAL'
(Con Conrad & Herb Magidson) Recorded 24 April, 1950. From Fred Astaire's 1934 film, *The Gay Divorcee*.

4. 'WHEN YOU'RE SMILING'
(Larry Shay, Mark Fisher & Joe Goodwin) Recorded 24 April, 1950. With almost anyone else this song sounds contrived, Frank made it convincing.

he was expected to sing, Frank gave his verdict: "I'm not going to do any of that crap." Now, given the fact that Frank would get to record some far worse material in 1951, it speaks volumes of how Frank must have been feeling. Then again, perhaps he still had not fully grasped the way things were going, either with the taste of the nation or his own career.

After Frank's refusal, Miller got hold of a young singer whom he had just signed and spent all day working on the songs; cutting them later that night. 'My Heart Cries for You' made No 2 in the chart and launched Guy Mitchell's career. The failure of the television series to excite anyone,

least of all Frank, must have made this a miserable time. Being away from California meant that Frank also saw little of his children, which hurt. Professionally, though not commercially, something good did happen, however: Frank began a new Sunday afternoon NBC radio show, *Meet Frank Sinatra*. There were signs at least in the songs, if not in the banal studio banter, that Sinatra's voice and eye for a good song were at least back to something like their best.

However, with the end of the year approaching, Frank's life took an unexpected turn. In September 1950, the FBI files show that Frank made an approach, through an intermediary, to broker an arrangement whereby he would supply the Bureau with "information with respect to subversives". The intermediary said that Frank could be contacted through the Hampshire House, where he was staying while looking for an apartment in New York. This was all very strange, given Frank's racial tolerance stance during the 1940s. Was it a measure of how desperate and perhaps harassed he felt? Perhaps he had got wind of something far bigger and potentially catastrophic for both his career and personal life. Whatever the case, the FBI was not interested in his offer. The Deputy Director wrote a note on the internal memo stating, "We want nothing to do with him." J Edgar Hoover, the Director, wrote on the same note "I agree."

CUBAN CLOSURE

In December, a Democratic Senator, Estes Kefauver, became Chairman of a Special Committee to Investigate Crime in Interstate Commerce. Appearing before the committee were some of the most powerful Mafiosi, men such as Meyer Lansky and Willie Moretti. They, along with the other Mafia dons, pleaded the Fifth Amendment, denying any knowledge of any crimes. Then, out of the blue, Kefauver decided that he wanted to question Frank. He had the picture of Frank in Cuba with Lucky Luciano taken back in 1947. The source of this picture may well have been one of Frank's old friends in the press, but then again it may have been the FBI. Rather than doing this in public, Frank's lawyer arranged for him to be interviewed at the Rockefeller Center in New York at 4:00 am on 1 March, 1951. It was the only time that Frank felt safe from the prying eyes of the media.

The transcripts of this interview make fascinating reading, with Frank denying that he knew any one of the suspected Mafia men, other than on a passing acquaintance basis. Frank summed up his relationship with these underworld characters by saying, "Hell, you go into show business, you meet a lot of people. And you don't know who they are or what they do." There is no question that it was a perfectly reasonable answer. It is doubtful whether anyone, singer, bandleader, or musician, didn't know similar characters from playing the clubs and theatres across the US. As Al Martino would later say, "We befriended them, we worked for them, they owned the night clubs." But Frank did, of course, know them somewhat better than most. Singing at Willie Moretti's daughter's wedding in Hasbrouck Heights in 1947, at the height of his fame, was more than you did for "a passing acquaintance".

After almost two hours of questioning, it was over. Fortunately for Frank, the committee decided not to call him before the televised hearings, which would have been a potentially career-wrecking move. Joseph Nellis, the lawyer who conducted the interviews, said that Frank was let off, "even though I recognized the inconsistencies in Sinatra's testimony and knew he was lying at times."

1950 ON THE JUKEBOX

FRANK ON THE US CHARTS

'THE OLD MASTER PAINTER'
(Beasley Smith & Haven Gillespie)
24 December 1949, No 13, 7 weeks

'SORRY'
(Richard Whiting & Buddy Pepper)
21 January, No 28, 1 week

'CHATTANOOGIE SHOE SHINE BOY'
(Harry Stone & Jack Stapp)
25 February, No 10, 7 weeks

'GOD'S COUNTRY'
(Beasley Smith & Haven Gillespie)
25 February, No 25, 1 week

'AMERICAN BEAUTY ROSE'
(Redd Evans, Mack David & Arthur Altman)
27 May, No 26, 2 weeks

'GOODNIGHT IRENE'
(Huddie Ledbetter & John Lomax)
5 August, No 5, 12 weeks

'ONE FINGER MELODY'
(Kermit Goell, Fred Spielman & Al Hoffman)
4 November, No 9, 16 weeks

'NEVERTHELESS
(I'M IN LOVE WITH YOU)'
(Harry Ruby & Bert Kalmar)
2 December, No 14, 5 weeks

Frank's 51 weeks on the charts failed to match his achievements during 1949. His best performing song, 'Goodnight Irene', could only make it to the middle of the Top 10, and it was well beaten by the Weavers and Gordon Jenkins, whose version topped the charts for 13 weeks. On the end of year ratings Frank could only make No 17, outstripped by Bing (back on top for the first time since 1946), and bandleaders Guy Lombardo and Ralph Flanagan. Both Perry Como and Frankie Laine finished the year above Frank.

It was of course the end of an era for Frank; Manie Sacks had quit Columbia and gone to RCA Victor. His replacement, Mitch Miller, took up his new post in February, shortly before Frank recorded 'American Beauty Rose' with Mitch Miller's Dixieland Band — it was an ominous sign. One of the first things Manie did when he got to RCA was to get everyone together to talk about signing Frank. No one felt that there was anything they could do with Sinatra. Manie had to tell Frank, which couldn't have been easy for either of the old friends.

COMPETING MASTERS
The competition to get a hit with many versions of the same song was intense. On both 'The Old Master Painter' and 'Sorry', The Modernaires, a four men and one girl vocal group signed to Columbia, backed Frank.

Almost all Frank's hits were out-performed by competing versions, a continuation of the trend from 1949. 'The Old Master Painter' fared better with Richard Hayes, and even Dick Haymes, while Red Foley's version of 'Chattanoogie Shoe Shine Boy' made No 1. As *Variety* said, "'Chattanoogie Shoe Shine Boy' is good without being standout." It kind of summed up Frank's year. Five other renditions of 'Nevertheless' climbed higher on the charts, including versions by The Mills Brothers and Frankie Laine. Frank's only real success was 'One Finger Melody'; his was the only version to chart. 'Sorry', and its b-side 'Why Remind Me', had attracted some negative comparisons by *Variety* in December 1949. "Frank Sinatra is top billed but more arresting are the jobs done by the Modernaires and Axel Stordahl. The Swoonster isn't catching on and besides there's a punchier Margaret Whiting version available."

Patti Page, who Mitch Miller signed at his former label Mercury, had the biggest hit of 1950 when her version of 'The Tennessee Waltz' topped the chart for nine weeks; it was another song Frank turned down. One of the year's big hits was Anton Karas and his zither-laden 'Third Man Theme' from the movie starring Orson Welles. 1950 was the start of "pop's dark hour", a spell of a few years where the quality of the records was markedly inferior to the 1940s. Novelty was the norm, and Frank didn't do novelty.

TO DIVORCE OR NOT TO DIVORCE

Frank must have felt that the separation agreement with Nancy would bring about a speedy divorce. Speculation about any marriage breakdown is just that; the truth is difficult to get at. Both sides have their own version that often gets in the way of resolution. Overlay that with emotions and there is a guarantee of confusion. Love often becomes a downgraded emotion, replaced by the desire to win.

Many have written of Nancy's efforts to "outlast" Ava, to win Frank back and to hope that he would eventually see the "error of his ways". All quite possibly true, but the reality was that Frank stayed with Ava. No matter how much he missed his kids, home comforts, and the order that such domesticity put into his life (something Frank definitely

THE EISENHOWER BOOM YEARS

"Frank was the cleanest man I ever knew, forever changing his clothes and underwear, always showering. If I'd caught him washing the soap it wouldn't have surprised me."

AVA GARDNER IN HER AUTOBIOGRAPHY

MR SLIM
Frank backstage at the Paramount with members of his Hoboken Fan Club. It's clear times were changing.

needed), he wanted Ava. But given all that was going on, or not going on, in his career, it must have sapped Frank's resolve. On-set outbursts could be put down to how he was feeling on any given day. His volatile relationship with Ava was both a cause and effect of everything that was happening. No doubt Ava was also getting tired of the whole dragged out divorce and she must have put pressure on Frank. It must have had an effect on his ability to concentrate on his work. For the first four months of 1951 there were no hit records, and the only bright spot was the fact that he had landed a movie role. Since being fired by MGM, Frank was hardly hot property, so it must have been quite a relief when Universal International signed him to play the lead in *Meet Danny Wilson*. Frank was to play a crooner who "sold" 50 per cent of his future earnings to a dubious nightclub owner with underworld connections.

Before filming commenced, Frank was tied to New York working on his TV series *The Frank Sinatra Show*. He also secured a couple of bookings, his first live work in over six months. The first was for two weeks at the Paramount, starting on 25 April, with his old friend from the Dorsey band Joe Bushkin and his Orchestra to back him. Also on the bill were Eileen Barton, comedians Tim Herbert and Don Saxon, and an actress named Dagmar, "a big buxom Southern gal" according to Eileen. It was all a far cry from the heady days of bobby-soxers; the audiences were smaller, older, and far more reserved. The movie that shared the bill was *My Forbidden Past*, starring Ava along with Robert Mitchum. *The New York Times* of 26 April ran a long review of the movie, and then a simple mention: "featured on the stage of the Paramount are Frank Sinatra…" with a list of the other performers. Frank just wasn't worth any more ink. Soon after the Paramount run ended, Frank had a week at a New York club, The Latin Quarter.

A DOG

Between the two bookings, Frank was in the studio cutting what most people consider to be the nadir of his recording career: the truly awful 'Mama Will Bark', complete with dog impersonations by Donald Baine. If that wasn't enough, Dagmar, popular more for her bust than her acting talents, lent a hand. According to Frank, "the only good business it did was with dogs".

From New York, Frank returned to Hollywood to begin filming *Meet Danny Wilson*. Frank did not get on well with his co-star, Shelley Winters, and his temper got the better of him on a number of occasions. On one notable take, Shelley got so cross that she punched Frank in the face. Needless to say, when Frank croons 'I've Got You Under My Skin' to her, it lacks a certain something. Shelley walked out at one point, and it is said that Nancy phoned to beg her to finish the film, because unless she did, Frank had no way of paying the mortgage on their Holmby house and she and the children would be out on the street.

During filming, Frank went back into the studio with Harry James and his Orchestra to record three songs, including 'Castle Rock', which would become Frank's biggest hit of 1951. Even given the waning appeal of the Big Bands, it was probably the combination of Harry and Frank, coupled with the nostalgia of it all, that got the record into the Top 10, because it was far from a classic. A week later, Frank and Ava attended the West Coast premiere of her new film, *Showboat*, at Hollywood's Egyptian Theatre. Public appearances were by now at least tolerated.

Nancy had finally agreed to a divorce while Frank had been playing the Paramount. She had given up all hope of getting Frank back and bowed to the inevitable. Almost immediately, Ava began badgering Frank about meeting his parents; but Frank had hardly spoken to Marty and Dolly for two years, and their mixed emotions over the Nancy

> 66 Dagmar, America's most prominent literary figure? 99
>
> *NEW YORK TIMES*, 25 APRIL, 1951

'I'M A FOOL TO WANT YOU'

THE 27 MARCH, 1951, was a pivotal moment in Frank's art/life series. He recorded 'I'm a Fool to Want You' in New York with Axel. Was this the greatest record Frank ever made? Well, it depends on who you talk to, but there is a good case to be made for it, and it is definitely one of the best. It is like an open letter to Ava, with Frank laying bare his emotions and his feelings. There is even a story that Frank rushed from the studio in tears after the recording, before returning to record the emotional 'Love Me'. Even before they married, Frank and Ava began their "dance of death", and there could be no better musical accompaniment to it than this. However, nothing can detract from Frank's performance of Jack Wool and Joel Herron's song, with added lyrical input from Frank himself. When it came out, it sold no more than 35,000 copies and reached only No 14 on the charts. To add insult to injury, Billy Eckstine released a version before Frank's came out, which

probably hurt Frank's sales. This song, along with 'Birth of the Blues', is the link between the Columbia and Capitol years, showing exactly where Frank was heading. He recorded the song again in 1957, this time with Gordon Jenkins for the *Where Are You?* album. Despite having a lovely arrangement, this later version lacks the emotional integrity brought on by Ava in the original.

situation had put an immense strain on relations. According to Ava, there were also problems over money because Frank was supporting them. When they eventually visited New Jersey, any concerns were soon forgotten as Dolly showed Ava album after album of photos of her Frankie. Ava's overriding memory of Dolly's home was how clean it was; Frank had clearly inherited his mother's fastidiousness.

LOCO IN ACAPULCO

A month or so later, Frank and Ava went to Acapulco on vacation after she finished filming *Lone Star*. They tried to leave unnoticed, but as usual the press were one step ahead. According to the *LA Times*, "The attempt to slip away quietly into Mexico by air last night became the most publicized romantic goings-on since the Rita Hayworth-Aly Khan trip before their marriage." In Mexico, Frank was even forced to say he had "no intentions of eloping with Ava".

In an effort to return to Los Angeles a week later without so much attention, they had the loan of a converted bomber belonging to baseball club owner Jorge Pasquel. They arrived at the non-commercial part of the airport, and the usual meeters and greeters were there. Frank was accused of deliberately trying to run over a photographer. The papers gleefully reported Frank's abuse: "Next time I'll kill you, you son of a bitch." He and Ava vehemently denied the story, saying the whole thing was a set-up. Whatever the truth it was yet more pressure, an unnecessary invasion of their privacy as they saw it. The argument of a celebrity's right to

privacy is one that has raged for as long as there has been a press, and more importantly for as long as there have been people whose career depended on the fame game. There is clearly a line that should not be crossed, but in reality Frank and Ava's own internal combustion engine worked just fine without the press. With hindsight, it is easy to see that their relationship was doomed.

On 9 August, Frank flew from Hollywood to Reno, and announced he would file for a Nevada divorce. When asked if he would marry Ava, Frank said, "I presume I will." In an unusual show of cordiality to the press, Frank invited them to his suite, saying, "I hope I'm going to get along with you fellows." Two days later, Frank opened at the Riverside Inn and Casino – his first-ever casino booking.

After Reno he went to Lake Tahoe for a few days before opening at the Desert Inn in Las Vegas. Frank stayed at the Cal-Neva Lodge in Lake Tahoe (the hotel was built along the California–Nevada state line). It may have been the scene of another suicide attempt. This time Frank was supposed to have overdosed on sleeping pills. Frank denied it, saying he was taken ill after mistakenly taking pills to which he was allergic. According to Ava, it was slightly different: "Frank made an offhand remark that hurt me so deeply that I decided to go back to Los Angeles", although at the time it was reported that MGM had summoned Ava back to Hollywood. After Ava got back to her house in Pacific Palisades, the phone rang. It was Hank Sanicola, "Oh My God Ava, hurry back. Frank's taken an overdose." Ava rushed to Lake Tahoe to find Frank in hospital but far from at death's door; he had not taken enough Phenobarbital for that. Frank's story? "I just had a bellyache."

A matter of days after the incident Frank opened at the Desert Inn, his first performance in Las Vegas; there would of course be many more. The *Las Vegas Morning Sun* reported on his appearance at the Painted Desert Room: "one of the greatest showmen ever seen in these parts". During his engagement he had some pretty disparaging things to say about another singer appearing in the town – in her autobiography Rosemary Clooney says that it hurt her deeply: she couldn't understand why Frank would bother to be so nasty. Apparently the *Morning Sun* thought so too and took him to task "with his mouth open and his capped teeth showing". Frank's personal problems had so often spoiled his public persona; they were now becoming career threatening.

Frank and Ava's relationship was continuing to be affected by Nancy's attitude towards divorce. She opposed Frank filing for a divorce in Nevada even after he established his six-week residency in the state. She wanted around $40,000 in unpaid alimony. With Frank's somewhat precarious finances he was unable or unwilling to pay. The former is more likely as the latter would seem to have been totally out of character. On 20 September, the *LA Times* ran a story saying Nancy had obtained a writ whereby a levy had been placed on a building Frank owned at 177 South Robertson

> ❝It wasn't the press who made me famous, it was my singing. You miserable crumbs.❞
>
> **FRANK TO THE PRESS WHEN IN MEXICO WITH AVA**

Boulevard in Hollywood. As far as the public saw it, Frank was not just a man who had deserted his wife, he now wouldn't pay her. All the talk over the years of Frank's huge earnings meant people assumed he was fabulously rich. They had no idea of the realities. A letter sent to columnist Hedda Hopper from New Orleans (addressed Miss Hedda Hopper, Hollywood, California) is a fascinating vignette of America in 1951. "No more money will we spend to see Frank Sinatra or Ava Gardner. We are all fed up with these immoral people whom we kids support. We used to think Frankie the best, but now we think of his poor kids when they grow up and what they'll have to hear of their dad." It was signed Charles, Bill, and Todd Jr. It held true for many others, but it was Frankie, rather than Ava, who was to suffer most.

Although probably not read by Charles, Bill, and Todd Jr, the *American Mercury Magazine* in August 1951 carried a story that set out to link Frank absolutely and completely with the Mafia. Under the title "Frank Sinatra Confidential – Gangsters in the Nightclubs" it described how Willie Moretti "kingpin of the Jersey rackets", had not only got Frank the gig at the Rustic Cabin but also how Moretti, "a respected and prominent Jersey citizen" managed to have the charges brought by Antoinette Della Pente in 1939 reduced to seduction. It also told of the time when Frank sang at Moretti's daughter's wedding, having been "escorted from New York by a delegation of New York motorcycle cops". The article went on to recite in detail the events of Frank's 1947 trip to Cuba. It was yet more mud designed to stick. The article neatly describes the whole underworld/show business link. "Show business also helps maintain the underworld's necessary social and political contacts. It may cause trouble if public figures allow their hoodlum friends to visit their houses, but the danger is minimal if they exchange a few words in a crowded nightclub. In the entertainment world, the gangsters can mix freely with politicos, tycoons, union bosses and newspapermen and build up priceless asset of good will in important strata," words that were to become prophetic for Frank and many who would come into his orbit. The writer was none other than Lee Mortimer.

THE LAST OF THE SHOWS

The second season of Frank's TV series began on 9 October, 1951. The sponsor was Ekco Housewares. The first sponsor, the Bulova Watch Company, didn't think the deal worth carrying on with. The one-hour show had been shifted to the less attractive slot of 8:00 pm on Tuesday, up against *The Milton Berle Show*. According to Frank, "It's like backing into the pennant. Berle's a big man to knock down." To get the show off to a good start, CBS booked Perry Como, Frankie Laine, and the Andrews Sisters. Despite being knocked from the top of the annual *Billboard* poll, Perry was still immensely popular, while Frankie Laine's 'Jezebel' had only just dropped off the charts after a run of 21 weeks (Frank only managed a total of 23 weeks on the charts in the whole of 1951). While the Andrews Sisters were in the last throes of their long career, they were still very popular. CBS must have been very worried to book such guests. To make matters worse, Perry Como stole the show according to the critics, who accused Frank of being under rehearsed, which he probably was. Jack Gould at the *New York Times* felt Frank was upstaged "effortlessly and smoothly by Perry Como", saying it was "a drab mixture of radio routine, vaudeville, and pallid pantomime". He felt Frank lacked "the dominant personality needed to sustain a 60-minute show." When the viewing figures came out, Frank lost out heavily to Milton Berle, whose guests were Tony Bennett, Rosemary

PAINTED DESERT ROOM
The menu from the nightclub and restaurant at the Desert Inn, Las Vegas, where Frank first performed in September 1951.

ON THE ROAD
Frank and Ava had travelled from Philadelphia to New York City by train, having taken out a marriage licence. Frank was as usual charming towards the waiting reporters. "All I'd let you do for me is press my pants," he said after one of them offered to help them with their luggage.

MR & MRS
Having married in Philadelphia on 7 November, Frank and Ava then went to Havana, via Miami where the picture below was taken on 9 November, 1951.

Clooney, and the Mills Brothers. But there is another side to this that's rarely mentioned. Two weeks before the show aired Ava had collapsed and had been rushed to hospital in Santa Monica where she was diagnosed with a severe viral infection and very low blood pressure. She was too ill to join Frank in New York until 28 October. Being in the public eye and having to keep up appearances is sometimes tough.

On 1 November, 1951, Frank and Nancy were finally divorced. "I wanted to be sure he knew what he was about," said Nancy after the hearing. Nancy cited Frank's "extreme mental cruelty" as grounds. The original terms of the separation were agreed as the divorce settlement. Now free to marry, Frank and Ava applied for a marriage licence the following day in Philadelphia – a safe distance from Los Angeles, New York, or Las Vegas, where the attention of the press would be more intense, and also the home town of Frank's old friend Manie Sacks.

WEDDING BELLS

The marriage, on Wednesday 7 November, took place at Manie's cousin Lester's home in West Germantown, Pennsylvania. Axel Stordahl was best man and his wife, June Hutton, was the matron of honour. Dolly and Marty were there, along with the usual coterie of friends. Interestingly, Frank gave his age as 34, which was a year older than his publicly quoted age, but a year younger than he really was. Despite the secrecy, the press were still there, and Frank was justifiably angry: "I'd been living through two years of high tension. Then we spend 45 minutes of our reception posing and that isn't enough! And they said I was uncooperative." For their four-day honeymoon, which Ava told a friend she paid for, they chose, of all places, Havana. Obviously Frank had no bad memories of Cuba, and perhaps he thought that there would be less intrusion from the press there. Given the attitude of some columnists, he was right to want to avoid them: "Frank Sinatra craves privacy… if it's privacy that Frank Sinatra wants, he should be kept out of the public eye permanently." Clearly he was not always the most sensible, tolerant, or gracious of men when it came to dealing with the press (even Ava reprimanded him about his attitude), but against the background of a fading career, Frank was

HONEYMOON
Corbis BE044428
Kvar pura radioj trinkis tri eta stratoj. Ses domoj rapide skribas kvar malbela bieroj, kaj la malalta

lashing out on all sides. It was a situation made worse because Ava was on the up – the perfect recipe for problems.

A month after the wedding, the *LA Times* reported that Frank was, in the opinion of some local churchmen, a bigamist. They were assuming his Nevada divorce was the only one and ignored the California proceedings initiated by Nancy. The situation calmed down as people began to realize that there was nothing particularly unusual in what Frank had done; his only mistake was the fact that he was famous.

Fortunately, Frank and Ava missed much of the fuss, having flown to London to appear before Princess Elizabeth and Prince Philip at a charity command performance for The National Playing Fields Association. By all accounts, Frank's performance was lacklustre; he also argued with the orchestra at rehearsals and, predictably, the press. To cap it all, the Sinatras' suite was burgled. The thieves got away with a diamond and emerald necklace, cameo cufflinks, and a ring. The necklace was a Christmas present to Ava from Frank, and one that he was probably hard pressed to afford.

During November, *Billboard* ran a piece saying that Frank had no intention of renewing his Columbia recording contract, which would run out in December 1952. It went on to say, "Sinatra has waged a long smouldering feud with Mitch Miller. Chief binge hinges on Sinatra claim that he isn't getting a fair shake on song material." It reported that Frank was talking with RCA and Capitol records. Clearly, Frank's hopes on RCA were more wishful than real, since it seems unlikely that Manie Sacks had not already told him that there was no hope of his being signed by RCA. As for Capitol, he may just have been sounding them out.

It would be interesting to know how Frank really felt at this point. Although his marriage should have made him optimistic about his personal life, it is hard to see how professionally he could feel anything but down. He must also have known that there was little chance of Columbia re-signing him, unless his television show really took off. With Miller and his old college friend, Goddard Lieberson, in charge at Columbia, he must have felt that the future was bleak. Miller was having hit records; Frank was not.

It was also in November that Frank met pianist Bill Miller. It would prove to be one of the most enduring relationships of his career. "I had a trio in the lounge (in Las Vegas). Jimmy Van Heusen called Frank's attention to what I was doing. I was in good shape, because I'd been on the job for a couple of months. And he heard me play, and he knew about me anyway, and his manager, Hank Sanicola, said 'You want to do a TV show?' And I said 'Hell yeah!' (laughs) That's how it all started."

When Frank returned to New York from London, he seemed anxious to ingratiate himself with the press. Frank's PR man, Mack Miller, insisted the only solution was to be nice, not confrontational. Unfortunately, Frank did not really get the chance, as no one was interested in talking to him or taking his photograph. In a staged interview with Fern Marja

1951 ON THE JUKEBOX

FRANK ON THE US CHARTS

'YOU'RE THE ONE'
(Victor Young & Ned Washington)
5 May, No 17, 1 week

'WE KISS IN A SHADOW'
(Richard Rodgers & Oscar Hammerstein II)
2 June, No 22, 2 weeks

'I'M A FOOL TO WANT YOU'
(Jack Wolf, Joel Herron & Frank Sinatra)
23 June, No 14, 7 weeks

'MAMA WILL BARK'
(Dick Manning)
23 June, No 21, 5 weeks

'CASTLE ROCK'
(Al Sears, Ervin Drake & Jimmy Shirl)
1 September, No 8, 8 weeks

Just 23 weeks on the charts was all that Frank could muster in 1951. Frank dropped one place to No18 on the Billboard year-end chart performance table, which was headed by the husband and wife team of Les Paul and Mary Ford. Les Paul's innovative multi-track recording technique can be heard to good effect on the couple's No 1 record, 'How High The Moon'. Guy Mitchell, who had his first hit in 1950, held the second spot and Frankie Laine made No 3 on the annual poll.

The two sides of one record can characterize Frank's dilemma. 'I'm a Fool To Want You' and 'Mama Will Bark' came out in early June and both made the charts. The contrast in the two songs is staggering. 'I'm A Fool To Want You' is one of his strongest performances from his Columbia years, yet sold fewer than 40,000 copies. Strangely Frank's biggest hit of the year was 'Castle Rock', recorded with Harry James. It is another lightweight song, arranged by Ray Conniff, that suited neither of them. There is some confusion as to whether or not Frank and Harry were at the session together. It is possible that the band tracks were recorded first and Frank added his voice later, whatever the truth it's a shame that he had to bother.

While Sinatra fans vilify Mitch Miller as the man who destroyed Frank's career it is clearly not that simple. Frank was not forced to make any of the dreadful records from this period, he agreed to them. In fact Frank had the power of veto on his releases; his contract gave him 48 hours to approve a master for release. The reality was that Frank was probably pretty desperate for hit records, not ones that languished in the lower reaches of the charts. Frank did as much to bring about his own fall from grace as all the Mitch Miller's in the world. But as Alan Livingston who signed Frank to Capitol later said "That was where Mitch made a mistake. He tried to put Frank in what he thought was the pop music business. And it was not for Frank."

THE PRINCE OF WAILS
While Les Paul and Mary Ford were the year's top sellers it was Johnnie Ray who had the single biggest seller. Frank had been 'the Sultan of Swoon', Johnnie became 'the Nabob of Sob'. His emotion-laden performances proved very popular and his ability to seemingly cry at will gave him a decided gimmick. His singing style was an important bridge between the crooners and rock 'n' roll. Many have made

the link between Frank and Elvis through Johnnie Ray. If Frank had been subtly sexual, Johnnie was at the other end of the scale, but it drew a similar reaction from the teens in the audience.

Johnnie Ray was born in Dallas, Oregon on 10 January 1927 and as a child became deaf in one ear. He began performing in the Detroit area when he was around 20 years old. Columbia signed him in 1951 and released 'Whiskey and Gin' on OKeh, a label normally restricted to black and R&B artists. His second record, 'Cry' credited to Johnnie Ray and The Four Lads, became a massive worldwide hit topping the *Billboard* chart for 11 weeks. Even the b-side, 'The Little White Cloud That Cried', made No 2 on the US chart. Over the next five years Ray's records sold in large numbers, without ever reaching the dizzy heights of 'Cry'.

Ray appeared as a singer-turned priest in the 1954 film, *There's No Business Like Show Business* and continued to find chart success with his gospel-influenced songs. By 1958 rumours about his sexuality and his drug-taking affected his popularity in the US. Alcoholism was a severe blow for him in the 1960s and from then on his work was limited to cabaret and nostalgia shows, although in Britain he still had a strong following. He died in 1990, aged 63, from liver failure.

THE CRY GUY
In Britain, where his chart success had been if anything better than in the US, Johnnie Ray continued to find an audience.

of the *New York Post*, Frank showed his desperation: "I lost control of my temper and said things. They were said under great strain and pressure. I'm honestly sorry."

In December, *Double Dynamite* was finally on US cinema screens. Apart from the studio's concerns about Frank's bankability, it may well have got mixed up with Howard Hughes's distaste for Frank because of his affair with Ava. According to Ava, Hughes maintained a sporadic campaign against Frank and her, even going as far as having them followed. The most unpleasant thing he did was on the eve of their wedding. A letter arrived for Ava at the Hampshire House from a hooker who claimed to be having an affair with Frank. According to Ava, it was full of pretty distasteful stuff and she decided after some consideration that Hughes was behind it. It had been yet more pressure.

To call *Double Dynamite* mediocre gives it an unwarranted status. It deserves to be forgotten and in truth pretty much has been, except by Sinatra completists. Frank's two songs in the movie are duets, 'Kisses and Tears' with Jane Russell and the mercifully short 'It's Only Money' with Groucho Marx. The latter was also the film's original title, and quite what the *Double Dynamite* refers to is unclear. Frank was not even on the poster; it just featured Marx and Russell. The omission may have had something to do with Hughes's animosity towards Frank over Ava. It also may have had something to do with the fact that Frank's face was not good box office. Around this time, Sammy Davis Jr talked of seeing Frank walking alone in Times Square. No one bothered him or seemed to even recognize him. Half a decade earlier, he couldn't walk anywhere in

the area without being mobbed. Sammy felt so sad for Frank that he didn't even go up and talk to him for fear of embarrassing the man who had helped him. And yet Frank still hadn't reached the bottom. There was still a little further to fall.

THE DARK AGES

If things had gone from bad to worse between 1950 and 1951, they turned truly awful in 1952. From the outset it had humiliation written all over it. Frank probably wished it was a year that never happened. In January Ava was away in Kenya filming *The Snows of Kilimanjaro*. She knew how fragile Frank's ego had become and how difficult he would find it if she was away too long so she persuaded the film's producer, Darryl F Zanuck, to condense her location shooting into as few days as possible. She was home in time for the opening of *Meet Danny Wilson* in early February.

Frank must have been anxious to get back on stage, having done so little over the past six months. What's more, he needed the money. Frank called Robert Weitman, the boss of the Paramount in New York, to ask him to book him and his new movie as a double bill. Back in 1942, Weitman had driven out to New Jersey when Frank left Tommy Dorsey and booked him into the Paramount, giving him his big break. Weitman had to pull some strings because *Meet Danny Wilson* was not a Paramount picture. Frank's booking began on 26 March; with him were comedian Frank Fontaine, June Hutton, and Buddy Rich.

FAMILY NIGHT OUT
Frank and Ava with Dolly and Marty at the New York premiere of Meet Danny Wilson.

Three weeks before he opened in New York City, Frank appeared on television's *The Dinah Shore Show* and reminisced about their "old days" together on radio. The show's producer, Bud Yorkin, remembered, "He was not the Frank Sinatra we all know and love."

Despite many of Frank's pals being at the Paramount night after night to give their friend support it made little difference; Frank wasn't able to fill the place. His failure was made more poignant by the fact that Bob Rolontz had given Frank a good write up in *Billboard*. "A mellow and friendly Frank Sinatra is a smash hit here. It is a show for Sinatra fans, for between the stage show and the movie there are over 15 Sinatra vocals." He added a guardedly prophetic note, "If the singer continues to act as warm as he does on this bill he could soon win back his once great following." Even so the take for the week was $62,000, around a third to a quarter of what would be considered a normal box office take for a similar booking. Frank and Ava went to see Johnnie Ray who was playing Frank's old stamping ground, The Copacabana. Ray was going down a storm, another thing to cast yet more doubts in Frank's mind. *The World Telegram & Sun* nailed it in a headline: "Gone on Frankie in '42; Gone in '52". To add to his woes, *Meet Danny Wilson* closed almost as quickly as it opened and United International decided not to exercise their option for a second movie. It was probably not just a lack of box office receipts that influenced them. Frank was paying the price for his on-set antics. Having an attitude is fine when you're at the top; on the way down it can be fatal. Frank's records were not cutting it either, according to *Downbeat*. "By every ordinary standard, 'London By Night' and 'April In Paris' are poorly sung... Frank Sinatra sounds tired, bored, and in poor voice, to boot." In the *Downbeat* end-of-year poll for 1951, Frank managed 276 votes to secure second place, a long way behind Billy Eckstine, who polled 1,354.

About the time Frank's desultory run at the Paramount was coming to an end, he heard that his TV series was being cancelled. He cannot have been surprised, but it must have disappointed him. It was originally a five-year contract, renewable annually, for which earned Frank around $250,000 a year; it was a costly loss. Everyone could see that Frank was not comfortable on television, but it is important to note that his singing throughout was his one saving grace.

TENT SHOW

In April, Frank went to Hawaii, almost it seems to distance himself from his problems. While there he played what was probably the strangest show of his entire career, in a leaky tent at the Kaua'i Country Fair. Daughter Nancy wrote that this "marked a turning point not only in his career but in his personal life". She leaves it at that, which is somewhat tantalising. Chris Cook, a journalist in Kaua'i, managed to unearth more of the story, and his findings were included in *The Kaua'i Reader*. Lillian Daily who hailed from New Jersey,

who had seen Frank at the Paramount in the early days, was by 1952 living on the island. The tent was set up on what are now the second nine holes of the Wailus golf course. "It was a rainy Sunday afternoon. He walked to the edge of the stage and sat down and looked out at the audience and said, 'What do you want to hear?' Whatever anybody called out he sang... he sang his heart out." There was no orchestra, just Bill Miller on piano to accompany Frank. Buck Buchwach, a reporter at the *Honolulu Advertiser*, later talked to Frank. "I wondered if the show really did have to go on. Then I peeked out at the audience. There were a few hundred tops. Their warmth and friendliness smacked me in the face. And when two brown-skinned young girls gave me a couple of handsome lei and little kisses, I almost broke down." According to Bill Miller, Frank "knew how to sing to an audience, he liked the idolatry". Frank was staying at the Kaua'i Inn and soon after the concert Ava flew in to join him. A DJ from KTOH went to the Inn to pick up Frank, as he wanted to play volleyball. When he arrived Frank and

---

MEET DANNY WILSON

IT CLOSED ALMOST AS QUICKLY as it opened and could well have been Frank's movie swan song. If art and life play such an important role in Frank's canon, then *Meet Danny Wilson* is just about the strangest chapter. It must have been difficult for Frank to play the part, so close was it to his own career (although Frank denied the similarity during a promotional spot, saying, "This is Frank Sinatra speaking to you from Hollywood. We just screened my new picture *Meet Danny Wilson* and the gang out here have been kidding me that it's the story of my own life. Actually I wish my life was as exciting as Danny Wilson's.")

Frank got $75,000 for playing Danny Wilson; it would be several years before he earned that kind of money for a movie again. Danny Wilson is a quick-tempered singer who sings and hustles for pool in lowly dives with his partner (Alex Nicol). Through Joy Carroll (Shelley Winters), they get a job at an upmarket nightclub owned by the crooked Nick Driscoll (played by Raymond Burr, who later played Perry Mason on television). Danny Wilson pledges 50 per cent of his future earnings, and then his career takes off. In the end, Wilson shoots Driscoll in the back and gets away with it, but loses Joy to Mike Ryan, while his own (fictional) career continues to flourish, in stark contrast to Frank's real one.

Frank sings 'She's Funny That Way', 'That Old Black Magic', 'When You're Smiling', 'All of Me', 'I've Got a Crush on You', 'You're a Sweetheart', 'Lonesome Man Blues', 'A Good Friend Is Hard to Find', and 'How Deep Is the Ocean?'

Time magazine commented that "Don McGuire's original screenplay cribs so freely from the career and personality of Frank Sinatra that fans may expect Ava Gardner to pop up in the last reel," while *Downbeat* claimed on 11 March that "It shows Danny Wilson becoming a character almost as obnoxiously arrogant and cocky as most newspaper reporters (and many others) now regard Sinatra."

THE EYES HAVE IT
The animosity between Frank and Shelley Winters seems evident in this poster for the movie.

ELLA FITZGERALD

"She was the best singer on the planet." MEL TORME

IF ELLA HAD HAD THE LOOKS TO GO WITH THE VOICE, THEN SHE WOULD HAVE UNQUESTIONABLY BEEN THE MOST TALKED ABOUT, ADMIRED, REVERED, AND LOVED FEMALE SINGER OF THE 20TH CENTURY. AS IT WAS, SHE WAS SIMPLY THE BEST.

Born in Newport News, Virginia, on 25 April, 1918, and orphaned at an early age, Ella was "discovered" after performing at the Harlem Amateur Hour aged just 16.

She was hired by Chick Webb to sing with his orchestra and had her first hit in 1936 with 'Sing Me a Swing Song (And Let Me Dance)'. Besides singing with Chick, she performed on records with The Mills Brothers in 1937. Her big break came singing with Chick in June 1938 when 'A-Tisket A-Tasket' spent 10 weeks at No 1. In a sign of the times, Ella and Chick had a hit a few months later with 'Wacky Dust', an unabashed opus to cocaine. Webb died aged 30 the next year, and for a while Ella continued to front his orchestra as well as recording solo.

She formed a successful short-term partnership with the Ink Spots, and they had two No 1 records in 1944. She also recorded successfully with Louis Armstrong and Louis Jordan in 1946. Her recording of 'I Love You for Sentimental Reasons' with the Delta Rhythm Boys was another big hit in 1947 while 'Baby It's Cold Outside' with Louis Jordan in 1949 from the Esther William's film *Neptune's Daughter* was her last Top 10 hit. During the late 1940s, Ella graduated from being a pop singer to a jazz singer.

As the 1950s rolled around, Ella's appearances on the *Billboard* charts became infrequent, but this was by no means a reflection of her talent and the quality of her recordings; Ella had simply risen above the charts. She became associated with Norman Granz's Jazz at the Philharmonic, which led to her becoming an international name. By 1956, she was recording for Granz's Verve label, and it is her recordings with this premier jazz company that have become the basis for her continuing popularity.

Ella recorded a series of albums of the best of the greatest American songwriters. These "songbooks" had arrangements by the likes of Nelson Riddle, Buddy Bregman, Billy May, Duke Ellington, and Paul Weston. The first of the songbooks was a double album of Cole Porter, which quickly sold 100,000 copies in 1956. Ira Gershwin paid tribute to her by saying "I never knew how good our songs were until I heard Ella Fitzgerald sing them."

In 1960, 'Mack the Knife', her last US chart success of any note, made No 27.

If Ella had a secret to her success it was her diversity. She had started out as a swing singer then moved to bebop; she sang perfect scat, was an extraordinary jazz vocalist, and had no fear of modern material as the 1960s and 1970s came along. From the blues to bossa nova and calypsos to carols, she imbued all with her unique voice, sounding forever young. She was blessed with a three-octave range and diction and enunciation that was, like Frank Sinatra's, as good as it gets. And Frank himself declared, "The best way to start any musical evening is with this girl. It don't get better than this."

In 1991, Ella, having famously once said, "the only thing better than singing is more singing", gave her final concert at New York's Carnegie Hall. In 1992, she had both legs amputated below the knees as a result of complications arising from diabetes. She died four years later, on 15 June, 1996.

BIGGEST HITS

'A-Ticket A-Tasket' (1938, No 1, with Chick Webb and His Orchestra)
'Into Each Life Some Rain Must Fall' (1944, No 1, with the Ink Spots)
'I'm Making Believe' (1944, No 1, with the Ink Spots)
'My Happiness' (1948)
'But Not for Me' (1959) Awarded a Grammy

For Ella, like many quality singers, what mattered was not so much which of the songs were her biggest hits but which were her best performances, which involved much more subjective criteria. 'How Long Has This Been Going On?', 'Manhattan', and 'Isn't It Romantic?' are pure Ella, and pure magic.

Ava were in the middle of what was described as "a very serious conversation". Frank gave the DJ "a negative wave" and Frank missed his game. Shortly afterwards Ava left and flew to Hawaii alone.

THAT'S IT FRANK

Columbia still needed hit records and while Frank had been in New York at the beginning of the year he cut three songs. Mitch Miller was under pressure to try and recoup the $109,997 that Columbia had advanced Frank to pay off the IRS. Miller approached this all but impossible task in the only way he knew how – find a "hit song" and get Frank to cut it, even if it didn't suit him. Given Frank's lack of public appeal it was probably the only way he was going to get a hit. Frank's views were somewhat different. But in fairness to Miller, they weren't all bad songs. During February in Hollywood Frank recorded 'My Girl', a song written by Clarence Freed. It proved that despite everything Frank could still come up with the goods; there's a smile in his voice throughout and you can't help thinking that things with Ava, at that point at least, were going well. Ava had just got back from Kenya. Frank was happy.

Frank's third recording session of the year was on 3 June and among the five songs he cut in Hollywood was 'The Birth of the Blues'. It's a musical signpost as to where Frank would be heading, although he of course had no idea where he would end up. While it is a link between the Columbia and Capitol years, it lacks much of the subtlety and added inspiration that would characterize Frank's output during the coming seven years. Mitch Miller was at the session, which was nominally being produced by Paul Weston, Jo Stafford's husband. One of the other songs Frank cut was 'Tennessee Newsboy', written by Percy Faith and Dick Manning; Wesley Ebb 'Speedy' West played pedal steel guitar on the recording. When the take finished, Miller apparently rushed into the studio smiling, and everyone presumed he was about to congratulate Frank. Instead he rushed over and slapped West on the back. While Frank was probably as flabbergasted as everyone else, it was amazing that he and Miller were even in the same room. On at least one occasion, Frank had Miller removed from the session. It was not just Miller who felt sore with Frank. His attitude apparently upset many working at Columbia. An engineer, Harold Chapman, said, "Sinatra was one of the meanest men we ever worked for, so we engineers and musicians just sat on our hands and let him go down." This is probably somewhat disingenuous, but there is little doubt that Frank's frustration was taken out on others. Still, it was not something he was going to have to worry about for much longer. Sometime in June Frank was told that Columbia would not renew his contract. Given

Frank's comments the previous year and everything else that had happened it was no bombshell. The last show of Frank's TV series aired on 11 June. He never did recover from being trounced in the ratings on his first show of the second series, nor from the mauling by most critics.

Losing his Columbia deal was a huge blow to Frank. To talk of wanting a new record deal as your contract is ending can be a great way of upping the ante; but only if there's someone willing to take the bait. No one was beating a path to Frank's door, not his old friend Manie Sacks at RCA or Capitol Records at this point. But of far greater significance to Frank was the loss of his agent. In February 1952, Lew Wasserman, the head of MCA, decided he no longer wanted to represent Frank. In the percentages game if a star is not earning the big bucks then there is little prospect of the agency getting a decent cut. They rationalized that it was better putting their efforts behind winners. Wasserman took out ads in *Variety* and the *Hollywood Reporter* saying MCA no longer represented Frank. For the trade press it was a bonanza; they called it "The Last Goodbye" and "The Final Indignity". Frank was incandescent: "Can you imagine being fired by an agency that never had to sell you?" But when you can't even give someone away it's all very predictable. MCA also let it be known that they had never really made any money from Frank because "everybody (including Tommy Dorsey) was getting a share of him". To rub salt into the wound, Ava got a new deal from MGM for 12 movies worth $1.2 million. She had what was termed a "Frank Sinatra clause" inserted in her contract. It stated that MGM agreed to do a picture with Ava in which Frank would appear. Frank must have felt humiliated.

With his career in free fall doubts about his relationship with Ava were beginning to surface; they had only been married for eight months. Frank couldn't even muster a half-decent crowd for a live show. At Chicago's Chez Paree, capacity 1,200 plus, he could only attract 150. There were new names, new faces, and new talent that didn't come with the baggage that Frank had accumulated. In September, he did get a booking at the Riviera in Fort Lee, New Jersey. A reporter for *Variety* noted, "Whatever Sinatra ever had for the bobby-soxers, he now has for the café mob. It adds up to showmanship rather than any basic singing appeal".

Frank's final recording session for Columbia took place in New York on September 17; he could hardly miss the irony of the single song he cut. 'Why Try To Change Me Now?' stands as Frank's epitaph for his years at Columbia. He had cut over 300 songs, most with Axel Stordahl, but at this last session the orchestra was directed by Percy Faith. Mitch Miller was at that final New York session and after Frank finished the song Miller flicked the switch on the studio intercom and said, somewhat flatly "That's it Frank." Joseph McCarthy's lyrics, to Cy Coleman's melody, were a better epitaph. A couple of years later, Frank talked of his relationship with Miller

and was more sanguine, "I'll admit he's a great musician, but I can't get along with him. One day he said to me 'Frank, we're going to make a record with a washboard' I looked at him and said 'Mitch you're kidding' I refused to do it. I guess I did a lot of refusing between 1949 and 1952." Miller was equally vocal, "take away the microphone and Sinatra would be slicing salami in a delicatessen". It's little wonder the animosity between the two men continued. One other thing that Frank didn't do for over a decade was to return to New York to record. From the moment he left Columbia, he recorded almost exclusively in Hollywood.

A month after that final session, Frank made a television appearance on old friend Jimmy Durante's *All Star Review*. A week later he appeared at the Hollywood Palladium singing 'The Birth of the Blues' and 'The House I Live In'. Frank earned nothing as it was a fund raiser for Democratic Presidential candidate Adlai Stevenson. The time when this would have helped Frank was long gone; it appears like the act of someone trying to keep themselves in the public eye.

SUPER SESSION
Frank cut three songs on 6 February, 1952, at Columbia's Hollywood studios. The first of the three was Axel's arrangement of Clarence Freed's 'My Girl', on which Frank sounded just about as good as it gets.

1952-1957

FRANK'S WORLD

EVERYBODY LOVES A COMEBACK — NOT THAT FRANK
ACKNOWLEDGED THAT HE HAD BEEN AWAY. FOR ALAN
LIVINGSTON AND CAPITOL RECORDS SIGNING FRANK
WAS SOMETHING OF A GAMBLE; ALTHOUGH FOR THE
THIRTY-SOMETHING, FAST-APPROACHING-FORTY,
FORMER POP IDOL THERE WAS NO REAL CHOICE AS
NO OTHER LABEL STEPPED UP TO THE PLATE. JUST AS
HARRY COHN TOOK A CHANCE IN GIVING FRANK THE
ROLE OF MAGGIO IN *FROM HERE TO ETERNITY*, CAPITOL'S
FAITH AND TRUST PROVED ABSOLUTELY CORRECT, AS
FRANK MADE HIS MOST CONSISTENTLY BRILLIANT
RECORDS AND SOME OF HIS BEST MOVIES DURING
THIS PERIOD. PREPARE TO ENTER FRANK'S WORLD.

SUNSET & VINE, HOLLYWOOD
*A sight that Frank was very familiar with during
his heyday at Capitol Records.*

THE NEW LOOK IN *VOGUE*, 1952

*F*RANK
COMES BACK

According to Ava, things between her and Frank became increasingly difficult during the summer and autumn of 1952. New York, Palm Springs, and Hollywood were all locations for Frank and Ava's fight scenes. The *Los Angeles Daily Mirror* ran the headline "Boudoir Fight Heralds Frankie and Ava to Courts."

It concerned a scene that took place at Frank's Palm Springs home. This one co-starred Lana Turner, but Lana appears to have sided with Ava; they were both former Mrs Artie Shaws. Frank's lack of any decent work at this time must have played havoc with his and Ava's relationship, particularly as her career was going so well (she had just landed a part in *Mogambo* alongside Clark Gable and Grace Kelly).

Frank always read a lot of books, and one that appealed to him especially was James Jones' best-selling

"The press generally has been wonderful to me, and I know that without their help I never could have become famous or earned more money than I ever believed existed."

A SHEEPISH FRANK TO *AMERICAN WEEKLY*, 1952

novel, *From Here to Eternity*. Frank heard that Columbia Pictures was going to turn it into a movie, and he was determined to play Angelo Maggio, a downtrodden, skinny Italian boy from New Jersey who, despite everything, kept his head held high. Frank identified with the man and instinctively "knew" that the part was written for him, although at this time he was the only one who thought so. Fred Zinnemann, who had previously directed *High Noon*, and Columbia's boss, Harry Cohn, had already slated Eli Wallach for the part. According to Ava, she set to work on Harry Cohn, initially through his wife, Joan, calling her to make a case for Frank. Ava then talked to Harry himself, who told her the role was cast.

"For God's sake, Harry, I'll give you a free picture if you'll just test him," Ava offered. Frank was also busying himself by sending Cohn, Zinnemann, and the film's producer, Buddy Adler, telegrams demanding the part; he signed all of them "Maggio". Unable to change their minds, and with no work demanding his presence at home, Frank accompanied Ava to Nairobi on 7 November — which happened to be their first wedding anniversary.

Location filming for *Mogambo* was in Uganda and, despite the rigours, things went very well. Prior to leaving Kenya for Uganda, the cast went to a party at the British High Commissioner's residence in Nairobi. During the evening, an incident happened that added to the Frank and Ava legend. With the party in full swing and in front of the High Commissioner and his wife, the film's director, John Ford, asked Ava what she saw in "the 120-pound runt". As quick as a flash Ava came back: "Well there's only 10 pounds of Frank and 110 pounds of cock." Luckily, the High Commissioner and his wife thought it was hugely funny. It's also an interesting

IN AFRICA
Frank and Ava pose at Nairobi Airport. Kenya would have been a romantic place to celebrate a year of marriage if Frank had not been so anxious.

remark by Ford, given recent disclosures about his sexuality. Fortunately, Frank had managed to find an agent who was happy to take him on. The William Morris Agency was MCA's great rival, a fact that heightened the stakes for all concerned.

After a week or so in Uganda, Frank got a telegram from his agent telling him to return to Hollywood immediately to screen test for the Maggio role. Frank left at once and flew back to California via London and New York. He shot two tests, of which the one where Maggio is drunk and AWOL in the grounds of the Royal Hawaiian Hotel was particularly impressive. So much so that Zinnemann called producer Buddy Adler, telling him to get over to the set, where he would "see something unbelievable". Over the years, Frank referred to this episode of the telegram summons many times: "I caught the next plane for Hollywood, 27,000 miles there and back, and at my own expense." Frank claims he did the test and then flew back to Africa the next day. This dramatic version of events all added to the myth, but in fact Frank didn't return to Africa, the round trip is under 20,000 miles and it seems likely that Ava paid for his ticket. To be fair to Frank, Columbia's Director of Publicity peddled the same story when the film came out.

The simple reason why Frank didn't fly straight back to Africa was because he had an all-too-rare nightclub booking, for which he had been due to return shortly after he came for the screen test. On 26 November, 1952, he began a two-week stint at the French Casino in New York. But at least Frank was earning again; he sorely needed the money.

OUT OF AFRICA

On the day that Frank opened at the French Casino, *Variety* carried a small piece saying that Frank had tested for a part in *From Here to Eternity*. It went on to say that the US Customs were tipped off by letter that Frank was smuggling diamonds when he came back from Africa. The US Customs reported that the letter was from a crank. A journalist covering Frank's appearance at the French Casino wrote somewhat more flatteringly than most had been recently: "The solution to the domestic problems makes him amiable and gracious.... Without the mental and emotional stress, he is completely relaxed and sings as of yore. Frankie is at ease." But another reporter picked up on Frank's anxieties and his desire for the Maggio role: "He just didn't have the time to sit down and talk." He found "a restless unhappy man in his middle thirties who wants very much to re-establish himself and who wants to be an actor, not just a singer playing himself."

While Frank was back in America, Ava found out she was pregnant. Not wishing to tell Frank, she secretly arranged for MGM to fly her to England. She left Nairobi on 23 November and went to a nursing home in

FRENCH CASINO
Frank's pay at the French Casino was just $10,000 per week. Around the same time, Dean Martin and Jerry Lewis were doing a series of one-nighters from Washington to New Jersey. Their guarantee was $10,000 per night, and with a percentage of the gross they earned $200,000 in 10 nights.

> **66** Stan Kenton may have a point when he says the kids have forgotten how to dance. Because there hasn't been enough sound dance music to which they could learn. They're so busy listening to gimmick records without any good dance music on them **99**
>
> **FRANK IN** *DOWNBEAT*, **FEBRUARY 1953**

Wimbledon, southwest London, for an abortion. The trauma of the experience can scarcely have helped Ava and Frank's relationship. Ava told the clinic, "At present my entire life is one mad whirl, and it is going to be like that for a few years to come." Ava must have felt the pressure of her career. She may also have felt that Frank's fortunes were not necessarily improving, despite his promising screen test.

Sometime in early December, Frank heard that he had got the part of Maggio. Even though his screen test was excellent, the real reason, or reasons, as to why he was chosen in favour of Eli Wallach are still a mystery. Some involved in casting thought that Eli looked too muscular; others claim that he was already committed to play in Tennessee Williams's play *El Camino Real* on Broadway and the dates conflicted. Frank was certainly helped by the fact that his new agent represented director Fred Zinnemann as well. Of course, rumours persisted that the only reason Frank got the part was down to Mafia involvement – an idea further fuelled by Mario Puzo writing about "the horse's head" incident in *The Godfather*. According to Bob Thomas, Harry Cohn's biographer, "Sinatra won it by default." In any

event, Cohn never owned a racehorse. Frank was ecstatic and headed back to Africa to spend Christmas with Ava. According to Ava, Frank was unaware of her trip to London and "those few weeks together were easygoing and fun".

HUMBLE PIE

During Frank's charm offensive earlier in the year, the *American Weekly*, a Hearst magazine, carried a two-part article entitled "Frankly Speaking", in which he apologized for some of the things he had done. Many years later, when daughter Nancy asked her father about the article, he said, "It's C-R-A-P. They made the whole thing up." Frank, of course, didn't write it – it was ghosted by a man named Irving Fein – but it still provides an insight into Frank's desperation that he agreed to it being published. The man with confidence to spare had eaten humble pie. "The press generally has been wonderful to me, and I know that without their help I never could have become famous or earned more money than I ever believed existed." At the end of the article it even had Frank say "I humbly apologize." There is

GARDNER AND FORD
Ava and John Ford go over the script on the set of Mogambo *in Uganda.*

something very sad in seeing a proud man brought down, but with Frank it really was pride before a fall. He, like everyone working in those changing times, was affected by the shift in the way things were done: the rise of television, Hollywood's metamorphosis, and the changes in radio. Add to all this the fact that most of Frank's professional support systems were gone: no George Evans, no Manie Sacks, no record deal, no studio, nothing that could springboard Frank back to the top. Then along came *From Here to Eternity*. To Frank, this was his passport back.

THE GLORY THAT WAS SINATRA

After celebrating Christmas and Ava's birthday in Africa, the couple went to Paris for a few days' respite from the heat. From there, Frank flew home, where even his old friend and newspaper ally Earl Wilson could find little to excite him about the homecoming. "Frank needed a haircut" was all Wilson could find to write about Frank's arrival at La Guardia airport.

A few days later, Frank was in Boston to play the Latin Quarter nightclub. On 21 January, the day he opened, *Variety* ran a piece saying that Frank had won the role he coveted in *From Here to Eternity*. During his Boston engagement, Frank did a stint as a DJ on WORL. Interestingly, two of the songs he played were Ella Fitzgerald's 'I've Got the World on a String' and Walter Huston's 'September Song', both of which would become important songs for Frank.

At the same time he told Nat Hentoff of *Downbeat*: "We've got to convince the accepted songwriters to come out of hiding and write again. The way things are now; they feel they'd be wasting their time. Another way is to record and revive more of the standards — like 'The Birth Of the Blues', my last release — that way we can at least balance the hokey tunes. It's murder now. Eventually the people who have something to say musically will be the ones who survive."

The Boston shows drew few patrons according to Duke Ellington's drummer Louis Bellson, who was playing at the nearby Storyville (opened by George Wein, who would start the Newport Jazz Festival a year later). One night Frank went over to the Storyville to catch Ellington's set. Pearl Bailey was there too, since she was married to Bellson. She told Frank, "You should do that movie even if you have to pay the studio."

From Boston, Frank went to Canada to fulfil another club booking, this time at the Chez Parée in Montreal. From Canada he flew to London, arriving on Tuesday 17 February, where he spoke somewhat guardedly to Tony Hall of the *New Musical Express*, who appeared to be one of the few press people to know that Frank was in England. Frank confirmed he would be touring Britain in the spring and early summer. He

1952 ON THE JUKEBOX

FRANK ON THE US CHARTS

'I HEAR A RHAPSODY'
(George Fragos, Jack Baker, Dick Gasparre & R Bard)
22 March, No 24, 3 weeks

'BIM BAM BABY'
(Sam Mysels)
13 September, No 20, 4 weeks

'AZURE-TE (PARIS BLUES)'
(Jack Wolf & WB Davis)
27 September, No 30, 1 week

'THE BIRTH OF THE BLUES'
(Ray O'Henderson, Buddy DeSylva & Lew Brown)
22 November, No 19, 2 weeks

By 1952 Frank's career as a chart performer seemed over, with just ten weeks on the chart and four very minor hits. During the year Frank only recorded 12 tracks at Columbia. His last was on 17 September with Canadian Percy Faith, and his Orchestra. Ironically, this last recording for Columbia is the wonderful 'Why Try To Change Me Now', and it has real poignancy. You get the feeling he wanted to make it count that day in the studio. It came out as the b-side of 'Birth of The Blues', an Axel Stordahl arrangement, which was a much better recording than its chart placing would suggest. It all underlined the desperate state of Frank's career.

The biggest song on the *Billboard* chart was Jo Stafford's 'You Belong to Me', but the year belonged to Eddie Fisher. He eclipsed his nearest rival, Johnnie Ray, by a huge margin. Eddie had 13 records on the chart (8 in the Top 10), including 'Wish You Were Here' which made No 1 in July. Eddie Fisher was only 19 when his first record made the charts in the early summer of 1948. Two years later his first solo hit 'Any Time' made No 2 on the US charts. By the end of 1954 he had four records that topped the *Billboard* chart. While Fisher was not in Frank's class as a singer there was no denying his popularity with the young, and especially young women, in America. Between 1952–3 he served in the military and upon his discharge he starred in a weekly TV show that took him back to the top.

He married Debbie Reynolds and the couple had a daughter, Carrie, who starred in *Star Wars* and *When Harry Met Sally*. Eddie later married Elizabeth Taylor and Connie Stevens; both marriages ended in divorce. By the end of the 1950s his chart career was all but over. Drugs played a part in Eddie's decline from popularity and despite several attempts at a comeback he never recaptured past glories. In truth he was only ever a pretender to the crown. Ironically his last chart hit was 'People Like You' in 1967, the orchestral accompaniment was by Nelson Riddle.

❝ You had to tell him when to start. It was amazing. He had a great voice, but he didn't have the feeling for a song the way Frank had. **❞**

ALAN LIVINGSTON, VP CAPITOL RECORDS, ON EDDIE FISHER

RHYTHM KING
Crooner Eddie Fisher surrounded by young fans in Brooklyn, New York.

ALAN LIVINGSTON

"Mr. Livingston, we don't understand why you won't put the Beatles out." BRIAN EPSTEIN

THE MAN WHO SAVED FRANK'S PROFESSIONAL SKIN WAS ALAN WENDELL LIVINGSTON, THE 35-YEAR-OLD HEAD OF ARTISTS AND REPERTOIRE FOR CAPITOL RECORDS IN LOS ANGELES.

He was born on 15 October, 1917, in McDonald, Pennsylvania. Alan gained a bachelor's degree in economics at the Wharton School, after his Army service, before moving to California, and started working at Capitol Records in 1946. He later recalled "I met Glen and Paul Weston who was music director at the time. We talked and talked and talked. I said 'Are you going to hire me or aren't ya?' They said OK. I said, 'I want $100 a week' which was big money then. They said OK. They gave me a job making children's albums." He later became vice-president in charge of Artists and Repertoire in 1950,

but left after five years to join NBC as vice-president of TV programming. He returned to Capitol Records in 1960 as president and Chairman of the Board, a position he held for eight years. He was instrumental in deciding to release the Beatles records on Capitol. Though they were signed to Capitol's parent company in the UK, the label had passed on their early releases. He later worked for Mediarts Inc and then Twentieth Century Fox-Film Corporation. As well as working with Frank Sinatra he created Bozo the Clown.

COUPLED FOR SUCCESS
Alan Livingston with his wife, actress Betty Hutton.

spoke also of *From Here To Eternity*, "his biggest film break to date". There was an interesting tailpiece to the article: "For those who say Frankie's finished – for all Sinatra fans we quote from *Metronome* Editor George T Simon's review of 'Birth of the Blues' and 'Why Try To Change Me Now', 'Wow! This is it! All of us who have been waiting for Frankie to come back and make some really great sides again need wait no longer.'" In *Metronome's* review of the year for 1952, 'Birth of the Blues' was one of their records of the year.

Why Frank was in London remains unclear. It may have been to finalize arrangements for the European tour, but it would appear to have been very much a private visit. It may have been connected with Ava's pregnancy or a miscarriage. Opinion is divided about exactly when Ava was pregnant, how many abortions she had, and what she told Frank at the time. Some have speculated that Ava was pregnant only once. In her autobiography, Ava talks of two occasions, one in November 1952 and then on another occasion when Frank was at her bedside when she came round from the anaesthetic. Daughter Nancy wrote in her book that there were two occasions, November and then another abortion in December, but this clearly must be wrong somehow. If indeed there were two occasions, it could have been November and then again in May/June when Frank and Ava were together in London during Frank's tour. Whatever the truth, we will never know for sure. The fact remains that it must have been a very harrowing experience for both of them.

The final screenplay for *From Here to Eternity* was finished on 24 February, 1953, and the interior shooting began on 2 March in Hollywood before the

LUCEY'S RESTAURANT

hundred-strong cast and crew decamped to Hawaii. At the same time that the film was getting underway, the issue of Frank's new record deal was being resolved. There remains some mystery surrounding the minutiae of the deal, and obviously such an important, life-changing, career-saving event is bound to attract comment. But one man who was pivotal in the whole thing was Alan Livingston.

A CAPITOL DEAL

The William Morris Agency was anxious to secure a recording deal for Frank. Without one, his earning potential, already severely curtailed, would go into a tailspin. Sam Weisbord at William Morris called everyone in an effort to get Frank signed. One man who took his call was Alan Livingston, the Vice President for A&R (Artists and Repertoire) at Capitol. According to Alan, "Mitch [Miller] finally let him go. He said 'I can't do anything with you. Music has changed. And you're not it anymore.' Frank went down lower and lower and no one cared about him anymore. One day and I got a call from Sam Weisbord. And he said 'We've just taken on Sinatra.' And I said 'Really?' because I was interested to hear that. And he said 'Yes. Would you be interested in signing him?' And I said 'Yes.' He said, 'You would?' Truly no one – not even his agent – had faith in him at that point." While Alan was *the* man at Capitol as far as a decision like this

was concerned, it's interesting to speculate on the role of Axel Stordahl, whose wife, June Hutton, was signed to the label. While Alan denies that Axel played any part in Frank's signing, his opinion may have helped. In an article in *Billboard* in 1998, another perspective emerged. Dave Cavanaugh, who produced some of Frank's later Capitol albums and was still working at Capitol in the 1990s, said, "The big Sinatra booster at Capitol was Dex. He kept insisting we ought to give him a try." Dave Dexter Jr had been a writer for *Downbeat* magazine before joining Capitol back in 1952. In the same *Billboard* article, he recalled, "We'd just signed Axel Stordahl and he and June kept telling me 'Frank's singing great again'

and suggesting we sign him. And at every A&R meeting, Alan Livingston would tell us that William Morris was submitting Frank to us."

Al Martino recalls being at KHJ Studio on 14 March when Frank arrived to meet Alan Livingston. "He was waiting in the lobby, I felt he was too big of a star to be waiting for anyone." The deal was finalized at Lucey's Restaurant situated right across the street from KHJ. It seems scarcely believable now, but so low was Frank that Capitol offered him only what was termed "a scale

LUCEY'S
This restaurant was the scene of Frank's historic signing to Capitol Records. In the bar (above), Frank sat with Alan Livingston for a drink after his first Capitol recording session on 2 April, 1953.

NELSON RIDDLE

"Nelson, who was a beautiful guy took things to heart."

JOHNNY MANDEL

NELSON SMOCK RIDDLE II WAS BORN IN ORADELL, NEW JERSEY, 10 MILES WEST OF NEW YORK CITY, ON 1 JUNE, 1921. HIS FAMILY ORIGINS WERE DUTCH, WHICH IS WHERE THE NAME "SMOCK" CAME FROM.

Nelson grew up in hard times. "We didn't feel the Depression at all. My father made his own depression... we were already in a depressed state by the time the Depression got here," is how Nelson remembers it. Indeed, Nelson appeared to be in a similar state, mentally, throughout his life. Friends and colleagues recalled him as a man who rarely smiled or laughed, and even when he did it was a very small smile.

Nelson's father was an amateur musician who inspired his son to take up the piano and later the trombone. Nelson learned arranging from Bill Finegan, who had worked with Glenn Miller. Nelson and his mentor were inspired by the work of Shostakovich, particularly his *First Symphony*, which premiered in 1937. His first band gig was with Charlie Briggs and his Briggadiers, before he joined Charlie Spivak's orchestra.

Nelson joined the Merchant Navy in 1943. His experiences there were to motivate his dislike of serving in the military. Nelson was not your average sailor, since he managed to join a Merchant Navy band started by Jack Lawrence, the lyricist on 'All or Nothing At All'. After serving for 17 months, Nelson joined the Tommy Dorsey band, first as a trombonist and then as an arranger. This all came to an end when Nelson was called up to join the Army in April 1945. After his demob, Nelson began working

as an arranger for Bob Crosby, among others, before he became a staff arranger for NBC radio.

In 1949, Nelson was writing for the CBS show *Carnation Hour*, which starred Tony Martin and later Dick Haymes, having been given this opportunity by Victor Young, the show's musical director, who much admired Nelson's talents. The pivotal moment that would eventually lead to Nelson working with Frank came in late 1949, when choral arranger Les Baxter got Nelson to arrange 'Mona Lisa' for Nat King Cole. Nelson also "ghost arranged" 'Too Young', and to this day Baxter often gets the credit. Nelson began working extensively with Nat Cole and did a great deal to hone his relaxed style of song delivery.

Besides working with Frank Sinatra, from 1953 Nelson was linked with many of Capitol's vocalists, including Dean Martin and Peggy Lee. Capitol signed Nelson as a solo artist and he had a No 1 with 'Lisbon Antigua' in early 1956. He wrote for TV shows including *The Untouchables*, *Batman*, and *Route 66*, as well as serving as musical director on *The Bob Newhart Show*, *The Smothers Brothers Comedy Hour*, and *The Julie Andrews Show*. Possibly one of his most challenging jobs was arranging 'Wandering Star' and giving voice lessons to Lee Marvin for his appearance in the film *Paint Your Wagon* (1969), which Nelson also scored.

His other film work included scoring *Ocean's Eleven*, *Robin and the Seven Hoods*, *Lolita*, and *Pal Joey*, before winning an Academy Award in 1974 for his work on *The Great Gatsby*.

A PARTIAL RETURN

By the late 1970s, Nelson was hardly working at all. In 1980, he was reduced to recording background music for a company that supplied "lift music". An offer of working with musicians Yehudi Menuhin and Stephan Grappelli in 1981 must have been a real boost

NELSON AND FRANK

Singer and arranger go over the charts prior to Frank conducting one of Nelson's pieces for 'Tone Poems of Colour'. At 6' 2" tall Nelson made Frank look even shorter than he was.

A GREAT ARRANGEMENT

In 1963 Nelson worked with Canadian virtuoso Oscar Peterson, one of the greatest jazz pianists ever.

at this time. A year later, an album with Ella Fitzgerald turned out to be less than impressive because Ella was in far from fine voice.

Shortly afterwards, an angel came along in the shape of Linda Ronstadt. After a career as a pop and rock singer, she had decided to make an album of the music that she grew up with. Her manager, and producer, Peter Asher, contacted Nelson about the possibility of him arranging 'Guess I'll Hang My Tears out to Dry'. When Nelson met Asher, his response was "I don't write arrangements, I write albums." Nelson urged Linda to listen to Frank's Capitol albums to see how he dealt with lyrics, and it was decided that he should do the whole record. *What's New* sold three and a half million copies and was followed by *Lush Life* and *Sentimental Reasons*. Nelson never got to see the release of the last album because he died on 6 October, 1985, before it came out. Sadly, Nelson Riddle never quite received the monetary rewards that his talents deserved. As is all too often the case, his particular genius has been more widely acknowledged only after it was too late for his own personal reward. Today, Nelson Riddle is recognized as one of, if not the, most talented post-war arranger-composers.

"My family are all very respectful of Linda because she brought our father back from what seemed to be obscurity. *What's New* was wonderful for its ingénue like quality." (Chris Riddle – Nelson's son). For more information, read the excellent book on Nelson Riddle, *September in The Rain* by Peter J Levinson.

COUNTRY ROCK MEETS THE STANDARDS

Linda Ronstadt made her name in country rock before working with Nelson on *What's New*, the first of their three collaborations.

deal" – the kind of deal that was offered only to new artists or one in whom there was little expectation. Frank got a five per cent royalty on every record he sold. According to Alan, it was "a one-year contract with six one-year options, and no advance. Nothing!" It meant that if Frank didn't work out in the first year, Capitol would drop him and move on. Hank Sanicola and Livingston's wife, the actress Betty Hutton (no relation to June), were at lunch and acted as witnesses. Although Frank was low, he should be given credit for taking it. Many people would have argued their way out of a deal by failing to acknowledge their plight. Frank was smart: he knew that this contract was his way back. In the final analysis it was Alan Livingston's decision and he deserves the credit. It's one that ranks alongside Sam Phillips selling Elvis Presley to RCA or George Martin having the vision of what he could do with John, Paul, George, and Ringo. "He was in the right place, at the right time," said Alan.

Either at lunch or soon afterwards there was discussion as to which arranger/conductor Frank was going to work with. Frank's reaction was immediate: "I've worked with Axel for practically my whole career, I can't leave Axel now." Livingston was anxious to put Frank with Nelson Riddle,

who had had considerable success with Nat King Cole for Capitol (Nat and Nelson's recording of 'Pretend' was sitting at No 6 on the *Billboard* chart as they lunched). According to the booklet that accompanied the boxed set of Frank's Capitol singles, a compromise was worked out. They would try a session with Frank and Axel, put out a record and see what happened. If nothing did, then Frank and Nelson would work together. The booklet goes on to say that the Sinatra/Stordahl partnership "had worn out its welcome, and this was probably the biggest single cause of the star's career nosedive". Clearly this is a further blurring of the legend, giving rise to some unfairly disparaging comments about Stordahl. In fact, Frank had a lot more to thank Axel for than he ever had to criticize.

When Alan Livingston announced that he had signed Frank at the Capitol Records National Convention in Colorado, the reaction was a resounding groan. Alan's response? "Look, I only know one thing, and that's talent. Frank is the most talented singer I've ever heard. He's had hard times but you watch. The sales force was not behind him. They didn't help him at all. They didn't think he would ever make it again." It made for an interesting

66 He sank lower and lower. No one was interested in him. He couldn't even get a job in a nightclub. 99
ALAN LIVINGSTON, 2003

FRANK'S FIRST SESSION
The first Capitol recording sessions with Axel Stordahl (far left) on 2 April, 1953. He is talking to Alan Livingston while Voyle Gilmore jokes with Frank.

CAPITOL SOUND

KJH studio, 5515 Melrose Avenue was where Frank made his first Capitol recordings. The label had bought the former radio station studios in 1949. It was close to the entrance to Paramount film studio. The studio was well equipped with new state-of-the-art tape machines and an early multi-channel mixing board. There were three studios, A B and C. A was on the upper storey and was the original radio theatre with excellent acoustics.

Downbeat and Frank had not forgotten it; another Capitol staffer, Voyle Gilmore, was brought in to do the honours.

Apart from a different Hollywood studio, it was business as normal. Along with Axel there were familiar faces in the band,

dilemma. Frank was really lucky. If anyone had a chance of getting him back it was Capitol. But the lack of support from the sales force was a problem and one that would remain largely unresolved for the remainder of the year.

Two weeks later, news of Frank's Capitol deal had reached Britain, and the *New Musical Express* ran a piece saying that Frank had signed a two-year deal. What's interesting about the story is that someone, either at Capitol or in Frank's circle, had put a much rosier hue on the story. "Various major companies including Columbia and RCA Victor are all reported to have made frantic bids to capture the echo of 'the Voice'. The betting was very heavily banked on RCA. Columbia also entered the running in a big way to retain the services of this top seller. A big factor that influenced Frank is that Capitol intend to use him to fill their name-singer gap, thus ensuring top exploitation." *Billboard* was closer to the truth, saying "that a coolness existed between Sinatra and Columbia was no secret". In the same article, datelined "Hollywood March 14", which appeared in the 21 March *Billboard* issue, they pointed out that "the bow-tied balladist joins Axel Stordahl, who moved to Capitol six months ago". Alan Livingston was quoted as saying "Capitol expects to cash in on Sinatra disk deals by tying in closely with tune material from his forthcoming movies." This was a brave statement indeed, since Frank's only movie was the forthcoming *From Here to Eternity*.

Frank's first Capitol session was on 2 April at the KHJ studios on Melrose Avenue, beginning at 8:30 pm and finishing three hours later. Livingston had originally intended that Dave Dexter would "produce" the session but Frank baulked at that one too. Dexter had written a bad review in

> **" Axel was a friend of mine, but I felt Nelson was what he needed. "**
>
> ALAN LIVINGSTON, 2003

including trumpeter Zeke Zarchy, sax player Ted Nash, and piano player Bill Miller, who had first played piano on a session for Frank a year before and would become an inexorable part of Frank's life for the next five decades. They cut four songs: 'Lean Baby' written by Billy May, with words by Roy Alfred (and orchestrated for Axel by Heinie Beau), 'Day In, Day Out', 'Don't Make a Beggar of Me', and 'I'm Walking Behind You', written by Englishman Billy Reid. The lyrics on 'Lean Baby' were not what Billy May had envisaged when he was writing the instrumental on which this song was based: "It was supposed to be Lean, Baby – you know, lean back or lean forward, baby!"

After that first session, Frank and Alan Livingston went across the street to Lucey's; according to Alan, it was one of the few times they ever socialized. "It was late and we were sitting in the bar having a drink, nobody else was in the place except for a man who was sitting across the bar. Frank and I were talking, I said 'Why don't you take it easy? Get a better image.' He said, 'Alan I don't do anything.' All of a sudden the man says 'What are you doing, buying a drink for your leech friend?' Frank said 'Knock it off.' The guy said 'Knock it off, knock it off…' And Frank didn't do a thing, but his kind of a bodyguard went up and grabbed this guy. I thought he was going to kill him. And threw him out of the restaurant. Frank said 'See? That's the trouble I get in. It's not my fault.'"

ETERNITY ROAD

After the first Capitol session, Frank went to Hawaii for *From Here to Eternity*. The locations described in the book, including Schofield Army Barracks, The Royal Hawaiian Hotel, and Diamond Head, were all used, adding to the movie's feeling of authenticity. Ava joined Frank shortly before he finished shooting. She did so against the wishes of MGM, so they suspended her. Shooting wrapped on the film on 26 April, giving Frank time to get back to Los Angeles for his next recording session four days later. One of the crew working on *Eternity* said that Frank had been "like a school kid playing hooky with the adults", on the first day of filming. By the end he "kind of filled out and his head went back and he started looking you straight in the eye again".

Capitol had decided to couple 'I'm Walking Behind You' and 'Lean Baby' as Frank's debut single, and it was just about to be released by the time of the second session. By 16 May it was on the charts and on its way to No 7, staying around for ten weeks. According to the Capitol Singles CD booklet, neither song "had the impact that Sinatra, Gilmore, and Livingston were seeking". This somewhat undermines the story that Nelson would work with Frank only if things didn't work out with Axel.

The fact that Frank's second Capitol session took place before his first single came out indicates that something else may have happened to change Frank's mind about Axel. Clearly the first record was not a smash, nor was it a radical change of direction. In fact Frank may have felt let down by Axel, betrayed in the worst way for someone with his Italian sense of values and honour – Axel had accepted a job conducting on Eddie Fisher's new television series. Not just another singer but a man who, in Frank's opinion, had little talent. Frank was reportedly madder than hell and there was a rift between the two old friends that lasted many years. To be fair to Axel, Eddie Fisher was hot; his recording of 'I'm Walking Behind You' topped the charts for seven weeks, easily out-selling Frank. Alan Livingston was still keen for Frank to work with Nelson, spurred on by his success with Nat King Cole. Some people have even suggested that Frank was unaware who Nelson was when he came to work with him at that first session. This is inconceivable. Nelson had arranged 'Mona Lisa'

❝A triumph of miscasting❞

HARRY COHN

TAKING DIRECTION
Fred Zinnemann (centre) directing Montgomery Clift (left) and Frank Sinatra (right) in From Here To Eternity.

and 'Too Young' for Cole, as well as arranging and conducting 'Unforgettable' and 'Pretend'. Nelson also worked with George Siravo, one of Frank's regular arrangers, in his last few years at Columbia. According to Alan, Frank "knew who he was, of course. I used Nelson at union scale to arrange and conduct orchestras behind singers."

But knowing of Nelson and agreeing to work with him was quite another thing. Frank wanted Billy May to succeed Axel, but with Billy on tour in Florida, Capitol hit on a novel solution. They got Riddle in to arrange four songs for Frank's next session: two in the style of Billy May and two as Nelson Riddle. To further the intrigue, the studio players were told that Billy had arranged 'I Love You' and 'South of the Border'. So good was Nelson the impersonator that most of the musicians thought they were genuine Billy May arrangements. Fifty years to the day, sax player Ted Nash, who was also a veteran of Billy May's Orchestra, recalled the session: "'South of the Border' – I thought that was Billy's arrangement – it's so typically Billy. I can't picture that Nelson would have done that in Billy's style – Nelson was SO ultra serious! All Billy's arrangements were written out for us. Billy was known for his special slides and slurps. There would be special coding on the paper, so the notes to slide on were known. We all knew how he worked and the sounds to aim for."

To complete the illusion, when 'South of the Border' and 'I Love You' came out later in the year, the label said 'Frank Sinatra with Billy May and His Orchestra'. Bill Miller insists they knew. "Oh yeah. Nelson made an announcement after we did his tunes. He said 'Now we'll make like Billy May.'"

According to Peter Levinson's book about Nelson Riddle, *September in the Rain*, this was not the first time that Nelson had worked for a Sinatra. Back in late 1951, he wrote some arrangements for Frank's cousin, bandleader Ray Sinatra, one of which was 'Ciribiribin', Harry James's theme song. As a young trombone player, Nelson was in the studio band at one of Frank's *Your Hit Parade* radio shows on 17 September, 1944.

The two songs that Nelson arranged in his own style were 'Don't Worry 'Bout Me' and 'I've Got the World on a String'. The fable of Frank's comeback could only have been better if 'I've Got the World on a String' had been his first recording for Capitol. Nelson's arrangement heralds Frank's arrival, while his perfect vocal phrasing sounds like a subtle fanfare. Some would have us believe that 'I've Got the World on a String' was like some triumphal moment in recording history: Frank was back, and back big. But this is a total misrepresentation of what really happened. Capitol were anxious to push Frank, even if their investment was almost

nothing, and released 'I've Got the World on a String' in June. The song only just managed to make the charts, reaching No 14, and staying there for just two weeks. Frank was simply not a hit with the public. It wasn't that people didn't like Frank's records; at this moment they didn't really like Frank. As little as a year later, *Downbeat* was referring to this as Frank's first Capitol recording, "the day his first two sides hit the disk jockeys his wax comeback was on its way". The fact is that 'I've Got the World on a String' is a superb recording, as is the B-side, 'My One and Only Love', on which Frank's personal problems are again reflected in song. It was the perfect down to the up of 'String'. While he hadn't yet hit the depths with Ava there is a world-weariness in his voice. It must have irked Frank that Eddie Fisher was still riding high in the charts that 4 July weekend when 'I've Got the World on a String' crept into the charts. Perry Como had two recordings in the Top 10, and to cap it all Mitch Miller's protégé, Frankie Laine, was doing so well.

Frank cut 'My One and Only Love' at his third Capitol session on 2 May along with 'Anytime Anywhere' and a song called 'From Here to Eternity'. The latter was heard in the film, but not with any words, and Frank certainly never sang it. Putting words to it and releasing it was pure opportunism, especially as Frank's Barton Music secured the publishing rights to the song. It's been said that Harry Cohn agreed to it because he paid Frank so poorly for his movie role. Bob Wells, who wrote it along with Fred Karger, went to the 2 May session and said that Frank was "down and out" and "insecure". At the end of the session, Frank spoke to Bob, asking humbly "Was that all right, Bob?" Bob told him "That was great, Frank." Next time Wells saw Frank he said "Hello Frank." "Hi Kid" was Frank's reply… he was, by then, already back.

EUROPE DECLINES

Not that Frank was around to witness in person his lack of "comeback" success on the *Billboard* charts. Even before signing to Capitol he had agreed to tour Great Britain and Europe. While the money was important to him, there was an additional incentive to make the trip. There were no American bookings coming Frank's way and according to Bill Miller, Ava

the music long awaited by the nation's dancers

the fresh approach of

BILLY MAY
and his orchestra

Capitol

BAND LEADER
Billy May was very popular at the time. He was even managing to chart records when most bandleaders were not, so it is easy to see why Capitol wanted to link him with Frank.

being in Europe was a big motivation. "We went because Ava was over there shooting a movie. And so they worked around that." Although this was put at risk after their short holiday in Hawaii during April, as MGM suspended Ava. It is important not to underestimate just how vital this European tour was given the miserable pay packet from *Eternity*, especially with his alimony payments to Nancy. News of the lack of success of Frank's new records would have reached him while he was away and none of it must have made him very happy.

Even in England, Ava's battle with the studio continued. On 7 May she met with MGM's Head of British Operations. He wanted Ava to stay in London and work on her horse riding; she flatly refused, deciding to go to Italy with Frank for the start of his European tour. They flew from London to Rome on Friday 8 May where Frank, true to form, had a scuffle with a photographer. And it didn't get any better. Frank played Rome, Milan, Florence, Turin, Genoa, and Naples, where he walked off the stage because the audience were chanting for Ava. Unbeknown to Frank, the over-eager promoter

had advertised the show as starring Frank AND Ava. Frank did not perform well. The "confidence boosting" injection that *From Here To Eternity* would bring had not kicked in, nor were things between him and Ava going well. One bright spot on the Italian leg of the tour was a radio show on 20 May for RAI when he sang three songs, just with Bill Miller's piano for accompaniment. 'Laura', 'Night and Day' and 'September Song' all sounded great. From Italy Frank went to Belgium, where he played the Knocke Casino before flying north to Scandinavia. If things had gone badly in Italy they were dire here. With a Dutch band called the Skyliners, under the direction of Harold Collins, Frank played to half-full venues, prompting the *New Musical Express* to comment, "Sinatra has been a flop in Denmark and Sweden". On calling his Copenhagen hotel the press were told that Frank was ill and had gone to bed. His concert at the Folkparken in Malmo, Sweden, attracted a total of 4,000 people to a venue that held 10,000. Frank walked off after half an hour of his scheduled 90 minutes, prompting the show organizer to complain, "It was awful to listen to." After this, further

ADVERTISING FRANK
The Melody Maker *carried regular advertisements throughout Frank's stay in Britain promoting the "extra" Sunday shows.*

FRANK LOVED A FIGHT
On 9 June, 1953, Ava and Frank and British bandleader Joe Loss sat in the front row at White City Stadium to watch Randolph Turpin fight Charles Homez for the World Middleweight Boxing title.

RELAXING FRANK
Frank in the apartment that he and Ava rented in St John's Wood in north London.

❝I saw the Birmingham Hippodrome shows – five nights in a row in the early 1950s – and you could have got a ticket any night!❞

EDDIE HAINES, DRUMMER

Swedish dates were cancelled, as were those scheduled for Norway. The hoped-for European cash injection was not to be.

Back in the US the news of Frank's performance in *to Eternity* had begun to leak out. There was a buzz around Hollywood. Frank was great. Frank *was* Maggio. How much of this filtered through to Frank in Europe is undocumented. Back in England by 8 June, Frank and Ava rented an apartment in St John's Wood, where their arguments continued. One night Stewart Grainger and Jean Simmons were visiting and Ava complained that Frank was impossible to live with. Ava's new film, *The Knights of the Round Table*, with Robert Taylor, had commenced shooting. This piece of period junk must have seemed like garbage even then, although it did earn her $17,500 a week. This too added to the rancour between Ava and Frank.

FRANKIE GOES TO TOOTING

In late May, adverts began appearing in the press for one-off Sunday concerts that Frank would be playing around London, although these told far from the whole story. Frank had managed to secure a full schedule of concerts in Britain that seemed to be added to the longer he stayed; no doubt, in part, to make up for Europe.

The Melody Maker reviewed his first British show at the Tooting Granada later that week. "Perhaps a few of us believed he was on his way out and came on a nostalgic pilgrimage... he was great as he swung into 'I've Got The World On A String'". It reported that Frank took requests, including 'September Song', which he performed to the accompaniment of just Bill Miller's piano. In Liverpool, according to Tommy Sheldon, it was a slightly different story. "I had paid six shillings for my ticket and was about half-way down the stalls in a fairly full Liverpool Empire, but certainly not a sell-out. People were shouting out requests in between numbers and at one point Frank paused and stood with one leg resting on the footlights and looked out and said 'whada ya think this is – an auction'. Someone shouted for 'Bim Bam Baby' (the b-side of Frank's November 1952 release of 'Walking in the Sunshine'). Frank fixed him with a look and said 'Columbia only made one mistake with that record – they put a hole in it'."

While Frank was at the Empire he went to Ma Egerton's pub which is just behind the theatre, but had to leave after too many people decided to join him. He retreated to Southport, where he stayed in a hotel overlooking Royal Birkdale golf course. Another who was at the Empire was Dorothy Webster who was the assistant to the stage manager. "At the second show on Frank's opening night he asked me for a cup of tea; singing so many songs he needed the lubrication. He said could he have it without milk and with some lemon. Back then we didn't keep a lot of lemons backstage so I told him we didn't have any. He was not worried and had it black. Before the next night's shows I went out and bought lemons so he had tea the way he liked it for the rest of the week." Frank very nearly didn't play a Sunday concert in Dundee, Scotland, as he Police Committee who authorized Sunday performances in the city doubted whether the one-third of receipts that had to go to a charity organization would actually be paid. Eventually, it was resolved and Frank performed at the Cairds Hall. He also played Green's Playhouse in Ayr but demand was such that people were shifted from the circle to fill the stalls. It would be 47 years, almost to the day, before Frank played again in Scotland.

For his appearances on radio the BBC Showband directed by Cyril Stapleton accompanied Frank. He also appeared on another radio programme with DJ David Jacobs "It was for a Radio Luxembourg show called *Portrait Of A Star*. It was recorded in London, and ran for 15 minutes. We did people like Ruby Murray and Alma Cogan, and was a star "chat" interspersed with some records. Frank was about an hour-and-a-half late – I think he had been playing golf – but he was worth waiting for! Before he started he was very pleasant, though he said that if I mentioned Ava Gardner he would push the mike down my throat! We played the two sides of his most recent single; he knew he had to plug... to pull his socks up."

SUNDAY AT THE OPERA HOUSE

A week after appearing on BBC radio Frank was on stage at the Blackpool Opera House. Accompanying him throughout his British shows, besides Bill Miller, was Billy Ternent and His Orchestra (recently voted the twentieth best band in Britain in the *NME* poll). Frank called Billy "the little giant". In mid-March, *The Melody Maker* had run a story saying that Ternent had been offered the job but "there is little I can tell you until I have made up my mind whether to accept or not." It gives a good indication of how low the Sinatra cachet had sunk.

The Blackpool concert was enthralling, a bridge from the old to the new. Frank opened with 'When You're Smiling', which he first recorded back in April 1950. He followed up with 'That Old Black Magic' first done with Axel back in 1946 before being redone for *Meet Danny Wilson*. Frank's first recording of the third song 'You Go To My Head', dates from 1945, a year after his fourth number at the show, his tour de force 'Ol' Man River'. The fifth song 'Sweet Lorraine', was recorded in 1946 with The Metronome All Stars, which included Nat King Cole on piano (Cole himself would do a great version of the song in 1957 for Capitol). 'The Birth of the Blues', which

UK TOUR DATES 1953

Thursday 11 June *BBC Showband Show*

Sunday 14 June *Granada, Tooting, South London*

Monday 15 June *The Hippodrome, Bristol (a week-long engagement)*

Sunday 21 June *Gaumont State, Kilburn, North London 6:00 pm & 8:30 pm*

Sunday 28 June *Regal, Edmonton, North London 6:00 pm & 8.30 pm*

Monday 29 June *Hippodrome, Birmingham (a week-long engagement)*

Sunday 5 July *Trocadero, Elephant & Castle, South London 6:00 pm & 8:30 pm*

Monday 6 July *The Empire, Glasgow (a week-long engagement)*

Sunday 12 July *Cairds Hall, Dundee*

Monday 13 July *Edinburgh*

Tuesday 14 July *Green's Playhouse, Ayr*

Thursday 16 July *BBC Showband Show*

Sunday 19 July *De Montfort Hall, Leicester 3:00 pm & 6:30 pm*

Monday 20 July *The Palace Theatre, Manchester (a week-long engagement)*

Sunday 26 July *The Opera House, Blackpool*

Monday 27 July *The Empire, Liverpool (a week-long engagement). Two shows on some days*

Sunday 9 August *Commodore, Hammersmith, West London*

FRANK IN LONDON

"I saw Frank Sinatra at the Commodore in Hammersmith, a half empty Flea Pit and the Trocadero at Elephant and Castle. He was in good shape, voice-wise." British singer, Dennis Lotis.

1952–1957

FROM HERE TO ETERNITY

HARRY COHN PAID FRANK $8,000 – for both men it was a great deal. Budget mad "King Cohn" got the movie made for a little over $2.5 million and grossed $19 million on release, and took $84 million by the end of 1954. It's probably why Frank always went for a percentage of the gross thereafter. Nominated for 12 Oscars, it won eight. Cohn had bought the film rights to James Jones's novel for $100,000 in March 1951 and many in Hollywood never thought he would get it made; people called it "Cohn's Folly". According to director Fred Zinnemann "it languished for many months until a young writer, Dan Taradash, found an original approach and wrote an exciting first draft screenplay."

While it would perhaps stretch credulity to say that without this film it would have been "from here to obscurity" for Frank, it was pivotal for his career. Just like the Harry James job, the Dorsey gig and then being signed by Alan Livingston. It is impossible to "what if" history but Frank could well not have become a legend; though it's doubtful he would have ever ended up on the cruise ships.

The story of Frank landing the part was given another twist in 2001 when Martin Jurow, who produced *Breakfast at Tiffany's* and *The Pink Panther*, told yet another version in his autobiography *Marty Jurow Seein' Stars*. "I consulted William Morris agent George Woods, after Harry Cohn refused to consider Sinatra. Cohn had screamed, 'I wouldn't let that bum in my studio.'" Woods in turn spoke to mobster Meyer Lansky and Lansky's "aide" Jimmy Blue Eyes. Jimmy simply said, "Cohn. He owes us. Expect a call."

This film was made against the background of McCarthyism, a decade before the Vietnam War and almost two before the Watergate saga. This was an America where questioning authority could still land you in a lot of trouble.

Frank was not the only one who nearly didn't get the part. Zinnemann wanted Montgomery Clift but Cohn was initially against the idea, wanting a contracted studio star (John Derek) to play the lead. Cohn was unconvinced, in part because Clift was homosexual. As it turned out, Clift was an inspired choice, making it a bitter disappointment when he didn't win an Oscar. Frank's respect for Clift was evident in that he went along with him in his persistence in getting a scene right. For Frank, one take was his preference, two at a pinch. For the female roles Joan Crawford had been linked with Deborah Kerr's part and Shelley Winters was at one time talked of instead of Donna Reed (Frank must have been glad!).

The scene in which Maggio is arrested was among the last to be filmed on location in Hawaii. Frank wanted to actually attack the arresting military policeman, but Cohn thought it too provocative towards the military. Zinnemann agreed with Frank and they were about to shoot the scene that way when Cohn arrived on set, having been tipped off. Cohn insisted that Frank

remain seated throughout the scene, which he did; it left a bitter taste in Frank's mouth. It was probably the right decision given the political climate in 1953, while the US Army allowed the film to be shown to troops, the US Navy banned it as "derogatory to a sister service".

"I was 19 years and I thought at the time, 'what is that "has been" doing in a movie with real movie stars? He is a singer' – a singer that I didn't like because he sang love songs and the girls screamed, which guys my age didn't understand." Ron Accosta, reminiscing in 2003.

> 66A picture so great in its starkly realistic and appealing drama that mere words cannot justly describe it. 99
>
> **SOUTHERN CALIFORNIA MOTION PICTURE COUNCIL**

THE STORY LINE

Published in February 1951, it was 29-year-old James Jones's first novel and ran to 800 pages and over 400,000 words. It is the story of army life in Hawaii prior to Pearl Harbor, a realistic gutsy story that for the first time portrayed service life as it really was. The climax comes as the Japanese attack on that fateful Sunday. Frank is not the only casualty in the film. Montgomery Clift's character is killed by his own buddies as he attempts to rejoin them after going AWOL. He is mistaken for a saboteur.

FILM NOIR?
Originally the Columbia sales people wanted the film to be made in colour but Zinnemann held out for black and white saying colour would trivialize it.

THE BOLDEST BOOK OF OUR TIME...
HONESTLY, FEARLESSLY ON THE SCREEN!

BURT LANCASTER·MONTGOMERY CLIFT

FROM HERE TO ETERNITY

DEBORAH KERR

FRANK SINATRA · DONNA REED

CAST & CREDITS

1st Sgt. Milton Warden	Burt Lancaster
Pvt. R. E. Lee 'Prew' Prewitt	Montgomery Clift
Karen Holmes	Deborah Kerr
Alma Burke (Lorene)	Donna Reed
Pvt. Angelo Maggio	Frank Sinatra
Capt. Dana 'Dynamite' Holmes	Philip Ober

Director	Fred Zinnemann
Producer	Buddy Adler
Screenwriter	Daniel Taradash
Art Director	Cary O'Dell
Cinematographer	Burnett Guffey
Composer	George Duning

followed, was cut at Frank's penultimate Columbia session in June 1952. The seventh number 'Embraceable You' was recorded a couple of weeks after 'Ol' Man River' in December 1944. Song number eight 'One For My Baby' was cut in 1947, and Frank would do it again in 1954 for his movie *Young At Heart*. His next two songs he'd recorded just before leaving California for Europe. 'Don't Worry About Me' and 'I've Got The World on a String' were cut at his second Capitol session and the former was released as a single in Britain in October (Frank's second Capitol release after 'I'm Walking Behind You' and 'Lean Baby' which had been released shortly before this date; interestingly he sang neither song). His eleventh song was 'It Never Entered My Mind', which Frank first recorded in 1947 (accompanied by Mitch Miller on oboe before he found 'fame' as an A&R man) and did it again for Capitol in 1955 for *In The Wee Small Hours*. The penultimate number 'All Of Me' featured in *Meet Danny Wilson* in 1951 and was reprised for Frank's second Capitol album. His closing song was 'Night and Day', first recorded by Frank in 1942 with Axel and issued as his first solo single for Bluebird when he was still Tommy Dorsey's boy singer. At the close of the concert Frank did a bizarre impersonation of Winston Churchill. The show was recorded by a doctor from Leeds who was a fan. The sound from the Opera House went to a central point in another theatre owned by the same company and the doctor had arranged through a contact to take his heavy old-fashioned reel-to-reel tape recorder into the theatre and placed a microphone next to the speaker so he could record this concert. It is one of the most fascinating recordings of Frank's entire career. It shows a man in transition, as well as one who was certainly not expecting his work to be captured for posterity.

TURNING POINT

On 5 August, 1953, *From Here to Eternity* opened at the Capitol Theatre in New York, a move seen as foolhardy by many. It was the middle of summer when no one released a picture in New York: without air conditioning in the theatre it would be stifling. Neither was there to be any pre-publicity, just one full-page ad in the *New York Times*. There was none of the usual opening night razzmatazz, which somehow seems to befit the movie, but against these odds it became a huge success. Within a week the film was showing round the clock, with just a short break for the cleaners to do their bit. *The New York Post* singled out Frank for special praise: "he proves he is an actor by playing the luckless Maggio with a kind of doomed gaiety that is both real and immensely touching." *Newsweek* was both fulsome in its praise for Frank and offered an interesting viewpoint. "Frank Sinatra, *a crooner long since turned actor*, knew what he was doing when he plugged for the role of Maggio." The italics show where they felt Frank's career was heading. Frank and Ava were still in London staying at the Savoy.

> 66 Good evening, ladies and gentlemen, and welcome to the Odeon or whatever this joint's called. 99
>
> **FRANK, AT THE BLACKPOOL OPERA HOUSE**

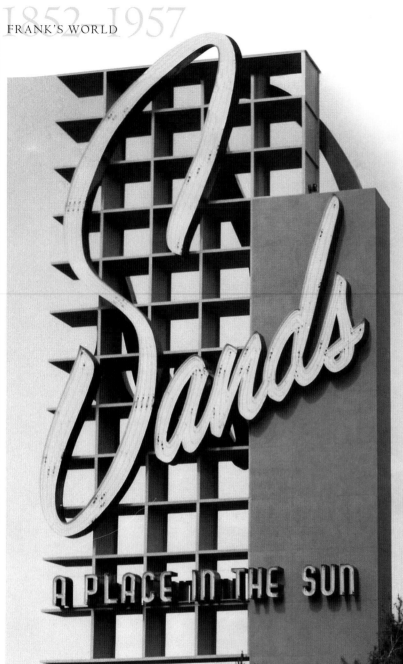

The day after the New York premiere, Earl Wilson and his wife had spent the evening with Frank and Ava. Reports of Frank's success in *Eternity* had reached them, so things went well, which must have been a relief for Wilson who wrote that Frank and Ava were "a two year soap opera with screaming fights heard all around the world", *The Sunday Times* in London commented that it seemed strange that an American film should portray American life as it did. Michael Foot MP thought it "the best piece of pro-American propaganda I have witnessed".

NICER TO COME HOME

In the middle of August Frank and Ava went their separate ways from London. Frank went back to the US while Ava took a three-week holiday in Spain. This sojourn in Europe, and the UK in particular, was incredibly important for Frank. It marked a turning point in his relationship with Ava as well as providing him with a good income at a time when he desperately needed it. Soon after he got back he played a week at Skinny D'Amato's Club 500 in Atlantic City in early September, before heading to northern New Jersey on 15 September for what became a sold out engagement at the Riviera in Fort Lee. Just four miles from the old Rustic Cabin it was a kind of a homecoming, and a world away from his disappointing shows in the autumn of 1952. Eddie Fisher described Frank's opening night at the Riviera as "electrifying". According to *Variety*, "Frank let loose a vocal *tour de force*, accompanied by Bill Miller at the piano and a seven-piece band. He held the floor a solid 60 minutes and while he might and should cut 10 minutes there was no gainsaying the consistency of his socko. He's in for $10,000 a week, for two weeks, and both he and Bill Miller owe a lot to Harry Cohn for what the Columbia picture did for all concerned. Oh

THE SANDS HOTEL
In 1953, there was little indication of what this desert icon would mean to Frank.

DESERT PLAYGROUND
An advertisement from 1952, in the very earliest days of Las Vegas as a resort. A far cry from its image today.

yes, he also sang 'From Here To Eternity' and wisely sh-sh'd some exuberant bobby-soxers who squealed an occasional 'Oh Frankie'."

Frank talked to *Metronome* a few weeks later, saying "If what I did at Bill Miller's [not Frank's pianist, but his namesake who owned the Riviera] did anything, it convinced me once and for all that you can still show good taste and be appreciated. You don't have to sing loud and raucously and belt them over the head all the time. You can use a little restraint and try to create a mood that you and they can both feel, sort of like being together in a small room, and if you really mean it, and show that you mean it, you can register all right." With Frank singing numbers such as 'Violets For Your Furs', 'Spring is Here', 'One For My Baby', and 'Someone To Watch Over Me', it must have been quite a show.

From Here To Eternity had its West Coast premiere in Los Angeles on 30 September at the Pantages Hollywood Theatre at RKO on Hill Street. "Blasts viewers with Atomic Power," was the *LA Times* headline on 1 October. "From Here to Eternity Oscar Contender", was *The Daily News* headline after the movie opened. *The Daily News* was high on Frank, too, staging that Maggio was the "best performance of his career and definitely stamps him as an actor of no little ability". The *LA Examiner* was even more effusive and predicted big things for Frank: "It is visible even from here that he will be among the first next academy time. He is simply superb, comical, pitiful, childishly brave, pathetically defiant."

Three days later, Ava and Frank went to the premiere of *Mogambo* in New York's Radio City Music Hall after pressure from MGM to get them there together. Shortly after *Mogambo*, Frank's new radio series began, in which he did not sing but played a private eye. *The Rocky Fortune Show*, created by the team who did the very much better *X-Minus One* science fiction series, was very definitely the radio equivalent of a B-movie. One wonders if Frank would have signed up for it if he could have predicted how successful *Eternity* was going to be. It ran for 26 weeks, finishing in March 1954, and included one episode in which Frank played a professional footballer's bodyguard, proving that radio is truly amazing. The first show of this NBC series, 'The Oyster Shucker', was a shocker. "Hi, I don't know what it is about me and employment, we start out together but sooner or later,

usually sooner, we reach the fork in the road. You take last week: the Employment Agency sent me out on a job as an oyster shucker, but someone tried to serve me up on a half shell, with a real crazy cocktail sauce – blood." Two weeks after the first *Rocky Fortune Show*, Frank was appearing at the Sands in Las Vegas for a week. The Sands, on Highway 91, had opened on 15 September, 1952. Frank's old friend from the Copacabana, Jack Entratter, was a Vice President at the hotel; he brought many of the big names to work there, including Dean Martin and Jerry Lewis, Lena Horne, Vic Damone, Tony Bennett, and even Louis Jordan in the early days. There was a whole raft of shareholders in the Sands, some from the seamy side.

Frank gave Louella Parsons an interview in which he bemoaned the fact that Ava was not with him, "I can't eat, I can't sleep, I love her." This admission may account for what *Billboard* reported the following week: "Frank Sinatra, the spindly crooner, who is not noted for his warmth towards an audience, this week tried hard to change his ways in the Copa Room, and succeeded, after drawing severe raps from local papers, for his rough treatment of musicians behind him on opening night." A declining relationship brings out conflicting, and often heightened, emotions, and Frank's reaction is far from untypical. According to reports, long-distance arguments on the telephone often kept Frank and Ava up through the night. Ava was also jealous, because she thought that Frank was having an affair in Vegas with a showgirl.

The situation got so bad that on 20 October Jack Entratter was forced to issue a memo to the hotel staff, on Frank's behalf, saying that Ava was banned from the hotel for the remainder of his engagement, and none of her phone calls was to be put through to Frank's suite. One week later, on 27 October, there was an announcement by Howard Sickling, MGM's publicist, on Ava's behalf, that "the separation is final and Miss Gardner will seek a divorce". They did in fact almost make it to two years – a year longer than Ava had been married to either of her previous two husbands.

Soon after finishing at the Sands, Frank appeared before the Nevada Tax Commission, as he too wanted to become a shareholder in the property, intending to take a two per cent stake. After some

INSIDE THE SANDS
The gaming rooms of the new hotel were not nearly as glamorous as you would imagine them to be.

questioning over Frank's back taxes, which he demonstrated had been repaid regularly from his earnings, they approved the transaction. It was, as an investment, probably the best $54,000 Frank ever spent, but it did nothing to enhance his reputation: it would be another link between Frank and the Mob.

Two days before his second wedding anniversary, Frank was at KHJ with Nelson Riddle. Among the songs he recorded over 5–6 November was 'My Funny Valentine'; Frank's ongoing soundtrack to his own life couldn't have worked out better. He also cut Rodgers and Hart's 'Little Girl Blue' from *Jumbo*, a melancholic song that makes some of the torch songs that Frank would later record seem positively upbeat. Frank also began another radio series, this one for NBC. It was a 15-minute twice-weekly show called *To Be Perfectly Frank*. Frank acted as a DJ as well as singing on the show. He pre-recorded over 60 songs for the series at NBC's Burbank studios with a five-piece band, almost a third of which he never recorded commercially. Within a week, Frank's personal life overwhelmed him. His feelings for Ava brought on another suicide attempt. Frank collapsed at Jimmy Van Heusen's New York apartment having apparently cut his wrists. For several years, Jimmy Van Heusen had been a constant source of support for Frank, and one whom he would pay back many times over through his singing of some of Jimmy's best songs. But even

ANOTHER SESSION, ANOTHER SONG
Frank at KHJ with Nelson conducting the orchestra, watched by arranger Dick Reynolds.

Jimmy must have been despairing at this point. The press put it down to a bad case of "Gardneritis". Frank was kept in hospital for three days.

A ROLLER COASTER RIDE

The roller coaster that was Frank's life took another unexpected turn two weeks later when he was back at KHJ studios for two late-night sessions on 8 and 9 December. Recording three songs on each night, on the second he cut Johnny Richards and Carolyn Leigh's 'Young at Heart'. The irony between Frank's recent suicide attempt and the lyrics and sentiment of what would be his comeback chart song is astonishing. What is also very noticeable on 'Young at Heart' is the clarity of the recording. When Frank starts singing after Nelson's gentle introduction, it is as though he's in the room with you. New equipment, better microphones, and the more sophisticated recording tape gives everything a gloss. It is an undervalued aspect of Frank's achievement at Capitol. Technology was at last a match for Frank's genius, and it all added up to an irresistible combination. At the same session he did the beautiful ballad 'I Could Have Told You', which is like a warm-up for the kind of songs Frank was to record two years later. It came out as a B-side to 'Don't Worry 'Bout Me' five months later. It's a measure of the quality of Frank and Nelson's work that it could be comparatively tossed away.

At this time Ava was away in Rome filming *The Barefoot Contessa*. It was ironic that while she looked radiant, Frank was down to 118 lb. According to Lauren Bacall, Frank asked her to take a coconut cake for Ava to Rome, where she was joining Humphrey Bogart. Bogie told Ava that the cake was in his suite, but she did nothing about it for two days. Lauren Bacall finally decided to deliver it herself. Ava didn't even bother to say thank you. "She couldn't have cared less," said Lauren Bacall. On their return from Rome, Bogie and Bacall went out of their way to spend more time with Frank. Both liked him – a feeling that was reciprocated – and Frank liked Humphrey Bogart's Rat Pack.

THE ORIGINAL RAT PACK

As far back as the early 1940s, the Bogarts used regularly to entertain a group of friends that included Spencer Tracy, David Niven, and John Huston. Later it included Frank, whom Bogie and Bacall befriended around the end of 1952. It was Bacall who christened them the Rat Pack.

The name owes its origins to a four-day trip to Las Vegas, headed up by Bogart and Bacall, Frank, along with Judy Garland and her husband, Sid Luft, Angie Dickinson, David Niven and his wife, Ernie Kovacs and his wife, and the Romanoffs, who owned a

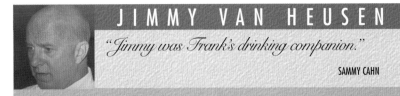

JIMMY VAN HEUSEN

"Jimmy was Frank's drinking companion."

SAMMY CAHN

THE FIRST OF JIMMY VAN HEUSEN'S SONGS THAT FRANK EVER RECORDED WAS 'SHAKE DOWN THE STARS' IN FEBRUARY 1940, JUST A MONTH AFTER HE JOINED TOMMY DORSEY. IT WAS FAR FROM HIS LAST.

For the next decade, Frank sang many of Jimmy's songs. Some, like the first, were written with Eddie de Lange, others co-written with Johnny Burke. It was Jimmy who co-wrote 'Nancy, With The Laughing Face' with Phil Silvers. Jimmy also wrote songs for Frank with Carl Sigman, Johnny Mercer, Mack Gordon, and Buddy Kaye. Some have said it was Bing Crosby that got Jimmy and Sammy Cahn to begin writing together; others have said it was Frank. Whatever the truth, the first songs that Jimmy and Sammy wrote for Frank were for the film *The Tender Trap* in 1955; it was the start of a decade-long partnership. "He's the man who invented using the word 'fuck' between syllables, like 'This melody is bea-fuckin'-utiful'", was how Sammy Cahn expressed it.

Jimmy was born Edward Chester Babcock on 26 January, 1913 in Syracuse, New York. He was 16 when he became James Van Heusen when he worked on radio station WSYR; the station manager thought his real name sounded obscene! He never legally became Van Heusen – a name he took from the shirt manufacturer – and most of his friends called him Chester.

His first song-writing assignment was for the Cotton Club revues in the 1930s, though his first real break came in 1938 when he met Jimmy Dorsey. It was soon after this that he met bandleader Eddie de Lange and they began writing together. Frank's recording with Tommy Dorsey of 'Polka Dots and Moonbeams' was an early successful collaboration between Jimmy and Johnny Burke. Soon Jimmy was in

Hollywood writing for films, which included the Hope and Crosby *Road to Zanzibar*. Ultimately, Jimmy wrote music for 18 Bing Crosby movies.

During World War II, Chester Babcock became a Lockheed test pilot, having learned to fly before the war. In this capacity he was not known as Jimmy Van Heusen, and neither did the Hollywood crowd know that he did such a risky job.

After the war, the hits just kept rolling, and only when Johnny Burke fell ill in 1954, which prevented him working for two years, did Jimmy begin working with Sammy Cahn. Their partnership produced memorable songs together, including the Grammy Award-winning 'September of My Years' and 'My Kind of Town' in 1964, which Frank sang as his penultimate song at his last concert in 1995. Van Heusen received 10 Oscar nominations for Best Song in a Motion Picture and won four Academy Awards in that category as well as an Emmy Award for Best Musical Contribution.

The man who listed "chicks, booze, music, and Sinatra" as his interests died on 7 February, 1990, having probably enjoyed all of them. As well as being Frank's drinking companion he wrote some damn fine songs.

GALA REHEARSAL
Frank rehearsing for JFK's Inaugural Gala in 1961, with Jimmy Van Heusen at the piano; Milton Berle is in the centre.

MARILYN MONROE

"I have never met anyone as utterly mean or as utterly fabulous on screen." **BILLY WILDER ON MARILYN**

THE TERM "SCREEN GODDESS" COULD HAVE BEEN INVENTED FOR MARILYN. HER FIRST HOLLYWOOD APPEARANCE WAS IN 1947'S *THE SHOCKING MISS PILGRIM*, IN WHICH SHE WAS FAR FROM SHOCKING AND BARELY NOTICED.

It wouldn't be until 1950 that she got her first part of any note in John Huston's thriller, *The Asphalt Jungle*. Marilyn was by then 24 years old, having been born Norma Jean Mortenson on 1 June, 1926 in Los Angeles. She was already divorced, having married her neighbour when she was just 16 years old. Her husband, Jimmy, joined up in 1944, and 18-year-old Norma began working in a munitions plant in Burbank, California. A photographer started taking her picture, and soon some modelling jobs came her way. When her husband returned from the service, they divorced, and almost immediately she signed a contract with Twentieth Century Fox, earning $125 a week. Shortly after, Norma Jean dyed her hair and became Marilyn Monroe (her grandmother's surname).

After appearing in *The Asphalt Jungle*, Marilyn's role in *All About Eve*, which starred Bette Davis, gave her career a real boost. Further films followed before her performance in *Niagara* in 1953 brought her real stardom. Further success came with *Gentlemen Prefer Blondes* with Jane Russell and *How to Marry a Millionaire* with Lauren Bacall and Betty Grable. On 14 January, 1954, Marilyn married Joe DiMaggio and then went to Tokyo for their honeymoon. Marilyn performed for US servicemen, which was something that Joe found difficult to cope with. The marriage lasted little over a year, ending in divorce on 27 October, 1955. Marilyn was keen to move away from her "dumb blonde" persona

and pursue more serious roles, but Hollywood was reluctant. In 1956, she married the playwright Arthur Miller and formed Marilyn Monroe Productions. Her company made *Bus Stop* and *The Prince and the Showgirl*, the latter co-starring Laurence Olivier. Both films boosted her career and in 1959 she won a Golden Globe for *Some Like It Hot*.

Miller wrote the part of Roslyn Taber in *The Misfits* (1961) for Marilyn, which co-starred Clark Gable and Montgomery Clift. Before the film came out, however, her marriage to Miller ended. The following year, she was named female World Film Favorite at the Golden Globes, but she would not live to reap the benefits. On 5 August, 1962, 36-year-old Marilyn died in her sleep at home in Brentwood, California. She had apparently committed suicide and died alone. However, rumours surrounding her death and her links to the Kennedys continue to this day.

66 When you speak of the American way of life everybody thinks of chewing gum, coca cola and Marilyn Monroe. **99**
RUSSIAN MAGAZINE *NEDVELA*, 1950s

Hollywood restaurant. Such was the level of indulgence on this booze, gambling, and envelope-pushing trip that everyone was totally wrecked by the time they had to go home. Lauren Bacall looked at the group on that final day and famously said, "You look like a goddamn rat pack." When they returned to Los Angeles, they arranged a reunion dinner at Romanoff's, and thereafter regular meetings took place. While Bogie was the head of the pack, Frank was named President.

By mid-December, Frank should have been at 20th Century Fox to begin shooting *Pink Tights*, a remake of Betty Grable's 1943 *Coney Island*. Shooting was postponed, then Frank's co-star, Marilyn Monroe, failed to show up for work because she had decided to marry baseball star Joe DiMaggio and flew to Japan on honeymoon. It wasn't just the marriage that caused the problem. Marilyn was a contract star at Fox but unhappy with her deal; she also felt she was being over-worked. Filming was postponed while Fox pondered substituting another contract player, but in the end they decided to shelve the project.

The first issue of *Playboy* came out in December, and included a nude shot of Marilyn Monroe as the centrefold of its 44 pages, along with a Sherlock Holmes story and an article on the Dorsey Brothers. Hugh Hefner, the publisher, wrote much of the copy himself and drew all the cartoons. Somehow it seems appropriate in Frank's comeback year.

Frank, with time on his hands, decided to fly to Rome and spend Christmas with Ava. But before he left, Frank appeared on Bob Hope's radio show and shared some sketches with Bob, poking fun at Eddie Fisher among others. Frank sang his current hit record, 'South of the Border', backed by Les Brown's Band of Renown.

By the time Frank arrived in Rome, Ava had left to spend Christmas in Madrid; she was having her second Spanish fling, following her earlier affair there with actor Mario Cabre in 1950. This second affair began during her summer holiday, this time with a bullfighter named Luis Miguel Dominguin; a man described by his friend Ernest Hemingway as "a combination of Don Juan and Hamlet". This was tough competition, even for Frank. Humphrey Bogart offered Ava an alternative view of Dominguin: "Half the world's female population would throw themselves at Frank's feet and here you are flouncing around with guys who wear capes and little ballerina slippers."

Frank arrived in Spain on Christmas Eve, and by all accounts they spent a far

BOGART AND AVA
Bogie and Ava on the set of The Barefoot Contessa *in Rome.*

from happy Christmas together. Ava said that there were downsides to *From Here to Eternity*, in that it brought back some of the less-lovable traits in Frank. His success as Maggio once again made him arrogant, although the New York suicide attempt in November shows that he was very confused at this time, possibly close to some kind of breakdown. After Christmas, Frank returned to Rome with Ava, where she was continuing work on *The Barefoot Contessa*. "A downcast and lonely looking Frank Sinatra sneaked out of Rome this afternoon on a New York bound plane after a five day attempt to win back his wife," is how one Rome-based correspondent saw it.

It's amazing that, against this backdrop, Frank managed to get his career back together. But possibly that's why he made the effort – thinking that it might bring Ava back. However, even Frank had to recognize the truth eventually: "I guess it's over if that's what Ava says. It's very sad… it's tragic…" said Frank, though, as usual, he said it much better in song. "It was Ava who did that, who taught him how to sing a torch song," said Nelson Riddle. In the end, Frank probably loved Ava more than she loved him. The outcome of all of this was that it was Ava who had turned The Voice into a legend.

> **❝I guess it's over if that's what Ava says. It's very sad… it's tragic…❞**
>
> **FRANK ON HIS BREAKUP WITH AVA**

1953 ON THE JUKEBOX

FRANK ON THE US CHARTS

'I'M WALKING BEHIND YOU' (Billy Reid) 16 May, No 7, 10 weeks	**'FROM HERE TO ETERNITY'** (Fred Karger, I Jones & Robert Wells) 26 September, No 15, 2 weeks
'I'VE GOT THE WORLD ON A STRING' (Harold Arlen & Ted Koehler) 4 July, No 14, 2 weeks	**'SOUTH OF THE BORDER'** (Michael Carr & Jimmy Kennedy) 12 December, No 18, 2 weeks

Appropriately, Frank's first hit of 1953 was his Capitol debut. 'I'm Walking Behind You' backed by 'Lean Baby'; it came out as Capitol F2450 in April, with the a-side making No 7 on the charts.

Frank hadn't had a hit record for almost six months, making it his longest spell off the charts in ten years. Statistically, it was also his biggest hit for three years, but it was not the triumphal comeback that everyone at Capitol was hoping for. It was more a turntable hit than it was a big seller. As is true with much about Frank it's not a straightforward story. 'I'm Walking Behind You' spent ten weeks at the top of the charts, having also been

PATTI PAGE
Patti's dog song was her fourth No 1 record in a string of hits from 1948 onwards. She continued to have hits up until the end of the 1960s.

recorded by one of Frank's least favourite singers, Eddie Fisher — the man about whom Frank would joke, saying he "warmed up with a snare drum"... his timing was that bad!

The rest of the year was a disappointment for Frank as his next three releases all failed to crack the Top 10 and could only manage two weeks apiece on the charts. Given the timing of Frank's contract and the fact that it ran for a year it was fortunate that *From Here to Eternity* did so well, that and the fact that albums were beginning to assume greater significance for record companies.

Perry Como was back at the top of the annual *Billboard* performance table having had two No 1 records during the year. He was closely followed by Patti Page who had a massive hit with 'The Doggie In the Window', which spent 8 weeks at No 1. If nothing else it proved that Mitch Miller was ahead of his time with his hunch that a barking dog could propel a record to the top. Then again it may have been the fact that Patti's dog barks were supplied by different canine impersonators to the one who had appeared with Frank on 'Mama Will Bark'.

FROM HERE TO MATURITY

By early 1954, Frank was living alone in the Wilshire Boulevard apartment he had hung on to in his divorce settlement with Nancy. Frank, who never much liked being alone, had asked Jule Styne to move into the five-bedroom apartment. According to Styne, Frank was not over Ava, and there were pictures of her throughout the place.

Styne stayed for eight months, until Frank asked him to leave for what he saw as a breach of his trust. (Styne had spoken about Frank and Ava to the press, and about how depressed Frank was.) Frank began spending more and more time with his neighbours, Humphrey Bogart and Lauren Bacall, and dinner parties arranged by Frank's neighbour in the apartment building, Swifty Lazar, an agent, often included the Bogarts. Frank enjoyed the company; he was not coping well without Ava.

ON BROADWAY, NORTH FROM 54TH STREET, NEW YORK, 1954

A NIGHT AT THE OSCARS
Frank Sinatra with daughter Nancy, 13, and Frank Jr, 10, at the Oscar ceremony, 25 March, 1954.

> *"That he is now 'the greatest thing since Sinatra' is a heartening sign for those of us who may lose faith in popular music now and then, a particularly rewarding sign for those of us who have never lost faith in a truly sincere and talented guy named Sinatra."*
>
> GEORGE SIMON IN *DOWNBEAT*, DECEMBER 1953

While Frank's weekly appearance in *Rocky Fortune* hardly promoted his acting credentials, it did give him the opportunity to plug his case for an Oscar. He had been nominated for a best supporting actor award, and as his radio show wound to a close, and the date of the Oscar presentations drew near, Frank was shameless. It became a running gag that Frank worked the phrase "from here to eternity" into almost every show.

AND THE WINNER IS...

In early February, Frank won an award for his portrayal of Maggio from The International Press in Hollywood. Then, on 13 February, 1954, 'Young at Heart' entered the *Billboard* chart. It made the Top 10 two weeks later, and from there went on something of a roller-coaster ride, rising up and down the Top 10 until it finally got as high as No 2 on 15 May, before drifting steadily down until it departed the Top 10 in the last week of June. It sold over a million copies and would have recouped everything (and a lot more) that Capitol had invested in Frank. It also marked the point from which the Frank and Nelson show really got on the road. If 'I've Got the World on a String' was the courtship, 'Young at Heart' consummated the marriage. It also proved to be very useful in Frank's film career. The release of the first Capitol album, *Songs For Young Lovers*, in January

was perfect timing, given the pre-Oscar publicity. Sales were very promising, and with the better return from albums than from singles, Alan Livingston and Capitol must have been delighted that their gamble had paid off.

A week before Oscar night, Frank was in New York with pals who included Jimmy Van Heusen. There was much discussion about whether or not Frank would win. He was up against opposition from both Brandon de Wilde and Jack Palance in *Shane*, Robert Strauss in *Stalag 17*, and Eddie Elbert in *Roman Holiday*.

On the night of the Oscars, Frank went for dinner with Nancy and the children before the ceremony. They gave him a small medal on the back of which was inscribed "Dad, we'll love you from here to eternity". Frank took 13-year-old Nancy and 10-year-old Frank Jr with him to the 2,800 seat Pantages Theatre for the 26th Annual Academy Awards hosted by Donald O'Connor. Mercedes McCambridge, who herself had won an Oscar for best supporting actress in the 1949 film *All The King's Men*, read out the nominations for best supporting actor. When she announced Frank as the winner, it brought a long, and loud, cheer from the crowd as he half ran to the stage to receive his statue. The grinning Frank was watched by millions on TV.

"Um... That's a clever opening! Ladies and gentlemen, I'm deeply thrilled and very moved. And I really don't know what to say because this is a whole new kind of thing, you know? I'm a song and dance man type. And, er, I'm terribly pleased and if I start thanking everybody I'll do a one-reeler up here, so I'd better not. I'd just like to say, however, that they're doing a lot of songs here tonight, but nobody asked me. I love you though. Thank you very much. I'm absolutely thrilled. Thank you." And that was it. Frank was off back to his seat.

Given the fact that Frank was far from the most popular man in Hollywood, his achievement that night was even more remarkable, and triumphant. His was the loudest cheer of the night, and it was from the hard-bitten and often cynical Hollywood crowd who just a year previously had thought Frank finished. *Downbeat* summed up how many people had been feeling about Frank when they wrote of his Oscar night success: "Frankly speaking, Frankie Sinatra was no sensational piece of merchandise."

Frank's was one of eight Oscars for *Eternity*, equalling the record set by *Gone with the Wind*. Ava was also nominated for her role in *Mogambo*, but she didn't win, nor did she attend the ceremony. She was in Spain, still in the arms of her bullfighter. Shortly after the ceremony, Frank expressed regret at one

GREAT SUPPORT
Frank and Donna Reed, who won best supporting actor and actress awards at the 26th Academy Awards for From Here to Eternity.

HERE AND THERE
It wasn't just in the US and in Britain that From Here To Eternity *was a success. It was dubbed into a number of languages, including Italian.*

WINNING OPENER
Frank recorded this Oscar-winning song, which is heard over the film's opening credits, with Victor Young. The version that made the chart was conducted by Nelson Riddle.

YOUNG AT HEART
Frank at Warner Studios in July rehearsing 'Young at Heart' with his pianist Bill Miller, watched by arranger Ray Heindorf, leaning on the piano, far right.

aspect of his acceptance speech: "I wanted to thank Monty Clift personally. I learned more about acting from Clift – it was equal to what I learned about musicals from Gene Kelly."

Everywhere there was talk of "comeback". *Variety* called it "the greatest comeback in history". Despite his joy at winning, Frank still felt the need to have a go at the press, who were eager to say how lucky he had been. Frank was just as eager to assuage their views, saying it was his talent. But of course in Hollywood, where the system supports winners, it brought offers from left and right for Frank to appear in more movies. After *Pink Tights* was shelved, Twentieth Century Fox kept him "on the books" waiting for a suitable film. Frank had already accepted another offer from producer Robert Bassler to appear in a thriller called *Suddenly*. Stanley Kramer had also made a commitment to put Frank as joint star billing with Robert Mitchum in *Not as a Stranger*, a deal that was signed while Frank was filming *Suddenly*. Between the Oscars and starting work on *Suddenly* in April, *Songs for Young Lovers* continued to sell well, and *Rocky Fortune* mercifully came to an end.

Frank was involved in another Twentieth Century Fox film project on the last day of March, but not one of his own. He was recording the soundtrack song for the film *Three Coins in the Fountain*, written by Jule Styne and Sammy Cahn. Frank had already recorded the song with Nelson for a Capitol single release at the beginning of March, which makes a mockery of Styne's claim that he tricked

Frank into recording the song, telling him he was going to make a demo and having Frank walk into the sound stage with the orchestra already set up. The second recorded version was used over the opening sequence of the film, accompanied by CinemaScope shots of Rome.

HOLLYWOOD "HEATWAVE"

Frank was busy recording with Nelson in April and May, but made the time to appear on Louella Parsons's radio show to talk about his film work, "the current Sinatra heat wave", as Louella put it. Frank confirmed his upcoming role in *Not as a Stranger*, and *Young at Heart*; he also plugged 'Three Coins in the Fountain', his new single. Frank, who was back to 135 lb from the 118 lb he had weighed in his dark days, sounded relaxed and happy. The revival in his career must have given him a boost. He told *Time* magazine around the time of the Louella interview, "Everything's ahead of me. Man I'm on top of the world. I'm buoyant." *Time* caught the mood of the moment, reflecting public opinion: "audiences decided that he was not just a mannered crooner but a mature pro". It wasn't just critical acclaim: by the end of June, sales of *Songs for Young Lovers* had passed the 150,000 mark (big sales for an LP at this time).

The first tentative, if somewhat irrelevant, moves in what was to be a long drawn-out divorce were made when Ava rented a house in the resort of Zephyr Cove on the Nevada shore of Lake Tahoe. Having returned from Italy, she was establishing her six weeks' residency in Nevada so that she could divorce Frank. "On the usual grounds (mental cruelty)" is what she told another *Time* reporter. She was also recuperating from two kidney stones and inevitably still arguing with MGM, who once again suspended her. Frank was busy mending fences. The *New York Times* speculated about a new production of *Guys and Dolls*. Samuel Goldwyn had spent several months securing the rights to Damon Runyan's stories, for around $1 million, despite Runyon's estate baulking at some of the terms. The role of Sky Masterton, said the *NY Times*, was "between Gene Kelly, Cary Grant, and Tony Martin with Burt Lancaster, Jeff Chandler, and Dean Martin as the 'dark horses'". Frank was said to be odds on to play Nathan Detroit, although several outsiders, including Phil Silvers and Sid Caesar, were being talked of. In fact, Frank's name had been linked with the part as early as February, well before his Oscar win. On 13–14 July, Frank was at Warner Brothers recording songs for *Young at Heart*. Two weeks later, Frank's second Capitol album, *Swing Easy*, came out.

If anyone wanted proof of Frank's phoenix-like rise from his career doldrums, nothing was more positive than the approval of Middle America's housewife's bible, *Good Housekeeping*. In August, it ran a long article entitled 'The Rise and Fall and Rise again

SONGS FOR YOUNG LOVERS

IT TOOK JUST 19 MINUTES AND 47 SECONDS FOR FRANK TO REALLY PROVE THAT HE WAS BACK; IT WAS THE RUNNING TIME OF HIS FIRST 10-INCH CAPITOL ALBUM.

IF FRANK'S CAPITOL SINGLES had been like canapés, this was the hors d'oeuvres, and if coupling Frank with Nelson Riddle was an excellent idea, the notion of using arranger George Siravo's band charts, adapted for a full orchestra added significantly to the end result. The sessions for the album were at a pivotal time in Frank and Ava's soap opera – a fact that ultimately worked in favour of the recordings. In Will Friedland's excellent book on the music of Frank Sinatra, *The Song Is You*, there is a detailed explanation of how Siravo's charts were used by Nelson. Among other things, it explains how Nelson was sorry that Siravo did not receive the credit he should have for his work on this album. This probably goes back to record company politics and the fact that Capitol had invested heavily in Nelson Riddle and he was part of their game plan. 'Like Someone in Love' was the only Nelson original arrangement; it includes a solo flute, which was something of a feature in Nelson's later recordings.

Its central theme was carefully crafted to appeal to Frank's fans, most of whom by 1953 were experiencing young married life. If there is any criticism to be levelled at the album it is that it has a sameness about it, but not the elevated sameness that would be achieved with subsequent releases. It was all part of Alan

Livingston's plan: "I was directing him toward an audience I thought would appreciate him. But the younger kids caught on, and he had a wide range of followers. He pretty much picked the songs he wanted to do, although I directed him to major composers to do albums of standards. He went along with it, and from then on I had very little to do with the choice of songs, because they were all acceptable. They were all standards. I couldn't object. And the albums were very, very successful."

> 66 At least I'm not using any gimmicks and they seem to be buying my records. This could be a transition – you know – from gimmicks to rhythm tunes and then on to real pretty ballads again, just the way it was when I was back with Tommy and when I was starting out on my own. 99
>
> **FRANK IN *DOWNBEAT*, 1953**

SONG LINES

Recorded: KJH Studios, Hollywood. Produced by Voyle Gilmore. Chart: US No 3 (31 weeks). First charted 27 February, 1954.

SIDE 1

1. 'MY FUNNY VALENTINE'
(Richard Rodgers & Lorenz Hart) Recorded 5 November, 1953. This song came from the 1937 Broadway show, *Babes In Arms*. It was a minor hit in 1945 for bandleader Hal McIntyre, who had played saxophone for Glenn Miller.

2. 'THE GIRL NEXT DOOR'
(Hugh Martin & Ralph Blane) Recorded 6 November, 1953. This came from Judy Garland's 1944

film, *Meet Me In St Louis*. Frank revisited this song with Gordon Jenkins in 1962.

3. 'A FOGGY DAY'
(George & Ira Gershwin) Recorded 5 November, 1953. This song won an Oscar in 1937 when it was featured in Fred Astaire's film, *A Damsel In Distress*. Fred's version was a hit that same year and another version by Bing Crosby also did well on the fledgling chart.

4. 'LIKE SOMEONE IN LOVE'
(Jimmy Van Heusen & Johnny Burke) Recorded, 6 November, 1953. Dinah Shore originally performed this song in the 1944 movie, *Belle of the Yukon*. It was another song that Bing had a hit with, a year after the film came out.

SIDE 2

1. 'I GET A KICK OUT OF YOU'
(Cole Porter) Recorded 6 November, 1953. Ethel Merman first performed this Cole Porter classic in the 1934 musical, *Anything Goes*, although Paul Whiteman and his orchestra had the bigger hit recording.

2. 'LITTLE GIRL BLUE'
(Richard Rodgers & Lorenz Hart) Recorded 6 November, 1953. Margaret Whiting had a very small hit in the early years of Capitol Records with this song from the 1935 musical *Jumbo*.

3. 'THEY CAN'T TAKE THAT AWAY FROM ME'
(George & Ira Gershwin) Recorded 5 November, 1953. Another song from an Astaire movie, in fact it appeared in

two: 1937's *Shall We Dance* and *The Barkleys of Broadway* from 1949, both co-starring Ginger Rogers. It was one of Astaire's biggest records topping the chart in 1937.

4. 'VIOLETS FOR YOUR FURS'
(Matt Dennis & Tom Adair) Recorded 5 November, 1953. But for the album's closing song, this could have been called 'Songs from the Films and the Shows'. It was also the only song that Frank had recorded before. He cut it twice during his tenure with Tommy Dorsey. Frank would go on to remake six of these songs later in his career ('Little Girl Blue' and 'Like Someone I Love' were the exceptions).

In 1960, Capitol released a 12-inch version of the album and added 'Someone To Watch Over Me', 'It Worries Me', and 'I Can Read Between The Lines'. The 1960 reissue is illustrated above.

SWING EASY

NELSON RIDDLE TOLD AT LEAST ONE INTERVIEWER THAT THIS WAS HIS FAVOURITE ALBUM WITH FRANK, AND IT'S NOT HARD TO HEAR WHY. "SWING EASY" IS SUCH AN APPOSITE TITLE.

FRANK MOST DEFINITELY SWINGS on this collection of up-tempo numbers, and he makes it sound oh so easy. His performances are noticeably more relaxed than on his first Capitol album.

Released on 2 August, 1954 this album was entirely arranged and conducted by Nelson Riddle, reinforcing the fact that Frank was now completely at ease with the arranger.

A SINATRA SESSION

A typical four-song session would take place in the evening from say 8:00 pm until midnight. During four hours usually four songs were recorded. According to Alan Livingston, "We couldn't afford to have them rehearse. They were all competent musicians – very good musicians – and they would sight read and if he didn't like something he would say so."

ALAN LIVINGSTON ON WHAT MADE FRANK STAND OUT

"First of all he was primarily interested in the lyric. He didn't pay much attention to the music. And if the lyric hit him, if he thought it was a good lyric, then he would do it. I think that was reflected in his success. He was a great interpreter of songs because he followed the lyric. And he sang with tremendous attention to what the song was saying. He would not just go into the studio and sing the song. He would spend time with the lyric and with the meaning of it and what it represented to him and he would rehearse it and rehearse it and rehearse it by himself. And then go into the studio with the orchestra and sing it. Most singers that I recorded – and most singers, in any event – did not pay that much attention. We'd pick a song; they'd go into the studio and probably sing it for the first time. Not Frank. He insisted that he study it and work on it, and study the phrasing. It was his phrasing and his attention to the lyric and what it was saying that made him a great artist."

... AND FRANK IN REPLY

"The melody should be like a back-drop for the lyrics. Sure, it should be good and musical. But it should be more like a guy reading poetry with organ music or something going on in the back. Of course the lyrics have to be something special, like the ones that Larry Hart and Oscar Hammerstein and Ira Gershwin and Johnny Mercer and Sammy Calm have been writing. You know I have a real, healthy respect for anybody who can write." December, 1953

> 66 Frank didn't just sing in tune – he had perfect pitch. He didn't need to hear the first note that he was to sing. He could start off and hit it, bam, just like that. 99
>
> **HARRY 'SWEETS' EDISON – TRUMPET PLAYER**

SONG LINES

Recorded: KHJ Studios, Hollywood. Produced by Voyle Gilmore. Chart: US No 3 (32 weeks), first charted 4 September, 1954; UK No 5 (17 weeks), first entered the UK chart as a 12-inch album on 29 October, 1960.

SIDE 1

1. 'JUST ONE OF THOSE THINGS'
(Cole Porter) Recorded 7 April, 1954. From the pen of the ever-reliable Cole Porter, it came from the 1935 Broadway show *Jubilee*. Recorded a year and five days after his first session for Capitol, it demonstrates Frank's greater confidence. He and the 14-piece band show just how to 'Swing Easy'. Three months later Frank did the song again for his movie, *Young at Heart*. This time the arranger was Ray Heindorf; it shows how good Nelson was for Frank.

2. 'I'M GONNA SIT RIGHT DOWN AND WRITE MYSELF A LETTER'
(Fred E Ahlert & Joe Young) Recorded 7 April, 1954. Originally a hit for the great Fats Waller in 1935, Frank recorded it again with the Count Basie Orchestra in 1962.

3. 'SUNDAY'
(Ned Miller, Bennie Krueger, Chester Conn & Jule Styne) Recorded 7 April, 1954. This song from 1925 has the distinction of being Jule Styne's first major song, albeit a collaboration with three others.

4. 'WRAP YOUR TROUBLES IN DREAMS'
(Harry Barris, Ted Koehler & Billy Moll) Recorded 7 April, 1954. This lovely song dating from 1931 was regularly heard on Frank's *Lucky Strike's Lite Up Time* radio shows, as well as on his TV show in 1951.

SIDE 2

1. 'TAKING A CHANCE ON LOVE'
(Vernon Duke, John Latouche & Ted Fetter) Recorded 19 April, 1954. This was originally from the 1940 musical *Cabin in the Sky*, and was sung in the movie version, three years later, by Ethel Waters. Ethel had begun life as a blues singer, with a sideline in saucy songs including the wonderfully naughty 'My Handy Man'.

2. 'JEEPERS CREEPERS'
(Harry Warren & Johnny Mercer) Recorded 19 April, 1954. This came from Dick Powell's 1938 movie *Going Places*.

3. 'GET HAPPY'
(Harold Arlen & Ted Koehler) Recorded 19 April, 1954. Another show tune, this was from a Broadway musical, *9:15 Revue*.

4. 'ALL OF ME'
(Gerald Marks & Seymour Simons) Frank had tackled this song before and would do again, but he was far from alone as it had already been recorded by numerous singers and orchestras since it was written for the 1931 film *Careless Lady*. Both Louis Armstrong and Paul Whiteman had best-sellers with it in 1932. Over the next 20 years, Ben Selvin, Count Basie, and Johnnie Ray all took 'All of Me' into the charts. Frank released it as a single in 1948 but it failed to chart. Four years earlier Frank recorded it for a V-Disc and cut another version for *Meet Danny Wilson*. Billie Holiday recorded 'All of Me' with Lester Young on saxophone in 1941 and all Frank's versions, but particularly the 1948 and this one have references to Billie's definitive version.

In 1960 Capitol released a 12" version of the album and added 'Lean Baby' and 'Why Should I Cry Over You'.

of Frank Sinatra' which ended by saying "The Crown Prince of Swoon has finally grown up." It was tempting fate, as was so often the case with Frank and others like him who lead their lives in the intense white light of the media spotlight. Events would conspire against Frank and prove that perhaps maturity was still something of an abstract concept.

THE DOORS OF PERCEPTION

On August 11 Frank was back at Warner Brothers recording 'One For My Baby' with Bill Miller at the piano. The song is the absolute manifestation of Frank – the saloon singer. But is this version the best or the one he recorded four years later for *Only The Lonely*? Then again, it could be one of the many live versions he did over the next five decades. Nor was it the first time he had recorded this Harold Arlen and Johnny Mercer classic. He did it with Axel Stordahl in 1947 with Allan Reuss's guitar to the fore, giving the song a far less haunted feeling than with Bill Miller's piano accompaniment.

On 3 September, *To Be Perfectly Frank* returned after the summer break. This show ran on Armed Forces Radio, which was ironic, given what was to happen. Two weeks later, Frank met the Adjutant General, Major General John A. Klein, at his office in Washington. Frank wanted clearance to appear at military bases in Korea during the Christmas holiday period. Permission had been denied, and Frank wanted to know why. The reason was simple: according to FBI files, the old red menace syndrome was rearing its ugly head. The Army couldn't countenance anyone visiting bases when there was the slightest hint of that person having communist sympathies and "serious questions existed as to Mr Sinatra's sympathies". Frank's reply was a new twist on an old theme: "I'm just as communistic as the Pope", but the Army wouldn't budge and Frank said he would take his case to the Attorney General to clear his name. One of the other generals at the meeting congratulated Frank on his performance in *From Here to Eternity*. But with no change of heart by the Army top brass, the meeting ended and Frank left feeling very angry.

Frank's agent, Abe Lastfogel, spoke to George Murphy, the man responsible for United Service Organization trips, asking him to plead Frank's case. Murphy contacted the FBI, having also heard from Lastfogel that they had somehow interfered with the process, though naturally the FBI denied any involvement. By the end of October, Murphy had backed out of the matter and Frank never did go to Korea.

By now Frank wasn't just big in the US. In mid-September, 'Three Coins in the Fountain' topped the UK charts. Frank was in Hollywood filming *Not as a Stranger* at Kling Film Studios when Maurice Kinn, Managing Director of Britain's *New Musical Express*, went to interview him. Frank told him he was glad that in *Young at Heart* he didn't have to die. He talked of playing the Copa at Christmas and "two weeks at the Sands Hotel in Las Vegas, in which I have a financial interest". He also said he was buying a new home in Palm Springs.

SUDDENLY

THE FILM PREMIERED on 24 September 1954, and it was the second successive movie in which Frank gets killed. The story revolves around three assassins who occupy pacifist Ellen Benson's (Nancy Gates) house in the small Californian town of Suddenly. They are there to try to kill the President, who is scheduled to pass through the town on a train. Of course, the attempt fails and it is pacifist Ellen who kills Frank. Screenwriter Richard Sale's story was, for its time, both daring and different. Casting Frank as ex-serviceman John Baron, the leader of the killers, was inspired; Montgomery Clift turned the part down. Given its subject matter, it's unusual in that Englishman Lewis Allen directed it.

INSPIRATION

Just before the attempt on the President's life, the words "Let's go to work" are uttered. These same words are used by Quentin Tarantino before the robbery in *Reservoir Dogs*.

Newsweek reported "As the assassin in the piece, Sinatra superbly refutes the idea that the straight-role potentialities which earned an Academy Award for him in *From Here to Eternity* was one-shot stuff. In *Suddenly*, the happy-go-lucky soldier of *Eternity* becomes one of the most repellent killers in American screen history."

Frank gives one of his most convincing on-screen performances, with Sterling Hayden and Christopher Dark as co-stars. While some critics had grumbled that

Frank had beginner's luck in *From Here to Eternity*, this proved it was nothing of the kind, even though there is more than a passing nod to *High Noon*.

After its initial release, the positive reception it received became largely forgotten, that is until Frank found out that John F. Kennedy's killer, Lee Harvey Oswald, had apparently watched the film before he shot the President. Frank had the film withdrawn from circulation, banning its showing on television. This ban remained in effect until 1994, when people could once again watch one of Frank's most skilful dramatic performances, with not a song to be heard. While Frank did perform well, the film failed to ignite public support, and it was a relative failure at the box office. Consciously or not, Frank never again played such an dislikable character in a movie.

HAT TRICK
Frank kept his hat on throughout the film, which saved him the trouble of having to be fitted with a hairpiece.

Joe DiMaggio and his team crashed into this house at 754 Kilkea Drive in L.A., hoping to nab Marilyn with a "guest." Score: one smashed door, one screaming woman — several red faces.

IN THE NEWS

"No Fiction — All Facts" is how Confidential *magazine promoted their particular brand of tabloid journalism. Below, Marilyn Monroe and Joe DiMaggio.*

After Frank's less-than-exemplary behaviour on the set of *Young at Heart*, he was far better behaved while filming *Not as a Stranger*, despite an incident in which he and his co-stars, Robert Mitchum and Broderick Crawford, got so drunk that they decided to remodel Frank's dressing room. They described their destruction of the room to director Stanley Kramer as "a spot of DIY."

Frank was due to be recording at KHJ on 22 October, but he cancelled the session. Maybe it was the day after the DIY or it may have had something to do with the fact that on the same day Marlon Brando was offered the lead in a film to be set in Hoboken, a role that Frank coveted. He had been lobbying hard for the starring role in *On the Waterfront* and could not have been amused to learn he'd been passed over. Further damage was done when the offer of a supporting role in the film, as a Catholic priest, was withdrawn because it had already been accepted by Karl Malden. Frank sued, and settled out of court five years later.

November brought further problems for Frank, but ones that wouldn't become public knowledge for almost a year. On 5 November, one of the more bizarre incidents of Frank's life took place. It's been said that Joe DiMaggio was to baseball what Frank was to singing, and few would argue that both men were among the greatest ever Italian-Americans. Joe's Ava was the beautiful Marilyn Monroe and their marriage mirrored aspects of the Sinatras' relationship. According to the story in *Confidential* magazine in September 1955, Frank and Joe were at the Villa Capri when Joe got a call from a private detective who had been tailing Marilyn to say she was in an apartment at 754 Kilea Drive belonging to a small-time actress, Sheila

Stewart. Joe told the guy, "Hold everything till I get there." He arrived soon after along with Frank and Billy D'Amore, the owner of the Villa Capri; "the latter pair were along for the excitement," said *Confidential*. Joe thought his wife was in the apartment with Hal Schaefer, her vocal coach. DiMaggio decided to break into the apartment where the supposed assignation was taking place. Frank's role in this is unrecorded, but he was very definitely there when DiMaggio broke down the door of the apartment. Unfortunately Marilyn was not inside, only a rather confused and probably very frightened older lady sitting bolt upright in bed, "her nightgown around her ribs and staring in utter terror".

SAMMY'S ACCIDENT

Two days after the "wrong door" incident, Frank appeared on a live NBC colour spectacular, *Max Liebman's Fanfare*. The 90-minute show starred Judy Holliday, Steve Allen, Dick Shawn, and the French comedian Jacques Tati. According to the advertising, Frank was "combining his vocal and dramatic talents in an outstanding presentation". In fact, his contribution was not as exciting as the billing promised: it was a 26-minute portion, broadcast from the El Capitan Theatre in Hollywood, and filmed in black and white, while the others were from New York and in colour. This would not, however, have affected 99 per cent of the viewers, since colour television was still a rare commodity at this time. To avoid short-changing those who did have colour, a split screen was utilized, with Steve Allen in colour

DEAN MARTIN

"Living high in the dirty business of dreams."

NICK TOSCHES, DEAN'S BIOGRAPHER

MARTIN–LEWIS
Dean Martin and Jerry Lewis were for a while one of the hottest acts in the US. Like almost every duo, they found it impossible to hold it together.

DEAN MARTIN MAY HAVE BEEN A MEMBER OF FRANK'S RAT PACK IN THE EYES OF ALMOST EVERYONE BUT HE WAS FIRST AND FOREMOST HIS OWN MAN. DEAN MANAGED TO PULL OFF THE IMPOSSIBLE: HE FOOLED MOST OF THE PEOPLE ALMOST ALL OF THE TIME.

Born Dino Paul Crocetti in Steubenville, Ohio, in 1917, he worked in a factory and briefly as a prize-fighter and card-shark. He then took up singing, emulating, like Frank, Bing Crosby. He formed a comedy duo in the 1940s with Joseph Levitch, better known as Jerry Lewis. In 1948, they made their film debut in *My Friend Irma*; Jerry was the comedic king and Dean the straight man. A whole rash of Paramount films followed, including *You're Never Too Young, Living It Up,* and *Hollywood or Bust*. By 1951, the duo had become one of the biggest box office draws. Their live shows, television, and radio series, along with Dean's recordings, made them both a lot of money.

Dean and Jerry had signed to Capitol in 1948, and after he and Jerry had a one-off hit, Dean carried on making solo records. His first big hit was 'That's Amore' (No 2) in late 1953. Two years later, he got to the top with 'Memories are Made of This.' This hit the top as Jerry and Dean were splitting up, which must have given Dean some confidence, despite most people feeling his career would slide. His solution was to create a drinking character that was close to the one perfected by Joe E Lewis. The first outing for his new persona and act was at the Sands Hotel in Las Vegas in April 1957. He was a huge success, many in the audience perhaps thinking his talent was less than his erstwhile partner. His singing career with Capitol continued through the 1950s, but was nowhere near as successful as Frank's. When Frank started Reprise, Dean became one of the label's first signings.

Dean's movie career flourished: he was great in *Rio Bravo* alongside John Wayne and in *The Young Lions* with Marlon Brando. Becoming embroiled in the whole Rat Pack/Summit syndrome elevated Dean still further, while he continued to make his own movies. Although it has to be said that Dean never seemed to pursue his career with the kind of vigour that others, notably Frank, did.

In 1964, Dean had the first No 1 for Reprise when 'Everybody Loves Somebody Sometime' knocked the Beatles off the No 1 spot. From there until the end of the decade, he had a string of *Billboard* hits, although few were that big. According to Joe Smith, who worked at Warner/Reprise from

1963, "Dean Martin was red-hot. However, he hated to learn songs! We had to set him up with new songs on an 8-track in his car, so he could hear them. We would keep trying to get him into the studio, then he'd call out of the blue and say, 'Hey, we should record some new records.' We'd ask when he'd like to do it, and he'd come back with 'How about 5:00 pm today?' We rush around trying to get studios and orchestra players…!!! I remember that on one occasion I bought out The Beach Boys' studio time!"

In 1970, he earned $7 million appearing in *Airport* and thereafter had a number of starring movies, although none were very substantial and he appeared to be just as happy to appear on television; although by this time his shows were a shadow of their former selves. He had first appeared on his NBC variety show in 1965, and his act of appearing to be drunk the whole show served him well. His act was helped by the fact that he hardly ever rehearsed so the ramshackle nature of his performance worked a treat: as Dean said, "It's only a TV show." Gradually, things started to tail off in every direction, and apart from appearances in the *Cannonball Run* movies with Burt Reynolds, his work rate slowed to a trickle. After he bowed out of the tour with Frank and Sammy Davis in 1988, Dean pretty much retired. His last years up until his death in 1995 were, it seems, far from happy.

For more on his life and times, read the brilliant Nick Tosches's *Dino*.

> **The man who defined modern celebrity (what exactly was he famous for?)**
>
> *I-D* MAGAZINE

1952-1957

YOUNG AT HEART

THE STORY IS OF three small-town sisters, played by Doris Day, Dorothy Malone, and Elizabeth Fraser, and their father, a Dean of Music (Robert Keith). Doris is meant to be marrying a singer (Gig Young), that is until she meets his gifted arranger Barny Sloan (Frank Sinatra). Frank takes a job singing in a bar – and a not very salubrious one. His story is of a nearly man who never exactly makes it, although it's clear that he has the talent. Doris, naturally, falls for Frank; they marry and head to New York, where Frank starts playing in a real dive. His gradual deterioration is complete when he tries to kill himself in a car crash, but he survives and learns that Doris is pregnant, and he recovers to deliver the final song.

Downbeat reviewed the film, saying that it was the craftsmanship of the music that underpinned "a pretty wobbly story". This seems a pretty fair statement. "The star of stars here is Sinatra." (*Downbeat*, 12 January, 1955). Other reviews were slightly less enthusiastic: "Hollywood has not lost its knack for making indifferent new pictures out of good old pictures." was the comment in the *Saturday Review*.

Directed by Gordon Douglas, who would work with Frank on more films than any other director, it was originally the 1938 film *Four Daughters*. After Frank's phenomenal chart success with 'Young at Heart', someone had the bright idea of changing the movie's name. Frank sings the song over the opening and closing credits with no discernible link between the lyrics of the song and the film itself. Warner

Brothers decided to cast Frank as much for the revival in his singing career as his acting. It was a clever pairing, and not a little lucky too. Frank and Doris had worked together on *Your Hit Parade* and so knew each other very well, which probably stopped the thing from completely coming off the rails when Frank began behaving badly on set. It was so bad that Frank refused to work if Marty Melcher, whose company was producing the film, was on set. Difficult for Doris, as she and Melcher were married!

DORIS DAY

It is impossible to underestimate the impact of Doris Day (born in 1924) on 1950s America. She was a huge star as both a singer and an actress. Her 1948 debut 'Love Somebody' topped the chart, and from then on there was a string of hits until she again made No 1 in 1952 with 'A Guy Is a Guy'. Her popular appeal reached its zenith during 1953–4, reinforced by her big hit, 'Secret Love', in January 1954, which stayed at the top for four weeks. It came from her movie *Calamity Jane*. Her pairing with Frank for *Young at Heart* in 1955 was as near a certainty of success as anyone in Hollywood could ask for. She later made a series of lightweight sex comedies with Rock Hudson, including *Pillow Talk* (1959), for which she was nominated for an Oscar as best actress.

QUEUE-SOME TWO-SOME!

DORIS DAY and FRANK SINATRA

Young at Heart

introducing Frank in black and white. That night, Sammy Davis Jr was at the Old Frontier Hotel in Las Vegas with the Will Mastin Trio. Nearly two weeks later, driving back to Los Angeles, listening to his own hit record 'Hey There' on the radio of his Cadillac convertible, Sammy crashed. He lost his left eye when his face was smashed against the pointed centre cone of the steering wheel. As Sammy lay in hospital, an article appeared in one of the scandal sheets with the headline "What makes Ava Gardner run for Sammy Davis Jr". It was nearly the end of a beautiful friendship before it had really begun. When Sammy found out, he was worried about what Frank would think, say, and do. The story was totally fabricated, but that was not really the point. In fact, Frank visited Sammy in hospital; he even arranged for Sammy to stay in his Palm Springs home for two weeks to convalesce. While Sammy Davis was in Palm Springs, Frank was in Hollywood working on another film, an animated version of *Finian's Rainbow* at Goldwyn Studios. The project was eventually shelved, but not before Frank had recorded a number of songs, including 'Ad Lib Blues' with Louis Armstrong and 'Necessity' with Ella Fitzgerald. Three days before his 39th birthday, Frank was cutting another song for the movie, 'If It Isn't Love'. The session ended around 4:00 pm, and later he went to the Crescendo on Sunset to see Mel Tormé perform. With Frank was Texan oilman Bob Neal, Cindy Hayes, and Judy Garland, who was heavily pregnant. As they were leaving, Jim Byron, the club's publicist,

ON SET VISIT
Veteran stage and screen actress Ethel Barrymore visited Frank on the set of *Young at Heart* with Lauren Bacall.

failed to recognize Judy and called over to Neal, asking him who the lady was with Frank. The next thing anyone knew was that Frank was on top of Byron, shouting abuse, and smashing his fist into his face. It once again turned into something of a media scrum. Frank claimed that two friends of Byron's held him while the publicist tried to knee him.

RESERVOIR FRANK

The day after Frank's birthday, he was in the studio with bandleader and trumpeter Ray Anthony, who had joined the Glenn Miller Orchestra at the same time as Billy May and was a Capitol recording artist, so it can be seen as another try-out. "I first met him when I was with Glenn Miller, we were down in Virginia Beach and he was with Tommy Dorsey. We'd party in a big ballroom, the public ballroom. And it was there, when I was dancing in front of him that I was first aware of his blue eyes," recalls Ray. They cut 'Melody of Love' and 'I'm Gonna Live 'Til I Die' together. The latter could have been a good candidate for Frank's theme song. "He was in great voice at that time. And naturally, I was excited about it too. I'd known Frank from years before — we were very close on a personal level. I used to go up to his house three, four times a week. In fact, we lived on the same street. On Beaumont Drive. He lived at the top house, and I lived on the bottom... He liked to show movies. Frank liked to have company. I'd bring Ginger Rogers one night, Tuesday Weld another night, along with all his other friends. Mostly the writers like Sammy Cahn, Van Heusen, and Natalie Wood. James Dean was there quite a bit. I was very pleased with 'The Melody of Love.' It was a very beautiful ballad. He sang very well, and I played pretty well too," said Ray, laughing. Exactly a week

1954 ON THE JUKEBOX

FRANK ON THE US CHARTS

'YOUNG AT HEART'
(Johnny Richards & Carolyn Leigh)
13 February, No 2, 22 weeks

'DON'T WORRY ABOUT ME'
(Rube Bloom & Ted Koehler)
8 May, No 17, 6 weeks

'THREE COINS IN THE FOUNTAIN'
(Jule Styne & Sammy Cahn)
29 May, No 4, 13 weeks

A year of "quality not quantity" for Frank on the *Billboard* chart included 'Young at Heart', his biggest hit for eight years. ('Mam'selle' had, in fact, topped the chart in 1947, but it was much less of a hit record.) By 1954, it was much more a case of the record being the hit, rather than the song or the sheet music. (In 1947 there were six other versions of 'Mam'selle' that made the charts.) And, of course, Frank was already aiming himself at a different audience, one that bought LPs rather than singles, but every artist loved a hit. Capitol, like every other record label, preferred long-playing records because they made them more money.

Eddie Fisher topped the *Billboard* artist performance chart for the year, with something akin to a new phenomenon in the No 2 spot — a vocal group. The Four Aces were the first group since the Andrews Sisters in 1948 to challenge the solo singers. It was their version of 'Three Coins in the Fountain', along with 'Stranger in Paradise', that propelled them to the top.

The Four Aces weren't the only vocal group to do well during the year: the Crew Cuts spent nine weeks at No 1 with 'Sh-Boom', and the Chordettes topped the charts for seven weeks, as 1954 became 1955, with 'Mr. Sandman'. It was all a sign of the changing times.

As a result of working with Frank, and others, Nelson Riddle was rewarded with a solo contract by Capitol. In 1954, he had his first solo hit, 'Brother John' (an adaptation of 'Frere Jacques'), which made No 23 on the *Billboard* chart in April just as 'Young at Heart' was making its way to No 2.

THE CREW CUTS
After their chart topper
'Sh-Boom', the band's
1955 follow-up
'Earth Angel' made
the No 3 slot.

after Frank thumped Jim Byron, *Young at Heart* premiered and everything was forgotten in a new round of acclamation for Frank. "Those who believed his excellent performance in *From Here to Eternity* was mainly a fortunate bit of type casting will find that in this picture he demonstrates that he is in fact a real actor, one capable of sustained creative characterization," said *Downbeat*. In addition, his singing abilities were once again drawing praise. He topped the *Billboard*, *Downbeat*, and *Metronome* polls for best male vocalist. In *Cashbox*, Frank trailed Eddie Fisher and Perry Como, but 'Young at Heart' was still the third best record of the year.

There is no question that Frank Sinatra was a strong man, but he was a strong man brought low by a strong woman. Frank used this low period in his life as a reservoir of despair from which he would draw and then pour into his songs. The next few years were to prove just how effectively he could use his draught of despondency.

ALONG WITH THE BEST
Frank at Capitol Studio with (left to right)
Hank Sanicola, Ray Anthony, Lee Gillette,
Alan Livingston, 13 December, 1954.

> **"**He has a Chrysler and two dogs — corgis bought in England. He plays a little golf and likes to spend Sundays in Palm Springs lolling beside someone's pool**"**
>
> *GOOD HOUSEKEEPING*, AUGUST 1954

SMALL HOURS AND BIG BUCKS

Frank's growing international reputation meant he was invited on his first tour of Australia. He arrived in Sydney on 17 January, 1955, with 14-year-old Nancy, to begin what impresario Lee Gordon was promoting as "The Big Tour". He opened at the West Melbourne Stadium two days later, supported by singer Anne McCormack and comedian Frank D'Amour.

Australian Dennis Collinson and his orchestra were augmented by Nick Bonny on guitar, Bud Shank on saxophone, drummer Max Albright, and Bill Miller on piano. Frank did six shows in Melbourne, then two nights in Sydney, before returning to Melbourne for five final shows, for which he earned $80,000. Frank was still performing the 'Ol' Man River' segment with the 'Ol' Man Crosby' parody, along with 'Young at Heart' and 'Three Coins in the Fountain', but there was also a fair smattering of Columbia-era tunes.

As Frank arrived back from Australia, there was an article in *Downbeat* with the headline "Sinatra Lands Lead in *Big*

A TRIP DOWN UNDER
Standing on the steps of the aircraft that would take Frank and Nancy to Australia.

DANCING AT THE EL MOROCCO, NEW YORK, 1955

"Frank Sinatra is one of the most delightful, violent, dramatic, sad and sometimes downright terrifying personalities now on public view."

TIME MAGAZINE, 29 AUGUST, 1955

Brass Band". This was to be a Jesse Lansky production, who produced *Miracle of the Bells*, and it was about "the development of military-style bands as an important part of undergraduate activities in the high school and colleges of the USA". The film never did get made and it seems likely that Frank decided that *Carousel* would be a better bet; he was also probably offered more money. In Britain, Phillips, who distributed Columbia, issued *Sing and Dance With Frank Sinatra*, which was his old Columbia album. In a review by the *New Musical Express* no mention was made of the fact that the recordings were five years old. It was the start of what was, for some consumers, a confusing period of Sinatra record releases; one that would continue for almost a decade.

SESSIONS IN THE STUDIO

Frank had been back from Australia for only a day or so before he flew to New York City to appear at the Manhattan Center for the 20th-anniversary tribute to Tommy Dorsey. Frank naturally reprised 'I'll Never Smile Again' and 'Oh Look at Me Now'. Five days later, on 8 February, Frank was in the studio for his first session of the year, but there would be 20 more at which he recorded over 50 songs. This first session was under the direction of Bill Miller rather than Nelson. It was a quintet with Bill on piano, along with Paul Smith's celeste, George Van Epps on guitar, Phil Stephens on bass, and Alvin 'Al' Stoler on drums. They did four songs, all arranged by Nelson, which would be included in what many people consider to be Frank's finest hour – *In the Wee Small Hours*. Bill Miller was firmly established as not just Frank's piano player but also his musical confidant and a pivotal part of the Frank/Nelson relationship. Frank and Bill would work together on songs before going into the studio, teasing out the subtle nuances, working on the phrasing and slight shifts in the timing that gave Frank his unique approach to what were in many cases old songs, and in others already standards. At the 8 February session, Frank cut 'Dancing on the Ceiling', which dated from 1930, 'Can't We Be Friends' (1929), 'Glad To Be Unhappy' from the Rodgers and Hart musical *On Your Toes* (1936), and Alec Wilder's 'I'll Be Around', which Frank had sung on a V-Disc in 1943. If ever proof of Frank's maturity were needed, take a listen to both versions... what a difference a decade makes.

At Frank's second session in February, he cut four more songs, including the title song for *In the Wee Small Hours*. Rita Kirwen attended the session and wrote about it a few months later: "Everybody listens to the playback. Sinatra, with his head in his arms, leaning against the glass paneled control booth, listens harder than anyone. An epidemic of yawns seizes the musicians. Frank looks up. 'Yeah. Yeah. I think that's the one. Whadda you think?' The producer nods and a few people in the audience laugh a little. They've ALL sounded good enough to be 'the one'. 'Well, then, that just about wraps it up, I guess.' Sinatra takes a gulp of the lukewarm coffee remaining in the cup most recently handed to him, and then he lifts the inevitable hat from his head a little, and plops it right back, almost as if he'd wanted to relieve pressure from the hat band. The studio empties fast; just music stands and chairs remain. Sinatra... waves to the night janitor now straightening up the studio and says, 'Jeez. What crazy working hours we got. We both should've been plumbers, huh?'"

The next night, Sammy Davis Jr was at Ciro's, his first engagement since his horrific accident. He was a sensation. Everyone was there, including Bogie and Bacall, Gary Cooper, Cary Grant, Spencer Tracy, and, of course, Frank, who had been pushing Sammy hard to get back to work as soon as possible. Sammy wore a patch, despite having been fitted with an artificial eye, because it made him feel "less nervous". According to *Downbeat*, "the audience were obviously out to cheer him on everything he did, but the cheers were well deserved."

Not every session was with Nelson Riddle, or for Capitol, during 1955. Frank cut songs for his abortive movie, *Carousel*, along with others for *Guys and Dolls*, *The Tender Trap*, and the theme song for *The Man with the Golden Arm*, by Cahn and Van Heusen. It is said that Sammy and Jimmy first worked together at the behest of Frank (others say Bing was the catalyst). According to Sammy, Frank called him on the phone and said, "Sam, I want you to write a song with Van Heusen called *The Tender Trap*. Then Van Heusen called, and we started to write." It was the first of many songs that they wrote together, becoming, as Sammy put it, "Frank's songwriters on call".

Frank's first work on *Guys and Dolls* was on 1 March, when he cut 'The Oldest Established...' and the film's title song; filming proper didn't begin for several weeks. Frank had been cast as Nathan

SAMMY'S COMEBACK
Sammy Davis Jr (centre), his father, Sammy Davis Sr (left), and Will Mastin (right), perform at Ciro's on the night of his comeback.

FRANKIE LP
Columbia decided to capitalize on Sinatra's success by releasing a new album in late February entitled Frankie. *It was made up of big hits from throughout his Columbia career such as 'You'll Never Know', 'Oh What It Seemed to Be,' and almost inevitably, 'Nancy'. As* Downbeat *said, "This one should sell well not only to old fans, but to those who have discovered Frank just since his comeback."*

IN THE WEE SMALL HOURS

"THERE IS NO SUNRISE, WHEN YOUR LOVER HAS GONE."

THESE LINES FROM THE SONG PERFECTLY EPITOMIZE HOW

FRANK WAS FEELING WHEN HE MADE THIS ALBUM.

FRANK SETS OUT HIS STALL the moment the album begins. "In the wee small hours of the morning, while the whole wide world is asleep, you lie awake and think about the girl." Frank, like just about everyone else, thought of this as one of his best albums, "I think the orchestrator's work and my work come together closely." There is no denying the closeness and the intimacy that it brings. It's almost as though we, as listeners, are somehow intruding into Frank's world. But then as has been claimed it is Frank's world... we just love in it.

When it was first issued it came out as a "double album", two 10-inch records with eight songs on each. But the days of the 10-inch album were numbered and it was soon re-packaged as a 12-inch record, as would be all of Frank's albums thereafter. Even with its dark overtones there are elements of jazz, but it is clearly *the* Frank ballad album. It combines impeccable song selection with stunning orchestration and vocal delivery; with Bill Miller's piano-playing adding immeasurably to the atmosphere. It is almost as though everything that had gone before was simply leading to this. Frank would make better recordings of individual ballads, but this is the greatest single album of romantic songs; the one to have stashed in case a romantic emergency threatens. Every song seems to include a reference to Frank and Ava. "I took each word she said as gospel truth, the way a silly little child would. I can't excuse it on the grounds of youth" (from 'Can't We Be Friends'). As *Downbeat* said in 1955, "The package should be a big seller for years" ... they weren't wrong.

> 66 And as he sang he created the loneliest early morning mood in the world. 99
>
> **FROM THE ORIGINAL LINER NOTES**

SONG LINES

Recorded: KHJ Studios, Hollywood, produced by Voyle Gilmore. Chart: US No 2 (33 weeks). First charted 28 May, 1955. Inducted into the Grammy Hall of Fame 1984.

SIDE 1

1. 'IN THE WEE SMALL HOURS OF THE MORNING'
(Dave Mann & Bob Hilliard) Recorded 17 February, 1955. Few albums can have begun with a more low key song. Dave Mann apparently bumped into Frank and Nelson in New York in late 1954 and "sold" them the song. He knew both men, and had played on many of Frank's sessions with Axel. Mann played them his song with words by Bob Hilliard and Frank was immediately enthusiastic. Frank took it as his "theme" and collected the other songs to match the mood.

2. 'MOOD INDIGO'
(Duke Ellington, Irving Mills & Barney Bigard) Recorded 16 February, 1955. The jazz credentials of the album are quickly established by the inclusion of Duke Ellington's classic from 1931.

3. 'GLAD TO BE UNHAPPY'
(Richard Rodgers & Lorenz Hart) Recorded 8 February, 1955. The first of three songs on the album from Rodgers and Hart came from the 1936 Broadway show *On Your Toes*.

4. 'I GET ALONG WITHOUT YOU VERY WELL'
(Hoagy Carmichael & Jane Thompson) Recorded 17 February, 1955. Originally from 1939 it was performed in the *Las Vegas Story* in 1951 by Hoagy Carmichael and Jane Russell.

5. 'DEEP IN A DREAM'
(Jimmy Van Heusen & Eddie de Lange) Recorded 4 March, 1955. Another song from the 1930s.

6. 'I SEE YOUR FACE BEFORE ME'
(Arthur Schwartz & Howard Dietz) Recorded 16 February, 1955.

7. 'CAN'T WE BE FRIENDS'
(Kay Swift & Paul James) Recorded 8 February, 1955. This song comes from the 1929 Broadway revue *The Little Show*.

8. 'WHEN YOUR LOVER HAS GONE'
Recorded 17 February, 1955. From the 1931 film *Blonde Crazy*, Frank cut it with Axel in 1944 for a V-disc.

SIDE 2

1. 'WHAT IS THIS THING CALLED LOVE'
(Cole Porter) Recorded 16 February, 1955. From the 1929 show *Wake Up and Dream*.

2. 'LAST NIGHT WHEN WE WERE YOUNG'
(Harold Arlen & EY 'Yip' Harburg) Recorded 1 March, 1954. First performed in the 1935 film *Metropolitan* by Lawrence Tebbitt and then by Judy Garland in 1949's *In The Good Old Summertime*. It is a gem of a song that Frank revisited with Gordon Jenkins for *The September of My Years* album in 1965. It's one of the few times Frank improved on a Capitol classic.

3. 'I'LL BE AROUND'
(Alec Wilder) Recorded 8 February, 1955. Frank originally recorded this for a V-disc in 1943.

4. 'ILL WIND'
(Harold Arlen & Ted Koehler) Recorded 16 February, 1955. Another ballad from the 1930s.

5. 'IT NEVER ENTERED MY MIND'
(Richard Rodgers & Lorenz Hart) Recorded 4 March, 1955. This was from the show *Higher and Higher*, but somehow or another it was not used in Frank's film version; although he did record it with Axel Stordahl in 1947.

6. 'DANCING ON THE CEILING'
(Richard Rodgers & Lorenz Hart) Recorded 8 February, 1955. From the musical *Evergreen*, staged in London in 1931 and made into a film in 1934 starring Jessie Matthews.

7. 'I'LL NEVER BE THE SAME'
(Matty Malneck, Frank Signorelli & Gus Kahn) Recorded 4 March, 1955. Dating from 1932, this is one of five songs on the album with an "I" in its title. Over half the songs are in the first person, emphasizing the personal nature of the material.

8. 'THIS LOVE OF MINE'
(Sol Parker, Hank Sanicola & Frank Sinatra) Recorded 17 February, 1955. Almost 14 years after Frank recorded this, he revisited one of his rare self-penned numbers.

Detroit, rather than his coveted role of Sky Masterton, who was to be played by Marlon Brando. In the original stage musical, which had opened on Broadway in late 1950, Detroit had only one song, 'Sue Me' – so Frank used his persuasive powers to get extra songs added for his character to sing.

A week after recording 'Learnin' the Blues', a song that would later top the *Billboard* disc jockey chart and make No 2 on the bestseller's list, Frank was back at the Pantages to present Eva Marie Saint with her Oscar as best supporting actress for her role in *On the Waterfront*. The irony must have fuelled Frank's irritation against the man he called "Mumbles". Losing out to Brando on both his Hoboken homecoming and *Guys and Dolls* was a constant source of irritation during the filming of the latter. To add further frustration, Brando won the best actor Oscar for his role in *Waterfront*.

On the set of *Guys and Dolls*, the crowning annoyance was Brando's endless demands for retakes. For "one-take" Frank, who liked to nail his scenes quickly, it must have been excruciating. Brando apparently did 135 takes on one scene, which, as well as annoying Frank, caused budgetary problems when the filming overran. Frank's frustrations boiled over when he and Vivian Blaine, Frank's love interest in the movie, were asked to stay on longer once too often. Frank just took Miss Blaine's hand and marched off set,

leaving director Joseph Mankiewitz speechless. However, it seems that Frank behaved himself most of the time, although after one Brando-instigated retake he demanded, "These fucking New York actors! Just how much cheesecake do you think I can eat?"

Despite Frank's dissatisfaction with the filming, there was good news: he'd knocked his old rival Eddie Fisher off the top of the *Downbeat* disc jockey survey for "Top Recording Personality of the Year". The 25 March poll had Perry Como in second place and Fisher back in third. The poll showed little evidence of the musical changes that were slowly taking place among the young, other than the Crew-Cuts taking seventh spot. 'Sh-Boom' had been a smash hit in 1954, and while they were for many "the acceptable face of rock 'n' roll", they were the advance guard for what was to come. Nelson Riddle did well in the poll, landing the No 2 spot on the "Best Conductor of a Studio Orchestra" survey.

MOVIE MANIA

In addition to filming, Frank had a radio show for Bobbi Home Permanent on which he premiered some of the songs from *In the Wee Small Hours*. There was also another appearance on an NBC TV colour spectacular, *Max Liebman's Kaleidoscope*, from which Frank earned $25,000. As Frank's earning potential grew, he was increasingly

MUMBLES SINGS
On the set of Guys and Dolls, *where Frank seems to be ignoring Marlon Brando.*

NOT AS A STRANGER

THIS FILM, DIRECTED BY Stanley Kramer, was his first independent production and has been described as a medical soap opera, and while there were some who admired its "tense excitement" there were others who thought it a dud. Most people agree that Frank comes out of it none too badly but then again he had only third billing to Olivia de Havilland and Frank's drinking buddy Robert Mitchum.

Filmed in black and white, it was released through United Artists and is the story of an arrogant doctor who accidentally kills a good friend during an operation, before finding redemption in the arms of his wife. This "moody and gritty screenplay" as the *Hollywood Reporter* put it was taken from a novel by Morton Thompson, which had been on the bestseller list for months.

Despite everything, there were high hopes for the film. Kramer had a budget of $2 million, his largest to that point. Kramer went for realism, getting his actors to attend real life operations at a hospital near the Chaplin studios where it was filmed. *Variety* decided that Mitchum was "considerably over his acting depth". There were some adverse reactions from doctors claiming that it showed them in an unfavourable light. It's probably best now described as a period piece that was typical of the era.

> 66 Sinatra [who] seems to become a better actor with each successive part, is simply terrific. 99
>
> **HOLLYWOOD REPORTER**

> 66 He's a great talent and can do no wrong as far as I'm concerned. The only thing Sinatra can ever do wrong is…stop singing. 99
>
> **TOMMY DORSEY, INTERVIEWED JUNE 1955**

focusing on what he did and how much he was paid. There was a story in *Variety* just before the special aired, stating how Frank had refused to appear on Ed Sullivan's show, *Toast of the Town*, as a sendoff for *Guys and Dolls*. Frank had demanded payment to promote his own movie. "TV is as much a business as motion pictures and I should be paid accordingly." MGM naturally disputed it, and Frank's lawyers went into battle; but he didn't appear on the show. As *Guys and Dolls* finished shooting, *Not as a Stranger* had its premiere on 2 July. Frank was also filming *The Tender Trap* during May and June, which meant there was some overlap with the *Guys and Dolls* schedule.

Frank, along with the Bogarts, Judy Garland, and Joan Fontaine, was at the Sands on 7 June to witness Noel Coward's desert debut. The man who had been described as "destiny's tot" had fallen on hard times and was now something of an anachronism. Somewhat against the odds, however, he was a great success – the four-week run earned him $160,000, securing his finances. Coward viewed the whole thing as something awful: it was like performing for "the Nescafé Set" in "the fabulous, extraordinary madhouse".

On 11 July, along with Dean, Sammy, and Humphrey Bogart, Frank went to Judy Garland's show in Long Beach, California. Frank was involved with Judy Garland in a romantic way, not a serious one like with Ava, more of a sexual flirtation. It certainly had little chance of going anywhere, since Judy was already showing signs of a self-destructive side of her personality, which Frank could neither understand nor deal with.

THE TWO FACES OF FRANK

In many ways Frank was a dichotomy. There were so many negatives that it is easy to overlook the fact that he was also an extraordinarily kind man. It was as though his temper, his outbursts, and his anger needed some kind of an antidote, and it was certainly through his compassion for others that he found some relief. Whether it was Frank's form of atonement, his public/private confessional, or just that, as is so often the case, his faults were closely mirrored by his strengths, no one can be certain, but there is no doubting Frank's legendary acts of kindness, even more so after his resurrection than before.

In 1955, he helped two men who were both in dire straits. One, the actor Lee J Cobb, Frank knew fairly well, having worked with him on *Miracle of the Bells*. The other, actor Bela Lugosi, Frank hardly knew at all, except through his movies. Lugosi was a heroin addict, and he eventually committed himself to hospital, where Frank sent him a huge box of delicacies. "It was a wonderful surprise. I've never met Sinatra, but I hope to soon. He was the only star I heard from," said Lugosi. Frank's kindness to Cobb was far more profound. Cobb had a serious heart attack in June 1955, and he also had very little work as a result of his involvement with the House Un-American Activities Committee. Besides having a near-death experience, Cobb was on the verge of bankruptcy. Frank paid Cobb's hospital bills, put him up in an apartment to recover, and spent time with Cobb talking about death, which Cobb was having difficulty facing. Cobb's future wife recognized the Good Samaritan in Frank: "Maybe he was so grateful for having made a comeback that he extended himself to someone in need."

Frank was scheduled to begin work on filming *Carousel* in the third week of August. On 15, 16, and 17 August, he was with Alfred Newman recording three songs for the movie: 'Blow High, Blow Low', 'If I Loved You', and 'You'll Never Walk Alone'. Immediately afterwards, he flew east to Boothbay Harbor, Maine, to begin filming, and on arrival with Hank Sanicola and his make-up man, Beans Ponedel, he was installed in a house overlooking the bay. Pretty soon he was engaged in a screaming match with the film's producer, Henry Ephron. Frank was angry because he had found out that he was going to have to shoot every scene twice – once in 35 mm CinemaScope and then again in 55 mm wide-screen process. This had either not been mentioned before or Frank had not read the contract too carefully. Whatever the case, Frank simply refused to shoot twice. Without even visiting the set, he simply declined to appear as Billy Bigelow opposite Shirley Jones. As a writer at the time said, "Walking out is as much a habit with Sinatra as it used to be with the Russians at the UN." Gordon MacRae was brought in to replace Frank, and within a couple of weeks they found that the film could, in fact, be converted between the different formats, and so everything was shot just the once after all. Ten days later, Fox announced that they were going to sue Frank for $1 million for walking out on the part that would have paid him $150,000 for 15 weeks' work. Fox eventually settled out of court. In the aftermath of the *Carousel* debacle, Frank gave an interview to *Time* magazine, which ran on 29 August: "I'm going to do as I please. I don't need anybody in the world. I did it all myself." Frank was already doing it his way. The article also noted that Frank's first three albums had each sold around 250,000 copies at $4.98 each. With Frank's standard royalty rate, that would have earned him around $100,000, which explains in part why the movies were so important to him. Frank also told *Time*, "Man I'm buoyant, I feel about 8 feet tall." A friend was reported as saying "He's got it made. He's come all the way back and still gone further.

He'll step right in when Bing steps out as the greatest all round entertainer in the business." Frank's earnings from movies in 1955 were around $800,000.

CONFIDENTIAL NO MORE

As September's *Confidential* hit the newsstands, breaking the story of Joe DiMaggio, Frank, and the "wrong door" incident from November 1954, Frank was appearing in Vegas. the Sands had recently bought the Dunes and Frank opened at this newly acquired property, riding in for his opening night on the back of a camel. Straight after, he made an unscheduled appearance on *The Colegate Comedy Hour* with Dean Martin and Jerry Lewis. The following night, Frank starred in another NBC TV special, playing the stage manager in Thornton Wilder's *Our Town*, also starring Paul Newman and Eva Marie Saint. Daughter Nancy wrote that this was song-writer Jimmy Van Heusen's first formal job for her father. This, of course, was far from true, since he had written a number of songs for Frank over the years, and, as recently as July, Frank had recorded Van Heusen's songs for *The Tender Trap*. In fact, Frank had cut the four songs that were used in *Our Town* at

JERRY, FRANK AND DEAN
Frank coming between the duo, who would soon go their separate ways.

1952-1957

GUYS AND DOLLS

THE NEW YORK premiere of *Guys and Dolls* took place at the Capitol Theatre on 3 November. It wasn't the first showing of the movie in New York. A few days earlier, at Loew's Theatre on 86th Street, there had been a press preview attended by, among others, Montgomery Clift. For whatever reason, though possibly connected with his own addictions, Clift hated the film. Talking loudly throughout the opening scenes, he eventually left well before the end: "This picture sucks, let's get out of here." A fortnight after the New York premiere, it was shown in San Francisco and then five days later at the Paramount in Hollywood. The public disagreed with Clift: it grossed $250,000 in its first ten days at the Capitol, which was a record for the theatre.

Frank Loesser, who wrote the music for *Guys and Dolls*, was less than impressed by some of Frank's interpretations of his songs during rehearsals for the film. Frank was predictably short with Loesser and did the songs his way. His four songs were 'Adelaide', 'Sue Me', with Vivian Blaine, 'Guys and Dolls', and 'The Oldest Established Permanent Floating Crap Game In New York'; the latter two songs were done with Stubby Kaye and Johnny Silver. They were not Frank's finest musical hour on celluloid, but they worked within the context of the film.

"Frank loved to hold court – to talk about movies, shows, and funny things. Once at the old MGM bar area, Frank was talking about his movie career to everyone. There was Tony Bennett, Vic Damone, and Steve Lawrence, and they were all mesmerized by Frank. Being a real movie fan myself, I'd chip in with various things, and he'd say 'How do you know that?' He talked about *Guys and Dolls*: 'What a terrible movie that was – Marlon Brando... what a joke! He wanted me to teach him to sing!' And then he went on about how the film had been miscast and how it should have been him as Nathan Detroit and Dean Martin as Sky Masterson. Then Tony Bennett piped up, 'Frank, I liked it....' Frank turned around and said, 'Who the hell said that?' to the throng. Tony said, 'It's me, Tony... I really liked it!' 'What the hell do you know? Go back to San Francisco and look for your heart!' The real joke is that recently I reminded Tony of this, and he said, 'You know what, Rich, I didn't like it! I was trying to get in with him – I really didn't like it. I just thought I was being nice!'" recalled comedian, Rich Little.

the same time as his *Carousel* sessions. Among these songs was 'Love and Marriage', which would prove to be an enduring song, even though Frank didn't much care for it. On 22 October, *Billboard* reported, "Since Sinatra's TV appearance this record has been selling steadily and at an ever increasing pace. Boston and New York now rate the disk among their Top 10." However, according to Frank, the TV special was a waste of his time: "*Our Town* requires four weeks of rehearsals, and for what? It had a lot of merit, I'll admit, but, after all that work you have nothing to show for it but a bad black and white kinescope... it's all burned up – poooof – in ninety minutes. I could make a good movie in that time." Given Frank's September schedule, you wonder how he would have fitted in the *Carousel* filming, even if there had just been one take of each scene. Fox had insisted he would have been finished location filming by 6 September in time for the Dunes opening on 9 September.

According to writer Dominic Dunne in his book *The Way We Lived Then*, in *Our Town* Frank was yet again uncooperative on set. "His behavior to the director and the cast was inexcusable. He refused to do the dress rehearsal for the live telecast, which we had to do with a stand in." (Dunne's memories of Frank were further clouded by an incident in the 1960s when he claimed that Frank paid a waiter to hit him in the face.) While many reviews of Frank's performance were positive, even allowing for the fact he retained his Hoboken accent, it has been said that Wilder disliked Frank's portrayal of the role more than that of any other actor.

HIS OWN PARADISE

In October, it was third time lucky for Frank in his personal battle with "Mumbles". He began filming what was perhaps his greatest film role (as a Chicago poker dealer in *The Man with the Golden Arm*), and he won it in preference to Marlon Brando. Midway through the month, he cut the first song for a new album project, George and Ira Gershwin's 'Love Is Here to Stay'. It demonstrates superbly how Frank's sound had changed. As Nelson said, "Where Sinatra used to sound like a muted violin, now he's like a fine cello."

Frank's last visit to a recording studio in 1955 was on 31 October, when he recorded the theme song for *The Man with the Golden Arm*. It was another Jimmy Van Heusen and Sammy Cahn film song, conducted by Elmer Bernstein: "He makes his own dreams, his own paradise, but paradise is just a false alarm. And no one's really sadder than the man with the golden arm. He buys every thrill and pays any price and thinks he's having fun and what's the harm. He's following the devil's plan, the man with the golden arm."

Far from being a love song, it neatly encapsulates the film, in which Frank plays a heroin addict. In the event, it

was not used in the film, perhaps because it was too explicit and could have fallen foul of the censors — it would certainly not have made the radio play lists.

Shortly after an appearance on Milton Berle's television show, Frank's base of operation shifted from Hollywood to Las Vegas for a while. He was back at the Sands for a two-week season, and while he was there he filmed a cameo appearance in an MGM musical, *Meet Me in Las Vegas*, in which he appears as a one-arm-bandit player; he also turned 40 while he was in the desert. While there was probably quite a party, no one seems to have been very talkative about it!

A little under two weeks later, *The Man with the Golden Arm* premiered, making this a successful end to a busy year for Frank. His Capitol contract was also renegotiated. It was reported that Frank's four-year deal was "torn up" in favour of

PREMIERE DATE
Frank and Deborah Kerr arrive at the Hollywood premiere of Guys and Dolls *in December 1955.*

AUTHOR'S VIEWPOINT
"I am writing the most beautiful play you can imagine. It's a little play with all the big subjects in it; and it's a big play with all the little things of life impressed into it." Thornton Wilder in a letter to Gertrude Stein, 1937.

a new seven-year deal. It had a guarantee of $200,000, which probably meant that Frank was given an advance at last, which seems eminently reasonable given his performance for the label.

Unfortunately, Frank still took issue with the press, despite his success. The frequent plaudits often referred to Frank's comeback, and he just wouldn't accept it… or see it. "I don't call it a comeback. I wasn't away anywhere," is how Frank saw it. His reaction offers a fascinating insight into his character. It shows his fear that it could, and might, happen again. By acknowledging his demise, Frank risked invoking the spirit of failure.

In fact, Frank had been the busiest actor in Hollywood during 1954 and 1955. Six movies were a lot, even for a seasoned actor. At the same time, he was exceptionally busy recording some classic songs for Capitol. A pivotal question in unravelling the mystery of Frank is why did a singer, such a brilliant singer, want to become an actor, and then work so hard at it?

THE *BILLBOARD* TOP 100 CHART
Frank was at No 16 with 'Love and Marriage' on the first ever Top 100, which was inaugurated on 12 November, 1955, having entered the bestseller's list at No 23 the week before. The Top 100 Record sides were "the combined tabulation of Dealer, Disk Jockeys, and Juke Box operator replies to *Billboard's* weekly popular record best seller and most played surveys. Its purpose is to provide Disk jockeys with additional programing material and to give trade exposure to newer records." The 100 has remained the yardstick of success ever since. The first No 1 on the Top 100 was 'Love is a Many Splendoured Thing' by the Four Aces and stayed there for two weeks. The Four Aces version of 'Three Coins in a Fountain' had out performed Frank's the year before.

THE TENDER TRAP

For New Yorkers, November 1955 must have felt like a return to the heady days of Swoonatra. *The Tender Trap* premiered within a week of *Guys and Dolls* opening. The film is based on a hit Broadway play by Max Shulman and Robert Paul Smith, and the pairing of Debbie Reynolds (age 23) and Frank (age 39) produced some nice moments.

Ostensibly, it is a light comedy but there are some dark overtones when Frank's character's friend (David Wayne) leaves his wife and children for Frank's on-screen ex-girlfriend, Celeste Holm. The film is directed by Charles Waters, who also directed *Easter Parade*. Apparently, making the film was a relatively relaxed affair, with Debbie even commenting on how nice Frank was to work with.

However, at around 110 minutes in length, most reviewers thought the material was "thinly spreading its trifles over nearly two hours", as *The New York World Telegram* put it. However, all agreed that it was a hit. Another thing all

were agreed on was the fact that hearing 'The Tender Trap' sung 5 times during the course of the film was an awful lot. Capitol, of course, was certainly not unhappy with the exposure. The *Hollywood Reporter* seemed to encapsulate just what the press felt about the film's box office appeal even if they were a little more fulsome in their praise than most. "Tender Trap is a cinch for top attendances everywhere; it's a great GREAT comedy, magnificently written, wonderfully directed and acted." It was during the filming that Debbie got engaged to Eddie Fisher. Frank apparently took her to lunch and gave her some advice. "You know, Debbie, your life may be difficult if you marry a singer. Please give this very deep and serious thought." According to Debbie, "I didn't. I should have!"

FRANK AND DEBBIE
The studio promoted the film as "Four Fabulous Funsters in Cinemascope and Gay Colour". Frank was happy as his publishing company owned the rights to the song 'The Tender Trap'.

If you go back to 1953, before his Oscar win, but after the success of *Eternity*, you'll probably find the answer. It is likely that Frank thought his singing career was effectively washed up, not just in terms of his popularity but in how much he could expect to earn from singing. Under his original scale deal from Capitol, his earning potential was severely limited, especially if he didn't sell records, and in 1953 he really didn't sell that many. Was his film career yet another example of Frank emulating his hero, Bing Crosby? In actual fact, films had been Frank's main source of income for the past two years, and back in 1953 he probably thought that his ability to earn big bucks from singing was one gamble too many.

There was also a historical factor. Prior to this time, singers didn't really have long-running "careers". It was the shooting star syndrome, where they rose quickly, and high, into the sky before burning out into a cloud of vapour and dust. In many ways, that description reflects Frank's time at Columbia. It wasn't just because Mitch Miller made him sing duff songs; Frank had simply run his course as a pop singer. "The Voice" had not been prepared to gamble everything

on his vocal chords lasting the course or continuing to soothe the ears and inspire the loins of 1950s America. However, Capitol had struck lucky, and been skilful too. The American dream was in full swing, and Frank was the soundtrack. Throughout America, there were others whose dream didn't include Frank, young people who sang to young people — people who were just like 1940s' Frankie in the eyes of the older generation. Their music was an attack on everything that Frank's songs stood for. While Frank sang of love, they sang of sex. Rock 'n' roll was about to be here to stay. As Frank had told *Downbeat* in 1953, "I expect to be making more pictures than before but all straight dramatic ones." Frank clearly thought it impossible to be a singer all his life. But Frank still reigned supreme on the *Downbeat* poll, getting 2,155 votes in the male singer category. His nearest rival was his Capitol label mate Nat King Cole, but he could muster only 670 votes. Frank also won the popular music personality of the year award, with Sammy Davis Jr as runner-up. In itself these were great results and take nothing away from Frank, but it should be remembered that *Downbeat*'s readership was the more sophisticated end of the market, and the market was polarizing. In Britain, Frank was voted "Outstanding Popular Singer in the World" in the *New Musical Express*: Frank polled 8,340; his nearest rival was Johnnie Ray on 5,963. All in all, a very good year.

ON SCREEN
The Tender Trap *was showing in British cinemas in the summer of 1956.*

THE MAN WITH THE GOLDEN ARM

BASED ON THE 1949 novel of the same name by Nelson Algren, the story of an ex serviceman with a drug habit is a dark tale. Frank's portrayal of the addict, Frankie Machine, earned him an Oscar nomination for "Best Actor" (he lost to Earnest Borgnine for his role in *Marty*). The film was refused a seal of approval by the Motion Picture Association of America for its subject matter, which probably helped rather than hindered the film at the box office.

Otto Preminger had bought the film rights to the story from the estate of John Garfield who had developed a script but then died (aged 39) before he could see the project through to the initial production phase. When Frank was sent the script he was said to have told friends that it was the "first role since Maggio that was written for him". Beating Brando to the part must have been the icing on the cake. The casting of Kim Novak,

CLUB LIFE
Like *Pal Joey*, the milieu of the film alluded to Frank's experience as an entertainer.

a discovery of Harry Cohn's, proved to be not without its problems. She was so inexperienced, and apparently terrified of the prospect, that it made filming very challenging. The film when finished pleased just about everyone concerned, although there were frustrations over the script, which was cumbersome in places.

Saul Bass, who designed the poster for the film, was born in New York in 1920. He came to prominence in 1949 after designing the print ad for Kirk Douglas' film *The Champion*. Having initially worked in New York and then in Los Angeles for a variety of advertising agencies, Bass had a strong working relationship with both Otto Preminger and Alfred Hitchcock. His direction of the shower scene in *Psycho* is Bass at his brilliant best. Later he worked on creating corporate identities for United Airlines, AT&T, and Exxon amongst many others. Bass, who died in 1996, has left his mark on today's print media.

STRONG STUFF
Frank gave a hard hitting performance as a flawed man driven by ambition.

CAST & CREDITS

Frankie Machine	Frank Sinatra
Zosch Machine	Eleanor Parker
Molly	Kim Novak
Louie	Darren McGavin
Sparrow	Arnold Stang

Director and Producer	Otto Preminger
Cinematographer	Sam Leavitt
Screenwriter	Walter Newman
Original story	Nelson Algren
Score	Elmer Bernstein

THE STORY LINE

Frankie Machine is the card dealer, who inspires the film's title, with a drug habit and a wife (Eleanor Parker) who is crippled from a car accident caused by her husband. He wants to move away from cards and drugs and become a drummer. His wife encourages him to play cards and Frankie meets Molly (Kim Novak); they have an affair. The film climaxes with Frankie playing cards, getting a fix and losing everything only to find out that his wife can in fact walk after all. She in turn has killed Frankie's dealer but it's all too late and Frankie tells her he's leaving. She kills herself by jumping from a window and Frankie walks off with Molly. You can see why the MPAA struggled with it!

BACKDOOR MAN
Frank's affair with Molly (Kim Novak) draws him into a web of deceit.

1955 ON THE JUKEBOX

FRANK ON THE US CHARTS

'MELODY OF LOVE'
(Hans Engelmann & Tom Glazer)
22 January, No 19, 4 weeks

'LEARNIN' THE BLUES'
(Delores Vicki Silvers)
7 May, No 1, 21 weeks

'SAME OLD SATURDAY NIGHT'
(Frank Reardon & Sammy Cahn)
24 September, No 13, 5 weeks

'FAIRY TALE'
(Jerry Livingston & Dok Stanford)
10 September, No 22, 5 weeks

'LOVE AND MARRIAGE'
(Jimmy Van Heusen & Sammy Cahn)
5 November, No 5, 17 weeks

'(LOVE IS) THE TENDER TRAP'
(Jimmy Van Heusen & Sammy Cahn)
10 December, No 7, 15 weeks

OUTSTANDING POPULAR SINGER IN THE WORLD

1.	FRANK SINATRA	8340
2.	Johnnie Ray	5963
3.	Doris Day	5042
4.	Dickie Valentine	4680
5.	Frankie Laine	4526
6.	David Whitfield	3239
7.	Sammy Davis, jnr.	3176
8.	Eddie Fisher	2927
9.	Nat Cole	2466
10.	Rosemary Clooney	2017
11.	Guy Mitchell	1763
12.	Bing Crosby	1665
13.	Ruby Murray	1383
14.	Perry Como	068
15.	Billy Eckstine	933
16.	Ella Fitzgerald	801
17.	Slim Whitman	638
18.	Sarah Vaughan	625
19.	Mario Lanza	620
20.	Alma Cogan	1383
21.	Peggy Lee	
22.	Caterina Valente	
23.	Dean Martin	
24.	Lena Horne	
25.	Dennis Lotis	
26.	Jo Stafford	
27.	Jimmy Young	
28.	Kay Starr	
29.	Al Martino	
30.	Eartha Kitt	

BIG IN BRITAIN
Frank topped the NME poll despite not topping the charts. His biggest UK single was 'Learnin' the Blues', which got to No 2. He graciously forwarded his thanks to his British fans (below).

Frank's first No 1 record of the 1950s, his first since 1947, was the fourth of his solo career and sold over 800,000 copies. It is credited as a No 1 in the *Billboard* book of hit singles but only actually ever made No 2 on the bestseller's list and No 1 on the DJ chart. It meant that, despite Frank's concentration on albums, it proved he could still cut it on the singles chart. He ended the year with three top 10 records, which hadn't happened since 1950, and spent a total of 67 weeks on the chart.

A look at the top selling records for the first half of the year gives no indication of what was about to happen. Records like 'Let Me Go Lover' by Joan Weber, 'Cherry Pink and Apple Blossom White' by bandleader Perez Prado and Bill Hayes's 'Ballad of Davy Crockett' are as ordinary as they sound. Then, on 9 July, a 30-year-old former yodelling cowboy from Highland Park, Michigan made No 1. '(We're Gonna) Rock Around The Clock' by Bill Haley and His Comets had been working its way up steadily since the middle of May. Haley had already scored with a cleaned up version of Big Joe Turner's 'Shake Rattle and Roll' the previous year and in actual fact 'Rock Around The Clock' had been recorded in 1954, before 'Shake Rattle and Roll'; it had originally been just a b-side. While 'Rock Around the Clock' was not the first rock 'n' roll record, nor the best, it was a seminal moment. The charts would never be the same again. Ironically it was Frank that vied with Haley for the top spot during the summer. 'Learnin' the Blues' was very much a case of the old versus the new. Ironically it was Frank's nemesis from Columbia that toppled both him and Haley: Mitch Miller's 'The Yellow Rose of Texas' spent six weeks at No 1 from early September.

Lest anyone think Frank's records were assured hits then just check out Capitol 3130. 'Not As A Stranger' did about as well as the movie from which it was taken. It failed to make any impression on the charts, despite *Billboard* saying, "interest has already reached an intense pitch, undoubtedly it will go much higher." It was actually competing head to head with 'Learnin' The Blues', and in fairness it was a more sophisticated song. 'Don't Change Your Mind About Me' which had a release in late March, backed by 'Why Should I Cry Over You' also failed to chart, despite *Downbeat* saying, "he's really got it once more and isn't about to let go." Interestingly, 'Don't Change Your

Mind About Me' smacks of Dorsey and the Pied Pipers, which may account for its lack of chart success; it was just a little too old fashioned.

FRANK AND THE BRITISH CHARTS
The first British Record Hit Parade was published on 14 November, 1952, and Frank was nowhere to be seen. Al Martino topped the first chart, which in keeping with Britain's non-decimal approach to life was a Top 12. Even during Frank's British tour in the summer of 1953 there were no hit records, despite Capitol pushing 'I'm Walking Behind You'/'Lean Baby'. Frankie Laine topped the charts for a record 18 weeks from April to August that year. Frank's first British hit single came with his fifth release, 'Young At Heart', which just scraped into the Top 12 for one week in July 1954. Two weeks later 'Three Coins in the Fountain' entered the chart and made the top by 18 September. It had the honour of being the first No 1 of the inaugural Top 20 on 2 October, 1954. Capitol must have been pleased that Nat Cole held the second spot with 'Smile' and three more Capitol records by Al Martino and Dean Martin were also on that chart.

In 1955, there were three hits, 'You My Love' (No 13/7 weeks), 'Learnin' The Blues' (No 2/13 weeks) and 'Not As a Stranger' (No 18/1 week). As in America, the critics didn't always get it right. In February 1955, 'Melody of Love' came out and according to the *New Musical Express*, "it will take a couple of atom bombs to prevent this from becoming a hit." It didn't.

BILL HALEY AND HIS COMETS
Looking back, it is difficult to see what all the fuss was about; Haley looked almost as old as Frank.

THE CAPITOL TOWER, HOLLYWOOD & VINE, LOS ANGELES, 1956

PARTY PEOPLE

On New Year's Eve, 1955, Frank hosted a party at his house in Palm Springs, but, as 1956 dawned, Frank ended up alone. His guests, including most of Bogie's Rat Pack and Noel Coward, all decided to go back to Los Angeles. It's ironic that just about anyone else in the United States would have jumped at the chance to stay.

Frank was riding high; his whole life seemed to be one long party. Precisely when this party, to which everyone wanted an invitation, began is a matter of debate. But one thing is for sure... it was Frank's party.

In early January, Frank was finishing filming *Johnny Concho* and he was also busy in the recording studio. Between 9 and 16 January, there were four sessions at KHJ, his last at the studio that had, for nearly three years, been so important in Frank's comeback. At these sessions, Frank recorded the bulk of the tracks for his next album, arguably the greatest of his career. One of the songs Frank wanted to include on *Songs for Swingin' Lovers* was Cole Porter's 'I've Got You Under My Skin'. During a break in recording between 10 and 12 January, Nelson Riddle was under considerable

CONDUCTING POETRY
Frank's idea for Tone Poems of Color *went back to the 1940s. While the results may not bear up to close scrutiny today, there is no doubting his motives and the sound basis for his idea.*

> "If I were to be around Laurence Olivier and John Gielgud for 30 years, some Shakespearean knowledge would have to rub off on me if I were a good student and listener. Now Frank was with James and Dorsey in the years when they had bands, that had jazz soloists and a jazz feel, and it would be impossible for a lot of that not to have rubbed off."

SAMMY DAVIS JR, *DOWNBEAT, AUGUST 1956*

pressure to finish this particular arrangement. There is an oft-repeated story of Mrs Riddle driving to the 8:00 pm session with Nelson still writing out the charts in the back of the car. Given the fact that there was another session on 16 January, when the last five tracks for the album were cut, it doesn't quite ring true. But it's a great story. The day after the sessions finished, Frank began filming *High Society*.

Six weeks after the *Swingin' Lovers* sessions, Frank's friend Humphrey Bogart was diagnosed with cancer. Some have speculated that Frank's love affair with Lauren Bacall began during Bogie's illness. This may have been true, but she was certainly not his only love interest during this time. Frank continued to see Judy Garland and he was also dating Kim Novak – an affair that began while filming *The Man with the Golden Arm* and one that would continue throughout 1956. Bogie's illness prevented him and Frank appearing together in a film called *Underworld USA*, based on a book about the infamous Brinks robbery.

His filming commitments meant that Frank couldn't travel to London to appear at the *New Musical Express* Poll Winners' Concert at the end of January. Instead, he sent a recorded message that was played – to ecstatic cheers – after Britain's Dickie Valentine had sung. "I hope to see all my friends in Great Britain some time in the very near future," said Frank. It would be six years before he performed in Britain.

Shortly before *Songs for Swingin' Lovers* came out, Frank was at the Capitol Tower – the first ever sessions in the new studio – working with a 50-piece orchestra. But Frank

wasn't singing, he was conducting an orchestra in an ambitious project featuring instrumental pieces by some of the leading arrangers and writers of the era. The dozen pieces were inspired by radio scriptwriter Norman Sickel's poems about colours.

Recorded over five sessions between 22 February and 15 March, the LP, *Tone Poems of Color*, came out in the summer. Saxophonist Ted Nash, who played on the album, recalled: "All he did was to conduct. He had worked hard with Nelson's conducting teacher, and he really enjoyed it. Frank asked me if I noticed anything not right to mention it to him. It was the only time I ever saw him a little hesitant…. I got a kick out of seeing him in that role. He did it real

> 66 Orange is the gay deceiver and I do deceive but nicely. 99
>
> **FROM NORMAN SICKEL'S POEM ABOUT FRANK'S FAVOURITE COLOUR**

THE CAPITOL TOWER

THERE'S NO MORE POTENT SYMBOL OF HOLLYWOOD THAN THE SIGN ON MOUNT LEE IN THE HOLLYWOOD HILLS, BUT THE CAPITOL TOWER, DESIGNED BY WELTON BECKETT, RUNS A VERY CLOSE SECOND.

CAPITOL REEKED OF CHIC and Frank just added to the style and sophistication after they signed him. The Tower was the embodiment of their image.

When songwriter Johnny Mercer, the lyricist on standards like 'That Old Black Magic' and 'Blues in the Night', and his partner Glenn Wallichs, who owned Music City on the corner of Sunset and Vine, started Capitol Records in 1942, they could not have dreamed how big their company would get. While other artists established the business, it was Frank who was putting the icing on Capitol's cake. Their first record had been 'The General Jumped At Dawn', by Paul Whiteman's Orchestra. With the Musicians' Union strike looming, Capitol worked hard to stockpile recordings including 'Cow Cow Boogie' and 'G.I. Jive'; both became big hits because Capitol was the only label with versions of the songs and they cleaned up.

The 13-storey building opened on 6 April, 1956 and was not, despite the legend, designed to look like a stack of records with a needle on top. It was the world's first round office building and the red light atop the needle flashed H.O.L.L.Y.W.O.O.D. in Morse code. The three studios were "floating rooms" encased in a layer of cork, cutting out external vibration. The studio's crowning glory are the four echo chambers designed by guitarist Les Paul. Problems with the studios took over a year to solve and Capitol spent somewhere near $1 million to make their new studios sound like the old Melrose

studios. Even then many still preferred the old KHJ facility, although it's still in use. The Capitol Tower's iconic image was kept well polished in the 1960s by The Beach Boys (although they rarely recorded in the tower), the Beatles, who Capitol distributed for their parent company, EMI, and many other artists became associated with the label. EMI bought Capitol in 1955, a good investment given the timing of the deal. A few years later, when Frank fell out of love with Capitol and started with Reprise, he told Mo Ostin "I helped build that, now let's build one of our own."

SONGS FOR SWINGIN' LOVERS

IF YOU HAVE JUST ONE OF FRANK'S ALBUMS THIS SHOULD BE IT; A PEERLESS VOCAL *TOUR DE FORCE* FROM FRANK MATCHED BY NELSON RIDDLE'S ARRANGING SKILLS AT THEIR BEST.

The *Metronome* Yearbook in 1957 called it an "Impeccable set of performances" while AA Gill in *The Sunday Times* later declared it: "The sexiest record ever made!" What more can you ask? With Frank under pressure on the singles chart, his albums were now his 'weapon of choice'. *Songs For Swingin' Lovers* came out in March 1957 and was soon sitting at No 2, remaining on the charts for almost a year. It was also Frank's last album to be recorded at KHJ Studios.

Sammy Davis Jr told *Downbeat* in August 1956 that "You can listen to him all night, and he never fires on your ears. That's why he's so successful an album singer." That simply describes what makes this album so long lasting; it has legs to die for. Put it on today and you'll find people instantly 'get it'. From the opening bars of 'You Make Me Feel so Young', you know where Frank is coming from. Love's not supposed to be some forlorn state, you're supposed to be happy; this was, and is, vinyl euphoria. In 2000 the album was inducted into the Grammy Hall of Fame. What's puzzling is that it took them so long.

From the original sleeve notes...

For teen-agers, when he himself was young and frail, Frankie stood in the theatre spotlight and sang with all his heart, till the throng of girls screeched their delight.

For adventure-loving moviegoers, he became the ill-starred soldier, Private Maggio, and his spirited, sensitive performance won a coveted Academy Award.

For sad romantics, singing bittersweet ballads, he gently caught the mood of the wee, small hours of the mornin', and created a best-selling record album.

For observers of the social scene, he courageously fashioned a new identity in his taut, dramatic film portrayal of the man with the golden arm.

> **❝** Frank seems to have co-invented a style of big band accompaniment that just took off like some big rocket. I could see it on his face, on stage, when the band started to blow on 'I've Got You Under My Skin'. He knew we were going to a place where man had never gone before. **❞**
> **JIMMY WEBB**

SONG LINES

Recorded : KHJ Studios, Hollywood, Produced by Voyle Gilmore. Chart: US No 2 (50 weeks) First charted 31 March, 1956. UK No 8 (8 weeks) First charted 15 November, 1958.

SIDE 1

1. 'YOU MAKE ME FEEL SO YOUNG' (Josef Myrow & Mack Gordon) Recorded 9 January, 1956. A song from the 1946 film *Three Little Girls in Blue* it became a feature of Frank's shows throughout his career. He often used it as an opener, including his White House concert in 1973 that brought Frank back from his retirement.

2. 'IT HAPPENED IN MONTEREY' (Mabel Wayne & Billy Rose) Recorded 12 January, 1956.

3. 'YOU'RE GETTING TO BE A HABIT WITH ME' (Harry Warren & Al Dubin) Recorded 10 January, 1956.

4. 'YOU BROUGHT A NEW KIND OF LOVE TO ME' (Sammy Fein, Pierre Norman Connor & Irving Kahal) Recorded 9 January, 1956.

5. 'TOO MARVELLOUS FOR WORDS' (Richard A. Whiting & Johnny Mercer) Recorded 16 January, 1956.

6. 'OLD DEVIL MOON' (Burton Lane & EY "Yip" Harburg) Recorded 16 January, 1956.

7. 'PENNIES FROM HEAVEN' (Arthur Johnson & Johnny Burke) Recorded 10 January, 1956. This had been a No 1 for Bing back in 1937.

SIDE 2

1. 'I'VE GOT YOU UNDER MY SKIN' (Cole Porter) Recorded 12 January, 1956. From the 1936 film *Born To Dance*, this is the one that most fans, critics and casual observers consider to be his best. It took 22 takes to nail it and according to Milt Bernhardt, who plays the famous trombone solo, there were some earlier ones that were more adventurous but he was asked to tone it down somewhat. At Christmas 2002, it was used in a basketball commercial for the NBA. A computer generated image of 1960s Frank is singing along with a small band on a basketball court in a packed arena, like he is doing a halftime concert. The ad keeps cutting back and forth between Frank and basketball players doing some amazing moves. It's difficult to imagine why Frank, and why the choice of song, but it all goes towards keeping Frank in front of yet another generation.

2. 'I THOUGHT ABOUT YOU' (Jimmy Van Heusen & Johnny Mercer) Recorded 9 January, 1956.

3. 'WE'LL BE TOGETHER AGAIN' (Carl Fischer & Frankie Laine) Recorded 16 January, 1956.

4. 'MAKIN' WHOOPEE' (Walter Donaldson & Gus Kahn) Recorded 16 January, 1956.

5. 'SWINGIN' DOWN THE LANE' (Isham Jones & Gus Khan) Recorded 12 January, 1956. This song from 1923 was one of the earliest Frank songs ever recorded.

6. 'ANYTHING GOES' (Cole Porter) Recorded 16 January, 1956.

7. 'HOW ABOUT YOU' (Burton Lane & Ralph Freed) Recorded 10 January, 1956.

well, good on all the retard passages and suchlike. He was very serious about it." In recent years, critics have been somewhat harsh on Frank for what they see as the album's overly kitsch approach. It was actually an interesting experiment and echoes Frank's words from 1949: "Artists and A&R men will have to pioneer in the use of script material in conjunction with music, the representation of musical sketches, commentary, narrative and mood music. 20 minutes of "time" on each side will call for much more of a production package."

QUALITY SOUND

Midway through recording *Tone Poems of Color*, Frank began work on his next vocal album, but it was to be a deviation from the traditional orchestral setting. Frank and Nelson had decided to work with a string quartet as the album's principal instrumentation, inspired by Frank's love of classical music. What is most interesting is the difference in the sound quality between KHJ and the new Capitol Tower studio. At Frank's last session at KHJ he recorded five songs, all of which appeared on *Songs for Swingin' Lovers*.

The very last song cut at KHJ was Carl Fischer and Frankie Laine's 'We'll Be Together Again'. This song shows a marked difference from the similarly paced 'Don't Like Goodbyes', which Frank worked on at that first Tower session. The difference in the ambience of the two rooms is clearly evident. Initially, the recordings in the new studio are much less alive than KHJ. It sounds like the players, and Frank, are standing in a line, whereas 'We'll Be Together Again' has depth, and shape as well as warmth, all of which were missing from the new studio. It took about a year for the engineers to get back to the marvellous tones coaxed from the KHJ facility.

If you fast forward to November 1, when Frank recorded 'Close To You', the title song for the album that includes 'Don't Like Goodbyes' you can hear that the sound has a much richer, more KHJ quality to it. In fact, the only song worked on at that March 1 session was 'Don't Like Goodbyes' and it was never used. The take that appears on 'Close To You' was made a week later. Some have said that Frank was unhappy with the Hollywood Quartet, but it seems just as likely that he was discontent with the overall sound. According to some of the musicians it was even worse "in the room" than it

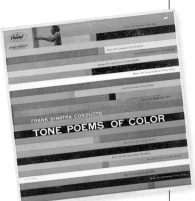

POETRY OF COLOUR
Not only was this an interesting experiment but also a great cover design redolent of the times.

WITH PEGGY CONNELLY AT THE OSCARS
Frank was nominated for the 1956 Academy award for his performance in The Man With The Golden Arm *but lost out to Ernest Borgnine in the Best Actor category.*

REUNITED
Frank on stage at the Paramount in New York City with Tommy Dorsey in August 1956.

It was one story too many for Frank, he declared war on Kilgallen. He sent her a tombstone with her name on it as well as working her into his act, criticizing her appearance, especially as he perceived she lacked a chin. It's been said the Frank coined the phrase "chinless wonder" about her. Dorothy Kilgallen, who died in November 1965, probably never got over the withering attacks from Frank, but neither did she stop attacking him in her column. While Frank was spiteful, he was also once again the victim of a press campaign that was nasty and vindictive. The unholy alliance between newspapers and stars had once more been stretched to the limit.

THE PAIN IN SPAIN

Such was Frank's complete detachment from Ava Gardner by this time that there was even some press speculation that he and Nancy might get back together. But Frank was less than predictable in love, just as he was in life. He flew to Spain on 17 April with Peggy Connelly, the actress he had taken to the Academy Awards in March, to begin work on a new film, *The Pride and the Passion*. Frank was cast as a Spanish cobbler's son who becomes a hero of the Napoleonic wars. Filming took place at over 20 different locations but Frank insisted on staying at the Castellana Hotel throughout. This meant he often drove for hours along difficult roads for his day's filming. He did see Ava in Spain, but she was under no illusions as to where their relationship stood. While he was in Spain, Frank's ire was mainly directed at the film's director, Stanley Kramer, but his sense of racial injustice was once again touched due to an event back home, when racists in Birmingham, Alabama, attacked Nat "King" Cole. As soon as Frank heard about it he called Nat to offer his support.

> 66 Sinatra's idea of paradise is a place where there are plenty of women and no newspapermen. 99
>
> **HUMPHREY BOGART**

sounded on the playback. In the midst of recording *Tone Poems of Color*, Frank was once again targeted by the press and while he can never felt "safe" he probably imagined that things had settled into a relatively comfortable co-existence. That is until Sunday 26 February when he saw the front page of the *Los Angeles Examiner* proclaiming, "The Real Frank Sinatra Story". Any doubts Frank had about the motives of the story would have been quickly dispelled when he read the opening sentences. "Success hasn't changed Frank Sinatra. When he was unappreciated and obscure he was bad tempered, egotistical, extravagant and moody." And from there? It got worse! The writer of the piece, Dorothy Kilgallen, "the voice of Broadway" accused Frank of being a 1956 version of Jekyll and Hyde, and of having a Napoleon complex. She dredged up just about every scandal that had ever touched him, named every lover (real and imagined) and where there were gaps in the story embellished things. But of course in substance it was true; Frank had plenty of skeletons in his closet. The story ran over the next six days finishing with words Miss Kilgallen must have felt very pleased with, "No matter how big a star you are, tomorrow is only maybe." Given Frank's status there can be one motive for such an article: to bring him down. Frank had real hatred for Kilgallen after what she wrote about Humphrey Bogart when he was seriously ill. The Kilgallen affair was a classic case of "big names sell newspapers". Gossip sells them too, and scandal adds circulation – put them all together and newspapers make a ton of money. It'll come as no surprise to learn that the *Los Angeles Examiner* was a Hearst paper.

HOLLYWOOD NOIR
Dorothy Kilgallen died from "an overdose" soon after interviewing Jack Ruby (killer of Lee Harvey Oswald, JFK's killer). She had told a number of people that she was going to blow the lid off the President's assassination.

ELVIS AND ROCK 'N' ROLL

SYNCHRONICITY IS SUCH A WONDERFUL THING. 'HEARTBREAK HOTEL', ELVIS
PRESLEY'S FIRST RECORD FOR RCA VICTOR, ENTERED THE TOP 100 ON 3 MARCH,
1956. IT WAS ELVIS'S FIRST APPEARANCE ON THE NATIONAL CHART.

ONE PLACE ABOVE him at No 67 was another
new entry, Frank's Capitol single 'You'll Get
Yours'. Two months later, Elvis reached No 1, where
he stayed for six weeks; Frank's record got no higher
than No 67 and drifted steadily down the chart
over the next four months.

Elvis had made his television debut on Saturday
28 January, 1956, one month before 'Heartbreak
Hotel' hit the charts. Ironically, in a bridge between
the old and the new, he featured on CBS's *Stage
Show* hosted by big band stalwarts Tommy and
Jimmy Dorsey. Choosing not to perform 'Heartbreak
Hotel', which had been released the previous day,
Elvis sang Big Joe Turner's 'Shake Rattle and Roll',
then segued into 'Flip Flop and Fly', another Turner
rock 'n' roll gem. Elvis was on the show again the
following week, but it wasn't until his third Dorsey
appearance – in mid-February, two weeks before
the song charted – that he performed 'Heartbreak
Hotel'. The Dorsey orchestra provided Elvis and his
group – Bill Black on bass and Scotty Moore on
guitar – with such a stilted accompaniment that it's a
wonder anyone bought the record. Cynics have
even muttered about attempted sabotage.

A NEW MUSICAL ERA

The arrival of Elvis on television and the *Billboard*
chart did not mean the end of Frank's chart career,
or others cast in a similar mould, but musically
things were about to change forever. By the time
'Heartbreak Hotel' had slipped from the No 1 spot,

there were other rock 'n' roll records on the charts:
Carl Perkins' 'Blue Suede Shoes', 'Long Tall Sally' by
Little Richard, Gene Vincent's 'Be Bop A Lula', and
Fats Domino's 'I'm in Love Again'. Naturally, rock 'n'
roll's takeover was not total, nor did it happen
instantly, but it clearly marked a shift in the tastes of
the nation. The young wanted their own heroes and
not ones that sang wearing a suit, and especially
not a dinner jacket.

Elvis, of course, was not the first rock 'n' roller
on the mainstream *Billboard* charts. Bill Haley had
already had hits in 1954 and 1955, as had Little
Richard with 'Tutti Frutti' and the Platters with 'The
Great Pretender'. Going further back, Chicago's
Chess Records, home of Muddy Waters, Howlin'
Wolf, Little Walter, and John Lee Hooker, released
Jackie Brenston and His Delta Cats' 'Rocket 88' in
1951, featuring a young Ike Turner on piano.
A debate has raged for five decades as to whether
this was the first rock 'n' roll record, but the
truth is that no one song has ever established
a musical genre – it was all a process of
evolution, not revolution.

A DANGEROUS NEW ARRIVAL

Whatever the lineage of the genre, initially many
people in the music business thought that rock 'n'
roll, which was about the whole package – the
clothes, the moves, as well as the music – was
nothing more than a passing fad. However, there
was growing concern in parts of American society

**CHUCK
BERRY**
A legend, an enigma
and an architect of
rock. His only
Billboard No 1 was
the appalling 'My
Ding-a-Ling'.

at signs that it was
actually more than fad
and was here to stay. In 1958, The Catholic Youth
Center's newspaper, *Contacts*, felt compelled to
issue a dire warning: "Smash the records you
possess which present a pagan culture and a
pagan concept of life. Check beforehand the
records, which will be played at a house party
or school dance. Switch your radio dial when
you hear a suggestive song."Perhaps Frankie
wasn't so bad after all....

**ELVIS COMES
HOME**
In 1956 the Lip went home
to Tupelo and gave what
for many was one of the
most outstanding
performances of his career.

1952–1957

HIGH SOCIETY

THIS FILM WAS A REMAKE OF the popular 1940 romantic comedy *The Philadelphia Story*, adapted from Philip Barry's stage play of the same name. The 1940 film starred Cary Grant in the role taken over by Bing Crosby, Katharine Hepburn preceded Grace Kelly as the female lead, and Frank Sinatra took the part that had won James Stewart an Oscar. Grace Kelly's wedding plans called for a tight schedule and so filming began on 17 January, 1956 and finished in early March. The most obvious difference between the two films is that *The Philadelphia Story* was not a musical. Jazz great Louis Armstrong appears in the 1956 remake as a kind of narrator, his performance being among the best in the film. Cole Porter supplied the songs. While most consider the acting in the original to be better, the remake achieved strong box office sales. Although it had mixed reviews on release, most felt Frank's performance was the best of the three stars. In any event his $250,000 fee was some consolation for his third billing.

GRACE KELLY

High Society was 26-year-old Philadelphia-born Grace Kelly's last film role before marrying Prince Rainier of Monaco. They had announced their engagement as filming started and the ring she wore in the film was the one given to her by the Prince. Grace knew the story well, having appeared in her school's stage version of *The Philadelphia Story* in her graduation year (1949). Her five-year film career had begun in 1951 in the film *Fourteen Hours* and from then on she captivated audiences with her beauty and charm.

COLE PORTER

Born into a well-to-do family in Peru, Indiana in 1891, Cole studied law at Harvard before switching to music. His first Broadway show was in 1916, but it opened and closed within a few days. Porter persevered but it wasn't until 1928 that he had his first major success with 'Let's Do It' from the show *Paris*. More triumphs quickly followed with songs like 'You Do Something To Me' and 'What is This Thing called Love'. The 1930s saw more Broadway success with 'Love for Sale', 'Night and Day', 'I Get A Kick Out of You', 'Anything Goes', and 'Begin The Beguine' being among his best-known songs.

> ❝Although Sinatra has the top pop tune opportunities, the Groaner makes his specialities stand up.❞
>
> *VARIETY*

FRANK AND THE PRINCESS
Directed by the 45-year-old Charles Walters, *High Society* is different from many film musicals of the era in that there are no big production song and dance numbers. The musical interludes are low key, complementing rather than punctuating the movie. "It misses the snap and crackle that the un-musical predecessor had", was the comment in the *New York Times* on 10 August, 1956.

THE STORY LINE

It is set in Newport, Rhode Island, against a backdrop of the newly established jazz festival, and the lives and homes of the rich and famous. Tracy Lord (Grace Kelly), the quintessential upper class "ice queen" has already discarded one husband, "jukebox hero", C K Dexter Haven (Bing Crosby) and is about to embark on a new marriage to boring businessman George Kittredge (John Lund). Two reporters from Spy magazine, Macauley "Mike" Connor (Frank Sinatra) and photographer Liz Imbrie (Celeste Holm), arrive to cover the wedding. Soon Bing Crosby arrives, determined to win back the woman he still loves. Amid the troubled wedding arrangements Louis Armstrong is on hand to help Bing get his way with Grace, but not before she and Frank have a romantic fling.

CAST & CREDITS

Grace Kelly	Tracy Samantha Lord
Bing Crosby	C K Dexter-Haven
Frank Sinatra	Macauley "Mike" Connor
Celeste Holm	Liz Imbrie
John Lund	George Kittredge
Louis Armstrong and his Band	Themselves

Director	Charles Walters
Producer	Sol C Siegel
Cinematography	Paul C Vogel
Music	Cole Porter
Vocal arrangements	Nelson Riddle/Conrad Salinger
Choreography	Charles Walter

There were arguments on set; Kramer frequently became furious with his star's behaviour. By 1 July, Frank was tiring of the whole process and although he had agreed to a 16-week shoot, he insisted that everything was wrapped up by 25 July – several weeks short of his commitment. Kramer needed longer, but Frank relented only until 28 July, when he simply left and flew back to America. Frank's scenes were not finished, and despite his co-stars Sophia Loren and Cary Grant doing their best to film, while pretending Frank was still there, it was not working. Eventually a compromise was reached where Frank agreed to film for a week on a soundstage in Hollywood. In one notable scene that was partially shot on location and then finished in Hollywood, the extras grouped behind Frank change from people who are obviously Spanish to a group who are clearly Americans; to compound the error, the shot then shifts back to the Spaniards.

It was a totally unsatisfactory situation, but Frank's priority was to be back in time for the release in early August of both his new movie, *Johnny Concho*, made by his own Kent Productions, and *High Society*. A 16-week shoot committed him beyond that point. Frank had told columnist Hedda Hopper before he left for Spain, "When I get there I'll talk to Cary Grant and see if we can tighten up the schedule, possibly to five or seven weeks. They are just digging the foundation for my new house and I'd rather be here [in Los Angeles]. It's a wonderful location, and what a view on a clear day." Megastar syndrome was beginning to kick in: Frank thought that things should, and would, revolve around him. *High Society* had its first showing in New York on 9 August. Frank flew to Chicago to sing the national anthem at the Democratic National Convention in Chicago three days later. From Chicago, it was on to New York for a week's booking at the Paramount with the

❝High finance film musical at anybody's box office…. The atmosphere is plush, the production and personalities lush in every respect… Director Charles Walters has kept his cast in top gear and the end result is as smartly paced as the dance numbers which he also staged.❞

HIGH SOCIETY

HIGH SOCIETY SOUNDTRACK

COLE PORTER'S SONGS AND MUSIC HELPED TO SELL OVER THREE MILLION COPIES OF THE SOUNDTRACK LP AROUND THE WORLD.

'HIGH SOCIETY (OVERTURE)'
Cole Porter Orchestra

'HIGH SOCIETY CALYPSO'
Louis Armstrong & His Band

'LITTLE ONE'
Bing Crosby

'WHO WANTS TO BE A MILLIONAIRE?'
Frank Sinatra & Celeste Holm

'TRUE LOVE'
Bing Crosby & Grace Kelly
US No 3 (31 weeks), UK No 4 (27 weeks)

'YOU'RE SENSATIONAL'
Frank Sinatra
US No 52 (15 weeks)

'I LOVE YOU, SAMANTHA'
Bing Crosby

'NOW YOU HAS JAZZ'
Bing Crosby & Louis Armstrong
US No 88 (4 weeks)

'WELL DID YOU EVAH?'
Bing Crosby & Frank Sinatra

'MIND IF I MAKE LOVE TO YOU?'
Frank Sinatra

The MGM Studio Orchestra conducted by Johnny Green. Orchestration by Nelson Riddle and Conrad Salinger.

Well Did You Evah? was the only song not written for the film having first been heard in the 1939 Broadway musical *Dubarry was a Lady* starring Ethel Merman.

US NO 5 (28 weeks)
Entered the album chart 25 August, 1956

UK NO 16 (1 week)
Entered the album chart 23 July, 1960

Frank on the set of High Society *with co-stars Grace Kelly (above) and, among others, Bing Crosby.*

JOHNNY CONCHO

INTERESTINGLY, FRANK'S FIRST movie from his new production company opened in Britain almost four months before its premiere in the United States. It premiered in London at the Leicester Square Theatre, and the *New Musical Express* reported, "In all categories Sinatra was excellent." The *NME* was in the minority. *Variety* called it, "only a fair mood western… passable for a first try." *The New York Times* was harsher: "Mr Sinatra, the actor, might mention to the producer, who happens to be Mr Sinatra, that he needs better writing and direction than he gets here."

Frank plays Johnny Concho, the cowardly younger brother of a gunslinger, who is tolerated by a small town – Cripple Creek – simply because his brother is feared. When two killers, played by William Conrad and Christopher Dark, take over the town and murder his brother, Frank is forced to flee. He eventually returns, rallying the townsfolk to get rid of the bad guys. Frank is wounded in the final shoot out and, as in all proper westerns, good triumphs over evil. It took 85 minutes to tell the story on screen, which is why the film failed – it was just too slow. One of the few people to come out of it with any real praise was Nelson Riddle; *Variety* applauded "the excellent background score."

the orchestrations, not the performer, that I loved. They were marvellous," recalled Seymour "Red" Press, alto sax, chuckling. There was even an outbreak of Sinatramania that would have really pleased George Evans. "The ushers, too, were helpless when, as Sinatra begged the crowd to take his arms – he'd never use them – a young woman leaped past all obstructions to rush up onstage and throw her arms around him in a fitting why-not-take-all-of-me mood. ('That's not fair!' remonstrated Frankie.)" Unfortunately, Frank lasted only three nights at the Paramount, because a bout of laryngitis forced the cancellation of the rest of the run. Even so, his appearance grossed $147,000 for the week, well up on the $62,000 taken at the box office back in 1952, when he appeared alongside *Meet Danny Wilson* (at a time when box-office takes were generally much better).

IT'S SHOW TIME

After his Paramount run was cut short, Frank appeared on the *Steve Allen Show* and the *Ed Sullivan Show*, to promote *Johnny Concho*. It was something of a coup, since both

Dorsey Brothers, starting Wednesday 15 August. The Dorseys were still a hard-working act appearing on TV in *Jackie Gleason's Show* every week and the original *American Bandstand*, as well as playing one-nighters. It had been Frank's idea to book Tommy for the New York shows, but it brought its own special set of problems: Nelson Riddle had to be dispatched to work with Tommy and the band on some of his more intricate arrangements. According to Peter Levinson's book on Nelson Riddle, things worked out very well. Over dinner one night at Tommy's house, Tommy praised Nelson's work with Frank and Nelson replied, "Much of the skill and ability to do these things came from my time with you." Tommy was also worried that Frank might embarrass him in front of his band, but Nelson assured him that Frank would never do such a thing, and he never did.

The crowd were lined up on Forty-Third Street west to Eighth Avenue and north to Forty-Fourth Street when the Paramount opened at 9:50 a.m. There were even a few people carrying placards. "We love Frankie" read one, another "Sinatra for President". Naturally, *Johnny Concho* was the movie on the double bill, and Frank, on stage, sang 26 songs, of which 'I've Got You Under My Skin' was the biggest hit that first night. According to Billy VerPlanck, who played trombone for the Dorseys, "It was four shows a day, 24 songs each time and it was filled every time! Red Skelton and lots of others came by; they were great shows. Tommy had said to us, 'Do whatever he says, but remember I taught him all he knows.'" "From where I was sitting Frank was a marvellous performer, but it was

OH, FRANKIE, I MEAN FRANK
At the Paramount, slightly older fans that matched the new, mature Frank.

programmes competed head-to-head and Frank had to go from Steve Allen at the Hudson Theatre to Ed Sullivan at the Old Broadway Theatre. In between he even appeared on ABC's *Famous Film Festival*. Three days later there was a cover story in *Downbeat* entitled: "The Frank Sinatra I Know" by Sammy Davis Jr. Sammy talked about a new film project he and Frank were working on for Kent Productions called *The Jazz Train*. "Sinatra got me a lot of loot for the picture plus 25 per cent of the picture." He also said they were talking about doing *The Harold Arlen Story*, with Sammy playing a composite role based on Cab Calloway and Bill "Bojangles" Robinson.

Back in Hollywood at his new Coldwater Canyon home, Frank was interviewed by Ed Morrow for another TV show – *Person to Person*. Frank opened in Las Vegas a few days later; Lauren Bacall was there with the Nivens, the Romanoffs, Cole Porter, and Swifty Lazar. It was Bacall's birthday, and Frank organized a cake for her that read: "Happy Birthday Den Mother." Frank's date around this time was Kim Novak, but while Lauren Bacall admits that Bogie was a little jealous of Frank, she insists in her autobiography that there was nothing between her and Frank at this stage, other than "I loved being with him." On 5 October, Frank was a guest on yet another show, this time *Dinah Shore's Show*. His appearance

coincided with starting work on his next movie, *The Joker Is Wild*, based on the life of comedian Joe E Lewis, for which Frank was to earn $125,000, plus a share of the box office. Frank and Lewis were old friends and shared MCA as an agent. Frank did a deal with Paramount through a new company he had set up named Bristol Productions. Frank's schedule at this point was a killer, since it included recording four songs for the movie on 3 October. One of

1956 ON THE JUKEBOX

FRANK ON THE US CHARTS

'FLOWERS MEAN FORGIVENESS' *(Al Frisch, Edward R. White & Mack Wolfson)* 25 February, No 21, 13 weeks	**'YOU'RE SENSATIONAL'** *(Cole Porter)* 14 July, No 52, 15 weeks
'YOU'LL GET YOURS' *(Jimmy Van Heusen & Dok Stanford)* 3 March, No 67, 5 weeks	**'JOHNNY CONCHO THEME (WAIT FOR ME)'** *(Nelson Riddle & Dok Stanford)* 28 July, No 75, 5 weeks
'(HOW LITTLE IT MATTERS) HOW LITTLE WE KNOW' *(Philip Springer & Carolyn Leigh)* 19 May, No 30, 14 weeks	**'WELL DID YOU EVAH'** *(Cole Porter)* 22 September, No 92, 2 weeks
'FIVE HUNDRED GUYS' *(Donald Canton & Ira Kosloff)* 2 June, No 73, 3 weeks	**'HEY! JEALOUS LOVER'** *(Bee Walker, Kay Twomey & Sammy Cahn)* 27 October, No 3, 19 weeks

In spite of the onset of Rock 'n' Roll, 1956 was Frank's best performance on the charts for over a decade, if weeks spent on the charts was the yardstick. Although to be absolutely fair the new consolidated Top 100 would have helped Frank notch up the 76 weeks. In terms of real "hit records" Frank had just one – 'Hey! Jealous Lover,' which climbed to No 3 at the end of the year.

Given the fact that Dean Martin had the first No 1 of the year with 'Memories Are Made Of This' it appeared, on the surface at least, to be business as normal. Songs were still to the fore, rather than the threat posed by rock 'n' roll. With names like Kay Starr, Tennessee Ernie Ford, Eddie Fisher, Al Hibbler and Gale Storm all in the top 20 this belief was further bolstered. Kay Starr's big hit was the patronizing 'Rock and Roll Waltz' which was about as far from Elvis as you could get. But by May it was all to change when Elvis Presley's 'Heartbreak

Hotel' made No 1, a feat emulated by 'I Want You, I Need You, I Love You,' Don't Be Cruel/Hound Dog', and Love Me Tender' before the year was over. 'The Voice' had been usurped by 'The Lip.'

Such was Frank's return to chart form since his arrival at Capitol that it was almost inevitable that he should be blessed with that new phenomenon – a greatest hits album. *This is Sinatra* came out in time for Christmas, 1956 and climbed to No 8 on the album chart, staying on the chart for six months.

DEAN MARTIN

66 The arrogance and kindness, force and gentleness, pride and helplessness of being a man is portrayed by this behatted, tie-loosened, after hours human with a precise artistry. 99

***METRONOME** ON FRANK*

these was another Jimmy Van Heusen and Sammy Cahn song called 'All the Way.' Before filming began in late October, Frank had a three-week run at the Sands. His film costumes had to be flown from Hollywood to Las Vegas for fittings to be done. At the same time, another movie featuring Frank came out. He had a cameo role as a bar-room pianist in *Around the World in Eighty Days*: appearing in the scene with Frank were Marlene Dietrich and George Raft. It was while filming *Around the World in Eighty Days* that Frank befriended actress Shirley MacLaine.

During the making of *The Joker Is Wild*, and again as the project wrapped, Frank spent a good deal of time in the studio. Between 1 November and 3 December, 1956, Frank did eight sessions, cutting 25 songs. Some were for *The Joker Is Wild*, but he also finished recording the songs for *Close to You*. Such was the demand for Frank's records that he also began work on his next album, recording three tracks for what would become *Swingin' Affair*. Towards the end of November, Frank made – for the time – one of the biggest ever television deals. The American Broadcasting Company signed a three-year contract worth $3 million (it would be worth 10 times that today). As well as beating

off competition from NBC and CBS, ABC bought into Frank's Kent Productions. Frank was back at the Sands on Wednesday 19 December for three weeks. It rounded off another stellar year – despite the onslaught from the young upstarts of rock 'n' roll. While at the Sands, Frank was questioned by a reporter about Ava's affair and rumoured marriage to Italian comedian Walter Chiari. "I loved Ava so much and I do not see why I should harass her happiness," he replied. The hectic year finally caught up with Frank during his engagement at the Sands. He was far from his best after the first couple of days and was reported as "singing listlessly". On Christmas Day at 7:00 am Frank chartered a plane and flew from Vegas to Los Angeles to spend the day with his children. He got back for the night's show with just 15 minutes to spare, and for the rest of his run he was superb.

The punishing schedule that Frank had kept up throughout 1956 was set to start all over again in 1957. Shooting for *Pal Joey* was timed to begin as soon as Frank got back from a tour of Australia, Manila, Hong Kong, and Tokyo in late February. Frank told Dick Williams of *The Mirror News*, "I've just got to be busy, that's all. I take a vacation for five days and I've had it. I get restless." That drive and energy were undoubtedly part of Frank's success.

A NIGHT AT THE SANDS

Actress Kim Novak, at a ringside table (foreground). Next to her is Cole Porter, then Lauren Bacall, and behind her, Hollywood hunk John Ireland. At the next ringside table is Jack Benny in the glasses.

CLOSE TO THE EDGE

Frank opened at the Copacabana in New York at the start of the second week of January, 1957, but he did only a couple of shows before the tragic news of 57-year-old Humphrey Bogart's death reached him. Frank cancelled five shows, but did not attend Bogie's funeral. He later returned to finish the engagement, performing two shows each night.

Fifty years later, Harry Agoratus recalls what it was like as a young New Yorker to witness Frank at the Copa: "It was a weeknight and snow was forecast. I had reservations for the early show, which started at ten. I picked up my date at about nine o'clock and we drove from Staten Island into

A DANCER BACKSTAGE AT THE COPACABANA

A NIGHT OUT
On 1 May, Frank took Lauren to watch a closed circuit broadcast of the World Middleweight title fight. After seeing Sugar Ray Robinson regain the title by knocking out Gene Fullmer, they left the theatre, only to run into a clutch of waiting photographers.

> *"He likes to change women the way he changes cuff links. Sometimes I think he picks them to match the colour in his tie."*
>
> A 'FRIEND' OF FRANK'S, QUOTED IN
> *LOOK* MAGAZINE, 11 JUNE 1957

Manhattan where we were lucky enough to find street parking near the Copa. We were given a table close to the stage; there were two more tiers of tables in a semicircle around the bandstand. Mr Sinatra was in excellent voice, very much at ease, establishing a marvellous rapport with the audience. After a few songs and a bit of chatter, he motioned with outstretched hand, thumb and forefinger a few inches apart, to a nearby table that had bottle and setup on it. Were they friends or strangers? I don't know. But someone poured a few fingers into a glass and handed it to him. I subsequently heard from others that he routinely did that and picked up the tab for the table. He was at the absolute top of his game. He had the audience, men as well as women entranced. There were hundreds in the room, but he sang to each of us individually. While he sang there was total silence, when he finished, the room erupted. Those same women, who as teenagers jammed the Paramount Theatre fifteen or so years earlier, now stood on the tables of the Copa to get a better view. When the show ended some tables did not want to leave. We left at close to midnight, and walked into a raging snowstorm."

Frank's failure to go to Bogie's funeral has caused great speculation. Some have said it was because he had begun an affair with Lauren Bacall during Bogie's illness. Others have pointed out that in those days Frank rarely went to funerals. Whatever the case, it would be about three and half months after Bogie's death that Frank and Lauren Bacall's very close friendship became public.

Just a week after Bogie's death, Frank's new album, *Close to You*, became the first of his albums with Capitol to fail to achieve what Frank and those associated with it would probably have hoped for (and expected). The combination of Frank and the Hollywood String Quartet, along with the very intimate feel of the LP, may even have frightened some fans; it was certainly very different to *Songs for Swingin' Lovers*.

PLANE STUPID

After the Copa engagement, Frank went home to Los Angeles to prepare for a tour that would take him back to Australia and from there to the Philippines, Hong Kong, and Japan for his first concerts. He found time to write to columnist Hedda Hopper after she had admonished him in her column, and signed off with "I shall miss you because you're a nice old broad."

Frank, Hank Sanicola, Jimmy Van Heusen, and five musicians left Los Angeles on Monday 4 February on the first leg of their flight to Sydney. Landing in Honolulu, they were met with the news that while there were berths on the Qantas aircraft for Frank and Hank, there was not one available for Jimmy. Frank saw red, turned around, and flew home to Hollywood. When he landed at Los Angeles, he told waiting newsmen "somebody goofed. We made reservations for eight people a year ago. The reservations

were confirmed but when we got on the plane there was no berth for Jimmy Van Heusen. They had no answer but to say someone had given it away." The Qantas manager in Honolulu disagreed, "We had confirmed two berths and hoped to get the third. But it never was confirmed at anytime." Frank was due to start filming *Pal Joey* on 4 March and was worried that he would not get back in time if they had to wait for the next plane, so delayed the start of the tour. Quite why he could not go without Jimmy Van Heusen is unclear, although petulance seems to have played the biggest part. The Australian promoter had to refund $50,000 in ticket sales while Frank paid his five musicians for their loss of earnings.

THE DISGRUNTLED
Frank, Hank and Johnny arrive back at Los Angeles after there was no berth on the aircraft for Van Heusen.

BROAD APPEAL

Back in Palm Springs, at 4:00 am on the morning of 16 February, Frank was at home in bed while outside, somewhat bizarrely, a 31-year-old brunette was crying out "Daddy, darling" and "Lover boy". The woman was a police officer, and the reason for this unusual activity was that she, along with a couple of other officers, were attempting to serve Frank with a subpoena. When her cries failed the police entered the house with keys that they had obtained from an informant. The officers shook Frank awake. According to one of them, Frank said "It's a good thing I was asleep. You could have got a bullet in you." According to the policewoman, the officer said, "If *I* had had a gun *you* might have got shot."

A little over a week later, the subpoena had done its job; the "wrong door" was reopened. The *LA Times* front-page banner headline said "Grand Jury May Call Marilyn In Raid Quiz", and underneath it said "DiMaggio and Sinatra also face summons". The following day, it got worse: "Sinatra Testimony On Raid Called A Lie", said the *LA Times*. Frank flatly denied taking part in the raid "that crashed the door". The article went on to relate Frank's testimony regarding that night, in which he denied ever getting out of his car. The view of the private detective who had been following Marilyn was very different: he said that Frank was the one who probably turned on the light in the apartment and then drove everyone away after they discovered their mistake.

CLOSE TO YOU

frank sinatra

close to you

NELSON RIDDLE ·
THE HOLLYWOOD STRING QUARTET

IT HAD BEEN FRANK'S IDEA TO TRY WORKING WITH A STRING QUARTET, INSPIRED BY HIS LOVE OF CLASSICAL MUSIC AND FRIENDSHIP WITH THE SLATKINS.

IT TOOK EIGHT MONTHS to make this album, longer than almost any other Frank ever recorded. It is not just the string quartet on the album – there are some other instruments used – but it is the Hollywood String Quartet, made up of violinist Felix Slatkin, his wife Eleanor on cello, Alan Dinkin viola, and Paul Shure on the other violin who dominate this album.

While it did take some while for the sound at the new Capitol Tower studio to rank alongside the old KHJ facility, that takes nothing away from what is probably Frank's most intimate album. While *In The Wee Small Hours* has a personal intimacy, it is Frank's voice and the delicacy of the quartet that imbues this album with qualities unique amongst the Sinatra canon.

"Sinatra still is the chairman of the board at the handling of material like 'Everything Happens to Me', 'With Every Breath I Take', 'It Could Happen to You', 'Blame It on My Youth', 'The End of a Love Affair', and the other seven quiet standards in the collection," said

Playboy magazine in May, 1957. Was this the first mention of Frank as fabled chairman? If it was, then it was a line that was taken up by just about everyone who had something to say about Frank – good or bad. Not that *Playboy* was entirely convinced by the coupling of Frank and the Hollywood String Quartet. "The writing for the quartet is unobtrusive and caressing enough; but with a singer who pulsates as surely as Sinatra, his background must have a rhythmic swing, too, even in ballads; especially in ballads. The Hollywood String Quartet doesn't. But, by all means, add the album to your Sinatra file. He himself is a model of mature craftsmanship in the not-at-all-easy art of popular singing."

The time taken to record the album, as well as Frank's hectic schedule, may have just taken the edge of this as a collection, although (and this is true of every one of Frank's Capitol albums) there are those who think that this is his finest hour.

> **❝It's real bedroom kind of stuff.❞**
>
> **FRANK**

I Couldn't Sleep a Wink Last Night

SONG LINES

Recorded: The Capitol Tower, Hollywood
Produced by: Voyle Gilmore. Chart: US No 5 (14 weeks),
First charted 2 March, 1957.

SIDE 1

1. 'CLOSE TO YOU'
(Al Hoffman, Jerry Livingston & Carl Lampl) Recorded 1 November, 1956. Frank first recorded this lovely song back in 1943 in an a capella arrangement by Alex Wilder, along with the Bobby Tucker Singers.

2. 'PS I LOVE YOU'
(Gordon Jenkins & Johnny Mercer) Recorded 8 March, 1956.

3. 'LOVE LOCKED OUT'
(Ray Noble & Max Kester) Recorded 8 March, 1956.

4. 'EVERYTHING HAPPENS TO ME'
(Matt Dennis & Tom Adair) Recorded 5 April, 1956. Frank must have identified with this song. He cut it four times, this being the second attempt. Listen to the words – he definitely related to this song at various times in his life.

5. 'IT'S EASY TO REMEMBER'
(Richard Rodgers & Lorenz Hart) Recorded 1 November, 1956. The song originally appeared in the 1935 film *Mississippi*

6. 'DON'T LIKE GOODBYES'
(Harold Arlen & Truman Capote) Recorded 8 March, 1956.

SIDE 2

1. 'WITH EVERY BREATH I TAKE'
(Ralph Rainger & Leo Robin) Recorded 5 April, 1956. Yet another of the many songs first performed by Bing Crosby that Frank remade. This one was featured in Bing's 1934 film, *Here Is My Heart*.

2. 'BLAME IT ON MY YOUTH'
(Oscar Levant & Edward Heyman) Recorded 4 April, 1956.

3. 'IT COULD HAPPEN TO YOU'
(Jimmy Van Heusen & Johnny Burke) Recorded 5 April, 1956.

4. 'I'VE HAD MY MOMENTS'
(Walter Donaldson & Gus Kahn) Recorded 4 April, 1956.

5. 'I COULDN'T SLEEP A WINK LAST NIGHT'
(Jimmy McHugh & Harold Adamson) Recorded 1 November, 1956. Rather than "Frank sings Bing", this was "Frank sings Frank". It had been a big hit for Frank in 1944. It had featured in Frank's film, *Higher and Higher*. Despite Frank's original a cappella version as well as his later V-Disc being arranged by the brilliant Alec Wilder Nelson's version puts them both in the shade.

6. 'THE END OF A LOVE AFFAIR'
(Edward C Redding) Recorded 5 April, 1956.
The solo trumpet on this exquisite reading by Frank is by Harry Sweets Edison.

Over the next week or so the papers were full of speculation, with claims and counter-claims around whether or not Frank would face charges of perjury. In the event it came to nothing, but it remained a blot on Frank's character, one that he probably ended up laughing about, but it could have gone the other way all too easily.

As things were calming down in the press, Frank was back in the studio cutting a couple of songs, one of which was called 'Crazy Love', which was recorded on 14 March. We can assume that Sammy Cahn did not especially tailor the lyric to this song ("It isn't normal or real to feel heaven's right inside your door"), although it was something he often did for Frank to celebrate special events.

CHANGING TIMES

A year after conducting *Tone Poems of Color*, Frank got the conducting bug once again. This time he worked with Peggy Lee, whom he had first met back in 1942 at the Paramount when she was Benny Goodman's girl singer. Frank did three sessions conducting the orchestra for Peggy's album, *The Man I Love*, arranged by Nelson Riddle.

Two days after finishing work on Peggy's album, Frank began work on his own next album, which would be his first for Capitol without Nelson Riddle. Gordon Jenkins was brought in to create a shift to Sinatra's sound. Almost as soon as the work was finished on what was to be called *Where Are You?*, Frank's latest LP was released. *A Swingin' Affair* came out just over two months after *Close to You* and performed much better on the album chart, reaching No 2.

(*Close to You* reached only No 5 and charted for just a third of the time.) In the early evening of 1 May, Frank went to see the boxing match at a Hollywood theatre on close-circuit TV with Lauren Bacall, before heading back to the Capitol Tower to finish work on the last songs for *Where Are You?*.

On 7 May, *Look* magazine published the first part of a three-part story on Frank. It was probably one of the most probing and thoughtful pieces that had been written so far. The writer, Bill Davidson, had been given access to Frank, but when the article was published, Frank was furious. The article revealed the truth regarding much of what made Frank tick, but unfortunately it failed to take a realistic view of Frank's achievements, and so presented a somewhat unbalanced view of the man. Frank was so angry that he sued the magazine's publishers, although the suit was dropped a few months later.

Soon after, Frank began a tour taking in Vancouver, Canada, along with Portland, Seattle, and San Francisco. *A Swingin' Affair* was in the album charts. Significantly, Frank wasn't in the Top 100, which was topped by Elvis Presley with 'All Shook Up'. On tour Frank was accompanied by a 26-piece orchestra made up of the cream of Los Angeles musicians, the same people that played on his albums. Listen today to the recording of Frank's 9 June show in Seattle and you hear a man in the form of his life. Frank is relaxed and the songs sound so fresh and exciting, it's like a run through of his Capitol greatest hits.

COVER STORY
You'd almost think it was Frank on the cover of Peggy Lee's album — which was no doubt the intention.

OFF THE CUFF
Frank being sworn in before the hearing over the "Wrong Door" incident. It was reported a year earlier that Frank had 1,000 pairs of cuff links.

GORDON JENKINS

"He had a way with strings that made it just gorgeous.
He had great heart in his arranging."

RAY ANTHONY

BORN IN WEBSTER GROVE, MISSOURI, ON 12 MAY, 1910, JENKINS WAS THE MASTER OF
LUSH. HIS ORCHESTRATIONS AND ARRANGEMENTS SOUND RATHER ANACHRONISTIC
TODAY, BUT THEY WERE AN ESSENTIAL PART OF 1950s' LISTENING.

By the 1930s, Gordon was working for Benny Goodman, Woody Herman, and Vincent Lopez. His composition 'Goodbye' became Benny Goodman's closing theme, as well as being recorded by Frank in 1958, ironically with Nelson Riddle arranging and conducting. This was not the first of Jenkins' compositions that Frank had tackled – that honour belongs to 'Homesick – That's All', cut in March, 1945.

Gordon moved to Hollywood and worked for Paramount Pictures from 1938 as well as working with Dick Haymes on his radio series. He signed to Capitol Records in 1942 and made the Top 20 with the label's sixth release, 'He Wears a Pair of Silver Wings'.

ROMANTIC SYNTHESIS
Frank and Gordon Jenkins in the studio.

In 1948 Gordon signed to Decca and, as well as backing Dick Haymes on some of his hits, began recording under his own name. His first record, 'Maybe You'll Be There', went to No 3 in the summer of 1948 and was followed by a number of other big hits over the next four years, including several with the Weavers folk group, which he persuaded Decca to sign.

In 1957, Gordon worked with Nat King Cole at Capitol on his album *Love Is the Thing*. It included one of Cole's biggest hits, the lovely 'When I Fall in Love'. On 10 April, 1957, Gordon began work with Frank on songs for what would become *Where Are You?*. Two years later, he worked with Frank again on *No One Cares*, and later still on *September of My Years* and *Trilogy*.

Gordon Jenkins worked very little in the 1970s, although he did cut an album of standards with Harry Nilsson. Entitled *A Little Touch of Schmilsson in the Night*, it had 12 songs, half of which had been recorded by Frank. He would probably have done little more of note without Frank's *Trilogy* sessions in 1979 and *She Shot Me Down* in 1981. Gordon died in Los Angeles on 1 May, 1984. Frank described him as "One of the modern geniuses of good pop music".

previous appearance in Seattle in 1935 during the Major Bowes' tour. As Ann Faber of *The Post-Intelligencer* wrote at the time: "Frank Sinatra demonstrated that pure professionalism can belt a nightclub act into the farthest corner of the Civic Auditorium."

"I'm about up to 'here' in Crown Royal", he boasted halfway through the show. There were songs from *Swingin' Lovers*, *Swing Easy*, and three from *In the Wee Small Hours*, including a brilliant version of 'When Your Lover Has Gone' in which, as Elvis Costello would later comment about his performance, "he learned to turn his then rare vocal frailty into an asset". Frank also sang four from his latest album, including the show-closer 'Oh Look at Me Now,' which he had first recorded back in the Dorsey days. As Frank left the stage, the orchestra played 'From Here to Eternity'. One of the show's promoters, Zollie Volchok, was asked by Sinatra's management to make three reservations for the after-show meal — one at a Chinese restaurant, another at an Italian restaurant, and one at a steakhouse. "They never knew what mood Sinatra was going to be in after a show," Volchok explained.

As Frank's tour finished, *The Pride and the Passion* opened in New York. The *New York Times* said of Frank that he was "possessed of an inner fire that glows but fitfully on rare occasions". Of the film they added, "A mighty canvas but it has virtually no human depth."

NEXT?
Ava's divorce from Frank was finalized in June 1957. She's pictured here with "textile millionaire" Robert Evans at New York's Harwyn club.

❝He learned to turn his then rare vocal frailty into an asset in 'When Your Lover Has Gone'**❞**

ELVIS COSTELLO COMMENTING ON SEATTLE 1957

Frank played two shows at Seattle's old Civic Auditorium, having already played an afternoon show in Portland. Each show was an hour long and, to be absolutely honest, by the second half of the last show Frank's vocals were not quite perfect. He missed some notes, joked of having "a shot glass stuck in my throat", and even fluffed his lines in 'The Tender Trap'. But none of this detracts from the magnificence of his performance. The most expensive tickets were $5.50, a good deal more than Frank's

THE GREATEST
According to Director Stanley Kramer, "If Sinatra really wanted to work, prepare for a role, research it, he'd be the best in the world." Unfortunately for this movie he didn't.

By mid-July, Frank's thoughts were a long way from Spain, since he was cutting an album of Christmas songs. And by the end of the month, he was recording songs for *Pal Joey*. Two weeks later, his next album, the Jenkins arranged *Where Are You?*, was released. It seems extraordinary looking back from today, when artists release an album every few years, that Frank released three in 1957, all of which made the Top 5. In every week of the year he had an album in the charts, and for most of the year there were two. In fact, when the soundtrack album to *Pal Joey* was released in November, it made No 2, giving Frank three simultaneous hit chart albums.

Frank's relationship with Lauren Bacall become ever more public, and the two stars were, as Bacall wrote in her autobiography, "a steady pair". They were together in Las Vegas for the opening of *The Joker Is Wild* at the end of August, and Lauren acted as hostess for Frank at dinner parties. While people talked, of course, at least Frank was divorced this time. According to Lauren Bacall, her friends did not think it would last, but she insists that they "were crazy about each other".

IT'S NEVER EASY
With Frank's career in high gear, an old wound was reopened with Mitch Miller in late August. During the previous year, Frank had testified before a House Judiciary subcommittee, claiming that Miller had tried to foist inferior BMI songs on him while he was at Columbia. (BMI was one of the two royalty-collecting organizations, the other being ASCAP. Both had been embroiled in a bitter dispute for years, with ASCAP accusing broadcasters and record companies of discriminating against them in favour of BMI.) Now Frank, in a telegram to Senator George A Smathers, accused Miller of accepting bribes. Frank even claimed that Miller had confessed in sworn testimony that he had received between $5,000 and $6,000. Miller, however, claimed that this money was for legitimate services such as "editing songs" and "fixing up lyrics". Given Frank's return to the top, it does seem both foolish and unnecessary to have carried on the war with Miller, but Frank never could forgive him for what he felt Miller had done to his career. Some people need to be able to blame someone else for what they

A SWINGIN' AFFAIR

THIS ALBUM OOZES finger snapping sophistication and epitomises Frank at the peak of his Capitol powers. It is ranked only second to *Swingin' Lovers* by many Sinatra aficionados, while others have called it the greatest of Frank's swing albums. However you rate it, there is no denying that it set the tone for Frank's swing style forever more. As *Playboy* put it in July 1957. "Like his first two albums this one swings... sung in such a way that all my best adjectives apply afresh."

There is fabulous energy throughout the album – in Frank's singing, Nelson's inspired arrangements, and the playing of musicians at the peak of their powers. From the opening bars of 'Night and Day' you know that you are in for a treat. If you don't "get" 'Night and Day', you won't "get" Frank, it's that simple.

If you listen hard to the four songs recorded on Wednesday 28 November, you can hear a slight nasal quality in Frank's voice, especially in 'From This Moment On'. He had a cold that day, as reported in the *LA Examiner* on 29 November in a story about Frank signing his $3 million ABC TV contract. But even with a cold, the Boice was still one hell of a Voice.

> 66I was layin' in bed one night and I thought of this title, 'A Swingin' Affair'; I think it'll go. 99
>
> **FRANK IN OCTOBER 1956**

SONG LINES
Recorded : The Capitol Tower, Hollywood.
Produced by Voyle Gilmore.
Chart: US No 2 (36 weeks). First charted 27 May, 1957.

SIDE 1
1. 'NIGHT AND DAY'
(Cole Porter) Recorded 26 November, 1956. "That was a driving arrangement, that was fairly impressive in its time. He would have been thinking about songs for days. I use to sit there and take notes. We had a sideways joke, which I think had some validity though. He said I was the best secretary he ever had. I would take notes and three months later we might do the album. You could never depend on him forgetting what he had said three months previously. I took the notes of what we discussed and that's what he got." Nelson Riddle on 'Night and Day'.

2. 'I GOT PLENTY O' NUTTIN'
(DuBose Heyward, George & Ira Gershwin) Recorded 15 November, 1956.

3. 'I WISH I WERE IN LOVE AGAIN'
(Richard Rodgers & Lorenz Hart) Recorded 20 November, 1956.

4. 'I GUESS I'LL HAVE TO CHANGE MY PLAN'
(Arthur Schwartz & Howard Dietz) Recorded 20 November, 1956.

5. 'NICE WORK IF YOU CAN GET IT'
(George & Ira Gershwin) Recorded 20 November, 1956.

6. 'STARS FELL ON ALABAMA'
(Frank Perkins & Mitchell Parish) Recorded 15 November, 1956.

7. 'NO ONE EVER TELLS YOU'
(Carroll Coates & Hub Atwood) Recorded 9 April, 1956.

8. 'I WON'T DANCE'
(Jerome Kern, Jimmy McHugh, Otto Harbuch, Oscar Hammerstein II & Dorothy Fields) Recorded 15 November, 1956. Featured in the 1935 Fred and Ginger film, *Roberta*. Frank's vocal elegance matches the dancing elegance of Astaire and Rogers.

SIDE 2
1. 'THE LONESOME ROAD'
(Gene Austin & Nathaniel Shilkret) Recorded 26 November, 1956.

2. 'AT LONG LAST LOVE'
(Cole Porter) Recorded 20 November, 1956.

3. 'YOU'D BE SO NICE TO COME HOME TO'
(Cole Porter) Recorded 28 November, 1956.

4. 'I GOT IT BAD (AND THAT AIN'T GOOD)'
(Duke Ellington & Paul Francis Webster) Recorded 28 November, 1956. Somehow this song seems to capture the essence of Frank during these marvellous Capitol years. It is sophistication personified.

5. 'FROM THIS MOMENT ON'
(Cole Porter) Recorded 28 November, 1956.

6. 'IF I HAD YOU'
(Ted Shapiro, Jimmy Campbell & Reg Connelly) Recorded 26 November, 1956. This song dates from the 1920s and Frank did it three times. This version is sandwiched between his two ballad renditions, the first with Axel in 1947 and the other with Robert Farnon in 1962.

7. 'OH LOOK AT ME NOW'
(Joe Bushkin & John DeVries) Recorded 28 November, 1956. Fifteen years after Frank first did this wonderful song by his old band mate Joe Bushkin with Tommy Dorsey, he and Nelson produced a sublime reading.

WHERE ARE YOU?

THIS IS AN ALBUM that may take a little more time to get into but when you do it's a deeply rewarding experience. As Frank said "I get an audience involved, personally involved in a song… I can't help myself." It is the first of three that Frank made with Gordon Jenkins for Capitol. Jenkin's string-laden arrangements envelop you and, with Frank's voice, provide an intensely personal listening experience. As *High Fidelity* magazine said in June 1957 "This is the pro singing again. Sinatra applies the polish of his voice to some excellent ballads. This collection doesn't have the sustained buoyancy of Frank's swinging sets, but it's an education in setting a vocal mood and in ballad singing of the highest caliber there is today."

This was the first of Frank's albums to be recorded in stereo, although it was first released in mono. When it came out as a stereo record it was deemed to be "Full Dimensional Stereo", Capitol's marketing name, in the same way as RCA had "Living Stereo." 'I Cover The Waterfront' was omitted from the original release as the new technology would not allow its inclusion for reasons of space. Capitol coined the term "Duophonic" for mono records that were remixed to sound like stereo; often achieved by putting the voice on one channel and the orchestra on the other. A number of Frank's earlier albums suffered this abomination. Prior to stereo recordings Capitol called their records "High Fidelity", which they were when compared with the old shellac 78 records.

SONG LINES

Recorded: The Capitol Tower, Hollywood, Produced by Voyle Gilmore.
Chart: US No 3 (21 weeks). First charted 23 September, 1957.

SIDE 1

1. 'WHERE ARE YOU?'
(Jimmy McHugh & Harold Adamson)
Recorded 1 May, 1957.

2. 'THE NIGHT WE CALLED IT A DAY'
(Matt Dennis & Tom Adair) Recorded 10 April, 1957.

3. 'I COVER THE WATERFRONT'
(Johnny Green & Edward Heyman) Recorded 29 April, 1957.

4. 'MAYBE YOU'LL BE THERE'
(Rube Bloom & Sammy Gallop) 1 May, 1957.

5. 'LAURA'
(Dave Raksin & Johnny Mercer) Recorded 29 April, 1957. Just listening to the lovely Gordon Jenkins introduction fills you with a sense of anticipation. If you are called Laura then this song's for you. If you're not, enjoy it anyway!

6. 'LONELY TOWN'
(Leonard Bernstein, Betty Comden & Adolph Green). Recorded 29 April, 1957.

SIDE 2

1. 'AUTUMN LEAVES'
(Joseph Korma, Johnny Mercer & Jacques Prevert) Recorded 10 April, 1957.

2. 'I'M A FOOL TO WANT YOU'
(Jack Wolf, Joel Herron & Frank Sinatra) Recorded 1 May, 1957.

3. 'I THINK OF YOU'
(Don Marcotte & Jack Elliott) Recorded 1 May, 1957.

4. 'WHERE IS THE ONE?'
(Alec Wilder & Edwin Finckel) Recorded 10 April, 1957.

5. 'THERE'S NO YOU'
(Hal Hopper & Tom Adair) Recorded 10 April, 1957.

6. 'BABY WON'T YOU PLEASE COME HOME?'
(Clarence Williams & Charles Warfield). Recorded 29 April, 1957. Written in 1922, making it one of the earliest songs Frank recorded. The first version was by Eva Taylor, then a few months later, in April 1923, by the legendary Bessie Smith. Ray Charles did a wonderful version in late 1949, but neither his nor Bessie's could have prepared us for Frank's rendition. Gordon Jenkins's arrangement transforms the song from its blues roots to a lush romantic ballad.

perceive as their misfortunes. Miller was not the cause of Frank's demise; it was just the way in which much of the recording business operated back then. Given Frank's newfound success, he should have let it go.

Having used Gordon Jenkins on *Where Are You?*, it apparently hurt Nelson Riddle deeply when Frank decided to go with Billy May for his next album. Nelson felt that Frank had betrayed him, not that this had anything to do with his opinion of Billy, whom he liked and admired. Frank's first session with Billy was on 1 October for the album that was to be called *Come Fly with Me*. Travel was the theme, and the first song they cut together was 'On the Road to Mandalay', with words by Rudyard Kipling. The album was finished a week later.

Five days afterwards, on 13 October, with *Where Are You?* sitting at No 3 on the album chart, Frank appeared on Bing's *The Edsel Show*. This television special was a kick off for Ford's new line of cars, which had been launched on 4 September. Appearing on the show with Bing were Frank, Bob Hope, Rosemary Clooney, Louis Armstrong, and The Four Preps, and *Variety* called it "a smooth, fast ride all the way…. Basically it was Crosby and Sinatra in a freewheeling sing-along. Working solo, duo and trio (with Rosemary Clooney) they covered several dozen songs." Louis Armstrong sang 'Birth of the Blues' with Frank. The show was a success, and this seemed like a good omen for Frank's own television series, which was to start just five days later. Despite the show, however, and the publicity campaign, the car soon turned into an expensive flop, and, just over two years later, Ford discontinued the Edsel.

A ROAD LESS TRAVELLED

Frank's contract for his ABC television series had been signed back in November 1956, and, at the time, much emphasis had been made of it being a series with a difference. There were to be 21, musically based, hour-long shows and ten 30-minute drama shows. Frank was the Executive Producer and had some very specific ideas on the format: "If I fall on my face, I want to be the cause… All of the years when I was taking advice from others they told me wrong 50 percent of the time" is what he told *New York World Telegram*.

The first thing he needed was an experienced television director. His choice was Kirk Browning, a contract director at NBC since 1949, who recalled how Frank had agreed to everything he suggested… and then changed his mind completely: "I did mostly arts programs like The NBC Opera series and a producers showcase which was a dramatic series – fairly elitist programming for those days. Actually, that's what networks did in those days! I got a call out of the blue in my office at NBC, and the caller said, 'This is Frank Sinatra.' After a beat or so I said 'Hello.' He was calling about the first show that he was exec producing, where he totally controlled the show – he was putting it together his way. He said, 'I'm doing a special and I want you to direct it.' I said, 'Mr. Sinatra, I, I, haven't done much in the pop world, I do a lot of classical stuff.' He said, 'I look at all the shows you do, and if you can do them, you can do me.' I said 'What network is it for?' 'I'm doing it on ABC.' 'Well, I'm under exclusive contract with NBC.' And he said 'Is that your only problem?' I said 'At the moment.' He said, 'Well, you keep thinking about it and I'll get back to you.' A couple days later I got another call from Frank and he said, 'OK, now I've done my end of the business.

I got you released from your contract. I called Sarnoff.' Sarnoff was the head of RCA. 'I called Sarnoff and he said I could have you for six weeks. So have you got any other objections?' I could think of nothing, so I said 'If you really think I'm the right director, at least I could come out and talk to you about it.' He said, 'Yeah, you do that. You come out and we'll talk and it'll all be OK.' So he arranged everything, he flew me out, and I remember our first meeting at his house in Coldwater Canyon. I rented a car and drove up to this gated estate, the gate opened up and a Filipino houseman greeted me at the door. He said 'Mr Sinatra wants you to come in and wait for him in the living room.' As I walked in I heard classical music (Frank's favourite composers were Ralph Vaughan Williams and Hector Berlioz). In the living room were shelves filled with classical albums. Frank waited long enough for all this to sink in before he came into the room, 'before we start talking, let me show you around a little bit.' So he took me outside 'Do you see all this landscaping? I did all the design. I did it all myself. I supervised it all myself.' I think he was trying desperately to find areas of common interest. He couldn't have been dearer or sweeter but I'm sure it was not the sort of conversation he has with people who normally come to see him. As we went back in Nelson Riddle arrived and we started talking about the show, and about the music Frank would sing. I had one thing I wanted to bring up, but I had to wait for the right moment. 'Frank, I have one idea. If I do the show, there's one song I want to open with, it's 'Lonesome Road'.' It starts out very quietly, with a slow, slow build up to a big ending. I had found out that when he goes in to recording session he sets the

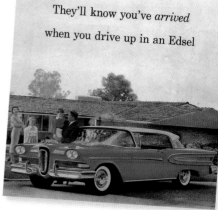

They'll know you've *arrived* when you drive up in an Edsel

FLOP CAR
Just about the biggest flop in the US automotive history, comedians began referring to it as "an olds sucking a lemon", as a result of the Edsel's distinctive grill.

CONCENTRATION
Frank and Billy May listen intently to the playback at a session at the Capitol Tower during the 'Come Fly with Me' sessions.

1952–1957

tempo for the number by clicking his fingers. 'I want to start with a close up of your fingers – nothing but a close up of your thumb and fingers clicking the tempo. And then I want the camera to go up to your face and when it pulls back, we discover that you're on the top of an enormous stairway. We come back further and reveal the universe. I thought we'd go from small to big.' Well, he adored that idea. We talked a bit and at some point I must have committed to it because I went home to New York and he arranged to bring my wife and me back to Los Angeles.

THE JOKER IS WILD

ALL THE WAY

From the Paramount Picture
FRANK SINATRA

MITZI   JEANNE
GAYNOR   CRAIN
EDDIE ALBERT

The Joker Is Wild

2/-

RELEASED AT THE END of August this was very much a Sinatra project. Frank had bought Art Cohen's story of a real life prohibition era nightclub comedian Joe E Lewis when it was still in galley proof form. He took the project to Paramount and worked with producer/director Charles Vidor. While there was no way Frank could be made to look like the diminutive funny man, he worked hard at aping his mannerisms. *Variety* said, "He's believable and forceful – alternatively sympathetic and pathetic, funny and sad." Lewis had started out as a crooner but had his throat cut by the mob to stop him singing, which is why he became a comic.

Jeanne Crain plays a girl who falls for Lewis in the film and it was a role she carried over into real life with Frank. Eddie Albert plays Lewis's long time friend and accompanist; Mitzi Gaynor also appears. The film introduced one song that would become a standard in the hands of Frank; Sammy Cahn and James Van Heusen's 'All The Way'. Although *Variety* could only bring themselves to say, "pleasantly OK via the Sinatra voice." Frank recorded the song again with Nelson Riddle two weeks before the film's release. It came out as a single in the autumn and climbed to No 2. It also won an Oscar the following March for Best Song which only goes to prove that *Variety*'s critic, like all critics, sometimes get it quite wrong.

Frank sang six more songs in the film and 'Chicago (That Toodlin' Town)', which is heard in the movie but not sung by Frank, was recorded as a Capitol single. Once again Nelson Riddle's work on the film is outstanding. The parody numbers that Frank sings, designed to evoke the 1920s capture the feel perfectly. With musical nods to Bob Crosby and Jimmie Lunceford's big bands they are extremely evocative.

PRESS APPROVAL
"Plays out in well organized and smooth fashion". Variety.

We put all the numbers together with Bob Hope; then Kim Novak and Peggy Lee came in, and we started rehearsing and everything was totally harmonious. We got within about a week of the show and we'd go in to rehearse and change little things, but basically Frank would approve everything we were doing. He behaved wonderfully! We were beginning to get into our run-throughs and everything, and one day he came in and said, 'I don't like some things about this show.' I said 'Well, Frank, we can change some things.' And that's when he decided to change *everything*. He kept the opening, but other than that he changed the numbers, the set, the order and the attitude. I remember the last few days of rehearsals when everything was different every day. Bob Hope came over to me and said 'Kirk, what's going on here? What's Frank doing? Things were going perfectly well, and suddenly he's changing everything!' I said 'Bob, if you don't know at this point in your career what is happening, don't look at me! I'm totally in the dark. I don't know what Frank's doing!' When you can throw Bob

Hope, you know that things are getting painful. Peggy Lee and Kim Novak didn't care much, because they had set numbers, but Bob Hope had a lot going on and wanted to be able to ground himself.

"It stayed pretty shaky right up to when we went into the studio for our camera rehearsals. We survived that process, and worked up to the dress rehearsal, which went OK. We were on the air at 9 and we were all ready by 8:30. Everything was in place. I said to the stage manager on the floor, 'Just keep track of Frank, so we can get him in place on the top of the big stair in front of the big crane camera which we had ready to take the opening shot.' The stage manager said 'Sure, fine, fine, fine.' So at 5 (minutes) of 9, when I'm about to get Frank on position, the stage manager says, 'Kirk, I can't find Frank.' 'What do you mean, you can't find him?' 'Well, he said he was just going to go out for a second and I can't see him anywhere.' 'Well, get everyone to find him and put him in place! I've got to have him there for the camera to focus and get on the air!' There was a total frenzy in the studio, everybody getting more and more hysterical. There was no Sinatra anyplace. One minute to airtime, no Sinatra. 45 seconds, thirty seconds, no Sinatra. At 20 seconds before nine, a side door

opens, Frank strolls in and slowly, slowly, slowly walks up those stairs. At 5, 4, 3, 2, 1 he hits the top stair, puts his hand in front of the camera and clicks his fingers.

He wanted to have the tension, and he wanted to feel that he was the one person totally in control. Obviously we went on the air, and survived. He was very sweet at the end of the show, and gave us all a big party, and by then the memory of the opening had already begun to fade. I remember he turned to me and said 'Kirk, we've had a good time working on this show. You know, I have a couple scripts for films that I'm doing, and if you'd like, you could do either one of them.' Well I took a long breath and said 'Frank that's so sweet of you, I think I'm just going to go back to TV.' I turned down his offer to do films!"

CRITICAL CRITICS

The opening show, aired on 18 October, was live from Hollywood, though the subsequent shows were mostly pre-recorded. Against all the odds, the predictions, and Frank's unqualified success in every aspect of his career, however, the opening show was a disappointment, with *Variety* comparing it unfavourably to *The Edsel Show*: "There's no disputing that Sinatra's own show lacked much of the spark and free wheeling quality of the automaker's presentation", although it did admit that "despite obvious faults, rewards could be manifold". Other reviews were generally encouraging, though opinion was very much divided.

As Frank's series was getting underway, he gave a rather bitter interview to *Western World*, saying "Rock 'n' roll smells phoney and false." He compounded it by adding, "It is sung, played and written for the most part by cretinous goons and by means of its almost imbecilic reiteration and sly, lewd, in plain fact, dirty lyrics it manages to be the martial music of every side burned delinquent on the face of the earth. It is the most brutal, ugly, desperate, vicious form of expression it has been my misfortune to hear." From that, we can take it that Frank was none to keen on the music of the young. In Peter Guralnick's brilliant book about Elvis Presley, *Last Train to Memphis*, he quotes Elvis's reaction, as told to reporters on 28 October, which is much more gracious than Frank's: "I admire that man, he has a right to say what he wants to say. He is a great success and a fine actor, but I think he shouldn't have said it. This is a trend, just the same as he faced when he started years ago." It's fortunate that Frank's career depended on neither his public utterances nor his TV shows.

Following the first musical offering was the half-hour drama show a week later, for which Frank's portrayal of a cabbie who adopts some war orphans got mixed reviews. Generally, they said that Frank did an acceptable job, but the material was poor. From there things went downhill fairly rapidly. Two weeks later, daughter Nancy appeared on the show with two school friends, Belinda Burrell and

> **66** Mr Sinatra's problems were those that seemed to be afflicting most vocalists who are going out on their own this fall. When he was singing the program held our attention and he did some excellent numbers…. But an hour's show cannot be sustained by one man alone and Mr. Sinatra's writers let him down badly. His patter with Bob Hope was second rate, and their sketch with Kim Novak never came off. **99**
>
> **JACK GOULD – *NEW YORK TIMES***

VERY PROPER
Frank recording one of his musical shows with some props that look very 1950s.

PAL JOEY

FRANK GOT $125,000 from Columbia Pictures for *Pal Joey*, plus a 25 per cent of the residuals; which made him a nice little bonus. It was a far cry from his measly pay packet on *From Here to Eternity* but then again Columbia adjudged Frank to be the hottest Hollywood property along with "Mumbles" Brando.

Columbia originally secured the film rights in the 1940s and Harry Cohn had thought about casting Gene Kelly along with Marlene Dietrich and Rita Hayworth. By the time the film got made, Hayworth was too old to play Linda, which is how Kim Novak got into the frame. There's no question that Novak was not really up to the part, and Hayworth was not at all happy at having to play the older woman.

The sequence featuring 'The Lady is a Tramp' was the outstanding moment in the whole show. At the press showing in

PERIOD PIECE
The film was based on a novella by best-selling novelist John O'Hara.

London, the audience broke out into spontaneous applause, which for the press was pretty much unheard of.

The press were largely unanimous in the praise for both Frank and the film. "It can't miss being a blockbuster", said *Variety* on 11 September, 1957. "This is largely Mr Sinatra's show, he projects a distinctly bouncy likeable personality into an unusual role", said the *New York Times* critic on 28 October, 1957. By the time the film reached Britain in January 1958 the *NME* took the view that "Sinatra dominates it from beginning to end".

Jane Ross. Calling themselves the Tri-Tones, they sang 'Someone Exactly Like You' and 'Side by Side', with Frank helping out on both numbers.

A week later a *Variety* headline asked the question, "Sinatra: Singer or Salesman?" in an attack on what they saw as Frank's "commercial prostitution". "Sinatra isn't the first and won't be the last of the entertainers to become a dollar happy commercial pitchman, though rarely has an actor or singer of his stature (and he's in the upstairs level in both depts) gone so heavy in personalizing the pitch. Does he need the money? Does Rockefeller?" It is possible that this attack was a contributory factor to the series being cancelled after just one series. *Variety* felt that Frank would have been very unlikely to have a show without such an overt sponsorship deal.

PRETENTIOUS, MOI?

On Friday 29 November, the show was broadcast live from the El Capitan Theatre in Hollywood. According to Variety, the show was "still wanting in smoothness and

LIKE FATHER...
Nancy pictured with her father at rehearsals for Frank's TV show in November 1957.

substance", and this was despite a guest appearance by Dean Martin singing 'They'll Never Believe Me' and sharing a medley of their hits with Frank, before Frank closed the show with 'The House I Live in'. By the 20 December show, on which Bing returned the compliment, the inevitable comparisons with *The Edsel Show* were once again made, and Frank's efforts were found to be sadly lacking. "Studied, pretentious and awkward" is how one review saw it.

It was the show's lack of a central theme, as well as sloppy production, that seemed to bother most critics. *Variety* called the show "common place". One particular aspect drew the sharpest rebukes: "Sinatra spouting a torrent of flip expressions that presumably are supposed to be sophisticated and hep but come across in a completely affected manner." Overall, it seemed as though Frank was still not comfortable in front of the television cameras. Lack of rehearsals may have played a part, but there is no law that says that being a great singer and performer makes you a television star. Fortunately, Frank probably felt the same and decided that television was not for him, or at least not a series of his own. He never again did a television series and contented himself with guest appearances and specials.

The last show of the series would be on 23 May, 1958, with Natalie Wood as his guest. Frank would have done well to remember what he told *TV Guide* back in 1955: "Television is too tough". But not everyone saw it that way, according to songwriter Jimmy Webb: "Of course like every other American Boomer I remember black and white images of Sinatra with Garland and Fitzgerald et al flickering on the screens of our first television sets. Not enough credit has been given to the 'Sinatra Smile'. Out in the Midwest it was the first time many of us had ever seen anybody having a real good time."

COMPETITIVE EDGE

While Frank's show was in full swing, so were a rash of others. Dean Martin, Patti Page, Nat King Cole, Eddie Fisher, Rosemary Clooney, Pat Boone, Guy Mitchell, Perry Como, and Dinah Shore all had their own shows. While Frank may have been under-rehearsed, he, and all the other old-style singers, was facing stiff competition from the young pretenders. Alan Freed's *Big Beat Show* went on the air in 1957, while Dick Clark's *American Bandstand* was on ABC. Not long after making his TV debut on the Dorsey Brothers TV show, Elvis Presley made his first appearance on *The Ed Sullivan Show*, which caused a bit of a stir. Frank's relative failure was, it seems, due in the main to his use of too-clever remarks, which meant that he did not embrace his audience in the way that the two most successful exponents from the old school of entertainers, Perry Como and Dinah Shore, did.

In the middle of the series, Frank celebrated his 42nd birthday at Patsy D'Amore's Villa Capri restaurant, and on the same day, *The Joker Is Wild* was released. Frank may have already made up his mind that from now on it was movies, recording, and concerts that were for him… though not necessarily in that order.

1957 ON THE JUKEBOX

FRANK ON THE US CHARTS

'CAN I STEAL A LITTLE LOVE'
Al Frisch, Edward R. White & Mack Wolfson
19 January, No 15, 19 weeks

'YOUR LOVE FOR ME'
Jimmy Van Heusen & Dok Stanford
19 January, No 60, 8 weeks

'CRAZY LOVE'
Philip Springer & Carolyn Leigh
27 April, No 60, 4 weeks

'SO LONG MY LOVE'
Donald Canton & Ira Kosloff
27 April, No 74, 5 weeks

'YOU'RE CHEATIN' YOURSELF
(IF YOU'RE CHEATIN' ON ME)'
Cole Porter
22 July, No 25, 1 week

'ALL THE WAY'
Nelson Riddle & Dok Stanford
28 October, No 2, 30 weeks

'CHICAGO'
Cole Porter
28 October, No 84, 5 weeks

Frank's appearance on the chart in the wake of rock 'n' roll was in itself an achievement. In actual fact, 'All the Way' from *The Joker Is Wild* turned out to be the record that spent longer on the *Billboard* charts than any other of Frank's career. It also narrowly missed out on the top spot, held off by Pat Boone's 'April Love'. Whereas most of Frank's single releases were fairly disposable, 'All the Way' broke the mould – it ranks up there with the best recordings of the 1950s and any other decade.

While Frank and some of the others, such as Johnny Mathis, Nat King Cole, and Tony Bennett, did well enough on the charts, the new breed of singers and groups was capturing the imagination of the younger record-buying public. Jerry Lee Lewis had his first hit in 1957 with 'Whole Lot of Shakin' Going on', as did Buddy Holly and the Crickets ('That'll Be the Day'), Sam Cooke ('You Send Me'), The Everly Brothers ('Bye Bye Love'), and Danny & The Juniors ('At The Hop').

BUDDY HOLLY
Aside from his 1957 No 1 'That'll be the Day', Buddy got to No 3 with 'Peggy Sue'.

THE SUMMIT AND BEYOND

BY 1958, FRANK HAD NOT JUST ARISEN, HE HAD
ARRIVED — ARRIVED AT THE SUMMIT FROM WHICH
HE COULD LOOK DOWN ON THE KINGDOM HE HAD
CREATED... THE KINGDOM OF COOL. AS THE 1960S
BEGAN TO TAKE SHAPE, OTHER PERFORMERS BEGAN TO
SCALE THE MOUNTAIN, TO STAKE THEIR CLAIM AS THE
ICON OF THEIR AGE, AND THE WORLD OF MUSIC AND
FILM TOOK ON A MORE DIVERSE ASPECT. AS FRANK
SLOWLY DESCENDED HE PASSED OTHERS ON THE WAY UP.
HIS JOURNEY TOWARD WHAT HE SAW AS HIS GRADUAL
RETIREMENT FROM THE WORLD OF TOP-FLIGHT
ENTERTAINMENT HAD MANY TWISTS AND TURNS. ONE
THING IS FOR SURE: WITH FRANK AROUND, THINGS
WOULD NEVER BE BORING.

THE STRIP, LAS VEGAS
*Without neon there would be no
Las Vegas, and without Frank it
wouldn't have burned so bright.*

CRUISING

The year 1958 began with Frank continuing work on his ABC televison series. His guests included Dinah Shore, Robert Mitchum, Louis Prima, Keely Smith, Pat Suzuki, Stan Freberg, and Jo Stafford. Frank also had a two-week booking at the Sands. Returning to Los Angeles one night in his brand-new Cadillac Eldorado, Frank was stopped by a Californian patrolman. Many years later, the car came up for sale and the patrolman's brother, a car collector, bought it for $120,000 and gave it to the former officer.

Frank appeared on *The Dinah Shore Show*, and on 1 February was Dean Martin's guest on *Club Oasis*. Frank joined Dean and his other guest, Danny Thomas, in an Academy Award medley that included 'I Fall in Love too Easily', 'Tender Trap', 'Three Coins in a Fountain', 'An Affair to Remember', 'All the Way', and 'Jailhouse Rock'. It would have been interesting to hear Frank's comments at having to sing such a "brutal, ugly, desperate and vicious form of expression" as 'Jailhouse Rock'.

Two days later, Frank's new album, *Come Fly with Me*, entered the charts, and a week later it became his first Capitol album to top the charts. This confirmed Frank as the label's "name singer" and completely justified Alan Livingston's foresight in signing him. Livingston was not at Capitol to share the pleasure, however, since he had moved to NBC. There is in any artist–label relationship a cycle, and while Capitol had improved the original 1953 contract, Frank took the view that, five years down the line, it ought to be much better. Not that the public knew anything of this, as it in no way affected Frank's output.

Having a No 1 record creates its own pressure, and Frank must have asked himself, "How long can this go on?" No popular singer had ever had a career that resembled Frank's to this point, either in its length or in terms of its success. Even his mentor, Bing Crosby, had long since stopped having real hit records; his last had been in 1956, when 'High Hopes' from *High Society* had done so well. Bing did not have a real hit LP either, other than a perennial Christmas album. When asked what was the biggest challenge of working with Frank, Alan Livingston commented: "When he became successful, his total independence. I didn't care, because I happened to agree with what he wanted to do. And it all happened when I was away, when I was at NBC. That's when the trouble started. Had I been there, I might have solved it. I don't know. But probably not." In mid-February,

AT WORK
Frank in the studio, January 1958.

**A NEW GENERATION ON THE MARQUEE,
PARAMOUNT THEATRE, NEW YORK, 1956**

"He was more than just a singer, he was a cultural expression of a whole nation's sense of style. He was our notion of class and elegance."

JIMMY WEBB, SONGWRITER

Frank flew to France to work on his new film, *Kings Go Forth*, which was directed by Delmer Daves and produced by United Artists. Location shooting was done around Nice, and of the film's three stars only Frank was there (Tony Curtis was finishing work on another movie and Natalie Wood was marrying Robert Wagner), which caused both shooting and editing conundrums. Early in the filming, Frank flew to Philadelphia to be at the bedside of his old friend and counsellor Manie Sacks, who had leukaemia. Frank got there in time to talk to Manie before he died, and paid for the two lost production days out of his own fee. While Frank was in Monte Carlo during filming, he got to shake hands with Winston Churchill, saying, "I've wanted to do that for 20 years."

Back in Los Angeles, work continued on *Kings Go Forth*, and on 3 March, Frank was in the studio for his first Capitol session of the year. He cut two songs with Billy May, 'How Are Ya' Fixed for Love?' and 'Nothing in Common' with Keely Smith, his first duet proper since signing with Capitol. When his single with Keely came out, however, it barely scraped into the charts, and stayed around for only a week.

"I select most of the music I record, primarily the standards. All the album work I do, I usually do myself.**"**

FRANK IN 1958

COME FLY WITH ME

FRANK SINATRA • COME FLY WITH ME

Come fly with me

FRANK SINATRA
with BILLY MAY and his orchestra

THIS WAS FRANK'S FIRST ALBUM WITH BILLY MAY AS ARRANGER AND CONDUCTOR. IT EXUDES STYLE AND SOPHISTICATION, A CLARION CALL TO MIDDLE AMERICA TO SEE THE WORLD.

AFTER SIX ALBUMS with Nelson Riddle and one with Gordon Jenkins, Frank at last got to work with his Capitol arranger of choice. It's not difficult to see why Frank wanted Billy as a partner. Mandalay, Hawaii, Capri, London, Paris, or Rome? Frank's enticing lyric "come fly with me" was an evocative invitation to 175 million Americans. Back in 1958 most people could only dream of air travel; foreign trips were for the rich and famous – Frank qualified on both counts. In actual fact, few Americans even owned a passport. The inspired selection of songs took the listener on a trip around the world. From the toe-tapping swing numbers (like 'Come Fly with Me' and 'Let's Get Away From It All') to the romantic ballads ('Autumn in New York' and 'Moonlight in Vermont') every song is crafted for maximum impact. The light-hearted humour of numbers like 'The Road To

B·O·A·C

SUNSET SPEEDBIRD TO

BERMUDA

BRITISH OVERSEAS AIRWAYS CORPORATION

Mandalay' and 'Isle of Capri' add an extra dimension to what some consider to be a strong contender for the title of 'the first real concept album' (a decade before it became an over-used notion in rock music).

It became Frank's first album to make the British album charts, which were inaugurated on 8 November, 1958. Although *Swing Easy* made the charts in 1960, six years after its American release, Billy May swears that he arranged 'Flying Down To Rio' for the *Come Fly With Me* album, but no recording has ever surfaced.

In their March 1958 review, *High Fidelity* thought it a great album. "Frank swings through a list of standards [as if on a trip], including 'Moonlight in Vermont', 'Autumn in New York', 'April in Paris', 'Brazil', etc. It is Sinatra at close to his very best, especially on the most bright-tempoed tunes like the title song and 'Isle of Capri', in which he amusingly tips his hat to a Hollywood restaurant in which he often eats, substituting these words: 'She wore a lovely meatball on her finger/t'was goodbye at the Villa Capri.'"

> ❝Once I get you up there, where the air is rarefied We'll just glide, starry eyed.❞
>
> **'COME FLY WITH ME'**

> ❝It is one of Sinatra's most exuberant sessions for the label, stimulated by Billy May's limber and often witty arrangements❞
>
> **NAT HENTOFF** *STEREO REVIEW*, DECEMBER, 1961

SONG LINES

Recorded: Capitol Studio A, Hollywood. Produced by: Voyle Gilmore. Chart: US No 1, 5 weeks, 71 weeks on the chart. First charted 3 February, 1958. UK No 2, 18 weeks on the Chart (8 November, 1958).

SIDE 1

1. 'COME FLY WITH ME'
(Sammy Cahn & James Van Heusen) Recorded 8 October, 1957. Frank asked Jimmy Van Heusen and Sammy Cahn to write some travel songs, and they came up trumps with 'Come Fly with Me' and 'It's Nice to Go Trav'ling'. "Credit should be given to the writers Sammy and Jimmy – good songs bring out good singers," said Billy May.

2. 'AROUND THE WORLD'
(Victor Young & Harold Adamson) Recorded 8 October, 1957. With music by Victor Young and words by Harold Adamson, this was the theme from *Around the World in 80 Days*. It had already been a hit in the summer of 1957

for Victor Young and his Orchestra, as well as Mantovani, Bing Crosby, and the McGuire Sisters.

3. 'ISLE OF CAPRI'
(Will Grosz & Jimmy Kennedy) Recorded 1 October, 1957. This was originally a hit in 1934 for Ray Noble, a British pianist and bandleader, and was revived in 1954 by the Gaylords, who took it to No 14 on the US chart.

4. 'MOONLIGHT IN VERMONT'
(Karl Suessdorf & John Blackburn) Recorded 3 October, 1957. Written by Karl Suessdorf (music) and John Blackburn (words), it was Capitol's 82nd release in 1945, by trumpeter Billy Butterfield, his Orchestra, and singer Margaret Whiting, becoming a million seller.

5. 'AUTUMN IN NEW YORK'
(Vernon Duke) Recorded 3 October, 1957. Frank first recorded this song in 1947 with Axel Stordahl, but it barely made a ripple on the chart when it came out in January 1949. Comparing the opening 30 seconds of Billy's and Axel's arrangements shows you how far Frank had moved on.

6. 'ON THE ROAD TO MANDALAY'
(Oley Speaks & Rudyard Kipling) Recorded 1 October, 1957. This was a Rudyard Kipling poem set to music by Oley Speaks, and was made popular by Frank Croxton in 1913. According to Billy May, "Frank had trouble getting the lyrics right" and changed Kipling's original words slightly. Later, the Kipling Society objected, asking Frank to re-record the song. Frank never did.

SIDE 2

1. 'LET'S GET AWAY FROM IT ALL'
(Matt Dennis & Tom Adair) Recorded 1 October, 1957. This had been a hit for Frank's old boss Tommy Dorsey along with the Pied Pipers in May 1941.

2. 'APRIL IN PARIS'
(Vernon Duke & E.Y. 'Yip' Harburg) Recorded 3 October, 1957. This became the second hit for bandleader Freddy Martin in 1933. Frank first recorded it in September 1950.

3. 'LONDON BY NIGHT'
(Carroll Coates) Recorded 3 October, 1957. First recorded in 1950, the same year as 'April in Paris', both times with Axel Stordahl.

4. 'BRAZIL'
(Ary Barrosa & Bob Russell) Recorded 8 October, 1957. Originally a samba, called 'Aquarelo do Brasil', 'Brazil' had been a hit for bandleader Xavier Cugat in 1943. Composed by Ary Barroso, with English words added by Bob Russell, it featured in the animated film *Saludos Amigos*.

5. 'BLUE HAWAII'
(Leo Robin & Ralph Rainger) Recorded 8 October, 1957. This was first a hit for Paul Whiteman and his Orchestra in 1929 and then Bing Crosby in 1937.

6. 'IT'S NICE TO GO TRAV'LING'
(Sammy Cahn & James Van Heusen) Recorded 8 October, 1957. The perfect ending to a perfect album, made all the more so by Sammy's brilliant lyrics.

A few weeks later, shortly before he left for an engagement at the Fontainebleau Hotel in Miami Beach, Frank proposed to Lauren Bacall; maybe 'Nothing in Common' had inspired him. It proved to be just another movement in his ongoing life's symphony. Their deeply affectionate relationship had gathered momentum throughout the second half of 1957, despite, as Bacall put it, their being a "combustible couple". Lauren had even sold the house she had shared with Bogie to dim the memories and make things easier for Frank. They decided to keep quiet, and not say a word to anyone — except, that is, mutual friend Swifty Lazar. According to Lauren, Swifty spilled the beans to Louella Parsons, the equivalent of an APB. The next day's *Herald Examiner* carried the story "Sinatra to marry Bacall". Frank was furious. He blamed Lauren, but strangely didn't call her for a few days. "I haven't been able to leave my room for days — the press are everywhere — we'll have to lay low for a while, not see each other," recalled Bacall in her autobiography. And that was it — the affair was over. "Frank, adoring one day, remote the next," she said. When Frank returned to Hollywood from Miami Beach, he and Lauren were invited separately to a dinner party, throughout which he completely ignored her, despite there being only one person sitting between them. Later Bacall admitted that she had been saved from what would have been a disastrous marriage. It was Frank who had recognized it; he just did not have the guts to face her. "But the truth is that he behaved like a complete shit," said Bacall.

Frank was looking to build his business portfolio, and, through his company, Essex Corporation, he brought three radio stations in the Northwest. Ten days later (perhaps to mend fences with the authorities after the "wrong door" subpoena incident in 1957), he played a benefit concert in Palm Springs for the local Police Department.

While Frank's recording schedule in 1958 was less than during recent years, his overall work rate was punishing. Confined to just the films and the recordings, it would have been considerable, but add the television series and the concert appearances, and most people would have wilted. It was the manifestation of Frank's persona; not wanting to be alone meant he needed to be kept busy. It was almost as though any gap in his schedule would, or could, cause him to remember the days when there was no work. It did, inevitably, mean that what Frank did was not always of the highest calibre, since quality invariably suffers from quantity, although this hardly ever affected his singing. Even Frank's friend, the director Billy Wilder, felt that he was spreading himself too thin: "Instead of involving himself in all those enterprises, television, records by the ton, four movies, producing, political things and all those broads — this talent on film would be stupendous." He had a point.

"He inspired you in a way that Nelson couldn't"

ELEANOR SLATKIN

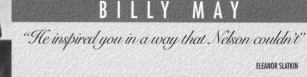

BILLY MAY ONCE SAID HE BECAME AN ARRANGER BECAUSE HE PLAYED THE TUBA IN THE SCHOOL BAND AND THEREFORE HAD PLENTY OF TIME TO OBSERVE WHAT THE OTHER INSTRUMENTS WERE DOING.

Billy, born in Pittsburgh in 1916, played trumpet and arranged for Charlie Barnet (including 'Cherokee', his biggest hit), Glenn Miller, and Les Brown before becoming a studio arranger for NBC. By the late 1940s he had formed a close relationship with Capitol Records, writing ghost arrangements for Paul Weston, and was soon musical director for many of the label's leading artists.

In 1951, May formed a recording band, gaining success with his novel glissando unison saxophone sound. His stylish, often witty arrangements soon put him in demand as a live act, which is why he couldn't work with Frank at his early Capitol sessions. Dick Nash, trombone player with Bill's band and a veteran of many Sinatra sessions, summed him up: "Some of Billy's work was tongue in cheek — he'd put in surprises along the line, to jolt you! He had a great command of brass, and was incredibly talented. Billy could hear everything about an arrangement in his head. He is a genius." In 2003 Billy had his own take on his talent. "With my arrangements I was not doing humour on purpose — we did a lot of work — some of the songs were good, some were crap. As arrangers we would sometimes make silk purses out of sow's ears!"

May was not a great conductor, according to many of the musicians that worked with him, but they felt he was an inspiration. Billy's album *Sorta-May* got to No 7 in 1955 and he won a Grammy in

BIG BILLY

On a track called 'Solving The Riddle' Billy emulates Nelson's arrangements. A kind of "anything you can do" moment, as a payback for Riddle's May imitation back in April 1953.

1958 for the album *Big Fat Brass*. Besides a reputation as a great arranger, he had one for his ability to drink copious amounts — he was known as the "guzzler." Not that any of this affected his musical abilities. While working with jazz pianist George Shearing there was an incident that exemplifies Billy's talent. George had run through a number he wanted Billy to arrange and started to go through it again to give Billy a second chance to hear it. Billy interrupted him, "Well, take it from after the bridge because I've got that much orchestrated already."

Billy later composed the music for the TV series *Naked City*, as well as writing the scores for *Johnny Cool*, *Tony Rome*, and *Sergeants Three*. His career slowed in the late 1960s, but he worked with Frank in 1979 on the first part of the *Trilogy* album. There was intermittent work in the 80s and he re-emerged in 1996 to contribute the band charts for comic Stan Freberg's album, *The United States of America, Vol 2*, 25 years after his work on *Volume 1*. In 1999 he visited Britain appearing in Edinburgh conducting the BBC Big Band; slurping saxes were back!

BIG MAN

Billy May died in January 2004, a few months after he was interviewed for this book.

1958-1962

"HE'S A GREAT ACTOR"
This is how the Los Angeles
Examiner *praised Frank in their
review of this WWII romance —
they were in the minority.*

DINNER DATE
*Princess Grace of Monaco
and Frank at the gala charity
dinner following
the world premiere of*
Kings Go Forth *on
14th June in Monaco.*

In Britain, Frank had been doing well on the charts, where 'All the Way' became his biggest hit since 'Three Coins in a Fountain' and 'Learnin' the Blues'. In February, 'Witchcraft' entered the UK charts and reached No 12, but there was far from unanimous praise for Frank's latest British release, an LP on Fontana called *Adventures of the Heart*, which contained old Columbia recordings. Comparing 'I Could Write a Book' to the *Pal Joey* version, *Disc* said, "In many ways it's a relief to listen to these older recordings of Sinatra's where he doesn't seem so bogged down with over-tricky arrangements." It went on to complain that the British market was swamped with Frank's recordings.

At the end of March, Frank appeared on British television as a guest on *The Dinah Shore Show*, which had been bought by the BBC following its American airing in January. In April, Capitol released a second greatest hits album in the US, *This Is Sinatra Volume 2*, which reached No 8 and stayed there for seven weeks, earning everyone involved a nice little bonus. Early in May, Frank and Nelson Riddle began work on an album to be called *Frank Sinatra Sings for Only the Lonely*. It was a step back into *Wee Small Hours* territory, but not one inspired by Frank's break-up with Lauren Bacall. At the first session on 5 May, nothing came of the three tracks he worked on, although he cut them successfully over the course of the next couple of months. The first song he attempted was 'Guess I'll Hang My Tears Out To Dry'. Frank certainly trawled his emotional depths on such songs as 'Blues in the Night', 'What's New', and 'Angel Eyes'. The dynamics on the latter song, especially, show how brilliantly the Capitol engineers had mastered the studio in the Capitol Tower. Of course, it helps that Frank was in perfect voice on the Matt Dennis and Earl Brent song; it remains a big favourite among Sinatra aficionados.

At the end of May, Frank recorded 'Monique' for the soundtrack of *Kings Go Forth*. At the same session, he cut three more songs before breaking off at 5:00 pm, only to return again at 8:30 pm to cut another four songs; it was a rare double session. Frank finished at around 11:30 pm, and the last song he cut was 'Willow Weep

GREATEST HITS TWO
This greatest hits package made No 8 on the US charts in the spring of 1958.

for Me', which means we can assume that it was put down around 11:00 pm. Not only does it show how strong his voice was at this time, but the length of the session and the time of night gave Frank's voice a very special quality that adds to the sadness of Ann Ronell's torch song.

SPRING IS HERE

In the spring of 1958, Frank took a decision that would change not just his life, but also Dean Martin's: he gave Dino a part in his new movie, *Some Came Running*. Dean had recently split up with his long-term partner, Jerry Lewis, and, while he had his own recording career, this gave him a chance to consolidate his solo work. Having helped Sammy Davis, and now Dean, Frank was, albeit unconsciously, laying the foundations for his own "Rat Pack" – one over which he had total control (although it is arguable that he ever had real "control" over Dean, who always remained his own man).

Before shooting began, Frank played his first concert in Europe since his disastrous trip with Ava in 1953, when he had performed badly and even been booed off stage in places. The show, at the Sporting Club in Monaco on 14 June, was a benefit for the United Nations Fund for Refugee Children. The patron for the evening was Frank's former co-star, Grace Kelly, now Princess Grace of Monaco. Quincy Jones, an American living in Paris, conducted the orchestra, and Noel Coward made the introduction. Coward, the master of high camp, speaking in both French and English, said "Fronk Sin-are-traa, Frank Sinatra"; he sounded not unlike Frank Sinatra impersonating Winston Churchill speaking French! Frank immediately launched into 'Come Fly with Me'; his 45 show was peerless. He was still doing his "Spain… oh Jeez" quip in the middle of 'I Get a Kick Out of You', and featured four songs from *Come Fly with Me*. He also sang 'Monique' from *Kings Go Forth*, which had a special European premiere in Monaco that night, and three weeks later had its first showing in Los Angeles on 4 July. While he was in Monaco, Frank even found time to appear in a British-made travel film called *Invitation to Monte Carlo*. Ever the opportunist, Frank never missed a chance for a little more self-promotion.

Back from Europe, Frank spent a couple of days working on songs for *Only the Lonely* before playing a

FRANK SINATRA SINGS FOR ONLY THE LONELY

A FRONT-RUNNER IN THE Frank's best album stakes and undeniably a masterpiece, Frank said *Only The Lonely* was his favourite album. But it was conceived in exceptionally sad circumstances. Shortly before Nelson had begun work on arranging the songs on this album his six-month-old daughter had died from bronchial asthma. Frank and Nelson went into the studio on 5 May to begin work on the album, but none of the three songs that were cut that night were used. Nelson's mother was critically ill and it must have affected the session. Four days later she died. Three weeks later Frank returned to the studio and, while the arrangements for the album were Nelson's, it was Felix Slatkin who conducted the orchestra on 29 May, before Nelson returned for the last two sessions.

While Frank delivers the sadness of the songs, the arrangements have an added dollop of despondency. It was a travesty that this album did so poorly at the inaugural Grammy awards. All it won was the award for the best cover. *Only The Lonely* was inducted into the Grammy Hall of Fame in 1999 partially to atone for the oversight. In December 1958, Peter Jones

IDEA AND EXECUTION
Frank's design idea for the cover was interpreted by Nick Volpe, and Frank, on winning his award, acknowledged the fact.

in the British music paper *Record Mirror* took stock. "This is the LP which my colleague on *Record Mirror* criticised when he wrote about an advance copy a week ago. I see his point, that Sinatra on some numbers lacks the necessary dramatic quality, I still feel the LP as a whole has so much magic it is a 'must'."

SONG LINES

Recorded: The Capitol Tower, Hollywood
Produced by: Dave Cavanaugh. Chart: US No 1, 5 weeks.120 weeks on the chart. First charted 29 September, 1958. UK No 5, 13 weeks (13 December, 1958).

SIDE 1

1. 'ONLY THE LONELY'
(Jimmy Van Heusen & Sammy Cahn) Recorded 29 May, 1958. Frank told author Robin Douglas-Home about pacing an album. "Tommy Dorsey did this with every band-show he played. Paced it, planned every second from start to finish. He never told me this; it just suddenly came to me as I sat up on that stand every night. This is what I've tried to do with every album I've ever made." This stands up as one of Frank's best "scene setting openers".

2. 'ANGEL EYES'
(Matt Dennis & Earl Brent) Recorded 29 May, 1958.

3. 'WHAT'S NEW'
(Bob Haggart & Johnny Burke) Recorded 24 June, 1958.

4. 'IT'S A LONESOME OLD TOWN'
(Harry Tobias & Charles Kisco) Recorded 25 June, 1958.

5. 'WILLOW WEEP FOR ME'
(Ann Ronell) Recorded 29 May, 1958.

6. 'GOODBYE'
(Gordon Jenkins) Recorded 25 June, 1958.

SIDE 2

1. 'BLUES IN THE NIGHT'
(Harold Arlen & Johnny Mercer) Recorded 24 June, 1958.

2. GUESS I'LL HANG MY TEARS OUT TO DRY'
(Jule Styne & Sammy Cahn) Recorded 29 May, 1958.

3. 'EBB TIDE'
(Robert Maxwell & Carl Sigman) Recorded 29 May, 1958.

4. 'SPRING IS HERE'
(Richard Rodgers & Lorenz Hart) Recorded 29 May, 1958.

5. 'GONE WITH THE WIND'
(Allie Wrubel & Herb Magidson) Recorded 24 June, 1958.

6. 'ONE FOR MY BABY'
(Harold Arlen & Johnny Mercer) Recorded 25 June, 1958. When he came to record this now-classic number, new producer Dave Cavanaugh created the right mood by putting the studio lights right down and illuminating Frank with a single spot. With Bill Miller beside him at the piano, Frank felt like he was in a nightclub.

benefit concert for the Cedars of Lebanon Hospital in Los Angeles. Dubbed "A Night with Sinatra", it exemplified his status as America's premier entertainer. A little under a month later, shooting began on Frank's next movie, *Some Came Running*, which was to be shot in an altogether less glamourous location than the South of France. Frank and over a hundred other cast and crew, including Dean Martin and Shirley Maclaine, descended on Madison, Indiana to begin filming. As shooting finished, *Frank Sinatra Sings for Only the Lonely* entered the chart and reached the top two weeks later, knocking Mitch Miller's *Sing Along with Mitch* off the top spot. Frank must have had something to say about that. Around this time, Frank was at a nightclub near Carmel in California when a woman who was slightly drunk sat at his table and said to him, "You know what we call you in our house? We call you the wop singer." There's little wonder that Frank felt the way he did about prejudice towards blacks and other minorities.

On the day that Frank topped the chart, 29 September, he was back in the studio conducting the orchestra for Dean Martin's album *Sleep Warm*. The title track was composed by Lew Spence, Alan Bergman, and Marilyn Keith, and this was the first time that Frank had worked with one of Alan and Marilyn's songs. They would later marry and became two of the most prolific quality songwriters in the US, working with Frank many times. In 1959, Frank would sing his first of their joint compositions, 'Love Looks so Well on You', on *Sinatra Sings of Love and Things*.

THE DAY THE MUSIC DIED

After several recording sessions, Frank began filming *A Hole in the Head* in Miami on 10 November. Once home from Miami, Frank went into the studio with Billy May on 9 and 11 December. The following night, there was to be another session, which did not go as planned, according to Billy May: "It was Frank's birthday and I had the band set ready at 8.00, the appointed time, and we had run down the music. Frank didn't show, and eventually came in an hour late. When we began he was not singing so well, and I asked if anything was wrong. He said, 'Which SOB booked this session for today? To Hell with this – let's go up to my house and party instead!' And he invited everybody up there – most went – and we had a great party!"

The year 1959 began much like 1958, with Frank playing the Sands, although this year Dean Martin joined him. At the same time, *Some Came Running* opened at Radio City Music Hall in New York City. Mid-way through the Sands engagement, on 2 February, Buddy Holly, Richie Valens, and the Big Bopper were all killed in a plane crash – a tragedy that would be remembered as "the day the music died" in Don Maclean's 'American Pie'. Back when Frank had been a band singer there was not much choice as to travel arrangements, but Buddy had opted to fly rather than endure another ride on the freezing cold tour bus.

A little over a week after the fatal crash, *Come Dance With Me* entered the *Billboard* album charts. It soon climbed to No 2, just failing to complete the hat trick of chart toppers for Frank's regular Capitol releases. Frank's appearance at the Sands was hastily arranged, because he was supposed to have been shooting *Never So Few* in the Far East. He'd grown a goatee in December, as dictated by the script, but shaved it off for his Sands appearance. Frank's transatlantic dominance continued when *Melody Maker* announced that he had scooped 71.7 per cent of the vote in the World's Best Male Singer category of their annual poll. His nearest rival, Jimmy Rushing, got just 10.2 per cent. (To put into perspective what type of person went for *Melody Maker*, Elvis got 0.4 per cent.)

Three sessions over three nights at the end of March with Gordon Jenkins almost wrapped up Frank's next album,

COME DANCE WITH ME

T HE VERY EPITOME OF up-tempo Frank and Billy, although a number of the charts were in fact written by Heine Beau. It was the most successful album of Frank's long career, spending over two and half years on the *Billboard* chart. As *Stereo Review* put it in 1959: "Sinatra swaggers his way with effortless verve through an appealing collection of bouncy standards, aptly described in the notes as 'vocals that dance'. The emphasis – in both his propulsive singing and in Billy May's buoyant orchestrations – is on danceability of the dozen selections. As usual, Sinatra's vocal wizardry is the whole show; he is apparently capable of transmuting the basest metal."

It took the Grammy award for Album of The Year, Best Male Vocal Performance for 'Come Dance With Me' and Best Arrangement for Billy May. It may have won album cover of the year but for Frank's choice of hat – it was far from his coolest.

66 A good set, but not up to Frank's best. 99
HIGH FIDELITY MAGAZINE, APRIL 1959

SONG LINES

Recorded: The Capitol Tower, Hollywood. Produced by: Dave Cavanaugh. Chart: US No 2, 140 weeks. First charted 9 February, 1959. UK No 2, 30 weeks. First charted 16 May, 1959.

SIDE 1

1. 'COME DANCE WITH ME'
(Jimmy Van Heusen & Sammy Cahn) Recorded 23 December, 1958. Compared to the opening of *Come Fly With Me*, this Cahn/Van Heusen number sounds like it's from a totally different era.

2. 'SOMETHING'S GOTTA GIVE'
(Johnny Mercer) Recorded 9 December, 1958. Another fairly contemporary song, it was from Fred Astaire's 1955 film *Daddy Long Legs*.

3. 'JUST IN TIME'
(Jule Styne, Betty Comden & Adolph Green) Recorded 9 December, 1958.

4. 'DANCING IN THE DARK'
(Arthur Schwartz & Howard Dietz) Recorded 22 December, 1958. Another song to feature in an Astaire film, 1953's *The Bandwagon*.

5. 'TOO CLOSE FOR COMFORT'
(George Weiss, Jerry Bock & Larry Holofeener) Recorded 23 December, 1958.

6. 'I COULD HAVE DANCED ALL NIGHT'
(Frederick Loewe & Alan Jay Lerner) Recorded 23 December, 1958. From the film *My Fair Lady*, it meant that every song on side one of this album was being performed on record by Frank for the first time.

SIDE 2

1. 'SATURDAY NIGHT (IS THE LONELIEST NIGHT OF THE WEEK)'
(Jule Styne & Sammy Cahn) Recorded 22 December, 1958. Having been all new on side one, Frank went back to very familiar territory for the opener on side two. He had first cut this tune for the *All Star Bond Rally* movie short in 1945 with Harry James.

2. 'DAY IN, DAY OUT'
(Rube Bloom & Johnny Mercer) Recorded 22 December, 1958.

3. 'CHEEK TO CHEEK'
(Irving Berlin) Recorded 22 December, 1958. From the Fred and Ginger classic *Top Hat*.

4. 'BAUBLES BANGLES AND BEADS'
(George Forrest & Robert Wright) Recorded 22 December, 1958. One of the best cuts on the album, it positively sizzles.

5. 'THE SONG IS YOU'
(Jerome Kern & Oscar Hammerstein II) Recorded 9 December, 1958.

6. 'THE LAST DANCE'
(Jimmy Van Heusen & Sammy Cahn) Recorded 23 December, 1958. Written specially by Jimmy and Sammy to close the album, this lovely ballad is totally different from the rest of the album and for that reason works perfectly.

WARM WORK
Frank working with Dean Martin on his album Sleep Warm *at Capitol Studios in September 1958.*

SOME CAME RUNNING

FRANK PROBABLY THOUGHT he was on to another winner with this second film adapted from a novel by James Jones. It is the story of a war veteran returning to his home town in Indiana. He befriends a teacher, played by Martha Hyer, who wants to help him with his creative writing; he is more interested in procreation. Dean Martin plays a poker player and Shirley Maclaine a prostitute from Chicago. The film has some excellent original music by Elmer Bernstein and Jimmy Van Heusen.

Director Vincente Minnelli, Judy Garland's ex-husband and Liza's father, coaxed some fine performances from Frank and Dean and a brilliant one from Shirley MacLaine, and press reviews were favourable. "Frank Sinatra is downright fascinating – or what the youngsters would probably call cool", said the *New York Times*; "Despite some minor flaws [it] is one of the most exciting pictures of the season", enthused *Variety*.

THE TWO FRANKS
Frank and veteran film director Frank Capra on the set of their co-produced movie Hole in the Head.

No One Cares. Time was tight, since he was off to Australia for another tour beginning in Melbourne on 31 March. Backed by Red Norvo, Frank's set was the usual mix of the old and the new. His last three albums were well represented, but so were his early days with 'Night and Day', as well as 'All of Me'. There was another brush with the past, because Ava was in Australia filming *On the Beach*. Ava went to a show in Melbourne and then apparently met Frank at his hotel for between 30 minutes and three hours, depending on which account you read; there was no reconciliation.

GRAMMY INJUSTICE

On the evening of 4 May, Frank picked up his date, the 25-year-old actress Sandra Giles, to go to the first Grammy Awards Ceremony, organized by the National Academy of Recording Arts and Sciences. Arriving at the Beverly Hills Hotel, Frank must have felt confident of picking up not one, but several awards. He had been nominated six times in four categories and indirectly in two other categories (two nominations in both the 'Best Engineered' and 'Best Arrangement' sections). In the end, Frank won just one award, for 'Best Album Cover' for *Only the Lonely*. He found it hard to hide his disappointment – and you cannot blame him.

It has been said that the Grammys were founded by a group of record company executives who were worried by the advances of rock 'n' roll and, by definition, the attack this new music was mounting on traditional popular music. It was a cause with which Frank had sympathy. It was very obvious that the awards were skewed towards the

established order. Despite having two No 1 records, Elvis did not even receive a nomination. Similarly, the Everly Brothers, who had had a great year and had two records nominated in the "Best Country and Western" category, failed to win anything; it was won by the Kingston Trio's 'Tom Dooley', which was even less C&W than the Everlys. Frank was beaten in the "Best Male Vocal" category, in which 'Witchcraft' and 'Come Fly with Me' were nominated, by Perry Como and 'Catch a Falling Star'. Henry Mancini's Music from *Peter Gunn* in the 'Best Album' category beat both *Come Fly with Me* and *Only the Lonely*. The winner of both the "Best Song" and "Best Record of the Year" was at least an Italian, Domenico Modugeno. His 'Nel Blu Dipinto Di Blu', better known as 'Volare', got both top spots, having managed only third place in the Eurovision Song Contest. Dean Martin also had a hit with this song but was nowhere near as successful as Modugeno, who spent five weeks at No 1. It was therefore not just rock 'n' roll that was unpopular with the judges. Four days after the Grammy ceremony, Frank was in the studio with Nelson recording another Van Heusen and Cahn film song, 'High Hopes', featured in *A Hole in the Head*. While it too failed to win a Grammy, it did win an Oscar for "Best Song" at the ceremony the following year.

DEATH OF A LADY

Recording was not at the top of Frank's agenda, because he was at last going to begin making *Never So Few*, a wartime drama set in Burma. The cast, which included Steve McQueen and Peter Lawford, headed to Burma, Ceylon, and Thailand in late June, which was a whole lot more glamourous than Madison, Indiana. Frank had wanted Sammy Davis Jr to be in the film too, and Sammy had been written into the story at Frank's insistence. However, Frank still had to battle with the Director John Sturgess and MGM to get Sammy on board, after it had been pointed out to him that there were no black soldiers in the Burma theatre of war. Sammy was almost as quickly written out, as Daniel O'Brian's wonderfully detailed book on Frank's movie career, *The Frank Sinatra Film Guide*, points out: "[Sammy] had committed virtual social and career hari-kari [by telling a journalist] 'I love Frank... but there are many things he does that there are no excuses for. Talent is not an excuse for bad manners.'" In actual fact, Sammy did not end things there, but went on to say that he had overtaken Frank as America's number one popular singer!

A Hole in the Head premiered in New York on 16 July. It was director Frank Capra's first movie since 1951, and it opened to considerable acclaim from the *New York Times*, who declared that "It is perfect entertainment on the screen." Frank played the widowed father of an 11-year-old boy who runs a Miami Beach hotel and is trying to

get together enough money to open a $5 million amusement park. It is an engaging comedy drama that is decidedly of its time. Edward G Robinson plays Frank's New York financier brother and turns in a polished performance. *Variety* claimed that "SinCap Productions, taken from Sinatra and Capra names, and distributor-financier United Artists have a finished commodity of wide appeal."

The day after *A Hole in the Head* opened, Billie Holiday, aged just 44, died in New York from the effects of excessive drug use. Only the year before, Frank had acknowledged his debt to Billie in an interview with *Melody Maker*: "Lady

NO ONE CARES

THERE ARE ONLY 11 SONGS on this album, and it was for the simple reason that the new stereo technology called for wider grooves on the album to accommodate the separation of both channels. Frank had recorded 'The One I Love Belongs to Somebody Else' as the 12th track but it was dropped. Even when technology

allowed for its inclusion, it was still left off subsequent LP re-issues. It wasn't until the CD re-issue that Capitol thought to restore it to its rightful place. It more than justifies its inclusion on *No One Cares*, rounding out the theme of the album perfectly.

In the album notes, Ralph J Gleason, editor of *Jazz* magazine, has this to say: "If I had my way (and the Comstock Lode to pay the bill), I would have Frank Sinatra record every song I have ever liked. I wouldn't care how he did it, with what accompaniment, with what interpolations or changes in tempo. I know I would like it. The fact that Capitol is gradually, through its series of Sinatra recordings, accomplishing this for me, I count as one of the greatest blessings of the decade."

❝It's all so beautifully simple that to me it's like being back in the womb.❞

FRANK ON GORDON JENKINS IN 1961

SONG LINES

Recorded: The Capitol Tower, Hollywood.
Produced by: Dave Cavanaugh. Chart: US No 2, 73 weeks. First charted 31 August, 1959.

SIDE 1

1. 'WHEN NO ONE CARES'
(Jimmy Van Heusen & Sammy Cahn)
Recorded 14 May, 1959. This album has been described as brooding, and this song fits that description perfectly.

2. 'A COTTAGE FOR SALE'
(Willard Robinson & Larry Conley) Recorded 26 March, 1959.

3. 'STORMY WEATHER'
(Harold Arlen & Ted Koehler) Recorded 24 March, 1959. Frank had originally recorded

this back in 1944, and while Axel's arrangement shows signs of age, it beats this Jenkins version hands down.

4. 'WHERE DO YOU GO?'
(Alec Wilder & A. Sundgaard) Recorded 26 March, 1959.

5. 'A GHOST OF A CHANCE'
(Victor Young, Ned Washington & Bing Crosby) Recorded 24 March, 1959.

6. 'HERE'S THAT RAINY DAY'
(Jimmy Van Huesen & Johnny Burke) Recorded 25 March, 1959. If Frank had decided to name the album after this song and changed two of the three songs he did, it could have been perfect. Frank nails this beautiful song from little-known 1953 Broadway musical *Carnival in Flanders*.

SIDE 2

1. 'I CAN'T GET STARTED'
(Vernon Duke & Ira Gershwin) Recorded 26 March, 1959

2. 'WHY TRY TO CHANGE ME NOW'
(Cy Coleman & Joseph A McCarthy) Recorded 24 March, 1959

3. 'JUST FRIENDS'
(John Klenner & Sam M Lewis) Recorded 26 March, 1959

4. 'I'LL NEVER SMILE AGAIN'
(Ruth Lewis) Recorded 14 May, 1959

5. 'NONE BUT THE LONELY HEART'
(P Tchaikovsky, B Westbrook, Edward Brandt & Gus Khan) Recorded 24 March, 1959

He's Here!

500 CLUB

10 WONDERFUL DAYS STARTING JULY 22ND

500 club

ATLANTIC CITY

CLUB NIGHTS
*The last show began at 5:00 am
at this legendary Atlantic City club.
Like all the other clubs in the East
Coast resort, it eventually succumbed
to the power of the hotel casinos.*

Day is unquestionably the most important influence on American popular singing in the last 20 years. With a few exceptions, every major pop singer in the United States during her generation has been touched in some way by her genius." Four months earlier, Billie had appeared on British television for the first time, and told *Melody Maker* that she was working in England because "I can't get my police card to work [in] New York, so how can I make it there? I'm Billie Holiday. Singing is |the only thing I know how to do. Do they expect me to go back to scrubbing steps – the way I started out?" It's interesting to compare the fates of Billie and Frank: both were brought low, in part from their own self-destructive tendencies, but whereas Frank battled against his, Billie succumbed. As a black woman in what was still a very prejudiced world, she was not so lucky.

Ten days later, Frank began a week's booking at Skinny D'Amato's 500 Club in Atlantic City. Red Norvo backed him again in a set that was almost identical to his Australian tour, although he had added 'High Hopes'. Frank's appearances at the club were becoming a regular summer occurrence, so much so that the club's hoarding announced his arrival with the laconic "He's Here", followed by the equally laconic "He's Gone" after he had left. The 500 Club, along with most of the small supper and nightclubs in Atlantic City, has long since disappeared, but it is commemorated in a tiny street that has been renamed 500 Club Lane, located just off the end of the Atlantic City Expressway, near Caesars Palace. The last show of the night at the 500 started at 5:00 am, and the club's patrons read like a who's who of the rich, the famous, the connected, and, of course, the Mob.

By the end of August, 'No One Cares' was out and already in the charts. Like its predecessor, it made it only to No 2, kept off the top spot by the Kingston Trio, who were themselves displaced in November by Johnny Mathis. Frank was also busy in the studio with Nelson recording songs for his next movie project, Can-Can, for which shooting proper started in September.

Not long after filming began, Frank, along with around four hundred other Hollywood luminaries, attended a lunch for Nikita Khrushchev after the Soviet Prime Minister had visited the Can-Can set. Apparently Khrushchev was less than impressed, announcing that it was "decadent western culture". With filming over, Frank was a guest on a Bing Crosby television special, this one sponsored by Oldsmobile. Three weeks later, Bing returned the compliment by appearing on Frank's Timex-sponsored television special along with Dean Martin. In the way of the incestuous world of television, Frank was then a guest two weeks later on Dean's NBC special. According to NBC executive Don Van Atta, it was a great scheme: "It was always a real picnic because they were so great together and they played it so loose. The audience loved it that way." It was one of the last programmes to be shot under the auspices of Alan Livingston, who was about to be enticed back to Capitol Records in a move that was to have interesting repercussions.

Frank's very last recording session of the 1950s took place on 13 October. Appropriately, given the amount of film work that Frank had done since his return to the top, it was a song from a movie. 'I Love Paris' was a duet with Maurice Chevalier and was slated to feature in Can-Can, but was dropped from the final picture. A few weeks later, Frank took a trip to Hawaii with a young woman named Judith Campbell, accompanied by Peter Lawford and his wife Patricia (née Kennedy). It was another of those seemingly unconnected events that would have far-reaching implications a few months later.

FRANK IN BRITAIN

FRANK AND THE BRITISH CHARTS 1956–1961

'LOVE & MARRIAGE'
Jimmy Van Heusen & Sammy Cahn
13 January, 1956, No 3, 8 weeks

'THE TENDER TRAP'
Jimmy Van Heusen & Sammy Cahn
20 January, 1956, No 2, 9 weeks

'ALL THE WAY'
Jimmy Van Heusen & Sammy Cahn
22 November, 1957, No 3, 18 weeks

'CHICAGO'
Fred Fisher
29 November, 1957, No 21, 2 weeks

'WITCHCRAFT'
Cy Coleman & Carolyn Leigh
7 February, 1958, No 12, 8 weeks

'MR SUCCESS'
Ed Greines, Hank Sanicola & Frank Sinatra
14 November, 1958, No 25, 4 weeks

'FRENCH FOREIGN LEGION'
Guy Wood & Aaron Schroeder
10 April, 1959, No 18, 5 weeks

'HIGH HOPES'
Jimmy Van Heusen & Sammy Cahn
28 August, 1959, No 6, 15 weeks

'IT'S NICE TO GO TRAV'LING'
Jimmy Van Heusen & Sammy Cahn
7 April, 1960, No 48, 2 weeks

'RIVER STAY AWAY FROM MY DOOR'
Harry Woods & Mort Dixon
16 June, 1960, No 18, 9 weeks

'NICE 'N' EASY'
Lew Spence, Marilyn Keith & Alan Bergman
8 September, 1960, No 15, 12 weeks

'OL' MACDONALD'
Lew Spence, Marilyn Keith & Alan Bergman)
24 November, 1960, No 11, 8 weeks

'MY BLUE HEAVEN'
Walter Donaldson & George Whiting
20 April, 1961, No 33, 7 weeks

'GRENADA'
Augustin Lara & Dorothy Dodd
28 September, 1961 No 15, 8 weeks

Frank's popularity in Britain continued unabated, despite his not appearing live in the country for almost a decade following the troubled tour of 1953. He was well served by his old friends Jimmy Van Heusen and Sammy Cahn, who wrote Frank's biggest British hits during this period. Frank had far fewer hits in Britain between 1956 and 1961 than in the US, but rather surprisingly he did better in Britain with 'High Hopes'. Singles that failed to excite British record buyers included 'The Johnny Concho Theme (Wait For Me)', 'Mind If I Make Love To You' and 'Talk To Me'.

Frank's best year in the British charts was undoubtedly 1956, when even his album Songs For Swingin' Lovers made No 12 in the singles chart and stayed there for two months. Three years later, Come Dance With Me also made the Top 30, but only for a week.

'Grenada' was the first British single for Reprise (the label was distributed by Pye). It made No 15 on the charts and stayed there for two months. From 5 October, 1961, Radio Luxembourg presented The Reprise Show with Kent Walton, a weekly 30-minute look at the company's recordings. Reprise's first album release was Ben Webster's The Warm Moods in January 1961.

BETTER TO TRAVEL
Nelson's arrangement did better in the UK than the US, where it only made No 7 on the Billboard Chart.

Frank's second Reprise single, 'The Coffee Song', was a minor hit in late 1961, but no thanks to the British singer John Leyton, who panned it on TV's Juke Box Jury saying, "Sinatra's version is square." His comments received a good deal of attention in the press and 18 months later Leyton was still being asked about "his feud" with Frank. "Today most of his stuff is square. He's passed his accepted peak. Everybody surely accepts that." Leyton later worked with Frank on Von Ryan's Express, though Frank graciously made no reference to the incident. Frank's fifth single for Reprise did surprisingly well in Britain ('I'll Be Seeing You' and 'Pocket Full of Miracles' both failed to chart: 'Everybody's Twistin' entered the charts in April 1962 and made No 22, staying around for three months; Frank was capitalizing on the twist craze. Chubby Checker's record, 'The Twist' had been a No 1 in 1960, and became the only record in US chart history to re-enter the charts and go back to the top. It was at No 1 again for the first two weeks of 1962, but only made No 75 on the Billboard chart in April 1962. In actual fact, the song was originally called 'Everybody's Truckin' and was written in the 1930s by Rube Bloom.

MAGIC
Nominated for five Grammys, this version of the synonymous Sinatra song was used in the film Scandal.

Still climbing up the hit parade
FRANK SINATRA
'WITCHCRAFT'
b/w 'Tell Her You Love Her'

Capitol 14429 CL.14511 — THE TENDER TRAP FRANK SINATRA With Orchestra conducted by Nelson Riddle

THE STRIP, LAS VEGAS

"Music has always been Frank's roots. For years he wanted his own record company. He was having his difficulties at Capitol and he began looking around."

MO OSTIN, FIRST GENERAL MANAGER OF REPRISE RECORDS

THE DECADE OF CADENCE

Never So Few had its premiere at New York's Radio City Music Hall on 22 January 1960. Steve McQueen and Peter Lawford were there and so were the critics, who were unimpressed. "Most sober people will sit there appalled," said the *New York Times,* and only Steve McQueen drew any praise. Frank missed it, as he was shooting yet another movie – but not just any movie.

Sammy Davis seems to be the one who actually coined the name "Clan", although according to Sammy Cahn, Davis "just wanted to belong to any clan that wasn't spelled with a K". Two years later, on a visit to England, Sammy told the press that "the only clan I know about is in Scotland". Frank and the rest of the "players" referred to themselves as "The Summit", calling their get-togethers a Summit meeting. It was all a little silly, but at the same time very redolent of the times. Frank's new film was *Ocean's Eleven,* the ultimate Summit meeting, which is what gives the film its iconic status with so many people. With the passing of time, and books like Shawn Levy's *Rat Pack Confidential,* published

THE CANDIDATE AND THE CLAN
Frank and JFK dining together brought on massive media interest, which was pleasing for both men.

in 1998, which has at its heart the making of the film and the antics of the delegates to The Summit, its legend seems assured. Levy's book is both evocative of the times and very informative about the film itself, along with seemingly trivial, yet fascinating, detail of these "summit meetings".

Setting *Ocean's Eleven* in Las Vegas was perfect for Frank, Dean Martin, Peter Lawford, Sammy Davis Jr, and their latest recruit, Joey Bishop. It was also very handy for Las Vegas, and all the hotel and casino owners. It was like an advert for the desert city and became a cash cow for many of the gambling establishments. According to Shawn Levy, the Sands alone turned away 18,000 bookings during the making of the movie. Not that the people were there to actually watch the filming. The other clever twist in proceedings was that Frank and the others performed nightly at the Sands in a freewheeling, somewhat anarchic show. Not that it was the "film all day, perform all evening, drink all night scene that has become the legend of the Summit," says Levy. Truth is, there were very few days that filming started before 3:00 pm, and as often as not there were just one or two of the principals on set.

SENATOR AT THE SUMMIT
On 7 February, the Summit had an unusual visitor in their midst, an honourary delegate. Senator John F Kennedy was busy campaigning for the Democratic

Presidential nomination, and he hung out at the Copa Room. According to Sammy Davis Jr, the hotel's owners gave JFK's election fund a gift of $1 million in cash. Judith Campbell, who had been Frank's girlfriend when she first met JFK at the Copa Room, soon became the future President's long-term girlfriend. A week later, there was another of Frank's Timex television specials, this one called *Here's to the Ladies*. The guests included Lena Horne, Juliet Prowse (Frank's latest flame), Mary Costa, Barbara Heller, and Eleanor Roosevelt. Becoming involved with the Kennedys and using Mrs Roosevelt in his show was a clear indication that Frank was once again back in the political arena, and politics would consume him for much of the next year. Frank sat on a bench and talked/sang the lyrics of 'High Hopes' to the dowager Democrat to a special Nelson Riddle arrangement .

Politics of the corporate variety were also playing on Frank's mind. Between 1954 and 1959, Capitol had released

NEVER SO FEW
The New York Times *called it "a romantic fabrication by which intelligence is simply repelled. Most sober people will just sit there appalled."* Variety *was more optimistic about the film's success, although they were forced to concede, "the film glistens agreeably, but it is far from pure gold". The main criticism was that it did not hang together as a credible story, possibly because it hinged around Frank's heroics. Gina Lollobrigida as the "love interest" hardly helps to make the film or the plot believable.*

1958–1962

11 Sinatra albums, excluding hit compilations, Christmas, and movie recordings; Frank was prolific. Then, after *No One Cares* came out in August 1959, the well went dry. Frank was unhappy with his deal, and he went on strike. With the level of success he was enjoying, he wanted to negotiate a new deal where he had a greater share of the profits. Capitol had baulked at this and by the time Alan Livingston returned to the label there was something of an impasse. Frank was refusing to record any more material until his demands had been satisfied. His last session for Capitol had been on 14 May, 1959, ignoring the *Can-Can* soundtrack sessions, which were for Twentieth Century Fox. "When I came back to Capitol – Frank had not had a record out for nine months. I said to Glen Wallichs, who was then Chairman of the Board, 'What happened? Where's Frank?' Glen said 'He came in to see me and wanted to rewrite the contract. And he wanted his own company, go 50/50 with Capitol, and Capitol would pay all the costs and expenses, and they would share the results.' And Glen said 'I can't do that! What would I do with Nat Cole? You're upsetting the whole structure of our business.' So Frank said 'the hell with you. I won't record anymore.' And he walked out and was not even willing to discuss anything. So I called him up and said 'Frank, I understand you had a problem with Capitol while I was gone. I'm back now. Can we sit down and talk about it?' He

HIP, LIP, AND VOICE
Frank and Elvis as they duetted on the Timex television special that welcomed back home the King from his military service in Germany.

said, 'No way. I don't want to talk to you. I'm going to tear down that round building.' He was threatening to do this and that and using every four-letter word in the book. And I was shocked. I said, 'Frank, I'm sorry. I didn't know you felt that way.' And I hung up. That was it. From there on we dealt with lawyers. Finally, I made a deal with Frank – with his lawyer, actually – saying that if Frank would come in and record five more albums, then we would cancel the contract. Frank said OK. So he came in and made the five albums, and walked. He started his own record company called Reprise – only we said it's not re-preeze, it's re-prize." It was the beginning of the end of one of the most important label–artist relationships in recording history.

To achieve his ambition, Frank instructed Mickey Rudin, his lawyer, to buy a small record label, and over the next few months he quietly tried to purchase the Verve label from Norman Granz, its founder. Frank had an affection for the label, not least because Ella Fitzgerald and Count Basie recorded for Verve, but in the end, the negotiations came to nothing because Granz sold Verve to MGM. Some good came out of the loss, however, because Rudin had spent some time dealing with Mo Ostin, an accountant at Verve, who Frank would later lure away to be the Head of Administration for his new label.

With the problem with Capitol resolved, Frank's first session for four and half months was on 1 March, and to reaffirm that it was business as normal, it was with Nelson Riddle. The first song they cut for what would become the aptly titled *Nice 'n' Easy* was Fred Coots and Haven Gillespie's 'You Go to My Head'. It had been 15 years since Frank first performed the song, and this new, superlative performance set the tone for the new record. Given the fact that Frank was at the studio finishing *Ocean's Eleven* during the day, his performances are even more remarkable.

THE PINKO PAST RETURNS

A week after the *Nice 'n' Easy* sessions, there was an announcement in the *New York Times* that Albert Maltz, who had worked on *The House I Live In*, had begun work on a new movie project with Frank. *The Execution of Private Slovik* had all the makings of a grade A controversy, because the storyline concerns the execution of a World War II American soldier for desertion, the first since the Civil War. Inevitably, some of the newspapers, especially those belonging to the Hearst empire, had plenty to say about this. As if his "pinko past" and the subject matter were not enough, the fact that he had chosen to work with

CAN-CAN

ACCORDING TO *VARIETY* on 16 March, 1960, *Can-Can* was "neither as bad as the remarks of Khrushchev would indicate nor as good as the drumbeating of the 20th Century Fox ballyman would have you believe". And that just about sums it up. It's a movie of its time that Fox hoped would emulate the success of MGM's *Gigi*. Frank did it under sufferance, as it formed part of his settlement over his walk-out from *Carousel*. Along with Frank were Maurice Chevalier, Shirley MacLaine, Louis Jourdan, and Juliet Prowse. Frank, despite being there under duress, got paid $200,000 and a healthy share of the profits. His star status was confirmed when he insisted they cast Shirley MacLaine, after Marilyn Monroe, Fox's choice, decided to do *Some Like It Hot* instead.

The storyline, which had Frank rather questionably cast as a French lawyer, concerns the banning of the Can-Can. Shirley MacLaine, a café owner, along with Frank and dancing Juliet Prowse, sets out to change the law, finally winning through by performing the dance in front of a judge in court. About the only real success from the film was the soundtrack, which made No 3 on the charts.

THE THREAT MEETS THE VOICE
Frank Sinatra greets Soviet Premier Nikita Khrushchev on the set of *Can-Can* watched by Louis Jourdan (on Khrushchev's right) and Shirley MacLaine.

NICE 'N' EASY

THIS ALBUM was to have been called *The Nearness of You*, a song Frank cut at a session on 2 March. Having got all 12 tracks down over three nights, subsequent discussion led to a change in the album's title. Everyone felt that a lead-off song that could double as a single was required. 'Nice 'n' Easy' was selected, making it definitely the odd one out – every other song was a standard and had already been cut by Frank during his time at Columbia. He was apparently less than keen on 'Nice 'n' Easy' but went along with it. In the event it fared no better than most of Frank's recent single releases and only managed No 60 on the *Billboard* chart. Paradoxically 'The Nearness of You' was one of the best recordings of Frank's Capitol years, and arguably a finer title song and opening track. Given the choice of material it may

have been better to have called it *That Old Feeling*. Whatever its title, it was still a very successful album, topping the charts for longer than any other Frank Sinatra album. It was highly praised by *High Fidelity Magazine* in September 1960. "The popular song in America, which at its worst is a dreary reprise of the sad dreams of children conditioned by the movie houses, can become in a performance by Sinatra a poem with meaning and reality that transcends its original triviality. It is this quality of creative interpretation that makes Sinatra the greatest singer of popular ballads this country has ever produced. He is a master of phrasing, that art which enables the lyric to come alive. Given such good material as he has in this album, Sinatra can and does make the definitive recordings of each song."

SONG LINES

Recorded: The Capitol Tower, Hollywood. Produced by: Dave Cavanaugh. Chart: US No 1, 9 weeks. 86 weeks on the chart (First charted 22 August, 1960). UK No 4, 27 weeks on the chart (First charted 21 January, 1961).

SIDE 1

1. 'NICE 'N' EASY'
(Lew Spence, Alan Bergman & Marilyn Keith) Recorded 13 April, 1960

2. 'THAT OLD FEELING'
(Lew Brown & Sammy Fain) Recorded 1 March, 1960. Frank had cut this in 1947 for Columbia, so it was fortunate that Nelson's arrangement was able to elevate this lovely

ballad to a new level. Maturity wins over innocence yet again.

3. 'HOW DEEP IS THE OCEAN'
(Irving Berlin) Recorded 3 March, 1960

4. 'I'VE GOT A CRUSH ON YOU'
(George & Ira Gershwin) Recorded 3 March, 1960. Frank is on classic form in this, with an edginess in his vocal that suits this lovely song perfectly.

5. 'YOU GO TO MY HEAD'
(Fred Coots & Haven Gillespie) Recorded 1 March, 1960. One of those songs that just about all the great singers have at one time had in their repertoire. Frank's interpretation of the lyrics lets you understand him perfectly, and when you add a Nelson arrangement that is nothing less than perfect:

you have one of Frank's best ballads from the Capitol (or any other) era.

6. 'FOOLS RUSH IN'
(Rube Bloom & Johnny Mercer) Recorded 1 March, 1960

SIDE 2

1. 'NEVERTHELESS'
(Bert Kalmer & Harry Ruby) Recorded 2 March, 1960.

2. 'SHE'S FUNNY THAT WAY'
(Richard Whiting & Neil Moret) Recorded 2 March, 1960. The orchestral playing on this album is indicative of musicians playing at the peak of their powers. There have been few better orchestras ever gathered together than the ones that backed Frank on these Capitol sessions.

3. 'TRY A LITTLE TENDERNESS'
(Harry Woods, Jimmy Campbell & Reg Connelly) Recorded 1 March, 1960

4. 'EMBRACEABLE YOU'
(George & Ira Gershwin) Recorded 3 March, 1960. You have to believe that over the years many people have fallen in love to this record, and this song in particular. Frank always seemed to have a special way with any of the Gershwin tunes.

5. 'MAM'SELLE'
(Edmund Goulding & Mack Gordon) Recorded 3 March, 1960.

6. 'DREAM'
(Johnny Mercer) Recorded Thursday 3 March, 1960.

Maltz, who was on the infamous Hollywood blacklist, made Frank guilty of treason in some people's eyes. It was made worse by the fact that Maltz, described by the *Hollywood Reporter* as "A sneaky, switch-hitting strike breaking FINK", had been to jail for declining to answer questions by the Senate Committee. Well-known Republican John Wayne could not resist linking Frank's action with those of "his crony" Senator Kennedy. According to FBI files, Senator Kennedy asked Frank, through Peter Lawford, to delay announcing his deal with Maltz until after the New Hampshire primary, which JFK later won. For Frank, it must have smacked of the bad old days, only this time he probably felt that he was on safer ground. But Frank, and JFK, should have been worried, because *Confidential* magazine had information about "an alleged indiscreet party", as the FBI files put it, at Frank's Palm Springs house the previous November. In the end, Frank found himself under pressure from the press, the film's sponsors, Joe Kennedy (JFK's father), and even the Church; and, aware of the potential downside for Kennedy

if he proceeded with Maltz, he paid Maltz for the entire job, and then sacked him. Matters became uglier still, with Frank having several public altercations with other Hollywood stars about his split loyalties to Maltz and Kennedy. Frank was linked with Kennedy because he was busy working on his campaign, even recording a reworked version of 'High Hopes' with new lyrics courtesy of Sammy Cahn ("Everyone is voting for Jack, because he has what all the rest lack" and "Jack's the nation's favourite guy" give you the general idea.) Frank never did make the film; he sold off his option and it was eventually made as a television movie in 1974 starring Martin Sheen.

THE KING'S HOMECOMING

With *Can-Can* having opened in mid-March, Frank was in Miami at the Fontainebleau, fending off the press over the Maltz affair and working on another television special, which was recorded on 26 March. *Welcome Home Elvis*, sponsored by Timex Watches ("from only $9.95"), celebrated Elvis's homecoming from the Army. "The

❝I make movies. I don't ask the advice of Senator Kennedy on whom I should hire. Senator Kennedy does not ask me how he should vote in the Senate.❞

FRANK, 25 MARCH, 1961

Pelvis" was being relaunched on the American public courtesy of Frank. Given his views on rock 'n' roll, it does seem like an odd call. Frank took the precaution of surrounding himself with most of the Summit, as well as daughter Nancy, who looked very demure in a cocktail dress and white gloves. The show opened with Frank doing a rewritten 'It's Nice to Go Trav'ling', after which he was quickly joined by Sammy Davis, Joey Bishop, and Nancy. The premise of the show was to recreate for Elvis what he had missed during his time in the Army, which gave Frank the chance to sing 'Witchcraft' and 'Gone with the Wind'. Before singing the latter, Frank lit up a cigarette and took a long draw on it. Frank introduced Elvis to a screaming audience, and then the King, looking ever so slightly incongruous in a tuxedo, sang 'Fame & Fortune' and 'Stuck on You' (which was at No 1 when the show aired on 12 May). Frank joined him for a shared set in which Elvis sang 'Witchcraft' and Frank crooned 'Love Me Tender'; it closed with both men harmonizing on 'Love Me Tender'. Rather lamely, the programme then went into a spoof version of 'You Make Me Feel So Young (Old)', with Frank and Nancy sharing the vocals. The show drew huge audience ratings and Timex must have sold a lot of $9.95 watches. Having paid Elvis $125,000 to appear, there was a good deal of pre-

screening hype that most considered had not been matched by the show itself. *Variety* summed it up best: "the show did not generate $250,000 worth of excitement", although it got over 40 per cent of the television audience when it aired on 12 May. Frank, though, had already moved on, concentrating on politics.

BANNER MAN

According to FBI files, Frank was working hand in glove with Mafia boss Sam Giancana to help Kennedy secure the West Virginia primary. Frank flew to Japan to play some shows in Tokyo, and by the time he returned, Kennedy was assured of winning the nomination. The Democratic National Convention was to be held in Los Angeles on 11 July, and Frank was asked to sing the 'Star Spangled Banner', which he duly did accompanied by Sammy Davis Jr, though racist delegates from some Southern states booed him. The night before the convention, there was a fund-raising dinner for almost 3,000 people at the Beverly Hilton; guests paid $100 to be in the presence of the candidate. Frank was there, of course, along with Sammy, Peter, Judy Garland, Tony Curtis, Angie Dickinson, and many others from among Hollywood's great and good. As soon as the hullabaloo in LA was over, Frank went east for a week to Atlantic City, performing two shows a night at Skinny D'Amato's Club 500. Then it was back to a summer of campaigning on behalf of Kennedy, as well as starting work on a new film, *The Devil at 4 O'clock*. Coincident with all this was the release of Frank's first album in almost a year: *Nice 'n' Easy* entered the charts on 22 August and reached No 1 on 24 October, where it stayed for nine weeks. Whether it was pent-up demand for a new Sinatra album, all the

HIGH SOCIETY
Patricia Lawford, Tony Curtis, Frank, and Peter Lawford share a joke at the Democratic National Convention on 11 July, 1960.

OCEAN'S ELEVEN

Wᴴᴱɴ ᴛʜᴇ ᴍᴏᴠɪᴇ ᴏᴘᴇɴᴇᴅ in August 1960, *Variety* said *"Ocean's Eleven* figures to be a money maker, despite itself."* The entertainment industry's "bible" succinctly captured the essence of this now legendary movie.

The idea for the movie stretched back to 1955, when Peter Lawford heard the story idea from a small-time Hollywood director named Gilbert Kay. Fast-forward three years and Kay sells Lawford the idea for $10,000, having been unable to sell it to a studio. Peter Lawford apparently had to get half the money from his wife as he was financially stretched. He had, by this time, been allowed to return to the Sinatra fold, having been ostracized, probably for being spotted on the town with Ava Gardner during one or another of Frank and Ava's temporary splits early in their relationship. It was lucky timing all round because Frank owed Warner Brothers a movie, and the deal with Jack Warner was done in double-quick time.

When the movie opened, it caused ripples with some critics who felt that the fact that Frank and his gang had succeeded in pulling off "the job" was not very good at all. "Frank should have a couple of his merit badges taken away," protested the *New York Times* on 11 August, 1960. "A surprisingly nonchalant and flippant attitude toward crime – an attitude so amoral it roadblocks a lot of valid gigs – is maintained throughout." However, the fact that it was cleverly written and funny did not go unnoticed, and it was acknowledged that the young would be less troubled than older filmgoers by the

studied nonchalance of the entire proceedings. *Variety* seemed concerned that none of the principals, including Frank, made any real attempt to get into their roles. Knowing Frank, he probably didn't, and the freewheeling production suffered accordingly.

The film's opening at the Capitol Theatre on Broadway broke the previous box office record set by *From Here to Eternity*. The lack of critical support for the movie did nothing to dent the public's enthusiasm. Frank's collateral had never been higher. He was placed at No 6 on the Hollywood Top 10 by *Fame* magazine: only Rock Hudson, Cary Grant, and James Stewart among male actors figured better.

The passing of time, and the appearance of books such as Shawn Levy's *Rat Pack Confidential* (1998) mean that the legendary status of *Ocean's Eleven* seems assured. The remake released in 2002, directed by Steven Soderbergh and starring George Clooney, Brad Pitt, and Matt Damon, proved so successful it spawned a sequel – *Ocean's Twelve*.

EIGHT FROM ELEVEN
The Rat Pack regulars with part-time partners in crime Richard Conte (first left) and Henry Silva (far right).

THE STORY LINE

The first task was to work the somewhat flimsy storyline into a screenplay, allowing Frank to set about casting his best friends in the key roles, along with other friends and acquaintances in bit parts and cameos. Frank plays Danny Ocean, who assembles a gang of wartime buddies to rob five Las Vegas casinos on New Year's Eve.

CAST & CREDITS

Danny Ocean	Frank Sinatra
Sam Harmon	Dean Martin
Josh Howard	Sammy Davis Jr
Jimmy Foster	Peter Lawford
Beatrice Ocean	Angie Dickinson
Anthony 'Tony' Bergdorf	Richard Conte
Director	Lewis Milestone
Written by	George Clayton Johnson & Jack Golden Russell (story)
	Harry Brown & Charles Lederer
	Billy Wilder (uncredited)
Original music by	Nelson Riddle & Jimmy Van Heusen
Cinematographer	William H Daniels

PETER LAWFORD

"They were taking bets that we'd all end up in a box."

PETER LAWFORD, AN ENGLISHMAN, WAS BORN IN 1923, THE SON OF SIR SYDNEY AND LADY LAWFORD. HE MARRIED PATRICIA KENNEDY, INTRODUCED MARILYN MONROE TO JFK, AND WAS PROBABLY THE LAST PERSON TO SPEAK TO HER. HE WAS THE LEAST WELL KNOWN OF ALL FRANK'S RAT PACK.

His first role was as a child actor in Britain aged seven in *Poor Old Bill*. He moved to the US just prior to World War II and became a contract actor for MGM in 1942. His aristocratic suave good looks made him perfect contract star fodder for the studio in need of British men in the Ronald Coleman mould. Peter met Frank at a party in 1944 and appeared in *It Happened in Brooklyn*, one of the numerous films he made during the 1940s and early 1950s. In 1954, he married Pat Kennedy, John and Robert's sister, which inadvertently became his route into the Rat Pack and his link to the American aristocracy.

His appearances with Frank helped sustain a flagging acting career but after they fell out Peter had to rely on character roles and television appearances.

By 1971, he was appearing on Doris Day's television show, having divorced Pat in 1966. He married three more times and as his career effectively disintegrated he spent much of his time battling his demons. It's sad but true that his memory lingers more for what he did off-screen than what he achieved in his professional life, which included 50 films. He died on Christmas Eve 1984 after a heart attack.

BEST FILMS
The Picture of Dorian Gray 1945
Royal Wedding 1951
Ocean's Eleven 1960
The Longest Day 1962

publicity by association with Kennedy, or the quality of the album itself (or a mixture of all three), it became Frank's longest-running album at the top of the charts.

For Frank, good publicity was almost always tempered by bad. Dorothy Kilgallen, the columnist on the *Los Angeles Examiner* was once again on the warpath – actually, she had never left it and continually sniped at Frank, while he vilified her from the stage. She set out to rubbish Frank's relationship with Jack Kennedy. She even attributed a direct quote to the Senator: "He's no friend of mine, he's just a friend of Pat and Peter Lawford." Kilgallen went on to report that Kennedy had been a guest of Frank's at a private dinner. The Republican press were clearly rattled.

On Wednesday, 3 August, 1960, the Summit reconvened in Las Vegas. They were there for the premiere of *Ocean's Eleven* at the Fremont Theatre. Just over a week later, Frank and Nelson were back in the studio cutting over a dozen songs that would feature on *Sinatra's Swingin' Sessions*. Mid-way through these sessions, which lasted two weeks, Frank flew to Chicago to appear at the Urban League Jazz Festival in Comiskey Park. Ten days after the last session for the new album, Frank gave daughter Nancy away at her wedding to singer Tommy Sands, who had had a run of hit records on the *Billboard* chart since 'Teen-Age Crush' made No 2 in 1957. A month later, and Frank was in Maui, Hawaii, filming *The Devil at 4 O'clock*.

Frank continued to campaign for JFK. Everything was wrapped in Hawaii on 1 November so that Frank could hotfoot it back to the mainland in time for the election. The following Sunday, John Fitzgerald Kennedy narrowly

won the election, which made him not just the 35th American President but also the youngest. A few days after this, Sammy Davis Jr married Mai Britt and Frank was the best man. Prior to their marriage, there had been a good deal of discussion, and press interest, because of their colour: many in America were still coming to terms with the idea of black and white people marrying. Sammy had decided that their wedding should not be held before the election, so as to avoid any adverse public reaction and backlash against Kennedy. Frank was apparently upset that there were people who even felt that it was an issue. Sammy took his decision after Joe Kennedy had put the squeeze on him and Frank.

Despite his filming commitments, the post-election period must have been somewhat anti-climactic for Frank, although he got a boost when he and Peter Lawford were asked to organize the Inaugural Ball in Washington in

STAR TAILOR

Sy Devore had mens' shops in Hollywood, Las Vegas, Palm Springs, and at the Cal-Neva Lodge on Lake Tahoe. As well as creating the suits worn in Ocean's Eleven, he was famous for dressing stars such as Liberace, David Niven, Laurence Harvey, Nat King Cole, William Holden, and Perry Como.

THE LAST CAPITOL SINGLES

FRANK ON THE US CHARTS

'WITCHCRAFT'
(Cy Coleman & Carolyn Leigh)
20 January, 1958, No 6, 16 weeks

'TALK TO ME'
(Stanley Kahan, Eddie Synder & Rudy Vallee)
19 October, 1959, No 38, 11 weeks

'HOW ARE YA' FIXED FOR LOVE'
(Jimmy Van Heusen & Sammy Cahn)
22 May, 1958, No 22, 1 week

'RIVER STAY 'WAY FROM MY DOOR'
(Harry Woods & Mort Dixon)
30 May, 1960, No 82, 2 weeks

'MR SUCCESS'
(Ed Greines, Hank Sanicola & Frank Sinatra)
27 October 1958, No 41, 11 weeks

'NICE 'N' EASY'
(Lew Spence, Alan Bergman & Marilyn Keith)
29 August, 1960, No 60, 6 weeks

'FRENCH FOREIGN LEGION'
(Guy Wood & Aaron Schroeder)
30 March, 1959, No 61, 7 weeks

'OL' MAC DONALD'
(Lew Spence, Alan Bergman & Marilyn Keith)
7 November, 1960, No 25, 9 weeks

'HIGH HOPES'
(Jimmy Van Heusen & Sammy Cahn)
15 June, 1959, No 30, 17 weeks

'THE MOON WAS YELLOW'
(Fred E Ahlert & Edgar Leslie)
17 March, 1962, No 99, 1 week

THE YEAR 1958 WAS REALLY the end of Frank's time as a serious and consistent chart contender, and this was made clear by the steady decline in his hit records over the next couple of years. While 'Witchcraft' made it to No 6, it was a far bigger "radio record" than it was a seller at 45 rpm. In 1959, 'High Hopes' spent over four months on the charts but could climb no higher than No 30. It was the first year in which Frank had failed to make the Top 10 since the dark days of 1952. However, neither he nor Capitol were probably very worried, given Frank's performance on the album charts. His market was increasingly older and more sophisticated, and one that preferred the more relaxing medium of the long-playing record. *Frank Sinatra Sings for Only the Lonely* spent all of 1959 on the album chart, joined by *Come Dance with Me* in February and *No One Cares* in August. This meant that as 1959 became 1960, Frank had three top albums on the chart. *Look To Your Heart*, a Capitol compilation issued in June 1960, spent almost four months on the chart. The 1950s had certainly ended a lot better than they began.

The last Capitol single that had any impact was 'Ol' Mac Donald'. After that, despite releasing 'My Blue Heaven', 'American Beauty Rose', 'Five Minutes More', 'Hidden Persuasion', and 'The Moon Was Yellow', Frank made the charts with only the latter.

Frank's strong views on colour and segregation extended to his backing musicians. In October 1958, he told *Melody Maker* "When I do a recording session the orchestra is picked for musical standards alone and the result is that [black] men like Harry Edison and Buddy Collette are invariably included and playing behind me." Harry's trumpet and Buddy's sax can both

be heard on Frank's classic version of 'Witchcraft'. On 4 August 1958, the first *Billboard* Hot 100 was published, and, fittingly, given his move away from singles, Frank was not represented. Hailed as "the industry's fastest and most complete programming and buying guide", it represented the best survey of what was popular across the United States. Like the Top 100, it took into consideration jukebox and radio plays as well as record sales.

The biggest hit of 1959 was 23-year-old Bobby Darin, a man whom some consider to be one of the great "nearly" men. His recording of 'Mack the Knife' spent 26 weeks on the chart, nine of them at No 1. The song, written by Kurt Weill, came from his *Threepenny Opera*, and was hardly the stuff of rock 'n' roll, yet that did not stop the fans buying it. It was also the first chart topper to carry the name of Ahmet Ertegun as producer.

HIGH HOPES
Lyrics by SAMMY CAHN · Music by JAMES VAN HEUSEN
From UA Picture "A HOLE IN THE HEAD"

FRANK SINATRA
EDWARD G. ROBINSON
ELEANOR PARKER
CAROLYN JONES
THELMA RITTER
KEENAN WYNN
FRANK CAPRA'S
'A HOLE IN THE HEAD'
also starring EDDIE HODGES
CinemaScope · COLOR by De Luxe
Released thru UNITED ARTISTS

95¢

SOLE SELLING AGENTS BARTON MUSIC CORP., 116 Central Park South, New York, N.Y.

January 1961. This would prove to be another test for Frank and Sammy's friendship. For the right-wing press, this was just kindling to reignite their anti-Kennedy, anti-Frank fire. Even *Time* magazine questioned the President's association with Frank: "some of JFK's biggest headaches may well come from an ardently pro-Kennedy clique known variously as the Rat Pack or the Clan". Professionally, however, things could not get much better: with *Nice 'n' Easy* atop the charts, Frank and Elizabeth Taylor were voted the Top Box Office Stars of 1960 by the Film Exhibitors of America.

SELF-EMPLOYED

With one album of the five he owed Capitol under his belt and another one already recorded, Frank now began working for his own label. His first session for Reprise was six days before Christmas 1960, and, appropriately it was not with any of the arrangers he had worked with at Capitol but Johnny Mandel, a 35-year-old New Yorker.

SAMMY'S WEDDING
Mai Britt and Sammy Davis Jr's wedding watched by Frank and Peter Lawford.

"Frank was at the Sands a lot, and I saw him there. I had written an act for Vic Damone, and Frank saw it and called me. I guess he liked my sound. My rhythmic arrangements were more like Billy May than, say, Nelson."

The first song they cut together was 'Ring-A-Ding Ding', which was to be the title of Frank's first Reprise album, as well as one of the hip sayings he was so fond of. Two more sessions over the next two nights completed work on the album, which would be released five months later. But it wasn't to be all change. Frank also cut 'The Second Time Around' and 'Tina' (dedicated to his younger daughter), with Felix Slatkin conducting two Nelson Riddle arrangements. The two songs became the first 45-rpm release on Reprise in February 1961. Frank had been putting his plan together for some time with Mo Ostin, the former Verve accountant. "Frank talked to me at great length on the Columbia set where he was making *The Devil at 4 O'clock*. He told me how important he felt it was to have a record company that reflected the artists as well as the businessmen's point of view. He wanted to encourage other artists to join him in what he felt would be a freer, more creative atmosphere. He wanted to build a better economic mouse trap for artists

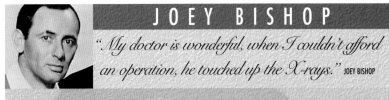

JOEY BISHOP

"My doctor is wonderful, when I couldn't afford an operation, he touched up the X-rays." JOEY BISHOP

STAND UP COMEDIAN BISHOP WAS ANOTHER PERFORMER WHO HAD MUCH TO THANK FRANK FOR. WITHOUT HIS INVOLVEMENT WITH THE SUMMIT, IT IS ARGUABLE THAT HIS CAREER MAY HAVE TAKEN A VERY DIFFERENT ROUTE.

Born Joseph Abraham Gottlieb in the Bronx on 3 February, 1918, Joey started out as a vaudeville-style entertainer in Philadelphia as one half of The Bishop Brothers, with... his brother. He went solo in the early 1950s and by the time he joined the other members of the Summit he was one of the hottest standup comedians in America. He became a regular on television, appearing on the *Tonight Show* before *The Joey Bishop Show* (which co-starred Bill Bixby, and Joe Besser of Three Stooges fame) ran from 1961 to 1965. After the sitcom format floundered, Joey began a two-year stint hosting his own late-night talk show, also called *The Joey Bishop Show*. Regis Philbin appeared on the show and he still has a daytime talk show on American TV. Joey Bishop also appeared in a number of films separate from the Rat Pack. They included *The Naked and the Dead* (1958), *The Valley of The Dolls* (1967), and *Delta Force* (1986). Bishop's last movie appearance was in *Mad Dog Time* in 1996.

having ownership in a record company so that they'd have not only idealistic but business motivations as well." *Billboard* on 5 December carried a piece about the new label, but at that time its new name was not revealed.

Shortly afterwards, it was announced that Sonny Burke was to handle A&R at Reprise; he stayed with Frank until he died in 1980.

In mid-December, for the fourth year running, Frank was voted favourite male singer in *Billboard*'s 13th annual disk jockey poll. Bobby Darin and Johnny Mathis came second, but, according to *Billboard*, "Sinatra still outdistances them all, with almost three times the number of votes in the favorite category, and with almost twice the number of votes as the most played. Nat Cole and Perry Como are two other veterans who still remain disk jockey favorites. A modified type of rock and roll appears to be strong as a programming trend, since almost all of the rock and roll artists who showed up on the various polls have changed to a sweeter style. This includes Elvis Presley, whose last record ('It's Now Or Never') and his current release ('Are You Lonesome Tonight') are on the ballad side." It shows how dangerous it is to predict anything in music.

> **"**All day long they lie in the sun. And when the sun goes down, they lie some more.**"**
>
> FRANK ON THE PRESS

$\mathcal{L}$ET'S GO TO WAR

Frank must have been full of confidence as 1961 dawned. His success on the *Billboard* poll and charts along with the launch of his new label all pointed to a man at the top of his game. Frank released six albums in 1961, three for Capitol and three for Reprise. Although one of the Capitol albums was a greatest hits package, it created a demand for Frank to be in the studio.

Having already recorded the material for his first two releases of 1960, he only went into the studio for the first time on 20 March. He and Sy Oliver began work on an album to be called *I Remember Tommy*. In all, during 1961, Frank did 17 sessions and cut 71 songs with five different conductors. "After 'Ring A Ding Ding', I think Frank wanted to try different guys. He was all over the place for a while – it was his store now!" said Johnny Mandel.

But before starting work on his own account there was the Inaugural Gala for President Kennedy on 19 January, that Frank was hosting and helping to organize. Those in

JFK'S INAUGURAL ADDRESS, JANUARY 1961

ALL THE PRESIDENT'S MEN (& WOMEN)
Frank rehearses for JFK's Inaugural Gala with (from left to right): Nat King Cole, Harry Belafonte, Kay Thompson, Jimmy Durante, Helen Traubel, Sammy Cahn, Joey Bishop, Gene Kelly, Janet Leigh, Peter Lawford, Milton Berle.

"A new happier, emancipated Sinatra… untrammeled, unfettered and unconfined."

ADVERT IN *BILLBOARD*, 1961 ON THE LAUNCH OF REPRISE

the Press opposed to Kennedy's politics used Frank's relationship with the President as fodder for their attacks; it was too early to have anything else to really criticize Kennedy for. The logistics of such an important one-off event would stretch anyone, and Frank and Peter Lawford, despite having a ton of professional help, probably felt the pressure. To cap it all, God appeared to have it in for them. On the day of the Gala, it began snowing heavily and didn't let up all day. While Jack and Jackie Kennedy managed to get to the Gala many guests didn't because Washington traffic was at a standstill. Neither did a whole lot of the orchestra. The show started half an hour late with Leonard Bernstein conducting the opening fanfare. Many of the stars had to wear borrowed clothes or the clothes in which they arrived. Frank appropriately sang 'The House I Live In', others who performed included Harry Belafonte, Joey Bishop, Nat King Cole, Ella Fitzgerald, Gene Kelly, and Juliet Prowse. But there was no place for Sammy; having married Mai Britt he was *persona non grata*. *Time* magazine commented, "Sinatra is to become Ambassador to Italy, Sammy Davis to Kenya or Italy, and Dean Martin Secretary of Liquor."

ON WITH THE SHOW

A week after the President was sworn in, Frank was in New York City for the Carnegie Hall Gala for the Southern Christian Leadership Conference. With many of the stars

SINATRA'S SWINGIN' SESSION

RELEASED IN LATE JANUARY 1961, this is the shortest 12-inch album Frank ever recorded. Every song is brief and really doesn't benefit from it. 'Should I?' clocks in at a mere 1 minute and 30 seconds and each side of the album runs a shade over 13 minutes. Arranged by Nelson Riddle, six of the songs were on the last Columbia album, *Sing and Dance With Frank Sinatra*. It has been mooted that Frank had asked Nelson to speed up the charts. But it was actually the case that Frank simply decided to shorten the songs, mostly by doing one-chorus versions. Maybe he felt he was getting at Capitol by delivering what the contract said but failing to give them value for money.

Despite its short length, the album did well on the American charts and impressed Nat Hentoff, writing in *Stereo Review* in March. "Again the great Sinatra wit and imagination bring new life to old standards. I think Sinatra interprets America's pop songs so memorably because he is an oversize personification of much in American life – gregarious and yet afraid."

SONG LINES

Recorded: The Capitol Tower, Hollywood, 1960. Producer: Dave Cavanaugh. Chart: US No 3, 36 weeks on the chart (first charted 13 February, 1961); UK No 6, 8 weeks on the chart (23 September, 1961).

SIDE 1
1. 'WHEN YOU'RE SMILING' (Fisher, Goodwin & Shay) Recorded 22 August.
2. 'BLUE MOON' (Lorenze Hart & Richard Rodgers) Recorded 1 September.

3. 'S'POSIN'' (Denniker & Razaf) Recorded 22 August.
4. 'IT ALL DEPENDS ON YOU' (Brown, DeSylva & Henderson) Recorded 23 August.
5. 'IT'S ONLY A PAPER MOON' (Arlen, Harburg & Rose) Recorded 31 August.
6. 'MY BLUE HEAVEN' (Donaldson & Whiting) Recorded 23 August.

SIDE 2
1. 'SHOULD I?' (Brown & Freed) Recorded 22 August.

2. 'SEPTEMBER IN THE RAIN' (Dubin & Warren) Recorded 31 August.
3. 'ALWAYS' (Irving Berlin) Recorded 23 August.
4. 'I CAN'T BELIEVE THAT YOU'RE IN LOVE WITH ME' (Gaskill & McHugh) Recorded 23 August.
5. 'I CONCENTRATE ON YOU' (Cole Porter) Recorded 22 August.
6. 'YOU DO SOMETHING TO ME' (Cole Porter) Recorded 22 August.

INAUGURAL DATE
Frank escorts the First Lady, Jackie Kennedy on the night of JFK's Inaugural Gala, 19 January 1961.

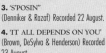

who had appeared at the Presidential Inaugural Gala taking up the first half of the event, the second half was given over to Frank, Sammy, and Dean. Sy Oliver conducted the orchestra for Frank, and the show closed with Harry Belafonte introducing Dr Martin Luther King to the rapturous crowd. (He had recently been freed from jail by presidential decree.) Looking back, it is difficult to comprehend how close the Kennedys allowed Frank to get to them, since aligning themselves with someone who had a far from perfect image was a high-risk strategy. Did it add votes? It is hard to say; but, as we now appreciate, things were not all they seemed in the Kennedy camp.

From New York, Frank flew straight to Las Vegas for a two-week run at The Sands beginning on 1 February, where the talk was all about Frank and the ex-Mrs DiMaggio, Marilyn Monroe. Marilyn was

RING-A-DING DING!

THE TITLE was one of Frank's hip expressions, one he would sometimes use on stage when he could not recall a song's lyrics. Considering that this was his first album for Reprise, it must have been a disappointment. Although it reached No 4 on the charts, he must have been hoping, even expecting, something higher. By way of a talisman, the album's title track was a Van Heusen and Cahn composition. Unlike the Capitol albums, there is no thematic template, and it's much like Frank's world at this time – more flash than substance.

This fact should not take anything away from Johnny Mandel's arrangements, however, which are great. He explained the background to the album: "The idea was to have an album with no ballads. There was one song 'Have You Met Miss Jones?' that they wanted to do, but it just didn't work as swing. Bill Miller, Frank, and I met to discuss things for the album – just keys, tempo, and feel. Frank detested rehearsals. He was very much a one-take man. He'd save up his energy, and use the adrenaline from the people that he would have there in the studio. He liked having an audience there to work off. He was still a café singer, and those guys are used to working without nets! I'd come from Buddy Rich and Count Basie, and much of my work was with the harmonics. I'd fool around harmonically. I'd try to make it so that you didn't notice things – keep the focus where it should be,

on the singer. So the focus would be on the words. And Sinatra was the greatest of the Twentieth Century! One good example of his musicality was to have the two bar break after the verse on 'Let's Fall in Love'. The verse of that song never usually gets done. He suggested the break, right off the cuff, and he was totally right."

Stereo Review compared *Sinatra's Swingin' Session* in a not entirely favourable way: "Frank Sinatra comes off a little bit better in the Capitol recording than he does in his initial effort for his own recently formed company. The lush romantic backgrounds furnished by the Billy May band for Capitol are much more compatible with Sinatra's warm, expressive singing than are jazz arranger Johnny Mandel's surprisingly routine orchestrations on the Reprise tape. This, however, is the major difference between the two collections, for Sinatra is at his effortless, propulsive best on both."

there on a number of nights, and whatever else went on between the two stars, there was talk of them appearing together in a musical remake of *Born Yesterday*. What was also interesting was how the public reacted to seeing Frank. According to band leader Ray Anthony, "I was walking with him from the main room to the lounge, and it was unbelievable how people liked to touch him, or they liked to call him Frankie like they knew him. He put up with it very well." But as Bill Miller saw it, rather than putting up with it, "Frank liked the idolatry." After two weeks off, Frank opened at the Fontainebleau, where he gave an interview to Joe Hyams in which he talked of how he saw his future. He acknowledged that by the time he was 50 (just five years away), entertainment would be taking a back seat to business: "The things I'm involved in personally, such as acting and recording, steadily earn less money while the things I have going for me earn most. And that's the way I want it to be." For the moment, though, there was no let up, as Frank went straight back to Los Angeles after his Miami gig to begin working on his next Reprise and Capitol albums. On 20 March, he and Sy Oliver began work on an album in memory of Tommy Dorsey. Later in the day he cut four more with Billy May for his follow-up to *Swingin' Session*. There has been speculation over the years that the cooling of relations between Frank and JFK that occurred around

SONG LINES

Recorded by: United Recorders, Los Angeles
Chart : US No 4, 35 weeks on the chart,
(First charted 5 January, 1961). UK No 8, 9
weeks on the chart (16 December, 1961).

SIDE 1

1. 'RING-A-DING DING'
(Sammy Cahn & Jimmy Van Heusen)
Recorded 19 December.

2. 'LET'S FALL IN LOVE'
(Harold Arlen & Ted Koehler) Recorded
19 December.

3. 'BE CAREFUL, IT'S MY HEART'
(Irving Berlin) Recorded 20 December,
arranged by Skip Martin.

4. 'A FOGGY DAY'
(George & Ira Gershwin) Recorded
19 December.

5. 'A FINE ROMANCE'
(Dorothy Fields & Jerome Kern) Recorded
20 December.

6. 'IN THE STILL OF THE NIGHT'
(Cole Porter) Recorded 19 December.

SIDE 2

7. 'THE COFFEE SONG (THEY'VE
GOT AN AWFUL LOT OF COFFEE
IN BRAZIL)'
(Bob Hilliard & Dick Miles) Recorded
20 December.

8. 'WHEN I TAKE MY SUGAR
TO TEA'
(Pierre Norman Connor, Sammy Fain &
Irving Kahal) Recorded 21 December.

9. 'LET'S FACE THE MUSIC
AND DANCE'
(Irving Berlin) Recorded 20 December.

10. 'YOU'D BE SO EASY TO LOVE'
(Cole Porter) Recorded 20 December.

11. 'YOU AND THE NIGHT
AND THE MUSIC'
(Howard Dietz & Arthur Schwartz) Recorded
21 December.

12. 'I'VE GOT MY LOVE TO
KEEP ME WARM'
(Irving Berlin) Recorded 21 December,
arranged by Dick Reynolds.

United Recorders
Located at 6050 Sunset Boulevard, on the
corner of the Columbia Screen Gems' lot, it
was an old sound stage built by Douglas
Fairbanks. Bill Putnam, who became Frank's
"engineer of choice", owned the studio,
along with Western Recorders. Frank did the
majority of his sessions in United's Studio A,
but sometimes worked in Western's Studio B.

this time was also part of a subtle shift in Frank's public persona. The whole concept of the "Clan" was an anathema to the White House, and to many in Democratic politics. It smacked of elitism, the world of gambling, playboys, hustlers, and ne'er-do-wells; it was an awfully long way from President Kennedy's vision of Camelot. Having said that, there was evidence to suggest that the whole Clan/Summit/Rat Pack concept took on a life of its own, inevitably fuelled by an over-eager press keen to feed their readers' fascination with seeing how the "other half" live, even if it is a very, very small half. Maybe Frank felt that it was his last fling at the high jinx for himself and his friends. If he really was going to become "a businessman", things would inevitably change; and he wasn't getting any younger. Around this time, Frank and the others went to one of Eddie Fisher's shows, and ended up on stage. This met with press criticism, although Eddie Fisher said that he had invited them on stage. Whatever the case, it appears that they were burning themselves out as a gang of friends hanging out together. The jokes inevitably got old and it was time for them to move on.

Before moving along, Frank had already committed to making another movie, a co-production between Frank's Essex productions and Dean's company, Claude. It was, in essence, *Ocean's Eleven* meets *Gunga Din* in the 19th-century US Cavalry. *Sergeants Three* began filming in May in Utah, and carried on both there and in Los Angeles over the next three months. Around this time (perhaps by way of atonement) Frank engaged in several benefit shows. He did one for the American Cancer Society, another for the LA County Sheriff's Rodeo, and would later do another for the Cedars of Lebanon Hospital in July. In April, Frank went to Mexico City. According to saxophonist Ted Nash, "We went to Mexico for a week to do charity dates for hospitals. He took Nelson's band and paid all the band expenses himself – he always liked to have guys around him that he was comfortable with." That's why Dean, Sammy, Joey, Peter, *et al.* were always around.

MOVIE MAN

Filming in Kanab, Utah, which is just north of the Arizona border and today has a population of a little over 3,000, cannot have been much

CONNECTED
Frank, Peter Lawford, and Robert Kennedy when relations were less strained – although given Bobby's expression, perhaps not.

THE DEVIL AT 4 O'CLOCK

RELEASED ON 16 JULY, this film went almost unnoticed by critics and public alike. On a small volcanic Pacific island, Father Donovan (Spencer Tracy) calls for volunteers to rescue a party of child lepers trapped in the hills. Frank plays a criminal who, along with two colleagues and Tracy, is parachuted in to affect the rescue. The film covers their journey back, Frank falling in love with a blind hospital worker, and a subtext about the existence of God!

If America was none too keen, there was one reviewer in Britain who was more enthusiastic. On its November release, the *NME* said, "Although slightly over-sentimental, the film comes off well, mostly due to messrs Sinatra and Tracy."

THE SCREEN ERUPTS WITH A NEW HIGH IN EXCITEMENT AND ADVENTURE!

COLUMBIA PICTURES presents

SPENCER TRACY AND FRANK SINATRA

THE DEVIL AT 4 O'CLOCK

fun. In the late 19th century, it was described as: "The village which had been started only a year or two was laid out in the characteristic Mormon style. The entire settlement had a thrifty air, as is the case with the Mormons. Not a grog-shop or gambling saloon, or dance hall was to be seen." This was not, however, the first movie shot around the town. In 1922, Tom Mix filmed *Deadwood Coach* here, with the nearby Vermillion Cliffs as a backdrop, and many other Westerns followed. Even so, Kanab had probably never seen anything like Dean Martin's 44th birthday party on 7 June, and probably has not since. Elizabeth Taylor and Marilyn Monroe, among others, were at the party, which halted filming for a couple of days.

In midsummer, Frank and Dean were in England filming cameo appearances as spacemen in Hope and Crosby's *The Road to Hong Kong*. On 7 August, the pair played a show in Frankfurt. Meanwhile, in the US, there was further press speculation at the demise of the Clan; there was even a televised debate featuring, among others, Toots Shor, Jackie Gleason, and Ernie Kovacs. Frank was getting more and more annoyed with the whole sorry mess. It got in the way of him being taken seriously – and not just by the President. Frank's desire to build a business base was clearly at odds with the high-school antics of the group. As an intelligent man, Frank could see that things were getting increasingly out of control. It may have begun to feel like a 10-year rehash of his earlier downfall. His share in The Sands increased to nine per cent in August, and he also

JULIET'S TONTO
Born in Bombay on 26 September, 1936, Juliet Prowse trained as a ballet dancer but grew too tall, and began working as a chorus girl at London's Palladium. She starred opposite Elvis Presley in GI Blues *in 1961, but became a more successful nightclub performer than film star before starring on stage in musicals such as* Sweet Charity. *She died in 1994, nine days short of her 60th birthday.*

> **"Soothing but exciting is how Sinatra sings swing."**
>
> **NEW MUSICAL EXPRESS, FEBRUARY 1962**

bought the Cal-Neva Lodge through his Park Lake Enterprises, 50 per cent of which was owned by Frank, a third by Hank Sanicola, and the remainder by another.

Frank's first session for his last Capitol album was on Monday 11 September; he cut six songs and did the same the following night. The orchestra was conducted by Axel Stordahl, which brought perfect symmetry to Frank's career at the label. Axel and Heine Beau, who both worked on Frank's first Capitol session eight years earlier, arranged all 12 songs. Others who had been at the first session included pianist Bill Miller, trumpeter Zeke Zarchy, saxophonist Ted Nash, and old friends the Slatkins, who had not worked that first session but had done nearly every other. Fifty years later, Ted Nash put into perspective what Axel did for Frank in the early days: "Axel really set Frank up on his own – he was a great strong writer who sent him into orbit." Two years after making this album, Axel would be dead. There is little doubt that Frank did this album for Axel, and he deserved it. It certainly would have been

lucrative work at a time when Axel was not doing much else. British author Robin Douglas-Home was at the first session, and commented: "All heads turned to the door. In sauntered Sinatra. He wore a well cut dark grey suit; a dark grey felt hat crowned him jauntily; a red and yellow handkerchief peeked perkily from his breast pocket." Douglas-Home goes on to describe Frank's wonderful involvement with each song; perhaps the most amazing revelation is that Frank kept his hat on throughout the recording. "His hat was a barometer of his feelings – pulled down over his eyes when he was concentrating, pushed back on his crown when he was relaxing between takes."

Frank's Dorsey album, *I Remember Tommy*, came out in October and reached No 3 on the album charts, one place better than his Reprise debut. It was the same position as *Sinatra's Swingin' Session*, and considerably better than his other mainstream Capitol album, *Come Swing with Me*, which reached only No 8. But there was a downturn in Frank's performance on the album charts. From the success of the last three or four years of the 1950s, when albums reached No 1, there was nothing to match it in 1961. The only album that spent time on the charts to match the longevity of those earlier albums was Capitol's *All the Way*, a collection of some of

SINATRA SWINGS

THIS ALBUM and *Come Swing With Me*, both Billy May arrangements, were released at the same time, and entered the *Billboard* album chart the same week. Capitol's album, with its familiar-sounding title *Come Swing With Me*, made No 8, two places below Frank's Reprise offering. Originally the latter was called *Swing Along With Me* but Capitol sued and Frank changed it to *Sinatra Swings*. In terms of sales the Capitol album did somewhat better, spending 39 weeks on the charts; *Sinatra Swings* notched up 22. *Sinatra Swings* sold around 150,000 copies whereas his Capitol albums were selling over 500,000, ample evidence of how clever Alan Livingston had been.

> **"Sinatra did not just swing, he overhauled the entire genre…his craft, discipline and approach… is impeccable and as yet unrivalled by any artist of comparable stature."**
>
> **ANDRÉ PREVIN**

THE CAL-NEVA

You could swim from Nevada to California if the urge took you, as the pool straddled the state line. Frank's company upgraded the Lodge soon after completing its purchase.

SONG LINES

Recorded: United Recorders. Chart: US No 6, 22 weeks on the chart. First charted 14 August, 1961; UK No 8, 8 weeks on the chart (28 October, 1961).

SIDE 1

1. 'FALLING IN LOVE WITH LOVE' (Lorenz Hart & Richard Rodgers) Recorded 19 May, 1961.

2. 'THE CURSE OF AN ACHING HEART' (Henry Fink & Al Piantadosi) Recorded 18 May, 1961.

3. 'DON'T CRY JOE (LET HER GO, LET HER GO)' (Joe Marsala) Recorded 23 May, 1961.

4. 'PLEASE DON'T TALK ABOUT ME WHEN I'M GONE' (Sidney Clare & Sam Stept) Recorded 18 May, 1961.

5. 'LOVE WALKED IN' (George & Ira Gershwin) Recorded 18 May, 1961.

6. 'GRANADA' (Dorothy Dodd & Agustin Lara) Recorded 23 May, 1961.

SIDE 2

1. 'I NEVER KNEW' (Ted Fiorito & Gus Kahn) Recorded 19 May, 1961.

2. 'DON'T BE THAT WAY' (Benny Goodman, Mitchell Parish & Edgar Sampson) Recorded 19 May, 1961.

3. 'MOONLIGHT ON THE GANGES' (Sherman Myers & Chester Wallace) Recorded 23 May, 1961.

4. 'IT'S A WONDERFUL WORLD' (Harold Adamson, Jan Savitt & Johnny Watson) Recorded 19 May, 1961.

5. 'HAVE YOU MET MISS JONES?' (Lorenz Hart & Richard Rodgers) Recorded 18 May, 1961.

6. 'YOU'RE NOBODY 'TIL SOMEBODY LOVES YOU' (James Cavanaugh, Russ Morgan & Larry Stock) Recorded 23 May, 1961.

Frank's greatest hits, including the title song, 'Witchcraft', and 'High Hopes'. And it was not a case of the younger artists dominating the charts – apart from Elvis, who had two chart-toppers, it was the music of Frank's generation that was the most successful, with Judy Garland, Lawrence Welk, Bert Kaempfert, Enoch Light, and a clutch of soundtrack albums all reaching No 1. Frank's performance on the Hot 100 was no better. His best performing single was 'Pocketful of Miracles', recorded for Reprise, which made No 34 in 196. Frank could only manage 19 weeks on the Hot 100 in 1961, the same as in 1960.

PLAY AND PLAY AGAIN

One could certainly argue that Frank's 1961 output represented quantity not quality, and the public must have been somewhat confused. The weeks that Frank's six albums spent on the *Billboard* Top 40 added up to 155, just one less than his outstanding performance in 1959, and 11 more than 1958. But it is irrefutable that the quality of his early 1960s albums did not compare to the Capitol classics. All the post-rationalisation by Sinatra's dedicated fans cannot change the facts: the diversity of Frank's career was probably to blame, that and the fact that artists should not run their own labels.

The issues that Frank and Reprise were facing went back to Frank's argument with Capitol and Alan Livingston over his deal in the summer of 1959. Frank wanted control but ironically ended up losing it, and this was no better illustrated than when Reprise signed the Electric Prunes in 1966. Alan Livingston was an astute businessman and went to work on Frank: "I killed him. I put out so many Sinatra albums. I'd go into the catalogue, find released masters and unreleased masters and put together combinations of records that were

COME SWING WITH ME

THIS ALBUM COMBINES the fun of *Come Fly with Me* and the dance rhythms of *Come Dance With Me*, but it lacks the overall appeal of either. The stereo mix on *Come Swing with Me* is not everyone's taste. There is too much boost on some of the brass punctuation that sends the sound way out "in front" of Frank's voice. That said, some tracks sound much better than others. 'That Old Black Magic' is a great, whereas 'Lover' has bouncing brass rather than slurping saxes! *Sinatra Swings* is the better set; it has a lightness of touch missing on the Capitol effort. It also features strings and saxes, whereas *Come Swing with Me* has neither.

SONG LINES

Recorded: Capitol Tower. Chart: US No 8, 39 weeks on the chart. First charted 14 August, 1961; UK No 13, 4 weeks on the chart (17 February, 1962).

SIDE 1

1. 'DAY BY DAY'
(Sammy Cahn, Axel Stordahl & Paul Weston) Recorded 20 March, 1961.

2. 'SENTIMENTAL JOURNEY'
(Les Brown, Bud Green & Ben Homer) Recorded 20 March, 1961. This is one of the tracks that works best on the album. It was a No 1 in 1945 for Les Brown and His Orchestra with Doris Day on vocals.

3. 'ALMOST LIKE BEING IN LOVE'
(Alan Lerner & Frederick Loewe) Recorded 22 March, 1961.

4. 'FIVE MINUTES MORE'
(Sammy Cahn & Jule Styne) Recorded 22 March, 1961.

5. 'AMERICAN BEAUTY ROSE'
(Arthur Altman, Mack David & Redd Evans) Recorded 21 March, 1961. Frank's first version was with Columbia in 1950 and this second version, arranged by Heine Beau, was better but it still sounds corny – made more so with the stereo effects.

6. 'YES, INDEED!'
(Sy Oliver) Recorded 21 March, 1961.

SIDE 2

1. 'ON THE SUNNY SIDE OF THE STREET'
(Dorothy Fields & Jimmy McHugh) Recorded 20 March, 1961.

2. 'DON'T TAKE YOUR LOVE FROM ME'
(Henry Nemo) Recorded 20 March, 1961.

3. 'THAT OLD BLACK MAGIC'
(Harold Arlen & Johnny Mercer) Recorded 21 March, 1961. This was the third recording of one of Frank's concert and radio perennials.

4. 'LOVER'
(Lorenz Hart & Richard Rodgers) Recorded 22 March, 1961.

5. 'PAPER DOLL'
(Johnny Black) Recorded 22 March, 1961. This song dates from 1930 and this was the only time Frank recorded it. It was not particularly worth it – it's a filler.

6. 'I'VE HEARD THAT SONG BEFORE'
(Sammy Cahn & Jule Styne) Recorded 21 March, 1961.

partly songs that had been released and some that hadn't been released. I'd do it by composer and say 'Frank Sings... Whoever' and put out a new album. I flooded the market with Sinatra albums, which they were willing to buy. And when Reprise came in, they said 'we don't need any more Sinatra records. We have more than we can handle.' That hurt him. And I didn't care because I was angry with him. Frank was upset and threatened to sue me and everything else – which he had no basis to do. His contract was very clear. I could put out whatever I wanted. We had total control and we killed Reprise Records." Things got personal, and naturally the lawyers had a field day. "Frank was the worst enemy you could possible have," said Livingston. "When I was having the trouble with him legally, people came to me and said, 'You'd better be careful. You're going to get your knees broken.' They were serious because Frank was not a grateful person, and if he didn't like what you were doing, he'd let you have it." Eventually it all blew over and Reprise had the new-release field to themselves. The last album that Frank owed Capitol was appropriately called *The Point of No Return*, and it would be released in 1962.

On 4 November, Frank flew to Las Vegas on his own plane for his second two-week engagement of the year at The Sands. Occupying the Presidential Suite, Frank held court throughout his stay. Reprise taped a number of shows with a view to releasing a live album, but, apart from several songs that have turned up on bootlegs, the tapes remain in the vaults. From Vegas, it was straight back to Hollywood to work with another new arranger/conductor, Don Costa, on Frank's next Reprise release – *Strings and Things*. A week after the last of the Costa sessions, Frank was down under, starting a new Australian tour at Sydney's Stadium. Frank's concerts were done "in the round", and combined the best from the Capitol years with his early Reprise material.

ALMOST

Back from his Australian tour, Frank spent time wooing Juliet Prowse. Their on-off relationship was very much on again, probably because Juliet had played it fairly cool. On 10 January, 1962, the newspapers carried news of their engagement the night before at Romanoff's. Coming just three days after the

JUDY'S SHOW
Frank and Dean were Judy's guests on her TV show, winter 1962.

premiere of *Sergeants Three*, it helped to diffuse some of the negative press generated by the film. Almost immediately, Frank went to New York to begin filming *The Manchurian Candidate*. The location shots were done at 67 Riverside Drive, at 79th Street, New York City (for Frank's character's apartment interiors/exteriors) and at Madison Square Garden. Long-time press friend Earl Wilson was even surprised to see how much Frank was acting like "an engaged man", a fact that others have disputed. The one thing every reporter agreed on was that Frank was behaving better. One even said, "He's become a lovable fellow."

At the end of January, Frank announced details of his summer world tour, which would benefit various charities in the countries he visited. There was talk of shows in South Africa, where Juliet's family lived, leading to speculation that she and Frank would get married there in June. Juliet returned from a family visit to be reunited with Frank in Los Angeles on Valentine's Day. Despite press speculation that Juliet would not agree to give up her career, which was Frank's condition of marriage, there was a party at Romanoff's. Then, two days later, it was all over. Frank issued a press release saying that their engagement was off; it had lasted a little over six weeks. By all accounts Frank was the most aggrieved of the two. He obviously had very strong feelings for her, but just could not reconcile himself to Juliet continuing to work while she was his wife. Clearly Ava had kept working, and Frank may well have felt that that was part of their problem. The odds are stacked heavily against celebrity marriages, but at the same time Frank's attitude was rooted in the past. He was, however, 46 years old and Juliet Prowse was just 25, only four years older than daughter Nancy. Some months later, Juliet had what were some of the last words on the subject: "I would have married Frank but I've always been a little too difficult for him." With no marriage to distract him, Frank threw himself into work. Sammy Davis Jr commented: "Frank's had longer engagements in Las Vegas".

All in all, 1962 would prove to be an interesting year in which there would be a notable event for Frank: he recorded outside the US for the first time, with foreign musicians. For Frank, who liked consistency, this was a bold move.

Three weeks into the year, in his new role as head of his own label, he addressed a meeting of his sales people, telling them that record companies would have to concentrate on better products and on "integrity in merchandising". He warned that "the public knows what it wants and it's up to the record companies and the entertainer to deliver". His remarks were obviously stimulated by the ongoing battle with Capitol, which was flooding the market with Sinatra records. A few weeks later, Livingston met Frank, who was working on Judy Garland's television special; the animosity between the two former colleagues was palpable. "I went over to NBC one day and... to Judy Garland's dressing room. Frank was in there, as well as Dean Martin. Dean

I REMEMBER TOMMY

Frank's third Reprise album of 1961, and the most successful, had advance orders of 200,000. At the time of its release, Frank said "I tried to sing the songs as he [Dorsey] used to play them on his trombone." You have to believe that he believed it, but with the perspective of time you realize that, despite Sy Oliver's excellent arrangements and the skilled playing of the band, they were no match for the originals.

SONG LINES

Recorded: United Recorders. Chart: US No 3, 42 weeks on the chart (First charted 6 November, 1961); UK No 10, 12 weeks on the chart (7 April, 1962).

SIDE 1

1. 'I'M GETTING SENTIMENTAL OVER YOU'
(George Bassman & Ned Washington)
Recorded 1 May, 1961.

2. 'IMAGINATION'
(Johnny Burke & Jimmy Van Heusen)
Recorded 1 May, 1961.

3. 'THERE ARE SUCH THINGS'
(Stanley Adams, Abel Baer & George Meyer)
Recorded 3/4 May, 1961.

4. 'EAST OF THE SUN (AND WEST OF THE MOON)'
(Brooks Bowman) Recorded 3/4 May, 1961.

5. 'DAYBREAK'
(Adamson & Grofe) Recorded 2 May, 1961.

6. 'WITHOUT A SONG'
(Eliscu, Rose & Youmans) Recorded 2 May, 1961.

SIDE 2

1. 'I'LL BE SEEING YOU'
(Sammy Fain & Irving Kahal) Recorded 1 May, 1961.

2. 'TAKE ME'
(Bloom & David) Recorded 1 May, 1961.

3. 'IT'S ALWAYS YOU' (Johnny Burke & Jimmy Van Heusen) Recorded 3–4 May, 1961

4. 'POLKA DOTS AND MOONBEAMS' (Johnny Burke & Jimmy Van Heusen) Recorded 2 May, 1961.

5. 'IT STARTED ALL OVER AGAIN'
(Bill Carey & Carl Fischer) Recorded 3–4 May 1961.

6. 'THE ONE I LOVE (BELONGS TO SOMEBODY ELSE)' (Isham Jones & Gus Kahn) Recorded 3–4 May 1961.

7. 'I'M GETTING SENTIMENTAL OVER YOU' (REPRISE) (George Bassman & Ned Washington) Recorded 1 May, 1961.

shook my hand. Judy gave me a kiss. Frank turned his back on me. He wouldn't talk to me. He was so angry at what I had done. We put out so many Sinatra records and had them on special price that the stores were loaded. When Reprise came in with their product, they would say we got all the Sinatra albums we can handle. They couldn't sell them." Just to rub salt into the wound, Capitol (we can assume it was Livingston) refused Judy Garland permission to record an album with Frank and Dean for Reprise.

Not that it was all work: comedienne Elaine Stritch recalled going to dinner at Frank's home in Palm Springs with a group of Hollywood's finest. They were gathered to watch Frank on television, and as he finished singing 'The Lady Is a Tramp', everyone whooped with delight. Stritch misjudged the mood of the moment and shouted "Yeah!... That man can still sing." An uneasy silence followed. As they were about to sit down to eat, Frank sidled up to Elaine and said "I hear that you're on Broadway... you just ain't goin' anywhere." She compounded her *faux pas* by saying "And tell me, Mr. Sinatra, where precisely are you 'going' these days?" "Get this broad out of here," said Frank, and she spent the rest of the evening eating hamburgers with Frank's chauffeur in a diner. Nearly 30 years later, when Elaine Stritch was big on Broadway, she ran into Frank at a restaurant. "Excuse me, Mr. Sinatra, but I wonder if you remember me?" "Sure, you're that broad who wasn't goin' no place." They then had a wonderful dinner together.

PRESIDENTIAL PROBLEMS

Frank's first sessions of the year had been in mid-January, when he was reunited with Gordon Jenkins cutting songs for an album to be called *All Alone*. Their first session was on 15 January; earlier in the day he had been a pallbearer at Ernie Kovac's funeral. The first song he cut around 8:30 pm was 'The Song is Ended'. Work continued over the next two nights. Around midnight on 27 February, Frank did 'Everybody's Twistin' (an early attempt to cash in on a younger generation's music) and 'Nothing But the Best' for release as a Reprise single. On 6 March, Frank's second session after his broken engagement, he once again provided his own soundtrack. He cut 'I've Got a Right to Sing the Blues' with Skip Martin and followed it with a Cahn/Van Heusen song called 'The Boys' Night Out'. The first song was needed for a Capitol album called *Sinatra Sings of Love and Things*. Frank recorded this one extra song at United Recorders because he refused to set foot inside the Capitol Tower. The album was another Livingston special of old Capitol singles, not one of the five to fulfil Frank's Capitol contract. Capitol had insisted that contractually Frank still owed them one more single; adding it to the album provided a useful extra selling point. In an almost identical, yet unconscious, reprise of Frank's last Columbia session, Frank finished his song with Skip Martin and said, "All right, that's all." According to author Chuck Granata, "Sinatra's petulance was plain to

THE END OF THE DREAM
The plot was thin, but as someone said, "It's a great film to watch if you ignore the antics of the actors." According to Variety, "his Cub Scout troupe are pioneering in a new art form: the $4 million home movie."... ouch!

PALM SPRINGS
The desert playground that Frank called home for more than 40 years.

1958–1962

CELEBRITY EATERY
Frank and Peter owned this Beverly Hills restaurant before they drifted apart.

❝He was not really a person, but a myth.❞
DAVID JACOBS, *NEW MUSICAL EXPRESS*, 8 JUNE, 1962

everyone at the studio that night." Frank was not just singing the blues, the air was blue and Frank was not just annoyed with Capitol. There was another situation that had got to Frank, got to him probably more than the broken engagement, the conniving of Capitol, and the bad press for *Sergeants Three* and the Rat Pack in general. Frank had been snubbed. President Kennedy was due to spend the night at Frank's home on Frank Sinatra Drive in Palm Springs; Frank had begun to refer to it as the "West Coast White House". The President's brother, Robert, who was also Attorney General, saw Jack and Frank's relationship as one fraught with potential pitfalls. Knowing what we know now he was probably right. While Jack loved the showbiz glitz Robert was more cautious. Others have said it was the Secret Service that vetoed Frank's home, but Robert was all in favour. After Frank had modified his home to accommodate the presidential entourage it was decided that they shouldn't stay there. If that wasn't enough the President went and stayed with Bing Crosby in Palm Desert. Who said what and who was to blame hardly mattered: Frank was mad, especially as Bing probably voted for Richard Nixon! To make it even worse, Jimmy Van Heusen had offered the Kennedy's "overflow" accommodation at his Palm Springs house. Granata interviewed Billy May about the incident: "Then it came to do the second song, 'Cathy', Frank did a rehearsal and then looked at Van Heusen and said, 'Tell you what, Chester, why don't you get Jack Kennedy to record this fucking song and see how many it sells." Frank walked out and never did cut the song. He also issued a snub of his own to the President when he asked Frank to sing at a dinner honouring Florida Senator George Smathers. After agreeing to be in Miami for the 10 March event Frank, with two days notice, cried off with laryngitis. Later in the month he did go to Miami and had dinner with his old friend Joe Fischetti at Puccini's Restaurant on 79th Street. We know all this because the FBI taped his conversation as part of their ongoing anti-racketeering investigations – Frank continued to fascinate the Bureau and its head, J Edgar Hoover.

FRANKIE'S PLANE

Four weeks after his late night walk-out, Frank was back at United Recorders, this time with Neil Hefti (who in 1966 would win a Grammy for composing the theme to *Batman*), to begin work on an album called *Sinatra and Swingin' Brass*. It would be Frank's seventh and last album with "swing" or "swinging" in the title, and would be the least successful. It made No 18 on the *Billboard* chart. Ironically, for everyone else the real "swinging sixties" were just beginning. The session was over in just two days, with Frank cutting six songs each day; his haste was necessitated by preparations for his "world tour".

On 18 April, Frank and some of his regular musicians flew to Japan. Their first date was two days later at Tokyo's Hibaya Park in front of 8,000 people, many of them children. Frank sang wonderful Neil Hefti arrangements backed by the Bill Miller Sextet featuring Emil Richards (vibraphone), Al Viola (guitar), Irv Cottler (drums), Ralph Pana (bass), Harry Klee (flute, sax, clarinet) and Miller on piano. Two more shows followed at the Mikado Theatre in Tokyo, and then it was off to Hong Kong, then Tel Aviv – where he played to 80,000 – followed by Athens, Rome, Milan, and Madrid, before they arrived in London on 30 May for a 1 June midnight show at the Royal Festival Hall. (He had arrived on board his own aircraft, the *Christina*, which he used throughout the tour. Somebody obviously misled the *New Musical Express*, as they reported that Frank's plane was called the *El Dago*!) This was Frank's first London appearance for nine years; his last one was in the immediate aftermath of signing for Capitol. The British press had written extensively about the concerts, creating a high degree of anticipation among the public, and tickets for the Festival Hall were changing hands for ten times their face value. There was not unanimous approval of Frank's performances, however. Pianist Russ Conway, who had seen Frank in concert in America, said, "Sinatra didn't go in for dynamics – he just stood there and sang." The *NME*'s managing director said "he seemed to have the greatest difficulty in retaining his voice for a complete act." But elsewhere in the *NME* the event was called "the musical highlight of the year". There had been talk of a special showing of *Sergeants Three* during Frank's London stay, but he categorically rejected the idea: the Rat Pack was definitely no more.

The DJ David Jacobs, who had interviewed Frank on Radio Luxembourg, was by this time on the BBC. "I was called upon to introduce him. Norman Vaughan did the first half, and it was televised by the ITV network (the following day). There was a problem when Sinatra wanted the first three rows for his guests and they had already been sold. He wanted them to put in another three rows in front of the ones already there. The hall saw this as a problem as the people who had already bought seats would not get what they wanted. I don't know

SPANISH RETURN
Frank played Madrid at the end of May with the Bill Miller-led sextet.

how that was resolved! Before the show, I was ready in my suit and I went to meet him in his dressing room and he was not yet ready, sitting there in his shirtsleeves and underpants with his valet. While I was there, the valet helped him up on to a chair and then onto a table. Then he helped him into trousers with really stiff legs, and a stiff jacket. Once back down he could only walk around like a penguin! It seemed really difficult for him to move well, so I asked him why he did it when he walked like that. He bent over and quietly said to me 'I know my voice is in good order, but when I go onto that stage I don't want to look like you do in your suit!' It was quite a rebuff! When he came onto stage he looked so relaxed, and even sat cross-legged on a stool! Later we shared the same Sackville Street tailor."

Frank's performance in front of Princess Margaret was excellent. "Captivating Sinatra" is how the *NME* saw it. During the concert, Frank talked of "how gratifying" it was to be doing this kind of work. Frank also told the audience that he really was drinking tea and honey, although he did say he would have preferred a whisky. He introduced the band, finishing up with 'Sun Tan Charlie', Bill Miller. After the Festival Hall, Frank played the following night at the Odeon Leicester Square, where actor Peter Sellers introduced him, and then the next night at the Gaumont Hammersmith. Ironically, Nelson Riddle was in England at

SINATRA AND STRINGS

Frank's first album with arranger Don Costa was one of the best of his early Reprise output and remains among the most popular of Frank's albums. It has been said that it is like an updated Axel Stordahl album. Every song is a standard and Frank turns in a really romantic performance with Costa's help. Despite the age of many of the songs, the arrangements make the songs sound much more contemporary. It is interesting that this album demonstrated very clearly the changes taking place between Frank's single releases and his preferred medium. 'Everybody's Twistin'' came out at the same time as *Strings*, and bombed.

SONG LINES

Recorded: United Recorders. Chart: US No 8, 31 weeks on the chart. First charted 17 March, 1962; UK No 6, 20 weeks on the chart (9 June, 1962).

SIDE 1

1. 'I HADN'T ANYONE TILL YOU'
(Ray Noble) Recorded 20 November, 1961.

2. 'NIGHT AND DAY'
(Cole Porter) Recorded 22 November, 1961.

3. 'MISTY'
(Johnny Burke & Erroll Garner) Recorded 21 November, 1961.

4. 'STARDUST'
(Hoagy Carmichael & Mitchell Parish) Recorded 20 November, 1961.

5. 'COME RAIN OR COME SHINE'
(Harold Arlen & Johnny Mercer) Recorded 22 November, 1961. This is one of Frank's best songs from his early Reprise career. The arrangement was so good that it was used on the first of the *Duets* albums in 1993. It was also one of his favourites. He was doing it live right up to his last but one concert, at the Fukuoka Dome, Japan, having first recorded it for a V-Disc in 1946 – that's almost 50 years.

SIDE 2

1. 'IT MIGHT AS WELL BE SPRING'
(Oscar Hammerstein & Richard Rodgers) Recorded 21 November, 1961.

2. 'PRISONER OF LOVE'
(Russ Columbo, Clarence Gaskill & Leo Robin) Recorded 21 November, 1961.

3. 'THAT'S ALL'
(Alan Brandt & Bob Haymes) Recorded 21 November, 1961.

4. 'ALL OR NOTHING AT ALL'
(Arthur Altman & Jack Lawrence) Recorded 22 November, 1961.

5. 'YESTERDAYS'
(Otto Harbach & Jerome Kern) Recorded 20 November 1961.

POINT OF NO RETURN

Far from most people's favourite Frank album of his Capitol years, it was also his least successful mainstream release for the label. It's a lovely collection of ballads and, while it does lack Nelson's Midas touch, it has Frank's hand all over it. The song selection is nostalgic, and totally out of step with the 1960s... but don't let that put you off. As the *NME* said in July 1962, "A collection of haunting ballads sung with the lonely-lost-empty feeling that Sinatra injects into his voice." Axel was very ill with cancer and this was Frank's goodbye to the man to whom he owed so much. Listen to it with that in mind and it sounds a whole lot different.

It's been claimed that Frank was so angry at having to do this album that he literally rushed it, doing just one take on everything and tearing up the music

after each song was finished. For a more accurate and thoroughly enlightening view of its making, read Robin Douglas-Home's book; it tells it like it really was.

SONG LINES

Recorded: The Capitol Tower. Producer: Dave Cavanaugh. Chart: US No 19, 29 weeks on the chart. First charted 21 April, 1962.

SIDE 1

1. 'WHEN THE WORLD WAS YOUNG'
(Johnny Mercer, M Philippe-Gerard & Angela Vannier) Recorded 11 September, 1961. Nostalgia is written all over this album and this song kicks it off perfectly.

2. 'I'LL REMEMBER APRIL'
(Gene DePaul, Pat Johnston & Don Raye) Recorded 12 September, 1961. This was the last song that Frank and Axel ever recorded together. It was written in 1941, a year after they had worked together for the first time in Tommy Dorsey's band.

3. 'SEPTEMBER SONG'
(Maxwell Anderson & Kurt Weill)

Recorded 11 September, 1961.

4. 'A MILLION DREAMS AGO'
(Eddy Howard, Dick Jurgens & Lew Quadling) Recorded 12 September, 1961.

5. 'I'LL SEE YOU AGAIN'
(Noel Coward) Recorded 11 September, 1961. From Noel Coward's musical *Bittersweet*, Frank gave his friend a nice little gift.

6. 'THERE WILL NEVER BE ANOTHER YOU'
(Mack Gordon & Harry Warren) Recorded 11 September, 1961.

SIDE 2

1. 'SOMEWHERE ALONG THE WAY'
(Kurt Adams & Sammy Gallop) Recorded 12 September, 1961.

2. 'IT'S A BLUE WORLD '
(George Forrest & Robert Wright) Recorded 12 September, 1961.

3. 'THESE FOOLISH THINGS (REMIND ME OF YOU) '
(Harry Link, Holt Marvell & Jack Strachey) Recorded 12 September, 1961. First recorded for Frank's Columbia album *The Voice of Frank Sinatra*, this is better than even that wonderful reading. Listening to the piano, you can see why Frank stuck with Bill Miller for so long.

4. 'AS TIME GOES BY'
(Herman Hupfield) Recorded 12 September, 1961. This was the first time that Frank recorded the song that will forever be associated with his friend Humphrey Bogart and the film *Casablanca*.

5. 'I'LL BE SEEING YOU'
(Sammy Fain & Irving Kahal) Recorded 11 September, 1961.

6. 'MEMORIES OF YOU '
(Eubie Blake & Andy Razaf) Recorded 11 September, 1961.

the same time touring with Shirley Bassey. They played an earlier show in London and so Nelson was able to see the Festival Hall gig. From London, Frank flew to Paris for a show on 5 June at the Lido and then one at Olympia two nights later. The last show of the tour was on 9 June in the open air in Monaco, at the invitation of Princess Grace.

OVERSEAS RECORD

From Nice, Frank flew to London to start work on a new album, appropriately to be called *Great Songs From Great Britain*. The first day of recording at CTS Studios, 46 Kensington Gardens Square in London W2 was on Tuesday 12 June. Frank had chosen Robert Farnon to arrange and conduct the 12 songs, all penned by British writers. Farnon recalled, "His voice was not quite at its best. It was tired. But everyone worth knowing was there, all the best musicians – the usual people I worked with that my contractor had called. Frank said 'This is my favourite way of working – in the studio with musicians I know!' When we ran it down, he learnt very quickly, and was easily able to sing with the arrangement, rather than against it. Only the very best can do that. Peggy Lee was one of the only others that could do that. Frank knew instinctively when to stay away from nice instrumental figures, like with the Harry Roche solo on 'Roses'. He could sing high, but when he was tired it just didn't happen. When we were recording 'Roses Of Picardy', his voice was tired and he couldn't get the top note, but after a short rest, he kept on until he had it. At one point he stopped, looked up to the ceiling and said 'Don't just stand up there, come down and help me!' Everyone laughed so much at that!" Clare Torry, a

FRANK IN GREECE
Frank at the Roman Amphitheatre in Athens on 19 May, 1962.

respected British singer and Harry Roche's partner, said "[Harry] played the trombone solo on 'A Nightingale Sung On Berkeley Square'. When they were recording the second take Sinatra fluffed a line near the end, and instead of doing it again, he said to pick it up on the recording, as 'The trombone solo was excellent, so let's save that'. Harry was really pleased!" Among the people at the sessions were journalists, radio people, arrangers, Pye executives (Pye distributed Reprise in Britain), and assorted others, including 22-year-old Tony Hatch, the composer, who supervised the session along with another Pye executive, Alan Freeman. "Sinatra in spite of his status is an extremely easy artist to work with," is how Tony talked about it a few days after the session. "I asked him if it was in order to stop him if he was wrong at any point. He fell over himself to assure me that he saw no point in continuing with a take if there was a slip up." Despite the occasional sense of humour failure in the studio, Frank was, as this shows, invariably very good during sessions. There is no doubt that he held fellow musicians and other professionals in the studio in great esteem, as was confirmed by Fred Deller, who ran the Frank Sinatra Appreciation Society in the 1960s: "There were perhaps up to 100 people sitting around – it was like a concert, but one where Sinatra would stop and start where necessary. I was in the control room with Tony Hatch. Sinatra would come in and listen to playbacks, and it was all very relaxed. What struck me most was his appreciation of the musicians." Even at the very last Capitol session, when he was very upset with the label, Frank remained cordial and polite to Dave Cavanaugh, the Capitol producer.

On both the first two nights, the musicians stood and applauded Frank as the session ended. When it was all over, he had a test pressing of the album delivered to his hotel, and flew to New York on Sunday 17 June. We tend to forget that making records in those days was a much simpler process. Frank always preferred to be in the studio, standing in front of the band singing his songs. In that way, the "mixing" process was vastly curtailed, and it was possible for an artist to make a record in a week, from start to finish. That is what helped to make it all so exciting. Capitol's parent company, EMI, decided to cash in on all the press interest regarding this album, and rush-released an album of their own in July entitled *London by Night*.

The continuing battle of the releases between Reprise and Capitol was having something of an adverse effect on Frank's career. Some in the press even began commenting that Frank was past his peak. In August, *The Melody Maker* noted "one gets the impression he's just recording for the sake of keeping his name on record."

Part of the reason behind the world tour could have been a conscious attempt to distance himself from the whole Rat Pack scenario. Being away for so long certainly kept Frank out of the press. Reporter Joe

CTS STUDIO
Sinatra recording at the CTS Studio, London, in June 1962 – his first recording session outside the US.

1958 1962

SINATRA AND SWINGIN' BRASS

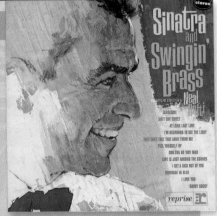

IT HAS BEEN SAID THAT FRANK working with different arrangers was on the advice of Bing Crosby, who believed it made sense to ring the changes, but always ensuring they were the best of the moment. Neil Hefti, who acknowledged Nelson Riddle as his "musical hero", had learned well and at the same time he produced a more modern sound. Hefti, who had arranged for Woody Herman and Count Basie, and Frank, produced some of the best Reprise efforts. Hefti's charts are much less "brassy" than Billy May's, relying heavily on the rhythm sections and innovative horn riffs. *Sinatra and Swingin' Brass* was made *Melody Maker's* album of the year. According to the *NME* in December 1962, it was "the dancingest album Sinatra has ever made". It came out at the same time as Capitol's *Sinatra Sings of Love and Things* and did a little better on the charts.

> ❝ He never removed his hat once during the two sessions, though occasionally he tilted it back on a head of hair that began thinning some years back. ❞
>
> ARNOLD SHAW – ROUGE MAGAZINE OCTOBER

SONG LINES

Recorded: United Recorders. Chart: US No 18, 16 weeks on the chart . First charted 1 September, 1962; UK No 14, 11 weeks on the chart (29 December, 1962).

SIDE 1

1. 'GOODY GOODY'
(Matty Malneck & Johnny Mercer) Recorded 11 April, 1962.

2. 'THEY CAN'T TAKE THAT AWAY FROM ME'
(George & Ira Gershwin) Recorded 10 April, 1962.

3. 'AT LONG LAST LOVE'
(Cole Porter) Recorded 11 April, 1962.

4. 'I'M BEGINNING TO SEE THE LIGHT'
(Duke Ellington, Don George, Johnny Hodges & Harry James) Recorded 10 April, 1962.

5. 'DON'CHA GO 'WAY MAD'
(Illinois Jacquet, James Mundy & Al Stillman) Recorded 11 April, 1962.

6. 'I GET A KICK OUT OF YOU'
(Cole Porter) Recorded 10 April, 1962.

SIDE 2

1. 'TANGERINE'
(Johnny Mercer & Victor Schertzinger) Recorded 11 April, 1962.

2. 'LOVE IS JUST AROUND THE CORNER'
(Lewis Gensler & Leo Robin) Recorded 10 April, 1962.

3. 'AIN'T SHE SWEET '
(Milton Ager & Jack Yellen) Recorded 10 April, 1962.

4. 'SERENADE IN BLUE'
(Mack Gordon & Harry Warren) Recorded 11 April, 1962.

5. 'I LOVE YOU'
(Cole Porter) Recorded 10 April, 1962.

6. 'PICK YOURSELF UP'
(Dorothy Fields & Jerome Kern) Recorded 11 April, 1962.

FRANK AND TONY
Frank in discussion at CTS Studios, London in 1962. The British composer Tony Hatch is seen far left.

Hyams, who often wrote stories "approved by Frank", wrote that "he also wants to play a role in the community, he's very serious about this." He quoted Frank as saying, "Now I'm slowing down. I don't know if it's because I'm getting older, but I'm getting mellower." Back home Frank spoke of how much he enjoyed the experience, and how happy he had been to raise over $1 million for the various charities. He talked of meeting a six-year-old blind girl in hospital. "The wind blew her hair into her eyes and she brushed it back and I told her it was the wind. 'What colour is the wind?' she asked me." Frank paid all the musician's costs, as well as his own, throughout the tour (amounting to $200,000), which considerably increased the benefits to the charities. The Tel Aviv shows were used in a special film called *Sinatra in Israel*, and his British shows were made into a short movie entitled *Frank Sinatra for All God's Children*. As the introduction to the TV special said, "A trip around the world for the benefit of under privileged children by an over privileged adult."

Frank was still causing more than a ripple among the more conservative members of the Southern states. Members of the Ku Klux Klan burned an effigy of Sinatra saying, "Death to nigger lover number one", not that this would have in any way have affected how Frank felt about Sammy or any other of his black friends or musicians. Neither was the devolution of the Rat Pack total. Frank, Dean, and Sammy remained friends, and colleagues at Reprise. Following the Kennedy snub things with Peter Lawford had significantly cooled; Frank saw Lawford as partly to blame for JFK failing to stay with him, although it is hardly credible to believe that he could have had any real influence. The Hollywood restaurant that Frank and Lawford owned had been sold earlier in the year.

When Frank got back from recording in London, he played at his own Cal-Neva Lodge before heading east to the Club 500 in Atlantic City. Frank appeared with Sammy and Dean to help his friend Skinny D'Amato. Atlantic City was on the wane, unable to compete with the legalized gambling in Vegas. It was the last time the three friends ever performed as a trio in Atlantic City. Around the same time, Frank told Joe Hyams "I'm narrowing the field of investments to show business. That interest me. I'm part of it. Anything else bores me and what bores me loses me." He also said "I've been performing about thirty years now and I'm getting lazy. I'd like to have something working for me for a change." Despite Frank's protestations, things at Reprise were not going well.

THE MANCHURIAN CANDIDATE

Aftar the criticisms of *Sergeants Three*, Frank buckled down to work hard on his new film. According to co-star Janet Leigh, "I was amazed how conscientious Frank is and how hard he worked. We had rehearsals before we started shooting and Frank always had suggestions. I think he's an actor who needs a challenge." *Variety* felt the same. "After several pix in which he appeared to be sleepwalking, Sinatra is again a wide awake pro, creating a straight quietly humourous character of some sensitivity." *The New Yorker* said "a thriller guaranteed to raise all but the limpest hair", and were matched by *Variety* in their praise: "Every once in a rare while a film comes along that 'works' in all departments."

Directed by John Frankenheimer, this is considered, by most people, to be Frank's best performance since *The Man with the Golden Arm*. The taut, classic thriller about a GI captured and brainwashed by the Communists into becoming a presidential assassin was released the year before Kennedy's assassination.

At the time, United Artists was worried that the film might encourage a would-be assassin. Conspiracy theorists have suggested that Lee Harvey Oswald, JFK's assassin, saw the film, probably in Dallas in November 1962. UA withdrew *The Manchurian Candidate* from theatres in 1964. In 1972, Frank bought the rights and by 1975 removed it from circulation altogether.

CAST & CREDITS

Bennett Marco	Frank Sinatra
Raymond Shaw	Laurence Harvey
Rosie Chaney	Janet Leigh
Mrs Iselin	Angela Lansbury
Chunjin	Henry Silva
Senator John Iselin	James Gregory
Director	John Frankenheimer
Writer	John Axelrod
	from the novel by Richard Condon
Original music by	David Amram
Cinematographer	Lionel Lindon
Producers	John Frankenheimer &
	George Axelrod

The label's track record of hits was not good. They had launched a lawsuit in the summer against Capitol alleging restraint of trade, but in the custom of such things it was slow moving. In the meantime, Reprise needed to sell records, but Livingston's tactics continued unabated.

In October, two Capitol albums, one of which was a three-record set entitled *The Great Years*, came out at the same time as Frank's new Reprise album. It was clever Capitol marketing and hurtful too, by implying that Frank's best days were over. The Reprise album, *All Alone*, could reach only No 25 on the *Billboard* album chart, and stayed there for just eight weeks. It was Frank's worst-performing album in a decade. While Capitol, in their deposition to the court, admitted that Frank had grossed $30 million for their label, the results at Reprise were far less impressive. Jack Warner, the head of Warner Brothers Pictures and Records, saw an opportunity.

He wanted to sign Frank to a movie deal. Negotiations began and moved slowly, but in the end Frank's share in Reprise was sold to Warner Brothers for $1.5 million, and Frank got a third of the new record company to be called Warner/Reprise. Frank, with Mickey Rudin's help, was turning into quite a businessman, even if things were not quite as he had envisaged them. The new company would officially start in September 1963.

VENICE IN ILLINOIS

During negotiations with Warners, it was business as normal at Reprise. On 2 October, Frank was at United Recording to cut an album with jazz legend Count Basie. On its release in early 1963 it sold better than any other for two years, easing some of the gloom in the Reprise camp. The Basie sessions took three days, and at

ALL ALONE
Arranged by Gordon Jenkins it was to be called 'Come Waltz With Me'. Five of the songs are by Irving Berlin. It made it to just No 25 on the US charts.

SINATRA SINGS GREAT SONGS FROM GREAT BRITAIN

THE IDEA BEHIND THIS ALBUM was a simple one: every song was written by a British composer. It was also unique among Frank's Reprise albums in that it did not get a US release at the time. It had to wait until the CD era before it was remastered to take its rightful place among his canon. According to the *NME*, at the time of the recording, "There was a flurry of activity a month before the album was due to be made when it was discovered that two of the songs Frank planned to record were not in fact written by Brits. 'White Cliffs of Dover' was from the pen of American Walter Kent, and a New Zealander, Clement Scott, wrote 'Now is the Hour.'"

According to the album's arranger, Robert Farnon, "Nelson Riddle was there most of the time. Frank would talk to Nelson and point out things to him like 'Hey, listen to the arrangements of those woodwinds there' – It was almost as if Nelson was in the role of a pupil! We would usually do just one or two takes, sometimes it was a bit longer, but then it was perhaps just redoing certain sections only."

As Frank walked into the studio for the third and final nights recording, he said "You guys are being great to me. It's almost a shame to think you've got to be paid too! Still, Reprise can afford it." When he finished that night he went around and thanked every musician personally.

On Sunday 21 October, Frank played the entire album on the BBC Light Programme with introductions. Despite all this promotion, it was not a big seller in Britain. Given that Frank had come off the back of a gruelling tour, you can hear how his voice struggles on this album. But Frank not quite on song is better than most singers when they are, and when you add Farnon's arrangements it produces a lovely

> 66 He gave, at last, to the handful of outstanding British popular songs, the kind of treatment their virtues deserve. 99

BENNY GREEN – *THE OBSERVER*

album. As Robert Farnon pointed out in 2003, "My arrangements are from the *heart*. I don't just write arrangements, there is also *composition* – much of my work is a complete composition, from my composer's background. [His stresses] Sometimes I would start from the beginning of the song, sometimes I would start from the coda and work back from there… it depended on the song. My arrangements were not geared to Sinatra – they worked from the tune, not the singer." The only disappointment for Frank was that he wanted a picture of his hero Winston Churchill on the cover but permission was refused.

Most reviewers, however, found it a disappointment – *The Melody Maker* was fairly typical: "Sinatra has not exactly pulled out the punches."

the end of the month Frank was again recording with Nelson, working on the soundtrack for his new movie *Come Blow Your Horn*. Early in 1963 Frank and Nelson cut it again for a Reprise single. He also did 'Call Me Irresponsible'. Frank's voice sounds far from good as he tackles a number of retakes. Mid way through one take he sings, "call me wrong note irresponsible" as his voice falters. Before take 16, Frank, who had been less than his best on the others, said, "If they don't get it, I'm gonna cry." Frank could not bring himself to criticize the players nor could he admit his own difficulties.

In October, one of Frank's longest relationships came to an end when he and Hank Sanicola parted company. Disagreements over the operation of the Cal-Neva Lodge was given as the reason. Frank took Sanicola's shares in the Cal-Neva and Sanicola got control of Barton Music. Nancy Sinatra expanded on this in her book saying that Frank and Hank had

SONG LINES

Recorded: CTS Studio London. Chart: UK No 12, 9 weeks on the chart. First charted 27 October, 1962.

SIDE 1

1. 'THE VERY THOUGHT OF YOU'
Recorded 12 June, 1962.

2. 'WE'LL GATHER LILACS IN THE SPRING'
(Ivor Novello) Recorded 14 June, 1962.

3. 'IF I HAD YOU'
(Jimmy Campbell, Reg Connelly & Ted Shapiro) Recorded 12 June, 1962.

4. 'NOW IS THE HOUR'
(Maewa Kaihan, Clement Scott & Dorothy Stewart) Recorded 14 June, 1962.

5. 'THE GYPSY'
(Billy Reid) Recorded 13 June, 1962.

6. 'ROSES OF PICARDY'
(Frederick Weatherly & Hayden Wood) Recorded 13 June, 1962.

SIDE 2

1. 'A NIGHTINGALE SANG IN BERKELEY SQUARE'
(Eric Maschwitz & Manning Sherwin) Recorded 13 June, 1962.

2. 'A GARDEN IN THE RAIN'
(James Dyrenforth & Carroll Gibbons) Recorded 12 June, 1962.

3. 'LONDON BY NIGHT'
(Carroll Coates) Recorded 13 June, 1962.

4. 'WE'LL MEET AGAIN'
(Hugh Charles & Albert Parker) Recorded 12 June, 1962.

5. 'I'LL FOLLOW MY SECRET HEART'
(Noel Coward) Recorded 12 June, 1962.

argued over Sam Giancana visiting the Lodge when the Nevada Gaming Commission had banned him from setting foot in Nevada. Frank was happy that Giancana was there, telling Sanicola that he was only visiting his girlfriend Phyllis McGuire. It obviously went very deep as it broke up a relationship that had lasted longer than any other in Frank's life. With Hank moving out of Frank's life, in came restaurateur Jilly Rizzo.

Frank's desire to be accommodating to Sam Giancana at the Cal-Neva Lodge was reciprocated when Frank, Sammy, and Dean played the Villa Venice Supper Club in Northbrook, Illinois. Apparently, Frank was acknowledging the debt he owed Sam over his help with Kennedy's election. Make no mistake, the Villa Venice is far from one of the great entertainment centres of America; Northbrook is an unpretentious suburb of northern Chicago. The club property covered eight acres and had been recently renovated, including canals with gondolas, each one manned by a gondolier. Two blocks away was the newly built Quonset hut, an illegal gambling casino; limousines shuttled customers back and forth between the club and the casino. Frank and the others worked for free and made Giancana a tidy profit and created great publicity for his opening. Sammy was the second act to play there, after Eddie Fisher. Frank and Dean joined him on November 26. Sixteen shows were recorded with a view to releasing a live album on Reprise. It never did happen and whether this was because the change of management at the label or Frank in any way worrying about the fall out from the Rat Pack days is unclear. Given what was about to happen on the music scene it seems more likely that the world just moved on. The Sinatra family did release it on CD. After the trio had played the club it was closed. Investigators had raided the hut; the crap game had broken up moments before. There was speculation from many quarters as to quite why the place had opened up in the first place. The State's Attorney General told *Variety* "I do not feel the entertainers were aware of the crap game." In Britain Reprise released Frank and Sammy's studio version of 'Me and My Shadow', which just made the Top 20 in December, some 40 places better than it did in the US. With mentions of Toots Shor, *Ring-A Ding Ding* and Bobby and JFK it's classic Rat Pack fodder.

ALL EYES ON FRANK
Frank standing at the mic and Count Basie seated at the piano facing the band on 3 October 1962 at United Recorders in Hollywood.

$\mathcal{T}$HE
MIDDLE AGES

WHEN YOU'VE DONE IT ALL, WHAT IS THERE STILL

TO PROVE? FOR FRANK THERE WAS THE LITTLE

MATTER OF HIS PERSONAL HAPPINESS, AND HE WANTED

TO SHOW THAT HE COULD STILL CONJURE UP SOME

GREAT RECORDS. FRANK STILL HAD COLLATERAL IN

HOLLYWOOD BUT, LIKE HIS RECORDS IN THIS PERIOD,

THE CONSISTENCY OF HIS MOVIES, WHICH WAS ALWAYS

AN ISSUE, BECAME SOMETHING OF A LIABILITY.

AS THE SIXTIES CAME TO A CLOSE FRANK WAS LESS IN

TUNE WITH THE REAL WORLD AND PERHAPS MORE

WILLING TO BE SEDUCED BY A NEW WORLD, HIS OWN

PRIVATE RETIREMENT PLANET.

SOUND STAGE
Frank recording The Concert
Sinatra *at Goldwyn Studios,
Hollywood, in February 1963. It
was the only studio big enough to
accommodate such a large orchestra.*

FILM FUN

According to Nancy Sinatra, Frank went east early in 1963 for Dolly and Marty's 50th wedding anniversary party. He was back in Los Angeles by 21 January for a studio session with Nelson Riddle, and two days later he opened at the Sands with Dean and Sammy; the Summit was once again in session. It would prove to be an eventful year in Frank's relationship with the Desert playground.

MARTIN LUTHER KING, ADDRESSING THE CIVIL RIGHTS
RALLY, WASHINGTON DC, 28 AUGUST, 1963

"Sinatra has managed to sustain his career through the era of the soft crooners, the blasting belters and the after-beat rock 'n' rollers. He is still the singer's singer, the favourite interpreter of show writers ... And he sings with a sense of involvement and an improvisational freshness that makes him the favourite vocalist of most jazzmen"

ROUGE MAGAZINE OCTOBER 1962

By mid-February, Frank was back home in Los Angeles and recording in the studio with Nelson, who was now contractually free of Capitol. The new album that the two old friends were working on was to be called *The Concert Sinatra*. The orchestra that was used was closer to a symphony-size ensemble than a regular studio band, and there were very few studios that could accommodate an orchestra of over 70 players. So, rather than use United Recorders, this and the three subsequent sessions took place on a Goldwyn film studio sound stage.

SERENADING BERLIN
Rosalind Russell, Groucho Marx, Frank, Dinah Shore, Dean Martin, and Danny Kaye singing to Irving Berlin (seated at the piano) at the Beverly Hilton, 3 March 1963.

NO REPRISALS?

Frank's second recording project of the year was a calculated dig at Capitol. When an artist changes labels, their former label has the benefit of retaining their old recordings, and with any luck there is a greatest hits package to be issued and exploited. Frank's novel solution was to remodel his greatest hits himself into a new Reprise album. On 29 April, he and Nelson went into United Recorders and cut some of his Capitol catalogue, along with some songs from the Columbia years too. To emphasize the point, the first song they did was 'In the Wee Small Hours of the Morning'. To prove that this was nothing personal against Capitol, he then did 'Nancy' (from the Columbia era). The recordings from that and the following night would all be included on a Reprise album artfully entitled *Sinatra's Sinatra*.

Coincident with his recording sessions, internal memos were flying back and forth between the FBI office in Los Angeles and the FBI Director's office in Washington. On 24 April, the Los Angeles office sent a detailed memo requesting permission to bug Frank's Palm Springs home. They argued that he was spending more and more time there and was continuing to maintain his friendship with "some of

the more infamous people of modern times". As Frank was cutting 'In the Wee Small Hours of the Morning', the FBI Director mailed his LA office chief saying "Bureau authority not granted." Three weeks later, Frank spent four days at the Surfrider Hotel in Hawaii with Mafia boss Sam Giancana (who would undoubtedly have been included as one of the "infamous people" referred to by the FBI) before starting work on his upcoming film.

Frank then flew from Hawaii to New York via Los Angeles to appear in a benefit for the blind at Carnegie Hall on 19 May. Four days later, he began shooting *4 for Texas*, which co-starred Dean, but not Sammy this time. To add some glamour to what turned out to be a dire movie, Anita Ekberg and Ursula Andress were hired. During the filming, George "Bullets" Durgom, Tommy Dorsey's old road manager, brought the 26-year-old Trini Lopez to meet Frank. Trini had just signed to Reprise and his record was due out in a few weeks. "The first thing on meeting Frank that impressed me was the way he wasn't a bit affected with being Mr. Frank Sinatra," said Trini. Of course he didn't need to be, because everyone else was.

MASKED MEN
John Huston made this film with a gimmick; a number of stars appeared heavily disguised. Frank was a gypsy, finally whipping off his mask to show it was, indeed, him. He was paid $75,000 for this job, which probably took no more than a couple of hours.

SINATRA-BASIE

❝I've waited twenty years for this moment.❞

FRANK, ENTERING UNITED RECORDERS ON 2 OCTOBER, 1962

APPROPRIATELY, THE FIRST SONG Sinatra and Basie cut was 'Nice Work If You Can Get It'. The band charts for this and the other songs were prepared by Neil Hefti. It marked the start of a three-year collaboration with the Count at a time when his reputation had never been higher. The Basie band cooks and swings like no other that Frank had ever sung with, and this was probably the best band that Basie ever put together. So good were the Count's boys that even Frank was put in the shade.

SINATRA-BASIE
AN HISTORIC MUSICAL FIRST

SONG LINES
Recorded : United Recorders, Hollywood
Chart : US No 5, 42 weeks on the chart
(First charted 2 February 1963).

SIDE 1
1. 'PENNIES FROM HEAVEN'
(Arthur Johnston & Johnny Burke) Recorded 3 October, 1962.
2. 'PLEASE BE KIND'
(Saul Chaplin & Sammy Cahn) Recorded 2 October, 1962 .
3. '(LOVE IS) THE TENDER TRAP'
(Jimmy Van Heusen & Sammy Cahn) Recorded 3 October, 1962.
4. 'LOOKING AT THE WORLD THROUGH ROSE COLORED GLASSES'
(Jimmy Steiger & Tommy Maile) Recorded 3 October, 1962.
5. 'MY KIND OF GIRL'
(Leslie Bricusse) Recorded 3 October, 1962.

SIDE 2
1. 'I ONLY HAVE EYES FOR YOU'
(Harry Warren & Al Dubin) Recorded 3 October, 1962.
2. 'NICE WORK IF YOU CAN GET IT'
(George & Ira Gershwin) Recorded 2 October, 1962.
3. 'LEARNIN' THE BLUES'
(Delores Silvers) Recorded 2 October, 1962.
4. 'I'M GONNA SIT RIGHT DOWN (AND WRITE MYSELF A LETTER)'
(Fred Ahlert & Joe Young) Recorded 3 October, 1962.
5. 'I WON'T DANCE'
(Jerome Kern, Dorothy Fields, Oscar Hammerstein II, Otto Harbach) Recorded 2 October, 1962.

THE CONCERT SINATRA

THIS ALBUM COULD ALMOST have been called *Frank Sings Richard Rodgers*, since six of the eight songs come from his pen and one of his writing partners, Oscar Hammerstein II or Lorenz Hart. For many this is one of Frank's most fulfilling albums of his early Reprise career. The huge orchestra cushioned Frank's vocals, and Nelson's effective arrangements offer a unique setting for some of the best songs from the American songbook. It was Nelson's favourite Reprise album, and it is easy to hear why. It is worth buying just for 'I Have Dreamed', one of Frank and Nelson's greatest collaborations.

THE CONCERT SINATRA
ARRANGED AND CONDUCTED BY NELSON RIDDLE
I HAVE DREAMED • MY HEART STOOD STILL • LOST IN THE STARS • OL' MAN RIVER
YOU'LL NEVER WALK ALONE • BEWITCHED • THIS NEARLY WAS MINE • SOLILOQUY
FROM CAROUSEL

reprise

SONG LINES

Recorded : Goldwyn Studios, Hollywood
Chart : US No 6, 35 weeks on the chart
(First charted 2 June 1963).
UK No 8, 18 weeks on the chart
(First charted 27 July, 1963)

SIDE 1

1. 'I HAVE DREAMED'
(Oscar Hammerstein & Richard Rodgers)
Recorded 19 february, 1963
The perfect opening number. Frank gets you in the mood with a vocal that hits the spot.

2. 'MY HEART STOOD STILL'
(Lorenz Hart & Richard Rodgers) Recorded

18 February, 1963

3. 'LOST IN THE STARS'
(Maxwell Anderson & Kurt Weill)
Recorded 18 February, 1963
Frank first did this beautiful song back in 1946. With its message of racial equality it was right on message back then, and so too in 1963. Two days after Frank recorded it, the Supreme Court released 187 black men jailed for protesting against segregation.

4. 'OL' MAN RIVER'
(Oscar Hammerstein & Jerome Kern)
Recorded 18 February, 1963

SIDE 2

1. 'YOU'LL NEVER WALK ALONE'
(Oscar Hammerstein & Richard Rodgers)
Recorded 19 February, 1963

2. 'BEWITCHED, BOTHERED AND BEWILDERED'
(Lorenz Hart & Richard Rodgers)
Recorded 20 February, 1963

3. 'THIS NEARLY WAS MINE'
(Oscar Hammerstein & Richard Rodgers)
Recorded 19 February, 1963

4. 'SOLILOQUY'
(Oscar Hammerstein & Richard Rodgers)
Recorded 21 February, 1963
Frank cut this on his fourth night on the trot at the Goldwyn Sound Stage — he sounds tired, but it's still one hell of a performance.

PARAMOUNT PANNED

Norman Lear's adaptation for Paramount of Neil Simon's first hit stage play met with a scathing press. New York Times was probably the worst: "a feeling of vapid boredom" is how their film critic summed it up.

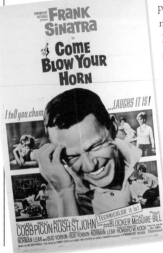

ever appeared on Broadway (with the exception of Sammy Davis Jr), but, since they were required only to sing, not to perform, this did not matter, and Frank had certainly chosen some of the best voices around. Besides Frank, Dean, and Sammy, there was Bing, Jo Stafford, Rosemary Clooney, The Hi-Los, the McGuire Sisters, and Debbie Reynolds. Frank's idea was to create the ultimate "cast album" for each of the shows; and if he did not entirely succeed, he got very close, even though he often switched a song's gender to suit his idea of who should sing what. One of the more interesting couplings was Phyllis McGuire singing 'I Hate Men' from *Kiss Me Kate*.

Recording on the Repertory Theatre project finished on July 31. Eight days later, Frank met with the Nevada Gaming Control Board in Las Vegas regarding his relationship with Sam Giancana, whose name was one of the eleven in the "Nevada Black Book", all of whom were forbidden from entering any casino in the state. If an establishment flouted the law, it risked losing its licence. The Board knew that Frank had transgressed. He spent

THEATRE CALL
Frank, Sammy, and Dean working together in the studio on the Reprise Repertory Theatre project, July 1963.

Ironically, 'If I Had a Hammer' became Reprise's best-selling single when it got to No 3 in September, just a few weeks before the Warner's takeover.

THE GREAT WHITE WAY

With filming of his latest cowboy caper almost over, Frank began work on one of his most unusual recording projects, one that he thought would give Reprise a much-needed boost. Throughout Frank's career in the 1940s and 1950s, much of his recorded output were songs that got their start in Broadway shows, some going back to the 1920s. His ambitious venture was the recording of the musical scores of four of the best Broadway musicals. The twist was to use not just Frank but also other Reprise artists on the recordings. The four shows were *Finian's Rainbow* (1947); *Kiss Me Kate* (1948), *South Pacific* (1949), and *Guys and Dolls* (1950). Frank's first session, along with Morris Stoloff, the project's MD, was on 19 July, when he cut 'We Open in Venice' from *Kiss Me Kate* and 'Guys and Dolls'; the same evening, Dean Martin also did a couple of numbers. Interestingly, none of the people who played on these four albums had

much of the next five weeks in Vegas, during which time he topped the *Cashbox* poll for Best Male Vocalist (Ray Charles was second, followed by Tony Bennett, Andy Williams, and Elvis). He was an ever-present item in the local press over the Board's investigation prior to the Summit being back at the Sands for two weeks on 23 September.

While Frank had been recording in Los Angeles, Giancana was staying at the Cal-Neva, which Frank admitted. He said he ran into him coming out of the cabin belonging to Phyllis McGuire, one of the McGuire Sisters. The Mob man from Chicago had been having an affair with Phyllis, and during his stay he got into a fight with the sisters' manager, which escalated into a mass brawl. The Nevada Gaming Control Board got wind of what had happened, courtesy of the FBI, and began an investigation. Frank's position was made worse when Skinny D'Amato, who was working for the Cal-Neva, offered a Board investigator a $100 bribe. At the Board meeting on

OFF BROADWAY

Frank saved most of the best songs for himself, including 'Old Devil Moon' from Finian's Rainbow and 'This Nearly was Mine' from South Pacific. He let 60-year-old Bing sing 'Younger than Springtime'.

8 August, Frank was both dismissive and truculent and was given two months to respond to the charges and to prove his innocence. If he failed, they told him that he would be stripped of his 10-year-old gaming licence.

By October, Frank had decided not to contest the Board's charges, in the certainty that he would lose. And so on 22 October, at Carson City, Frank's licence was revoked and he was given until 5 January, 1964 to divest himself of his holdings in Las Vegas and Lake Tahoe. As usual, some columnists revelled in Frank's problems, while others took a more lenient view, saying that it was all rather hypocritical. One of the most indignant was, rather surprisingly, Robert Ruark, the man who had broken the Havana story in 1947. "For Nevada to go high and mighty and bust the Voice's license is the absolute Chinese end." He went on to mix his metaphors still further, and managed to get morality, bigotry, and harlotry in the same column! You really have to wonder why Frank was singled out, other than to set him up as an example of what could happen if people stepped out of line: if it happened to Frank, it could happen to you.

LIKE FATHER

Before Frank's final humiliation in Nevada in October, he had other, more pleasant things on his mind. On 9 September, the Americana Hotel in Manhattan was the scene for the opening night of Sinatra — not Frank, but Franklin — 19-year-old Frank Jr. Like sister Nancy, who had already recorded her first record for Reprise, Junior had decided to give singing a

COUNT BASIE

You could play whatever you wanted, as long as you were swinging HARRY 'SWEETS' EDISON, TRUMPET SOLOIST

BORN IN NEW JERSEY ON 21 AUGUST, 1904, WILLIAM BASIE LEARNED THE PIANO FROM MEN SUCH AS JAMES P JOHNSON AND FATS WALLER. HE BEGAN PLAYING IN VARIOUS TOURING BANDS BEFORE SETTLING IN KANSAS CITY IN 1927.

After playing with a number of different bands in Kansas, he formed his own nine-piece band, the Barons of Rhythm, in 1935, which included the brilliant saxophonist Lester Young. It was while they were broadcasting on radio that the announcer called Basie "Count", and the name stuck. He signed to Decca, and the Count Basie Orchestra had a number of big hits, including 'One O'clock Jump' (1937) and 'Jumpin' at the Woodside' (1938).

Basie enjoyed hits through the 1940s, and his orchestra was always considered to be one of the best to come from the swing era. When the big bands were struggling in the early 1950s, Basie disbanded his, but reformed it in 1954 to embrace a whole new legion of fans. Neil Hefti arranged extensively with Basie's band in the 1950s. Count Bill Basie died in Hollywood on 26 April, 1984, working to the end.

don't-type scenarios for Frank. He did go to watch his son on 11 September, and commented, "the kid sings better than I did at that age". Two nights later, Frank appeared at the General Assembly Hall of the United Nations in a show for UN staff, with Frank's old friend Skitch Henderson providing the backing.

On the day *Sinatra's Sinatra* entered the charts, Frank played Carnegie Hall with Lena Horne, but refused to do any duets with her, claiming that there was not enough rehearsal time. There were also arguments regarding the running order, but eventually Frank did the second half both nights and Lena the first; rank has its privileges.

FRANK THE PRODUCER

Frank's old sparring partner, Gene Kelly, had been named producer of Frank's new film, *Robin & The Seven Hoods*, earlier in the year, but by the time filming began on 31 October in Chicago, Kelly was no longer on the payroll. He and Frank had fallen out over how many musical numbers there should be. Frank's solution was to take over the role of producer himself; with no day-to-day involvement at Reprise, he probably felt that he had the time. (It had been announced that under Reprise's new arrangements with Warner Brothers, Frank would have some executive responsibilities to Jack Warner, but no one took this very seriously.) Frank cut the first of the musical numbers for the film on 18 October, and then six days later he cut another, called 'I Like to Lead When I Dance', with Nelson Riddle. Many years later, Sammy Cahn, who wrote the lyrics for Jimmy Van Heusen's music, recalled how it came to be dropped from the film: "Frank really loved it. We'd go to parties; he'd say 'Play that marvelous new song.' He told everybody everywhere. So, now comes the day to shoot it. The producer Howard Koch says, 'We're having a problem; he's not doing the song.' It turned out that Frank didn't have the patience to learn the lip sync. The song was supposed to be reprised three times in the movie. So I wrote Sinatra a note that just said 'God will punish you'".

Three weeks after beginning work on *Robin & The Seven Hoods*, Frank, like the rest of the US and much of the rest of the world, was stunned by the news of the assassination of the President. If you are around 50, you can probably recall exactly where you were when you heard that John Fitzgerald Kennedy had been shot. Frank was filming in a cemetery in Burbank, California. America virtually came to

LIKE SON
Frank Jr playing with the reincarnated Tommy Dorsey Band at Disneyland. Junior and the band toured Europe in 1964.

shot. He first appeared at Disneyland a year earlier, when he sang some old Dorsey-era Sinatra songs with bandleader Bill Elliott. Over the course of the next year there were further appearances including Dallas, Lake Tahoe, and even the Flamingo Hotel in Las Vegas.

Shortly before his New York appearance, there was an article in *Life* magazine featuring father and son. On the first night, at the Hotel Royal Box, the junior crooner's reviews were mixed. Most people, correctly as it turned out, recognized that his father was as big a hindrance as he was a help. The fact that he had chosen some of his father's signature songs, such as 'Night and Day' and 'I'll Never Smile Again', was ill advised. Interestingly, Frank Sr was not there. The press tried to link his absence with his ongoing problems with the Nevada Gaming Board, but it seems just as likely that Frank did the sensible thing and stayed away so as not to distract attention from his son. Frank had also been playing the Sands up until the wee small hours of 8 September along with Dean and Sammy. It was another of those damned if you do, damned if you a halt over the next few days as the nation tried to come to grips with the tragedy. It was some days before Frank was back at work. A Martin Luther King benefit that he and Count Basie were to play in Santa Monica four days after the assassination was cancelled. Two weeks after this national calamity, Frank had to face up to a personal challenge of his own.

THE PRICE OF FAME

On 3 December, Frank was in Los Angeles recording with Don Costa. Five days later, fame extracted a payment from Frank that was cruel and ill-deserved. Frank Jr was appearing at Harrah's Club in Lake Tahoe with the Tommy Dorsey Band. Around 9:00 pm, Junior was having a chicken dinner in his room at a motel in Stateline Nevada with John Foss, a trumpet player with the band, when there was a knock at the door. "It's room service," said a voice. Junior opened the door to a man carrying a box, but as he put it on the table he turned to show that he was holding a gun. Then two other men came in and bound and gagged Foss before taking Junior to a car. They drove off into the night. Foss eventually broke free and called the police.

Nancy, who was at home in Los Angeles, was the first to be told about what had happened to her son. She called Frank, who was in Palm Springs. There followed a series of frantic phone calls, culminating in Frank flying to Reno to meet the FBI. The first contact from the kidnappers was the next afternoon, when they called Frank. There was talk of a deal, and Frank spoke briefly to his son. The next call told Frank to go to a service station in Carson City, where the kidnappers again called him. They demanded $240,000 in small, used bills, which was arranged over the next 24 hours. Frank spent most of that time at Nancy's Bel-Air home along with Tina and Nancy Jr. Around 9:00 pm the call instructed Frank to take the money to a petrol station in Beverly Hills. Once there, another call told him to have a courier take the money to a phone booth at LA's airport. An FBI man doubled as the courier, and after several more phone calls, at different locations, he was told to place the 23-pound bag between two parked school buses and then check into a hotel.

All this time, Junior was being held at a house in San Fernando Valley. He heard about the money drop from the kidnapper who was guarding him. At the last minute, the man who had gone to pick up the money was frightened and ran. The kidnappers had arranged a pick-up for Junior, and Frank left Nancy's house to go to meet his son. Unfortunately, the remaining kidnapper also got scared and did not take Junior to where he was supposed to meet his father. He did, however, let him go

SEE IT SOON.....

AT MOST ⒶⒷⒸ AND OTHER LEADING CINEMAS

4 FOR TEXAS
Ursula Andress was big box office after her scene-stealing antics in Dr. No *(the first James Bond movie). In actual fact it was so bad it made* Sergeants Three *seem good.*

shortly after the intended pick-up point, but obviously not where Frank could see him. Junior ran off and at first hid before deciding to walk home to Bel Air. A car went by with some men in it, but it had gone before Junior realized that it was probably FBI men. Shortly after, another car went by, and he recognized it as belonging to the Bel Air Patrol. He shouted, and they stopped and took Frankie home, smuggling him in the boot of the patrol car to avoid the throng of reporters camped out in Nancy's

> ❝Maybe Frank is not quite so assured these days in handling those sustained notes, but he still projects with the old magic.❞
>
> *NEW MUSICAL EXPRESS,*
> **26 OCTOBER, 1963**

SINATRA'S SINATRA

Frank's ninth album for Reprise charted as control of his own label was switching to Warner's. It proved to be the most successful album, in terms of chart longevity, of his Reprise career so far; unsurprising since it is effectively a greatest hits package. It is hard not to enjoy, and it sounds unbeatable if you don't play it alongside the originals. Nelson's arrangements cleverly disguise Frank's ageing voice by shortening the length of the songs and setting them in a lower key. Virtually no artist has ever been able to return to material and offer something better than the originals, and Frank was no different.

Given Reprise's financial situation it is possible that this was an album born of necessity, although when you own the label there is no one telling you what you should and shouldn't do. Frank's taste, impeccable during his years at Capitol, had begun to seem questionable. By this time, only one

other singer had a career that had lasted longer – Bing Crosby. And Frank signed him to Reprise in July 1963 (probably out of nostalgia for his old hero). The album was one of many issued as a series of EPs.

SONG LINES
Recorded United Recorders, 29 & 30 April 1963 (except where indicated) Chart : US No 8 43 weeks on the chart (First charted 5 October, 1963) UK No 9 24 weeks on the chart (5 October, 1963).

SIDE 1
1. 'I'VE GOT YOU UNDER MY SKIN' (Cole Porter)

2. 'IN THE WEE SMALL HOURS OF THE MORNING' (Bob Hilliard & Dave Mann)

3. 'THE SECOND TIME AROUND' (Sammy Cahn & Jimmy Van Heusen)

4. 'NANCY (WITH THE LAUGHING FACE)' (Phil Silvers & Jimmy Van Heusen)

5. 'WITCHCRAFT' (Cy Coleman & Carolyn Leigh)

6. 'YOUNG AT HEART' (Carolyn Leigh & Johnny Richards)

SIDE 2
1. 'ALL THE WAY' (Sammy Cahn & Jimmy Van Heusen)

2. '(HOW LITTLE IT MATTERS) HOW LITTLE WE KNOW' (Carolyn Leigh & Phillip Springer)

3. 'POCKETFUL OF MIRACLES' (Sammy Cahn & Jimmy Van Heusen) Recorded 22 November, 1961

4. 'OH! WHAT IT SEEMED TO BE' (Bennie Benjamin, Sammy Cahn & George Weiss)

5. 'CALL ME IRRESPONSIBLE' (Sammy Cahn & Jimmy Van Heusen) Recorded 21 January, 1963

6. 'PUT YOUR DREAMS AWAY (FOR ANOTHER DAY)' (Ruth Lowe, Paul Mann & Stephen Weiss)

DON COSTA

Don Costa was one of the greatest orchestrators ever to put pen to paper. JIMMY WEBB

DON COSTA WAS THIRTY-SIX WHEN HE FIRST WORKED WITH FRANK IN NOVEMBER 1961. HE HAD PRODUCED TWO NO 1 SINGLES FOR PAUL ANKA, 'DIANA' (1957) AND 'LONELY BOY' (1959).

Born in Boston on 10 June, 1925, Costa left school at 15 to play guitar on a local radio station, before moving to New York to work as a studio musician. His first taste of fame was playing on Vaughn Monroe's 1949 No 1 'Riders in the Sky'. Don then began working at ABC–Paramount Records in the early 1950s, which is where he met Canadian Paul Anka. Before Anka, Costa worked with Steve Lawrence and Eydie Gorme, writing charts for their recordings on Coral and eventually signing them to ABC–Paramount. He had another No 1 with Lloyd Price and 'Stagger Lee' in 1958, which is far enough away from Frank Sinatra to make the fact that they ended up working together very interesting.

In 1959, Costa joined United Artists and recorded in his own name. 'I Walk with the Line', only reached No 59, but in early 1960

he got to No 27 with the 'Theme from The Unforgiven', a film starring Burt Lancaster and Audrey Hepburn. He also had a Top 20 hit with in the US with 'Never on Sunday', which is probably what attracted Sinatra to his work. Soon after working with Frank for the first time, Costa produced Trini Lopez's 'If I Had a Hammer', which reached No 3 on the Hot 100 in the summer of 1963, making it Reprise's first top three single. Costa also co-wrote Duane Eddy's 'Because They're Young', and contributed to the success of Little Anthony and the Imperials, Trini Lopez, Barbra Streisand, Perry Como, Dean Martin and the Osmonds.

Costa worked as Frank's touring conductor, as well as arranging for him, until he began having heart problems in the early 1980s. He died in New York in 1983.

driveway. It was 11 December; no doubt Frank had never had a better birthday present. A few days later, Frank took actress Jill St John to his birthday celebration at the Sands. Naturally, press speculation was rife that this was another serious romance.

Junior's abduction was obviously not the kind of punishment that Sammy Cahn had had in mind when he wrote his "God will punish you" note, and he was reported to "feel terrible" over it. The three kidnappers were caught on 14 December and, as if the ordeal of the kidnap wasn't bad enough for Frank Jr and the family, what would happen during the trial was almost as bad. John Irwin, Joseph Amsler, and Barry Keenan went on trial in Los Angeles on 16 February. Their defence case rested largely on the fact that it was all a set-up to try to boost Frank Jr's collateral as a performer, and so that "he might make the ladies swoon like papa". Their defence tried, unsuccessfully, to needle Frank Sr on the witness stand, and after a trial lasting just over three weeks they were found guilty. Amsler and Keenan got life and Irwin got 16 years, although the sentences were later drastically reduced.

FRANK AND BING SING

After a hectic 1963, 1964 was a far less active year for Frank. There were the inevitable sessions, and some filming, but there was less live work than for a number of years. His first session of the year was on 2 January, when he cut three tracks with Fred Waring and His Pennsylvanians, including a remake of 'The House I Live In'. The tracks were for an album of patriotic songs that Frank made with Bing Crosby called *America I Hear You Singing*. At the end of the month, Frank and Nelson were back in the studio working on an album of movie songs, before Frank and Bing finished their patriotic duty. Frank also appeared on Bing's television special in the middle of January, along with Dean and Rosemary Clooney. To round out the month, 'Stay With Me', the theme from *The Cardinal*, sneaked into the charts and got no higher than No 81. It was arranged by Ernie Freeman and had been recorded early in December 1963. Ernie was also a pianist who, among other things, masqueraded as B Bumble on a recording produced by Kim Fowley. Kim recalled the December session:

YOUNG SINATRA SPEAKS
Frank Jr and mother Nancy facing the press outside their home on 11 December, 1963 after his release by the kidnappers.

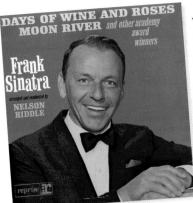

WINNERS

The concept seems like a good one, and it did manage to scrape into the album charts Top 10. However, it was the least successful Sinatra album since All Alone, two years earlier. It is too nebulous a record and the songs don't hang together to produce a cohesive work. Frank and Nelson revisit some of the Capitol classics and you have to say why bother; other than it was a way of getting recordings into the Reprise catalogue.

"There we were, a whole crowd of us sitting waiting and Sinatra shows up with all his entourage. His hat and coat are hung up on the stand real carefully, and he says 'Hi'. The orchestra is ready with the song and they start recording. After a bit, Sinatra stops them. He has heard something with the bass drum. He notices that the drummer has a bandaged foot and he says to him that he is somehow getting an extra sound with the bandage. Everything is stopped while the guy has to get it re-strapped, which makes it OK. But then again, Sinatra hears something with one of the horn players. He realizes that the man's lips are chapped and it is spoiling the note. Sinatra says that everything has to be just right on one of his sessions, and tells the man to put on some Lip Salve, and after he has done this it is OK and they manage to finish the song. I tell you that the man [Sinatra] didn't need a producer – who needs a fucking producer with ears like those?"

A NEW DEAL

As Frank finished up his recording with Bing and Fred Waring in February, *4 For Texas* came out and was met with apathy at best. As *Variety* put it, "Sinatra and Martin carry on in their usual manner, the latter getting most of what laughs there are."

Two months later, Frank finished recording the soundtrack album for *Robin & The Seven Hoods*, just prior to starting work on his new film, *None But The Brave*, in which he was not only starring but directing. Shooting started at the end of April, and the locations were in Hawaii. It turned into something of a family affair, since the cast included Nancy's husband, Tommy Sands, and Frank's second cousin, Dick Sinatra, whose father was band leader Ray. The producer was again Howard Koch, and he and Frank flew to Japan to finalize the funding for the film,

'NAPPERS NABBED

An uncharacteristically grim-looking Sinatra meets the press after the sentencing of Junior's kidnappers. In what resembles a scene from one of his 1960s crime movies, the headlines say it all.

70

EXTRA
THE SATURDAY PICTORIAL
HERALD EXAMINER
NIGHT EDITION
The Full FBI Report
KIDNAPERS JAILED
Sinatra Ransom Recovered

ROBIN & THE SEVEN HOODS

This film, released on 27 June, 1964, became the fourth and final film in what had been planned as the Rat Pack quintet. It was not a great success, and this is reflected in the fact that the soundtrack album managed to make only No 56 on the album charts.

FLOPSVILLE

Coming out at the end of May, Frank and Bing's album was a total flop; well, it did make No 116, but that's as good as a flop!

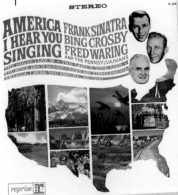

and to audition Japanese actors, since it was an American/Japanese co-production. When they arrived in Tokyo, Frank had some problems with customs because they suspected him of drug smuggling! Then, when filming finally got underway, Frank almost died. After a couple of weeks of filming on an isolated beach north of Moloa, Frank was relaxing one Sunday afternoon at the house he had rented along with Koch, his wife Ruth, Jilly Rizzo, and some of the other cast members. Chris Cook, editor of *The Garden News*, interviewed Koch shortly afterwards: "Frank, Ruth Koch and Howard had all gone in swimming, despite the fact that the surf was well up. A big set of waves dragged Frank about 200 yards out to sea." After almost 20 minutes in the water, Frank was eventually rescued by several locals, along with Brad Dexter, who was also in the film. According to Lt. George Kaewe of the Fire Department, "in another five minutes he would have been gone, his face was starting to turn blue". The next day, Koch acted as director, but Frank was back the day after to complete the filming. Dexter's relationship with Frank continued for a while – he even became a vice president of Sinatra Enterprises – but the two men eventually stopped speaking to each other.

CHANGING TIMES

Apart from an appearance on Ed Sullivan's show in late June and a benefit concert for the NAACP at San Francisco's Cow Palace a month later, Frank was almost invisible during the summer of 1964. It was the summer of "The British Invasion" and the sound of young America, with bands such as the Beach Boys, The Four Seasons, and the first chart-topper from Tamla Motown's Supremes. In the words of Bob Dylan's song from his 1964 album, "the times they are a-changing". It seemed for a while that Frank had rather lost the fight. His single 'My Kind of Town' had sunk without trace, despite featuring in *Robin & The Seven Hoods*. According to Warner/ Reprise's Joe Smith, it was not for want of trying: "It had a long orchestral intro, and I wanted to cut the intro to make it better for radio and DJs. We had an argument about it, and I had to say to him, 'Frank, it's a different world out there now!' I got my way, and I specially packaged it in gold and I had Playboy Bunnies deliver it to DJs and radio stations – he liked that!"

Early in June the British music press had been filled with stories of Frank definitely visiting the UK for a series

of concerts in the autumn. Promoter Harold Davison, confirmed there would be four shows in London, but, for whatever reason, they never took place. In early June, Frank had been in the studio working on another album with Count Basie, called *It Might as Well Be Swing*. It was completed over the next four days, and before June was out there were some more sessions with Bing Crosby and Fred Waring for a Christmas album.

At the end of July, Frank was in the studio with a new conductor, Ernie Freeman. Two of the songs they cut, 'Softly as I Leave You' and 'Then Suddenly Love', came out as a single in August, and after a

BRAVE MOVE

Frank on the set of None But the Brave *in 1964, which was his directorial debut.*

slow start it would finally climb to No 27 by the end of October. In doing so, it became Frank's most successful 45 for four years. Given what else was in the charts during the summer, this must have been as big a surprise to Frank as to anyone – although in mid-August Dean Martin's 'Everybody Loves Somebody' had knocked The Beatles' fifth No 1 of the year, 'A Hard Day's Night', off the top of the charts. Dean's record was, naturally, on Reprise, and it became the label's first record to top the charts, just a year after the take-over by Warner's. Nearly 17 years earlier, in December 1947, Frank had cut 'Everybody Loves Somebody', written by Ken Lane and

PANAVISION

Irving Taylor, with Axel Stordahl. Frank missed his success at home because he spent late July, August and September travelling. He spent a month visiting Sweden, Tel Aviv, Paris, and the French Riviera. In Stockholm, he planned to go to a boxing world title fight, but he never saw the fight because he apparently collapsed from "overstrain".

WHEN IN ROME

Soon after this tour, Frank began work on *Von Ryan's Express* in Italy. It was a welcome return to traditional film-making after what some have dubbed the Clan's "home movies". There were some initial difficulties because Frank did not want to stay in Rome and opted to stay at the Villa Apia on the outskirts. It created logistical problems, since Frank had to be flown north to the location by helicopter. In addition, Frank's relationship with the director, Mark Robson, has been described as among the worst of his career. Not so his relationship with another of the film's stars, John Leyton, who recalled: "I had got a three picture deal with Fox on the basis of being in *Guns at Batasi*. I was to get good co-billing for the size of my role under Frank Sinatra and Trevor Howard. My first scene was to be with Frank and Trevor – just the three of us – and I had never met either of them before. It was to be a night scene, and I was collected by car and taken across to the other side of Rome to some railway sidings. All the lights were already set, and I went straight into wardrobe and make-up, and eventually the director Mark Robson came up and said 'Hi'. He looked at my rather modern hair, but didn't actually change anything, and then took me over to between two railway carriages where he introduced me to Frank Sinatra and Trevor Howard. Within two minutes the cameras were rolling. It was overpowering! I had been a little worried about meeting Sinatra as, a little while before, I had been a panelist on *Juke Box Jury*. They had played Frank's version of 'Old MacDonald' and I had been rather unkind about the record. I couldn't believe that someone of his ilk and standing would do it. I didn't criticize him as a singer, just that he had done that record. Well, it had got me some press and static about it, but he never mentioned it! Frank Sinatra had an extraordinary *aura* – with his piercing blue eyes. He was *more* than I had expected. He was terribly nice to me, but I always had the feeling that he could explode, though I never saw it. He was very professional. He'd walk in and everyone would go quiet. He was not overly gregarious, and he always had folk around him, so he was not approachable." Filming later switched to Malaga, and Frank's mood seems to have improved, possibly because he distanced himself from Ava Gardner, who visited him in Italy and upset him; she appears to have been drinking too much.

THE ENGLISH SINATRA
Matt Monro was a great talent who had considerable success in Britain, but never quite made it in the way that he should have. He had his first British hit, 'Portrait Of My love', aged 28 in 1960. Over the next five years he had ten hits but could never really make the breakthrough against the competition of the beat boom. Frank's recording of 'Softly as I Leave You' was a cover of Monro's version – many consider Matt's to be superior. He died aged 53 in 1985.

SECOND TIME AROUND
This album was the second collaboration between Frank and the Count. Some consider it a stronger effort than their first; others feel the addition of strings hampers the sound.

SOFTLY, AS I LEAVE YOU

RELEASED TO COINCIDE with the Christmas sales rush, this didn't do well and the title track seemed to sum up Frank's year – and possibly his future. It seemed like an album designed to cash in on the single's success – and it was. You can't somehow imagine it being released if Frank had still been running Reprise, yet he still had control over his own records. All in all, it was typical of Frank's post-kidnap blues, where for a while he seemed to lose interest. It lacks cohesion, and is not helped by the assortment of arrangers and conductors. Without a defining style, it doesn't work as a whole, and it has not been released on CD.

SONG LINES

Recorded: United Recorders
Producer: Jimmy Bowen
Chart: US No 19, 28 weeks on the chart
(First charted 19 December, 1964)
UK No 20, 1 week on the chart
(20 March, 1965).

SIDE 1

1. 'EMILY'
(Johnny Mandel & Johnny Mercer) Recorded
3 October, 1964 arr. & cond. Nelson Riddle.
2. 'HERE'S TO THE LOSERS'
(Jack Segal & Robert Wells) Recorded 31 July,
1963 arr. and cond. Marty Paich.
3. 'DEAR HEART'
(Ray Evans, Jay Livingston & Henry Mancini)
Recorded 3 October, 1964 arr. and

cond. Nelson Riddle.
4. 'COME BLOW YOUR HORN'
(Sammy Cahn & Jimmy Van Heusen)
Recorded 21 January, 1963 arr. and cond.
Nelson Riddle.
5. 'LOVE ISN'T JUST FOR THE YOUNG'
(Bernard Knee) Recorded 31 July, 1963
arr. and cond. Marty Paich.
6. 'I CAN'T BELIEVE I'M LOSING YOU'
(Don Costa & Phil Zeller) Recorded 8 April,
1964 arr. Don Costa cond. Nelson Riddle.

SIDE 2

1. 'PASS ME BY'
(Cy Coleman & Carolyn Leigh) Recorded
3 October, 1964 arr. Billy May
cond. Nelson Riddle.

2. 'SOFTLY AS I LEAVE YOU'
(Giorgio Calabrese, Antonio DeVita & Hal
Shaper) Recorded 17 July, 1964 arr. and
cond. Ernie Freeman.
3. 'THEN SUDDENLY LOVE'
(Roy Alfred & Paul Vance) Recorded 17 July,
1964 arr. and cond. Ernie Freeman.
4. 'AVAILABLE'
(Sammy Cahn, LB Marks & Ned Wyan)
Recorded 17 July, 1964 arr. and cond.
Ernie Freeman.
5. 'TALK TO ME BABY'
(Robert Dolan & Johnny Mercer) Recorded
3 December, 1963 arr. and cond. Don Costa.
6. 'THE LOOK OF LOVE'
(Sammy Cahn & Jimmy Van Heusen)
Recorded 27 August, 1962 arr. Nelson Riddle
cond. Neal Hefti.

Frank returned to Los Angeles in late September and was in the studio with Nelson by 3 October; he was also finishing *Von Ryan's Express* at Twentieth Century Fox. With the success of 'Softly, as I Leave You', Frank cut some tracks to complete an album to trade off the name recognition of the single. A month later, he went back into the studio with Ernie Freeman to cut another single, 'Somewhere in Your Heart'. It did not do quite as well, reaching only No 32, but it did stay on the charts for ten weeks. This meant that Frank's 1964 releases spent 24 weeks on the Hot 100, six weeks more than in the previous two years put together. In part, this was due to a subtle shift in his singles: they were more modern, less backward-looking, which helped him to do better on the Hot 100. But "better" is a relative term, and Frank's main focus continued to be albums.

ENTER MIA

While Frank was filming at Fox, a young actress began to drop by the set regularly. She was working on the television show *Peyton Place*, and her name was Mia Farrow. According to John Leyton, Mia came to see him: "I had

got to know her when she replaced Britt Ekland on *Guns At Batasi* after which we had exchanged a couple of letters. She came over to visit me, I saw Frank's eyes flash from just behind me – It was like… yow, what's that hitting me in the back? I think I introduced them then, and then she went back to *Peyton Place*. A little later she called me and said 'He's asked me to Palm Springs – What do I do?' We talked about it and I said I didn't know and that it was her decision. She was nervous, saying things like 'How Do I Get Out Of It?' and seeking my advice. She was in awe of him too, as he was such a powerful figure, but she was also concerned and apprehensive about going. She knew what it meant… he was interested. Eventually she did go." Shooting on *Von Ryan's Express* ran well into November, which concerned Frank because he was booked for a stint at the Sands starting on the 27th. This would be his

first show in Las Vegas for over a year. John Leyton was at the opening night, at which the Count Basie Orchestra, with Quincy Jones conducting, accompanied Frank. "I was with my future wife Diana. We were shown to a table right at the front. It was as if it had been put there especially for us. I noticed people looking over, wondering who we were. We had our meal, and the show began. It was a terrific show and in between songs he acknowledges me. Now everyone is looking! Who is that guy? At the end I went for the bill and found it was all paid for by him! Afterwards he was around at a table surrounded by masses of people. He saw me, left them and walked over to us and said hello. Diana was literally speechless! He took us over to the table and introduced us to some people one of whom was Sam Giancana – I called him Sir! Frank said to

HAPPY DAYS AT THE SANDS
A gathering of friends and family including Nancy (far left), Yul Brynner, Jack Entratter (standing), Edward G Robinson, Tommy Sands and Nancy Sinatra (bottom right).

me to ask him what he did for a living. I wasn't sure… but Frank insisted with a smile…. Well, I asked him… and sure enough he stood up and shouted it out 'I own Chicago, that what I do for a living!' He realized that Frank had put me up to it, so it was said with a smile on his face!" News of Frank and Mia broke while Frank was in Las Vegas. Mia told the *Herald Examiner* that she was merely discussing the possibility of playing Frank's daughter in a movie he was planning called *Community Property*. Soon after, it was confirmed that Mia would not have a part in the film, which had been retitled *Marriage on the Rocks*. The news about their relationship was soon all over town, as well as the papers: Frank was in love. Despite the age gap (Frank was 49, Mia only 19), it was the perfect scenario, for, as Frank's press friend Earl Wilson put it: "Mia was a non-sleeper (four hours a night), Frank was a can't sleeper."

SINGING ACTOR
John Leyton started out as an actor and sprang to fame performing 'Johnny Remember Me' as pop star Johnny St Cyr on British TV's Harpers West One (1961).

MIA FARROW

Congratulations! He's a great director, just don't have babies by him. MIA, TO ACTOR JIM BROADBENT, ON WORKING WITH WOODY ALLEN

MIA IS THE DAUGHTER OF ACTRESS MAUREEN O'SULLIVAN AND DIRECTOR JOHN FARROW. HER FATHER DIED IN JANUARY 1963, AND SHE REVEALED IN HER AUTOBIOGRAPHY THAT BOTH HE AND FRANK WORE THE SAME AFTERSHAVE.

Born on 9 February 1945 in Los Angeles, she was christened Maria de Lourdes Villiers Farrow and her godmother was the columnist Louella Parsons. Mia's early career received an early boost when actress Vivien Leigh (a friend of her mother) made calls to ensure that agents and directors saw her off-Broadway debut in *The Importance of Being Earnest*.

Moving back to Hollywood, Mia worked on TV's *Peyton Place*, where she met Frank. Her breakthrough came in Roman Polanski's *Rosemary's Baby*. She then turned down a role in *True Grit* playing opposite John Wayne, and cites this as the worst decision of her career. After she divorced Frank she married pianist and conductor André Previn, with whom she had

three children as well as adopting three more. She then lived with actor/director Woody Allen for many years and they had a child. Further adoptions meant that Mia ended up looking after fourteen children following her acrimonious break up with Allen.

THE TRENDY GAP
When Frank and Mia first met, she had long flowing blonde hair, but later cut it short. "Mythical suicide" is how Salvador Dali saw Mia's haircut. It may have had something to do with not being invited to Frank's 50th.

MARRIAGE AND MUSIC

It was plain to see that for the early part of 1964 Frank struggled. The kidnap of Frank Jr, the loss of his Nevada gaming licence, the sale of Reprise, and the onset of a new musical era all played their part in affecting Frank's career. Often people assume that stars operate in a vacuum in which they are somehow artistically cocooned, unaffected by what goes on around them.

We often make the mistake of thinking that art somehow rises above the day to day; nothing could be further from the truth. After the troubles of 1964, 1965 was to be very different; Frank was "back to work"; no doubt spurred on by Mia being around. *None But The Brave* opened in late January and by and large the critics liked it. Frank had little time to think too much about reviews as he opened at the Eden Roc Hotel in Miami with comedian Joe E Lewis on 1 February for two weeks. Three days after pocketing $115,000 Frank and Joe began a two-week engagement at the Sands. It was probably around this time that Frank reportedly said to Jimmy Van Heusen as he was about to go on stage "Look at the that [the audience], why don't they

MID-LIFE ANTHEM
Frank working in the studio with Gordon Jenkins on his homage to the male menopause 'September of My Years'.

SOUTH BEACH, MIAMI

"Frank Sinatra is a happening. When he eats in a restaurant, the normally blasé get all-aflutter ... When he makes a movie, no matter how bad, legions pay to see the cool of the man. Sinatra is a man separated from others by more than money, talent and fame. He has the rare and mystical ability to fascinate."

JOSE M FERRER, *LIFE* MAGAZINE, DECEMBER, 1966

buy my records?" Frank had not managed to crack the Top 20 of the Hot 100 since 1958 and with the fierce competition from all and sundry that was unlikely to change. From there it was Hollywood, to start work on *Marriage on The Rocks*; another movie that Frank probably wished he never made. Ironically, he gets to play a conventional family man, with Deborah Kerr as his wife. Daniel O'Brien's seminal work, *The Frank Sinatra Film Guide* sums it up. "A witless blending of material, the film is further doomed by incompetent direction, tatty sets, an unbearable 'swinging' score and some truly desperate acting." Enough said, other than that Frank's daughter Nancy played his on-screen daughter, and did little to enhance the movie.

MID-LIFE CRISIS

Frank must have been glad to get back to the nightshift after *Marriage on the Rocks*, which he must have realized was a worthless film even before its release. His first session of 1965 was on 13 April; it was also his first for five months. Frank was with Gordon Jenkins, and the first song they cut was the inappropriately titled 'Don't Wait Too Long', which would appear on *September of My Years* — which is, quite simply, the best-ever album as homage to the male mid-life crisis. Frank must have decided on the concept for the album

before his relationship with Mia Farrow became serious, and yet the whole notion of looking back, reaching for youth, as shown in many of the songs, seemed so relevant to his current situation: "As a man, who has always had the wandering ways. Now I'm reaching back for yesterdays, till a long forgotten love appears." These words are from 'September of My Years', which Frank cut six weeks later, by which time he had already been seen with Mia at a Hollywood charity luncheon. It was just what the papers loved, and every comedian in Hollywood got in on the act too. Even Dean had to apologize after he cracked, "I've got scotch older than Mia Farrow."

During April and May there were several sessions at which Frank cut further tracks for *September of My Years*, along with songs that would appear on *Sinatra '65* and others destined for single release. 'Tell Her (You Love Her Each Day)' and 'Forget Domani' with Ernie Freeman were aimed at the Hot 100, but neither made the Top 50.

Meanwhile, Frank had some fatherly duties to attend to: he took Tina to Europe after she graduated from high school. They flew back to New York and spent time together at his apartment on East 72nd Street in New York City. In her book *My Father,* Tina tells of their visiting Hoboken together and Frank showing her the site of the old Paramount Theatre. One night, they went for dinner, and when they left the restaurant there were around 500 people waiting outside. "Dad still moved around without security in those days, it was just us and the driver. When you were with him in public, you adapted and moved with him, you didn't dare fall behind. 'Stay close, stay close to me, let's go.'" The crowd were all very Italian-looking, according to Tina, and Frank spoke with people before getting into the car and driving off. "This is where I came in," he said proudly.

SINATRA'S COMING

In June, Frank, Dean, and Sammy played a Teamster's Benefit for a convict rehabilitation centre at the Kiel Opera House in St Louis. A few days later, Frank flew to Israel to film a cameo appearance in *Cast a Giant Shadow*. Just a week later he played the Newport Jazz Festival with Count Basie's Orchestra, conducted by Quincy Jones. The festival's organizer, George Wein, had asked Basie if he could get Frank to play the festival, and Frank readily agreed. "The news — Sinatra is coming — started a gold rush matched only by teenagers in search of seats to a Beatles bash," said one newspaper. Some of the jazz purists were less enthusiastic, but then again they always have been.

NOT BAD, NOT GOOD
Frank's directorial debut was known in Japan as Yusha Nomi. The film did not receive bad notices, but neither did it get any really good ones. The original music was credited to Johnny Williams — none other than John Williams of Star Wars, Jaws, Indiana Jones, Superman, and Close Encounters of the Third Kind fame. While not the 32-year- old's first movie score, it was very early in his career.

> **❝ If I had as many love affairs as you give me credit for, I would be speaking to you from a jar in the Harvard Medical Centre…**
>
> **… I believe in some quarters of the Hearst Empire I am known as the Eichmann of song. ❞**
>
> FRANK AT THE PUBLICISTS' GUILD LUNCHEON AT THE BEVERLY HILLS HOTEL, 2 APRIL 1965

BESTSELLER

Entering the chart's on Independence Day weekend 1965, this became Frank's best performing chart album for a couple of years. It made No 9 and stayed in the US charts for 10 months.

I'M TELLING YOU

Some of the Walter Cronkite interview had already been shot while Frank was recording September of My Years *earlier in 1965; he was at his best in his natural environment.*

The festival was, as usual, an eclectic mix, and two nights before Frank, Blues legend Muddy Waters had appeared with Dizzy Gillespie.

On Sunday 4 July, Independence Day, the show opened with the Oscar Peterson Trio (at Frank's request), followed by the Count Basie set, before Frank joined to close the show. *Time* magazine reported Frank's arrival and performance: "7:51 pm: The baby-blue helicopter chopped through the warm, clear sky. Beards wagged and stretch pants stretched. Is it or isn't it? It was. Without a smile or a wave, Frank briskly walked 75 ft into a special trailer. 9:35: 'Here he is,' said Basie, 'the chairman of the board.' The audience moaned. Out stepped Frank, lyric book in hand, looking a little bald. 'Jump,' said Frank, shoulders hunched, left hand flicking rhythm, right hand flicking mic. Saved by the lyric book when he forgot words, Frank sang a set of old favourites such as 'Get Me To The Church on Time,' 'Street of Dreams', and 'I've Got You Under My Skin.' He spoke only once to Basie, 'Cook, cook, cook, cook, baby, cook.'"

Wein described Frank's arrival in his autobiography, *Myself Among Others*, as "the festival's *deus ex machina*. A god stepping out of the machine." Mid-show, Frank quipped, "with all those beards out there it looks like a state home for the hip," before launching into 'You Make Me Feel so Young'. Two minutes after 'My Kind of Town' finished, his helicopter was airborne, and he was at dinner at Jilly's in New York before midnight. "It makes you believe in God" said a guy in the audience (quoted in *Time*). Frank had made another successful conquest. Frank stayed in New York for the next week because he had three sell-out shows at Forest Hills Tennis Stadium in Queens; they grossed over

$270,000, of which Frank got $125,000. After more gigs in Chicago, Baltimore, and Detroit, Frank flew home to Los Angeles to appear on the Joey Bishop Show. In all, the tour grossed $600,000, which was a great deal of money.

After the success of Newport and his tour, Frank took a short holiday with Mia. He hired a 168-ft yacht, the *Southern Breeze*, for a cruise off the New England coast. Speculation was rife that Frank and Mia were going to marry. There was further press interest when Frank visited Joe Kennedy, who was unwell, while another paper claimed that Jackie Kennedy had visited Frank and Mia on the yacht. But all this was nothing compared to what happened on the second night of the boat being anchored off Hyannis Port. Two crewmen who had spent the night ashore, took a dinghy and, along with two girls they had met, started to head for the *Southern Breeze*. The seas were a little rough and the boat capsized, drowning one of the sailors. The tragedy brought an end to Frank and Mia's plans for a peaceful cruise; as *Time* magazine put it "the most closely observed cruise since Cleopatra floated down the Nile to meet Mark Antony". They sailed back to New York and flew home to Los Angeles. Frank was about to start work on yet another film, which may have prompted his boat trip. *Assault on a Queen* began location filming on 20 September. It was the story of modern-day pirates and their attempt to board and rob the *Queen Mary*. Come October Frank was in Hollywood for studio filming, where he also appeared in Joey Bishop's TV show twice and hosted the *Hollywood Palace* show. There were also sessions for an ambitious TV project, rather grandly entitled *A Man and His Music*. It was to be yet another trawl through Frank's greatest hits.

SMALL SCREEN

Frank had agreed to appear on CBS TV, being interviewed by Walter Cronkite for a show called *An American Original*. As filming the non-interview segments continued, several things made Frank nervous as to how the final programme

A MAN AND HIS MUSE
Frank and Mia on board the Southern
Breeze *before the tragedy that cut short
their holiday.*

might portray him. One scene in
particular worried him. Daughter Nancy
is on camera at Jilly's and says, "sometimes
you want a daddy to be a daddy all the time.
Sometimes when he's with his friends they
carry on like a bunch of kids." *The Journal
American* called her remarks "plaintive, even
poignant", though they regarded the finished
portrait of the almost 50-year-old Frank as
"institutional advertising". He was also
interviewed for *Esquire Magazine*, where Gay Talese
had some interesting observations: "*A Man And His
Music* would require that he sing eighteen songs with
a voice that at this particular moment, just a few
nights before the taping was to begin, was weak and sore
and uncertain. Sinatra was ill. He was the victim of an
ailment so common that most people would consider it
trivial. But when it gets to Sinatra it can plunge him into a
state of anguish, deep depression, panic, even rage. Frank
Sinatra had a cold. Sinatra with a cold is Picasso without
paint, Ferrari without fuel — only worse. For the common
cold robs Sinatra of that uninsurable jewel, his voice."

Eight days later, there was some real hardcore
institutional advertising when Budweiser sponsored Frank's
NBC show *A Man and His Music* for a cool $500,000.
This Thanksgiving weekend special concentrated on what
Frank was best at and garnered unqualified rave reviews.
'I've Got You Under My Skin', 'I Get a Kick out of You',
'Nancy', 'Come Fly with Me', 'I've Got the World on a
String', and 'Witchcraft' were just some of the dozen and
a half songs he sang. Interestingly, almost every one was
from his Capitol years, with just a few Columbia songs
thrown in for good measure. He closed with 'Put Your
Dreams Away', the song that ended 1940s radio shows,
which was co-written by Ruth Lowe, who also wrote
Frank's first No 1, 'I'll Never Smile Again'.

Five days after *A Man and His Music* aired, work began on
yet another album, one with more of a well-defined theme
than anything since *Come Fly with Me*. The first song he cut
was 'Moon Song', then 'Moon Love'… the album was to be
called *Moonlight Sinatra*. Two weeks after the second *Moonlight*
session, Frank turned 50, and his new single came out.
Appropriately entitled 'It Was a Very Good Year', it summed
things up fairly well. A week later, it was in the charts and
climbed up to No 28. Frank must have felt that this was
about the best he could do on the Hot 100, what with all
that competition from the long hairs, the Merseybeat
merchants, and the new-style home-grown talent.
Frank's 50th birthday party was hosted by his ex-wife,

VON RYAN'S EXPRESS

DIRECTED BY MARK ROBSON, the film
premiered in New York on 25 June,
1965. Anything positive that Frank had said
about directors regarding his own efforts in
None But The Brave had been forgotten when
it came to making this film. It has been
said that Robson was the only director that
Frank actively ever disliked, which must
have meant he really disliked him because
he had been uncooperative, difficult and
downright rude
on other sets.
According to
John Leyton,
it wasn't open
warfare:

"Frank would arrive in a helicopter. He'd
step out, do the scenes that were set up
for him, and he'd be in and out in an hour!
On one occasion Frank called out, 'Hey,
where are you gonna get this [film]
developed — Schwab's?' So there were these
sort of asides rather than too many direct
confrontations. With all of that
background you had to be on your mettle!"

Frank plays a US Army colonel in an
Italian POW camp from which he and
Trevor Howard (pictured left) organize
an escape. In the closing scene, as he is
desperately trying to board a train
commandeered by the prisoners he is
shot by German troops. It's a simple yet
effective story that still works.

SEPTEMBER OF MY YEARS

THE SLEEVE NOTES OF this wonderful album announced, "Tonight will not swing. Tonight is for serious". Released shortly after *Sinatra '65*, it was a return to the thematically orientated albums of the Capitol years. Against the musical odds, against the background of beat, it became Frank's most artistically and commercially successful album since starting Reprise. However, only in America — it failed to even chart in Britain.

"Frank Sinatra sings of days and loves ago…. September of My Years" is what it says on the cover. It stands as both a reflection of a life lived and at the same time looks to the future. By Frank's standards, many of the songs he chose were new songs and not standards at all, but in Frank's hands they sound like they are. Arranged and conducted by Gordon Jenkins it is a synthesis of their romantic talents. The settings allow Frank to be

totally open with his feelings, illustrating what Frank had told *Playboy* in 1963: "When I sing, I believe, I'm honest. If you want to get an audience with you, there's only one way. You have to reach out to them with total honesty and humility."

Nancy, at the Beverly Wilshire Hotel. According to the newspapers, the guest list was the cream of Hollywood society, but since Frank was showbiz royalty, you would expect nothing less. Mia Farrow was noticeably absent, but, despite this, she and Frank were now very much a couple. One couple that wasn't were Nancy and Tommy Sands: they had split mid-way through the filming of *Marriage on the Rocks*. Several months later, with their marriage definitely over, Nancy had her first *Billboard* chart hit, admittedly a small one, but 'So Long Babe' did make No 86, staying around for a month in October 1965. She was no overnight sensation — since being signed to Reprise in 1961 she had released well over a dozen singles. To continue the theme, the next single Nancy cut was 'These Boots Are made For Walkin', but this was a very different record from 'So Long Babe'. Lee Hazlewood, who wrote and produced the song, lectured Nancy before she began recording, telling her that she was no "sweet young thing" but a grown woman who had been married and divorced. "Let's do one for the truck drivers, bite the words," ordered Hazlewood. Nancy was 25 years old, and gorgeous to boot, and her new single made No 1 on the Hot 100 on 26 February. Britain thought that Nancy was gorgeous too, and 'Boots' made the top of the charts there a week earlier than in the US. This would be a very good year for Nancy, spawning

SONG LINES

Recorded: United Recorders
Producer: Sonny Burke
Chart: US No.5 69 weeks on the chart
(First charted 21 August, 1965).
Grammy Awards:
1965 — Album of The Year: September of My Years (Sinatra)
1965 — Best Vocal Performance: It Was A Very Good Year (Sinatra)
1965 — Best Album Notes: September of My Years (Stan Cornyn)
1965 — Best Arrangement: It Was A Very Good Year (Gordon Jenkins)

SIDE 1

1. 'THE SEPTEMBER OF MY YEARS'
(Sammy Cahn & Jimmy Van Heusen) Recorded 27 May, 1965.

2. 'HOW OLD AM I?'
(Gordon Jenkins) Recorded 22 April, 1965.

3. 'DON'T WAIT TOO LONG'
(Sunny Skylar) Recorded 13 April, 1965.

4. 'IT GETS LONELY EARLY'
(Sammy Cahn & Jimmy Van Heusen) Recorded 22 April, 1965.

5. 'THIS IS ALL I ASK'
(Gordon Jenkins) Recorded 22 April, 1965.

6. 'LAST NIGHT WHEN WE WERE YOUNG'
(Harold Arlen & Yip Harburg) Recorded 13 April, 1965.

7. 'THE MAN IN THE LOOKING GLASS'
(Bart Howard) Recorded 22 April, 1965.

SIDE 2

1. 'IT WAS A VERY GOOD YEAR'
(Ervin Drake) Recorded 22 April, 1965. This was originally recorded by the Kingston Trio in 1961 but was covered by the Modern Folk Quartet and came out as a single on Warner's in 1963. Chances are that this

was the route by which this song came to be covered by Frank.

2. 'WHEN THE WIND WAS GREEN'
(Don Hunt) Recorded 14 April, 1965.

3. 'HELLO, YOUNG LOVERS'
(Oscar Hammerstein II & Richard Rodgers) Recorded 13 April, 1965.

4. 'I SEE IT NOW'
(William Engvick & Alec Wilder) Recorded 14 April, 1965.

5. 'ONCE UPON A TIME'
(Lee Adams & Charles Strouse) Recorded 14 April, 1965.

6. 'SEPTEMBER SONG'
(Maxwell Anderson & Kurt Weill) Recorded 13 April, 1965. Frank first recorded this with Axel in 1946. Compare the two versions. The first is like a young man trying to appreciate a good single malt — they're just not going to get it.

A MAN AND HIS MUSIC
This LP sneaked into the American album chart at Christmas and capitalized on the success of the TV show. It also became Frank's highest placed chart album in Britain for three years when it got to No 9 (the same position as the US). In 1966 it won the Grammy for Album of The Year.

two more Top 10 singles. Best of all, her growing success meant that she was her own woman – not Frank's daughter, Junior's sister, or any other epithet.

EASY LISTENING

'It Was a Very Good Year' was also doing well on the Hot 100, and it became Frank's first record to top *Billboard*'s Easy Listening chart. The chart had been inaugurated in July 1961, when Brook Benton's 'Boll Weevil Song' was listed as No 1. The chart was solely based upon airplay, and Dean Martin had already topped it three times. 'It was a Very Good Year' went on to win a Grammy award for best male vocal performance.

While Nancy was cruising up the British and American charts, Frank was in his spiritual home, the Sands, with the Count and Quincy Jones. Three weeks after the run finished, he was at his Miami Beach house, the Fontainebleau, for a two-week booking during which he took to introducing himself as "Nancy's father".

On 11 April, Frank was at United Recorders working with conductor Donnie Lanier on a song arranged by Ernie Freeman. It was his first session of the year and his first time in the studio for over four months. In almost 30 years of recording, Frank had cut over 1,000 songs, although he had probably given up any serious thoughts of topping the charts again. He cut just one song on this day;

'Strangers in the Night' had a melody by Bert Kaempfert and English words by Charles Singleton and Eddie Snyder… and Frank hated it! The song was to be used over the end credits of a little-known James Garner movie, *A Man Could Get Killed*. In Jimmy Bowen's autobiography, he tells how Frank had difficulty getting the half-tone key change two-thirds of the way through. In the end, he was given explicit instructions on how to cope with it: "'Frank, sing it right up to the key change and cut. Then we'll give you a bell tone and we'll go from there in the new key to the end.'" It worked, and Bowen edited it, mastered the song, and then got it out to radio stations within 24 hours. He had heard that Jack Jones was recording a version that same day and wanted to be sure that Frank's version was the first to get on the radio.

A month later, and four days after 'Strangers in the Night' entered the Hot 100 at No 90, Frank was back in the studio with Nelson cutting more songs for an album. At this point it is doubtful whether anyone could have envisaged just how big 'Strangers' would become. One man who certainly took something from that session was guitarist Glen Campbell: "I started listening to a lot more Sinatra. I'd never really paid that much attention to it, because I'm really a musician at heart. Singin' was, like, secondary. But when I heard the way he

FRANK SINGS THE SHOWS

Not content with one attack on the Christmas charts in 1965, Reprise released this lacklustre album of Broadway songs. The public felt the same, and it only made No 30.

BIRTHDAY DAD

Tina and Nancy arriving at the Beverly Wilshire hotel on 12 December with their father for his 50th birthday party.

MOONLIGHT SINATRA

FAR BETTER than the Broadway album, *Moonlight Sinatra* was released in March and made the top 40 for just a couple of weeks in June. Frank is reunited with Nelson Riddle whose excellent arrangements have the feel of a warm summer's evening. Bing Crosby recorded many of the songs featured in this collection, including 'I Wished on the Moon' (No 2 in 1935) and 'Moonlight Becomes You' (No 1 in 1942). Its lack of commercial success belies its content — it's a real gem of an album but, unlike many of Frank's LPs from this period, it had no hit single to provide that extra sales boost. *Downbeat* reviewed it at the time and liked it too: "Moonlight Sinatra, however, is all sensitivity and passion and, despite the preponderance of lunar lyrics, never gets sticky or mushy."

MOONLIGHT SINATRA
arranged and conducted by **NELSON RIDDLE**

MOONLIGHT BECOMES YOU / MOON SONG / MOONLIGHT
SERENADE / REACHING FOR THE MOON /
I WISHED ON THE MOON / OH, YOU
CRAZY MOON / THE MOON GOT IN
MY EYES / MOONLIGHT MOOD /
MOON LOVE / THE MOON
WAS YELLOW
(And The Night
Was Young)

SONG LINES

Recorded United Recorders,
29–30 November 1965
Producer Sonny Burke
Chart: US No 34, 14 weeks on the chart
(First charted 23 April, 1966)
UK No 18, 8 weeks on the chart
(First charted 21 May, 1966)

SIDE 1

1. 'MOONLIGHT BECOMES YOU'
(Johnny Burke & Jimmy Van Heusen)
From Bing's movie *The Road to Morocco*,
it's a great opening track.

2. 'MOON SONG'
(Sam Coslow & Arthur Johnston)

3. 'MOONLIGHT SERENADE'
(Glenn Miller & Mitchell Parish)
Without a doubt one of the best ballad recordings from the Reprise years, with a lush and evocative Nelson Riddle arrangement that's as good as anything he ever did. Just before the first take Frank said to no one in particular "Gee, this is a nice tune." With various problems on several more takes — including Frank, Sonny Burke, and Nelson discussing whether it should be a little faster, it finally gets done on take 9. It was worth the wait!

4. 'REACHING FOR THE MOON'
(Irving Berlin)

5. 'I WISHED ON THE MOON'
(Dorothy Parker & Ralph Rainger)

SIDE 2

1. 'OH, YOU CRAZY MOON'
(Johnny Burke & Jimmy Van Heusen)

2. 'THE MOON GOT IN MY EYES'
(Johnny Burke & Arthur Johnston)

3. 'MOONLIGHT MOOD'
(Harold Adamson & Peter DeRose)

4. 'MOON LOVE'
(Mack David, Mack Davis & Andé Kostelanetz)

5. 'THE MOON WAS YELLOW'
(Fed Ahlert & Edgar Leslie)

TOTAL ANTITHESIS
The Rolling Stones — Charlie, Mick, Bill, Keith, and Brian — represented everything Frank didn't. He hated their kind of music and was probably none too keen on their dress sense.

phrases, I said 'Wow, that's really cool.'" (Campbell went on to have well over 30 Hot 100 hits, topping the American charts twice.)

In the week that Frank entered the charts, eight other singles had their *Billboard* debut, including, 'I Am a Rock' by Simon and Garfunkel (No 62), The Lovin' Spoonful's 'Did You Ever Have to Make Up Your Mind?' (No 65), and Dean Martin's 'Come Running Back' (No 83). A week later, Dean's record was still nine places higher than 'Strangers', but seven weeks after that, Frank was at No 1, having toppled the Beatles' 'Paperback Writer', which had, in its turn, ousted 'Paint It Black' by the Rolling Stones. Middle (aged) America must have thought that the cavalry had arrived in relief of the wagon train. Their euphoria lasted only a week, however, because the Beatles quickly returned to the top. Frank spent the rest of his career

hating the song and having to sing it night after night. "He thought it was about two fags in a bar!" said Joe Smith from Warner/Reprise. In concert thereafter, Frank would often have something to say about it, as he did in Jerusalem on 27 November, 1975: "Here's a song I cannot stand, I just cannot stand this song, but... what the hell."

What makes the achievement so much more significant is the fact that it was the first time Frank had made the Top 10 since early 1958. In Britain, it topped the singles chart for three weeks, ousting the Stones and then being replaced by the Beatles. The pop papers felt that the new order had been re-established after this minor blip, but could not help commenting on the situation. *Disc*'s view was typical: "We say 'no comment' about this type of music, Sinatra shouldn't make singles aimed at the chart — he's strictly an LP bloke." Ironically, if Frank himself had been asked, no doubt he would have said that he was not really making records for the charts either. It just goes to prove that the public are the arbiters on such things, and all that is debatable is our taste. By the time the year was over, 'Strangers' had become Britain's second biggest hit single of the year, beaten comfortably by Jim Reeves and 'Distant Drums'; Nancy's 'These Boots Were Made For Walking' took the No 3 spot.

...AND MORE AGAIN

Frank was scheduled to star in another movie in July; this was to be filmed in London and looked a great deal more promising than *Assault on a Queen*. Shortly before flying to London, he and Nancy taped another television special for CBS; it was to be called *A Man and His Music II*. The opening of the show with 'Fly Me to the Moon', 'The Most Beautiful Girl in the World', 'Moonlight in Vermont', and 'You're Nobody Til Somebody Loves You' is just great. Frank spends much of this section in the orchestra pit with Nelson Riddle conducting. Author and Sinatra expert Ed O'Brien has called this "the most exciting 15 minutes of Frank's TV appearances," and it is pretty hard to disagree. You can see what a good time Frank is having surrounded by the brilliant orchestra in full cry. As Frank succinctly put it during the show, "Bless the musicians".

Soon afterwards, Frank flew to Prestwick in Scotland and then on to London to work on *The Naked Runner*. There were stories in the pop press of Frank's people talking with people at Pye about another record being made in London after filming was finished. Back home, headlines in the papers told the story of Frank and Mia's continuing romance, with "Sinatra buys Mia the ring". Soon after arriving in London, Frank broke off his script meetings and flew back to New York for a couple of days, where he was seen around town, mostly at Jilly's, with Mia. He then announced that he was flying back to London,

A BANK RAID
Released on 27 July 1966, this was a flop too far. It had "low budget" written all over it – apart from Frank it had no names that would ring a bell with anyone. The soundtrack featured Duke Ellington's music.

but instead flew to Las Vegas and married Mia in a five-minute ceremony in Jack Entratter's suite at the Sands. They honeymooned in Palm Springs and no doubt took a few calls from members of both families, none of whom had been invited. Frank was then supposed to return to London to continue filming, but instead he and Mia went to the South of France to stay at Jack Warner's house in Cap d'Antibes. Frank and Mia eventually got back to London around the end of July, where they stayed at the Grosvenor Square flat of the singer Marion Ryan. Pretty soon, Frank was arguing with Brad Dexter, who was producing the film, insisting that they return to California. After a spell shooting in Copenhagen, Frank once again deserted the film, this time to host a fund-raiser for Governor Pat Brown, the Democratic Governor of California (who lost the election to former Hollywood star Ronald Reagan). He then refused to return to Europe again, where the rest of the cast and crew shot around Frank using footage that was already in the can. Dexter delivered the film to Warner's and never worked with Frank again.

It was not just on filming that Frank let someone down, according to Tony Hatch: "He called me in London and asked me to compose, arrange and produce more songs specifically for him. It was agreed that I (with Jackie Trent) would write seven new songs and we would re-record 'Downtown' as a swinger and add his versions of 'Call Me' and 'Subway' to make a ten-track *Sinatra Sings Tony Hatch* album. The songs were written and Sinatra came to London where we rehearsed and set keys in the comfort of an apartment in Grosvenor Square. He was pleased with all the songs and my orchestrating ideas and our relationship was warm and productive. The sessions for the new recordings were to be in London at Pye No 1 rather than the old CTS Studios in Bayswater where we had recorded *Great Songs from Great Britain*. The first date was cancelled by Sinatra but the MU kindly allowed me to re-schedule without penalty. The new dates were cancelled again by Sinatra and, once again, the MU kindly allowed me to reschedule without penalty. By this time I was getting pretty angry and nearly called off the project myself. I had a chat, however, with Claus Ogerman who said, 'It's such a great honour to work with Sinatra

STRANGERS IN THE NIGHT

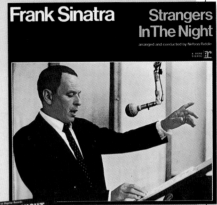

THERE IS NOTHING LIKE a hit single to propel an album into the charts, and when it is a No 1 single, then the eponymous album usually does very well. Even Frank must have been surprised that it went all the way to No 1, but it was the season for middle-of-the-road music. Frank knocked another record-company-owning artist from the top – Herb Alpert and his Tijuana Brass had been there for two months with *What Now My Love*. *Strangers in the Night* spent just a week at No 1 before being replaced by the Beatles' *Yesterday... and Today*. It was Frank's first chart-topper for Reprise and his first No 1 since 1960's *Nice 'N' Easy*. It would also be the last album he made with Nelson Riddle. Nancy later claimed that the album spent 73 weeks at No 1, which would have driven everyone mad, and possibly none more so than Frank.

British composer Tony Hatch had two songs on the album. According to him, it was "A sort of 'if you can't beat 'em then join 'em' idea, 'Downtown' had been a global hit for Petula Clark and was therefore an obvious choice for inclusion. Nelson Riddle's arrangement, however, is quite bizarrely 'pseudo-oriental'. Sinatra invited Petula Clark to the recording session but found he couldn't really work out how to sing the song with this ghastly and pointless arrangement. Anyway, with the original artist sitting in the studio I

think he found it all quite embarrassing so, lacking any better ideas, he decided to 'send it up'. Hence the vocal 'yuk's' preceding the word 'Downtown'. The song works very well as a 'swinger' (I have done it myself like that) and I cannot fathom out why neither Sinatra nor Riddle could envisage it that way."

Also on the album is the quite awful 'Yes Sir, That's My Baby', along with the sublime artistry of 'Summer Wind'. As singer Scott Walker said when interviewed in NME in July 1966, "Sinatra degrades himself by doing this rubbish. Listening to him doing numbers like 'Downtown' is like trying to watch an old man jive."
Downbeat's viewed the album as a "happy and free-wheeling affair". Whatever the case, it made a lot of money.

SONG LINES

Recorded: United, and Western Recorders
Producer: Jimmy Bowen
Chart: US No 1 (1 week), 71 weeks on the chart (First charted 18 June 1966)
UK No 4, 18 weeks on the chart (First charted 2 July 1966)
Grammys (all 1966)
Record of the Year
Best Vocal Performance, Male
'Strangers in the Night' (Frank Sinatra)
Best Arrangement
'Strangers in the Night' (Ernie Freeman)
Best Engineered Record
'Strangers in the Night' (Eddie Bracket and Lee Hershberg)

SIDE 1

1. 'STRANGERS IN THE NIGHT'
(Bert Kaempfert, Charles Singleton & Eddoe Snyder)
Recorded 11 April, 1966

2. 'SUMMER WIND'
(Hans Bradtke, Heinz Meier & Johnny Mercer)
Recorded 16 May, 1966

3. 'ALL OR NOTHING AT ALL'
(Arthur Altman & Jack Lawrence)
Recorded 16 May, 1966

4. 'CALL ME'
(Tony Hatch)
Recorded 16 May, 1966

5. 'YOU'RE DRIVING ME CRAZY'
(Walter Donaldson)
Recorded 11 May, 1966

SIDE 2

1. 'ON A CLEAR DAY (YOU CAN SEE FOREVER)'
(Alan Lerner & Burton Lane)
Recorded 16 May, 1966

2. 'MY BABY JUST CARES FOR ME'
(Walter Donaldson & Gus Kahn)
Recorded 11 May, 1966

3. 'DOWNTOWN'
(Tony Hatch)
Recorded 16 May, 1966

4. 'YES SIR, THAT'S MY BABY'
(Walter Donaldson & Gus Kahn)
Recorded 11 May, 1966

5. 'THE MOST BEAUTIFUL GIRL IN THE WORLD'
(Lorenz Hart & Richard Rodgers)
Recorded 11 May, 1966

1963–1973

you simply have to hang in there'. So I did but when Sinatra cancelled for the third time the MU (quite rightly) would not agree to further re-scheduling. As the big orchestra had to be paid (Reprise Records picked up the entire bill for studio, musicians and scores, by the way) the sessions went ahead with Mike Redway demo-ing all the new songs. Most of them were subsequently recorded by artists such as Matt Monro and Val Doonican. I then heard rumours that I wasn't the only songwriter/arranger/producer being dangled at the end of a piece of Sinatra string and that Les Reed and Burt Bacharach were also waiting to record albums they had individually written and arranged."

Mia and Frank, whom she called "Charlie Brown", settled into a life of domesticity, spending much of their time in Palm Springs as well as buying a house in Bel Air. By November, Frank was back in Las Vegas, accompanied by Mia. They also appeared on the popular TV show *What's*

My Line?; with Dorothy Kilgallen dead, there was no hindrance. Mia was on the panel, Frank the mystery guest.

Frank's follow-up to 'Strangers in the Night' was the wonderful 'Summer Wind', which only made it to No 25 on the Hot 100. It became a concert favourite from 1986 to the end of Frank's touring days. During the autumn, there were sessions with Ernie Freeman for an album to be called *That's Life*. The title track was cut on 18 October and came out a couple of weeks later. It made the Hot 100 a week before Frank and Mia appeared on *What's My Line?* Unlike 'Strangers in the Night', 'That's Life' was the highest new entry of the week. According to *Life* magazine, the song was "an absolute corker". Eight places below it was another new entry, Nancy's 'Sugar Town'. Being featured on *A Man and His Music II* on 7 December helped 'That's Life' to reach No 4 on Christmas Eve 1966, with Nancy two places behind. The following week, Nancy climbed to No 5, right behind her father.

SINATRA AT THE SANDS

Two MONTHS AFTER *Strangers in the Night* came out, this album, recorded with Count Basie in January, nosed its way into the chart. A few months later it made the Top 10, and it stuck around for most of the next year. Arranged by Quincy Jones, it is totally reflective of Frank's live shows with the Count in the mid-1960s, including a couple of Sinatra's concert monologues.

Stephen Thomas Erlewine, in the *All Music Guide*, calls this album "the definitive portrait of Frank Sinatra in the '60s". This, of course, doesn't make it the best. Frank sounds tired, and that may be because recording didn't begin until three weeks into his run. But don't let that put you off — it's still very enjoyable, and features many of the songs from earlier shows before Frank took up with Bill Basie. One thing that definitely doesn't work, however, are some of Frank's jokes.

BRAZILIAN MAGICIAN

In the last three years of the 1960s, Frank was slowing up: he was making half the albums he had made in each of the first seven years. The type of albums changed, too. He came to the realization that the standards repertoire that he had made his own had pretty much run its course. Having already recorded many of these classic songs for Columbia, Capitol, and Reprise, there was no way they would stand a fourth outing. The problem for Frank was: what to record? And the solution was the most unusual collaboration of his career. On 30 January,

NUMBER 3
A very large wedding cake for such a low-key wedding — maybe they sent a piece to all their friends.

SONG LINES

Recorded at the Sands Hotel, Las Vegas, 26–29 January & 1 February, 1966.
Chart: US No 9, 44 weeks on the chart
(First charted 20 August, 1966)
UK No 7, 18 weeks on the chart
(First charted 18 October, 1966)
Grammy in 1966 for Best Album Notes, written by Stan Corwyn

SIDE 1
1. 'COME FLY WITH ME'
2. 'I'VE GOT A CRUSH ON YOU'
3. 'I'VE GOT YOU UNDER MY SKIN'
4. 'THE SHADOW OF YOUR SMILE'
5. 'STREET OF DREAMS'
6. 'ONE FOR MY BABY (AND ONE MORE FOR THE ROAD)'

SIDE 2
7. 'FLY ME TO THE MOON (IN OTHER WORDS'
8. 'ONE O'CLOCK JUMP'
9. 'THE TEA BREAK'
10. 'YOU MAKE ME FEEL SO YOUNG'

SIDE 3
11. 'ALL OF ME'
12. 'THE SEPTEMBER OF MY YEARS'
13. 'LUCK BE A LADY'
14. 'GET ME TO THE CHURCH ON TIME'
15. 'IT WAS A VERY GOOD YEAR'
16. 'DON'T WORRY 'BOUT ME'
17. 'MAKIN' WHOOPEE!'

SIDE 4
18. 'WHERE OR WHEN'
19. 'ANGEL EYES'
20. 'MY KIND OF TOWN'
21. 'A FEW LAST WORDS'
22. 'MY KIND OF TOWN'

❝ When things swing, he's the happiest man in the world. ❞

PHIL RAMONE,
PRODUCER OF *DUETS*,
WHO WAS AT THE SANDS IN 1966

1967, Frank went into Western Recorders to begin work on an album with Brazilian composer, singer, and guitarist Antonio Carlos Jobim. The first song they cut, along with an orchestra conducted by Claus Ogerman, was a minor standard – 'Baubles, Bangles and Beads'. Frank knew the song well, having recorded it with Billy May for *Come Dance For Me* in 1959. This version was a beautiful bossa nova done as a duet with Antonio, who sang partially in Brazilian. Over the next three nights, they recorded 12 songs; at 51 years old, Frank had never sounded so cool. According to pianist Bill Miller, "It was his idea to do the album with Antonio Carlos Jobim. Jobim suggested Claus Ogerman, and Frank said 'Fine – use whoever you want.' He said he had no particular ideas on routines, except to try to keep them under three minutes, if possible."

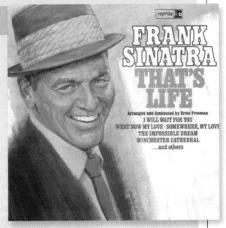

THAT'S LIFE

THIS MADE THE VERY last album chart of 1966, eventually getting to No 6 and staying on the chart for well over a year. The title song was found for Frank by Russ Regan: "I was a recording artist at Capitol for a little while in 1959 – as a singer – but I didn't have anything to do with Frank Sinatra. I did work at Warner/Reprise for about a year, and I worked at Loma Records, which was an R&B Warner arm with a lot of artists. While I was there, one of the writers, Kelly Gordon, brought the song to me, and wanted to record it himself. I said right away that it wasn't a song for him and that it was a Frank Sinatra song, so I took it to Mo Ostin. He agreed and passed it through to Frank and within two days Frank said he wanted to do it. It went to No 25 on *Billboard*'s R&B chart, and No 4 on the main pop chart. Frank was delighted and I was the hero for a time!" OC Smith had already cut a version when

Frank first sang it for *A Man and His Music* in July. Nelson Riddle arranged it then, while Ernie Freeman arranged the hit version and the rest of this album.

Once again, witness the power of a big hit single to sell what is, at best, an average album: it sold well over a million copies when first released, and was the last of Frank's albums to make the US chart Top 10 for a quarter of a century.

SONG LINES

Recorded United and Western Recorders
Producer Jimmy Bowen
Chart: US No 6, 61 weeks on the chart
(First charted 31 December, 1966)
UK No 22, 12 weeks on the chart
(First charted 25 February, 1967)

SIDE 1

1. 'THAT'S LIFE'
(Kelly Gordon & Dean Kay Thompson)
Recorded 18 October, 1966

2. 'I WILL WAIT FOR YOU'
(Jacques Louis Demy, Michel Legrand & Norman Gimbel)
Recorded 18 November, 1966

3. 'SOMEWHERE MY LOVE'
(Maurice Jarre & Paul Francis Webster)
Recorded 17 November, 1966

4. 'SAND AND SEA'
(Gilbert Becaud, Maurice Vidalin & Mack David) Recorded 18 November, 1966

5. 'WHAT NOW, MY LOVE?'
(Gilbert Becaud & Carl Sigman)
Recorded 17 November, 1966

SIDE 2

1. 'WINCHESTER CATHEDRAL'
(Geoff Stephens)
Recorded 17 November, 1966
Ridiculous... and there is nothing sublime on the album to compensate.

2. 'GIVE HER LOVE'
(James Harbert)
Recorded 17 November, 1966

3. 'TELL HER (YOU LOVE HER EACH DAY)'
(Gil Ward & Charles Watkins)
Recorded 17 November, 1966

4. 'THE IMPOSSIBLE DREAM'
(Mitch Leigh & Joe Darion)
Recorded 18 November, 1966

5. 'YOU'RE GONNA HEAR FROM ME'
(André Previn & Dory Previn)
Recorded 18 November, 1966

NOT SO STUPID

After recording the last two tracks with Antonio on 1 February, Frank cut a great Johnny Mercer/Doris Tauber song called 'Drinking Again', which would come out on an album later in the year. He also recorded a duet with Nancy, who later said, "Mo Ostin bet him [Frank] two dollars it would bomb." The song was written by Carson C Parks, who had come out of the early 1960s folk boom, and by 1966 was working with Gaile Foote as Carson & Gaile. Both had been in the Greenwood County Singers with Carson's brother, Van Dyke Parks, who collaborated with Brian Wilson (of the Beach Boys). Carson commented, "'Somethin' Stupid' came from the material for my duet album with Gaile. I had realized that the songwriters get more money from records, so I had written seven out of

*Performing and preparing at the
Fontainebleu, Miami Beach, Frank's
home-from-home on the East Coast.*

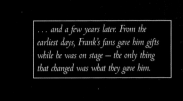

THE FONTAINEBLEAU
Frank's Miami home away from home epitomised the allure of Miami Beach to the "snowbirds".

CLEVER PAIR
"Ought to make it's mark" was the NME's verdict in their review of 18 March 1967.

the twelve tunes, and of these six were recorded by others! The Carson & Gaile version was the original recording of the song done in November 1966, but as Christmas was upon us, we did not release it then. My manager Wally Brady knew Mo Ostin and Wally said to me 'Do you want to pay the bills, or take a chance on being a star?' He got a tape of the song to Mo and asked him to put it on top of the pile! Frank used to fly up every Friday from Palm Springs to Burbank to do the business things. Well, it seems that Frank called Nancy and said 'We gotta do this!' Mo thought it was a dog, but Frank thought it was top 10. The song was in the right place at the right time – Nancy was on the teen rock stations, a market Frank hadn't cracked, and at that stage Nancy hadn't cracked the MOR market. They did a whale of a job with it!" According to Nancy, in May 1967, it was not quite like that: "Him influence me, you're joking! Do you think it was an easy job getting him to record commercial songs? It's like pulling teeth. I had to drag him bodily into the studio. The first three takes we were completely messed up because we couldn't sing for laughing. I was trying to listen to Dad's crazy phrasing with one ear and follow the orchestra with the other and remember the words." It was referred to within Reprise as the 'Dumb, Dumb Song.'

Two weeks after recording 'Somethin' Stupid', Frank was in Miami at the Fontainebleau for another two-week run. The night after he finished at this Miami Beach landmark, Frank had his most successful night ever at the Grammy Awards. He won Record of the Year for 'Strangers in the Night'; Album of the Year for *A Man and His Music*, and Best Male Vocal Performance again for 'Strangers in the Night'. To round out a great night, Ernie Freeman won Best Arrangement for 'Strangers', *Sinatra at The Sands* won Best Liner Notes, and 'Strangers' also won the Best Engineered Record award. While not belittling Frank's achievements, it is worth putting into perspective how these somewhat strange "industry awards" work by pointing out that the New Vaudeville Band's 'Winchester Cathedral' won Best Rock 'n' Roll Recording, beating in the process the Beach Boys' 'Good Vibrations', the Beatles' 'Eleanor Rigby', and the Mamas and the Papas' 'Monday, Monday'.

Frank was back in Miami for another two-week stint at the Fontainebleau in early April (where he was also filming *Tony Rome*); and he was still there when 'Somethin' Stupid' went to No 1 on 15 April, knocking the Turtles' 'Happy Together' from the top of the Hot 100. It stayed at No 1 for four weeks, giving both Frank and Nancy their biggest hit of the modern chart era.

At the end of June, Frank did something he had not done since his Columbia days: he recorded in New York, for the first time in almost 15 years. The three songs were for a new album with Gordon Jenkins. He then "worked his passage" back to Los Angeles by playing shows in Pittsburgh, Cleveland, Madison, Detroit, Chicago, Philadelphia, and Baltimore, before continuing the recording for the new album on 24 July in Hollywood. The first song Frank did was 'Born Free', written by English writers John Barry and Don Black. "I had won the Oscar for that song that year, so

JOLLY JOBIM
ACJ was revered in Brazil and when he died, in 1994, three days of official mourning were declared in honour of the father of Bossa Nova.

FRANCIS ALBERT SINATRA & ANTONIO CARLOS JOBIM

WAS THIS FRANK'S MOST AMBITIOUS ALBUM? The most unusual of his career? With hindsight it was definitely one of the most outstanding of his Reprise era, although under-appreciated at the time. It also marked the start of Frank's slow but steady decline as a force on the album charts. It managed to reach No 19 and remained in the Top 40 for just six weeks.

This is not an album that grabs you and forces you to listen. Its strength lies in the subtlety of Ogerman's soft and sensuous arrangements and the choice of material, including seven songs composed by Jobim. If you want a romantic soundtrack to a warm summer's evening, look no further. It is music for sipping cocktails in the setting sun. While Frank's Capitol classics are the most often cited as his best work, this album ranks alongside them and is certainly very near the top for serious fans and critics alike.

SONG LINES
Recorded Western Recorders. Producer: Sonny Burke. Co-produced: Ray Gilbert. Chart: US No 19, 28 weeks on the chart (First charted 15 April, 1967)

SIDE 1
1. 'GIRL FROM IPANEMA' (Antonio Carlos Jobim, Vinicius de Moraes & Norman Gimbel) Recorded 31 January, 1967
2. 'DINDI' (Antonio Carlos Jobim & Aloysio de Oliverira) Recorded 30 January, 1967

3. 'CHANGE PARTNERS' (Irving Berlin) Recorded 30 January, 1967
4. 'QUIET NIGHT AND QUIET STARS (CORCOVADO)' (Antonio Carlos Jobim & Gene Lees) Recorded 31 January, 1967
5. 'MEDITATION' (Antonio Carlos Jobim, Newton Mendonça & Norman Gimbel) Recorded 31 January, 1967

SIDE 2
1. 'IF YOU NEVER COME TO ME' (Antonio Carlos Jobim & Ray Gilbert) Recorded 31 January, 1967

2. 'HOW INSENSITIVE (INSENSATEZ)' (Antonio Carlos Jobim, Vinicius de Moraes & Norman Gimbel) Recorded 1 February, 1967
3. 'I CONCENTRATE ON YOU' (Cole Porter) Recorded 30 January, 1967
4. 'BAUBLES, BANGLES AND BEADS' (Robert Wright & George Forrest) Recorded 30 January, 1967
5. 'ONCE I LOVED (O AMOR EN PAZ)' (Antonio Carlos Jobim, Vinicius de Moraes & Ray Gilbert) Recorded 1 February, 1967

it was almost compulsory for people to record it then. There were 600 recordings within a year! I was thrilled that Sinatra had done it. It was a thrill just to be in his canon. But I was disappointed that he did it in a swing version. I'd have preferred a soulful ballad," said Don Black.

TWO CAP IT ALL

After taking August off at home in Palm Springs Frank played the Sands for two weeks, starting on 30 August, although he missed the last three nights because he was suffering from "fatigue". His "fatigue" followed an altercation with the management of the Sands, who had cut off Frank's credit because "when Frank won, he took his chips, and when he lost he didn't pay his markers", according to Eleanor Roth, Jack Entratter's assistant. When Frank was refused credit in front of some of the Apollo astronauts, who were visiting the hotel, he completely lost his temper. He pulled all the wires out of the hotel switchboard and

LAST NAILS
Thanks to Frank's antics this became one of the final nails in his movie coffin. Sidney J Furie had directed The Ipcress File *in 1965, and he probably expected better.*

1963–1973

FRANK SINATRA AND THE WORLD WE KNEW

THIS IS FRANK'S ATTEMPT to produce a contemporary album for an audience which was pretty confused about what was going on in the world. Mot people failed to get it and it didn't even make the Top 20 (the four before this one all had). It sounds like a collection that has been thrown together, which indeed it is.

There are three songs that Frank had released as singles during the previous year along with three more that were big hits for other people. Five different arrangers contribute to the album and Nancy's mentor, Lee Hazlewood, along with Jimmy Bowen, pulled it all together.

SONG LINES

Recorded: United and Western Recorders.
Producers: Jimmy Bowen & Lee Hazlewood.
Chart: US No 24, 23 weeks on the chart
(First charted 16 September, 1967)
UK No 28, 5 weeks on the chart
(First charted 7 October, 1967)

Frank with Phil Ramone, who worked as an engineer on several tracks.

SIDE 1

1. 'THE WORLD WE KNEW (OVER AND OVER)
(Kaempfert, Herbert Rehbein & Sigman)
Recorded 29/30 June 1967, arr. Ernie Freeman

2. 'SOMETHIN' STUPID'
(Carson C Parks) Recorded 1 February 1967, arr. Billy Strange

3. 'THIS IS MY LOVE'
(James Harbert) Recorded 24 July 1967, arr. Gordon Jenkins

4. 'BORN FREE'
(Barry & Black) Recorded 24 July 1967, arr. Gordon Jenkins

5. 'DON'T SLEEP IN THE SUBWAY'
(Hatch & Trent) Recorded 24 July 1967, arr. Ernie Freeman

SIDE 2

1. 'THIS TOWN'
(Lee Hazlewood) Recorded 29/30 June 1967, arr. Billy Strange

2. 'THIS IS MY SONG '
(Charles Chaplin)
Recorded 24 July 1967, arr. Ernie Freeman.

3. 'YOU ARE THERE'
(Sukman & Webster) Recorded 29/30 June 1967, arr. Gordon Jenkins

4. 'DRINKING AGAIN'
(Mercer & Tauber) Recorded 31 January 1967, arr. Claus Ogerman

5. 'SOME ENCHANTED EVENING'
(Oscar Hammerstein II & Richard Rodgers)
Recorded 24 July 1967, arr. HB Barnum

drove a golf cart through a plate-glass window. According to Nancy, "it was all Entratter's fault for not telling Frank about the problem in the first place". Things got worse as the casino manager hit Frank in the mouth and knocked two caps off his front teeth. The District Attorney was far from happy, saying that Frank would be "run out of town if he doesn't stop behaving like he owns it".

Frank had problems at home too: he and Mia were not getting on well, and this had not been helped by the fact that Mia had been out on the town in Los Angeles and had innocently danced with Bobby Kennedy. Tina Sinatra talks affectionately of the Mia years and of how fond she was of "Mama Mia". She also points out in *My Father* how little Mia liked the kind of life that Frank enjoyed. He liked the nightlife, but she loathed it, or at least the kind of nightlife that involved sitting in restaurants with a bunch

of friends drinking and telling tall stories. Mia preferred the club scene on Sunset, dancing to Motown. As if to prove that bad things really do come in threes, Howard Hughes bought the Sands mid-way through Frank's engagement. Among those listed as owning shares in the property were Dean Martin, Jack Entratter, and Frank's old Cal-Neva partner, Sanford Waterman. It was the end of a 14-year engagement; Frank never again played the Sands. It eventually closed in November 1996, a month after being used in a Nicholas Cage movie, *Con-Air*, in which a plane full of convicts crashes into the front of the casino. Frank had made marginally less of a mess of the building with the golf cart.

PRELUDE TO THE END

In mid-October, Frank was in New York filming the follow-up to *Tony Rome*, to be called *The Detective*. At least no one would be confused. Frank had originally wanted Mia to appear with him in the movie, but she was well behind in filming *Rosemary's Baby* with Roman Polanski. The delay caused Frank a great deal of irritation, mostly because Mia refused to walk off the picture to join him.

While in New York, Frank played a benefit for the Italian American League at Madison Square Garden with Sammy Davis Jr. Sammy was having problems with his marriage to Mai Britt, and the old friends probably shared tales of woe.

Just prior to leaving Hollywood, Frank taped the third in his *A Man and His Music* series, featuring Antonio Carlos Jobim, and Ella Fitzgerald. Amazingly, he was still doing 'Ol' Man River', accompanied by just Bill Miller on piano. Frank even managed to get "cotton" and "taters" the wrong way around – which he left in even though the show was recorded. He also did medleys with both Antonio and Ella, and the show closed with the perennial 'Put Your Dreams Away.' According to *Downbeat*, "[It] was one of the best music shows ever presented on television. In marked contrast to the singer's previous 'specials,' the key to this hour was relaxed and unrestrained performance. The star and host was in superb voice. Gone was the rather forced vitality that has marred some of his more recent work; in its place, there was warmth, mellowness, and assurance without a trace of arrogance."

A week or so after *A Man and His Music* aired, Mia was served with divorce papers on the set of *Rosemary's Baby*. Frank had, it could be argued, come to his senses over a

THE BEST
Frank and Ella Fitzgerald on the set of A Man and His Music, *where they performed with Antonio Carlos Jobim.*

TONY ROME

IT WOULD HAVE BEEN SAD if *The Naked Runner* had been Frank's movie swan song. While it undoubtedly reduced his Hollywood collateral, it came out too late to affect Frank being cast as a down and not-quite-out private detective named Tony Rome.

It was directed by veteran actor/director Gordon Douglas, who had made almost 90 films before Tony Rome and who turned 60 just after the movie came out. He had last worked with Frank on *Robin & The Seven Hoods*, which did not bode well for this film, and had also directed *Young at Heart*. Although Frank did not have the distraction of Sammy and Dean during filming, both Jilly Rizzo and Michael Romanoff had bit-part cameos. Nancy Sinatra sang the title song, which

was written by Lee Hazlewood, and it got to No 83 on the *Billboard* chart. Also on the soundtrack was a song called 'Hard Times', with music by Billy May and lyrics by a young unknown songwriter, Randy Newman. Newman was working for a Californian music publisher and would go on to write 14 Academy Award-nominated songs and write Three Dog Night's No 1 'Mama Told Me Not to Come' in 1970.

marriage that was doomed from the start. Mia was just too young and her world was entirely at odds with Frank's world, and she, unlike others, was far from happy living in it. The restrictions, the rules, and the claustrophobic atmosphere would be tough for anyone, but impossible for someone so young. There is, however, ample evidence to suggest that it hurt Frank greatly, he obviously loved her, even if it was in his own way. The break-up was going to be tough.

A few weeks later, Frank, together with Dean and Sammy, was a guest on Nancy's television special. It aired on 11 December, the same day that Frank went into the studio with another giant from the jazz world. Having played with the Count he was now working with a Duke – Edward Kennedy Ellington, the 68-year-old composer, pianist, and bandleader. Frank must have really enjoyed it because he worked the next night too, which was his 52nd birthday. The first song they cut was Stephen Sondheim and Jules Styne's 'All I Need Is the Girl'. It was not a song of longing for Mia, but it is uncanny how Frank's material seems always to be so apposite. Meanwhile in Britain, a story had been reported in the *NME* on 2 December, which claimed that singer Long John Baldry had been lined up to star in a series of 13 one-hour colour television shows. "Baldry would sing and act in the shows in which he would play a Sinatra-like show business tycoon," said his manager, Simon Napier Bell. It never did come to anything, but it is interesting to see how Frank was beginning to be viewed by people in the entertainment world.

THE END IS NEAR

Frank and Mia were not quite over, and they spent Christmas 1967 together, but it proved only a temporary reunion. She admitted as much in a *Playboy* interview shortly after Christmas, before flying to India with her sister Prudence. They went to Rishikash, where they joined the Beatles, Mike Love of the Beach Boys, and the singer Donovan. They were all there to "study" with the Maharishi; this was much more Mia's scene than Palm Springs.

In January 1968, Frank was back at the Fontainebleau entertaining the snowbirds who had flown south to escape the New York winter. In actual fact, he spent the first quarter of the year in Miami, both performing and filming. At the end of February/beginning of March, he began work on his new movie, *Lady in Cement*. This overlapped

IN THE GROOVE
From left to right: "Dear" Prudence Farrow, John Lennon, Mike Love, the Maharishi, George Harrison, Mia, Donovan, Paul McCartney, Jane Asher, and Cynthia Lennon.

THE WHITE HOUSE, WASHINGTON DC

"No one ever to this date was more impressive. He had more colour, more controversy, more style than anyone — he was a walking bureau of activity of every type, with all the charisma. There were things only he could sing."

PAUL ANKA

with his second run at the Fontainebleau, which began on 3 March. Frank's preferred method of working was to begin filming at around noon at the earliest and carry on until about 7:00 pm. This gave him time to get back and do his show at the hotel in the evening. The film's director, Gordon Douglas, set up shots with Frank's stand-in so that Frank could film with the minimum of waiting around.

Frank's first public appearance on the West Coast for quite a while was when he hosted the annual Emmy TV Awards on 19 May in Hollywood. Three nights later, Frank headed north on the Californian coast to Oakland for a fund-raising event for Democrat Senator Hubert Humphrey at the Oakland Coliseum. Frank gave a wonderful performance that night, running through the usual selection of Capitol classics, along with 'Nancy' and 'Ol' Man River' from the 1940s. There was a clutch of Reprise-era songs, including one of his newest recordings, the wonderful 'All I Need Is the Girl' from the Ellington sessions. Unusually, Frank also sang a song that he had not yet recorded. 'Goin' Out of My Head', by Teddy Randazzo and Bobby Weinstein, had been a big hit for Little Anthony and The Imperials in 1964, and The Lettermen, a close-harmony group on Capitol, had had a Top 10 hit with a cover version in early 1968, when they

combined it in a medley with 'Can't Get Used to Losing You'. Frank introduced the song as being arranged by Nelson Riddle and gave an impassioned performance of this very sensual song. Was it for Mia? It could well have been. At the show's end, Frank said, "Ladies and gentlemen, I am quite grateful for your attendance and your applause and your reason for being here. I hope that in the very near future I will be back here with the candidate."

Two weeks later Robert Kennedy, who had won the California primary, was shot at the Ambassador Hotel in Los Angeles; he died in hospital the next day. While Frank had clearly been supporting his opponent, he must have been upset as he remembered how the younger Kennedy had helped him during the kidnap of Frank Jr. On the other hand, his support for Humphrey was perhaps initiated by his antipathy towards Bobby for what he saw as meddling in his relationship with JFK. In Frank's world loyalty counted, and the Kennedys were not loyal – at least not to him.

COP SHOW
The second film in the detective trilogy is better than the first. It was released in June to some of the better reviews of Frank's latter-period film career. "Sinatra has honed his laconic, hep veneer to the point of maximum credibility" said the Hollywood Reporter.

AN EARLY CHRISTMAS

In the wake of Bobby's assassination, Frank's support for Humphrey continued with a series of fund-raisers throughout the country in Cleveland, Minneapolis, Baltimore, Detroit, and Philadelphia between 18 July and 3 August. While Frank was on the road, he had only his second recording session in New York in almost 16 years. It was also his first session of the year, and the year was half over. On the evening of 25 July, he cut three songs all arranged by Don Costa, one of which was 'Cycles', the title song of Frank's next album. He also did 'Whatever Happened to Christmas?', a song written by Jimmy Webb, which would feature on another album, *The Sinatra Family Wish You a Merry Christmas*. (A month earlier, 'MacArthur Park', another of Jimmy's songs, had gone to No 2 on the Hot 100 sung by the charismatic Irish actor Richard Harris.) "I was driving across a causeway near my home in the icy depths of winter this last December (2002) and chanced to hear 'Whatever Happened to Christmas?' in its entirety and I was pretty much blown away", remembers Jimmy Webb. "It was a beautiful record, exquisitely arranged, and sung with great tenderness by

TUNESMITH
Jimmy Webb has helped carry the torch lit by the writers of the Great American Songbook. He is a multiple Grammy award-winner, and a true musical innovator.

FRANCIS A & EDWARD K

THIS UNIQUE COLLABORATION went almost unnoticed at the time of its release, failing even to make the Top 40 album chart in early spring 1968. It was a collection arranged and conducted by Billy May, who, in 1999, described Frank's voice to Scottish singer Vance Adair: "There's no airiness there, it's all pure sound – layer upon layer of it," which aptly describes *the* voice alongside one of *the* great jazz orchestras.

Listen to 'Indian Summer', and you can't help feel how perfect it is for both Frank and the Duke. The arrangement is reflectively modern, and at the same time old-fashioned, as befits a song from 1919 – the "Ellington Effect" à la Billy May. Some have gone as far as saying that it is one of the best songs Frank ever recorded for Reprise. Johnny Hodges' sax solo certainly adds to the overall effect, and so enthralled was Frank during the recording that when it ends he's half a second late coming in. It was an album that was not without its problems – not least the fact that the

Ellington orchestra had not done all the prep work they should have before they got to the studio which, coupled with the fact that they were not the best sight readers, meant that there were a few headaches for Billy May, who was conducting the rehearsals at Western Recorders on 8 December.

SONG LINES

Recorded: Western Recorders
Chart: US No 78, 13 weeks on the chart
(First charted 24 February, 1968)

SIDE 1

1. 'FOLLOW ME'
(Frederick Lowe & Alan Jay Lerner)
Recorded 12 December, 1967

2. 'SUNNY'
(Bobby Hebb)
Recorded 12 December, 1967

3. 'ALL I NEED IS THE GIRL'
(Jule Styne & Stephen Sondheim)
Recorded 11 December, 1967

4. 'INDIAN SUMMER'
(Victor Herbert & Al Dubin)
Recorded 11 December, 1967

SIDE 2

1. 'I LIKE THE SUNRISE'
(Duke Ellington)
Recorded 12 December, 1967

2. 'YELLOW DAYS'
(Alan Bernstein & Alarcon Carrillo)
Recorded 12 December, 1967

3. 'POOR BUTTERFLY'
(Raymond Hubbel & John Golden)
Recorded 12 December, 1967

4. 'COME BACK TO ME'
(Burton Lane & Alan Jay Lerner)
Recorded 11 December, 1967

LADY IN CEMENT

This was a first for Frank: it was given an "R" classification upon its release in November 1968. The combination of violence and bare flesh was too much for the censors.

one of the greatest musical figures of our century. Tears came to my eyes and ran down my face. And just how was it that an unknown teenage songwriter from Oklahoma came to be recorded by this giant? The Lord works in mysterious ways."

When Frank got back to California, he and his three children had an early Christmas recording songs for their family album at Western Recorders on 12 August. Four days later, Frank was taping a television special with Don Costa when he got a call from his lawyer, Mickey Rudin, who told him that his divorce from Mia was final. According to Nancy, who was with him, "It was as if someone had turned the lights out in his

eyes." It is reported that Frank was too upset to continue the taping of the show, and so what everyone saw when it aired a few months later was the dress rehearsal. According to Don Van Atta, who was the executive producer, "We always taped the dress-rehearsals with an audience, then taped the show with an audience and then made cuts from the best of everything. So we had done one rehearsal with Frank, and shot the whole thing. Then there was the usual hour, hour and a half break between the rehearsal and the show tapings so everybody could get something to eat and take a rest and refresh their make-up, change their wardrobe, change the audience, et cetera et cetera. And, well, Frank thought that the dress rehearsal that we taped was pretty darn good. So he said 'I think I'll go home now.' And he did. True, the show was great, so no one was going to say 'C'mon Frank, you can't do that! We've got to do better.'" Interestingly, Mia asked for no settlement and in time became a firm friend of Frank's; this was definitely not another Ava.

Three days after taping the show, Frank was on the front page of the *Wall Street Journal*. Nicholas Gage, a staff reporter, wrote a barbed piece about Frank, signalling his intent from the very first line – this was personal: "Frank Sinatra is rather sensitive about his baldness." He then went on to name several Mafia bosses as close enough friends to be allowed in his presence without a hairpiece. A central theme to the piece was that Frank had been identified by JFK's aides as too closely associated with the Mob (for aides, read Robert Kennedy, Humphrey's opponent). Gage had attempted to contact Frank for a comment before the article went to press, but was told by his PR man "Mr. Sinatra is taping his next television special." The spokesman denied that Frank associated with undesirables, suggesting they should concentrate on the Presidents, heads of states and hundreds of personalities much more interesting and copy worthy." It's possible this is what stopped Frank taping the show proper – he was probably incensed. Frank didn't work again until November, when he spent three days cutting the remaining tracks for *Cycles* with Don Costa. He also recorded a couple of songs with Nelson that would end up as the b-sides of singles. After the euphoria of 'Strangers in The Night' and 'Something Stupid', Frank's performance on the Hot 100 had once again slipped back into the familiar 60's pattern. The three singles that followed 'Somethin' Stupid' all struggled to make the middle reaches of the chart. 'Cycles' came out in advance of the album and actually did fairly decently by getting to No 23, staying on the charts for two and half months. Five days before Frank went into the studio, Humphrey, having won the Democratic nomination, was narrowly defeated by Richard Nixon at the polls on November 6. After the *Wall Street Journal* article, the Humphrey team had made some attempt

NICE

This album is very much a product of its time. Frank sings just two songs solo, which are unquestionably the musical highlights. Besides 'Whatever Happened to Christmas?' he does 'The Christmas Waltz'.

to distance themselves, although Frank's support never wavered. With the holiday season looming, Frank's TV special aired over Thanksgiving. Called *Francis Albert Sinatra Does His Thing*, Frank did just that, along with medleys with his guests, Diahann Carroll and the 5th Dimension. In an effort to put Frank into the mood of the time, he became the 6th Dimension and sang 'Sweet Blindness'. He wore a Nehru jacket and had beads around his neck. The day after the show aired, Frank had his debut at Caesars Palace in Las Vegas. The 700-room, 14-storey hotel and casino had opened in 1966, with each guest being welcomed by the official greeter, a blonde, statuesque "Cleopatra". The first show at Caesars was *Rome Swings*, which featured Andy Williams. Even before Frank played there, it had become famous when Evel Knievel almost killed himself trying to jump the hotel's fountains on his motorbike. In Caesars Forum, the world's largest crystal ceiling fixture dominated the interior; Frank played the 1,200-seat Circus Maximus.

MIDDLE-AGED ANTHEM

With Christmas over, Frank was back in Western Recorders on the day before New Year's Eve for a rare event, an afternoon recording session. Starting at around 3:00 pm, 40 musicians conducted by Bill Miller began working on what would become an anthem for Frank — and a whole generation. In a review of Frank's Reprise CD box set in the 1990s, *Downbeat* said, "'My Way' helped Frank reinvent himself." Composed as 'Comme d'Habitude' ('As Usual'), it was written by Jacques Revaux and Gilles Thibault, along with Egyptian-born French singer Claude François.

GROOVY FRANK

The Nehru jacket, the beads — maybe only the hair was missing. The hippies had a lot to answer for.

CYCLES

Released just before Christmas 1968, there were ten months between the release of his Ellington collaboration and Cycles — the longest period without an album since Frank's falling out with Capitol almost ten years earlier. The material is a reflection of Frank's personal life, and also demonstrates the challenge of finding material with which he felt comfortable.

Canadian singer Paul Anka, Don Costa's old protégé, provided the English words.

"I had a house in France, which was where I heard the Claude François record," said Paul Anka. "I liked the melody, but not the words so much. I knew the French publisher and they gave me the song, and I thought I would re-construct the feel of the song. I met Frank where he was filming *Tony Rome*, and he said he was retiring. The song became a composite of my life and his, but mostly his. I made a demo with a session singer, called him; I said that I thought I had something pretty sensational. Don saw the worth of it — Frank stayed cool, but I knew he liked it. Three, four, five weeks later, I had a phone call and they said 'listen to this' and played the record over the phone to me. They were very excited! I'd never had a song quite of that substance. It was pressed up, but they threw the first run copies away because they didn't like the mix."

Anka's attempt at an English lyric was not the first. A few months earlier, David Bowie had had a crack at the song, calling it 'Even a Fool Learns to Love', but his demo was not acceptable to the publisher:

"There was a time, the laughing time
I took my heart to every party
They'd point my way
'How are you today?'"

from 'Even a Fool Learns to Love'

'My Way', entered the *Billboard* chart in the last week of March 1969 at No 69; it was the highest new entry of the week. Six weeks later, it had climbed to No 27, where it stalled, which is somewhat surprising given its subsequent fame. It made No 5 in the UK, which accounts for the fact that the LP of the same name did significantly better in Britain in the summer of 1969.

Besides being a karaoke classic, 'My Way' has been recorded by a whole mass of artists. It made the US charts in 1970, having been covered by Brook Benton, and again in 1977, when it got to No 22, in the first posthumous Elvis Presley release. In Britain, the Sex Pistols took it to No 7 in

1963–1973

MY WAY

THIS IS ANOTHER ALBUM full of contemporary material along with a few standards, but a better one than most of his recent efforts. Yet it's still hard to get excited about this Don Costa arranged and conducted album. It's almost as though Frank's trying too hard, and too anxious to appear contemporary. But there are good songs, and Frank performs well with some sparkling Costa work. *My Way* became the first of Frank's regular albums to do significantly better in Britain than in the US. It failed to reach the top in the UK only because of a Ray Conniff album – it was Conniff who arranged 'Castle Rock', which Frank sang with Harry James back in 1951.

SONG LINES

Recorded: Western Recorders
Producer Sonny Burke
Chart: US No 11, 19 weeks on the chart
(First charted 10 May, 1969)
UK No 2, 59 weeks on the chart
(First charted 7 June, 1969)

SIDE 1

1. 'WATCH WHAT HAPPENS'
(Michel Legrand, Jacques Louis Demy, and Norman Gimbel). Recorded
24 February, 1969.

2. 'DIDN'T WE'
(Jimmy Webb) Recorded 18 February, 1969.

3. 'HALLELUJAH, I LOVE HER SO'
(Ray Charles) Recorded 24 February 1969.

4. 'YESTERDAY'
(John Lennon & Paul McCartney)
Frank became one of the thousands of artists to cover Lennon and McCartney's 'Yesterday', and his reading is one of the best, again proving that Frank could handle songs with poignancy and pathos better than almost anyone during this period (or indeed any period).

5. 'ALL MY TOMORROWS'
(Sammy Cahn & Jimmy Van Heusen)
Recorded 18 February, 1969.

SIDE 2

1. 'MY WAY'
(Anka, Francois, Revaux, and Thibault)

2. 'A DAY IN THE LIFE OF A FOOL'
(Luiz Bonfa, Antonio Marez, and Carl Sigman). Recorded 20 February, 1969.

3. 'FOR ONCE IN MY LIFE'
(Ronald Miller and Orlando Murden)

4. 'IF YOU GO AWAY'
(Jaques Brel & Rod McKuen)
Recorded 24 February, 1969.

5. 'MRS. ROBINSON'
(Paul Simon) Recorded 24 February, 1969.
Paul Simon had originally written the line "Jesus loves you more than you'll ever know". Frank changed Jesus to Jilly, no doubt in honour of his friend Jilly Rizzo. Frank also leaves out any mention of Joe DiMaggio in his version; he was probably still smarting over the "wrong door" incident.

follows 'My Way'. Clearly their logic was chronology, but it throws up as bad a piece of programming as you can imagine, one that you cannot envisage Frank allowing if he had been in control.

There is a sadness about 'Wave' that Frank's delivery nails perfectly. In fact it was recorded just three weeks after Frank's father Marty, in the company of Dolly, had been flown to Houston to consult the best heart specialists available. Marty had been having health problems for some time, but they could do nothing – Marty's heart simply gave out. He was 74.

The funeral, back in New Jersey, attracted a large number of celebrity watchers, along with huge floral tributes from Frank's friends in Hollywood and Las Vegas. It took 75 limos to transport the guests. Dolly and Marty had been living in Fort Lee, New Jersey, and soon after his father died Frank began lobbying Dolly about moving to Palm Springs. Dolly was not at all keen – she felt it was too far from her Jersey friends, and she was not happy about living in the desert during the searing summer heat. Frank countered every one of her arguments against leaving Jersey. He offered to fly friends to California to see her; he even said he would get her another home near the ocean for the summer. Eventually Dolly gave in and moved west to live in a five-bedroom house Frank had specially built for her.

1978, and almost 20 years later Shane MacGowan, the lead singer of Irish band The Pogues, briefly made the Top 30. Frank himself cut it again as part of his *Duets* project in 1993. It was released as a bonus cut on a Capitol CD, *Sinatra 80th: Live in Concert*, with Italian tenor Luciano Pavarotti sharing the vocals. This was not the only duet version attempted; one was done with country legend Willie Nelson and another with singer Jon Secada; neither was released. The producers of TV talent show *Opportunity Knocks* had to tell hopefuls "Give you music to the pianist, but please, no more 'My Way's". And as proof of his despotic insanity, Saddam Hussein chose Frank's version of 'My Way' as the theme song for his 54th birthday.

Six weeks later, Frank was back at Western Recorders. It was to prove a huge contrast to the bombast of 'My Way'. He began working on another set of Brazilian subtleties with Antonio Carlos Jobim. At the first session on 11 February, he recorded the lovely 'Wave', only this time the arranger was not Claus Ogerman but another Brazilian, 27-year-old Eumir Deodato. On the Reprise four CD career retrospective issued in the 1990s, 'Wave'

WITH ROD McKUEN
Teaming up with West Coast poet Rod McKuen was another step in Frank's progress towards elder statesman of "popular" music.

A MAN ALONE

Following his father's death, Frank threw himself into his work. Besides the 11 February session, there were five more during February at which he recorded sixteen songs. As well as more songs with Jobim, Frank did a number of contemporary songs including Jimmy Webb's 'Didn't We', Paul Simon's 'Mrs. Robinson', and 'If You Go Away', a French song by Jacques Brel with English words by Rod McKuen. A month later, on 19 March, Frank began working on what would be another of his more unusual albums, a whole album written by Rod McKuen, to be called *A Man Alone*; it's another that divides both critics and fans. McKuen's simple melodies are made very effective by Don Costa's arrangements but it is the poetic lyrics, as well as some poems that are spoken by Frank, that cause people the most difficulty. Many feel uncomfortable with Frank reciting what is far from the greatest poetry. There seems little doubt that Frank identified with McKuen's lyrics. His relationship with Mia had ended when they first started working on the idea. Marty's illness and death made Frank acknowledge his own mortality, what better way to say that than in song? As Frank said "real singing is acting."

With the exception of the Jobim songs, the others that Frank recorded in February came out on *My Way* in May. The album entered the US charts the day after Frank opened at Caesars Palace for a two week run. After that

Frank retreated to Palm Springs for the summer to oversee Dolly's move and to no doubt recharge his batteries in preparation to begin work on yet another album, well before *A Man Alone* was ready for release.

GREAT CONCEPT

This was to be another unusual LP, a concept album that was as far removed from the mother-lode of the Great American Songbook as it is possible to be. On 14 July at Columbia studio in New York, work began on the orchestral tracks for *Watertown*. Singing against a backing track was something that Frank was not keen to do, and it was another factor that made the album different. It was similar to *A Man Alone*, only this time it was two young songwriters who wrote every track; 27-year-old Bob Gaudio and 29-year-old lyricist Jake Holmes. Gaudio takes up the story: "*Watertown* was conceived as a total project – initially it was planned as a one-man TV special about a small town average Joe with the wife leaving – all very contrary to his image! Frank had heard a fair bit of my music (things like 'Can't Take My Eyes Off Of You' and 'The Sun Ain't Gonna Shine Anymore'), and through his friendship with Frankie Valli he contacted me and said 'send me some songs'. I was under the impression that it was to be a song concept. When Jake and I were writing it, we didn't have any pictorial concept in mind, though we realized it could be a good TV special. We wrote it and sent him the demos that Jake had sung, which were pretty good as Jake is a fine singer. A little later we got the call from his man George Weiss, and he said 'Guess what kid, he wants to do them all!' Frank had got the story straight away – his focus was on the whole story."

Frank was in New York in July when the tracks were laid down, which caused Gaudio just a few headaches. "I got in early – the orchestra was there all set up. I had asked the contractor to get the best that New York had to offer. We were in the old church studio that Columbia had on 32nd St. The booth there was a couple of stories up, above the orchestra, and I was there going through with the strings before he got there. I'm listening to them, and they are *really* not on it! I thought 'Oh My God!' I was very edgy and I started panicking, and I told the contractor that this was certainly not an 'A' team! I'm still up in the booth when Frank walks straight

LYRICISTS
Paul Anka (top) and David Bowie (bottom) were very much "of their generation". And both did it their way.

POETIC LIBRETTIST
A rare book of the poetry that formed the lyrics to Rod McKuen's songs on Frank's A Man Alone *album.*

1963-1973

THE FOUR SEASONS
Left to right: Tommy DeVito, Frankie Valli, Bob Gaudio, and Nick Massi. While Frankie's falsetto was the "voice" of the group, it was Gaudio, along with the band's producer Bob Crewe, who wrote many of their hits, including their first No 1 'Sherry' in 1962. Charlie Calello, who conducted and was co-arranger of the Watertown *sessions, was also briefly a member of the band.*

GOING TO THE MOON
When the Astrodome opened in 1966, it was considered one of the world's engineering marvels. Its infrastructure was the perfect setting for Robert Altman's quirky film Brewster McCloud *(1971).*

in and says straight away, 'Right, let's do one.' And they run it down *perfectly*! He had set them up!"

The writing of *Watertown* was a total collaboration between Holmes and Gaudio. Holmes recalled, "Bobby and I had worked on the Seasons' album *Genuine Imitation Life Gazette*. First we did 'Lady Day' as a one-off, as a single I guess, and then we worked on the album. We decided it would be a concept – a story album. *Watertown* is a fakey place, though there is a Watertown in New York, but I don't think it has a train line through it. I envisaged that Frank Sinatra could do it as a TV special, with the wig off, and do it as an old man. Some people at the time, and since, have asked if it was meant as a metaphor for him and Mia Farrow, but it was conceived more as a character thing of a restless girl and a man who had 'settled in'. When we came to record it with him, we did I believe present it as a 'character' idea, but I recall that Frank pretty well batted that one aside straight away. Bobby basically had the music first, but I sat with him, and the work was very much integrated. We stayed in our main areas, but we did cross-collaborate. During the time I stayed with him, and we'd both decide things. We really liked the end result – there are a lot of the songs that I still really like. Bob Gaudio is a very melodic writer, and he knows how to write for voice. I'm good at character/ theatrical writing, and I wanted to put Frank in a character place. I did the vocals on some rough tracks that we presented for him, and then we were into the studio."

Gaudio felt that Frank was totally at ease with the concept: "He was very confident and comfortable taking risks with it – to the extent of having the cover without his face on it. Once finished, he elected not to do the TV special – he wasn't looking or feeling that great at that point, so we thought and suggested that we could put it on ice until later when maybe he felt better about doing the TV show. However he said, 'No, I'm proud of it – Let's put it out!' So out it came, but without any real launch, and it didn't do too well even though he did have an AC No 1 hit at the time." The fact is that *Watertown* was poorly marketed, and, given the background to what else was going on – Woodstock, the dawning of the rock generation – it is perhaps not surprising to see its small sales. What is so interesting is the fact that Frank had the nerve at this stage in his career to try something so new and so completely different.

During the orchestral sessions, there was a very funny incident. According to Gaudio, "We had been rehearsing at the Waldorf for keys. I was walking with Frank to the elevator when I said, 'Why don't you come out to Jersey next weekend, and have a good relaxing time.' I had a nice new house. Frank said, 'Yes, maybe I will.' Then he said that if I were providing the house, he would bring everything else and that we would have a great day. So I said 'Great, remember to bring your trunks…' On the way down the elevator, I suddenly remembered that I didn't have a pool. I had just sold a house that *did* have one, and I had forgotten. What was I going to do? I called my friend the Police Chief of Montclair – an Italian of course – and he said – 'If its Frank Sinatra, all things can be done!' He called a contractor he knew, and some other guys, and all he wanted from it was to shake Frank Sinatra's hand! The pool was built some 200/300 metres away from the house in a sort of natural dip, with 30 or so steps leading down to it. They managed to get it done… just. The day Frank was to come, an old man was still finishing the steep grass surround a half hour before he was due to get there. He gives me the signal that all the sloping sides are finished just in time! Frank arrives, and the cars pull into the driveway, and just at that moment there was the most torrential downpour… really, really heavy rain! And the new grass had all slid down into the pool!! It was a total mess that took weeks to clean up! Anyway Frank took the time to go out and meet the old man who had finished the pool for him, and shook his hand. Frank really laughed!! And I got a new pool out of it, so I was happy too! Frank and his bunch stayed all day and we had a great time."

Just prior to doing the vocal overdubs for *Watertown* in Hollywood, Frank finally got around to recording 'Goin' out of My Head'. It would become Frank's fourth chart single of 1969, following 'Love's Been Good to Me' into the Hot 100, although neither song managed to crack the Top 70. Like 'My Way', 'Loves Been Good to Me' did very well in the UK, although it failed to match the amazing chart run for 'My Way' of 42 weeks on the singles chart in 1969. It did, however, reach No 8 and stayed around for four months. It meant that Frank did really well on the annual NME chart survey, prompting Derek Johnson to comment: "It's always good to see Sinatra in the hit parade with the younger element. I can't help wondering how many of today's pop stars will still be around when they are in their fifties." Few will emulate Frank's achievement with 'My Way': it re-entered the British charts eight times after its initial release, the last occasion being in 1972. In 1994, Reprise once again reissued it and it still crept into the charts at No 45, staying there for two weeks. Altogether, 'My Way' spent 124 weeks on the UK singles chart.

FLY ME TO THE MOON – AND BACK

During the summer of '69, Frank appeared at the Astrodome in Houston in an all-star tribute to the Apollo 11 astronauts. Frank's recording of 'Fly Me to The Moon' had been played to the space travellers while en route to the moon. Two weeks later Frank was back in Vegas appearing at Caesars (where he closed a show for the first time with 'My Way'), at the same time as Nancy was booked into the Hilton and Junior was at the Frontier.

Frank's last studio session of the 60s was on November 7 when he cut 'Lady Day' with Don Costa conducting. It would be another 51 weeks before he set foot in a recording studio; the longest gap in his whole career to

A MAN ALONE

FRANK WAS VERY MUCH A TRADITIONALIST in all he did, and so to wait until he was 53 to do an album of material written by just one man was perhaps a strange choice – stranger still in that Rod McKuen was not someone many would consider a songwriter, he was more a poet. He had met Frank at a party, which is how the album came to be made. It's another that polarizes the opinion of Frank's dedicated fans; some find it almost unlistenable, and others love it. It was helped immeasurably by the brilliant Don Costa arrangements and Frank does a great job interpreting the song lyrics even if he struggles with the poetry. Chart-wise it was helped by 'Love's Been Good To Me', especially in Britain where it made No 8. Yet another look back over a life that clearly struck a chord with some, and made others wonder.

SONG LINES
Recorded: Western Recorders
19. 20 & 21 March, 1969
Producer Sonny Burke
Chart: US No 30, 16 weeks on the chart
(First charted 6 September, 1969)
UK No 18, 7 weeks on the chart
(First charted 4 October, 1969)

SIDE 1
1. 'A MAN ALONE' (Rod McKuen)
2. 'NIGHT' (Rod McKuen)
3. 'I'VE BEEN IN TOWN' (Rod McKuen)
4. 'FROM PROMISE TO PROMISE' (Rod McKuen)
5. 'THE SINGLE MAN' (Rod McKuen)
6. 'THE BEAUTIFUL STRANGERS' (Rod McKuen)

SIDE 2
1. 'LONESOME CITIES' (Rod McKuen)
2. 'LOVE'S BEEN GOOD TO ME' (Rod McKuen)
3. 'EMPTY IS' (Rod McKuen)
4. 'OUT BEYOND THE WINDOW' (Rod McKuen)
5. 'SOME TRAVELING MUSIC' (Rod McKuen)
6. 'A MAN ALONE' (Rod McKuen)

this point. 'Lady Day' was intended to be the title track of a tribute album to Billie Holiday that for one reason and another got dropped. Two days before the 'Lady Day' session Frank's latest TV special aired. Unusually almost every song was a contemporary one – even the Great American Songbook was ditched. The *New York Times* headline about the TV special was another small kick in the teeth for Frank: "CHARM OUTLIVES VOICE". George Gent went on to say "Frank Sinatra has long since passed beyond the point of formal criticism. It is one of the privileges of living legends… the famous Sinatra voice, once so redolent of sex and longing, is all but gone, and what remains is dry and without timbre. What is still without flaw and even seems to grow with the years is the Sinatra techniques, the impeccably intelligent phrasing that sips every fragrant nuance from overly familiar lyrics and convinces each listener that Frankie is singing for just him – or her."

Frank's first real work of the 1970s was on *Dirty Dingus Magee* which

JAKE HOLMES
The classic 1960s folkie pose – but it failed to really launch Holmes' career as a solo artist.

WATERTOWN

IF *A MAN ALONE* was ambitious and different, then Frank clearly thought it was a trend worth continuing with *Watertown*. Where his classic Capitol albums had been thematic, this is a concept, in reality a song cycle, play, or story about an imaginary New England town. Bob Gaudio and Jake Holmes created the story of a man who has been left by his wife to look after their children. Each song adds to the imagery and at the same time conveys the sadness of a man without hope. Frank handles it brilliantly, and conductor/arranger Charlie Calello creates a musical backdrop that is both retro and modern, a perfect counterpoint to Frank. It is a brilliant, underrated album that bombed at the time, and still causes tempers to fray in heated debate among serious Sinatraphiles. The measure of its commercial failure is in the fact that over 400,000 copies were pressed at the time and it sold only around 35,000 – about 40 per cent of sales for *A Man Alone*. It became his third album in a row to do better in Britain than in the US. One aspect of *Watertown*'s failure was its lack of obvious single material. As a concept album, it was very definitely the sum of its parts.

Once Frank began the concert years, material from *Watertown* was hardly heard. He attempted 'Michael and Peter,' 'Elizabeth', and 'I Would Be in Love Anyway' a few times, but was unhappy with the orchestral sound. He felt that he could not recreate the album's sound, so he dropped them.

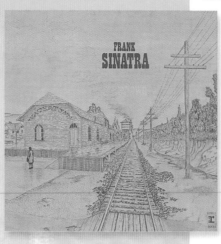

> **❝** It is a story, It's an attitude. I love the material. I think the kids did a great job. **❞**
>
> **FRANK, JUNE 1970**

SONG LINES

Orchestra recorded in New York,
Vocals recorded at Western Recorders
Producer Bob Gaudio
All songs written by
Bob Gaudio & Jake Holmes
Chart: US No 101, 10 weeks on the chart
(First charted 11 April, 1970)
UK No 14, 9 weeks on the chart
(First charted 9 May, 1970)

SIDE 1

1. 'WATERTOWN'
Recorded track 15 July, 1969
Vocal 26 August, 1969

2. 'GOODBYE (SHE QUIETLY SAYS)'
Recorded track 14 July, 1969
Vocal 27 August, 1969

3. 'FOR A WHILE'
Recorded track 13 October, 1969
Vocal 31 October, 1969

4. 'MICHAEL AND PETER'
Recorded track 13 October, 1969
Vocal 31 October, 1969

5. 'I WOULD BE IN LOVE (ANYWAY)' Recorded track 14 July, 1969 Vocal 25 August, 1969

SIDE 2

1. 'ELIZABETH'
Recorded track 15 July, 1969
Vocal 31 October, 1969

2. 'WHAT A FUNNY GIRL (YOU USED TO BE)'
Recorded track 17 July, 1969
Vocal 27 August, 1969

3. 'WHAT'S NOW IS NOW'
Recorded track 16 July, 1969
Vocal 26 August, 1969

4. 'SHE SAYS'
Recorded track 16 July, 1969
Vocal 25 August, 1969

5. 'THE TRAIN'
Recorded track 14 July, 1969
Vocal 25 August, 1969

began location filming in Tucson, Arizona on 24 February, 1970. He broke off to fly to Washington to make an appearance at the White House in a tribute to Senator Everett Dirksen. Interestingly, Dirksen, who had died a few months previously, and President Nixon were, of course, both Republicans. For Frank, the confirmed Democrat, it marked a shift in his politics, and one that was to become a huge jump over the coming decades.

Filming and the White House were a welcome relief as he had just been called to testify before the New Jersey State Committee investigating organized crime on 17 February; you cannot help but marvel at the incongruity. Frank had already refused a subpoena to attend, saying that he was "not going to be a part of a three ring circus". When he finally did appear, he was once again put on the spot about his relationship with the usual suspects, Luciano, Moretti, Fischetti, Lansky, *et al.* Once again, Frank denied knowing that any of these men were members of any illegal organization. In other cases, he claimed barely to have known people whose names were put to him. The chairman dismissed the contempt charges and announced that Frank had cooperated. This did not, however, stop the headlines and press banter. It would also have another, somewhat unlikely repercussion.

LONDON CALLING

On 10 March, Hoover and the FBI had an unusual request from the American embassy in London: "On March nine last John Waldron Commissioner Metropolitan Police, Scotland Yard advised Sinatra and Count Basie appearing at London's Royal Festival Hall on May seven and eight next in charity performance for benefit of Society of Cruelty to Children. Society holds annual performance, is one of Royal Family's favorite charities. They are usually invited and usually attend. The Commissioner is extremely concerned over recent publicity afforded Sinatra over testimony re Mafia connections in New Jersey. Commissioner must make recommendations for or against appearance of Queen. If Queen attends Sinatra will be presented to her and he fears unfavourable press may result."

The FBI responded two days later with details of Frank's "affiliation over the years with such well known hoodlums and members of the La Cosa Nostra". The FBI recommended that the American Embassy furnish Scotland Yard with the information. Despite this information, Frank was fêted at an Embassy party with Ambassador Walter Annenberg, although the Queen was notable in her absence from the Festival Hall.

The 2 May edition of the *Melody Maker* reported that Frank was flying in with the Count Basie Orchestra and would be backed by an additional 24 British musicians. "Impresario Harold Davison lashed out at the reported black market tickets. 'Naturally I am disgusted with it all. It's just that some people have got hold of two tickets for £5 and maybe they're asking and getting £30 for them.'" A couple of weeks later the same paper announced that the concerts had made £120,000 for the charity. Earlier in the year hopes of Frank playing outside London were dashed when a bid by the Wakefield

Theatre Club to stage some Sinatra/Basie shows was turned down by Frank over what the club alleged were "tax problems".

Preparation for the concerts was meticulous, as was everything with Frank. According to Don Lusher, who played on this date and many other European dates, they followed a pretty set pattern: "We would meet up and there was a set routine – there would be four rehearsals – standard 3-hour ones. There were always all the original parts with names and parts written on. We were all very good readers. The next day, Frank Sinatra would come in and pull it to pieces, especially any tempo variations. He hated a band that played with just one dynamic – the loud sections had to be loud, and we had to be just a whisper when it should be quiet. He was a very artistic person, and he would hate it if people would try to jazz

it around. Once, when playing with the Basie band, a very fine jazz trombonist, who shall remain nameless, did some improvised playing and FS growled, 'Stop the Be-Bop Shit'. He liked set solos!"

The concerts were a triumph for Frank. He had lost weight during the filming of *Dirty Dingus Magee*, which probably helped his vocals. He opened the first night with 'I've Got the World on a String', after which there followed a show that took in his whole career: 'Try a Little Tenderness' from 1945, some of his late 1950s Capitol classics, and 'I Would Be in Love Anyway' from *Watertown*, before closing with 'My Way'. A month later, Frank appeared on a radio show for KGIL with Paul Compton, on which he called the London concerts his "finest hour". He also revealed that he was going to confine his concert appearances to just those for charity. It was a hint as to Frank's future plans – heading towards 55, he was now planning to slow down. *Watertown*'s disappointing chart showing may have been at the back of Frank's mind, although he was always at pains to praise the project.

TRIUMPH
The programme from Frank's London shows at Festival Hall, 4–8 May, 1970.

LIGHT UP TIME
Constant smoking over the years did little to help Frank's voice.

CHARITY MAN

True to his word, Frank's concert appearances over the coming few months were all for charitable causes. On 30 May, he played the Coliseum in Memphis, Tennessee, as a benefit for a children's research center. In mid-August, he was at the Civic Opera House in Chicago. The following day, 16 August, he was at the Hollywood Bowl and two weeks later in Richmond, Indiana. Another five days on, Frank was back to doing "his thing" in Vegas for a two-week run at Caesars. Frank then did three benefit shows of a very different kind that formally announced Frank's move to the right politically. (One wonders what Dolly had to say about this.) Frank appeared in Los Angeles, San Francisco, and San Diego in support of Ronald Reagan's quest for re-election. Reagan introduced Frank, who naturally included 'Nancy' in his show, in honour of Nancy Reagan. One reason for Frank's reduced appearances at this time is that

1963-1973

BARBARA MARX
Frank with Barbara Marx at the Century Plaze Hotel, Los Angeles, attending the American Film Institute's tribute to James Cagney.

WITH THE V-P
Spiro Agnew, Nixon's vice-president, out on the links with Frank at Palm Springs.

his right hand was giving him a lot of pain when he held the microphone. He underwent surgery around this time for Dupuytren's contracture, a problem with the muscular tissue.

At the end of October, Frank was back in the studio for his first session in almost a year. The first song he recorded was 'I Will Drink the Wine', a song by English writer and former pop star Paul Ryan. At the same session, he cut 'Bein' Green' from television's Sesame Street and 'My Sweet Lady', written by John Denver, who had a year before released his first solo album. This included 'Leaving on a Jet Plane', which became a big hit for folk trio Peter, Paul, and Mary.

Over the next few days, Frank cut another batch of songs, including another by Paul Ryan along with John Denver's 'Leaving on a Jet Plane'; they were included on his next album, *Sinatra and Company*. On 2 November, Frank and Nancy recorded a couple of duets to try to emulate 'Somethin' Stupid', although neither did; it was Frank's last recording session for almost 30 months. Shortly afterwards, Frank flew to London for a couple of charity shows at the Festival Hall.

On 13 and 14 November, the mainly British band were rehearsing with Bill Miller. According to saxophonist Bobby Lamb, they were working on the second day and the number was going great, when "Suddenly the atmosphere in the room changed dramatically. Not knowing why I looked up – and there he was, standing right near the saxophones, the man himself." Everyone just stopped playing and Frank just said "Hi guys", turned around, and walked out. His old friend Princess Grace of Monaco introduced him on the shows, and both were

SINATRA & CO
An album of two halves, but better than its performance on the US chart suggests (US No 73, UK No 9). Side one features collaborations with Antonio Carlos Jobím, intended for a follow-up to their 1967 album; Eumir Deodato arranged the Brazilian half. The pop side was a set of excellent Don Costa arrangements.

Sinatra & Company*

*Antonio Carlos Jobim
Don Costa
Eumir Deodato

Drinking Water
Somone To Light Up My Life
Triste
Don't Ever Go Away
This Happy Madness
Wave
One Note Samba
I Will Drink The Wine
Close To You
Sunrise In The Morning
Bein' Green
My Sweet Lady
Leaving On A Jet Plane
Lady Day

taped by the BBC and edited into one television programme. Amongst the chat from Frank was a wonderful vignette about his visit to old friend Noel Coward in hospital; Coward had been booked to appear alongside Frank and Bob Hope. Coward had asked Frank how old he was, to which Frank had replied he would be 55 next month. "You pitiful youth" was Coward's pithy retort. The shows were far less successful than those in May, with some of the expensive (£40 and £50) seats at the first show remaining unsold. Frank included many of the same songs from May but also sang, in the first show, 'This Love of Mine', which he had co-written nearly 30 years earlier. "It's my only claim to fame as a lyric writer," said Frank, before proceeding to forget the words; it was dropped from the second show. *Melody Maker* commented, "But for all that, Sinatra produced 55 minutes of the kind of singing which lovers of the best in pop vocal music have come to expect." The shows raised over £100,000 for the United World Colleges Fund.

A few weeks after returning from London, it was the "pitiful youth's" 55th birthday. Nancy claimed that "Dad liked to give presents on his birthday", and so she decided that "he should give me to Hugh Lambert": Nancy got married for the second time at the Catholic Church in Cathedral City, Los Angeles. After Christmas, Frank sang at a gala in Los Angeles to celebrate Ronald Reagan's re-election, and then, before the month was out, he was at a Democratic fund-raiser at the Beverly Hills Hotel. In between, there was the opening of the Martin Anthony Sinatra Medical Education Center in Palm Springs, in memory of Marty. It was the most conspicuous example of Frank's philanthropy. Ronald and Nancy were there, along with Vice President Spiro Agnew, and, of course, Dolly; it would have been wonderful to be a fly on the wall. For the remainder of the spring of 1971, Frank virtually disappeared from public life apart from a couple of celebrity events. The release of *Sinatra and Company* in the US went almost unnoticed by any but serious fans. While it did better than *Watertown*, it still failed to climb higher than No 73. It was possibly the last straw for Frank. After 32 years, he decided to retire. In keeping with his announcement that his appearances would only be for charity, his "Last Show" was in support of the Motion Picture and Television Relief Fund on 13 June. Produced by Gregory Peck, it was at two theatres – the Ahmanson and the Dorothy Chandler Pavilion – in downtown Los Angeles. Frank had played golf earlier in the day, and the smaller theatre was full of his friends and family. Word had got out that this would be his last show, and $250 tickets were changing hands for a great deal more than face value. It was actress Rosalind Russell who introduced Frank, and she could not keep from crying. "Here's the way it started," said Frank and sang 'All or Nothing at All.' Before long, it was Frank's eyes that filled with tears as he sang 'Nancy', 'I'll Never Smile Again', 'Ol' Man River', and 'Fly Me to the Moon.' 'My Way' appeared to be the closer, before Frank did the ever so appropriate 'That's Life'. Then he did just one more song. He had probably thought about this for a long time, since the obvious song to sing to represent what he felt was the cornerstone of his career as a saloon singer would be 'One For My Baby'. Instead, he did 'Angel Eyes', which finishes with the line, "'scuse me while I disappear". And that was it: he did just that as the stage went black. It does not get any more dramatic than that. Afterwards, Frank, his family, and friends went to dinner at Chasens, where it was the retiree who seemed the least affected. Even then, Sammy Davis Jr couldn't resist quipping that "He'll be doing a whole series of comebacks now after the retirement".

THIRTY VERY GOOD YEARS

Retirement for Frank didn't of course mean retirement. He did a benefit show at Madison Square Garden for the Italian American Civil Rights League just five months later. But he spent much of the time at home in Palm Springs playing golf and painting. He continued his charity work in 1972, often helping out old friends on their particular projects and at the same time his ties with the Republican Party strengthened. Vice President Agnew had spent a Thanksgiving weekend at Frank's house in Palm Springs and in May 1972 Frank went to Washington and grew close to the Nixon administration. But just as Frank and politics were often linked, so was his supposed link with racketeers. In July 1972 he was again put on the block about his 1963 investment in Berkshire Downs racetrack in Massachusetts, one that was part owned by several known Mafia bosses. Not that this was new news; in the *Wall Street Journal* article in 1968 they took him to task for this investment. Initially Frank seemed to be reluctant to testify before the Senate Select Committee on Crime, resulting in a round of ever more extravagant demands for his attendance by Senators who took it personally. The newspapers, of course, poured fuel on the fire, saying Frank was "hiding out" in London: he was there but hardly hiding. Then they said he taken off to go gambling in Monte Carlo.

Frank finally testified on 18 July and six days later wrote to the *New York Times* defending his position. He was particularly upset that the Committee wouldn't hear his testimony in private, "without all the attendant hoopla". He also took them to task over the sort of attention given to stars, "but it is complicated in my case because my name ends in a vowel." The letter was one full of self-righteous indignation, but, of course, Frank had hardly been the innocent victim that he proclaimed. It's a dirty business and he was caught in the crossfire of Senate politics. But you can't link yourself with the re-election of the President without others seeing you as a way of harming his chances with the voters. If there's any moral in the whole story, it's that celebrity and politics don't mix. The essential aspects of each cancel out the other, and when you add the magic ingredient of Frank then it's bound to be volatile. Mind you, he was the consummate politician when in October he sang at a Young Voters for Nixon rally in Chicago; he performed 'My Kind of Town' and a Sammy Cahn parody of 'The Lady Is a Tramp' for Agnew (The Gentleman Is a Champ).

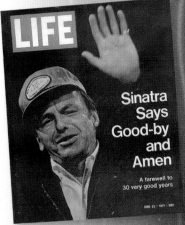

AMEN TO ALL THAT
Like many before, and many since, Sinatra's farewell concert in 1971 was anything but.

1963-1973

Nixon and Agnew demolished the Democratic challenge of George McGovern and Sargent Shriver (John and Bobby Kennedy's brother-in-law). Nixon was elected with the biggest winning margin in the popular vote of any President to that time, although it was the lowest turnout since 1948. How much of the result was down to Frank's support is conjecture.

Since his divorce from Mia, Frank's love life had been low profile. There had been a number of temporary girlfriends, including the actress Victoria Principal, but there was no one who even approached the serious category. It was on New Year's Eve 1972 that 42-year-old Barbara Marx publically appeared on the scene, though according to daughter Tina she had gone on a trip to Monaco with Frank back in June 1971. She attended a party at Walter Annenberg's home in Palm Springs with Frank. Not long afterwards, Frank got himself back into the fray with the gossip columnists, whom he saw as targeting Barbra to get to him and his friend Spiro Agnew. Barbara was born in Missouri in 1930 before her family moved to California. She won several beauty contests and then married and had a son in 1951. By 1959 she had married Zeppo Marx; her marriage allowed her to move in the best circles in both LA and Palm Springs, where Zeppo had a house. By the early 1970s her marriage was over and soon after she began her relationship with Frank. She began divorce proceedings four days before the Annenberg's party.

THE HOUSE HE LIVED IN

Having attended President Nixon's inauguration as a guest, Frank was asked by the President to come and sing at the White House three months later. It was an offer that Frank couldn't refuse, as the event honoured the Italian Prime Minister, Giulio Andreotti. In fact, President Nixon's thoughts were elsewhere on that glittering night at the White House. Two weeks after Frank sang, HR Haldeman (Nixon's Chief of staff), John Erlichman, Richard Kleindienst (the Attorney General), and John Dean (the President's legal consul) all resigned on 30 April. Nixon's end game had began back in January, when two men had been convicted over the Watergate scandal. Sixteen months later Nixon resigned. Just six months after Frank's appearance at the White House, Spiro Agnew resigned as Vice President, having been given three months' probation for income tax evasion. Frank continued his friendship with Agnew; when he wanted to be he was intensely loyal.

But on that night, 17 April, probably no one, other than possibly the President, had an inkling of what could and would happen. Backed by Nelson Riddle, Frank opened up with 'You Make Me Feel So Young' and sang nine of his greatest hits, including the ubiquitous 'Ol' Man River',

'I Have Dreamed', and 'I've Got You Under My Skin'. Rather appositely, he also sang 'I've Got the World On A String', before finishing with 'The House I Live In'. Before singing his homage to racial equality, Frank spoke about his rehearsal earlier in the day: "I was looking at the paintings of President and Mrs Washington and thinking about what a marvellous dignity has come from this one particular man up through the years, all the way down to this moment with our own President; the dignity that has been given to the office."

Frank flew home from Washington to play host to Princess Grace and Prince Rainier at his home in Palm Springs. Shortly afterwards, he was best man at Dean Martin's wedding. Five days later, Frank went to MGM studios on the Monday evening of 30 April, the day of the mass resignation of Presidential aides. For his first

AFORE YE GO
Even the UK satirical magazine Punch *picked up on Frank's significance, and noted his retirement.*

> This house is honoured to have a man whose parents were born in Italy, who from humble beginnings went to the very top entertainment. "

PRESIDENT RICHARD MILHOUSE NIXON,
17 APRIL, 1972

session in two-and-a-half years, Frank was backed by Bill Miller on piano, three guitarists, bass, drums, and percussion. Conducted by Don Costa, they did Kris Kristofferson's 'Nobody Wins' and Joe Raposo's 'Noah (Walk With The Lions)'. For whatever reasons, the tapes were destroyed. Maybe Frank was not just struggling with being back in the studio but also with the shock news from Washington. They were going to record the next day, too, but the session was cancelled. It was another month before Frank actually finished some tracks. His first was on 4 June with Gordon Jenkins, when he recorded two Joe Raposo tracks, including 'Noah' and 'Bang Bang (My Baby Shot Me Down)', composed by future Mayor of Palm Springs, Sonny Bono, and a 1966 No 2 hit for

Cher. Over the course of the rest of the month, Frank cut eight more songs. they would form the backbone of his comeback album.

While this comeback was self-imposed, and twenty years since his first one, it needed careful handling to ensure that Frank had something to come back for. Being encouraged to record again was one thing, but there was no point unless the records sold. With plans well advanced for a TV show, there was also the question of live gigs. In 1970, Bill Miller had said, "The one thing Frank wouldn't want to do is appear in a big stadium or something. Because then you don't get the intimacy with the audience", so that seemed to suggest it would be business as normal and a trip to Vegas.

ALL THE WAY UP
On 18 April 1973, Frank performed at the White House during a dinner for Italian Prime Minister Giulio Andreotti. From left to right: Spiro Agnew, Andreotti and his wife, Frank, Pat Nixon, President Nixon, and Mrs Agnew.

1973-1998

ℱOREVER, OL' ℬLUE EYES

HAVING DECIDED ON A "COMEBACK", FRANK NEEDED TO
MAKE IT COUNT, AND CAPITALIZE ON WHAT WAS HIS LAST
BIG OPPORTUNITY. HE PROBABLY WONDERED FOR JUST
HOW LONG HE COULD KEEP HIS CAREER GOING; HE WAS
WELL INTO UNCHARTERED WATERS. FRANK HAD ALREADY
HAD DIFFICULTIES IN FINDING NEW MATERIAL, AND SO
TO BEGIN WITH, HE SETTLED INTO A FAMILIAR PATTERN
OF RECORDING AND PERFORMING LIVE. HE CUT TWO
ALBUMS WITHIN A YEAR, BUT IT SOON BECAME OBVIOUS
THAT CONCERTS WERE THE FUTURE. WHILE FRANK'S
SECOND COMING WAS TO BE BE VERY DIFFERENT FROM
THE FIRST TIME, IT WOULD LAST JUST ABOUT AS LONG.

"The sound system was not the best
and the desert winds howled before the
well-lighted Pyramids and Sphinx, but
Frank, like that other Italian, Caesar,
conquered all."
THE LA HERALD EXAMINER

ROMAN OPULENCE, CAESARS PALACE, LAS VEGAS

$\int$TADIUMS & PALACES

According to Nancy Sinatra, there was much debate on what to call Frank's new album. Her choice, *Let Me Try Again*, met with derision from her father. Frank himself wanted *Ol' Blue Eyes Is Back*, a great call as the phrase has become synonymous with the man. But then Frank for the most part was always in touch with his legend.

To celebrate Frank's return, *Ol' Blue Eyes Is Back* became an NBC television special. Frank took some lessons from opera singer Robert Merrill to get his voice in shape prior to taping the show in Hollywood on 20 September, 1973. The invited audience was there to honour Frank, but they also got to see his special guest, Gene Kelly. They sang some of their film songs together, and Frank did a selection of old and new numbers, including Steven Sondheim's 'Send in the Clowns', along with 'Let Me Try Again' and 'You Will Be My Music'. When the show was first aired on 18 November, however, the ratings were a disappointment: it came in third behind the premiere of *The Hospital* and a Dinah Shore special.

SELF-PROMOTION
Frank, with his keen eye for what sold, missed no opportunity to let people know he was back. 'Ol' Blue Eyes' was thought up by Frank's PR man Lee Solters. Rarely in the field of showbiz epithets has one fitted so perfectly.

"Well, it seemed like a good idea... to loaf and play golf. After several years, I have a 17 handicap. And the other day, I made an overseas call and the operator asked me how to spell my name. I told her... and she asked my first name. Then she said, 'Junior?'"

FRANK AT THE TAPING OF HIS COMEBACK SPECIAL

Frank's comeback album came out two weeks after the special was recorded, and when the show aired it reached No 13 on the album chart, helped too by an expensive and lavish promotional campaign. 'Let Me Try Again' was picked as the lead off single but it did badly on the American charts and didn't chart atall in the UK. Things had not changed: Frank was still not going to excite the younger buyers that made big hit singles.

Ten days after taping the special, Frank was at The Dorothy Chandler Pavilion for a benefit for the Los Angeles Music & Art School. After being introduced by Bob Hope, he did just 20 minutes, telling the audience "I just took a rest for awhile." Leonard Feather, writing in the *LA Times*, said, "He promised to offer a saloon song ('Drunks love 'em') that turned out to be 'Here's That Rainy Day.' For the first 16 bars he was accompanied only by his perennial pianist-conductor Bill Miller; then the strings came in. I wasn't drunk, but I loved it. Closing with 'I Get A Kick Out Of You,' he seemed to be reminding us that as long as there is Sinatra to sing them, lyrics and melodies of this quality shall not perish from the earth."

With the album doing well and the encouragement of a warm glow of press plaudits for the television show, Frank and Don Costa were in the studio on 10 December to work on a follow-up album. They did Jim Croce's 'Bad, Bad Leroy Brown', along with 'I'm Gonna Make It All the Way'. Neither were standards, and their choice demonstrated Frank's difficulty in finding songs that he could make his own, or for that matter relate to. On Frank's return to work, Reprise issued a press release saying that he would "record an album every six months and make a few personal appearances", but Frank's next two albums were to prove that there was little money, and precious little acclaim, for his recordings. It was to be the concert arenas where the big bucks were to be made: Bill Miller had got it totally wrong.

ONCE MORE TO THE ROAD

No sooner were Christmas and New Year out the way than Frank's attention turned to performing live. Apart from the "Retirement Show" and the "Comeback Show", Frank had not performed seriously since his London shows in November 1970. He opened at Caesars Palace on 25 January, 1974. His shows were billed as "when the man sings, the whole world is in love" and he opened with 'Come Fly With Me'. Frank certainly had a great sense of what worked – most of the time. During his week-long run with the Nat Brandwynne Orchestra conducted by Gordon Jenkins, he did about half new songs and half old, mostly Capitol classics. Interestingly, he dropped 'My Way' as the closer (and from the show), preferring to end with 'I've Got the World on a String.' On the afternoon following Frank's opening night, Tina married Wes Farrell, a songwriter; that night, Frank nostalgically added 'The

OL' BLUE EYES IS BACK

ol' blue eyes is back

THE FIRST SESSION for Frank's comeback album was on 30 April 1973, a Monday night. Frank walked into MGM studios where Bill Miller and a small rhythm section including guitarists John Morell, Alvin Casey and Al Viola were ready and waiting. The room as was so often the case was filled with friends. Frank stood at the music stand, raised his arms, smiled, and said, "The Chairman is back." When the album came out it was relatively successful, but no return to the glory days. It is a mish-mash of songs, four from the pen of Joe Raposo. Gordon Jenkins arranged six of the tracks, Don Costa the others. Having Jenkins seems a strange choice given the material; it certainly baffled many critics. Gordon's forte were lush, string-laden settings in a consciously romantic style, which really didn't suit some of the songs.

SONG LINES

Recorded: Goldwyn Studios, Hollywood Producer: Don Costa. Chart: US No 13 22 weeks on the chart (first charted 27 October, 1973); UK No 12 13 weeks on the chart (1 December, 1973)

SIDE 1

1. 'YOU WILL BE MY MUSIC' (Joe Raposo) Recorded 4 June, 1973
2. 'YOU'RE SO RIGHT (FOR WHAT'S WRONG WITH MY LIFE)' (Roger Joyce, Victoria Pike & Teddy Randazzo) Recorded 20 August, 1973

3. 'WINNERS' (Joe Raposo) Recorded 21 June, 1973 Arranged Don Costa
4. 'NOBODY WINS' (Kris Kristofferson) Recorded 5 June, 1973
5. 'SEND IN THE CLOWNS' (Stephen Sondheim) Recorded 21 June From the Broadway show *A Little Night Music*, wiht a lovely Jenkins arrangement on a song better suited to his style.

SIDE 2

1. 'DREAM AWAY' (John Williams & Paul Williams) Recorded 20 August, 1973

2. 'LET ME TRY AGAIN (LAISSE MOI LE TEMPS)' (Francois Caravelli, Michel Jourdan, Paul Anka & Sammy Cahn) Recorded 21 June, 1973 Arranged Don Costa
3. 'THERE USED TO BE A BALLPARK' (Joe Raposo) Recorded 21 June, 1973. Another great Jenkins arrangement that improves on the song.
4. 'NOAH (WALK WITH THE LIONS)' (Joe Raposo) Recorded 4 June, 1973. This may well be the worst song Frank ever did.

House I Live In' to his set. *Billboard* reviewed his opening night, saying "Sinatra was nervous and tense. It became apparent that even more than the crowd wanting Sinatra back, was Sinatra's desire to be back. It was his own personal triumph. The most impressive thing about his presentation was the obvious amount of thought and hard work that went into the song selections and arrangements. Some of Sinatra's notes weren't what they once were. He looks his age and he looks good. He picked songs that were reflective, romantic and fitting his age. Mid-way through he sat down on a stool and began to relax. He became the Sinatra whose singing knows no peer."

Apart from a few benefit shows, early 1974 was quiet until Frank began a tour on 8 April at Carnegie Hall to raise money for Variety Clubs International. Tickets were being bought for $125 and resold for $1,000. His set was similar to his Caesars show, and he played to almost 200,000 people in Uniondale, Providence, Philadelphia, Atlanta, Detroit, Washington DC, and Chicago. According to the *New York Post*, "Frank

MY WAY AGAIN
Paul Anka and Sammy Cahn's English words to this French song were an attempt to replicate 'My Way.' It could only make No 63 on the US charts.

US on the big screen, but not in a dramatic role. Someone at MGM had had the bright idea of reprising the studio's greatest musical hits in a two-hour spectacular. Frank was one of the hosts of *That's Entertainment* which included Crosby, Astaire, Gene Kelly, Liz Taylor, and Liza Minnelli. Frank appears in the opening segment standing in front of the old MGM lot; his film clips included *Take Me out to the Ball Game*, *It Happened in Brooklyn*, *High Society*, *Anchors Aweigh*, and *On the Town*.

Frank's interest in the movie was probably negligible, since he was back in the studio working with Gordon Jenkins on more tracks for an album. Since his comeback, Frank had abandoned United and Western Recorders and shifted to Burbank Studio. At his first session on 7 May, he cut 'Empty Tables', along with 'The Summer Knows', by Michel Legrand and the Bergmans' and David Gates's 'If' for an album to be called *Some Nice Things I've Missed*. Before the month's end, there were several more sessions with Bill Miller conducting.

Two days before the last session, on 24 May, Nancy gave birth to a baby girl, Angela Jennifer. According to Nancy, her father was predictably overcome by his first grandchild, but could not resist joking, "All I ask is that Nancy never let the child grow up and see *The Kissing Bandit*."

Two weeks later, Frank was back at Caesars for his second run of the year. Although clearly happy to be a grandfather, he shocked the *Variety* critic Bill Willard with some bad-taste jokes. "Ella Fitzgerald and Count Basie didn't find it at all funny when he said 'The Polacks are deboning the coloured people and using them as wet suits." You have to wonder if Frank's entourage helped to distance him from reality at times. Bob Hope's jokes were in better taste "He found Caesars paid better than social security".

A LAND DOWN UNDER

Two weeks after finishing in Vegas, Frank flew to Japan for five shows in Tokyo's Budokan and a 4 July show on the USS *Midway*. Frank was travelling with Bill Miller, Al Viola (guitar), Irv Cottler (drums), Gene Cherico (bass), Billy Byers (trombone), Marvin Stamm (trumpet), and Bud Shank (saxophone); the arrangements had all been written for this small combo. From Japan, Frank went to Australia on 8 July to open the following day in Melbourne's Festival Hall. He added two of the songs he'd recorded at his May sessions: 'You Are the Sunshine of My Life'

LIVE IN JAPAN
Frank "in the round" on a central stage at Tokyo's Budokan with his band led by Bill Miller. He was still opening with 'Come Fly With Me' but closed with 'My Way'.

Sinatra was a religious event." Not everyone was so complimentary, however. Ralph J Gleason, who had written the sleeve notes for Frank's 1959 album *No One Cares*, wrote in *Rolling Stone* "There are those of us who still dig his voice, but for whom Ol' Blue Eyes is a drag that Frankie never was." Much of Gleason's rhetoric was aimed at Frank's coterie of hangers-on, bodyguards, and the like. He felt it all detracted from Frank the singer. Reprise recorded the shows, but Frank was unhappy with what he heard, so the idea of a live album was shelved. Almost as soon as the tour ended, Frank was being seen across the

and 'If'. But for the most part it was old songs such as 'I've Got You Under My Skin', 'I Get a Kick out of You', and the ubiquitous 'Ol' Man River'.

This tour would, however, be remembered not for what Frank sang as much as for what he said. All through Frank's sabbatical, Barbara Marx had been his constant companion, a situation that apparently upset Dolly Sinatra.

Barbara arrived with Frank in Australia onboard his Gulfstream jet. Frank and Barbara had planned to have some free time in Melbourne, and they were dismayed to discover that the tour's promoters had planned press conferences. Barbara, who was also looking forward to some time off with Frank, may have encouraged him to be uncooperative, resulting in a serious spat in which Frank was accused by a female reporter of "verbally abusing" her. There followed a typical Frank versus the press match, in which the usual subtleties were traded. Frank's trump card was to call the Aussie press "a bunch of fags", not smart at all in the land of all things macho. A New South Wales politician asked, "Who the hell does this man Sinatra think he is?" Bob Hawke, the Head of the Council of Trade Unions, and later the Prime Minister of Australia (1983–1991), announced that Frank "will never get out of the country unless he apologizes" – a not unreasonable threat since the unions were refusing to refuel Frank's aircraft. As comedian Don Rickles said at the time, "Frank's just called me – he's declared war on Australia". Eventually, Frank's lawyer, Mickey Rudin, stepped in, and after some discussion a joint statement was issued on behalf of Frank and the unions. The tour continued with shows in Sydney's Horden Pavilion, and Frank closed them with 'My Way'; you have to admire his self-belief. It would be 15 years before Frank went back down under. The aftermath of this disastrous tour would be reflected at Christmas, when The Hollywood Women's Press Club awarded Frank the Sour Apple Award in recognition of his "achievements".

MAIN MAN

Back home, Frank, Nancy, and Junior were booked into Harrah's South Shore Room in Lake Tahoe, Nevada. What should have been a nice family show was marred, according to *Variety*, by Frank continuing to lambast the press over his Australian trip, calling them "a bunch of god damn liars" and heaping much venom on women reporters in particular. It seems extraordinary that no one was telling Frank to calm down. Certainly members of the audience were unhappy – *Variety* reported "some hisses, catcalls, and boos". The result of all this was that more and more Frank jibes were appearing in the press, and for stand-up comics it was manna from heaven. It has been reported that Frank even sued a comedian for $10,000 for a bad-taste joke directed against him. There was a sense of *déjà vu* hanging around Frank, and the media. As soon as the family show ended, Frank and Gordon Jenkins began work on some songs, including 'Just as

Though You Were Here', which he had first recorded in 1942 with Tommy Dorsey and the Pied Pipers. This new version of the John Brooks and Eddie DeLange song is beautiful and showed just what Frank could still do with a great song.

Recording came a poor second to touring, however, and Frank's focus was on his forthcoming shows with Woody Herman and the Young Thundering Herd, which opened in Boston on 2 October, 1974. Billed as "The Main Event", the tour coupled Frank with boxing, which, given his recent experiences, probably appealed to his ego. After Buffalo, Philadelphia, and Pittsburgh, where the high ticket prices meant that not every seat was filled, the climax of the tour took place at Madison Square Garden on 12 October, where a television special was taped. According to Jerry Weintraub, the promoter, the build-up to the show was typical Frank: no rehearsals, a seeming lack of attention to what was happening, and, what was worse for Weintraub, a reluctance to perform his biggest songs. (Apparently, Frank

SOME NICE THINGS I'VE MISSED

Some Nice Things I've Missed

IF *BLUE EYES* was a lightweight, this album is a featherweight, offering almost nothing of substance to suit either Frank's voice or intelligence. The "concept" of the album may be OK; it's just that it misses on every level. Only the Bergmans' and Michel Legrand's 'What Are You Doing For The Rest Of Your Life' and 'The Summer Knows' are worthy of Frank's talent; particularly the former. 'Tie A Yellow Ribbon' and 'Bad, Bad Leroy Brown' rank up there with 'Mama Will Bark' in the dog song stakes. Frank's need to be seen as contemporary is partially understandable. However, the material selected for this album offered no assistance. It's a no hoper.

SONG LINES

Recorded: Burbank Studios
Producers: Jimmy Bowen & Don Costa
Chart: US No 48 12 weeks on the chart (first charted 3 August, 1974);
UK No 35 3 weeks on the chart (17 August, 1974)

SIDE 1

1. 'YOU TURNED MY WORLD AROUND'
(Kim Carnes, Dave Ellingson, Bert Kaempfert & Herbert Rehbein) This was a minor hit making No 83 on the US chart. Co-writer Kim Carnes would top the Hot 100 with 'Bette Davis Eyes' in 1981 for nine weeks. She had been in the New Christy Minstrels.

2. 'SWEET CAROLINE'
(Neil Diamond) Recorded 8 May, 1974 It's one of the songs that works as a pop song in its original setting by its composer Neil Diamond but as soon as you put Frank and "an arrangement" near it, it falls apart. A perfect example of the type of song Frank should not have gone near.

3. 'THE SUMMER KNOWS'
(Marilyn Bergman, Alan Bergman & Michel Legrand) Recorded 7 May, 1974 This haunting song was first heard in the 1971 film, *The Summer of '42*.

4. 'I'M GONNA MAKE IT ALL THE WAY'
(Floyd Huddleston) Recorded 10 December, 1973

5. 'TIE A YELLOW RIBBON ROUND THE OLE OAK TREE'

(Russell Brown & Irwin Levine) Recorded 21 May, 1974

SIDE 2

1. 'SATISFY ME ONE MORE TIME'
(Floyd Huddleston) Recorded 21 May, 1974

2. 'IF'
(David Gates) Recorded 7 May, 1974

3. 'YOU ARE THE SUNSHINE OF MY LIFE'
(Stevie Wonder) Recorded 21 May, 1974.

4. 'WHAT ARE YOU DOING THE REST OF YOUR LIFE'
(Marilyn Bergman, Alan Bergman & Michel Legrand) Recorded 21 May, 1974

5. 'BAD, BAD LEROY BROWN'
(Jim Croce) Recorded 10 December, 1973 This also made No 83 in the charts but it didn't deserve to.

was just teasing the panicking Weintraub and fully intended to do his normal set.) In the end it all worked out, and the capacity Garden crowd was ecstatic, although the television show filmed there proved not as popular as the *Ol' Blue Eyes* special. The stop-start nature of the recording to accommodate the commercials did nothing to enhance Frank's performance, and tapes of the Garden show reveal him telling Bill Miller that it was "bad".

Two days before filming at the Garden, one of Frank's oldest friends and one of the most important people in his life, died. Hank Sanicola and Frank had not really been reconciled after their disagreement over Sam Giancana, but his loss must have hit him hard.

1975 was to be a busy year for Frank, beginning with a two-week booking at Harrah's Casino in January. He played another week at Harrah's in the middle of February as well as recording Paul Anka's 'Anytime (I'll Be There)' in Hollywood, with Bill Miller conducting, on 5 March. It made the Hot 100 a little over a month later, but went no higher than No 75. 'I Believe I'm Gonna Leave You', also

THE MAIN EVENT

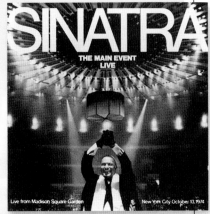

FRANK'S LOVE OF BOXING went way back and so the idea of the concert certainly appealed. The introduction by commentator Howard Cosell was a good idea, if a bad one in the execution. Frank performs well throughout and so do the Young Thundering Herd. The album was in fact not one single event, but an amalgam of a number of shows. The majority of the songs are taken from the Madison Square Garden shows and added to theses are the best bits from the tour; disingenuous, maybe, but far from unusual. Given its make-up it vastly improves on the TV show, with a dynamic that was far more representative of the tour than the TV special. What's most surprising is the fact that Frank didn't release another live performance during the remainder of his concert years; although there are hundreds of bootlegs in circulation.

SONG LINES

Recorded: Madison Square Garden, New York City, or as indicated below Producer: Don Costa. Chart: US No 37 12 weeks on the chart (first charted 7 December, 1974); UK No 30 2 weeks on the chart (15 February, 1975)

SIDE 1

1. 'OVERTURE: IT WAS A VERY GOOD YEAR/ALL THE WAY/MY KIND OF TOWN.'
(Sammy Cahn, Ervin Drake & Jimmy Van Heusen) Recorded New York, 13 October, 1974

2. 'THE LADY IS A TRAMP'
(Lorenz Hart & Richard Rodgers) Recorded New York, 13 October, 1974

3. 'I GET A KICK OUT OF YOU'
(Cole Porter) Philadelphia, 7 October, 1974 (verse); New York, 13 October, 1974 (chorus)

4. 'LET ME TRY AGAIN (*LAISSE MOI LE TEMPS*)'
(Francois Caravelli, Michel Jourdan, Paul Anka & Sammy Cahn) New York, 12 & 13 October, 1974.

5. 'AUTUMN IN NEW YORK'
(Vernon Duke) New York, 12 October, 1974

6. 'I'VE GOT YOU UNDER MY SKIN'
(Cole Porter) Buffalo, 4 October, 1974

SIDE 2

1. 'BAD, BAD LEROY BROWN'
(Jim Croce) New York, 13 October, 1974

2. 'ANGEL EYES'
(Earl Brent & Matt Dennis) Buffalo, 4 October, 1974

3. 'YOU ARE THE SUNSHINE OF MY LIFE'
(Stevie Wonder) New York, 13 October, 1974.

4. 'THE HOUSE I LIVE IN'
(Lewis Allan & Earl Robinson) Boston, 2 October, 1974.

5. 'MY KIND OF TOWN'
(Sammy Cahn & Jimmy Van Heusen) New York, 13 October, 1974

6. 'MY WAY'
(Paul Anka, Claude Francois, Jacques Revaux & Giles Thibault) Boston, 2 October, 1974.

---

recorded on 5 March, came out in July and became Frank's highest-placing US single since 'My Way', although it still reached only No 47. It also did fairly well in Britain, reaching No 34 in early 1976.

Following a week at Caesars in March, Frank embarked on a mini world tour in late April, beginning at San Francisco's Civic Arena. After more American dates, as well as one in Montreal, he flew to London to rehearse ahead of his European tour. Arriving on 14 May, he headed to Claridges, where he frequently stayed after he sold his London flat. An important issue for Frank was to get the right musicians to play on these live shows. Travelling with Bill Miller, drummer Irv Cottler, and some other key players helped. It became the norm for Frank to pick up the same musicians where he performed regularly, and this included London. He was in London, ahead of his European shows, to rehearse. Two days after he arrived and prior to working with Don Costa and the British musicians, he went to Downing Street to meet Prime Minister Harold Wilson. British Sax player Vic Ash was

one of Frank's regulars: "He got so he recognized us. Initially he'd attend rehearsals, but on later tours he didn't. We did several nights at the Albert Hall, and he'd give out my name, though he often got it wrong. He probably got it right only half the time! In rehearsals, he'd often ask 'How's Bob Farnon?' We loved the rehearsals — he was the guy! — aura, charisma, magic… and wonderful arrangements! We were treated well by his management. We'd do the songs a couple of times each — we were all good readers. Frank would go through with us and be very polite — we saw none of his supposed bad side." After rehearsals it was off to Monaco for a Red Cross Gala on 19 May before playing Paris, Vienna, Munich, Frankfurt, Brussels, and Amsterdam. Frank cancelled a planned show in Berlin following a kidnap threat, though the German press was unimpressed, accusing him of cancelling because of poor sales (his other German shows did not sell out either). Frank

FRONT PAGE
Frank could still make the front page of the UK's Melody Maker, a paper that, at the time, would have more likely featured David Bowie; it speaks volumes.

CALIFORNIA COUPLE
Beach boy Bruce Johnston, pictured with his wife, Harriet, around the time he wrote 'I Write The Songs'. He had joined the Beach Boys after Brian Wilson retired from touring.

FIRST DATE
Frank and Jackie Kennedy Onassis, accompanied by Jilly Rizzo, on their way to dinner at New York's Club 21 after he had performed at the Uris.

returned to London for two shows at the Royal Albert Hall, and the reviews there were brilliant. "Is he now a fifty-nine-year-old short winded has-been living on nostalgia? They needn't have worried. The voice is in great shape, the breath control still extraordinary. The obituaries have been distinctly premature," said Ray Wright in the *Evening Standard*. Frank sold out both nights, with £30 tickets selling for eight times their face value. So taken was Frank by the good reviews for his opening night show that, during the second night, he even thanked the press midway through 'The Lady Is a Tramp'. Such was Frank's appeal that he would be back in London in November along with Sarah Vaughan and Count Basie for a week-long booking at the London Palladium – the venue for his first British shows a quarter of a century earlier. The demand for tickets would be amazing: over 350,000 people applied for the 15,000 available seats.

The London shows were in the wake of two weeks at New York's Uris Theatre, and one-nighters in Philadelphia, Cleveland, and Chicago during September with Ella Fitzgerald, Count Basie's Orchestra, and a 20-piece string section. Frank even insisted on being billed beneath the other two legendary performers on the marquee. Frank and Ella duetted on 'The Song Is You', 'They Can't Take That Away From Me', and 'The Lady Is A Tramp'. This dream team concert was another of the unusual ideas that Frank had during the year, not that there was anything wrong with unusual as the two weeks at the Uris grossed over a million dollars. During August, he played a week in August at Harrah's with John Denver; 672,412 people tried to get tickets for the week's shows. It was a very clever idea because at this point John Denver was hot. Given Frank's less than ecstatic notices for his shows earlier in the year, it was an inspired pairing. During 1974, Denver had two No 1 singles, another in March 1975, and a week after the Harrah's booking was over, 'I'm Sorry' took over from David Bowie at the top of the US charts. It was the perfect marriage of the old guard and the new, although after 1975 John Denver never even made the Top 20 of the Hot 100 again.

While Frank was in New York with Ella and the Count, he had a date with Jackie Kennedy Onassis. Jackie, who by this time was working for the publisher Viking, contacted Frank about writing his memoirs. He told Jackie that she should come to one of his shows at the Uris, and she readily agreed. After a backstage party, Frank and Jackie, along with Jilly Rizzo, went to the Club 21 for dinner. From there it was back to the Waldorf, where Jackie spent

DREAM TEAM II
*Frank's idea of working with Sarah Vaughan and
Count Basie followed on from the idea of working
with Ella who was unavailable for the London
shows. The programme is below right.*

the night. That was the extent of their
"relationship": one date. Thereafter they didn't
speak or have anything to do with each other,
least of all discuss a book for Viking.

Before Frank played his London Palladium shows
he had bookings at Harrah's and at Caesars, but his
most unusual bookings of the year were in Tehran
and Israel. Spiro Agnew, Vice President under
Nixon and now a friend of Frank's, joined Frank
in London and they flew to Tehran for a charity
show. In Jerusalem, he played two concerts in aid
of Jewish and Arab children. Apart from the usual
songs, Frank sang Eric Carmen's 'All By Myself',
which had just come out as a single. Carmen's
song, based on Rachmaninov's Piano Concerto
No 2 and arranged by Don Costa, seems like a
perfect song for Frank, but he did not record it.

The culmination of a very busy year was
Frank's 60th birthday, a year that included 140
performances to over 500,000 people, which
would be increased by 17,000 with a sell-out
New Year's Eve show at the Chicago Stadium.
Two weeks later, Frank was back to work in
Vegas with a week-long Caesars engagement
followed by another at Harrah's. The Sinatra
show was turning into the never-ending tour.

SINGER OF SONGS

Recording continued to come a poor second to live
shows during 1976, although Frank and Bill Miller
did cut three songs on 5 February. One of these was the
Grammy award-winning 'I Write the Songs' written by Beach
Boy Bruce Johnston; it had recently topped the charts sung
by Barry Manilow. "I've been alive forever and I sang the very
first song" was Frank's subtle change of lyric that made it
autobiographical. Bruce Johnston later recalled, "Frank was
talking about my song to Gail Martin, Dean's daughter, after
they heard it on the radio. Gail said that I was an old friend
of hers and that we had gone to school together. Frank asked
her if I would mind if he recorded it, and she assured him
that I would be thrilled. Sarge Weiss called me shortly after
the first session and invited my wife Harriet and I to Sinatra's
opening night at Caesars. We had a table right in the front
and Frank introduced and shook hands with me. It made me
very proud that one of my favourite singers sang my song." 'I
Sing the Songs' and 'Empty Tables' came out as a single but
failed to chart. For two days following the recording session
Frank was at ABC in Hollywood recording John Denver's
television special. Frank's segment was a 15-minute medley in

which he
worked with the Harry
James, Tommy Dorsey, and Count
Basie Orchestras, along with another
conducted by Nelson Riddle. It was apparently
fairly tense, since Frank's aversion to rehearsing
meant that for much of the time he, the musicians,
and John Denver were flying blind, especially since
Denver seemed less than familiar with Frank's
songs. In the end it all worked out, although Frank
hit a real bum note and did an eight-bar retake
that was slotted into the middle of the medley.
Just a few days after the taping, Frank was back on the
road playing the Latin Casino in Cherry Hill, New Jersey;
this was not in fact a gambling casino but a supper club.
It was located just a few minutes from downtown

The
CONCERT

Philadelphia and across the road from the Garden State Park Racetrack. Frank would stay at the Hyatt Regency Hotel, where he reserved an entire floor, leaving by the back door for the short limo ride to the Latin. Ten days later he was at Caesars before moving on to Harrah's. Early April brought a run at the Westchester Premier Theatre in Tarrytown, New York. May was a very busy month, with 17 shows in a number of cities, including one at Nashville's Grand 'Ole Opry with Count Basie; it seemed as though Frank was on a mission.

While the summer months were less busy, there were one-nighters and another Caesars booking. At the Casino on 6 September, Frank was involved in a telethon for muscular dystrophy. By careful planning, Frank had got Dean Martin to agree to a surprise reunion with his former partner, Jerry Lewis. While onstage with Jerry, Frank brought Dean out, and the former partners met for the first time in 20 years. From Vegas it was a short move to Harrah's for another double-header with John Denver.

One reason for Frank's slower work rate in the summer was his marriage. His relationship with 46-year-old Barbara Marx had been somewhat strained during 1975 but, having turned 60, perhaps Frank felt that it was time he stopped his wandering ways. Frank and Barbara married at Sunnylands, the former ambassador to Great Britain Walter Annenberg's home in Rancho Mirage, on 11 July. Among the guests were Spiro Agnew, Sammy Davis Jr, Ronald and Nancy Reagan, and Frank's second granddaughter, aged 4 months. Dolly was there, although it appears that Frank got Micky Rudin to break the news of his getting married, rather than tell her himself. In October, after another run at the Westchester Premier Theatre, Frank began a tour that took in Hartford, Buffalo, Bingington, Pittsburgh,

> 66 After Sinatra closed his show with his powerful version of 'My Way', a woman came from the audience and offered the king a beautiful crown. To the cheers of the audience, Sinatra put it on. He wore it well. 99
>
> BILLBOARD, MAY 1976

BARBARA MAKES FOUR
Frank and Barbara tied the knot in front of 130 "carefully selected guests" at Rancho Mirage.

WITH THE GUYS
After a show at Westchester in 1976, Frank with Gregory de Palma, Tommy Marson, Carlo Gambino and, seated, Richard Fusco.

Providence, New Haven, Montreal, Syracuse, Norfolk, Richmond, Murfreesboro, Birmingham, and Atlanta. He opened every night with his latest single, 'I Sing the Songs', and closed with 'My Way'. Before the end of the year, there were two more shows and a recording session, at which Frank cut 'I Love My Wife', which subsequently came out as a single. He also attempted 'Evergreen', written by Barbra Streisand and Paul Williams; Nelson Riddle provided the accompaniment on both songs. In Westchester, Frank sang 'See the Show Again', a Barry Manilow song, for the first time. He planned to record it but was perhaps talked out of it by Streisand.

A new year brought another Vegas booking at Caesars. For Frank, it was becoming a habit, but this year it would be tragically different. Frank's opening night was Thursday 6 January, 1977, and in the morning he took the short flight from Palm Springs. Dolly Sinatra had been due to accompany her son but had decided to fly to Vegas later instead, and so Frank charted a Lear jet to fly his mother and Ann Carbone, a New Jersey friend. The plane took off at 5:00 pm in very poor visibility, and, due to a misunderstanding between the pilot and the air traffic controller, it failed to gain the required height to clear Mount San Gorgonio: it flew straight into the mountain, killing everyone on board. During the early evening, it was unclear what had happened to the aircraft and there was some hope that perhaps it had crash-landed and there might be survivors. Amid the uncertainty, Frank decided to open at Caesars. He flew home to Palm Springs on the next day, hoping for news, but none came: the crash site had still not been located. It was not until Saturday that

the wreck was found, and Frank had to accept what he probably already knew. Dolly's funeral took place in Palm Springs on 12 January, and she was laid to rest beside Marty; she was 82 years old.

Frank didn't wait long to get back to work when he opened at the Sunrise Musical Theatre in Fort Lauderdale on 24 January for a week-long booking. Two weeks later, he was recording in New York, adding vocals to some orchestral tracks. He tackled Paul Anka's 'Everybody Ought to Be in Love', and went all the way back to his early days to revisit 'Night and Day' and 'All or Nothing at All', but these were no typical Frank remakes. It was Frank Sinatra goes "disco", and it seems that Don Costa was the man responsible for trying to bring Frank bang up to date. The motivation on the one hand was obvious. The Bee Gees were just getting in step with disco, having topped the charts with 'You Should Be Dancing' a few months earlier. Abba's homage to the disco divas 'Dancing Queen' was heading for No 1, and so it seemed like the right thing to do…but not for a 61-year-old.

LEAR JET

Frank's Lear Jet with his personalised registration was similar to the one in which Dolly Sinatra tragically lost her life.

ROYALTY

Frank meets Princess Margaret before one of his Royal Albert Hall shows. The proceeds from one of the concerts went to the NSPCC. The programme is below.

Arranged by Joe Beck, they turn classics into crap. Nevertheless, they stuck around in Frank's live shows for far too long, although Frank referred to 'Night and Day' as "a hustle" rather than use the word "disco" at many of his live shows. Two weeks later, Frank crossed the Atlantic to Britain and Holland for concerts at the Royal Albert Hall and Amsterdam's Concertgebouw. Playing the first half of the shows were the Fifth Dimension and comedian Pat Henry. Shortly after Frank played London, his Reprise greatest hits album, *Portrait of Sinatra* topped the UK album charts. From Amsterdam, Frank flew straight home and into the studio to begin work on a new album project with Nelson Riddle.

FUTURE IMPERFECT

Although Frank had spoken to Tito Puente about collaborating on an all-Latin album, nothing came of it, as they were both too busy on the road. And so it was that, following on from 'I Love My Wife', Frank decided to make an album of songs based on women's names.

THE ALADDIN HOTEL, LAS VEGAS

He asked Jimmy Van Heusen and Sammy Cahn to write one called 'Barbara', and then set about deciding which others he should do. For three days in March 1978, Frank cut some of his old favourites for the album, which he planned to call *Here's to the Ladies*; there were songs such as 'Nancy', 'Laura', and 'Sweet Lorraine'. He also did 'Emily', 'Tina', 'When Joanna Loved Me', and 'Linda'. The latter had been written by Jack Lawrence about 4-year-old Linda Eastman, who was by this time Mrs Paul McCartney. Nelson also recorded a number of backing tracks, but Frank lost interest, and so the project was shelved.

Nelson recalled, "I think Frank thought it was an old-fashioned premise." It all went to prove how difficult it was for Frank to find anything meaningful to record that he had not already done better, that had any appeal to his ageing legion of fans, or that might somehow interest a younger audience. In an interview a few years later, Nelson got it just right when he said "I think he realized reluctantly that one

REPRISE
Frank performing 'All or Nothing at All' with Harry James in the Universal Amphitheatre, Los Angeles, in June 1979.

"As the show concluded with, 'New York, New York,' he raced into the dressing room, changed clothes and left. The audience was still on its feet as Sinatra jumped into the driver's seat of a station wagon. His friend Jilly took the shotgun seat. Within seconds, the pair of cronies drove off."

MITCHELL FINK, *LA HERALD EXAMINER* AFTER A SHOW AT THE
UNIVERSAL AMPHITHEATRE, LOS ANGELES.

cannot reach over the decades forever, so he just decided to sing good songs." Sadly, this was the last time that Frank and Nelson worked together in a studio, the end of the most perfect partnership. Two days after the girl songs sessions, Frank was back at Caesars doing what he did best – singing the old songs. He had not entirely given up on the new stuff, however, and he included Elton John and Bernie Taupin's recent Top 10 hit, 'Sorry Seems to Be the Hardest Word'.

Back-to-back with Caesars and another stint at Harrah's was the taping of an ABC television special with the inspired title of *Frank Sinatra & Friends*. The friends were Tony Bennett, Dean Martin, Natalie Cole, Robert Merrill, Loretta Lynn, John Denver, and Leslie Uggams. It was live work that sustained Frank, however, and he worked the Circle Star Theatre in San Carlos, California, the Latin Casino in Cherry Hill, the Westchester in Tarrytown, and the Sabre Room of the Ambassador Hotel in Hickory Hills, just outside Chicago before the middle of June. In Tarrytown and Chicago, Frank tried something he had not done in a long time – working with Dean Martin. Dean opened each show and Frank had the middle section, before the two old friends did their double-act with comedy and a medley that would as often as not comprise 'I Can't Give You Anything But Love' – 'My Kind of Town' – 'Pennies From Heaven' – 'A Foggy Day' – 'Embraceable You' – 'The Lady Is a Tramp' – 'Where or When' – 'They Can't Take That Away From Me' – 'Oh Marie' – 'When You're Smiling'.

Almost as soon as the Frank and Dean shows finished, Frank began shooting a new film in New York, although, strictly speaking, it was only a made-for-television movie. Frank was cast as a New York cop in *Contract on Cherry Street*, an adaptation of a favourite book of Dolly Sinatra's, which is probably what made Frank break his vow of never appearing in a television movie. When it aired in November 1977, Frank's performance was just about the best thing in an average affair.

With filming over, Frank played the Forest Hills Tennis Stadium in New York, Alpine Valley, Wisconsin, and a benefit for the University of Nevada at the Aladdin Hotel in Las Vegas. About the only remarkable aspect of these concerts was Frank's live "disco" renditions of 'Night and Day' and 'All or Nothing at All'. Most of the autumn was spent playing week-long bookings at Caesars and Harrah's. In August,

Variety noted "excellent demo of his newest disc Paul Anka's 'Everybody Ought To Be In Love.' (Anka joined him onstage for duet of the same.) Highly effective is Sinatra's 'I Concentrate On You,' accompanied only by guitarist Al Viola. Sinatra is probably the only cabaret singer who generously credits the composer and arranger of every song he offers in a most satisfying vocal hour."

With Frank now 62 years old, one had to wonder how long this could continue, or how long Frank would want to keep doing it. But continue he did: 1978 opened with another Caesars booking and the first three months of the year saw Frank play the hotel for 18 nights, mostly two shows a night. However, having opened at the Sunrise Musical Theatre, Fort Lauderdale, in mid-March, he had to cancel the rest of the booking because of a sore throat, and he took off to Barbados for a ten-day vacation.

Dolly's death produced an unexpected reaction in Frank: he became closer to his Catholic faith. He began thinking of, and then talking about, having his marriage to Nancy annulled so that he and Barbara could marry in church, which was something that he thought his mother would have approved of. He received his annulment in 1978, but apparently it became the cause of great upset within the family.

In early April, Frank went to Israel, accompanied by Gregory Peck, Johnny Carson, and over 100 of Hollywood's finest. He dedicated the Frank Sinatra

GREAT PAIR
Frank and John Denver was the perfect coupling. John was absolutely at the peak of his fame and at the same time was appealing to many of Frank's fans.

PAUL AND LINDA
Before Paul and Linda married, Paul had sent a song to Frank for his consideration. Frank, of course, had sung other Lennon & McCartney compositions so he thought he might be onto a winner. "I once sent Frank Sinatra a song called 'Suicide'. I thought it was quite a good one – but apparently he thought I was taking the mickey out of him and he rejected it," said Paul.

NEW YORK, NEW YORK

FROM THE POINT THAT FRANK first began performing this song, just about everyone wanted to hear it at his shows. And for the rest of his career, Frank pretty much obliged, often using it as his closing number. Written by John Kander and Fred Ebb, who also wrote *Cabaret*, it was the title song for Martin Scorsese's 1977 film of the same name. Although Scorsese's Liza Minnelli/ Robert De Niro film flopped, New Yorkers quickly picked up on the song, and it was heard all over the city — especially at ball games. Soon, it was the city's unofficial theme song.

The recording on 20 August, with Vinnie Falcone playing the piano, wasn't quite right and another attempt, in Hollywood on 19 September, is the version that appears on *Trilogy*. It's been said that the song exemplifies both New York and the Man. It's swagger, and bounce, it's soft and sassy, triumphal and tender — it's much more Sinatra than 'My Way' could ever be.

Released in April 1980, this became Frank's last single to chart on the *Billboard* Hot 100. Between 1940 and 1980, 146 Sinatra records made the *Billboard* charts — only Elvis Presley charted more singles.

FRANK SINATRA — Theme from New York, New York

US No 32, 12 weeks on the chart (First charted 3 May 1980). UK No 59, 4 weeks on the chart (First charted 9 Aug 1980); re-entered 22 February 1986 and got to No 4 spending 10 weeks on the chart.

66 I know what you wanna hear baby, and I think you're gonna hear it now. 99

FRANK INTRODUCING THE SONG AT HIS 1986
NEW JERSEY HOMECOMING CONCERT

International Student Center at the Hebrew University on Mount Scopus. After Israel, it was back to work at Caesars, Harrah's, the Latin Casino, and a series of one-nighters. Frank also stepped back into the studio to record three songs with Vincent Falcone at TBS Studios in Hollywood on 17 July. 'That's What God Looks Like to Me', by Lois Irwin and Lan O'Kun, Elton John and Bernie Taupin's 'Remember' (written especially for Frank), and 'You and Me' by Carole Bayer Sager and Peter Allen all failed to make it out of the studio at the time. This session also marked the last time that Frank and Bill Miller, his accompanist of three decades, would work together for a long while. "We had a falling out. I don't want to get into the whole…. It was just one of those things. We probably got tired of looking at each other", said Bill Miller recently. Their relationship had worked because "I learned how to accommodate him. Let's put it that way. Sometimes it was easy, sometimes it wasn't so easy. He was a little picky now and then."

Vinnie Falcone, who had been working as Frank's regular live pianist since 1973 when Bill Miller was more often conducting than playing, had given up a successful career in retailing to pursue his dream of becoming a professional musician. He was

66 Sinatra's tribute to the big band era is a rich and rewarding experience. His best singing has always been done when he works with great material. His lack of respect for some of the recent material recorded has certainly hurt his performances. This is not the case with Part One of *Trilogy*. Sinatra has not sung this well in years. 99

ED O'BRIEN — SINATRA SOCIETY OF AMERICA
MAGAZINE, MAY 1980

LONDON AGAIN
At the Royal Festival Hall in London in September 1978, he opened with 'Night and Day' and closed with 'My Way'.

"discovered" playing in the lounge at the Dunes, and playing for Frank must have felt like the proverbial dream come true. According to Falcone in Will Friedwald's book *The Song Is You*, the 17 July session was a set-up: "Sinatra told me later that the whole recording session was bogus; he just wanted to test me out."

Frank's performances around the US in August included a ten-day stint at the Universal Amphitheatre. "The man they call Ol' Blue Eyes, the Chairman of the Board, the Voice, but more simply, Francis Albert Sinatra, put on a spellbinding concert last night," said the *Herald Examiner*. According to *Billboard*, "He snaps his fingers during 'Something' to accent the line 'ain't gonna leave her now.' He sways his shoulders in a sensuous way during 'At Long Last Love'. He contorts his face with intensity during 'All of Me'. Sinatra's music embodies all the aspirations for the good life."

Frank made one of his now more frequent forays to the UK and played six nights at London's Royal Festival Hall. On his return from London, Frank played Radio City Music Hall, selling 62,000 tickets for nine shows, as well as his first show in Atlantic City since Skinny D'Amato's Club 500 had closed down. These shows were notable in that it was the first time that Frank performed 'New York, New York'. Don Costa had written an opening orchestral medley of New York songs, and the Kander and Ebb song was its closer. Frank would walk on and begin singing it as the song was finishing.

While many of the people who went to see Frank in these bigger venues were new fans, many more were from the old days. Harry Agoratus had seen Frank at the Copacabana in the 1950s, and he commented: "In spite of the difference that singing in a large venue as opposed to the coziness of the Copa, Sinatra was still able to sing to each person in the audience." This is what you hear from everyone: Frank was singing just to them. Before the year was out, Frank was again back at Caesars but he was forced to cancel his last night of a mid-November run because he was exhausted. Once fit again, Frank was back at Florida's Sunrise Theatre to complete a week's run that would straddle the New Year. It was his first year since his comeback that he didn't start out the year in Vegas, although he was back there in mid-March following short runs at Chicago's Arie Crown Theatre and Valley Forge Music Fair in Pennsylvania. In April, Frank played a week-long booking at Resorts International in Atlantic City with Sy Oliver. Between then and mid-June, Frank was busy playing shows in Vegas, California, and Denver. Most important of all, Frank was in great voice, adding songs like

'The Tender Trap' and 'You Make Me Feel so Young', which he had not performed in a long while. On 14 June, Frank performed at his own "40th Anniversary In Show Business Celebration" at the Universal Amphitheatre in Los Angeles. Following more shows in New Jersey, New York, Clarkston, Michigan, and Washington DC, Frank was about to begin work on the most ambitious recording project of his entire career, even though he was just five months short of his 64th birthday.

Back in December 1978, there had been an article in the *Wall Street Journal* by David McClintock urging Frank to record again. Three days after Frank's 63rd birthday, McClintock asked for three things: for Frank to stop worrying "about competing against anyone except his own high standards"; the people who paid $25 to see him perform at the Radio City Music Hall were "not representative sampling of the vast and perpetual audience for his records"; and since Frank "has far less reason to concern himself with rock", he shouldn't be singing new songs that are not worthy. He implored Frank to record again, saying, "there is plenty of material for several albums and they would sell well. These recordings would meet Sinatra's deep obligations to himself and the millions who admire his talent." The article struck a chord with Frank and those around him, but the idea for *Trilogy* per se came from Frank's long-time producer, Sonny Burke, one of the first men hired by Reprise back in 1960.

THREE'S A CROWD

Sonny had the whole concept worked out before he presented it to his boss, who thought it was an amazing idea and one to which he became totally committed. The idea was simple – a musical past, present, and future. McClintock's article had borne fruit after all.

But there was a weak link. Frank decided to use his good friend Gordon Jenkins to arrange and compose the *Future*. The choice to handle the *Present* section was probably the easiest – Don Costa. The *Past* for many people would ideally be represented by Nelson Riddle, but the task went to Billy May – a pretty good first reserve! Nelson and Frank were not talking Following their last session together, things had come to a head when Frank had failed to show up at a dinner to honour Nelson, despite it having been arranged around Frank's schedule. So bitter was Nelson that even when asked to do a chart for Frank, he flat refused, at a time when he was far from busy. Work on *Trilogy* appropriately began with the *Past* on 16, 17, and 18 July. In the event, only one of the songs from these sessions would be used, and later

VIEW FROM THE BLUES

In a recent interview with the New York Times, *BB King recalled his first meeting with Frank., "To play the lounge (in Las Vegas), a performer needed the approval of the main act. Frank Sinatra was the headliner at Caesars Palace, and we sent him a message asking him if he would permit us to come to the lounge. His answer came back in a telegram – 'Hell yes'. I liked that." BB King was taken to Frank's suite for a party. "I'm the only black guy in there, so guess he couldn't miss me. So he said, 'Hi B, how are you? I'm tired tonight. Thank you for coming by. I got some booze and some broads and some friends. Help yourself.' But I wasn't looking for no booze and no broads. I was so happy."*

DOWN IN BRAZIL

The Maracaña was principally a football stadium. Its capacity of 180,000 was perfect for Frank. There was no risk of him not selling out.

❝It was like the old days at the Paramount Theater in New York City when Frank Sinatra made his South American debut last night in the convention room of the New Rio Palace Hotel on Copacabana Beach. Women of all ages screamed and sighed, a dozen of them walking onstage during his performance to hand him roses.❞

JAMES BACON, *LA HERALD EXAMINER*

versions of the same songs appear on the album. The first number they tried was Victor Young and Sam Lewis's 'Street of Dreams', which neatly summed up this period: "Love laughs at a king/Kings don't mean a thing, on the street of dreams. Dreams broken in two, can be made like new/On the street of dreams".

A month later Frank was in New York with Don Costa working on the *Present*, fittingly the first song they cut was the anthemic, 'New York, New York'. The next day they did three more songs including Billy Joel's 'Just The Way you Are'. Session singer Marlene Ver Planck, whose husband had played trombone in Tommy Dorsey's band with Frank at the Paramount back in 1956 recalls the session: "I got the job of being the contractor for the 16 singers, especially for 'Just The Way You Are'. It was such a thrill to hire all the singers, but I didn't tell them who it was for until we all assembled. I walked them to the music stand, and showed them Frank's name – they too were thrilled. It was 55 musicians and 16 singers, with an arrangement by Don Costa – all at Columbia Studios on 30th Street. Frank walked in at the stroke of 8.00. We did the song, and took a break to listen, and then the producer Sonny Burke said that we would do it one more time. After we had done it, we wanted to get a photo of the singers with Frank, so I asked some of the guys if they would ask him. None of them would do it, so I peeked around the baffles that Frank worked within, sort of 'air-knocked' and asked him. He agreed and I pushed the camera at the viola player to take the shots."

A month after that it was back in Hollywood with Billy May to nail the songs that they'd previously worked on. The trickiest section with Gordon Jenkins conducting "the philharmonic symphony orchestra and mixed chorus", as it says on the album, took place on December 17 and 18 at the massive Shrine Auditorium in Los Angeles. During rehearsals there was feedback from the hall and so the stage curtain was closed and the orchestra was made to face the wall. It was a massive undertaking for Frank to learn the all-new Jenkins material. He and Vinnie Falcone spent many long hours at the piano going through what would not be easy task for a younger man. For 64-year-old Frank it was a daunting challenge. In the end it was largely to no

avail. The orchestra sounds great, Frank sings well, but there is a vacuous quality to the songs with their bogus lyrics. It was a collective disaster.

In between recording Frank was still playing live shows. Five days after recording at Western Recorders with Bill May, Frank and Barbara Sinatra were having dinner with the President of Egypt prior to one of the more unusual concerts of Frank's career. On September 27 Frank appeared in the open air, with the pyramids in Cairo as a backdrop, in a charity concert. "It's the biggest room I've ever played, and the toughest act I have ever followed". This was no ordinary gig; the 1,000 strong audience paid $2,500 each for the privilege.

On December 12, five days before beginning work on the *Future*, Frank was at Caesars Palace for a show that was taped for TV. Called *The First 40 Years* it celebrated Frank's career. There were friends Don Rickles, Harry James, Red Skelton, Cary Grant, Rich Little, Sammy Davis Jr., Dean Martin and family too – Frank and Nancy. While many in the press were complimentary some couldn't miss the opportunity to "have a go". The Washington Star found the whole thing filled with "vulgarity". They even accused Frank of choosing charities to support that made him look good. It only goes to prove that while times don't change, nor do some sections of the press.

BENEATH AN AMBER MOON

The 1980s for Frank began, as many years in the past two decades had done, with a Vegas booking. He played Caesars Circus Maximus room, tickets $35, and followed this with an appearance together with Paul Anka on a charity telethon. At Caesars, Frank previewed the new album, singing 'I've Been There', calling it "an excerpt from a 36-minute operetta by Gordon Jenkins." He also did 'It Had To Be You', telling the audience that it was a song he had never before recorded. But most of the show was a canter through Frank's much-loved back catalogue, causing one reviewer to remark "There is much love in the room when Francis Albert performs."

A few days later Frank flew to Rio de Janeiro to play four nights at the Rio Palace, with the well-heeled Brazilians paying $500 for the privilege. Right afterwards Frank played the biggest concert of his career at the Maracaña Stadium in Rio. Frank performed in the round and opened somewhat appropriately with 'The Coffee Song', which he first recorded in 1946 and did again with Johnny Mandel for his first album on Reprise.

In daughter Nancy's book, according to Frank it had been raining all day but the moment he began to sing the rain stopped, only to start again the minute he finished singing 'New York, New York', which was the encore. Some of the Brazilian press complained that Frank was siphoning money out of the Brazilian economy, not least because he took his entire orchestra from the United States to Brazil. Frank's retort was to tell them that Pelé had been doing the same in America.

A couple of days after getting back from South America Frank was at Santa Clara University in California to inaugurate the Frank Sinatra Chair in Music and Theater Arts. It was just one of the many diverse gigs that Frank performed during 1980, a year in which he didn't set foot inside a recording studio – he was probably burnt out from all the *Trilogy* sessions.

The immediate legacy of *Trilogy* was the unexpected death of Sonny Burke from cancer in May. Frank was in New York filming his appearance in *The First Deadly Sin* when he spoke with Sonny on the phone. He told his boss he was in hospital having some check ups; a week later he was dead. "I'll miss him as a friend. We'd been friends for so many years. He was a wonderful man and bright. *Damn*, he was bright. And he really worked his tail off on *Trilogy*. He mixed and mixed and mixed and mixed" said Frank a couple of months later. Besides regular shows at Atlantic

City's Resorts International (one of several during the year), Carnegie Hall, the Universal Amphitheatre (with Sergio Mendes and Brazil '88), two more stints at Caesars, there were a number of benefit shows. The first was for Ronald Reagan's presidential campaign, along with Dean Martin. Others included the Desert Hospital in Palm Springs and another Red Cross benefit in Monaco for Princess Grace.

In September he did a number of shows in London, some at the Albert Hall and others at the Festival Hall, with the orchestra was conducted by Vinnie Falcone, as were all of his dates throughout the year. As usual the band featured many British musicians including trombonist Don Lusher. "The band would first play a seven-minute overture. We would get applause and bow, then there would be a short silence and then he just walked on and sang. There was never any big announcement – it was magical and it had enormous impact! He always looked the part – immaculate in a really good dinner jacket and bow tie…no extra jewellery or anything else…just absolute class. It was wonderful to feel

> 66 The old man is still capable of doing his best work when he tries. Don't hold him down for the count. Not yet. Not by a longshot 99
>
> **THE *NEW YORK DAILY NEWS*, APRIL 1980**

TRILOGY QUARTET
Billy May, Frank, Don Costa and Gordon Jenkins at the 1979 Reprise recording session. Only Nelson was missing.

TRILOGY

WHATEVER THE RESULTS, and they are mixed, there is no doubting the ambition. It was almost as though Frank felt he had one last "big one" in him. Maybe if it had been anyone but Gordon Jenkins writing *Future* it may have worked.

Amazingly, Frank found some very good standards for *Past* that he had not recorded before; they were 'But Not for Me', 'I Had the Craziest Dream', 'It Had to Be You', 'All of You', 'More Than You Know', and 'They All Laughed'. The fact is that *Past* is by far the best part of the project, and Billy May was very proud of it.

Although bits of *Present* also work well, the Costa-arranged songs suffer a similar fate to some of Frank's other 1970s "modern" song output: when it is a song that works (lyrically) for Frank, then it works; 'Something', and 'Summer Me, Winter Me' rank up there with the best from his later years. Although Frank and Nelson had stopped working together, it was the arranger's old charts that were used on 'Something'. Then of course there's 'New York, New York', which sounded absolutely nothing like the present, which is precisely why it worked so well. Somehow the album is best summed up by what it says on the sleeve: "The Future: Reflections on The Future in Three Tenses." Ultimately it was an overblown idea. David McClintock was rewarded for his *Wall Street Journal* article by being commissioned to write the album's sleeve notes, for which he won a Grammy; Saul Bass designed the cover. The album was nominated for a Grammy as "Album of the Year" but failed to win.

the reaction." In London there was a radical departure from Frank's normal concerts – he conducted. He did 'Bosa Nova For C', although the players probably got themselves through it without a lot of help from Frank. Teleprompters were not available for concerts back in 1980 and so Frank had a book to which he would occasionally refer. At one London show he read out what it said on the page and held it up. It said "TALK", and Frank went into his monologue. He also used the book when he did songs from *Trilogy*.

KING OF THE HILL

For much of the last half of 1980 Frank was involved in supporting Reagan's bid for the Presidency, which he duly won in November. As a reward Frank was asked to help produce the Presidential Inaugural Gala in Landover, Maryland on January 19 1981. Besides Frank there was Bob Hope, Ethel Merman, Johnny Carson and Rich Little. Little recalled the rehearsals. "I was working on my impression of Frank with the orchestra, doing 'My Kind Of Town', and I hadn't realized that he was watching me! He walked up and showed me more of the mannerisms – telling me how to do him! Especially showing me the pointing – there was a lot of pointing! He did it with a twinkle in his eye! Frank had definite movements. Vinnie Falcone would say, 'Frank's a furniture mover – he's always moving something on stage.'" Frank himself sang 'My Kind Of Town', 'New York, New York', 'America The Beautiful' and 'Nancy (With The Reagan Face)'. A few days later he received a nice note from the President saying, "Every minute was sheer magic, and that was due to you."

No sooner had Frank got over the success of the Inaugural than it was back to Caesars in Vegas. Once his week was over he switched to Caesars in Lake Tahoe for another week but not before he spent two hours in front

SONG LINES

Recorded: Western Recorders, Hollywood/Columbia Studios, New York/Burbank studios, Hollywood/Shrine Auditorium, Los Angeles.
Chart: US No 17, 24 weeks on the chart (First charted 12 April, 1980)

PAST
Arrangements by Billy May

1. 'THE SONG IS YOU'
(Jerome Kern & Oscar Hammerstein) Recorded 18 September, 1979

2. 'BUT NOT FOR ME'
(George & Ira Gershwin) Recorded 18 September, 1979

3. 'I HAD THE CRAZIEST DREAM'
(Harry Warren & Mack Gordon) Recorded 17 July, 1979

4. 'IT HAD TO BE YOU'
(Isham Jones & Gus Kahn) Recorded 18 July, 1979.

5. 'LET'S FACE THE MUSIC AND DANCE'
(Irving Berlin) Recorded 19 September, 1979

6. 'STREET OF DREAMS'
(Victor Young & Sam M. Lewis) Recorded 18 September, 1979

7. 'MY SHINING HOUR'
(Harold Arlen & Johnny Mercer) Recorded 17 September, 1979

8. 'ALL OF YOU'
(Cole Porter) Recorded 17 September, 1979

9. 'MORE THAN YOU KNOW'
(Vincent Yeomans/Edward Eliseu/Billy Rose) Recorded 17 September, 1979

10. 'THEY ALL LAUGHED'
(George Gershwin & Ira Gershwin) Recorded 18 September, 1979

PRESENT
Arrangements by Don Costa & Nelson Riddle

1. 'YOU AND ME (WE WANTED IT ALL)'
(Carol Bayer Sager & Peter Allen) Recorded 20 August, 1979

2. 'JUST THE WAY YOU ARE'
(Billy Joel) Recorded 22 August, 1979

3. 'SOMETHING'
(George Harrison) Recorded 3 December, 1979.

4. 'MACARTHUR PARK'
(Jimmy Webb) Recorded 20 August, 1979

5. 'THEME FROM *NEW YORK, NEW YORK*'
(John Kander and Fred Ebb) Recorded 19 September, 1979

6. 'SUMMER ME, WINTER ME'
(Michel Legrand/Alan Bergman/Marilyn Bergman) Recorded 20 August, 1979

7. 'SONG SUNG BLUE'
(Neil Diamond) Recorded 22 August, 1979

8. 'FOR THE GOOD TIMES'
(Kris Kristofferson) Recorded 21 August, 1979 (with Eileen Farrell)

9. 'LOVE ME TENDER'
(Elvis Presley & Vera Matson) Recorded 21 August, 1979

10. 'THAT'S WHAT GOD LOOKS LIKE TO ME'
(Lan Kuhn & Lois Irwin) Recorded 21 August, 1979

FUTURE
A musical fantasy in three tenses for Frank Sinatra, Philharmonic Symphony Orchestra and Mixed Chorus. Composed, arranged, and conducted by Gordon Jenkins

1. 'WHAT TIME DOES THE NEXT MIRACLE LEAVE?'
Soprano solo by Diana Lee, narration by Jerry Whitman. Recorded 17 December, 1979

2. 'WORLD WAR NONE!'
Recorded 18 December, 1979

3. 'THE FUTURE'
Alto solo by Beverly Jenkins. Recorded 17 December, 1979

4. 'THE FUTURE (CON'T.): I'VE BEEN THERE!'
Recorded 18 December, 1979

5. 'FUTURE (CONCLUSION): SONG WITHOUT WORDS'
Soprano solo by Loulie Jean Norman, alto solo by Beverly Jenkins. Recorded 17 December, 1979

6. 'FINALE: BEFORE THE MUSIC ENDS'
Recorded 18 December, 1979

SHEAR TALENT
George Shearing was born in London in 1919, and blind from birth. His best-known work was the wonderful 'Lullaby of Birdland'.

of the Nevada Gaming Commission answering questions so that he could get a licence to once again become a shareholder in a Vegas casino. Appropriately three of Frank's opening songs at Lake Tahoe were 'I've Got The World On String', 'Pennies From Heaven' and 'The Best Is Yet To Come' – the soundtrack was back on track.

When the Tahoe run ended Frank was again before the Gaming Commission and for most of March Frank was at Caesars in Vegas. He cancelled his last show following the attempted assassination of President Reagan. A week later he was at Wally Heider's studio in Hollywood working with Gordon Jenkins. For almost anyone, other than Frank Sinatra, an album like *Trilogy* would have heralded the end of their recording career, despite its relatively good showing on the charts. There was a feeling among many critics, fans and others that Frank had lost the plot. Even with the passing of two decades most people still haven't caught up with *The Future*. The studio sessions were to start work on a new album, to be called *She Shot Me Down*. This came from the lyric of the first song that Frank recorded on April 8, Sonny Bono's 'Bang Bang'. It was an album that those in Frank's orbit referred to as "The Saloon Singer" album, and it had been on the cards since the first half of the 70s. He'd even cut 'Bang Bang' back in 1973, along with Jimmy Van Heusen and Johnny Mercer's 'Empty Tables'. It was three months before Frank did any more work for the album, spending two days at Columbia in New York. Between the sessions he was all over the US playing in Fort Lauderdale; Valley Forge, Pennsylvania; Atlantic City, Caesars Palace (a couple of runs); The Metropolitan Center, Boston and San Francisco. He'd taken to joking about his prolific touring "If you've seen me work before, and if you haven't you've been living under a rock. I've been everywhere."

As if to prove his point Frank flew from New York to South Africa to open at the Sun City Resort on July 24. The old democrat with principals had done another one eighty. Sun City was in Bophuthatswana, an "independent homeland", under the watchful eye of the Apartheid-dominated regime of President Marais Viljoen. Most entertainers gave South Africa a wide berth, but according to daughter Nancy Frank saw it differently, "I play to all people of any colour, creed, drunk or sober."

From South Africa Frank flew across the South Atlantic for shows in Buenos Aires's Luna Park Stadium, for which he reportedly earned a cool $2 million, before heading north for three shows in São Paulo. From there he flew to New York, did a recording session and played a week in Atlantic City, before doing two weeks at Carnegie Hall with pianist George Shearing. This meant that between July 20 and September 20 Frank did four studio sessions and

played 37 concerts. Just to top it all off he recorded a car commercial for Chrysler and did a Muscular Dystrophy telethon – it was a prodigious and lucrative work rate. Frank worked really hard at keeping his voice in good shape during the early 1980s. He cut down on his drinking and even his smoking, both of which helped him cope with the type of punishing schedule that would have floored many a younger singer. Vinnie Falcone matched Frank's dedication by always being there for him. It's been said by some of the musicians from before and after Vinnie that he worked harder for Frank than any of his other conductors. Falcone, from his perspective was in the dream job. He was also in awe of Frank's lung capacity, which was so great the he could make the piano vibrate during rehearsals. Perhaps with Vinnie's encouragement Frank would often drop the strings from his shows, making the whole show take on a much jazzier feel.

The Carnegie shows did not mark the end of 1981's live shows. Besides concerts and benefits there was another week at Caesars in Vegas. According to Peter Altschuler, son of the legendary Murray The K, the DJ who ruled the airwaves of New York from 1958 to 1967, his father ran into Frank in Vegas. "Though Murray opened every single show with a Sinatra tune, the only time they were seen together was in Las Vegas... and no one took a picture. Murray was with Tony Orlando, who was performing on the Strip, and they bumped into Frank (plus entourage) in one of the hotels. Sinatra, according to Tony, spread his arms, said, "Murray the K! Man, do we owe you," shook hands, exchanged a few words, and... that was it."

In late October Frank was back in a TV studio for two

FRANK WITH THE LAUGHING FACE
US president Ronald Reagan cuts in on Frank as he dances with first lady Nancy Reagan during a party in the East Room of the White House on 6 February, 1981.

FRANK CONDUCTS
Sylvia tried to persuade Frank to do at least one chorus of 'Honeysuckle Rose' with her, but he wouldn't. It would certainly have helped sell some more copies of the album.

CITY IN THE SUN
Sun City somehow personifies old South Africa. Many performers simply refused offers to play there.

days, along with Count Basie doing another *A Man and His Music*. It was Frank's first TV special in five years. On the day Frank went into the studio in Hollywood to cut 'To Love A Child', a Joe Raposo–Hal David song, *She Shot Me Down* entered the *Billboard* chart but it was far from the hoped for success.

As New Year inevitably follows Christmas so Frank, almost inevitably, began 1982 with a booking at Caesars in Vegas. There followed another week in February before a two week booking with daughter Nancy. Then Frank performed at another White House Gala in honour of another Italian President, Alessandro Pertini. He shared the stage with another Italian American, his old rival Perry Como. The two sons of immigrants performed alone and then sang together. Through the spring and on into the summer there were one off shows across the States as well as engagements in Atlantic City and Las Vegas. Frank also took up the conducting baton again, this time for his old friend Sylvia Syms; with most of the arrangements written by Don Costa. They had known each other since meeting in 52nd Street clubs where they marvelled at Billie Holiday and Mabel Mercer. Costa unfortunately suffered a heart attack just before the session in New York in early April.

In July Frank with Cary Grant, Charlton Heston, Dorothy Lamour, James Stewart, Ernest Borgnine and Angie Dickinson opened the newly enclosed Universal

Amphitheatre in a gala charity evening. Right afterwards Frank and Nancy were booked into the same venue on what was becoming their year-long family tour. Soon after Frank went back into the studio to cut a couple of tracks, one arranged by Billy May and the other by Costa; neither got a release at the time. Many, including Billy May himself, have proffered the opinion that the reason that he and Frank lasted so long was the fact they didn't have a lot to do with each other socially. Billy was also less in awe of Frank than Nelson and he remained his own man; as he succinctly put it, "you simply did the job!" The day after recording Frank flew to the Dominican Republic to appear in The Concert for the Americas, with the Buddy Rich Orchestra. There was a black tie audience of 5,000 for the televised show, South and Central America's most prominent, and well-heeled, citizens. Frank was on top form and the finale of 'New York New York' was choreographed to a spectacular firework display at the outdoor arena.

On September 11 Frank was in Ottawa for a hospital benefit concert, it was a favour for Rich Little. "I used to do lots of benefits for Frank, and he would always say 'If ever I can do anything for you...' I was involved with fund raising in my hometown for the Civic Hospital, where I was born. I had been trying to get Paul Anka, who was also born there, to commit to the date, but diaries were difficult. I thought I'd mention it to Frank and he agreed right away. He got out his Miss Piggy Diary, with different pictures of Miss Piggy on each page, and wrote the date saying that he would be there with his musicians! It was set some five months ahead. I was there in Ottawa, and we had pulled some 20–25,000 people on the strength of Frank coming, including Prime Minister Trudeau. Well, time went by, and Frank hadn't arrived for the pre-show dinner, and I was getting ready to renounce my citizenship! But he turned up just in time to say a few words at the dinner, and then he insisted that I should

close the show, not him! He had brought his key rhythm section, to which we added local people. It was really generous of him to let me close, though I suspect that he was also anxious to get back to New York as soon as he could! He got a huge reaction, then asked 'Do I have to do it all again now in French?'" A few days later, Frank and The Buddy Rich band opened for ten days at Carnegie Hall. On the third day of the engagement Frank's old friend Princes Grace was killed in a car crash in France, on a hairpin bend, a few miles from Monaco. For the rest of the year it was the same ol' same ol', with shows in Los Angeles, at Caesars in Las Vegas, and in Atlantic City. This included a week at the East Coast's newest casino, Steve Wynn's Golden Nugget (Frank did TV ads with Steve Wynn to promote its opening). After having his, by now normal, Christmas holiday, which this year included a week in Acapulco, Frank was true to form and did a week at Caesars in Vegas, this time followed by a week at their sister establishment in Lake Tahoe to start the year.

BACK TO THE OFFICE

On the recording front Frank began the year with an unusual assignment. He conducted the orchestra on a session for Charlie Turner. Frank's first vocal sessions of the year were on January 19 in New York City with Joe Parnello conducting. Don Costa, "that dear, decent and talented man", as Frank described her father in a letter to Nikka Costa, died around the time of this session. He had been too sick for some while to contemplate working with Frank again. At the second session a few days later Parnello, who had worked with Vic Damone among many others, contributed a couple of arrangements, one of which, 'Here's To The Band' became the only tune to get a release at the time. It came out as a single and predictably failed to worry the single's chart in either the UK or the US.

After another run at the Golden Nugget and Caesars in Las Vegas Frank, Dean Martin, Sammy Davis and Nancy did a hometown benefit for the Desert Hospital at the Palm Desert Country Club on February 12. It was the first time in many years that the three old friends had done their Rat Pack/Summit/Clan (delete as appropriate) show, although they had appeared at other celebrity or charity shows. Shortly afterwards Frank went into the studio to do something he'd never done before. He cut 'It's Sunday', a song by Jule Styne and Susan Birkenhead, with just Tony Mottola's guitar as accompaniment (Frank and Tony often did songs *à deux* in concert). Frank had tried it a month earlier, using one of Costa's last arrangements, with a full band but he was unhappy with it. 'It's Sunday' became the b-side to 'Here's To The Band' and is a subtle alternative to the over-blown nature of this homage to his fellow musicians. 'It's Sunday' is musically just a few miles down the road from 'Watertown' – a lovely song. 'It's Sunday' was recorded the night after Frank and others entertained

SHE SHOT ME DOWN

USING ARRANGEMENTS BY JENKINS, Riddle, and Costa, this was "the album that got away" according to Will Friedwald in *The Song Is You*. It has in Nelson Riddle's 'The Gal That Got Away/It Never Entered My Mind' one of the truly great Frank Reprise recordings. Old friend Alec Wilder's 'A Long Night', arranged by Jenkins, is another triumph. It is a song that perfectly fits Frank's age, verifying the album's torch-song status. Given the fact that Frank was working so hard, his voice sounds great, and this can only be attributed to his regime of care during this period.

Chart-wise this record did nothing of significance, failing to make the Top 50 in the US and not even making the charts in Britain. The truth is that you had to be a Sinatra fan of some commitment to buy his albums by this time. It was before the nostalgia boom had kicked in, and, while people respected Frank, they were not yet suitably aware of his mortality, which, given his work rate, is hardly surprising.

SONG LINES

Recorded April & July, 1981, in New York and Hollywood. Arranged and conducted by Gordon Jenkins. Producer: Don Costa

SIDE 1

1. 'GOOD THING GOING' (Stephen Sondheim) From the musical, *Merrily We Roll Along*. Recorded 19 August 1981

2. 'HEY LOOK, NO CRYING' (Jule Styne & Susan Birkenhead) Recorded 10 September, 1981

3. 'THANKS FOR THE MEMORY' (Leo Robin/Ralph Rainger) Recorded 20 July, 1981

4. 'A LONG NIGHT' (Alex Wilder/Loonis McGlohon) Recorded 20 July, 1981

SIDE 2

1. 'BANG BANG (MY BABY SHOT ME DOWN' (Sonny Bono) Recorded 8 April, 1981

2. 'MORNING MORNING QUARTERBACK' (Pamela Phillips/Don Costa) Recorded 10 September, 1981

3. 'SOUTH – TO A WARMER PLACE' (Alec Wilder/Loomis McGlohon) Recorded 21 July 1981

4. 'I LOVED HER' (Gordon Jenkins) Recorded 20 July, 1981

5. 'THE GAL THAT GOT AWAY/IT NEVER ENTERED MY MIND (MEDLEY)' (Harold Arlen/Ira Gershwin/Rodgers/Hart) Recorded April 8, 1981

Queen Elizabeth at a special show at Twentieth Century Fox. After playing Caesars and Harrah's Frank went back into the studio, and was professionally reunited with Bill Miller. The two old friends hadn't worked together in five years and with Don Costa gone and Vinnie Falcone having moved on and Nelson Riddle still out in the cold it was perhaps logical to call on 'Sunshine Charlie'. According to Miller "I ran into him accidentally, and he said 'Did you get a call from Mickey Rudin?' I said 'No.' Next day I got a call, saying Frank wanted me to come back I said 'Yeah, why not.' Things were forgotten by then." They worked on Michel Legrand and the Bergmnan's 'How Do You Keep The Music Playing' from the Burt Reynold's film, *Best Friends*. Despite the reunification there was not enough magic in the air to allow the recording to surface either then, or

BATON MAN
Charlie Turner had been Frank's regular lead trumpeter since 1976. They worked together on the tracks in January and February 1983.

CHARLES TURNER, trumpet
conducted by: Frank Sinatra
arranged by: Billy May, Nelson Riddle, and Don Costa

"What's New"

THE CHAIRMAN AND THE PRINCE

Frank and Michael Jackson together in New York City at one of Quincy Jones's sessions for 'LA is My Lady'.

A TENOR, TWO DIVAS AND A VOICE

Frank, Diana Ross, Luciano Pavarotti, and Monserrat Caballe at New York's Radio City Music Hall on 18 March 1984 before a benefit concert for cancer research; they raised $3.5 million.

since. After that session there were no more in 1983, in fact it would be over a year before Frank was in a studio; but he was far from idle. His touring schedule was, if not quite as hectic as previous years, still very full. He played almost 50 concerts from April through the end of 1983. Among the highlights was a show with Sammy Davis in Monaco as a tribute to Princess Grace and another with Dean and Sammy along with Diana Ross for the University of Nevada.

Having recorded a song from a Burt Reynold's film Frank now had a cameo in one of his movies, *Cannonball Run II.* Sammy, who was in the movie, asked Frank to appear and whatever they paid him it must have been one of his better hourly rates. He flew to the location on his aircraft in the morning, worked for four hours, and flew home that evening. A few days later Frank went to the funeral of his old boss, Harry James. Frank and Barbara then flew to France and spent a month on the Riviera, there were some signs of Frank taking a little more time away from work; for a workaholic like Frank it must have been a challenge, even approaching 69 years of age. In November the *Variety* Club honoured Frank with an all-star party filmed by NBC at Burbank Studios. Among the tributes was a Sinatra medley

performed by Vic Damone and Steve Lawrence, with Nelson Riddle conducting the orchestra. Almost simultaneously a 16-LP boxed set of Frank's Capitol classics came out and failed to make the charts, but then it did cost a cool $350. Two weeks after the Variety Club event Frank was at the Reagan White House to receive a Lifetime Achievement Award from the Kennedy Center.

RAZZMATAZZ

Frank rang the changes in 1984 by having as his first date of the year, a benefit show, in Houston with the Buddy Rich band. There followed a small number of one off dates through the early part of April before he went back into the studio. There was also a new conductor, in Quincy Jones, who Frank had last worked with in the mid-60s when he was with the Count Basie Orchestra. While life had moved on for Frank it had radically altered for Quincy. From an established jazzman Quincy had found mainstream fame working with Michael Jackson on the *Thriller* album in 1982. Quincy produced the album, as well as co-writing one of the songs with James Ingram. It earned him a small fortune; at last count *Thriller* has sold over 26 million copies worldwide. But Frank was not a Michael Jackson fan; it was through Quincy's work with Lena Horne that he came to get this very different gig. There had even been talk of Quincy producing an album

of duets with Frank and Lena, along with Lionel Ritchie, Barry Manilow and even Michael Jackson. The first session in New York City with Quincy yielded three songs that would appear on Frank's next album, including the title song, co-written by Quincy, 'LA is My Lady'. Frank's old habit of asking people to work on material for an album continued, one he talked to in the early to mid 1980s was Jimmy Webb "Mr. Sinatra asked me specifically to compose an "opera" for a record. It was to be a "four seasons" theme with a song for every month of the year. I finished about half of them and played them for Mr. S. at the MGM Grand Hotel in Las Vegas. He was quite excited and said to Frank Jr. "I think we can make a hit out of this don't you Frank?" It had reached the point where he was suggesting arrangers. Unfortunately he was having difficulty at that time in assimilating new music. I might tell you that while I was working on this project I became friends with Joe Raposo who warned me that *he* had written an album of songs for Mr. Sinatra and had run into difficulty at the recording stage and that he was still sitting on the songs."

By the time 'LA is My Lady' came out in August Frank was playing a gala in Monte Carlo with Elton John, fresh from playing shows all over America. Frank cancelled a week long booking at the Golden Nugget with Willie Nelson when he became ill, straight after a two-week booking at Carnegie Hall, but apart from that it was a year much like the previous one. Back in May he had taken to dedicating his concerts to Count Basie and Gordon Jenkins. A month later he added Don Costa to that tribute. Among the regular shows during the remainder of 1984 there was campaigning on behalf of Reagan's re-election. Frank also went to Vienna for a charity show for blind children at the request of the American Ambassador. The Austrian concert for 11,000 people followed a week at the Albert Hall in London; in London his closer was 'Mack The Knife' instead of 'NY, NY'.

Around the time of his 69th birthday Frank decided to call Nelson Riddle. According to Nelson's son, Chris, in an interview with British writer and broadcaster Spencer Leigh it worked out fine. "He asked my father to be the music director on Ronald Reagan's second Inaugural in Washington DC. The last time my father and Frank had worked on a similar project was John F Kennedy's in 1961. My father lived in Los Angeles and Frank was calling from Washington DC. At one point he realized it was 6.15 in the morning where my father was, and 9.15 where he was. Frank was a little uncomfortable about calling him so early. He said, 'Nelson, I am really sorry.' My father had a dry wit and he said, 'That's alright, Frank, I had to get up to answer the telephone anyway.'" The Inaugural on 19 January went off without a hitch, apart from some niggling from the press about some of Frank's connections. Frank got mad at some of the comments and it's reported

LA IS MY LADY

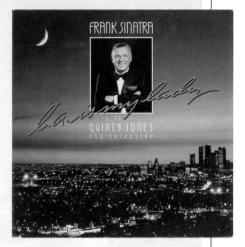

THE OBVIOUS COUNTERPOINT to 'New York New York', 'LA is My Lady' failed to galvanize California as Frank's homage to the Big Apple had done. As a single, it failed even to dent the Hot 100, and as an album it was even less successful than *She Shot Me Down*. Quincy Jones employed a very different crew of people from Frank's regulars. There was jazz pianist Bob James, playing synthesizer (the first use of the ubiquitous 1980s instrument on a Sinatra album), guitarist George Benson and other notable session players such as Marcus Miller (bass), Ralph MacDonald (percussion), Randy Brecker (trumpet), ex-Blood Sweat and Tears man Lew Soloff (trumpet), Lionel Hampton (Vibes), and drummer Steve Gadd. All of them contributed to the very different sound of this album.

Quincy's production is both a weakness and a strength, depending on which song you are listening to. But as one commentator noted, "everyone involved, from Sinatra and Jones to the band themselves, sounds like they're having fun". In retrospect, it does not sound half as bad as it did at the time. Frank did 'Mack the Knife' on 16 April with George Benson's lovely guitar, but he was never happy with his vocal. After singing it on the road for two years he gave it another go, using the same backing track. This new vocal got a release on a CD boxed set in the 1990s. It stands as the last truly great Sinatra vocal.

The failure of the album to do anything on the charts hastened Frank's recording decline.

SONG LINES

Recorded A&R Studios, New York City
Producer: Quincy Jones
Chart: US No 58, 13 weeks on the chart
(First charted 25 August, 1984)
UK No 41, 8 weeks on the chart
(First charted 18 August, 1984)

SIDE 1

1. 'LA IS MY LADY'
(Quincy Jones, Peggy Lipton Jones, Alan & Marilyn Bergman) Recorded 13 April, 1984
2. 'THE BEST OF EVERYTHING'
(John Kander & Fred Ebb)
Recorded 16 April, 1984

3. 'HOW DO YOU KEEP THE MUSIC PLAYING?'
(Michel Legrand, Alan & Marilyn Bergman)
Recorded 17 April, 1984
4. 'TEACH ME TONIGHT'
(Gene de Paul & Sammy Cahn)
Recorded 17 April, 1984
5. 'IT'S ALL RIGHT WITH ME'
(Cole Porter) Recorded 16 April, 1984
6. 'AFTER YOU'VE GONE'
(Turner Layton & Henry Craemer) Recorded 13 April, 1984

SIDE 2

1. 'MACK THE KNIFE'
(Kurt Weill, Bertold Brecht & Marc Blitzstein)

Recorded 16 April, 1984.
2. 'UNTIL THE REAL THING COMES ALONG'
(Holiner, Nichols, Freeman, Cahn & Chaplin)
Recorded 13 April, 1984.
3. 'STORMY WEATHER'
(Harold Arlern & Ted Koehler)
Recorded 17 April, 1984
4. 'IF I SHOULD LOSE YOU'
(Ralph Rainger & Leo Robin)
Recorded 17 April, 1984
5. 'A HUNDRED YEARS FROM TODAY'
(Victor Young, Joe Young & Ned Washington)
Recorded 16 April, 1984

that he warned a roomful of reporters: "You're dead, every one of you!" Even vice-president George Bush senior was moved to tell some journalists to "just leave him alone." The Inaugural was the last time that Frank and Nelson publicly worked together although they talked of recording an album. According to Chris Riddle "They were working on a three-record album of standards, none of which they had done before. My father was very excited about that, and he was working on that project when he passed away. I'm glad that it didn't end with negativity between them." By the time Nelson died on October 6 1985 he had completed two arrangements.

THE EMPIRE STATE BUILDING AND FIFTH AVENUE
LIT UP TO CELEBRATE FRANK'S 80TH BIRTHDAY

*"Sinatra's work is his legend,
his legend is his work"*

JOHN LAHR IN *THE NEW YORKER*

THE FINAL CURTAIN

During the first quarter of 1985, Frank was much less busy than he had been for a while. In April, he embarked on a tour to Japan, playing the Budokan in Tokyo as well as a one-off show in Hong Kong. Back from the East there was a week-long booking at the Golden Nugget in Vegas.

There were also more accolades, at very different ends of the awards spectrum. First Frank was given an Honourary Engineering Degree from the Stevens Institute of Technology in Hoboken; the place he had thought of attending as a youth. It resulted in one of his very rare visits to the town of his birth. Then Ronald Reagan gave Frank the Medal of Freedom. Amongst this good stuff was a family tragedy when Nancy's husband, Hugh Lambert, died from throat cancer in August. There was

CARNEGIE COMEBACK
Frank performing with the Peter Duchin Orchestra at the re-opened Carnegie Hall in New York, 16 December 1986.

also a return to "Frank and the Mob" when following the Medal of Freedom, cartoonist Gary Trudeau mocked Frank over his Mafia connections in his Doonesbury cartoon strip. Frank immediately had his lawyers fire off a broadside. "Mr. Sinatra believes that you've misrepresented the facts of an event that took place in such-and-such casino,'" Trudeau later recalled. "My editor called me and said, 'What about it?' And I said, 'Well, of course I misrepresented the facts. I made it up. It was a comic strip. So, it would have been a very short trial.'"

In the last months of the year, running up to his 70th birthday, Frank was definitely taking it easy. In the four months from 1 September he played just 20 dates, and these were mostly at Carnegie Hall and the Golden Nuggets in Vegas and Atlantic City. In keeping with the slower pace Frank didn't open the year in Vegas but holidayed in Switzerland. But from then on the work rate stepped up a gear. With a mix of shows, ranging from one-off dates to the regular casino bookings, he performed on 75 days during the year, and on a number of these it was two shows a night, which is none too shabby for a septuagenarian. Bill Miller was also back, playing some piano, and conducting on many of these dates.

Not necessarily linked with his work rate Frank was taken ill when playing the Golden Nugget in Atlantic City

during November. He was flown back to Palm Springs for emergency surgery, for diverticulitis, at Eisenhower Medical Center. Having spent a week in hospital he was back five days later at the Atlantic City's sister casino in Las Vegas.

January 1987 came and went with Frank not performing anywhere. He did spend five days in Hawaii specifically to appear in an episode of Tom Selleck's TV show, *Magnum PI*. Frank played a retired police officer tracking down the killer of his granddaughter. A few days before the episode aired on CBS Frank appeared at a benefit at the Century Plaza in Los Angeles, several other benefits followed before the first proper engagement of the year on 3 April at the Golden Nugget in Las Vegas. From then on Frank really got into his stride, playing one-off shows, week-long bookings at both Golden Nuggets and then in June he embarked on a five-city tour of Italy. Frank had planned to play some dates in Scandinavia but the Swedish government decided to tax him, when foreign performers were normally exempt, for playing in Bophuthatswana in 1981.

The spectre of the Sun City dates returned when some people objected to Frank receiving an NAACP Life Time Achievement Award. The NAACP president defended the decision "Frank Sinatra has made significant outcries against segregation, discrimination and bigotry". Fifty years after *The House I Live In* it seemed somehow appropriate, but as often with Frank there was a dichotomy, and some found it difficult to fathom him. Sammy Davis Jr made a tribute speech and even allowing for any personal bias put it well. "He was my friend long before it became fashionable to be my friend. You wouldn't see black dealers or black people living in hotels in Las Vegas if Sinatra hadn't spearheaded it all in 1946".

Frank and Sammy played shows at the Greek theatre in Los Angeles in August before Frank began a hectic round of shows taking up the last third of the year. He had over fifty engagements between the opening night at the new Bally's Grand (formerly the Golden Nugget) in Atlantic City on 3 September and the New Year's Eve show at Bally's in Las Vegas (formerly the MGM Grand). Frank, Dean and Sammy had opened the renamed Las Vegas Bally's on 29 October. It had been one of Dean's first appearances since the death of his son, Dean Paul, who crashed his USAF Phantom jet into the same mountain as Dolly Sinatra. As Nancy Sinatra later said "I believe this tragedy changed Big Dean's life forever." The events of the

MARTY'S BOY
Frank's father would have been proud as his son received an honourary degree at Stevens Institute of Technology in Hoboken on 23 May 1985.

FRANK LIVE IN 1986

Frank sang many of the same songs that he had at his concerts over the previous few years. At his "New Jersey Homecoming Show" at the Meadowlands in New Jersey on 14 March the set was:

1. 'Without A Song'
2. 'Where Or When'
3. 'For Once In My Life'
4. 'Nice 'N' Easy'
5. 'My Heart Stood Still'
6. 'The Best Is Yet To Come'
7. 'Change Partners'
8. 'April In Paris'
9. 'It's All Right With Me'
10. 'It Was A Very Good Year'
11. 'You Make Me Feel So Young'
12. 'The Gal That Got Away'
14. 'Come Rain Or Come Shine'
15. 'Bewitched'
16. 'Moonlight In Vermont'
17. 'LA Is My Lady'
18. 'I've Got You Under My Skin'
19. 'Someone To Watch Over Me'
20. 'New York, New York'

Interestingly, only half of these songs appeared in the set Frank played at the Bernabeu Stadium in Madrid, Spain, in September. 'My Way', off the set list for years, was a bigger hit in Europe and so was sung as the closer.

**THE SUMMIT'S
IN SESSION**
*Dean, Sammy and Frank at
Sammy's Beverly Hills house on
9 March, 1988, just prior to
their proposed 29-city tour.*

coming year were to
bear this out.

Frank began 1988 with
shows at Bally's in Las Vegas
before heading to Australia
for a concert on 9 January
at Sanctuary Cove, Sydney.
It was his first trip back
there since the troubled tour
of 1974; this time all went
without a hitch. Bob Hawke,
who had been so critical of
him 14 years earlier, was
now the Prime Minister;
whether he was invited to
the concert is anyone's guess. There were also more shows
at Bally's in Vegas and Atlantic City. At the same time
Frank's people were working on an ambitious plan to
reenergise the concerts. Part of the plan was for Frank
Sinatra Jr, by then 44 years old, to begin
conducting for his father, with Bill Miller
returning to the piano stool full time. Many
people fail to recognize that Junior is a
trained musician, an expert reader
and an accomplished pianist. Such
is so often the fate of the sons
of famous fathers.

Shortly before Frank's
72nd birthday he held a
press conference, along
with Sammy and Dean,

at Chasen's in Los Angeles. They announced that in the
new year they were to tour together for the first time in
twenty years — the Summit was to reconvene. It was a
slight fudge as they had performed together at various
times. The first show was on 13 March 1988 at the
16,000-seat Oakland Coliseum, sold out in two hours.
Dean opened the two-hour show and ran through seven
numbers including 'Everybody Loves Somebody' and
'That's Amore'. Sammy's eight numbers included his
'theme songs' 'What Kind Of Fool Am I' and 'Mr
Bojangles'. Frank's set went right back to the 1940s for
'It Never Entered My Mind' and spanned his whole
career. He finished with 'New York, New York' before all
three of them did a medley that closed with 'You're
Nobody 'Til Somebody Loves You', before the trio
returned for an encore of 'The Old Establishment'. As
one fan said, "this is like the super bowl!" And it seemed
like the 29-city tour, sponsored by American Express, was
set for huge success. That is until 20 March when
Dean Martin decided he had had enough after

Liza is called up as Dean Martin is rocked by the Rat Pack sack

**From PHILIP FINN
in New York**

SUPERSTAR Liza
Minnelli joined the
Rat Pack yesterday
—after Frank Sinatra
was said to have axed
Dean Martin follow-
ing a row over Dino's
drinking.

Liza will appear with
Sinatra and Sammy
Davis junior when the
old stagers team up
again later this year.

Little Ol' Wine Drin-
ker Martin clashed with
Ol' Blue Eyes after the
Rat Pack's return debut
in Oakland, California.

A critic wrote: "If his
drunk act is an act, it's
mighty believable—he
was teetering through
the show. He was an
embarrassment.

Martin opened the
shows singing alone, and
Sinatra is said to have
been upset by the way he
altered the words of his
opening number, Pennies
from Heaven.

Dino substituted Bour-
bon for pennies and as he
sang he lit a cigarette

which he tossed, still
burning, into the
audience.

He put his hands over
his ears as though the
cigarette was going to
explode.

Said one insider:
"Maybe Dean thought it
was funny, but Frank was
furious. Backstage he re-
ally let Dean have it—he
bawled him out."

Loss

It is thought his
renewed drinking is over
the loss of his son, Dean
Paul Martin, in a plane
crash.

*Friends say Martin knew
he was sad when he had to
make his way to the
sold-out concerts in his
own limousine, while
Sinatra and Davis
travelled together.*

Martin left the Rat Pack
after just six shows, app-

arently blaming an old
kidney problem.

He entered Cedars Sinai
medical centre in Los
Angeles on March 21 and
his old pals said they
were concerned for his
life.

But he was quickly
released, and everyone
said he would be back in
July. But those concerts
have been cancelled and
yesterday Martin, now 70,
said he was going solo in
Las Vegas next week.

Sinatra's agents still
maintain the trio remain
friends.

But Martin was repor-
ted last night to be
distressed at being shown
the door after a partner-
ship lasting 30 years.

"How can they do this?"
he asked one relative.
"We're the three mus-
keteers. I thought they'd
show some respect and
wait for me to get well
again.

"I blame Frank for this.
He's been picking on me
ever since he went on the
road."

In: Liza Minnelli

Out: Dean Martin

❝ This was before our time said Sammy to
Liza during 'All Or Nothing At All'. It was
before everybody's time, replied Frank. **❞**

their third night at the Chicago Theatre. Dean's heart had not really been in it from the start, he just couldn't ignore the tensions between them. According to Ricci Martin in his book about his father "Dad was reluctant to do the tour. It was difficult transferring their intimate Vegas showroom act to venues that seated crowds for hockey and basketball games. Adding to Dad's aggravation was Frank's well-meaning attempts to turn back the clock on the Rat Pack routine."

Dean chartered a plane, flew to Los Angeles and checked into the Cedars-Sinai Medical Center. From there it was announced that he had a recurrence of his "old kidney problems". It was clear that Dean had no intention of rejoining the tour and two nights later Frank and Sammy played the Metro Center Arena in Minneapolis. After a few more shows as a duo, Liza Minnelli was drafted in for the rest of the tour. Frank had known Liza since she was born and she called him Uncle Frank. They had already played some shows together in the previous couple of years). It was the beginning of 'The Ultimate Event', a world tour starring the three of them that would run until spring 1989.

Frank interrupted the 'Ultimate Event' tour to perform at George Bush's Inaugural Gala in Washington DC on 19 January. Away from the music Frank was branching out. He launched his own range of pasta sauces in July 1989, or rather Armanino Foods did. On 13 November Frank, along with a whole host of stars, taped a TV special at the Shrine Auditorium to honour Sammy Davis Jr's 60 years in showbiz; Sammy himself was already too riddled with cancer to perform. After completing the 'Ultimate Event'

THE ULTIMATE EVENT
Frank, Liza Minnelli and Sammy at the first of five sell-out concerts at London's Royal Albert Hall on 19 April 1989. (Far right) the programme for the 23-concert 'Ultimate Event' tour.

THE ULTIMATE EVENT

1988

18 September
Phoenix, Arizona

19 September
Phoenix, Arizona

22 September
Atlanta, Georgia

24 September
Miami, Florida

25 September
Tampa, Florida

27 September
Philadelphia, Penn

28 September
Philadelphia, Penn

30 September
New Jersey

1 October
New Jersey

3 November
LA, California

8 November
Houston, Texas

11, 12 & 13 November
San Carlos, California

26 November
Los Angeles, California

30 November
Detroit, Michigan

1, 2, 3 & 4 December
Detroit, Michigan

1989

17 January
Dallas, Texas

18 January
New Orleans, Louisiana

20, 21 January
Miami, Florida

23 February
Osaka, Japan

25 February
Tokyo Bay, Japan

28 February
Melbourne, Australia

1 March
Melbourne, Australia

3 March
Sydney, Australia

4 March
Sydney, Australia

7, 8 March
Honolulu

6 April
Milan, Italy

8 April
Rotterdam, Holland

11 April
Sweden

13 April
Oslo, Norway

15 April
Gothenburg, Sweden

16 April
Helsinki, Finland

18, 19, 20, 21, 22 April
London, England

25 April
Paris, France

27 April
Amsterdam, Holland

29 April
Munich, Germany

30 April
Vienna, Austria

3, 4 May
Dublin, Ireland

For the 29 April show in the Olympiahalle in Munich, Frank Sinatra Jr conducted the orchestra for his father's set and the medley.

Sammy Davis Jr
'Here I'll Stay', 'Begin The Beguine', 'It Could Happen To You', 'The Candy Man', 'What Kind Of Fool Am I', 'Bad', 'Mr. Bojangles', 'The Music Of The Night', 'One' (to introduce Liza Minnelli).

Liza Minnelli
'The Sound Of Your Name', 'God Bless The Child', 'Some People', 'Sailor Boys'. Medley: 'I Can See Clearly Now – I Can See It', 'I Love A Piano', 'Mein Herr', 'Cabaret'.

Frank Sinatra
'For Once In My Life', 'Come Rain Or Come Shine', 'The Best Is Yet To Come', 'I Have Dreamed', 'Where Or When', 'Bewitched', 'Strangers In The Night', 'Soliloquy', 'Mack The Knife', 'My Way'.

Frank, Sammy, and Liza
(some as solos, 'Witchcraft' a Frank and Sammy duet, and some all together)
'Style', 'Witchcraft', 'Liza With A "Z"', 'Talk To The Animals', 'All Or Nothing At All', 'Money Makes The World Go 'Round', 'Once In A Lifetime', 'I've Got You Under My Skin', 'Maybe This Time', 'I Gotta Be Me, All The Way', 'Old Friends', 'The Birth Of The Blues', 'The Lady Is A Tramp', 'And The World Goes Round', 'There's A Boat That's Leaving Soon For New York', 'New York, New York'.

tour Frank's live shows for the second half of 1989 were much reduced. Apart from playing Bally's a few times there were just a few one-off shows. Frank's association with the Vegas resort came to a temporary end in November when a strike by the local Las Vegas Musicians' Union took hold. The hotels wanted to get rid of their contracted musicians, which is what sparked the strike. Frank naturally supported the musicians and after he cancelled some shows he was "fired" by Bally's for a short while. Come March 1990 the strike had petered out and Frank was back, and by May he was even playing their new property in Reno.

The first shows of 1990 were in Florida at the Sunrise Musical Theatre and the Orlando Arena on 23 January. Two days later Ava Gardner died in London following the stroke she had suffered during the previous year. By March Frank's concert schedule was on the up and through April and early May he did one-off dates and played Bally's again. He began a run at Radio City Music Hall on 14 May but after playing that night, and the following one he cancelled the rest. Sammy Davis Jr had died. It was just six months after taping the tribute show. Probably after his mother and father, this was the death that affected Frank the most. The loss of Hank Sanicola, Nelson, Don Costa and Gordon Jenkins had all been awful, but Sammy was Frank's brother. "He was a class act, and I will miss him forever". There must too have been thoughts of Ava.

When Frank resumed working on 24 May he was at Bally's in Reno and between then and mid-December he was busy all over the United States. He also played shows in London, Glasgow (where he hadn't performed since 1953) and Stockholm; the Swedish Government had relented over Sun City. The night before Frank's 75th birthday he was spotted in New York by Pete Hamill, a columnist for the *New York Daily News*.

"So you're walking along Second Ave. on a Friday night. And at 52nd St. the doors of Rocky Lee's restaurant open, and an old man walks out, surrounded by his guys. And it's the Chairman of the Board! Frank Sinatra! He has just eaten dinner at his favorite table with his wife, Barbara, and stepson Bobby Marx and pal Jilly Rizzo. He's wearing a blue satin warm-up jacket. His thinning hair is combed just so. And he's heading slowly, slowly to a waiting pale blue Caddie with the license plate NY, NY. Much too marvelous, too marvelous for words." For his birthday show Frank was at the Meadowlands, where it was billed as the opening night of his world tour and appropriately the first number was 'You Make Me Feel So Young'. The show closed with everyone, including his co-stars, Liza Minnelli, Steve Lawrence and Eydie Gorme, singing 'Happy Birthday To Frank'.

TOMORROW, THE WORLD

The world tour proper, sponsored by Chivas Regal, didn't really get going until March when Frank, Steve and Eydie played Sydney, Australia. In between times Frank had played some dates in Miami, Orlando, Tampa and San Diego. During every month of the rest of the year Frank was playing shows somewhere in the world, often with Steve and Eydie. After Australia he was in Japan, Mexico City, Spain, Belgium, Italy, Norway, Sweden, Germany, Holland, Ireland and Canada. Frank was not away from home continually but interspersed his trips abroad with numerous shows in Vegas, Atlantic City and at other US

cities. There is no questioning his stamina, even if at some of the performances the voice was far from what it was, or some hoped it would be. But when the voice let him down, his timing rarely did. You could be churlish and say he should have stopped, but getting a ticket for these shows was never easy so it seems that most people wouldn't subscribe to that view.

After Irv Cottler, who had been Frank's drummer since 1955, died, Gregg Field took over in 1991 and saw things from close to. "True, the Old Man's voice isn't what it once was, but so what? People should listen to what's there, not what isn't. Even on bad nights, like if he's hoarse, he'll sing through it. He doesn't have it in his mind that he can't do it. And on the really good nights, he's so powerful. But he's always rhythmically intense. That strong phrasing hasn't diminished at all. If anything, it's better." For some years Frank had been using teleprompters, his old lyric/running order book having long gone. There are some who are critical of what he did, but it made sense; many far younger singers sometimes have trouble with the words. The phenomena of performers of Frank's age going on to perform in the type of locations that he did was a totally new concept.

The Sinatra Celebrity Cookbook
Barbara, Frank & Friends

FRANK SINATRA ENTERPRISES
To go along with the pasta sauces, Frank and Barbara published this cookbook. Frank was also a regular on the cover of his local magazine. He was, after all, the King of Palm Springs.

Just as in most things he did Frank was even then ploughing his own, new furrow. But by this time performances were beginning to get patchy; there were good shows, and there were plain awful shows. Harry Agoratus who had been a fan since the 1940s and who saw Frank at the Copa in the 1950s. "It was still Sinatra, but somehow he wasn't there. Shirley MacLaine, who was on the bill with him, had to point out the monitors. It got to the point that I wanted him to stop singing so I could listen to the marvelous orchestra that was backing him with those magnificent arrangements in the acoustically perfect Radio City Music Hall. It was very quiet on the way home. Finally my wife said, 'He should retire'. I don't think another word was said the rest of the trip."

In August 1991 Frank even went back into the studio, the first time since his abortive attempt at nailing 'My Foolish Heart' with Billy May in June 1988. Frank cut 'Silent Night' with Junior playing the piano. The song was to be used on a Christmas charity album. Ten days later Frank again worked with Billy May on a Maurice Jarre/Sammy Cahn song called 'The Setting Sun'. The song was for a Japanese movie and was an extremely complicated melody, courtesy of Mr Jarre, and Frank didn't like what he heard. Ella Fitzgerald ended up singing it to Billy May's backing track.

Frank began his 53rd year since he joined Harry James on the road with a fund-raising show for mayoral candidate Andrew Stein at the Waldorf Astoria in New York with Shirley Maclaine and Liza Minnelli. The rest of the year was much like the previous one with shows all over America and a tour to Europe that included shows in London at The Royal Albert Hall where Frank Jr conducted the John Dankworth Orchestra. There were also shows in Spain, Portugal and Greece. While he was in London he spent most of his time in his suite at the Savoy, possibly mourning the death of his great pal Jilly Rizzo. Just before Frank left for England Jilly had been killed in a horrific car fire near his home in Palm Springs.

JUST THE TWO OF US0

Given Frank's failure to nail the Jarre/Cahn song most people probably thought that it was the end of the road for Frank and recording, but there was to be one more spin of the tape. Given his hectic touring schedule Frank didn't even step foot inside a studio during 1992 or for the first half of 1993 (where even his concert dates had been cut down). Behind the scenes there had been much activity working on an idea for a new album. Phil Ramone had the idea to team Frank with the best (and the best known) singers in various

OLD FRIENDS
Frank and his longtime friend Shirley MacLaine duet on 'You Make Me Feel So Young' at Radio City Music Hall, on 8 October 1992 — the opening night of their eight-day stint in New York.

THE DUETS ALBUMS

DUETS I WENT TRIPLE-PLATINUM, WHILE DUETS II WENT PLATINUM. THEY WERE THE FIRST OF FRANK'S ALBUMS TO BE RECORDED SPECIFICALLY FOR THE CD GENERATION.

Besides being Frank's last studio recordings these albums helped to introduce Frank to people who had never dreamt of buying a Sinatra album. For many long-time fans these albums were something of an abomination. Why did Frank need to work with all these inferior talents, and rock singers at that? The fact is that the younger CD buyers who liked what they heard then bought many of his classic albums. For Capitol it was a shrewd marketing concept and Reprise probably did pretty well too.

The albums were made at the Capitol Tower, and it was the first time that Frank had worked in the studio for over 30 years. His last session had been in September 1961 with Axel Stordahl. The first session for *Duets* had Patrick Williams conducting the orchestra and the first song that the orchestra worked on was appropriately 'Come Fly With Me' shortly after 2:00 pm on 18 June 1993. Frank arrived around 6:30 pm while the orchestra was rehearsing 'South of The Border'. It was one of the songs that he and Nelson had done at their first session together in April 1953, but despite rehearsing it with the orchestra over several more sessions Frank didn't actually record it again. According to Gregg Fields, Frank's drummer, it all went a little differently on the second night. "The doors to Capitol A are locked and 70 or 80 of us are in the hallway. And the recording light is on. Door opens up, out comes Frank. He stepped out. Phil said he had tried to convince Frank to put on headphones to sing to what we had recorded the day before. He tried it and the quote was 'This is hokey.' He left." On the third night Frank stood out front and sang with the band. "He did 'Come Fly With Me' in one take. We finished it then he said 'That's great. Let's keep goin'.' I thought 'You gotta be kidding me. I need another one.' Pat Williams said 'You better get yours because if he gets his, we're going to use whatever you played.' He got into his groove and – I'll tell ya, that was one of the most amazing feats I've ever seen a conductor pull off."

SONG LINES – DUETS 1

Recorded: The Capitol Tower. Producer: Phil Ramone. Chart: US No 2, 38 weeks on the chart (First charted 20 November 1993). UK No 5, 14 weeks on the chart (first charted 6 November 1993. The dates with the songs refer to when Frank first recorded them.

1. 'THE LADY IS A TRAMP'
November 1956 (with Luther Vandross)

2. 'WHAT NOW, MY LOVE?'
November 1966 (with Aretha Franklin)

3. 'I'VE GOT A CRUSH ON YOU'
November 1947 (with Barbra Streisand)

4. 'SUMMER WIND'
May 1966 (with Julio Iglesias)

5. 'COME RAIN OR COME SHINE'
June 1946 (with Gloria Estefan)

6. 'THEME FROM NEW YORK, NEW YORK'
August 1979 (with Tony Bennett)

7. 'THEY CAN'T TAKE THAT AWAY FROM ME'
November 1953 (with Natalie Cole)

8. 'YOU MAKE ME FEEL SO YOUNG'
January 1956 (with Charles Aznavour)

9. 'GUESS I'LL HANG MY TEARS OUT TO DRY'/'IN THE WEE SMALL HOURS OF THE MORNING'
July 1946/February 1955 (with Carly Simon)

10. 'I'VE GOT THE WORLD ON A STRING'
April 1953 (with Liza Minnelli)

11. 'WITCHCRAFT'
May 1957 (with Anita Baker)

12. 'I'VE GOT YOU UNDER MY SKIN'
January 1956 (with Bono)

13. 'ALL THE WAY/ONE FOR MY BABY'
October 1956/August 1947 (with Kenny G.)

SONG LINES – DUETS II

Recorded: The Capitol Tower. Producer: Phil Ramone. Chart: US No 9, 18 weeks on the chart (First charted 3 December 1994). UK No 29, 6 weeks on the chart (first charted 26 November 1994) Frank won an Emmy for best traditional pop vocal performance for Duets II; his first competitive Grammy for 29 years. Frankly, it was nothing but nostalgia.

1. 'FOR ONCE IN MY LIFE'
February 1969 (with Gladys Knight & Stevie Wonder)

2. 'COME FLY WITH ME'
October 1957 (with Luis Miguel)

3. 'BEWITCHED, BOTHERED AND BEWILDERED'
August 1957 (with Patti Labelle)

4. 'THE BEST IS YET TO COME' June 1964 (with Jon Secada)

5. 'MOONLIGHT IN VERMONT'
October 1957 (with Linda Ronstadt)

6. 'FLY ME TO THE MOON'
June 1964 (with Antonio Carlos Jobim)

7. 'LUCK BE A LADY'
July 1963 (with Chrissie Hynde)

8. 'A FOGGY DAY'
November 1953 (with Willie Nelson)

9. 'WHERE OR WHEN'
January 1945 (with Steve Lawrence & Eydie Gorme)

10. 'EMBRACEABLE YOU'
December 1944 (with Lena Horne)

11. 'MACK THE KNIFE'
April 1984 (with Jimmy Buffett)

12. 'HOW DO YOU KEEP THE MUSIC PLAYING'/'MY FUNNY VALENTINE'
March 1983 (with Lorrie Morgan)

13. 'MY KIND OF TOWN'
November 1963 (with the Sinatra family)

14. 'THE HOUSE I LIVE IN'
May 1945 (with Neil Diamond)

Right: Frank with Al Schmitt, the engineer who worked on both *Duets* albums.

musical genres to produce an album of duets. Naturally there were no shortage of takers to work with Frank, but the only problem was none of them actually got to work with Frank live in the studio. All Frank's vocals were recorded completely separately from his vocal partners.

The concept was tried and tested. Julio Iglesias had done an album in 1984 working with artists as diverse as Diana Ross, Willie Nelson and the Beach Boys. Frank's concept took it one stage further. Phil Ramone had first worked with Frank in 1967 and by the 1980s he had become one of the hottest producers in America.

The first session was fixed for late June and Phil had a simple technique for capturing Frank's vocals. "I'd start rolling the tape and would not stop the tape from the time he started down the hallway into the studio, until he left". On the first two nights things didn't go according to plan and Frank didn't get anything recorded. "After the third night finally things started rolling correctly, and we got a take of 'Come Fly With Me' and played it back, and he was turning around and starting the next tune, and the mike didn't work. My whole body dropped. I'd never felt more nervous and more upset by something as simple. He just stood there for about 10 seconds, and dropped the mike on the floor. Went off stage. There was a hush in the crowd. There was a quiet scramble where, God knows what's going to happen. Then it started again. The pre-announce from backstage, "Ladies and gentleman, Francis Albert Sinatra." He came out with a different mike, absolutely working, and didn't mention it, didn't talk about it." Patrick Williams was conducting the orchestra, which included many of Frank's regulars and of course Bill

Miller. Frank recorded the songs "live" with the orchestra, his preferred method of working. There were obviously some post-edits before the vocals of Frank's duet partners were added. "He hadn't lost his voice. In fact, many people have accused me of stealing the voice tracks from the '50s and I laughed. Technology. Why would I do that? People are suspicious."

According to Ramone, choosing the songs for Frank to sing was easy. "I took the library of what he was doing on stage and I decided there's no point of trying to introduce new songs. I only had one or two songs that he wanted to do but then it just didn't feel right to do them. One was 'South of the Border' and he loved that tune. But to relearn it after 40 years is crazy. I'd picked out one or two that he hadn't done in concert or in any way other than that." When it came to adding the other voices Phil was amazed at people's reactions. "It was going to a graduation of students. Not one – from Luther Vandross who was the first duet I did – or Natalie Cole… I've never seen anybody behave as childlike as Aretha Franklin. People who are wonderful professionals just rose to another occasion. Hearing his voice coming down their headphones and singing – oh my God, what am I doing here? Genuine. I think you can hear it in their voices. They had lots of time to practice. A week. To me, that's lots of time. Once they chose…I gave them a choice of two or three songs. Then it was like one of those crossword puzzles. You start to cross off the names from one side (then the other)." Almost as soon as Frank had finished his sessions he went back on the road opening at the Desert Inn in Vegas on July 14 for a week. After shows

> ❝He held the patent, the original blueprint on singing the popular song, a man who would have thousands of imitators but who, himself, would never be influenced by a single, solitary person…❞
>
> MEL TORME

THREE GENERATIONS
Bruce Springsteen, Frank and Bob Dylan were to their generation what their parents' generation most hated.

1973 1998

around the United States and Canada Frank went back into the Capitol Tower to cut some more songs to make up enough for a second *Duets* album. More shows before the year's end ran into shows in Fort Lauderdale in January 1994. On 1 March Frank went to the Grammys to receive a lifetime achievement award. Almost immediately Frank was back on the road, in Richmond. Frank collapsed on stage, and at first people suspected the worst. But it was probably just the heat.

For the rest of the year Frank conducted what amounted to a "Grand Tour" of America, playing Tulsa, Moline, Omaha, Wilmington, Boston, Dallas and Houston among other cities. He also played his favoured casinos in Vegas and Atlantic City as well as the Philippines in late July. In November it was officially announced that Frank would stop touring by the end of the year. His last show on American soil was appropriately New Jersey at the Sands in Atlantic City on 20 November, 1994. A month Frank went to Japan to play the Fukuoka Dome for two nights with Natalie

BIRTHDAY BASH

Frank's 80th birthday celebration was hosted for TV by Gregory Peck and Sharon Stone, amongst others. There were guest appearances by Little Richard, Hootie and The Blowfish, Salt 'n' Pepa, Paula Abdul and Natalie Cole and many more. Somehow you have to believe it was more to do with TV ratings than giving Frank a good time. But doesn't he look great!

Cole. By all accounts Frank was often showing his age through 1994, and none more so than in Japan. These were his last concerts proper, just a few days after his 79th birthday.

However, on 25 February, 1995 Frank did appear live in his hometown of Palm Springs, after his annual charity golf tournament, with an orchestra conducted by Frank Junior and Bill Miller at the piano. Frank launched into 'I've Got The World On A String'…and frankly you had to believe it. Frank even jokes over the intro of 'String' saying, "what's the name of this one?" Where he had sung with a teleprompter for years on this date he did without – perhaps he had a point to prove. Frank sang just seven numbers and ironically finished with 'The Best Is Yet To Come'. After the concert Bill Miller was sitting around with Frank watching TV. "We're listening to someone singing on TV. And he says 'Oh, I love that song. If we ever go back to work I'm going to include that.' I said, 'Well, they're waiting for you, Frank.' He said, 'Nahhh. It's too late, too late. We've done a lot of work.'

"Frank was old school. He had passion." *Luther Vandross*

"On behalf of all New Jersey, Frank, I want to say 'Hail Brother, you sang out our soul'." *Bruce Springsteen*

"The master is gone, but his voice will live forever." *Tony Bennett*

"His songs are not only his biography but ours, as well." *Peter Bogdanovich*

"He was the godfather of the musical depths of their sorrows, their lonely nights, their passionate silliness." *Shirley MacLaine*

"Let's face it – Sinatra is a king." *Bing Crosby*

He was the epitome of what singing is all about, beautiful sounds, smooth as silk, effortless, impeccable phrasing, stylish, intelligent and full of heart. *Barbra Streisand*

"He was motivated by the song and the lyric and what it meant. And very often it related to his life and what he was going through." *Alan Livingston*

"Frank has musical integrity and he does it so very well that he's the musical end." *Sammy Davis Jr*

"Frank demanded a lot." *Nelson Riddle*

"There are any number of tunes that people call Sinatra songs, even though many of them are not. But once he put his signature on 'em that was it. They became his." *Frank Sinatra Jr*

"He just wanted to be Frank Sinatra, and he became Frank Sinatra." *Bill Miller*

"LADIES AND GENTLEMEN, MAY YOU ALL LIVE TO BE 102 YEARS OLD AND THE LAST VOICE YOU HEAR BE MINE" *Frank*

"You only live
once, and the
way I live, once
is enough."

"Thank you for
letting me sing
for you."

FRANK

HE'S HERE
12 December 1915

HE'S GONE
14 May 1998

INDEX